ISBN 978-0-428-74766-4
PIBN 11306220

ANNUAL REPORT of program activities

MENTAL HEALTH INTRAMURAL RESEARCH PROGRAM -
Division of Clinical and Behavioral Research,
Division of Biological and Biochemical Research, and
Division of Special Mental Health Research

US NATIONAL INSTITUTE OF MENTAL HEALTH

July 1, 1974 - June 30, 1975

VOLUME II

INDIVIDUAL PROJECT REPORTS

ANNUAL REPORT
MENTAL HEALTH INTRAMURAL RESEARCH PROGRAM -
Division of Clinical and Behavioral Research,
Division of Biological and Biochemical Research, and
Division of Special Mental Health Research
NATIONAL INSTITUTE OF MENTAL HEALTH

July 1, 1974 - June 30, 1975

TABLE OF CONTENTS

VOLUME II - INDIVIDUAL PROJECT REPORTS

Unit on Childhood Mental Illness (cont'd)

Unit on Perceptual and Cognitive Studies

Unit on Studies of Drug Abuse

Section on Psychobiology

Section on Neuropsychopharmacology

Section on Neuropsychopharmacology (cont'd)

ADULT PSYCHIATRY BRANCH (cont'd) Page

Section on Neuropsychopharmacology (cont'd)

Section on Psychogenetics

Section on Biochemistry

Section on Family Studies

LABORATORY OF CLINICAL SCIENCE (cont'd) Page

Section on Medicine

Section on Histopharmacology

LABORATORY OF CLINICAL SCIENCE (cont'd) Page

Section on Psychiatry

Section on Clinical Neuropharmacology

Section on Experimental Therapeutics

LABORATORY OF DEVELOPMENTAL PSYCHOLOGY

LABORATORY OF DEVELOPMENTAL PSYCHOLOGY (cont'd) Page

LABORATORY OF DEVELOPMENTAL PSYCHOLOGY (cont'd) Page

LABORATORY OF PSYCHOLOGY AND PSYCHOPATHOLOGY

LABORATORY OF PSYCHOLOGY AND PSYCHOPATHOLOGY (cont'd) Page

LABORATORY OF SOCIO-ENVIRONMENTAL STUDIES

DIVISION OF BIOLOGICAL AND BIOCHEMICAL RESEARCH | Page

LABORATORY OF BRAIN EVOLUTION AND BEHAVIOR

Section on Comparative Neurophysiology and Behavior

LABORATORY OF NEUROBIOLOGY | Page

LABORATORY OF NEUROCHEMISTRY

LABORATORY OF NEUROPHYSIOLOGY

LABORATORY OF NEUROPHYSIOLOGY (cont'd) Page

DIVISION OF SPECIAL MENTAL HEALTH RESEARCH

Section on Neurochemistry

LABORATORY OF NEUROPHARMACOLOGY

LABORATORY OF NEUROPHARMACOLOGY (cont'd) Page

LABORATORY OF CLINICAL PSYCHOPHARMACOLOGY

LABORATORY OF PRECLINICAL PHARMACOLOGY

LABORATORY OF PRECLINICAL PHARMACOLOGY (cont'd) Page

LABORATORY OF PRECLINICAL PHARMACOLOGY (cont'd) Page

Project No. Z01 MH 00092-01 AP
1. Adult Psychiatry Branch
2. Office of the Chief
3. Bethesda, Maryland

PHS-ADAMHA-NIMH
Individual Project Report
July I, 1974 through June 30, 1975

Project Title: Central Amines and Psychiatric Illness

Previous Serial Number: None

Principal Investigator: Gerald L. Brown, M.D.

Other Investigators: Frederick K. Goodwin, M.D., Victor M. Holm MC, Capt., USN, James C. Ballenger MC, LCDR, USNR, Orren L. Royal MC, Capt., USN

Cooperating Units: Department of Psychiatry, National Naval Medical Center Lab. of Clinical Science, DCBR, NIMH; Adult Psychiatry Branch, DCBR, NIMH

Man Years:

Total:	0.45
Professional:	0.25
Other:	0.20

Project Description:

Objectives: A growing body of evidence obtained in recent years indicates that the biogenic amines, norepinephrine, dopamine and serotonin, act as central nervous system neurotransmitters and/or modulators of central nervous system transmission. Although considerable indirect pharmacologic evidence has linked functional abnormalities in these amine systems with psychiatric illnesses (particularly affective illness and schizophrenia), the relative lack of direct data in man has limited the applicability of these hypotheses to improved diagnosis and treatment of the major psychiatric disorders. Relatively little direct data from man can be immensely valuable in making use of the massive data from animals and assessing the differences and similarities between man and animals. As well, recent data suggests that affective disorders and psychoses may yield to biological sub-typing which would enable a more effective choice of pharmacological therapy for individual patients. Direct passive data from relatively few patients could be of more value than many times that number of patients' data resulting from active pharmacological manipulations and inferences therefrom. In addition, there is virtually no data on central neurochemical function in the various characterological disorders - a rather striking deficit in our knowledge, considering the evidence suggesting that some character disorders have patterns of family history transmission suggestive of a genetic component. Recent evidence from animals suggesting a close correlation between aggressive behavior and biogenic amines, for example, renders this a particularly interesting area for exploration at this time. The purpose of this present project would be to extend the studies of central amine turnover into larger populations of psychiatric patients including manic depressive psychosis, schizophrenia and various characterological and personality disorders.

Methods Employed: Recently at the NIMH a technique has been developed which allows for the direct estimation of brain amine turnover in psychiatric patients. This method involves the administration of probenecid, a drug which blocks the process by which the amine metabolites are removed from the brain-cerebrospinal fluid system into the blood. Following blockade of their removal, the metabolites of the amines accumulate in the spinal fluid at a rate which is in direct proportion to their synthesis or turnover rate in the brain. Experiments with this technique conducted over the last six years at the Clinical Center of the NIH have led to the following conclusions: (1) experience in over 200 patients has indicated that both the lumbar puncture and the administration of probenecid are safe procedures not associated with significant side effects of toxicity; (2) studies of this technique in conjunction with specific amine precursors and synthesis inhibitors has provided direct evidence that the probenecid induced accumulation of amine metabolites does reflect amine synthesis and turnover rates; (3) application of this technique has been shown to be capable of uncovering differences in central amine function among subgroups of patients with manic-depressive illness and other functional psychotic states. These differences were not detectable by measurement of amine metabolite baseline levels without probenecid.

Major Findings: Though 25 patients have participated in the study to date, because of various difficulties in applying the methodology consistently, in sustained cooperation from the patients, in medications prescribed by the patients' doctors, and mixed diagnoses, the most pertinent finding at this time relates to a group of personality disorders with problems secondary to poor impulse control, high levels of anger and hostility, and poor judgment. The metabolites studied were 5-hydroxyindoleacetic acid (5-HIAA), homovanillic acid (HVA), and 3-methoxy-4-hydroxyphenylglycol (MHPG), the major CSF metabolites of brain serotonin, dopamine and norepinephrine, respectively.

There were no significant differences in 5-HIAA or MHPG between the groups of patients with character disorders and normal controls. However, the HVA in the patients with character disorder was significantly elevated, both in comparison with our normal control group and in comparison with a group of healthy young military volunteers studied by the same method elsewhere.

Significance for Mental Health Research: HVA changes in the CSF are especially interesting since it is the only CSF amine metabolite apparently derived exclusively from amine metabolism in the brain. Data suggest that age, sex, or activity cannot explain the elevated HVA found in this group of patients. Thus, the possibility that these patients have an alteration in brain dopamine metabolism must be considered. This possibility, although based on preliminary evidence, is intriguing in light of animal studies suggesting a close association between central dopamine systems and aggressive behavior.

Proposed Course of Project: The preparation for this project began in January 1973 and the preparation of the protocol and its approval at various levels, both in terms of scientific merit and the protection of rights of patients, required until July 1974. The first lumbar puncture was performed in September 1974. This project is re-evaluated on a yearly basis by the U.S. Navy. We hope to renew this collaborative effort in July 1975. We believe this collaboration is of mutual benefit to NIMH and NNMC.

Key Word Descriptors:

Amine metabolites; cerebrospinal fluid; psychiatric in-patients; personality disorders; U.S. Navy

Honors and Awards:

Commendation-Citation - U.S. Navy: for teaching and administration of training programs (residents and medical students) 1974.

Publications:

Brown, G.L., Goodwin, F.K., Ballenger, J.C., Holm, V.M.: CSF Amine Metabolites in Personality Disorders. Presentation, 128th Annual Meeting of the American Psychiatric Association, 1975.

Project No. Z01 MH 00102-09 AP
1. Adult Psychiatry Branch
2. Office of the Chief
3. Bethesda, Maryland

PHS-ADAMHA-NIMH
Individual Project Report
July 1, 1974 through June 30, 1975

Project Title: Evaluation of Family Dynamics with Conjoint Family Art Procedures

Previous Serial Number: M-AP(C)-14-10

Principal Investigator: Hanna Yaxa Kwiatkowska

Other Investigators: None

Cooperating Units: None

Man Years:

Total: 0
Professional: 0 (inactive)
Other: 0

Project Description:

This project has been reported each year for the last nine years, under the above serial number. The objectives, methodology, and major findings have been contained therein. The project has been terminated. However, the findings are being written in a book commissioned by Charles Co. Thomas, Co., to be published in the latter part of 1975.

Honors and Awards: None

Publications: None

Project No. Z01 MH 00103-09 AP
1. Adult Psychiatry Branch
2. Office of the Chief
3. Bethesda, Maryland

PHS-ADAMHA-NIMH
Individual Project Report
July 1, 1974 through June 30, 1975

Project Title: Family Art Therapy

Previous Serial Number: M-AP(C)-14-11

Principal Investigator: Hanna Yaxa Kwiatkowska

Other Investigators: None

Cooperating Units: None

Man Years:

Total: 0
Professional: 0 (inactive)
Other: 0

Project Description:

This project has been reported each year for the last nine years, under the above serial number. The objectives, methodology, and major findings have been contained therein.

The project was terminated at the time of departure from the Adult Psychiatry Branch of the principal investigator.

Honors and Awards: None

Publications: None

Project No. Z01 MH 00105-07 AP
1. Adult Psychiatry Branch
2. Office of the Chief
3. Bethesda, Maryland

PHS-ADAMHA-NIMH
Individual Project Report
July 1, 1974 through June 30, 1975

Project Title: Systematic Analysis of Family Art Evaluations

Previous Serial Number: M-AP(C)-14-12

Principal Investigators: James K. Dent, Ph.D. and Hanna Yaxa Kwiatkowska

Other Investigators: None

Cooperating Units: None

Man Years:

Total: 0.01
Professional: 0.01
Other: 0.00

Project Description:

Objectives: The overall objective is to explore systematically the materials available from the Family Art Evaluations which have been introduced by Ms. Kwiatkowska and conducted for several years. Such an analysis is aimed at improving diagnostic procedures and increasing our understanding of the social psychological dynamics of psychopathology. In presenting the specific objectives, the longer-range of objectives are listed first; the immediate objectives are listed last.

a. Family dynamics and psychopathology. (1) To differentiate, through the characteristics of their art productions, families in which the index is diagnosed as process schizophrenic, reactive schizophrenic, psychoneurotic, and so forth. (2) To distinguish role positions in the family (father, mother, sibling, etc.), as revealed by their pictures (such as family portraits).

b. Diagnostics (A Manual for the use of the Family Art Evaluations). (1) To specify the relation of the diagnosis of the index to the characteristics of his own art productions and those of his family. (2) To determine which characteristics of the art productions appear to represent transient symptoms and which represent more enduring personality characteristics.

c. Measurement objectives. (1) To develop objective rating systems for pictures and family transactions in the Family Art Evaluation method.

(2) To determine the interrater agreement and the internal consistency of the scales used. (3) To construct by combining scales, variables having stronger metric power. (4) To analyze the significance of variables like artistic talent and intelligence which may confound the relation between diagnostic variables and characteristics of the art productions. It is important to separate the evidence of psychopathology in a picture from the inference of intelligence or artistic talent.

Methods Employed: The pictures are blinded, randomized, and rated; one picture in four is check rated for studies of interrater agreement. A variety of statistical techniques are being used, depending upon specific objectives.

'Blind" ratings of pictures represent an independent measure of the mental status of an individual at a particular point in time. It is our plan to correlate these ratings with other data. Correlation with diagnosis and family characteristics such as socioeconomic status will be greatly facilitated because some of these data have already been compiled in connection with research done by other investigators in the last decade in the Branch.

Major Findings: Factor analysis across pictures reveals that there are some expected dimensions which are prominent and stable. For example, there is a dimension that might be labeled "bizarreness" which is always first or second in explaining variance regardless of how the factor analysis is conducted. However, there are many more independent dimensions than was anticipated; that is, even though interrater agreement is high, relations among dimensions tend to be low. The characteristics of the pictures are not easily summarized in a few dimensions.

Factor analysis across individuals indicates that there are a few dimensions which might be labeled "trait" dimensions. They extend across the various procedures, across two FAE's, and are correlated with intelligence and artistic talent. An example of such a dimension is the use of color. However, unexpectedly, "bizarreness" is not such a dimension; that is, an individual who produces a bizarre "first free" picture is not more likely to show "bizarreness" in his last picture.

There are a large number of dimensions which show significant differences between patients and siblings. These differences are almost always as one would predict: for example, patients' pictures are more likely to be "bizarre." Comparisons between offspring and their parents are difficult because the parents tend to show less artistic talent. Further analyses of talent-free dimensions are required.

Significance to Biomedical Research and the Program of the Institute: Since the art production is an independent, enduring representation of the mental status of an individual (or family) at a moment in time and in a structured family setting, it is a valuable datum both for enhancing our diagnostic methods and for investigating family dynamics in relation to mental disorder.

The usefulness of "drawing tests" for individual diagnosis is widely recognized. Considerable research has been done on the Draw-A-Person test. More recently there have been efforts to use other types of art productions. Although the literature is full of ideas about how to diagnose mental illness from pictures, most of the research has been concerned with a much simpler and less useful task, viz.: To predict whether a person is mentally ill. Only a few systematic studies (e.g., those of Dr. Robert Kaye) have been concerned with trying to specify what aspects of a picture are predictive of what kinds of mental disorder, and there have been no statistical studies of family dynamics as seen through the art productions of the whole family.

Proposed Course of Project: Further analyses of diagnostic groups will be conducted.

Honors and Awards: None

Publications: None

Project No. Z01 MH 00106-07 AP
1. Adult Psychiatry Branch
2. Office of the Chief
3. Bethesda, Maryland

PHS-ADAMHA-NIMH
Individual Project Report
July 1, 1974 through June 30, 1975

Project Title: Systematic Analysis of Brazilian Family Art Evaluations: A Replication

Previous Serial Number: M-AP(C)-14-T3

Principal Investigators: Hanna Yaxa Kwiatkowska and James K. Dent, Ph.D.

Other Investigators: Dr. Carlos Paes de Barros, Dr. Aroldo Rodriques, Vera Pollo Flores, Vera Lemgruber Garcia, Junia Novaes

Cooperating Units: Institute of Psychology, Catholic University, Rio de Janeiro, Brazil; Department of State Committee on International Exchange of Persons (Fulbright Commission)

Man Years:

Total:	0.01
Professional:	0.01
Other:	0.00

Project Description:

Objectives: To explore the differences and similarities appearing in the systematic analysis of pictorial material obtained from Brazilian families with the material obtained from American families here, in the identically structured situation of the "Family Art Evaluation." The specific objectives are: (1) To investigate and compare the characteristics of pictures drawn by Brazilian families where a family member has a specific psychiatric diagnosis, with the characteristics of pictures of diagnostically similar families in the United States. (2) To define if eventual differences observed through this analysis could be attributed to cultural variations. (3) To study the differences in roles of nuclear and extended family member in both countries, as seen in the different procedures of the Family Art Evaluations. (4) To investigate and compare the interrater agreement on the same items of the rating system in the United States and Brazil. This could also shed light on cultural differences.

Methods Employed: The manual used for the NIMH study was translated into Portuguese by the Staff of the Institute of Psychology at the Catholic University in Rio de Janeiro. It was edited by Ms. Kwiatkowska; staff members were personally trained by her to conduct a study parallel to the NIMH study.

A psychologist, Ms. Vera Pollo Flores, with the consultantship of Ms. Sylvia Beatriz Machado Joffely, is in charge of the study and under the direction of Dr. Carlos Paes de Barros, Chairman of the Department of Psychology. Other staff members of the Institute were designated as coordinators and trainers of the raters. The ratings were done by students as part of their regular curriculum for credit. Dr. Aroldo Rodriques, Research Psychologist, is a consultant for the statistical aspect of the study. Another staff member of the Institute, a psychologist, Vera L. Garcia, personally visited us at NIMH in order to discuss the study.

The patients referred to the Clinic at the Institute of Psychology are mostly children or adolescents in their early teens. Jointly with their families they all have a Family Art Evaluation as part of their routine psychological work-up. A considerable amount of material has been accumulated since the evaluations were introduced there. In selecting sample families for the present study we were, nevertheless, limited by the age group; we do not want to include families where the index would be less than ten years old. Diagnostically, the sample includes families of severely neurotic or behavior problem children, all outpatients at the Clinic. Records of all investigated Brazilian families were obtained and translated from Portuguese into English in order to obtain data (symptoms, onset, premorbid history) to be used to establish diagnoses of the Brazilian subjects.

Major Findings: Factor Analyses reveal that there are some similarities with, and some differences from, the factor structure of pictures drawn by our families here at NIMH. The clarification of omissions and discrepancies in the Brazilian data was helped by the assistance of Ms. Junia Novaes, psychologist, guest worker at the Adult Psychiatry Branch, who secured additional data while on a trip to Brazil in 1973. It was possible to fill in most of the gaps in communication which were necessary to finish statistical analyses. The first objective described above is complicated by the fact that most Brazilian indexes are outpatients, and few of the severe disorders in our NIMH patients are found among the Brazilian sample.

Significance to the Program of the Institute: Family Art Evaluations provide a situation which offers a good deal of stability in the manner in which material is gathered for comparative studies. The basic material (pictures) is collected in an experimental setting structured as identically as possible with the NIMH setting. The methods used for the computer analysis of these data are also identical. The possible flaws in the translation and interpretation of the scoring manual, whether of linguistic or cultural nature, are being investigated in a separate study, Z01 MH 00107-07 AP.

Proposed Course of Project: Final completion of analyses and publication of results. The Brazilian group plans to elaborate and refine the data there. The principal investigator, Ms. Kwiatkowska, has been officially invited to Brazil to supervise further research. During the past year additional FAE's were gathered in Brazil by Ms. Novaes and have been returned for analysis. Some further data are needed. For example, we need to know the ages of the siblings in these families. Fortunately, Ms. Kwiatkowska's planned trip to Brazil is now possible through a grant to the University from the Brazilian government.

Honors and Awards: None

Publications: None

Project No. Z01 MH 00107-07 AP
1. Adult Psychiatry Branch
2. Office of the Chief
3. Bethesda, Maryland

PHS-ADAMHA-NIMH
Individual Project Report
July 1, 1974 through June 30, 1975

Project Title: Sources of Variance in the Crosscultural Application of an Objective System for Analyses of Pictures Drawn by Patients and Their Families

Previous Serial Number: M-AP(C)-14-14

Principal Investigators: James K. Dent, Ph.D. and Hanna Yaxa Kwiatkowska

Other Investigators: Dr. Carlos Paes de Barros, Dr. Aroldo Rodrigues, and Vera Pollo Flores

Cooperating Units: Institute of Psychology of the Catholic University of Rio de Janeiro, Brazil

Man Years:

Total: 0.01
Professional: 0.01
Other: 0.00

Project Description:

Objectives: A system has been developed for objectively classifying pictures drawn by patients and by members of their families in the Family Art Evaluations at NIMH (see Project No. Z01 MH 00105-07 AP). This rating system, which consists of about fifty dimensions, has been translated into Portuguese and is being used to describe pictures drawn by mental patients and their families in Brazil (see Project No. Z01 MH 00106-07 AP). In application, the two measurements may not be equivalent for several reasons: (a) Various pictorial symbols may have different significance in culture A (American) from those in culture B (Brazilian). (b) The English and Portuguese translations may not be equivalent. (c) Research group A may have particular frames of reference not common to their own culture. (d) Research group B may also have particular frames of references. The objective of this project is to begin to sort out some of these various sources of error and variance.

Methods Employed; Sixty-eight pictures selected at random from about one thousand pictures (American families) have been rated as follows:

Ratings 1 and 2: Two members of research group A have independently rated each of the pictures using the English translation.

Rating 3: These raters discussed their differences and prepared a check rating representing the best judgment of research group A for each picture.

Rating 4: Using the English translation, the pictures have been rated by two American college student volunteers working alone (no contact with the research group), each doing about half of the pictures.

Rating 5: Using the Portuguese translation, a bilingual American college student volunteer rated the pictures alone (no contact with the research group).

Ratings 6, 7, and 8: These are like ratings 1, 2, and 3, but are being done by Brazilian members of research group B in Brazil, from slides of the same pictures rated at NIMH.

For the fifty dimensions in the rating system, comparison among these ratings should permit us to isolate translation difficulties and some of the group effects. Presumably differences not attributable to these two sources of variance represent cultural factors in interpretation or individual rate biases. Because of the small number of pictures and of having only one bilingual rater, the results will have to be considered tentative. This project is essentially a pilot study for this type of investigation.

Major Findings: The Brazilians were able to rate only about half of the pictures sent them. Analysis of this half indicated clearly which dimensions have a constant meaning in both centers, which have different meanings but are reliable within centers (group frames of reference), and which are so poorly defined that they have little meaning in either center. Ms. Novaes, guest worker and graduate student from Brazil, has studied the various dimensions and has concluded that the differences between the Brazilian ratings and the NIMH ratings cannot be attributed to a lack of equivalence between the Portuguese and English versions of the rating systems.

Proposed Course of Project: Findings are being written up.

Significance to the Program of the Institute: The precise description of mental disorders across cultures is hampered by a paucity of culture-free methods of assessment. Frequently the problem is dealt with by using the inferential judgments of particular clinicians who evaluate patients in two or more cultures. Agreement among them about particular patients is interpreted as constancy in measurement. This system - which is biased by language, dialect, and status problems - may not provide replicable descriptions; i.e., there are no assurances that another group of clinicians with differing backgrounds would provide the same description, or even a common one.

At the other extreme, one is impressed by the almost universal understanding and appreciation of works of art. The messages of enduring representations of art seem, on the one hand, to be an expression of the different cultures and, on the other hand, to convey emotions universally accessible. One is also impressed with the high quality of communication in pure science. Where ideas are precisely defined in observable terms, crosscultural communication is facilitated. For these reasons objective descriptions of art productions may be an important way of achieving crosscultural communication in describing mental disorders. In addition to being tangible, the communication is not limited and/or biased by the language or dialect problem, and the professional has a direct access to the experience of the patient.

Honors and Awards: None

Publications: None

Project No. Z01 MH 00108-07 AP
1. Adult Psychiatry Branch
2. Office of the Chief
3. Bethesda, Maryland

PHS-ADAMHA-NIMH
Individual Project Report
July 1, 1974 through June 30, 1975

Project Title: Intellectual Factors in Mental Disorders

Previous Serial Numbers: M-AP(C)-14-15 and M-AP(C)-14-16

Principal Investigator: James K. Dent, Ph.D.

Other Investigators: None

Cooperating Units: None

Man Years:

Total:	0.01
Professional:	0.01
Other:	0.00

Project Description:

Part A:

Objectives: To relate WAIS, IQ, and subtest patterns to diagnosis of mental disorders among adolescents and among unipolar and bipolar depressed adults.

Methods Employed: Data were obtained from the files of the (since terminated) Section on Clinical Psychology and are being analyzed by means of several multivariate techniques.

Major Findings: Preliminary findings indicate some consistencies with studies that are reported in the literature. Further analyses are needed to confirm these relationships.

Significance to Biomedical Research and the Program of the Institute: Efforts to find WAIS patterns for various diagnostic groups have a long, discouraging history. It is generally believed that a major problem is the unreliability of diagnoses. The clinical and research records of the Adult Psychiatry Branch are a rich source of diagnostic material. For a number of years, in connection with this project (and with a now-terminated project, previously reported under Serial Number M-AP(C)-14-16), the investigator extracted information to form relatively homogeneous symptom patterns. The result is a large number of groups with small numbers in each. However, this permits comparisons with other studies which have similarly defined narrow diagnostic groups. Preliminary findings are encouraging. Discovery of such patterns would (1) provide a relatively objective aid to diagnosis, and (2) shed light on intellectual factors associated with various disorders.

Proposed Course of Project: Analyses will be continued: It is expected that these findings will be written up during the next fiscal year.

Honors and Awards: None

Publications: None

Part B:

Objectives: To relate WAIS, IQ, and subtest patterns to family role and mental disorders among adolescents.

Methods Employed: Same as Part A above.

Major Findings: The conceptualization of intellectual factors in mental disorders appears to shift radically when one passes from the individual to the family constellation. Although there is evidence of intellectual factors (positive intercorrelations) within families, still the important findings probably surround the constellations of factors rather than these homogeneities. All present analyses are preliminary.

Significance to Biomedical Research and the Program of the Institute: There are probably very few research sites that have IQ measurements for whole families. Some work has been done on the IQ's of siblings of schizophrenics. But, otherwise, practically nothing is known. In fact, a major problem has been to search out whether certain observed patterns for these families are also found among normals (e.g., the correlation between parents' IQ's).

Proposed Course of Project: Further searches of the literature will be conducted. It is doubtful that the investigator will have time to complete this work in the coming fiscal year.

Honors and Awards: None

Publications: None

Project No. Z01 MH 00021-10 AP
1. Adult Psychiatry Branch
2. Unit on Sleep Studies
3. Bethesda, Maryland

PHS-ADAMHA-NIMH
Individual Project Report
July 1, 1974 through June 30, 1975

Project Title: Studies of Sleep

Previous Serial Number: M-CP(C) 18-3

Principal Investigators: J. Christian Gillin, M.D., and Richard J. Wyatt, M.D.

Other Investigators: William E. Bunney, Jr., M.D., Dennis L. Murphy, M.D., Frederick K. Goodwin, M.D. Robert M. Post, M.D., and Monte S. Buchbaum, Ph.D.

Cooperating Units: Laboratory of Clinical Science and Laboratory of Clinical Psychopharmacology

Man Years:

Total: 6
Professional: 1
Other: 5

Project Description:

Objectives:

Experimental findings over the past decade promise understanding of the basic biochemical processes underlying sleep and increasingly clear demonstrations of the severity of sleep disturbances in many psychiatric patients indicate the need for better means of alleviation. To whatever extent understanding of sleep can be achieved, more effective treatment of its disturbance will surely follow.

Major Findings: Pharmacological

A. Relationship of Cholinergic Activity to REM Narcoleptic Attacks

In order to explore the possible relationship between levels of cholinergic activity and REM narcoleptic attacks, we have begun therapeutic trials of the cholinergic blocking agent, Artane (trihexyphenidyl 2 mg, tid). Results from the first three narcoleptic patients have been encouraging in that all three appeared to show clinical improvement, especially in terms of less frequent attacks of cataplexy. The converse procedure of administering physostigmine (0.5 mg i.v., q 5 minutes to a total dose of 1.5-2.5 mg) in an effort to determine whether increased cholinergic activity induces REM narcoleptic cataplexy did not have any discernible effects in the same three patients. In addition, physostigmine had no apparent effects on the mood of these patients, contrary to recent reports involving psychiatric patients.

Effects of L-Histidine on Sleep

There is considerable indirect evidence suggesting that histamine may function in the brain as a neurohumor in sleep-waking mechanisms. To test the possible role of histamine in the control of waking in man, we administered its amino acid precursor, L-histidine, to human subjects and evaluated their electrographic sleep patterns. L-Histidine was given to three patients with intractable narcolepsy (20 gm per day for 2 weeks), to four normal volunteers (32.4 gm per day for 5 days) and to a patient with progressive systemic sclerosis (48.6 gm per day for 16 days). No effects were observed on nocturnal EEG sleep patterns in any of the subjects or on the symptoms of the narcoleptic patients. Although the degree to which histamine levels in the brain were elevated in this study is not clear, these results do not encourage the hypothesis that histamine is an alerting or waking factor in the brain.

Differential Effects of D- and L-Amphetamines on the Sleep of Depressed Psychiatric Patients on and off Lithium Treatment

Since there is evidence suggesting that D-amphetamine preferentially blocks norepinephrine re-uptake as compared with L-amphetamine, and that lithium carbonate enhances norepinephrine re-uptake, sleep patterns of four depressed psychiatric patients were examined on nights when they had been given D- or L-amphetamine on and off lithium therapy. The data indicate that both D- and L-amphetamine suppressed REM sleep and REM %, but that only D-amphetamine suppressed total sleep time. Lithium carbonate did not alter the above-mentioned effects of D- or L-amphetamine.

Effects of Cocaine

Cocaine was administered orally on a double-blind basis to depressed patients. In doses which did not produce consistent effects on vital signs or mood, cocaine significantly reduced total sleep and REM sleep. The REM sleep suppression with cocaine administration and rebound upon cocaine discontinuation was dose related; there was a greater effect at higher doses. Two properties of cocaine appear to closely correspond to those of many other drugs which suppress REM sleep in man--enhancement of functional catecholamines and/or high drug-abuse potential.

E. Adrenal Cortical Insufficiency

The effects of decreased adrenal cortical steroids on sleep were investigated during six studies in four patients with adrenal cortical insufficiency before and after withdrawal of hormonal replacement therapy for five days and in five normal male volunteers before and after administration of metyrapone. In both groups, Delta Sleep (Stages III and IV) and Delta % rose following reduction of adrenal cortical steroids.

F. Effects of ACTH

ACTH (40 IU) was administered intravenously over a period of 8 h to nine healthy volunteers beginning at 8 a.m., 3 p.m., or 11:30 p.m., and to three patients with Addison's disease beginning at 8 a.m. ACTH produced a significantly greater reduction in REM sleep in the normal volunteers after infusions beginning at 8 a.m. and 3 p.m.; it did not do so when ACTH was infused during sleep. Delta Sleep was also reduced after the 8 a.m. infusion in the volunteers.

These results suggest that ACTH affected sleep through its effect on adrenal corticosteroid secretion. Time appears to be an important aspect in the effects that ACTH and adrenocorticosteroids have upon the central nervous system.

Major Findings: Clinical Disorders

A. Unipolar and Bipolar Illness

This study compares the EEG sleep patterns of Unipolar depressed patients (history of depression only), Bipolar I depressed patients (history of hospitalization for both depression and mania), and Normals selected on the basis of age and sex.

From a large number of normals and depressed patients studied, three groups of subjects were formed: 18 Normals (1 male, 17 female, mean age = 40, range 20-52), 21 Unipolar (1 male, 20 female, mean age=37, range 20-52), and 14 Bipolar I (3 male, 11 female, mean age=41, range 17-52). Each individual was selected so that at least one subject of the same sex and age (same 5-year age block) was represented in both of the other two groups. Subjects were selected without knowledge of sleep data. In order to control for intensity of clinical symptoms, psychotic patients (presence of delusions or hallucinations) and recovered patients were excluded. No subject had received psychoactive or sleeping medication for two weeks prior to the study.

For each subject sleep data from three to eight consecutive nights were averaged.

	Normals	Unipolar	Bipolar I
Total Sleep	379 ± 11	320 ± 19	339 ± 21
Sleep Latency	25 ± 5	48 ± 9	64 ± 17
REM Latency	79 ± 5	52 ± 5	34 ± 7
REM	91 ± 4	86 ± 5	92 ± 10
REM Density	1.8 ± 0.1	2.1 ± 0.2	1.9 ± 0.3
REM%	23.8 ± 0.8	25.6 ± 1.2	26.5 ± 2.4
Delta	30 ± 6	15 ± 5	20 ± 7
Awake	24 ± 5	39 ± 7	35 ± 7
EMA	6 ± 3	27 ± 6	29 ± 9

Means ± SEM

Data are in minutes/night except for REM% and REM density (units/minute of REM, a measure of eye movement activity, scored on a scale of 0 to 8). EMA = early morning awake, time awake in bed before arising after last sleep.

Depressed patients exhibited significantly less total sleep and less Delta sleep, shorter REM latencies; more intermittent awake time; and more early morning awake time than normals. REM and REM% were not significantly different. REM latency was the only sleep measure which significantly differentiated between Bipolars and Unipolars ($p < .05$, Newman-Keuls test).

The finding of a short REM latency in Bipolar as compared with Unipolar depressed patients, if confirmed, would supplement genetic, pharmacologic, clinical and psychophysiologic data suggesting that Bipolar illness is different from Unipolar depressive illness.

B. Schizophrenia

Eight actively ill schizophrenics and eight nonpsychotic controls were deprived of REM sleep by the awakening method for two nights. Sleep patterns during five postdeprivation nights were analyzed by a variety of univariate and multivariate techniques.

Data suggest that actively ill schizophrenics are less likely than control psychiatric patients to exhibit a normal REM rebound. They require fewer awakenings than controls to achieve REM deprivation. They show little or no change in REM time or REM% during recovery as compared with base line, and, compared with controls, have significantly less REM time, REM%, and change in REM time and REM% on early postdeprivation nights.

The two patient groups also differed in their pattern of stages III and IV during recovery. Considerable overlap existed in REM compensation between actively ill schizophrenics and controls. Additional information suggests that REM compensation may be related to Rod and Frame testing: the more field independent a subject is, the better REM compensator he is.

C. Restless Leg Syndrome

A patient with restless leg syndrome had very unpleasant sensory and motor symptoms, occurring mainly in the legs at rest and relieved or avoided only by leg movement, as well as the aggravation of these symptoms during pregnancy. The great likelihood that the patient's father and sister were similarly afflicted exemplifies its often-reported hereditary basis. Insomnia was severe.

The laboratory sleep-electroencephalographic data not only clearly establish the quantitative extent of her insomnia and its relationship to the restless legs symptoms but also highlight the extreme night-to-night variability of her sleep, a finding emphasized in recent studies of primary insomniacs.

Our patient had no evidence of peripheral vascular disease, anemia, diabetes, avitaminosis, or central nervous system trauma. Her weakness on neurologic examination was subtle and was elicited only by push-pull examinations of individual muscles. Our patient had obvious abnormalities on the EMG and muscle biopsy specimen that were indicative of neurogenic disease, in addition to the mildly but definitely abnormal results of clinical neurologic examination. There were strikingly high calcium and magnesium levels and slightly low bicarbonate level in the CSF.

Major Findings: Normal Studies

A. Effects of Sleep Stage and Stimulus Intensity on Auditory Evoked Responses

The purpose of this study was to evaluate the effect of sleep stage and stimulus intensity on the auditory evoked response (AER). Nine normal volunteers (age 18-22; 6 M, 3 F) slept in the sleep lab for three nights each; the first night was adaptation and was not included in any calculations. Four intensities of clicks (50, 60, 70 and 80 dB) were generated by the LINC computer in pseudo random order. EEG was sampled at 250 Hz for 1 second and AER was computed on line for each intensity for each minute of the night. Each minute was visually scored for sleep stage. AER from the minutes of each sleep stage were then averaged. AER amplitude tended to increase little from 50 to 80 dB in waking subjects but increased markedly in sleeping subjects in stages 3 and 4 ($p < 0.05$, 2 way analysis of variance). Rapid eye movement (REM) and stage I sleep had small amplitude AER's in comparison with other sleep stages. Individuals who showed decreases in amplitude at high intensities while awake slept significantly longer during the experimental night ($r = -.76$, $p < 0.05$). The loss of inhibitory mechanisms during stages 3 and 4 is well known. It is therefore not surprising to see the disappearance of the paradoxical AER amplitude reduction at high intensities and a more linear EP amplitude/stimulus intensity function; stage 1, 2 and REM sleep resembled the waking state. Of interest was the finding that waking AER amplitude/stimulus intensity functions predicted sleep duration in this noisy environment. This suggests that individual differences in sleep duration may be related to differences in inhibition of sensory processing.

Significance to Mental Health Research:

These studies contribute to the present extensive national and international efforts to unravel the complex relationships of clinical disorders, biochemistry and sleep.

Keyword Descriptors:

pharmacology, psychopathology, depression, schizophrenia, narcolepsy, and biochemistry

Publications:

Gillin, J.C.,Fram, D.H., Wyatt, R.J., Henkin, R.I. and Snyder, F.: L-histidine: Failure to affect the sleep-waking cycle in man. Psychopharmacologia, in press.

Gillin, J.C., Jacobs, L.S., Snyder, F. and Henkin, R.I.: Effects of ACTH on the sleep of normal subjects and patients with Addison's disease. Neuroendocrinology 15: 21-31, 1974.

Gillin, J.C., Buchsbaum, M.S., Jacobs, L.S., Fram, D.H., Williams, R.B., Jr., Vaughan, T.B., Jr., Mellon, E., Snyder, F., and Wyatt, R.J.: Partial REM sleep deprivation, schizophrenia, and field articulation. Arch. Gen. Psychiat. 30: 653-662, 1974.

Frankel, B.L., Patten, B.M., and Gillin, J.C.: Restless legs syndrome: Sleep, electroencephalographic and neurologic findings. JAMA 230: 1302-1302, 1974.

Post, R.M., Gillin, J.C., Wyatt, R.J., Goodwin, F.M.: The effect of orally administered cocaine in sleep of depressed patients. Psychopharmacologia 37: 59-66, 1974.

Gillin, J.C., Wyatt, R.J.: Schizophrenia: Perchance a dream? Int. Rev. Neurobiol., in press.

Gillin, J.C., Jacobs, L.S., Snyder, F. and Henkin, R.I.: Effects of decreased adrenal corticosteroids: Changes in sleep in normal subjects and patients with adrenal cortical insufficiency. Electroenceph. Clin. Neurophysiol. 26: 283-289, 1974.

Wyatt, R.J.: Human sleep - adrenergic and serotonergic systems. In: Proceedings of World Congress of Psychiatry, in press.

Kaplan, J., Dawson, S., Vaughan, T., Green, R., and Wyatt, R.J.: Effects of prolonged chlorpromazine administration on the sleep of chronic schizophrenics. Arch. Gen. Psychiat. 31: 62-66, 1974.

Mendelson, W., Guthrie, R.D., Guynn, R., Harris, R.L. and Wyatt, R.J.: Rapid eye movement (REM) sleep deprivation, stress and intermediary metabolism. J. Neurochem. 22: 1157-1159, 1974.

Mendelson, W., Guthrie, R.D., Frederick, G. and Wyatt, R.J.: The "flower-pot technique" of rapid eye movement (REM) sleep deprivation. Psychophysiology, in press.

Wyatt, R.J. and Gillin, J.C.: Biochemistry of Human Sleep. In Karacan, I. (Ed.): Pharmacology of Sleep. New York, Academic Press, in press.

Project No. Z01 MH 00097-01 AP
1. Adult Psychiatry Branch
2. Unit on Childhood Mental Illness
3. Bethesda, Maryland

PHS-ADAMHA-NIMH
Individual Project Report
July 1, 1974 through June 30, 1975

Project Title: Re-evaluation of Adults Hospitalized Fifteen Years Previously as "Hyperactive" Children

Previous Serial Number: None

Principal Investigator: Gerald L. Brown, M.D.

Other Investigators: W.E. Bunney, Jr., M.D., Judith Rapoport, M.D., Walter Sceery, MSCW, Ralph J. Gemelli, M.D.

Cooperating Units: Office of the Chief, Adult Psychiatry Branch; Unit on Childhood Mental Illness, APB

Man Years:

Total:	1.9
Professional:	1.7
Other:	0.2

Project Description:

Objectives: The purpose of this study is to follow up longitudinally a group of people who as children had symptoms of hyperactivity within a heterogeneous group of behavioral disorders. We intend: 1) to assess the psychosocial outcome of the assigned specific diagnostic categories of childhood psychopathology; 2) to investigate the persistence of hyperactivity and associated symptoms thought to be associated with minimal brain dysfunction (MBD); 3) to examine the relationship between adult psychopathology and the emotional and behavioral problems previously identified in childhood.

A need exists for more data concerning both the outcome of the specific diagnostic categories of childhood psychopathology, and the relationship between the emotional and behavioral problems of childhood and adult psychopathology. One such childhood diagnostic category in which the outcome in adulthood is unclear is the "hyperkinetic syndrome", sometimes called "hyperactivity" or "minimal brain dysfunction".

Methods Employed: All patients will be located and asked to come in for an initial outpatient evaluation, which will include a social history and a psychiatric evaluation in which the data will be systematized. A chart review of the childhood evaluation will be carried out by one of the investigators who will remain blind to the findings of these children as adults and the adult investigator who will remain blind to the childhood chart review.

General interim social, medical, and psychiatric history will be gathered and systematized. This will include a familial-genetic history and life events inventory, as well as socio-economic status utilizing the Hollingshead-Redlich Rating Scale. A physical examination and a neurological examination will be done. Stigmata (minor physical anomalies) which have been associated with MBD will be noted and rated. Routine laboratory examinations, such as CBC, UA, SMA-12, T3 and T4 will be performed.

A current Research Diagnostic Criteria (RDC) will be made; followup IQ and psychological assessments of cognition will be arranged. The instruments to be used are the WISC, WRAT, Porteus Maze, Goodenough Test, ITPa, Bender Gestalt, "Stimulus Seeking Behavior" Test, Lincoln Oseretsky Motor Development Scale; Halstead-Reitan Battery for assessment of organic brain dysfunction, and experimental tests of cognition, such as the paired associate learning, continuous performance test, and recognition learning. EEG's, both routine awake and sleeping, will be obtained. AER will be measured.

Initially, clinical blood and urine tests will be obtained as above. In addition, monoamine oxidase (MAO), catechol-O-methyl-transferase (COMT) and serotonin (5-HT) will be measured in platelets, COMT in erythrocytes, dopamine-β-hydroxylase (DBH) and MAO in plasma, and 3-methoxy-4-hydroxyphenylglycol (MHPG), vanillylmandelic acid (VMA), homovanillic acid (HVA), 17-hydroxysteroids, and 17-Ketosteroids in 24-hour urine collections.

Major Findings: Double-blind evaluation of childhood charts, work on location of patients, and some social history interviews of those patients residing in the Washington Metropolitan Area have been accomplished to this point. There are not yet any findings to report.

Significance to Mental Health Research: Follow-up studies all support the observation that the child with symptoms of and similar to MBD remains at risk for academic, emotional, and social problems in later development. Certain research questions need further clarification. A need exists for assessing the various adult outcomes of MBD children. Of interest would be the persistence of MBD characteristics or their change, and adult psychopathology: 1) will these adults show perceptive, cognitive, and/or memory deficits even if an alteration in hyperactivity occurred? 2) will the type and length of treatment affect outcome in terms of adult psychopathology? 3) do MBD characteristics in children correlate with specific adult psychopathology? 4) given the previous follow-up reports of decreased self-esteem and poor self-image, along with inadequate reporting of the incidence of depressive illness and type of psychosis, how many of these adults develop symptoms of affective disorders and how many with histories of psychoses are affective vs. schizophrenic? As central amine aberrations are postulated in affective and schizophrenic illnesses and in MBD, one might expect to find more of these illnesses in this adult population than in a normal adult population.

Proposed Course of Project: We plan to conduct this study over a two-year period.

Project No. Z01 MH 00097-01 AP

Keyword Descriptors:

hyperactivity, hyperkinetic syndrome, minimal brain dysfunction, MBD, childhood psychopathology, affective illness, schizophrenia, central amine aberrations.

Honors and Awards: None

Publications: None

Project No. Z01 MH 00098-01 AP
1. Adult Psychiatry Branch
2. Unit on Childhood Mental Illness
3. Bethesda, Maryland

PHS-ADAMHA-NIMH
Individual Project Report
July 1, 1974 through June 30, 1975

Project Title: Study of Children and Grandchildren of Patients with Unipolar and Bipolar Depressive Illness

Principal Investigators: Leon Cytryn, M.D. and Donald H. McKnew, Jr., M.D.

Other Investigators: Alina Efron, M.D. and Walter Sceery, M.S.W., J.D.

Cooperating Units: Laboratory of Clinical Science

Man Years:

Total:	1.
Professional:	0.8
Other:	0.0

Project Description:

Objectives: (1) To determine the frequency of affective disorders in the children and grandchildren of adults with unipolar and bipolar depressive illness, (2) to identify biological markers of a genetically-transmitted predisposition to affective disorders, and (3) to study the interaction between genetic predisposition and environmental factors in children with affective disorders.

Methods Employed: This project is part of a larger study directed by Dr. Elliot S. Gershon (Z01 MH 00084-01 AP). We plan to study all available children and grandchildren (ages 4-15) of the probands. All children, with or without affective disturbance, will undergo biological studies identical to those in the patient group. A second examination with repeat enzyme studies will be done after a 3-month interval. Blood will be drawn at each visit; the amount will not exceed 10 ml/40 lbs. of body weight for children weighing less than 90 pounds. All children will be considered as short-term outpatients admitted for tests only. Those in whom an affective disorder or other psychopathology warrant treatment will be referred either to a private psychotherapist or a facility such as the psychiatric outpatient department of Children's Hospital in Washington, D.C.

A social worker will obtain a developmental history from the parents using a modified version of Medical and Social History Section of the ECDEU (Early Clinical Drug Evaluation Unit, compiled and published by Psychopharmacology

Research Branch, NIMH). Upon completion of the questionnaire, the social worker will follow-up by obtaining more detailed information where relevant.

Every child will have two psychiatric interviews at three-month intervals. During the interview there will be a structured portion which will aim at eliciting fantasy material by the use of free drawing, story-telling, TAT cards, and play material. This will be followed by an unstructured interview which will attempt to elicit any psychopathology with emphasis on affective disorders. Following the interview, the children will be observed through a one-way mirror in order to record their spontaneous behavior. Following the interview and observation period, the children will be rated on all three scales of the Children's Psychiatric Rating Scale of the ECDEU. All of the procedures above have been used for several years by many investigators and pose no hazards for the children.

Major Findings: The study only began recently and we have seen to date seven children. Thus, no conclusions can be drawn at this time.

Significance to Biomedical Research and the Program of the Institute: There is much interest in determining whether affective disorders can be rated to predict biochemical and other physiological measures which may be genetically determined. Also, there is a considerable interest presently in the nature and prognosis of affective disorders in children and their relationship with affective disorders in adults. It is to be hoped that our present study will help to clarify some of the issues mentioned above.

In addition to the potential significance of clarification of the problem of affective disorders in children, this study has the potential of developing preventive measures in children and perhaps (psychotherapeutic and pharmacological) measures to reduce and forestall, or reduce the frequency of, affective disorders in adults.

Proposed Course of Project: We contemplete at this point to study 100 children and a similar number of suitable controls. Upon completion of the data collection, the affective symptom patterns will be compared to the results of the biochemical and physiological determinations to see whether a meaningful relationship exists.

Honors and Awards: None

Publications: None

Project No. Z01 MH 00099-01 AP
1. Adult Psychiatry Branch
2. Unit on Childhood Mental Illness
3. Bethesda, Maryland

PHS-ADAMHA-NIMH
Individual Project Report
July 1, 1974 through June 30, 1975

Project Title: Pharmacokinetics of Methylphenidate in "Hyperactive" Children

Previous Serial Number: None

Principal Investigator: William E. Bunney, Jr., M.D.

Other Investigators: Irwin J. Kopin, M.D., Michael H. Ebert, M.D., Gerald L. Brown, M.D., Robert D. Hunt, M.D.

Cooperating Units: Office of the Chief, Adult Psychiatry Branch; Unit on Childhood Mental Illness, APB

Man Years:
Total: 1.9
Professional: 1.6
Other: 0.3

Project Description:

Objectives: The purpose of this study is: 1) to evaluate the clinical pharmacology of methylphenidate in hyperactive children; 2) to compare clinically and pharmacologically responders with non-responders; 3) to elucidate the neurochemical mechanisms of minimal brain dysfunction (MBD); 4) to compare cognitive and motoric dysfunction during active treatment and placebo phase; 5) to explore the familial relationship between MBD and other psychiatric disorders.

At this time very little is known about the pharmacokinetics of methylphenidate in man. Assay techniques for identifying methylphenidate in the urine using flame detector gas chromatography have been available for years. However, assay techniques sensitive enough to measure methylphenidate levels in blood have been published recently using electron capture gas chromatography and mass fragmentography. The metabolism of methylphenidate in man is largely unexplored. Data currently available in the literature indicates that methylphenidate is rapidly metabolized to ritalinic acid and eliminated renally.

Methods Employed: Over the course of two years we expect to admit approximately 50 children who are referred from pediatricians, schools, and mental health clinics for evaluation of hyperactivity. The children will have their own treating physician who will follow them after discharge with our active participation in diagnosis and treatment consultation. The children will be under age 14, not severely retarded (I.Q. 80 or above on WISC), have no major medical illnesses other than the neuropsychiatric constellation of minimal brain dysfunction (MBD). We will give preference to children who have not had a trial of methylphenidate.

Medical history and physical examination including history of birth trauma and age of onset of hyperactivity will be reported on the form "Physical and Neurological Exam for Soft Signs." Familial-social history will be obtained by social worker. This will include a family history of psychiatric illness in relatives and a Life Events Inventory which explores the child's experiences with separation and object loss.

Biological parameters to be measured include routine blood examinations and determinations of plasma norepinephrine, erythrocyte catechol-O-methyltransferase (COMT), and platelet monoamine oxidase (MAO), COMT, and serotonin (5-HT). Routine urinalysis will be done plus 24-hour determinations for 3-methoxy-4-hydroxyphenyl-glycol (MHPG), vanillylmandelic acid (VMA), homovanillic acid (HVA).

Major Findings: Three children have been admitted and evaluated to this point. There are not yet sufficient data to report.

Significance to Mental Health Research: Though hyperactive children have been considerably studied in the last few years, there are still a number of diagnostic and psychopharmacological questions to be answered. The pharmacokinetics of methylphenidate, a drug to which well selected cases respond 84% of the time, is poorly understood with no correlation between its pharmacokinetics and the behavorial responses. More importantly, for the future, basic biological factors in hyperactive children which might explain the psychopharmacological responses are, at this point, only hypotheses. The degree to which these hypotheses are validated or refuted could play a significant role in understanding the biological contributions to childhood mental illness.

Proposed Course of Project: We plan to conduct this project over a two-year period with the possibility of continuance and expansion thereafter.

Keyword Descriptors: Hyperactive children, methylphenidate, pharmacokinetics, central amine aberrations.

Honors and Awards: None

Publications: None

Project No. Z01 MH 00034-05 AP
1. Adult Psychiatry Branch
2. Unit on Perceptual and Cognitive Studies
3. Bethesda, Maryland

PHS-ADAMHA-NIMH
Individual Project Report
July 1, 1974 through June 30, 1975

Project Title: Psychological and Physiological Correlates of the Average Evoked Response.

Previous Serial Number: M-P-C(C) - 36

Principal Investigator: Monte Buchsbaum, M.D.

Other Investigators: Thomas Bittker, M.D.; Stephen G. Landau, M.D.; and Redford Williams, M.D.

Cooperating Units: All Adult Psychiatry Branch, NIMH.

Man Years:

Total:	1.0
Professional:	0.5
Others:	0.5

Project Description:

Average evoked response (AER) techniques provide a kind of mathematical depth electrode which in humans has the potential of getting closer to measuring the specific function of a specific brain area in a non-invasive way than any other current biochemical or physiological method. Two areas of development have been necessary for the application of AER techniques to large scale patient testing and clinical studies. These are basic psychophysiology of the AER and computer techniques.

Our major psychophysiological theme has been the study of the neurophysiology of sensory input regulation. Coping with sensory overload is perhaps the major perceptual problem of 20th century urban man, and individuals differ widely in their relative success in coping. Average evoked responses to sensory stimuli that are loud, repetitious, or meaningless showed wide variation across normal subjects and psychiatric groups.

Our early discovery that some subjects paradoxically showed actual decreases in AER amplitude with increasing stimulus intensity led to the development of a perceptual style concept known as "stimulus intensity control" or "augmenting/reducing" and to a variety of clinical and more basic investigations.

Based on the results of a number of studies here and at other centers, we have found AER augmentation (increasing AER amplitude with increasing stimulus intensity) to be correlated with a tendency to tolerate pain and noise poorly. In contrast, evoked response reducing (decreasing amplitude with increasing stimulus intensity) seems to be associated with a tendency to decrease the perceived intensity at intense levels and to be relatively pain and noise tolerant.

Methodological issues involving recording sites, measurement techniques, and stimulus parameters have also required much basic investigation. Advances in meeting these problems have been essential to understanding the differences between people in their sensory AER and the clinical applications. During the past year the relation of AERs to muscle tension and autonomic responsiveness and attention have been analyzed, and two reviews of our work over the past eight years have been prepared.

The Unit has also played a key role in planning a new computer system for the NIMH Intramural program. The current Systems Engineering Laboratory 81B has been used for on-line experimental control and data analysis for about four years. Two separate AER recording rooms operate independently, allowing us to carry on studies both in basic psychophysiology and in clinical psychiatry. However, with the rapid advances (and price reductions) in computer technology as well as increasing maintenance tasks for the SEL, it has been important to plan the replacement of this facility. The new distributed system will not only offer enhanced capability and reliability but also occupy far less floor space. In conjunction with DCRT's DECsystem 10, the design will provide a potent data collection and analysis facility. Further, by maintaining compatibility among the individual computers being acquired, much development can be done in common. The new system will also allow for extension to a truly portable facility (under-airline-seat size) utilizing the same basic software and design. This will permit patient testing off the NIH campus at other psychiatric hospitals, in subjects' homes or in foreign field studies.

Keyword Descriptors: Evoked response, electroencephalography, psychophysiology, perception, noise tolerance, pain, computers.

Publications:

Buchsbaum, M.: Self-regulation of stimulus intensity: Augmenting/reducing and the average evoked response. In Schwartz, G.E. and Shapiro, D. (Eds.): Consciousness and Self Regulation: Advances in Research. Plenum Press, (In Press).

Landau, S.G. and Buchsbaum, M.: Average evoked response and muscle tension. Physiological Psychology, 1: 56-60, 1973.

Williams, R.B., Bittker, T.E., Buchsbaum, M and Wynne, L.C.: Cardiovascular and neurophysiologic correlates of sensory intake and rejection I. Effect of cognitive tasks. Psychophysiology, (In Press).

Bittker, T.E., Buchsbaum, M., Williams R.B. and Wynne, L.C.: Cardiovascular and neurophysiologic correlates of sensory intake and rejection II. Interview behavior. Psychophysiology, (In Press).

Project No. Z01 MH 00035-03 AP
1. Adult Psychiatry Branch
2. Unit on Perceptual and Cognitive Studies
3. Bethesda, Maryland

PHS-ADAMHA-NIMH
Individual Project Report
July 1, 1974 through June 30, 1975

Project Title: Biochemical and Psychopharmacological Correlates of the Average Evoked Response in Psychiatric Patients.

Previous Serial Number: M-AP(C) - 21-2

Principal Investigator: Monte Buchsbaum, M.D.

Other Investigators: Frederick Goodwin, M.D.; Dennis Murphy, M.D.; Eugene Redmond, M.D.; Daniel van Kammen, M.D.; and Richard Wyatt, M.D.

Cooperating Units: Laboratory of Clinical Psychopharmacology, Laboratory of Clinical Science, NIMH.

Man Years:

Total:	1.8
Professional:	0.6
Others:	1.2

Project Description:

The objective of this project is to relate individual differences in electrophysiological function to individual differences in human neurochemistry and to the neurobiology of psychiatric illness.

Neurochemical and evoked response techniques have two complementary defects in approaching the problem of human psychiatric dysfunction. While many basic biochemical mechanisms are understood, measurement in intact human subjects is often indirect, depending on metabolic products and reflecting slow responses of the whole brain (and often body as well). The evoked response is a more empirical measure for which the underlying neurophysiology is not fully understood. It has the advantage, however, of enabling us to examine the response of specific brain areas to brief psychological events.

Last year, we found that the combined multivariate use of platelet MAO level and AER allowed us to successfully separate the four groups; normal, schizophrenic, bipolar, and unipolar affective illness, with 72% accuracy. However, since hospitalization stress, sensory isolation, dietary changes, etc. might complicate both MAO and AER, we planned to locate normal individuals with extreme values of MAO and to study them with AER measures. This then represented a kind of biochemical "high-risk" study for the major psychoses.

Blood samples were drawn from 400 college student volunteers. Individuals with platelet MAO levels in the upper and lower 10% were brought to NIMH for four two-hour sessions. MAO levels in these extreme groups were roughly comparable with those obtained previously in patient samples. We obtained AER data, IQ, personality scales, interview material, biographic information, sleep reports, detailed family history information, height and weight, and performance on eye-tracking and psychophysical tasks (rod-and-frame, continuous performance task, channel capacity, Stroop). Initial phases of analysis have revealed not only AER differences between high and low MAO groups but also a tendency for the low MAO males to show greater incidence of psychological adjustment problems both in themselves and in their kindred. During the coming year, the data will be analyzed, and a follow-up survey of the original 400 will be completed by mail and telephone.

Individual differences in drug response to d- and l-amphetamine were also examined as part of this program. AER parameters, measured at baseline, were predictors of mood changes on amphetamine, and AER changes associated with amphetamine closely paralleled the extent of mood change. Baseline off-medication AER parameters as predictors of clinical response to lithium, imipramine, and amitriptyline are also being examined in patients with affective disorders.

Taken together, these studies indicate that AER techniques may yield useful indicators of the functional states of certain catecholamines or of baseline states of responsiveness to psychopharmacologic intervention. Projected work for the next two years involves projects with methylphenidate in hyperkinetic children and continued pharmacologic studies of patients with affective illness.

Keyword Descriptors: Evoked response, electroencephalography, psychophysiology, perception, neurochemistry, affective illness, schizophrenia.

Publications:

Buchsbaum, M.: Average evoked response augmenting/reducing in schizophrenia and affective disorders. In Freedman, D.X. (Ed.): The Biology of the Major Psychoses: A comparative Analysis. Raven Press. (In Press).

Landau, S.G., Buchsbaum, M., Carpenter, W., Strauss, J. and Sacks, M.: Schizophrenia and stimulus intensity control. Archives of Gen Psychiatry, (In Press).

Redmond, D.E., Borge, G.F., Buchsbaum, M. and Maas, J.W.: Evoked potential studies of brain catecholamine alterations in monkeys. J. of Psychiatric Research, (In Press).

Belmaker, R., Beckman, H., Goodwin, F., Murphy, D., Pollin, W., Buchsbaum, M., Wyatt, R., Ciaranello, R. and Lamprecht, F.: Relationships between platelet and plasma monoamine oxidase, plasma dopamine-beta-hydroxylase, and urinary 3-methoxy-4-hydroxy phenylglycol. Life Sciences, 16: 273-280, 1975.

Project No. Z01 MH 00036-01 AP
1. Adult Psychiatry Branch
2. Unit on Perceptual and Cognitive Studies
3. Bethesda, Maryland

PHS-ADAMHA-NIMH
Individual Project Report
July 1, 1974 through June 30, 1975

Project Title: Individual Differences in Sleep and the AER.

Previous Serial Number: NONE.

Principal Investigator: Monte Buchsbaum, M.D.

Other Investigators: Robert Coursey, Ph.D.; J. Christian Gillin, M.D.; and Robert Post, M.D.

Cooperating Units: Department of Psychology, University of Maryland; Laboratory of Clinical Psychopharmacology, NIMH.

Man Years:

Total:	0.5
Professional:	0.2
Others:	0.3

Project Description:

The sleeping organism is able to respond to environmental stimuli. This capability sets sleep apart from coma, anaesthesia and other similar behavioral states. Perceptual ability is, therefore, an important aspect of the definition of sleep. It has, in addition, evolutionary significance for species which must respond during sleep to threats (e.g. predators), to positive opportunities (e.g. prey) and to other needs (e.g. a crying infant). The widely known presence of sleep disorders in psychiatric illness, and our findings of perceptual tendencies to regulate incoming stimulation in unusual ways have suggested that the study of AER augmenting/reducing during sleep and in insomniacs might furnish valuable information.

Auditory average evoked responses (AERs) to clicks ranging from 50 to 80 dB were studied in nine normal adults while awake and during sleep. AER amplitude tended to increase little from 50 to 80 dB in waking subjects, but they increased markedly in sleeping subjects during stages 3 and 4. Rapid eye movement (REM) and stage I sleep had small amplitude AERs in comparison with other sleep stages. Individuals who showed decreases in amplitude at high intensities while awake slept significantly longer during experimental nights with tone stimulation.

In clinical studies, eighteen chronic insomniacs, whose sleep problems were confirmed by all-night EEG recordings, were matched with normal sleepers for age, sex and education. Insomniacs were significantly more depressed than normals on Zung's Depression Scale and the MMPI D scale. Secondly, insomniacs showed more anxious worrying behavior; they were high on the MMPI Pt, Hy, Hs, Taylor Manifest Anxiety and Eysenck's Neuroticism scales, toward the sensitization end on Byrne's Repression-Sensitization Scale, and overly concerned about the past and future on the Time Competence Scale. Thirdly, insomniacs appeared to be sensory reducers, as evidenced by lower evoked potential responses to sound and by low scores on Zuckerman's Sensation Seeking Scale. They were also less proficient in perceptual-motor skills on the WAIS. A step-wise regression analysis showed that the sensation-avoiding dimension accounted for the most variance in predicting an EEG sleep-efficiency criterion.

Studies of the effects of sleep deprivation on the AER are currently in progress.

Keyword Descriptors: Evoked response, electroencephalography, psychophysiology, perception, sleep, insomnia, noise tolerance.

Publications:

Buchsbaum, M., Gillin, J.C. and Pfefferbaum, A.: Effect of sleep stage and stimulus intensity on auditory average evoked responses. Psychophysiology, (In Press).

Coursey, R.D., Buchsbaum, M. and Frankel, B.L.: Personality measures and evoked responses in chronic insomniacs. J. Abnormal Psychology, (In Press).

Project No. Z01 MH 00037-03 AP
1. Adult Psychiatry Branch
2. Unit on Perceptual and Cognitive Studies
3. Bethesda, Maryland

PHS-ADAMHA-NIMH
Individual Project Report
July 1, 1974 through June 30, 1975

Project Title: Genetic Factors in Psychiatric Illness and the AER.

Previous Serial Number: M-AP(C)-21-4

Principal Investigator: Monte Buchsbaum, M.D.

Other Investigators: Elliot Gershon, M.D.; Victor Gindilis, M.D.; and Marat Vartanian, M.D.

Cooperating Units: Institute of Psychiatry, Academy of Medical Sciences, Moscow, USSR.

Man Years:
Total: 0.4
Professional: 0.2
Others: 0.2

Project Description:

The application of average evoked response (AER) techniques in human genetic studies of behavioral disorders is an especially promising area. Most psychophysiological effects can only be observed after much statistical data reduction, but the great similarity in evoked response waveform in twins can be seen at a glance; familial patterns are also often clearly visible.

The visual AER augmenting/reducing measure that we have found distinguishing patients with schizophrenia and affective disorders from normals appears to be partially set genetically. Heritability estimates for this measure on a group of 30 Mz and 30 Dz normal adult twins ranged from 0.52 to 0.68, depending on the technique used. These heritabilities reflect relatively high intraclass correlations in monozygotic (Mz) twins and often absent or negligible correlations in dizygotic (Dz) twins. Other AER investigations have supported this, suggesting that the augmenting/reducing similarities in Mz twins do not result from a single gene but more likely from disassortative mating, two or more genes showing epistasis or dominance interactions at several loci. Additive genetic or dominance effects would be less likely candidates since they would create similarities between Dz twins as well. Alternatively, some common environmental factors might act to increase similarity in Mz twins and decrease similarity in Dz twins.

A study of augmenting/reducing in 30 patients with affective disorders, normal controls, and their first-degree relatives has also been carried out to help assess the relationship between the genetics of affective illness and the AER measure.

Since amplitude/intensity slopes, amplitudes, and AER peak latency from different AER components all show significant heritability but are not all highly intercorrelated, some multivariate analysis seemed especially appropriate.

The relationship of the AER measures to schizophrenia, their apparent multigene dependence, and the need for multivariate analysis have intrigued Dr. Vartanian and Dr. Gindilis at the Institute of Psychiatry (IOP) in Moscow. As part of the joint US-USSR studies on the biology and genetics of schizophrenia, AER data on 34 Mz and 30 Dz normal twin pairs was sent to the IOP. Multivariate distances between twin pairs were calculated and multivariate strategies developed. Further multivariate comparisons between schizophrenics and normals, using dimensions of tested heritability, are now being planned, again based on AER data collected at NIMH. Dr. Buchsbaum will visit the IOP in Moscow to consult on these analyses, to plan a proposed visit by Dr. Gindilis in Fy76 and to discuss evoked potential recording techniques with IOP staff.

Keyword Descriptors: Evoked response, electroencephalography, psychophysiology, perception, genetics, affective illness, twins.

Publications:

Buchsbaum, M.: Average evoked response and stimulus intensity in identical and fraternal twins. Physiological Psychology, 2: 365-370, 1974.

Project No. Z01 MH 00038-01 AP
1. Adult Psychiatry Branch
2. Unit on Perceptual and Cognitive Studies
3. Bethesda, Maryland

PHS-ADAMHA-NIMH
Individual Project Report
July 1, 1974 through June 30, 1975

Project Title: Laterality, Psychopathology and the AER.

Previous Serial Number: M-P-C(C) - 36

Principal Investigator: Monte Buchsbaum, M.D.

Other Investigators: John Docherty, M.D.; Dorothy Drago; Paul Fedio, Ph.D.; Samuel Siris, M.D.; and Daniel van Kammen, M.D.

Cooperating Units: Adult Psychiatry Branch, NIMH and NINDS.

Man Years:

Total:	0.4
Professional:	0.2
Others:	0.2

Project Description:

The left cerebral hemisphere has long been recognized as the major processing area for verbal information and the right hemisphere as the area for certain nonverbal spatial information. Recently, several psychophysiologic and neuroanatomic studies have suggested that a lateralized deficit may occur in schizophrenia. By presenting visual stimuli in the right and left visual field and recording EEG from the left and right hemisphere, AER techniques can take advantage of the anatomical arrangement of the human visual system to study abnormalities in lateralization. In normal subjects, AERs are highly asymmetrical and differ markedly with the task assigned the subject. AERs from the left temporo-parietal area seem especially sensitive to changes in the attention given to the stimulus by subject. Since attentional deficits have been one of the most widely postulated psychological deficits in schizophrenia, the application of this AER technique seemed promising. A group of 20 off-medication schizophrenics and comparison groups of affective disorder patients and normal controls have been tested. As a further comparison, testing of patients with right or left temporal lobectomies has been accomplished.

Our current AER procedure utilizes an automated television eye position monitoring system to insure stimulus delivery to the right or left retina. In an effort to simplify the procedure, bilateral visual stimulation studies have been begun in schizophrenic patients and normals. Psycholinguistic function as measured by the Illinois Test of Psycholinguistic Ability is also being assessed in both schizophrenic patients and a normal control group.

Keyword Descriptors: Evoked response, electroencephalography, psychophysiology, perception, attention, laterality, schizophrenia, affective illness.

Publications:

Buchsbaum, M. and Drago, D.: Hemispheric asymmetry in the effects of attention in the visual evoked response. In Desmedt, J. (Ed.): Cerebral Evoked Potentials in Man. (In Press).

Project No. Z01 MH 00039-01 AP
1. Adult Psychiatry Branch
2. Unit on Perceptual and Cognitive Studies
3. Bethesda, Maryland

PHS-ADAMHA-NIMH
Individual Project Report
July 1, 1974 through June 30, 1975

Project Title: Sensory Thresholds and Averaged Evoked Responses

Previous Serial Number: NONE

Principal Investigator: Monte Buchsbaum, M.D.

Other Investigators: Arnold Anderson, M.D.; William E. Bunney, Jr., M.D.; Thomas Chase, M.D.; Frederick Goodwin, M.D.; Robert Post, M.D.; Daniel van Kammen, M.D.; and Marion Webster.

Cooperating Units: Adult Psychiatry Branch, Laboratory of Clinical Science, NIMH and NINDS.

Man Years:

Total:	0.9
Professional:	0.3
Others:	0.6

Project Description:

In 1974 we found strong support for our concept of sensory augmenting/reducing (see Project report No. Z01 MH 00034-01 AP). Individuals who were relatively pain tolerant as indicated by subjective shock ratings exhibited AER to electrical stimuli which decreased in amplitude with increasing stimulus intensity (reducing). This year's development of a nonparametric signal detection analysis of subjective shock ratings has increased the precision of our AER-shock-rating relationships. This form of analysis is a powerful tool for analyzing experiments and evaluating audioanalgesia and acupuncture. It is currently being used in clinical studies of patients, in combination with AER techniques.

Another especially important approach to pain response has been the investigation of neurochemical differences between individuals. Baseline visual AERs were recorded, followed by shocks of varying intensity both for subjective pain rating and somatosensory AER. Urinary 3-methoxy-4-hydroxyphenylglycol (MHPG) during this period was collected for comparison with the same time period on another "non-stress" day. In this group of 18 normals, AER augmenters tended to have significantly greater increase in MHPG excretion on the stress day than did reducers.

Taken together, these findings illustrate the interrelationships between individual differences in response to pain stress as measured by a central norepinephrine metabolite, a psychophysiological variable, and subjective response ratings. These stress responses in normals will be compared to similar data obtained from hospitalized depressed patients. We expect to refine further our AER technique during the current year by better localizing the central areas involved.

Keyword Descriptors: Evoked response, electroencephalography, psychophysiology, perception, stress, neurochemistry.

Publications:

Project No. Z01 MH 00111-01 AP
1. Adult Psychiatry Branch
2. Unit on Studies of Drug Abuse
3. Bethesda, Maryland

PHS-ADAMHA-NIMH
Individual Project Report
July 1, 1974 through June 30, 1975

Project Title: Developmental Phase of Drug Abuse Treatment and Research Program

Previous Serial Number: None

Principal Investigators: William E. Bunney, Jr., M.D. and Arnold E. Andersen, M.D.

Other Investigators: Robert M. Post, M.D., Daniel P. van Kammen, M.D., Gerald LaVonne Brown, M.D., and Dennis L. Murphy, M.D.

Cooperating Units: Section on Psychobiology and Section on Neuropsychopharmacology, Adult Psychiatry Branch; Section on Clinical Neuropharmacology, Laboratory of Clinical Science

Man Years:

Total:	1.5
Professional:	1.0
Other:	0.5

Project Description:

Objectives: To develop a treatment and research program for drug abuse. The ability of lithium and AMPT (alpha-methyl-para-tyrosine) to block the euphoria associated with amphetamine, cocaine, heroin, marijuana, alcohol, and barbiturates will be studied in experienced drug users.

Methods Employed: Drug treatment centers have been informed about the development of the drug abuse program in the Adult Psychiatry Branch in order to refer patients. A screening questionnaire has been developed. Several potential patients have been interviewed. Protocols are being written for the testing of each drug abuse with each blocking agent. Some protocols have been approved by the Food and Drug Administration, some are under consideration by the FDA, and some are being written. Informed consent documents are being developed for each protocol.

Major Findings: This is a developmental phase. Patients will be admitted to the program shortly.

Significance to Biomedical Research and the Program of the Institute: This study will be useful in testing the ability of lithium and AMPT to block the euphoria associated with drug abuse, and may therefore result in more effective treatment of drug addicts. Additional information about the neurochemical mode of action may lead to additional effective treatments. Information about the euphoria associated with drugs of abuse may aid in the treatment of the naturally occurring abnormalities in mood states, such as the manic-depressive illness.

Proposed Course of Project: Experienced drug users will be admitted to the psychiatric units of the NIH Clinical Center in order to study and test the usefulness of administering lithium and AMPT as agents in blocking the euphoria associated with drugs of abuse. We anticipate developing an effective treatment methodology in helping addicts withdraw from drugs.

Honors and Awards: None

PUblications; None

Project No. Z01 MH 00070-02 AP
1. Adult Psychiatry Branch
2. Section on Psychobiology
3. Bethesda, Maryland 20014

PHS-ADAMHA-NIMH
Individual Project Report
July 1, 1974 through June 30, 1975

Project Title: Psychological and biological interactions in manic-depressive and schizophrenic psychoses

Previous Serial Number: M-AP (C)-22-1

Principal Investigator: Robert M. Post

Other Investigators: David Jimerson, Robert Gerner, Harvey Fernbach

Collaborating Scientists: W. E. Bunney, Jr., F.K. Goodwin, J.C. Gillin, Monte Buchsbaum, D. Van Kammen

Psychiatric Consultants: H.A. Meyersberg, J. Smith, E. Silber

Cooperating Units: Nursing personnel on 3-West and Occupational Therapist (Eleanor Stapin, 1/2 time), Social Work personnel (Robert Savard); and Psychologist Elizabeth Sherwood

Man Years: Total 6.7
Professional 5.2
Other 1.5

Project Description:

Objectives and Strategies Employed: The objectives of the program in the broadest sense include the precise delineation of the psychological and biological determinants and concomitants of the major psychoses. A guiding principle of our clinical research program is that not only do biological variables affect behavior, but behavior can exert profound influences on biology as well. Such an interaction makes the separation of state-dependent and state-independent biological concomitants of psychosis and the assessment of primary and secondary relationships imperative to an understanding of the role of a given biological variable in a psychiatric disorder. Longitudinal study of the patient during an acute episode, the process of recovery, and during the "well interval" helps clarify such interactions. Behavioral-biological relationships can also be teased out more systematically using animals models of the psychoses. In this fashion, environmental events, including biochemical and psychological stresses, can be manipulated and their effects on behavior assessed. Thus, an active animal bio-behavioral research laboratory is maintained for testing and generating new hypotheses regarding etiology and treatment of the major psychoses, as well as the development of new techniques for their study.

Methods Employed:

1. Patients with manic-depressive illness and schizophrenia, who meet formal research diagnostic criteria developed by the American Psychiatric Association, and modified by Spitzer, et al., are admitted to the Section on Psychobiology, 3-West Clinical Research Unit for intensive treatment and study. Precise behavioral and biochemical data are collected on a longitudinal basis during drug-free evaluation periods, as well as during different psychological and pharmacological treatments.

2. The physicians on the unit see patients in individual psychotherapy two to three times weekly, as well as in group therapy three times a week. Precise records of individual therapy sessions are recorded and patients are rated on global items as well as on a Brief Psychiatric Rating Scale. A clinical case presentation conference is held weekly by the clinical associates in collaboration with Arnold Meyersberg. Clinical associates in addition have two hours a week of individual supervision with consultants and the unit chief. Patient care and research issues are discussed in a weekly three hour staff conference. A social worker or psychologist maintains close contact with families and spouses of patients and obtains detailed family and genetic histories. Where indicated, spouses or members of the family are seen in conjoint therapy.

3. Behavioral Data. Patients are rated twice daily by a trained nursing team on global items of depression, mania, anxiety, psychosis, and anger, as well as on a detailed 34-item scale designed to distinguish precise subcategories of altered cognitive and affective function. For procedures involving acute changes in behavior, patients are rated on a two-hourly basis. In addition, patients rate themselves on a variety of items on a twice daily basis so that subjective changes and diurnal mood fluctuations can be compared with objective nurses' ratings and be used for assessment of drug response. Videotaped records of selected clinical interviews are obtained for evaluation of the patient and his response to treatment.

4. Telemetric Activity Study. The level of physical activity of selected patients is monitored longitudinally by means of a telemetric system which provides continuous read out of activity counts 24-hours per day. This system, which has proved effective in dissecting out the relationship of biological variables to motor activity and clinical state, is being updated and redesigned in collaboration with the Plant Engineering Branch.

5. Electrophysiological data is collected on a longitudinal basis using all-night EEG sleep monitoring techniques in collaboration with J.C. Gillin. In addition, patient's cortical evoked potentials and sensory thresholds are studied during various phases of their hospitalization in collaboration with Monte Buchsbaum.

6. Biochemical Data.

a. Aliquots of 24-hour urine specimens are collected for measurement of biogenic amines, metabolites, and electrolytes. The pineal neurohumor, melatonin, is being measured in collaboration with R. Wurtman.

b. Assessment of neuroendocrine function, receptor sensitivity, and competency of the biogenic amine systems is being assessed by measuring various endocrine parameters in blood. Assays are being performed for prolactin luteinizing hormone, growth hormone, follicle stimulating hormone, in collaboration with J. Skylar.

c. Systematic assessment of electrolytes in blood, urine, and cerebrospinal fluid is carried out.

d. Measurement of amine metabolites in cerebrospinal fluid is conducted during baseline drug-free intervals and during various treatments. 5-Hydroxyindoleacetic acid (5HIAA) and homovanillic acid (HVA) are measured by fluorometric techniques and 3-methoxy-4-hydroxyphenyl glycol (MHPG) and vanillylmandelic acid (VMA) are measured by gas chromatographic and mass fragmentographic techniques respectively. In this fashion assessment of serotonin, dopamine, and norepinephrine metabolism can be made. Cyclic AMP and cyclic GMP, which may provide reflections of receptor function in the central nervous system, are also measured in cerebrospinal fluid.

e. In order to measure a more dynamic aspect of central amine metabolism, amine-metabolites (5HIAA and HVA) in CSF are measured after probenecid administration. Since probenecid blocks the outflow of these metabolites, their accumulation in CSF reflects "amine turnover."

7. Pharmacological Studies. Drugs with known antidepressant, antimanic, and antipsychotic efficacy, such as lithium carbonate, as well as other experimental compounds, are administered on a "double-blind" basis utilizing identical placebo substitution. The mechanism of action of these drugs can then be systematically studied by the above techniques. Agents with relatively specific pharmacological effects on the central nervous system are also being administered in therapeutic trials. In this regard, the noradrenergic receptor stimulator, clonidine, and the dopamine receptor stimulator, piribedil, are being administered to selectively test amine hypotheses of the major psychoses.

8. Sleep Deprivation Studies. The effect of one night's sleep deprivation on mood and amine metabolism is systematically assessed in patients with different levels of depression. Paradoxically, marked antidepressant response has been associated with one night's sleep deprivation in severely depressed patients.

9. Cognitive and memory studies are conducted in collaboration with H. Weingartner in order to assess state-dependent learning during different psychiatric states and in relation to therapeutic response.

10. Pharmacological Interviews. Focused interviews by a "blind" physician are conducted during intravenous administration of amphetamine and placebo in order to provide diagnostic clarification, to develop a possible predictor of subsequent pharmacological response, and evaluate the effects of stimulants on mood.

11. Animal models. An active primate facility is maintained in collaboration with the Laboratory of Clinical Science for the development of new methodologies and detailed assessment of cerebrospinal fluid techniques employed in clinical assessment of patients. A series of ongoing studies of chronic stimulant administration to monkeys are in progress, in order to provide a pharmacological model for affective and schizophreniform behavior, since chronic stimulant use in humans has been associated with profound affective changes and the development of a syndrome very closely resembling paranoid schizophrenia. Studies are also being conducted on the effects of cocaine and related compounds on the progressive development of hyperactivity, stereotypy, and seizures in other animals as a model for the progressive development of pathological behavior in man.

Major Findings:

A. Studies of receptor function.

1. Clonidine, which specifically stimulates norepinephrine receptors has been shown to be an antidepressant in some patients while, contrary to current theoretical formulations, it appears to exacerbate schizophrenic symptomatology. These findings lend additional support to the role of norepinephrine in depression, but also suggests its possible involvement in schizophrenia. These data and others, question the utility of hypotheses of single neurotransmitter deficits in single illnesses and suggest that multiple neurotransmitter alterations may be implicated in a given clinical syndrome.

2. Piribedil, which specifically stimulates dopamine receptors, has been associated with antidepressant effects in patients with affective illness. While, in sensitive or predisposed patients, it may activate mania, it also may be associated with antimanic effects at low doses. Manic behavior may be suppressed by the administration of pimozide, a compound which relatively specifically blocks dopamine receptors. Thus, pharmacological alterations in dopaminergic receptor function can be closely linked to manic illness and its treatment.

3. Cyclic AMP and cyclic GMP have been measured in cerebrospinal fluid and C-AMP has been shown, in contrast to urinary studies, to be slightly elevated, rather than reduced, in depression. Both compounds have been shown to increase dramatically after probenecid administration and such measurements may provide an index of central nervous system receptor function in man. Preliminary data suggest that lithium may affect the probenecid-induced accumulation of cyclic AMP and GMP.

B. Amine metabolism in patients with affective illness and schizophrenia.

CSF metabolite studies have documented that norepinephrine metabolism may be reduced in some depressed patients, while it is not different than controls in mania, schizoaffective illness, and schizophrenia. Although this data is consistent with the catecholamine hypothesis of affective illness, recent data suggest that decreases in norepinephrine metabolism may reflect a predisposing or state-independent biological change in depressed patients, possibly reflecting a trait or marker for depression-prone patients rather than a specific relationship to depression per se.

In collaboration with W. Carpenter and E. Fink we have demonstrated decreased HVA accumulations in patients recovered from acute schizophrenic episodes. Again, one interpretation is that reduced dopamine turnover may occur in patients who are predisposed to the illness. While alternative explanations are possible, many non-specific effects can be ruled out since patients recovered from other acute episodes, such as mania, do not have a reduction in dopamine turnover. This finding, if substantiated by further work, would have very significant implications for the diagnosis and treatment of schizophrenic patients and is consistent with a wide body of data suggesting that dopamine function may be altered in schizophrenic patients.

The phenothiazine compounds with known antipsychotic efficacy have been demonstrated to increase dopamine turnover in manic and schizophrenic patients. For the first time in man, tolerance phenomena to these compounds have been demonstrated. While patients studied early in the course of phenothiazine treatment have substantial elevations in HVA accumulations, those studied later in the course of phenothiazine administration have reduced or no HVA accumulation compared with baseline levels. This evidence of tolerance to the neurochemical effects of the phenothiazines on the dopamine system in the face of lack of tolerance to the clinical antipsychotic effects of the phenothiazines, represents an important clinical and theoretical issue for further study. The data may indicate that both pre- and post-synaptic dopamine mechanisms are maximally reduced with chronic phenothiazines, possibly coinciding with the time course of maximum antipsychotic effects.

Similar time-dependent effects of the tricyclic antidepressant compounds have been demonstrated on the accumulation of 5HIAA in cerebrospinal fluid of depressed patients. Reduction in serotonin turnover is more marked early in treatment of the tricyclics compared to those patients studied later. Study of such long-term biological changes are of critical importance in psychiatry because of the observations that the behavioral effects of various psychotropic drugs often take weeks to months before they become fully manifest. Thus, the intensive study of the chronic, adaptive, and compensatory biological changes induced by pharmacological treatments may be most relevant to the elucidation of behavioral-biological relationships.

All of the treatments associated with acute antidepressant effects have been demonstrated to reduce serotonin turnover utilizing the cerebrospinal fluid probenecid technique. The tricyclic antidepressants (amitriptyline and imipramine) as well as lithium, and electroconvulsive shock therapy all decrease 5HIAA, while the major antipsychotic treatments such as clorpromazine, thioridazine, and pimozide, all substantially increase HVA accumulations. Thus, there is consistent pharmacological differentiation of the therapeutic tools utilized in the treatment of the depressive versus manic and schizophrenic disorders.

Measurement of the accumulation of amine metabolites in cerebrospinal fluid may be of value in predicting subsequent clinical response to pharmacological treatment. Patients with low accumulations of 5HIAA and HVA in CSF tend to respond to antidepressant effects of lithium, while patients with higher accumulation of these metabolites tend to be better responders to the tricyclic antidepressants.

The new finding that depressed women have higher 5HIAA and HVA accumulations in cerebrospinal fluid than do men may be of particular significance since females have a much higher incidence of depression than males.

Quantitative measurement of patient's psychomotor activity by telemetric device has revealed substantial differences in activity during depressed compared to manic and schizophreniform states. In addition, we have documented with these measurements that urinary MHPG varies with affective state independently of its relationship to motor activity. This is the first documentation that this biochemical measure of central norepinephrine metabolism can be reliably related to mood and dissociated from secondary variables such as activity.

C. Studies of specific antipsychotic compounds.

A new neuroleptic, pimozide, has been shown to be the most specific of the currently used neuroleptic treatments in blocking dopamine receptors (although it does affect norepinephrine-induced increases in cyclic AMP in the limbic system). This drug, with relatively selective dopamine receptor blocking function has been shown to be efficacious in patients with manic disorders and of some value in the treatment of acute schizophrenia. Its lack of a full therapeutic spectrum in the acute schizophrenic syndrome again suggests that neurotransmitter systems other than dopamine may be involved in such psychopathology.

D. Sleep deprivation studies.

In the most severely depressed patients one night's experimental sleep deprivation is associated with profound, global antidepressant effects usually lasting one day. After one night's recovery of sleep most patients return to their baseline depressed state or rebound to a more intense level of depression. The acute antidepressant response and subsequent return to baseline depression provide a model for the study of the rapid offset and onset of depressive illness. The sleep deprivation procedure produces changes in the diurnal rhythms of patients' mood, electrolytes, temperature, and related parameters. One hypothesis is that it is the disruption of these circadian patterns and abnormal rhythms that may be responsible for the onset and offset of the antidepressant response. The sleep deprivation procedure may also be of help in diagnosis and prediction of subsequent responders to other therapeutic modalities.

E. Electrolyte studies.

Decreases in both serum and cerebrospinal fluid calcium have been documented during and following successful electroconvulsive shock therapy of depression. Significant decreases in CSF calcium have also been documented following sleep deprivation. A wide variety of antidepressant treatments alter calcium metabolism and recently several patients with episodic or cyclic mood disorders have been shown to have concomitant fluctuations in serum calcium. A calcium mechanism may serve as a marker or, less likely, a pace-setter of the cyclic mechanism involved in these disorders. Alteration in behavior and calcium can be dissociated, however, since it has been demonstrated that the behavioral changes can be successfully treated pharmacologically while the underlying calcium cycles persist for some time. Preliminary evidence suggests that lithium may interfere with the calcium cycles.

The section has continued to document that lithium carbonate has acute antidepressant effects as well as its better known prophylactic efficacy in manic-depressive illness. Preliminary studies have demonstrated that serum calcium-magnesium ratios are predictive of subsequent antidepressant response to lithium and that early assessment of antidepressant responders can be made from the initial increases of calcium and/or magnesium during the first five days of lithium treatment.

In order to further clarify the role of calcium metabolism in the mood disorders, a hypercalcemic agent, parathormone, is being administered to patients on and off lithium, and a hypocalcemic agent, thyrocalcitonin, will also be studied. Preliminary evidence suggests that significant increases in serum calcium can be produced without inducing major alterations in mood in depressed patients.

F. Stimulants.

Patients with affective illness experience marked affective changes in response to intravenously administered amphetamine. Mood elevation, activation, and hypertalkativeness, have been produced in some depressed patients, while others experience an affective catharsis with tearful reminiscences. Depressed patients have a marked reduction in total sleep the night following the infusion. Amphetamine responses in patients with schizoaffective and schizophrenic illnesses have been more variable, but clearly distinguished from those in patients with affective disorders in that no major sleep reduction is produced. Thus, amphetamine infusions may serve as a diagnostic and therapeutic adjuvant, as well as helping predict subsequent pharmacological responsiveness. It is significant that affective responses are produced by the same drugs (amphetamine and cocaine) that can produce a schizophreniform disorder when taken chronically by addicts.

In order to clarify the behavioral-biology of this progression from affective to schizophreniform symptomatology, cocaine has been administered chronically to rhesus monkeys. Striking behavioral changes evolve with chronic administration. Initially monkeys display hyperactivity and stereotypy in response to cocaine, but after three to five weeks of administration, animals enter an inhibitory phase characterized by catalepsy (catatonic-like waxy flexibility) and abnormal glancing and visual tracking of non-existent objects. Concomitantly with this transition from an activated to an inhibitory state with many bizarre behaviors, the cocaine seizure thresholds decreases. Thus, there is clear-cut evidence for increasing effects of cocaine over time, a concept which contrasts with the generally accepted notion that chronic administration of the stimulants is associated with tolerance. Progressive development of bizarre behavior and seizures has also been documented with chronic lidocaine administration. Animals treated with lidocaine indiscriminately place objects in their mouth and display coprophagia, apparently very like that described by Arieti in chronic, "terminal stage" schizophrenics.

The cocaine and lidocaine models for increasing effects of a drug over time may have important implications for the development of psychopathology in patients. These drug models may help conceptualize a mechanism by which intermittent and repetitive stress in psychiatric patients may be associated with progressive alterations in limbic system function critical for normal emotional and cognitive function. These pharmacological models for the psychoses may help in the development of new conceptual frameworks integrating biochemical, physiological, and neuroanatomical approaches to behavior. Such models for the progressive development of pathological behavior are also consonant with our clinical observations of considerable overlap in affective and schizophreniform symptomatology in the major psychoses. A continuum model for affective and schizophreniform behavioral changes has thus been suggested on the basis of a variety of clinical and pharmacological data.

Psychobiology: In collaboration with Dr. Arnold Meyersburg current psychological and biological observations are being integrated with more classical analytic concepts in the hopes of documenting that the two major approaches to current psychiatric theory and practice are not mutually exclusive but are parallel and interrelated ways of viewing the same phenomena. Possible neurobiological mechanisms and substrates for analytic concepts such as fixation, regression, and unconscious determinants are being suggested. In a similar fashion, detailed clinical observations of patients with psychotic disorders are being related to disorders with known biological determinants, such as Parkinson's Disease. Comparison of psychiatric and neurological syndromes may provide the basis for understanding similarities in neurochemical and neuroanatomical deficits in these illnesses.

Proposed Course of the Project: The Section on Psychobiology will continue its multiphase study of manic-depressive illness and schizophrenia and their treatments. Studies of specific receptor stimulating drugs and the role of receptor sensitivity changes in psychiatric illness will be continued. The study of neuroendocrine, electrolyte, and amine mechanisms in these illnesses will also be pressed further. In addition, new emphasis will be placed on models for the acute psychoses and particularly the phenomena of tolerance and reverse tolerance or increased sensitivity to a drug over time. The psychopharmacology of stimulant and narcotic induced mood changes will be studied with particular emphasis placed on investigation of drugs, such as lithium carbonate, which may block these effects and be of therapeutic value in the treatment of patients addicted to stimulants and narcotics. Major focus will continue to be given to the interaction of multiple neurotransmitters in relationship to each other in the different psychiatric illnesses, rather than previously emphasized "one drug-one neurotransmitter models" of psychoses. Study of patients in different phases of their illness will be continued in order to try to assess state-dependent and state-independent variables, as well as acute versus chronic compensatory changes following pharmacological treatments.

Particular focus will be given to the study of biological variables which may predict subsequent therapeutic response to a specific pharmacological treatment. New treatment strategies will be initiated, such as the study of specific electrolyte manipulations in affective illness (thyrocalcitonin), investigation of the possible antipsychotic effects of diazepam and clozapine, and the alteration of receptor site sensitivity as a method for potentiating antidepressant responses to the tricyclics.

Honors and Awards:

Dr. Post will present two papers at the Annual Meeting of the American Psychiatric Association in Anaheim, California entitled "A Dopamine receptor stimulator in depression" and "Cocaine, kindling, and psychosis." He is also the co-author on two other papers being presented at this meeting including studies of vanillylmandelic acid in cerebrospinal fluid and the effects of sleep deprivation on mood.

Dr. Gerner will present the paper relating to sleep deprivation entitled "Antidepressant effects of sleep deprivation" at the Annual Meetings.

Dr. Jimerson will also present the fourth paper at the American Psychiatric Meetings entitled "Central norepinephrine function in man: VMA in CSF."

At the Society of Biological Psychiatry in New York on May 30th, a paper entitled "Progressive effects of cocaine on behavior and central amine metabolism in rhesus monkeys" is being presented by R. Kopanda and Dr. Post.

Dr. Post was also an invited lecturer at the Symposium on Anxiety and Depression, Jan. 27-31, 1975, in New Orleans, Louisiana by the Division of Mental Health of the State of Louisiana. The title of his talk was "New developments in the psychopharmacology of the depressive disorders." At this lecture, Dr. Post was awarded an honorary State Senatorship for his contribution to the symposium. Dr. Post was an invited lecturer at the Washington School of Psychiatry for a special course and gave a lecture entitled "Treatment of the affective disorders." He was also an invited co-presenter of a paper at the 54th Annual Meeting of the Association for Research in Nervous and Mental Disease (ARNMD), New York, December, 1974.

Project No. ZOI MH 00070-02 AP

Key Words

manic-depressive illness
schizophrenia
psychomotor activity
behavioral rating
neurophysiology
sleep deprivation
antidepressants
neuroleptics
lithium
amine metabolites
cerebrospinal fluid
electrolytes
stimulant model psychoses
receptor stimulators
neuroendocrine
cyclic nucleotides

Publications:

Post, R.M., and Goodwin, F.K.: Studies of cerebrospinal fluid amine metabolites in depressed patients: Conceptual problems and theoretical implications. In Biological Aspects of Depression, J. Mendels (Ed), Spectrum Publications, 1974.

Post, R.M., and Goodwin, F.K.: Estimation of brain amine metabolism in affective illness: Cerebrospinal fluid studies utilizing probenecid. Psychother. Psychosom. 23: 142-158 (1974).

Carman, J.S., Post, R.M., Teplitz, T.A., and Goodwin, F.K.: Divalent cations in predicting antidepressant response to lithium. Lancet ii: 1454 (1974).

Goodwin, F.K., and Post, R.M.: Brain serotonin, affective illness, and antidepressant drugs: Cerebrospinal fluid with probenecid. In: Advances in Biochemical Psychopharmacology, Raven Press, New York, Vol. 11, 1974.

Gillin, J.C., Post, R.M., Stoddard, F.J., Snyder, F., and Bunney, W.E., Jr: Changes in sleep and activity in a bipolar patient with regualrly occurring manic and depressive phases. In: Sleep Research, Chase, M.H., Stern, W.C., Walter, P.L. (Eds), Vol. 3, Brain Information Service/Brain Research Institute, University of California, Los Angeles, 1974. p. 124.

Post, R.M., and Kopanda, R.T.: Cocaine, kindling, and reverse tolerance. Lancet i: 409-410, 1975.

Post, R.M.: Cocaine psychoses: A continuum model. Am. J. Psychiatry 132: 225-231 (1975).

Post, R.M., Fink, E., Carpenter, W.T., and Goodwin, F.K.: Cerebrospinal fluid amine metabolites in acute schizophrenia. Arch. Gen. Psychiatry, in press.

Post, R.M., Kotin, J., and Goodwin, F.K.: Effects of sleep deprivation on mood and central amine metabolism in depressed patients. Arch. Gen. Psychiatry, in press.

Goodwin, F.K., and Post, R.M.: Studies of amine metabolites in affective illness and in schizophrenia: A comparative analysis. In: The Biology of the Major Psychoses: A Comparative Analysis, D.X. Freedman (Ed), Raven Press, New York, 1975, in press.

Project No. Z01 MH 00045-01 AP
1. Adult Psychiatry Branch
2. Section on Neuropsychopharmacology
3. Bethesda, Maryland

PHS-NIMH
Individual Project Report
July 1, 1974 through June 30, 1975

Project Title: Cortical Laterality and Psychological Functioning

Previous Serial Number: NONE

Principal Investigators: Samuel Siris, M.D.
John Docherty, M.D.

Other Investigators: Daniel P. van Kammen, M.D.
Monte Buchsbaum, M.D.

Cooperating Units: Unit on Perceptual and Cognitive Studies, APB

Man Years:

Total:	0.4
Professional:	0.2
Other:	0.2

Project Description:

This project aims at investigating differences which may exist between the two cerebral hemispheres in processing basic informational input. Investigations in post-commissurotomy patients have demonstrated a capacity for striking independence of function in the two hemispheres. This study represents an attempt, utilizing average-evoked-response techniques, to demonstrate discrepancies of function of the hemispheres in the intact brain which could have relevance to clinical psychiatric syndromes. Specifically studied are habituation, contrast effect, and augmentation to light stimuli under varying attentional sets: light attention, sound attention, verbal attention (dominant hemisphere task) and spacial attention (nondominant hemisphere task).

Series of normal controls who are right-handed and have only right-handed first-degree relatives are tested on two separate days. Active electrode placements are over the right and left Warnicke's area with the ipsilateral ear as a reference electrode.

Preliminary data indicates greater stimulus response to light over the dominant hemisphere, while there is greater response to sound over the minor hemisphere. Differences in contrast effect, with the minor hemisphere being more responsive to the absolute stimulus magnitude and the dominant hemisphere more responsive to the relative magnitude, are suggested.

Many of the clinical phenomena of schizophrenia could be explained by the model of information of one cerebral hemisphere inappropriately intruding int the other. Interruptions of the normal patterns of verbal production and affectivity could be explained on this basis as could misinterpretations of various pieces of intrapsychic content for external reality (i.e., secondary symptoms as hallucinations and delusions). In this study, reproducible electrophysiological correlates of normally occurring lateral specialization are being sought which could then be used to study possibly deviant functioning o these mechanisms in the schizophrenic population.

A larger series of normal controls is being evaluated. If reproducible electrophysiological correlates of lateral specialization are found, studies will be initiated with schizophrenic and other psychiatric patients.

Keyword Descriptors:

Laterality, AER, attention, Warnicke's area, habituation, contrast, augmentation.

Project No. Z01 MH 00046-01 AP
1. Adult Psychiatry Branch
2. Section on Neuropsychopharmacology
3. Bethesda, Maryland

PHS-NIMH
Individual Project Report
July 1, 1974 through June 30, 1975

Project Title: Endocrine Effects of Pimozide

Previous Serial Number: NONE

Principal Investigators: John Docherty, M.D.
Samuel Siris, M.D.
Ethel Siris, M.D.
Daniel P. van Kammen, M.D.
William E. Bunney, Jr., M.D.

Cooperating Unit: 4-East Nursing Unit, Clinical Center, NIMH

Man Years:

Total:	.15
Professional:	.10
Other:	.05

Project Description:

The purpose of these studies is to examine hypothalamic-pituitary function in male and female schizophrenic patients and to determine the effects of pimozide, a central dopamine receptor blocker, on this function. Pituitary hormones, including growth hormone (hGH), prolactin (hPRL), follicle stimulating hormone (hFSH) and luteinizing hormone (hLH), appear to be controlled by hypothalamic releasing and inhibiting factors, which are in turn mediated by monoamines, including dopamine. Since a central dopamine hyperactivity has been postulated as a mechanism for schizophrenia, an attempt to examine hypothalamic-pituitary function in untreated and in pimozide treated patients seems warranted. Alterations in hormonal control, if they exist, might serve as endocrine markers of the disease, might help to explain certain behavioral manifestations of the illness, and more generally might serve to define physiologically some aspects of the role of dopamine in hormonal regulation.

Currently, two projects are in progress. Daily 24-hour urines are being collected on all patients to be assayed for hFSH and hLH; such samples over a long period of time--both in untreated and in treated states--should offer a good estimation of gonadotropin activity in schizophrenia. A second project involves serial sampling of blood in the basal state to determine baseline serum levels of hFSH, hLH, hGH, and hPRL in schizophrenic patients.

The urine samples obtained thus far have been held for assay and results will be forthcoming. Serum levels of the hormones listed have been obtained in 5 patients off therapy and initial review of the data shows the levels to be within normal limits for hPRL and hGH. The data on hFSH and hLH is as yet not conclusive for normality.

The dopamine hypothesis of schizophrenia is one of major current interest and requires physiologic testing. Alterations in levels of pituitary hormones or in their response to provocative testing in patients with schizophrenia might reflect a disturbance in control secondary to excess dopamine, and might further offer a marker to be followed in treatment. In addition, it is important to investigate the endocrine effects of drugs such as pimozide, in search of markers which might define effective dopamine blockade by the drug. Finally, as noted earlier, such testing may reveal new information on endocrine regulation and in a more general way be of great usefulness to the endocrinologist.

Following assessment of basal levels of the four pituitary hormones in untreated and pimozide treated patients, it is hoped that we can perform prolactin tests, including use of luteinizing hormone releasing hormone (LHRH) to measure response of hFSH and hLH, use of L-DOPA as a blocker of hPRL and stimuli for hGH release, and use of thyrotropin releasing hormone (TRH) to assay hPRL release in these patients. It is possible that basal levels of hormones may not be altered in schizophrenia, but response to provocative tests may well be abnormal.

A second proposed project would entail monitoring of serum levels of these pituitary hormones during sleep, to compare response of our patients on and off drug with the human nocturnal and/or sleep related patterns of secretion.

Key Descriptors:

Acute schizophrenia, hypothalamic-pituitary function, FSH, LH, prolactin, growth hormone, pimozide.

Project No. Z01 MH 00047-01 AP
1. Adult Psychiatry Branch
2. Section on Neuropsychopharmacology
3. Bethesda, Maryland

PHS-NIMH
Individual Project Report
July 1, 1974 through June 30, 1975

Project Title: Schizophrenic Thought Disorder: A Quantitative Study of Information Processing Disturbance

Previous Serial Number: NONE

Principal Investigators: John Docherty, M.D.
Herbert Weingartner, Ph.D.

Other Investigators: Daniel P. van Kammen, M.D.
Samuel Siris, M.D.

Man Years:

Total:	0.2
Professional:	0.1
Other:	0.1

Project Description:

(1) Most generally we are attempting to observe the phenomenon of cognitive disorder in schizophrenia from the vantage point of a theory generated to account for normal information-processing, and emphasizing the measurable organization and recall of experience.

(2) More specifically we are attempting to take into account the important, salient, but little understood observation that disordered thinking in schizophrenics is not a constant phenomenon, and we are trying to specify some of the conditions determining the appearance or disappearance of cognitive dysfunction.

(3) We are interested in observing the effects of (a) treatment with psychoactive drugs and (b) different phases of the illness upon this quantified measure of thought disorder.

(4) We also plan to test family members of schizophrenic patients to determine the presence and degree of disordered thinking in these relatives.

A card-sorting task has been devised to provide a measure of information processing activity. Two decks of cards have been generated: I. The first deck is a set of 32 highly-structured words. There are 4 words from each of 8 toxonomic categories. II. The second deck consists of 32 random, common words.

The subjects are given a deck and asked within a 5-minute time limit to assign each word to a category. They are told that they may form as many or as few categories as they choose. Following trial a record is made of the imposed organization; the cards are collected, and the subjects are asked to recall the words.

We have analyzed the results of this procedure with 10 acute schizophrenic patients and with 10 normal controls. The results are very encouraging. For this sample (a) there was no difference in the pattern of organization used for the highly-structured deck. (b) However, there was no overlap between the groups for the unstructured deck. The normal subjects organized the cards into 5-6 categories; the schizophrenic subjects into 9-12 categories.

Using the information processing model an Uncertainty Analysis was performed on these data, which yielded highly significant findings: (a) Both the schizophrenics and normals reduced the 5-bit uncertainty of the highly-structured deck to approximately 2.28 bits. (b) For the unstructured deck, the normals reduced the uncertainty to 1.98 bits; the schizophrenics to only 3.28 (an amount in excess of channel capacity). This difference was significant at $p < .001$. Also, (c) cluster analysis of the recall sequence revealed that the structure imposed on the words in the sorting was reflected in the recall.

Key Descriptors:

Acute schizophrenia, information processing (human, abnormal), thought disorder, cognition.

Project No. Z01 MH 00049-01 AP
1. Adult Psychiatry Branch
2. Section on Neuropsychopharmacology
3. Bethesda, Maryland

PHS-NIMH
Individual Project Report
July 1, 1974 through June 30, 1975

Project Title: Psychosocial Aspects of the Progression of Malignant Melanoma

Previous Serial Number: NONE

Principal Investigators: Nicholas Rogentine, M.D.
John Docherty, M.D.
William E. Bunney, Jr., M.D.

Other Investigators: Daniel P. van Kammen, M.D.
William D. Terry, M.D.
Enser Cole, M.D.
Steven Rosenberg, M.D.

Cooperating Units: National Cancer Institute

Man Years:

Total: 0.5
Professional: 0.3
Other: 0.2

Project Description:

This study is aimed at developing a detailed characterization of the psychosocial factors which distinguish those patients who suffer recurrence of malignancy from those who remain disease-free or who have a delayed recurrence. Data is to be gathered which will permit the testing of several current hypotheses concerning psychosocial antecedents of the onset of physical illness and predisposing psychobiological states.

Fifty to 100 patients with "surgically-cured" Stage II Melanoma will be studied. We plan a multi-level assessment of each patient. In addition to the biological measures gathered on the patient, we will characterize the patient's genetic history, past psychosocial history, level of personality development, current life stress and present psychological state. We will accomplish this by (1) psychiatric interview; (2) objective assessment of a 5-minute speech sample, and (3) standardized questionnaires including MMPI, Holmes and Rahe Schedule of Recent Experience, SCL-90, Rotter Internal-External Locus of Control Scale, and Beck Depression Inventory.

The patients will be seen shortly after their "curative" surgery and will be followed up at 2-month intervals, at which time we will obtain the Holmes-Rahe

Scale, the SCL-90, Helplessness-Hopelessness Index and Beck Depression Inventory.

Keyword Descriptors:

Melanoma, psychosomatics, disease onset, psychological precursors of illness.

Project No. Z01 MH 00050-01 AP
1. Adult Psychiatry Branch
2. Section on Neuropsychopharmacology
3. Bethesda, Maryland

PHS-NIMH
Individual Project Report
July 1, 1974 through June 30, 1975

Project Title: Stages of Schizophrenic Psychosis

Previous Serial Number: NONE

Principal Investigators: John P. Docherty, M.D.
William E. Bunney, Jr., M.D.

Other Investigators: Samuel Siris, M.D.
Daniel P. van Kammen, M.D.

Project Description:

An important, although somewhat neglected, feature of schizophrenic decompensation is that it is not a unitary event but rather a multi-staged phenomena. There is, however, no currently available clear definition of these stages.

It is, however, apparent that a clear delineation of these stages is of great importance since it may considerably reduce the variance of numerous indices of the disorder and provide a more powerful method for the differentiation of state vs. trait features of the disorder.

We have, therefore, undertaken a two-part project:

I. We have reviewed the literature which describes staging of onset and resolution of schizophrenic psychosis. We are currently writing up this review including illustrative cases from our own patient population.

One of the major findings of this review led to the second project. Although this literature is not extensive, it is remarkably consistent. Moreover, each of the stages preceding psychotic decompensation can be described in rather easily discriminable form.

II. We have, therefore, developed a list of eight descriptive phases of the schizophrenic decompensation, and each day ask the Nursing Staff to select their first and second choice for the phase which seems to best fit the patient for that day. We have called this the Stage-of-Illness Scale.

Preliminary results indicate that the staff is able to accomplish the stage discrimination readily and that inter-rater reliability is extremely high. Validity studies with other standardized measures will be carried out.

Project No. Z01 MH 00050-01 AP

Keyword Descriptors:

Schizophrenia, psychosis, state of illness, stage of illness, decompensation, phase of illness.

Project No. Z01 MH 00051-01 AP
1. Adult Psychiatry Branch
2. Section on Neuropsychopharmacology
3. Bethesda, Maryland

PHS-NIMH
Individual Project Report
July 1, 1974 through June 30, 1975

Project Title: HL-A Typing in Acute Schizophrenia

Previous Serial Number: NONE

Principal Investigator: Daniel P. van Kammen, M.D.

Other Investigators: Nicholas Rogentine, M.D.
William E. Bunney, Jr., M.D.

Cooperating Units: National Cancer Institute

Man Years:

Total:	0.2
Professional:	0.1
Other:	0.1

Project Description:

HL-A antigens are genetically determined human cell membrane antigens found on a variety of cell types. The genes controlling their expression are found on chromosome 6 and are thought to be linked closely to genes controlling immune responses to a number of antigens. In recent years associations of certain HL-A types and certain diseases have been found. These diseases are frequently those with associated or causal disorders of immunity, possibly the result of aberrant immune response genes--thus their association with HL-A.

Schizophrenia may have causal or secondary immune abnormalities, thus a study of HL-A antigen frequencies in this disease seemed worthwhile. If found, this would constitute more evidence for the role of the immune system in schizophrenia.

To date we have typed 17 patients with acute schizophrenia. Of note in this small series is the elevation in frequency of HL-A2. Twelve of 17 have this antigen whereas in the normal population 8 of 17 would have it. This is significant at about p = .05. More cases are needed to draw any conclusions.

Keyword Descriptors:

HL-A antigens, linkage, schizophrenia.

Project No. Z01 MH 00052-01 AP
1. Adult Psychiatry Branch
2. Section on Neuropsychopharmacology
3. Bethesda, Maryland

PHS-NIMH
Individual Project Report
July 1, 1974 through June 30, 1975

Project Title: Amphetamine in Acute Psychotic Patients With and Without Pimozide Pretreatment and Blood Levels of d-Amphetamine

Previous Serial Number: NONE

Principal Investigator: Daniel P. van Kammen, M.D.

Other Investigators: John Docherty, M.D.
Michael Ebert, M.D.
William E. Bunney, Jr., M.D.

Cooperating Units: Section on Psychobiology, APB
Section on Experimental Therapeutics, LCS

Man Years:

Total: 0.5
Professional: 0.3
Other: 0.2

Project Description:

In order to test the dopamine hypothesis, which states that there is a dopamine receptor sensitivity in schizophrenia, we propose to use a relative selective dopamine receptor blocker, pimozide, as an antipsychotic agent and a relative dopamine agonist, d-amphetamine. d-Amphetamine has been reported to briefly increase psychosis in some psychotic patients but not in others. This could be a test to separate patients with increased dopamine sensitivity from those whose dopamine system is stabilized. The blockade of pimozide would allow us to tease out the rather specific dopamine effects in those patients. Pimozide has been shown in animal studies to block some amphetamine behavior, while some schizophrenic patients did better with the combination.

Patients admitted to the Unit will have one placebo and one amphetamine infusion during the test week, after a two-week period off medication ("washout period"). After a clinical response on pimozide has been established, or after side effects have occurred, patients will have another amphetamine infusion, where double-blind ratings will take place. Behavior observation by nurses and self-rating forms for the patients will be employed. Dr. Ebert will determine the blood levels with a radioimmuno assay developed by him. Blood levels of amphetamine will tell us the influence of metabolism on late effects of the drug compared to depressed patients.

This project has just begun. Four out of six patients who received their amphetamine infusion (20 mg) responded with some increase of psychosis. These four also became dysphoric and displayed some lability of affect, while the other two patients became euphoric, more able to relate to their environment, displaying sensitivity and warmth to other people. The acute effect lasted not longer than 20 minutes and subsided over the next three hours. An interesting finding is the relatively little effect on sleep, while from a previous study d-amphetamine in depressed patients showed a significant decrease in total sleep time and REM sleep.

Presently there are numerous studies showing improvement with amphetamine in psychotic (schizophrenic) patients from 10-75%, which are in contrast with the reports that psychosis can be intensified. This discrepancy will be examined. It may well be that the activation of the dopamine system leads to an increase in psychosis only during the acute phase. Presently we are correlating the stages of the psychosis with the effect of the drug. The effect of pimozide on the response to amphetamine should be able to give us some extra informatio

After collecting our data, we will then compare it with data from other studie done with the same patients, hoping to develop some critical variables which may be state or trait related. Blood level results will be correlated with response and blockading effects of pimozide.

Keyword Descriptors:

Pimozide, d-amphetamine, d-amphetamine blood levels, acute schizophrenia.

Project No. Z01 MH 00053-01 AP
1. Adult Psychiatry Branch
2. Section on Neuropsychopharmacology
3. Bethesda, Maryland

PHS-NIMH
Individual Project Report
July 1, 1974 through June 30, 1975

Project Title: Sleep Parameters in Acute Psychotic Patients With and Without Pimozide, an Antipsychotic Agent

Previous Serial Number: NONE

Principal Investigator: Daniel P. van Kammen, M.D.

Other Investigators: Christian J. Gillin, M.D.
William E. Bunney, Jr., M.D.
John Docherty, M.D.
Samuel Siris, M.D.
Robert M. Post, M.D.

Man Years:

Total:	.04
Professional:	.03
Other:	.01

Project Description:

It has previously been shown that the sleep of acute psychotic patients without medication is disturbed. At the onset of the psychosis, patients frequently do not sleep or they experience disturbed sleep. Pimozide, a relative major dopamine receptor blocking antipsychotic agent, will be studied during the sleep period. Frequently, two to seven days after the drug is discontinued, the sleep of one night is diminished. By using sleep EEG recordings, we will be able to see the influence of this dopamine receptor blocker on the sleep parameters. This may well give us a measure to separate the patients with hypersensitive dopamine receptors from those psychotics without this hyperactive system.

A series of patients presently on the unit and also those who will be admitted over the next year will be put on sleep recordings after a 2 1/2 week drug washout period. Patients will be on pimozide or a matched placebo throughout the recording period. The length of administration will not go beyond two months, and will depend on the clinical efficacy of the drug and occurrence of side effects. After discontinuation of pimozide, patients will continue sleep study for ten days. The medication will be administered in a double-blind placebo-controlled form, in which the patient is his own control.

So far, only the first patient on this project has completed the sleep recording. Three other patients have just started. We have found in most previous patients that sleep dropped from 7 1/2 to 1 hour per night within one to seven days after discontinuation of pimozide.

This method will give us another parameter in the biochemical, neurophysiological profile of the psychotic patients which will be correlated with symptoms, prognostic variables and other biochemical findings to detect diagnostic subgroups with major consequences for drug response.

A larger series of patients will be admitted over the next year. On completion of the data collection, symptom patterns, biochemical data, etc. will be compared to see whether a meaningful relationship exists.

This project interlocks with:

Amphetamine in acutely psychotic patients
Pimozide in acutely psychotic patients
Endocrine effects of pimozide in acutely psychotic patients
Endocrine effects of amphetamine in acutely psychotic patients

(See Projects Z01 MH 00046-01 AP and Z01 MH 00052-01 AP for further details).

Keyword Descriptors:

EEG recorded sleep, acute schizophrenia, pimozide, pimozide withdrawal, amphetamine.

Project No. Z01 MH 00054-01 AP
1. Adult Psychiatry Branch
2. Section on Neuropsychopharmacology
3. Bethesda, Maryland

PHS-NIMH
Individual Project Report
July 1, 1974 through June 30, 1975

Project Title: CSF Amine Metabolites in Acutely Schizophrenic Patients

Previous Serial Number: NONE

Principal Investigators: Daniel P. van Kammen, M.D.
Robert M. Post, M.D.

Other Investigators: William E. Bunney, Jr., M.D.
David Jimerson, M.D.

Cooperating Units: Section on Psychobiology, APB

Man Years:

Total:	.25
Professional:	.15
Other:	.10

Project Description:

The objectives of this study are: (1) to utilize the probenecid technique to study dopamine, serotonin and norepinephrine metabolites in acutely psychotic patients; (2) to restudy the same patients when they are recovered.

Consecutively admitted patients are studied during acute psychosis after being off medication for 2-3 weeks. First lumbar puncture (LP) takes place at 8:30 a.m., followed by a second LP at 3:00 p.m. the next day, after 100 mg/kg probenecid over 18 hours pre-LP. The same procedure is repeated after two weeks of medication prior to discharge. Data are collected on psychosocial, behavioral states of illness and other biochemical indices like platelet MAO. Results have not been analyzed yet.

Keyword Descriptors:

Lumbar puncture, CSF, monoamine metabolites, acute schizophrenia.

Project No. Z01 MH 00055-01 AP
1. Adult Psychiatry Branch
2. Section on Neuropsychopharmacology
3. Bethesda, Maryland

PHS-NIMH
Individual Project Report
July 1, 1974 through June 30, 1975

Project Title: Platelet MAO Activity in Schizophrenia

Previous Serial Number: NONE

Principal Investigators: William T. Carpenter, Jr., M.D.
Daniel P. van Kammen, M.D.

Other Investigators: Dennis L. Murphy, M.D.
Richard J. Wyatt, M.D.

Cooperating Units: Section on Clinical Neuropharmacology, LCS
Unit on Sleep Studies, APB

Man Years:

Total: 0.3
Professional: 0.2
Other: 0.1

Project Description:

The object of this study is to determine if platelet MAO activity is impaired in acute schizophrenia and, if so, if it is a state or trait phenomena.

Blood was collected during the third drug-free week while the patient was psychotic. Platelet MAO activity was determined using ^{14}C-tryptamine as substrate as described by Murphy. Sixty-five clinical variables routinely and independently assessed in each patient were recorded. Data analysis was done by diagnostic groups (e.g., schizophrenic versus normal), by diagnostic subgroups (e.g., acute versus chronic), and by dichotomizing the schizophrenic cohort into high normal ($\geq$ 5.0) and low (< 3.0) platelet MAO activity (expressed as nanomoles per milligram per hour).

We found normal monamine oxidase (MAO) activity in 40 acute schizophrenic patients, in contrast to previous reports of a genetically linked platelet MAO deficit in chronic schizophrenia. Variations in MAO activity were not significantly associated with the 65 clinical variables analyzed, although there was a tendency for patients in the low-MAO group to have more severely impaired reality testing, more paranoid and grandiose delusions, better prognostic scores, and less restlessness.

Deficit platelet MAO activity may be a genetic "Tag" for chronic schizophrenia. This study makes it clear that it is not a marker of acute schizophrenia and suggests that platelet MAO activity is not a function of clinical state per se This will guide investigators as to the appropriate application of platelet MAO data.

Keyword Descriptors:

Monamine Oxidase, platelets, enzyme activity, acute schizophrenia, biologic marker of schizophrenia.

Publications:

Carpenter, W.T., Jr., Murphy, D.L. and Wyatt, R.J.: Platelet Monoamine Oxidase Activity in Acute Schizophrenia. Am. J. Psychiatry 132: 438-441 1975.

Project No. Z01 MH 00056-01 AP
1. Adult Psychiatry Branch
2. Section on Neuropsychopharmacology
3. Bethesda, Maryland

PHS-NIMH
Individual Project Report
July 1, 1974 through June 30, 1975

Project Title: Viral Antibodies in Schizophrenic Patients

Previous Serial Number: NONE

Principal Investigator: Daniel P. van Kammen, M.D.

Other Investigators: E. Fuller Torrey, M.D.
William E. Bunney, M.D.
Michael Peterson, M.D.

Cooperating Units: 4-East Nursing Unit, NIMH

Man Years:

Total:	.02
Professional:	.01
Other:	.01

Project Description:

Since slow-growing viruses have been found in diseases like Jacob Creutzfeldt Disease and are suspected in others like multiple sclerosis, there is reason to assume that in psychosis a slow-growing virus may be involved. It has been hypothesized that a panencephalitis as connected with measles could then mediate some of the schizophrenic symptoms.

Patients admitted to the 4-East Unit will have 2 cc of spinal fluid collected during the two admission lumbar punctures and two during discharge testing, which will be tested for antibody titers by Dr. Peterson.

This is a quite different approach to the study of the etiology of schizophrenia. A positive finding would have major implications for treatment and research.

Of the patients studied so far, only one had an increased antibody titer. The study is expected to last five years.

Keyword Descriptors:

Acute schizophrenia, viral antibodies.

Project No. Z01 MH 00058-03 AP
1. Adult Psychiatry Branch
2. Section on Neuropsychopharmacology
3. Bethesda, Maryland

PHS-NIMH
Individual Project Report
July 1, 1974 through June 30, 1975

Project Title: Psychobiology of Cortisol Metabolism

Previous Serial Number: M-AP(C)-16-8

Principal Investigator: William T. Carpenter, Jr., M.D.

Other Investigators: Edward B. Fink, M.D.

Cooperating Units: Unit on Perceptual and Cognitive Studies, APB
Unit on Psychophysiology, LCP

Man Years:

Total:	.20
Professional:	.15
Other:	.05

Project Description:

The objective of this study is to study the interaction between cortisol metabolism, behavior, and psychophysiologic variables in drug-free acute schizophrenic patients.

Cortisol excretion will be estimated by determining urinary output of free cortisol and 17-hydroxycorticosteroids. Standardized clinical assessment techniques are used to gain detailed clinical information. Perception, cognition, and arousal are measured in collaboration with Drs. Zahn and Buchsbaum.

Cortisol metabolism changes with mental state and behavioral changes. Furthermore, alterations in cortisol metabolism affect psychophysiologic responsivity. Thus, it is important to determine whether adrenal cortisol activity underlies or reflects behavioral disturbance, and which is the best predictor of psychophysiologic responsivity.

Studies of cortisol metabolism are being incorporated into the 4-East clinical unit's research program. In keeping with the major thrust of the work on 4-East, there will be careful attention to the clinical variables related to altered steroid metabolism and the possibility of using biological variables such as steroid metabolism as validating criteria to test classification systems. The relationship between cortisol, psychopathology and psychophysiology is being investigated in collaboration with the Laboratory of Psychology. An evaluation of cortisol excretion as a predictor of suicides has been submitted for publication.

Project No. Z01 MH 00058-03 AP

This project terminates 1975.

Keyword Descriptors:

Cortisol, steroids, schizophrenia, suicide, psychophysiology.

Project No. Z01 MH 00059-04 AP
1. Adult Psychiatry Branch
2. Section on Neuropsychopharmacology
3. Bethesda, Maryland

PHS-NIMH
Individual Project Report
July 1, 1974 through June 30, 1975

Project Title: WHO International Pilot Study of Schizophrenia

Previous Serial Number: M-AP(C)-16-1

Principal Investigators: William T. Carpenter, Jr., M.D.
John S. Strauss, M.D.

Other Investigators: John Bartko, Ph.D.
Alan B. Hawk, M.D.

Cooperating Units: Biometrics Branch, NIMH
University of Rochester Medical School
Prince Georges General Hospital
Spring Grove State Hospital
Morris Cafritz Memorial Hospital
World Health Organization and its Field Research Centers in Colombia, Czechoslovakia, Denmark, Great Britain, India, Nigeria, Taiwan, and Union of Soviet Socialist Republics

Man Years:

Total:	2.6
Professional:	1.3
Other:	1.3

Project Description:

The objectives of this study are: (1) To develop standard interview and rating schedules that can be used cross-culturally for the evaluation of psychotic patients. (2) To evaluate a cohort of patients from the catchment area of Prince Georges County, Maryland with these instruments and to compare these findings with similar evaluations being carried out by investigators in eight other psychiatric centers in Colombia, Czechoslovakia, Denmark, Great Britain, India, Nigeria, Taiwan and the USSR. (3) To work toward a consensus with investigators from these other countries about criteria derived from the interview instruments, for classifying patients as schizophrenic. (4) To compare these WHO diagnostic evaluations with clinical evaluations and ratings of the same patients made with other methods such as the Lorr IMPS scale and projective tests. (5) To compare social and demographic data on patients evaluated by the standard instruments to understand more completely how these factors are related to schizophrenia as defined through the use of the standard

Diagnostic Schedules. (6) To compare course of illness in patients from the collaborating centers by conducting a follow-up study on patients seen in the original sample.

Standardized forms have been developed for evaluating mental status, history, social function, and outcome. Initial evaluations were completed using these forms of 135 patients from each center. Data is being analyzed to compare the patients from the nine centers in terms of initial diagnosis, social function, and follow-up status. Alternative diagnostic techniques have been applied to evaluate their validity.

Analysis of variance techniques including the profile analysis of variance and stepwise discriminate function analysis have been used to identify discriminating features of schizophrenic diagnosis and the comparability of the schizophrenic diagnosis and subtype diagnoses across centers. Cluster analytic methods have been used in seeking new diagnostic groupings and an attempt to replicate subtype diagnoses commonly used.

Volume One of the IPSS report has been published. This report described methods and findings of the first phases of the IPSS. These phases include (1) the preparation, translation, pretesting, and revision of the data collection instruments; (2) the application of these instruments to 1,202 patients in nine different centers; (3) the evaluation of reliability of the interview schedules; and (4) diagnostic comparisons of the patients seen in the nine centers.

The preparation and translation of data collection schedules of this kind with collaboration of psychiatrists from nine centers is, in itself, a significant contribution to the methodology available to future cross-cultural studies. In evaluating the applicability and reliability of the schedules, two findings were especially significant. First, it was possible to use the same standardized mental status interview (in translation where necessary) in all of the collaborating centers and reliability of ratings within each of the centers was high. The reliability of the ratings across centers was at a lower but still acceptable level. Because history and social description data had to be collected in different ways in the different centers, and because these data depend so much for their psychiatric significance on the cultural milieu, it was more difficult to evaluate the comparability of these kinds of information from center to center. However, the schedules provided a useful means of collecting these data and represent a first step towards the development of comparable methodology in this area as well.

The comparison of similarities and differences in patient types seen in the different centers has been given considerable attention. The inherent complexity of such a comparison, even of patients within one center, is often underestimated, but was highlighted by the cross-cultural nature of this project. Three different methods for defining diagnostic types were used. The results of these three different methods were then compared. In the first diagnostic method, the interviewing psychiatrist assigned the patient to one of the commonly used clinical diagnostic categories. The categories defined by the

International Classification of Diseases were those most frequently used; however, some centers tended to use special diagnostic categories. Analysis of symptom profiles of the different diagnostic types showed broad similarities across centers for the general diagnostic categories such as schizophrenia and manic-depressive psychosis. It indicated further that patients with some of the common defining characteristics of these diagnostic categories were seen in all centers. Comparison of symptom profiles to diagnostic labels applied by investigators from the centers also clarified many differences in the way in which psychiatrists from different centers used symptom information in reaching a diagnosis.

A second diagnostic method used to analyze the types of patients seen in this study was a computer program developed to simulate clinical diagnoses as they might be made by the psychiatric school led by Kurt Schneider. Using data from the mental status examination and psychiatric history, this computer method (Catego) was able to duplicate, to a large extent, the broad clinical diagnoses such as schizophrenia and psychotic depression given to the patients by the investigators in the centers. This method represents considerable progress in developing a technique for applying diagnoses to patients, which can be applied in different centers with complete reliability.

The third method used for assigning patients to diagnostic categories employed cluster techniques. With these mathematical techniques for defining groups of patients, it was possible to arrive at categorizations that were somewhat similar to both clinical and Catego diagnoses. The cluster techniques also provided a means for defining certain subgroups of patients that were seen in only one or two centers. The results of these three methods were compared and combined to describe basic similarities and differences among patients seen in the different centers.

Data from the IPSS is used in other projects previously described under M-AP(C)-16-3 and 4. Major findings have been (1) that Schneider's first-rank symptoms are discriminating of schizophrenia but fall short of the pathognomonicity claimed; (2) using Schneider's first-rank symptoms to increase the certainty of the schizophrenic diagnosis does not add predictability of poor outcome to the diagnosis of schizophrenia; (3) Langfeldt's diagnostic approach to schizophrenia has been found by a number of investigators to predict poor outcome. In this investigation, we are able to make a clean separation between discriminating symptoms and outcome and fail to find any evidence that Langfeldt's symptoms predict poor outcome; (4) the use of analysis of variance techniques has made it possible to determine the most discriminating symptoms of a schizophrenic diagnosis. A flexible diagnostic approach has been developed using the nine symptoms most discriminating for schizophrenia and three symptoms most discriminating of the nonschizophrenic psychiatric diagnoses. This system has the advantage of giving an estimate of the diagnostic error one could anticipate as well as being based on relatively few items of information that can be obtained with high reliability.

Project No. Z01 MH 00059-04 AP

The Section on Neuropsychopharmacology has evaluated subtypes of schizophrenia using profile analysis of variance. We found that traditionally defined subtypes were not distinguishable using sign and symptom data. The application of cluster analytic techniques has resulted in defining four new subgroups of schizophrenia which are readily distinguished from one another and from traditional subtypes.

In addition to investigating signs and symptoms as diagnostic criteria and as predictors of outcome, we have used correlational, multi-regression, and discriminate function techniques to examine the relationship of prognostic variables with each other and their ability individually and collectively to predict outcome. The major finding is that they are relatively autonomous predictor outcome systems, so that past work performance predicts future work performance but is not a good predictor of overall outcome, and past social adjustment predicts future social adjustment without being a good predictor of work function or general outcome. Past hospitalization predicts future hospitalization and can be generalized, to some extent, as a predictor of total outcome. Past hospitalization, past work performance, and past social adaptation have almost as much predictive power collectively as the entire 17-item prognostic scale.

The five-year follow-up on the IPSS patients was conducted last year. We have successfully replicated findings in the two-year follow-up demonstrating the poor predictive value of a schizophrenic diagnosis, whether made by DSMII criteria, Langfeldt's system, or Schneider's system. Paranoid-nonparanoid status does not predict outcome; neither does the degree of certainty of diagnosis based on our 12-point flexible diagnostic system. At the five-year point, the schizophrenic patients have a slightly worse outcome as a group than the non-schizophrenics. This is largely accounted for by the few patients with extremely poor outcome being placed in a schizophrenic group. An outcome scale has been further developed to include items on the patient's ability to care for himself and an estimate of "fullness of life." All items on the outcome scale have interrater reliability of .75 or better with the overall reliability being .97. Using this data, we have replicated our findings on prediction of outcome. That is, various areas of outcome are only modestly associated, and any single measure (e.g., rehospitalization) is grossly inadequate. The best predictors are found in past history rather than current status information, and predictors tend to be fairly specific (e.g., work history predicts work future) rather than global.

The difficulty in comparing psychiatric patients from different cultures has made it impossible to evaluate accurately the etiological importance of cultural factors in psychiatric disorder. The absence of standard methods for evaluation and diagnosis of psychiatric patients has also made it difficult to compare incidence and prevalence rated in different cultures and to compare usefulness of treatment methods employed in different centers. Until these comparisons can be performed, it is not possible to test many crucial hypotheses regarding the nature and etiology of psychiatric disorders. The difficulties in establishing standard instruments are considerable, not only in the writing and testing of such instruments, but in the extensive negotiations and communications necessary with the various investigators from different countries with diverse backgrounds and orientations. Nevertheless, in this study it has been possible to develop such instruments that can be applied in a useful way in a variety of cultural settings. These instruments were used with patients in nine different countries and proved to be applicable and useful for this purpose.

While methods of evaluating patient characteristics must be developed in order to perform cross-cultural studies, it is also essential to develop methods for categorizing patients once their characteristics have been elicited and rated and to compare patient types among the different centers. Through applying these methods, it is possible to show in what sense patients seen in the different centers are similar and in what sense they are unique. The combinations of these methods can also be used to determine in what sense the statement, "schizophrenia is found in all of the nine centers," is true, and in what sense the statement omits recognition of real differences in "schizophrenic" patients from the different centers.

The two-year and five-year follow-up evaluations add a critical dimension to an assessment of schizophrenia. Finding a heterogeneous outcome cross-culturally of patients diagnosed schizophrenic and demonstrating the failure of accepted diagnostic systems to predict poor outcome provide a serious challenge to the postulate accepted in much of the world that a properly made schizophrenic diagnosis carries with it a poor outcome. Investigation of prognostic variables has challenged the confidence and the number of criteria believed predictive of poor outcome and has suggested that relatively few items can be used for prognostication, and each tends to predict future function in its own area rather than general function of the individual patient. Assessment of diagnostic criteria has challenged several systems but, most importantly, has provided an operationalized reliable system for identifying schizophrenic patients which is flexible enough to be adaptive to various settings and provides an estimate of the diagnostic error. Assessment of outcome is demonstrably complicated and the critique of this area has assisted in developing an outcome evaluation form which is easily applied and highly reliable.

Volume II of the IPSS Report has been drafted and revised and will go to press some time in 1975. Each of the nine Field Research Centers has completed collection of five-year follow-up data. Data analysis and writing of the joint report of five-year follow-up will commence during fiscal year 1975 and publication is anticipated in 1976.

With Dr. Carpenter's scheduled departure in July 1975, it is not anticipated that the Intramural Research Program will participate further in IPSS collaboration with the World Health Organization.

Project No. Z01 MH 00059-04 AP

Keyword Descriptors:

Schizophrenia, cross-cultural, WHO, diagnosis, prognosis, outcome, schizophrenia subtypes, research interview techniques.

Honors and Awards:

Dr. Carpenter made presentations on the diagnosis of schizophrenia, subtypes of schizophrenia, and outcome in schizophrenia at the following medical centers and meetings:

Dept. of Psychiatry, Medical University of South Carolina; Dept. of Psychiatry, University of Chicago Medical School; Yale Psychiatric Institute, New Haven, Conn.; Dept. of Psychiatry, Bronx Municipal Hospital Center, New York, N.Y.; Dept. of Psychiatry, University of Michigan Medical Center, Ann Arbor, Mich.; Dept. of Psychiatry and Behavioral Sciences, Johns Hopkins Hospital, Baltimore, Md.; Suburban Maryland Chapter of the Washington Psychiatric Society; Georgetown University School of Medicine, Washington, D.C.; Annual Meeting of the American Psychiatric Association, Anaheim California, 1975. Dr. Carpenter was the discussant on schizophrenia for Mental Health Matters, a NIMH radio program distributed nation-wide.

Publications:

Strauss, J.S. and Carpenter, W.T., Jr.: The Evaluation of Outcome in Schizophrenia. In Ricks, D., Thomas, A. and Roff, M. (Eds.): Life History Research in Psychopathology, Vol. 3. Minneapolis, Minn., University of Minnesota Press, 1974.

Strauss, J.S. and Carpenter, W.T., Jr.: Characteristic Symptoms and Outcome in Schizophrenia. Arch. Gen. Psychiatry 30: 429-434, 1974.

Strauss, J.S. and Carpenter, W.T., Jr.: The Prediction of Outcome in Schizophrenia. II. Relationships Between Predictor and Outcome Variables: A Report from the WHO International Pilot Study of Schizophrenia. Arch. Gen. Psychiatry 31: 37-42, 1974.

Carpenter, W.T., Jr. and Strauss, J.S.: Cross-cultural Evaluation of Schneider's First Rank Symptoms of Schizophrenia: A Report from the International Pilot Study of Schizophrenia. Am. J. Psychiatry 131: 682-687, 1974.

Carpenter, W.T., Strauss, J.S. and Bartko, J.J.: Use of Signs and Symptoms for the Identification of Schizophrenic Patients: A Report of the International Pilot Study of Schizophrenia, to be published in Schiz. Bull.

Bartko, J.J., Strauss, J.S. and Carpenter, W.T., Jr.: Similar Groups of Schizophrenia--Some Concepts and Findings, to be published in Schiz. Bull.

Strauss, J.S., Carpenter, W.T., Jr. and Bartko, J.J.: Towards an Understanding of the Symptom Picture Considered Characteristic of Schizophrenia: Its Description, Precursors and Outcome, to be published in Schiz. Bull.

Strauss, J.S., Carpenter, W.T., Jr. and Bartko, J.J.: A Review of Some Findings from The International Pilot Study of Schizophrenia, to be published in Cancro, R. (Ed.): Ann. Rev. Schizophrenic Syndrome.

Hawk, A.B., Carpenter, W.T., Jr. and Strauss, J.S.: Diagnostic Criteria and 5-Year Outcome in Schizophrenia: A Report from the International Pilot Study of Schizophrenia. Arch. Gen. Psychiatry 32: 343-356, 1975.

Strauss, J.S. and Carpenter, W.T., Jr.: The Key Clinical Dimensions of the Functional Psychoses, to be published in Freedman, D.X. (Ed.): Association for Research in Nervous and Mental Disease. New York, Raven Press.

Editor: World Health Organization (Eds.): International Pilot Study of Schizophrenia, Volume II. To be published, Geneva Switzerland, World Health Organization Press.

Project No. Z01 MH 00060-04 AP
1. Adult Psychiatry Branch
2. Section on Neuropsychopharmacology
3. Bethesda, Maryland

PHS-NIMH
Individual Project Report
July 1, 1974 through June 30, 1975

Project Title: The Recovery Process and Research Data in Acute Psychosis

Previous Serial Number: M-AP(C)-16-10

Principal Investigator: William T. Carpenter, Jr., M.D.

Other Investigators: Michael Sacks, M.D.
John S. Strauss, M.D.
Marion Richmond, M.D.

Cooperating Units: University of Rochester Medical School, Rochester, N.Y.
Veterans Administration Hospital, New York, N.Y.

Man Years:

Total:	.20
Professional:	.18
Other:	.02

Project Description:

The objectives of this study are: (1) To define the different phases of the psychotic process as the patient moves from severe decompensation toward recovery. (2) To describe the kinds of research investigations the patient is able to participate in as he passes through these phases, and the implications of this phasic process for interpreting results of research on psychosis. (3) To examine the relationship of the patient's research participation to his therapy.

Acutely psychotic patients were observed during the course of their illnesses as they participated or failed to participate in different research projects. These observations were supplemented by interviews with the patient, held prior to discharge, regarding his views on the research procedures.

Distinct phases of patient's illness have been identified. The three phases are: (1) The delusional phase during which patients typically were unaware of research expectations. Thought processes are fragmented and delusional. During this time the patient is unavailable for any kind of research or therapeutic activity that involves active cooperation with another person or cognitive engagement in a task. (2) Double-awareness phase during which the patient is still delusional, but has become aware of the ward research and therapy programs. A capacity for insight of his symptoms has begun and the patient begins to modify his behavior despite severe symptoms. Participation and co in complex research tasks, although tedious, are now possible even th delusional interpretations of procedures may suggest a danger to the and, in fact, influence the way in which he takes the test. (3) The phase during which the patient is able to realistically perceive and the research and his participation in it comes with significant clini provement. When the patient fails to cooperate in research procedure has clear reasons for refusing--which reflect his attitude toward the his therapy and his doctor. Themes about the research which were pre delusional form during earlier phases may continue, but are now expre more rationally in a therapeutic relationship. Research that can be out is restricted by the phase through which the patient is passing. more disturbed phase, no information is obtainable about either respo other measures requiring active collaboration of the patient; as the improves, more aspects of his function can be evaluated. (4) Researc influences psychotherapy and concepts of research transference and co transference are useful.

The major focus of experimental research on psychosis in the past has been on chronic patients. Only recently has greater attention been d toward the acute patient. This study attempts to define phases of th process and to demonstrate their interrelationship to the research fi the conclusion that can be drawn from them, and the patient's therapy fying the psychological set during collection of data provides a fram interpreting results which enriches the disease model or simple behav rating approach. Awareness of the patient's research experience is v the therapist since patients will often utilize their research partic to express thoughts and feelings that otherwise might not be availabl

Keyword Descriptors:

Schizophrenic, research and treatment, psychotherapy, recovery proces research transference, research countertransference.

Publications:

Sacks, M.H., Carpenter, W.T., Jr. and Strauss, J.S.: Recovery f Delusions: Three Phases Documented by Patient's Interpretation o Research Procedures. Arch. Gen. Psychiatry 30: 117-120, 1974.

Sacks, M.H., Carpenter, W.T., Jr. and Richmond, M.B.: Psychothe in Hospitalized Research Patients, to be published in Arch. Gen. Psychiatry.

This project terminates June, 1975.

Project No. Z01 MH 00061-04 AP
1. Adult Psychiatry Branch
2. Section on Neuropsychopharmacology
3. Bethesda, Maryland

PHS-NIMH
Individual Project Report
July 1, 1974 through June 30, 1975

Project Title: Psychiatric History Study: The Nature and Reliability of the Data

Previous Serial Number: M-AP(C)-16-6

Principal Investigators: William T. Carpenter, Jr., M.D.
John S. Strauss, M.D.

Cooperating Units: John Bartko, Ph.D., Biometrics Branch, NIMH; Nursing Units 4-East, 4-West, 3-East, 3-West, NIH, Clinical Center; University of Rochester Medical School, N.Y.

Man Years:

Total:	0.1
Professional:	0.07
Other:	0.03

Project Description:

The objectives of this study are: (1) To identify different types of data ordinarily obtained in psychiatric history interviewing; (2) To study the reliability for these data as obtained from the patient compared to that obtained from his relative; (3) To study the effect of when in the course of hospitalization data is obtained on the nature of the data elicited; (4) To learn how psychiatric history is obtained in various psychiatric settings. These data will be used to examine the hypothesis that there is a greater variability in psychiatric history information than is usually expected and that the nature of the data obtained relates to the degree of variation.

Standardized psychiatric history and social description interview schedules developed for the International Pilot Study of Schizophrenia were utilized in interviewing. The first 20 admissions to one of the psychiatric nursing units who also had relatives available as informants were interviewed. The patient and relative were interviewed within one week of admission and again six weeks later. The same interview schedules were used in each interview and the interviewing was rotated between the three investigators listed above in an effort to keep the interviewer as naive as possible to patient information other than that obtained during the interview.

A questionnaire was sent to a large number of facilities that admit psychiatric patients in the United States. This questionnaire requested information about who interviews whom and at what time to obtain psychiatric history information. Data has been collected from 20 patients and their relatives and is being analyzed to determine reliability. Narrative summaries of the interviews and certain key items are being examined by the investigators in order to determine comparability of the less structured aspect of psychiatric history evaluation.

Results show that data obtained by structured questions is most reliable. Several areas of data such as duration of illness, acuteness of onset and precipitating factors have low reliability. These findings challenge the validity of many concepts of psychiatric disorder that are based on results from unstructured collection of these data.

The relationship of past experience to present behavior is fundamental to most psychological theories of behavior and mental function. There is a paucity of data testing the reliability and validity of background information obtained from psychiatric patients and their families. This study will attempt to identify the various means of collecting past history from psychiatric inpatients in various settings and to identify the pitfalls involved in interpreting this information.

The findings are being prepared for publication.

This project terminates 1975.

Keyword Descriptors:

Reliability, psychiatric data, clinical methodology, interview techniques.

Project No. Z01 MH 00062-03 AP
1. Adult Psychiatry Branch
2. Section on Neuropsychopharmacology
3. Bethesda, Maryland

PHS-NIMH
Individual Project Report
July 1, 1974 through June 30, 1975

Project Title: CSF Amine Metabolites in Acutely Schizophrenic Patients

Previous Serial Number: M-AP(C)-16-16

Principal Investigators: William T. Carpenter, Jr., M.D.
Robert M. Post, M.D.

Other Investigators: Frederick K. Goodwin, M.D.
Edward B. Fink, M.D.

Cooperating Units: Section on Psychobiology, APB
Section on Psychiatry, LCS

Man Years:

Total:	.25
Professional:	.15
Other:	.10

Project Description:

The objectives of this study are: (1) To utilize the probenecid technique to study dopamine, serotonin, and norepinephrine metabolism in a drug-free, acutely psychotic patient population; (2) To restudy the same patients when they are recovered; (3) To investigate the relationship of the measures of amine turnover to standardized ratings of signs, symptoms, premorbid factors and outcome.

Consecutively admitted schizophrenic patients are studied during acute psychosis after a minimum of 2 weeks off medications. A baseline LP is performed at 9:00 a.m. after 9 hours bedrest, followed by probenecid administration (100 mg./kg.) over 18 hours, after which a second LP is performed at 3:00 p.m. During a drug-free, recovery period about 4 months after admission, the baseline and post-probenecid LP's are repeated in identical fashion. An 8 cc CSF specimen is assayed by photofluorometry for serotonin and dopamine metabolites, 5HIAA and HVA, and by gas chromotography for the norepinephrine metabolite 3-methoxy-4-hydroxyphenyl glycol (MHPG). Data is systematically collected regarding daily clinical symptomatology, premorbid psychiatric, social, and work history, family history of mental illness, and outcome.

Results from 17 patients reveal that mean values for baseline and probenecid-induced accumulation of 5HIAA (28.4 $\pm$ 2.6 and 145.1 $\pm$ 14.3), and HVA (21.2 $\pm$

2.3 and 248.6 $\pm$ 28.9) are not significantly different from comparably studied normal controls (baseline only) and affective disorder patients. Mean baseline MHPG (17.7 $\pm$ 2.3) is not significantly different from the normal and manic groups, but the previously reported depressed group had lower MHPG.

Correlation coefficients revealed no significant relationship demonstrated between levels of 5HIAA, HVA, or MHPG and the presence or severity of symptoms or premorbid and family history items.

To date four patients have been studied during both admission and recovery test periods. Paired t-test revealed significantly lower probenecid-induced HVA accumulation ($p < .05$) and significantly lower baseline MHPG ($p < .025$) during recovery phase testing.

Among the several important biological hypotheses which attempt to account for schizophrenic symptoms are those postulating altered CNS amine metabolism. Amphetamine psychosis and phenothiazine receptor blockade implicate dopamine, the 6-hydroxydopamine self-stimulation model emphasizes norepinephrine, and the effects of LSD, PCPA, and DMT implicate serotonin. Despite the serious shortcomings of each of these as a model for schizophrenia, they deserve clinical investigation.

The above data for baseline and probenecid-induced determinations in drug-free, acute schizophrenics suggests that dopamine, serotonin, and norepinephrine metabolism is not significantly different from healthy or affective illness subjects. Preliminary evidence suggests that changes in amine metabolism do take place after recovery from the acute episode. It is possible that the reductions in HVA and MHPG after improvement indicate that, for a given patient, the levels observed during acute schizophrenia are elevated and reflect altered CNS catecholamine neurotransmission. Whether such an abnormality is of etiological significance, or an epiphenomena of an acutely disorganized psychotic state, or whether an underlying amine deficiency predisposes one to psychosis, should be further clarified by the continuing investigation of our patient population.

Following the above protocol, data continues to be collected from patients on 4-East and 3-West during both admission and discharge test periods. It is expected that the increasing number of patients in the study will help to clarify the significance of the present findings which suggest that within-patient changes in amine metabolism are dependent on clinical state.

This project terminates 1975.

Keyword Descriptors:

CSF, biogenic amines, schizophrenia, probenecid, catecholamines, indoleamines, diagnosis.

Project No. Z01 MH 00062-03 AP

Publications:

Post, R.M., Fink, E.B., Carpenter, W.T., Jr. and Goodwin, F.K.: CSF Amine Metabolites in Acute Schizophrenia, to be published in Arch. Gen. Psychiatry.

Project No. Z01 MH 00063-04 AP
1. Adult Psychiatry Branch
2. Section on Neuropsychopharmacology
3. Bethesda, Maryland

PHS-NIMH
Individual Project Report
July 1, 1974 through June 30, 1975

Project Title: The Group Processes on Clinical Research Units

Previous Serial Number: M-AP(C)-16-15

Principal Investigator: William T. Carpenter, Jr., M.D.

Other Investigators: Michael Sacks, M.D.
Edward Fink, M.D.
Carol Langsner

Cooperating Units: Department of Psychiatry, VA Hospital, New York, N.Y.

Man Years:

Total:	.20
Professional:	.18
Other:	.02

Project Description:

The objective of this study is to identify and conceptualize group processes on a clinical research unit and examine their relationship to therapeutic and research tasks.

Study group techniques have been used to make observations on ward functioning vis-a-vis therapeutic and research work tasks.

(1) The concepts of emergency and crisis have been defined and applied to a psychiatric unit. The crisis is said to exist when the unit is dominated by a covert work task. Evidence for crisis may be subtle but include the breakdown of ordinary work structures. For example, meetings fail to begin and end on time, absenteeism increases, cohesiveness between staff is lost, role function becomes diffuse, personnel are stereotyped, and therapeutic patterns, such as the giving of medication, are altered. Emergency is defined as a gross disruption of the unit requiring immediate management. Aspects of crisis recognition and emergency prevention are discussed in the publication listed below. (2) Conceptualized from a group-process orientation, five prominent, anti-therapeutic trends have been identified. They are (a) the absence of a therapeutic standard; (b) assignment of irresponsibility; (c) establishment of an anti-therapy leader; (d) the absence of therapeutic leadership, and (e) maintaining a pathogenic environment (the community double bind). (3) Emphasis on definition of a work group task and the organization structure for pursuing it

are relevant to successful collection of psychobiological data in acute schizophrenic patients. In addition to individual behavior based on intrapsychic conflict, we found that group expectations are perhaps the most important determinant of a patient's behavior vis-a-vis research expectations. Increasing attention to group phenomena as related to the research endeavors was accompanied by increasing success in patient participation in a variety of psychobiological investigations. Individual patient differences do not account for the increased success. (4) Informed consent is a difficult concept applied in any medical setting and special complications in doing research with schizophrenic subjects have been noted. An approach to informed consent which has some success in engaging the patients and advocating on their own behalf is described in the publication listed below. A specific role for nurses in informed consent has been proposed.

The observations and concepts related to these projects have general applicability across psychiatric units and probably on most medical units. Enhancing the recognition of the crisis is fundamental to the prevention of an emergency. Awareness of important anti-therapeutic tendencies on psychiatric units provides an opportunity to enhance the consistency with which a unit can accomplish its therapeutic work. A new approach to informed consent provides an opportunity for fuller participation by the patient in understanding the risk and benefits and his role in investigative and/or therapeutic studies. Increased sensitivity to the relationship between organization and work task provides an opportunity for enhancing psychobiological investigations of acutely psychotic patients.

Keyword Descriptors:

Group process, organizational principles, inpatient units, therapeutic milieu (community), informed consent, research wards.

Honors and Awards:

Dr. Carpenter made presentations on the research milieu and psychosocial treatment of schizophrenics to the Dept. of Psychiatry at Yale University, New Haven Connecticut; the Dept. of Psychiatry, Medical University of South Carolina; Dept. of Psychiatry at the University of Rochester, Rochester, N.Y.; Dept. of Psychiatry at the University of Pittsburgh, Pittsburgh, Pennsylvania, and at the Annual Meeting of the American Psychiatric Association, Anaheim, California, 1975.

Publications:

Sacks, M.H., Carpenter, W.T., Jr. and Scott, W.H.: Crisis and Emergency on the Psychiatric Ward. Comprehensive Psychiatry 15: 79-85, 1974.

Sacks, M.H. and Carpenter, W.T., Jr.: The Pseudotherapeutic Community: An Examination of Antitherapeutic Forces on Psychiatric Units. Hosp. Community Psychiatry 25: 315-318, 1974.

Carpenter, W.T., Jr.: A New Setting for Informed Consent. The Lancet 1: 500-501, 1974.

Carpenter, W.T., Jr. and Langsner, C.A.: The Nurse's Role in Informed Consent, to be published in Nurs. Times.

Carpenter, W.T., Jr. and Langsner, C.A.: Informed Consent: The Problem and Partial Solution (Abstract). Psychosomatic Med. 37: 88, 1975.

Sacks, M.H., Fink, E. and Carpenter, W.T., Jr.: The Clinical Research Meeting, to be published in Am. J. Psychiatry.

This project terminates 1975

Project No. Z01 MH 00064-04 AP
1. Adult Psychiatry Branch
2. Section on Neuropsychopharmacology
3. Bethesda, Maryland

PHS-NIMH
Individual Project Report
July 1, 1974 through June 30, 1975

Project Title: Serum Enzymes in Acute Psychotic States

Previous Serial Number: M-AP(C)-16-5

Principal Investigators: William T. Carpenter, Jr., M.D.
John S. Strauss, M.D.
Herbert Meltzer, M.D.

Cooperating Units: University of Rochester Medical School, Rochester, N.Y.
University of Chicago Medical School, Chicago, Illinois

Man Years:

Total:	0.2
Professional:	0.1
Others:	0.1

Project Description:

In an attempt to determine relationships between biochemical findings and psychotic conditions, Dr. Meltzer has demonstrated that creatine kinase and serum aldolase levels are often elevated in acute psychotic states. The objective of this project is to determine more precisely in which psychotic conditions these enzymes are elevated. By the use of standardized and diagnostic interviews to obtain information on a wide variety of symptoms and environmental conditions, it will be possible, using a sample of patients, to define more clearly the correlations of individual symptoms with enzyme elevations. It will be possible in this way to evaluate how reliably these enzyme methods differentiate schizophrenic patients from other psychotic and borderline conditions.

A series of patients is being interviewed using standardized mental status, history and social description interviews. Blood is drawn at the time of the mental state interview and analyzed employing methods currently in use by Dr. Meltzer for determining serum aldolase and creatine kinase.

An initial sample of patients has been tested with the techniques described, and preliminary findings suggest that degree of "cognitive disorganization," as defined by a group of mental status items, correlates more closely than other parameters with elevated enzyme levels.

There is much interest in determining whether schizophrenia and other psychoti conditions can be related to particular biochemical and other physiological measures. Although there is some evidence for such relationships in regard tc certain affective psychoses, evidence for similar relationships in schizophren is more controversial. Dr. Meltzer has been able to demonstrate relationships between creatine kinase and serum aldolase in psychotic conditions but it is not clear yet to what extent elevations in these enzymes are related to (1) th acuteness of the psychotic conditions and (2) particular clinical pictures. In the present study, it will be possible to help clarify some of these relationships as well as to evaluate by replication Dr. Meltzer's earlier work.

Data collection on the 4-East Clinical Research Unit has been discontinued. Analysis of clinical data has been deferred. The Section's participation in this work has ceased.

Keyword Descriptors:

Schizophrenia, serum enzymes, creatine kinase.

Project No. Z01 MH 00065-04 AP
1. Adult Psychiatry Branch
2. Section on Neuropsychopharmacology
3. Bethesda, Maryland

PHS-NIMH
Individual Project Report
July 1, 1974 through June 30, 1975

Project Title: Evaluation of Urinary Bufotenin and Dimethyltryptamine (DMT) and Serum Methyltransferase in Acute Schizophrenia

Previous Serial Number: M-AP(C)-16-12

Principal Investigator: William T. Carpenter, Jr., M.D.

Other Investigators: N. Narasimbachari, Ph.D.
Edward Fink, M.D.
Harold E. Himwich, M.D.

Cooperating Units: Galesburg State Research Hospital

Man Years:

Total: .2
Professional: .1
Other: .1

Project Description:

In previous investigations, Dr. Himwich has consistently found hallucinogenic substances in the urine of schizophrenics, while absent in normal controls. More recently, his laboratory has found a probable transmethylating enzyme in the serum of schizophrenics, while absent in normals. The objective in this investigation is to test the hypothesis that schizophrenics abnormally transmethylate hallucinogenic compounds.

Drug-free acute schizophrenic patients subjected to intensive clinical evaluations provide urine and blood samples for biochemical determinations. Non-schizophrenic patients and normal volunteers provide control urine and blood specimens. The schizophrenic patients are studied during sick, recovered and follow-up periods. Biological specimens are shipped frozen to Galesburg, Illinois for assay.

Psychiatric Assessment interview schedules are used in the evaluation of patients hospitalized for study at the Galesburg State Research Hospital. These chronic schizophrenic patients are taken off drugs for periods ranging from 6 to 12 weeks with the biologic investigations being carried out during this extensive drug holiday.

Project No. Z01 MH 00065-04 AP

Hallucinogenic substances, bufotenin and dimethyltryptamine, are found in the urine of acute and chronic schizophrenic patients. A substance in serum which is probably a transmethylating enzyme is found in the serum of acute and chronic schizophrenic patients. However, we have now found urinary bufotenin and DMT as frequently in normal controls as in our schizophrenic subjects. These findings are contrary to those hypothesized and significantly weaken this aspect of the transmethylation hypothesis in schizophrenia. A transmethylating enzyme has been found in serum of nonschizophrenics by three other groups and this finding is replicated in our normal volunteers. Normals had the same enzyme activity as acute schizophrenic subjects. Enzyme activity did not change from sick to recovery assay.

These findings demonstrate the necessity of a rigorous clinical methodology in psychobiological research in schizophrenia. The refutation of previous work requires a reconsideration of hypotheses that have received considerable attention in recent years.

Data analysis has been completed and a report submitted for publication.

Keyword Descriptors:

Bufotenin, dimethyltryptamine, transmethylating enzyme, transmethylation hypothesis, schizophrenia, diagnosis, hallucinogenic compounds in schizophrenia.

Honors and Awards

Dr. Fink presented a paper on New Research at the Annual Meeting of the American Psychiatric Association in Anaheim, California, 1975.

Publications:

Narasimbachari, N., Baumann, P., Pak, H.S., Carpenter, W.T., Jr., et al.: Gas Chromatographic-Mass Spectrometric Identification of Urinary Bufotenin and Dimethyltryptamine in Drug-Free Chronic Schizophrenic Patients. Biological Psychiatry 8: 293-300, 1974.

This project terminates 1975.

Project No. Z01 MH 00067-04 AP
1. Adult Psychiatry Branch
2. Section on Neuropsychopharmacology
3. Bethesda, Maryland

PHS-NIMH
Individual Project Report
July 1, 1974 through June 30, 1975

Project Title: Investigation of the Schizophrenic Process Through Art Productions of Acutely Psychotic Patients

Previous Serial Number: M-AP(C)-16-11

Principal Investigators: Harriet Wadeson
William T. Carpenter, Jr., M.D.

Cooperating Units: 4-East Nursing Unit, Clinical Center, NIMH

Man Years:

Total:	1.0
Professional:	.9
Other:	.1

Project Description:

This study obtains art productions from acutely psychotic patients at intervals during the course of their hospitalization and follow-up, and compares and studies the art productions and the patients' associations to them in order to gain a greater understanding of the schizophrenic process.

All patients on a research ward for the study of acute schizophrenia are evaluated in individual art therapy sessions shortly after admission, just prior to discharge, and at follow-up. Patients are provided with simple media and encouraged to express themselves freely and to free associate to their pictures. At each session, they are requested to make the following pictures: (1) whatever they want to draw; (2) a self-portrait; (3) a picture of the illness; (4) pictures of any hallucinations they have had; (5) pictures of any delusions they have had. If there are other pictures that patients particularly want to produce, either during the session or at any other time, they are encouraged to do so and to discuss them with the investigator. To date 62 patients have been studied. Each session is recorded on audiotape and a summary is written by the investigator. All pictures are photographed and catalogued for study purposes.

The following are specific areas that have been investigated in this project:

"Subjective Experience of Schizophrenia," paper presented at the 1975 Annual Meeting of the American Psychiatric Association. This study covers expression of feeling in representations of the psychosis; the unexpected finding of almost universal depression among the schizophrenic patients; perception of the origin of the illness as external or internal, biological or psychological; the surprising number of occurrences of representations of an improperly functioning brain to depict the illness; somatization; and the unexpected representations of pleasurable aspects of the psychosis.

"Prevalence of Universal Themes and Motifs in Psychotic Delusions," paper presented at International Congress of Social Psychiatry, Athens, Greece, and published in proceedings of meeting. This paper links universal themes in mythology, history, and psychotic delusions.

"Meaning and Experience of Seclusion Room for Acute Schizophrenic Patients," completed paper. This paper points up the importance of the seclusion room experience for the patients. In a number of instances, a representation of the seclusion room was used to symbolize the experience of the entire psychotic episode. The paper focuses on delusions about seclusion, the many hallucinations occurring in seclusion, and the patients' expression of feelings about seclusion.

"A Comparative Study of Art Expression of Schizophrenic, Unipolar Depressive, and Bipolar Manic Depressive Patients," completed paper. Although there were some general characteristics applicable to each diagnostic grouping, there was so much overlapping of characteristics among the groups that it was impossible to delineate distinguishing criteria. Such was the case, as well, when the total sample of 166 patients was broken down into subsamples matched for age and severity of illness.

"Depression in Schizophrenia," paper in progress, reporting the high incidence of depressive characteristics in the art productions of schizophrenics during the acute phase as well as at recovery and follow-up.

"Delusions of Power and Passivity," paper in progress, reporting the high incidence and nature of such delusions as portrayed in patients' drawings.

Blind raters have evaluated expressiveness in art productions of acute schizophrenics to test hypotheses regarding recovery style conceptualized as "integrating" or "sealing-over." Data is being analyzed.

Literature review on art productions of schizophrenia is in progress.

Sub-groups of acute schizophrenics have been delineated according to richness and paucity in art expressiveness. This distinction is being compared to possible distinctions of these two groups found by means of other psychological measurements. Data is being analyzed.

"The Influence of TV in Delusion Production," paper in progress reporting on the incidence and nature of delusions stimulated by TV programs depicted in patients' drawings.

We have developed the first systematic collection of psychotic patients' graphic depictions of their hallucinations and delusions. A representative sample has been exhibited at the American Psychiatric Association Annual Meeting, the 7th International Congress of Psychopathology of Expression, the Annual Meeting of the American Art Therapy Association, and the U.S. Public Health Service Professionals Association Annual Meeting. At the request of the Japanese Journal of Art Therapy, a paper has been published on hallucinations and delusions which notes the following findings: (1) incidence of occurrence of hallucinations and/or delusions in over 95% of our patients; (2) the fleeting nature of hallucinations compared with the more enduring experience of delusions; (3) prevalence of religious themes and transformations of real objects; (4) differences in hallucinatory and delusional experiences along variables of paranoia, grandiosity, organization of ideas, and conviction of the realness of the experience.

From these studies have come the following findings of significance to the mental health field:

Delusions and hallucinations frequently embody a universal struggle between good and evil, taking religious, mythological, and historical forms. These psychotic experiences are often grandiose and/or persecutory in nature. There is a high incidence of delusions of power and passivity.

The expression of feeling in the pictures indicates almost universal depression in the schizophrenic population studied, occurring during the acute phase of illness as well as at recovery and follow-up. In addition, approximately 25% expressed pleasurable feelings associated with the psychosis.

Depictions of the seclusion room were employed by many patients to symbolize the entire experience of the psychosis, thus highlighting its prominence in the patients' experience. For many, it was the locus of hallucinations and delusions, and some expressed very strong feelings about being in seclusion in commenting on their pictures. In reporting these findings, the focus has centered on the importance of the seclusion room in the patients' experience of their psychiatric treatment.

In contrast to reports in the literature which characterize the art expression of schizophrenics, manic-depressives, and depressives, a controlled comparison of the art work of 166 psychotic patients produces some general patterns, but so much overlapping and individual exceptions are evident that it is impossible to delineate specific graphic criteria to distinguish the patient groups. It appears, from a literature review in progress, that most of the reports are derived from general impressions, rather than empiric investigation.

Although the relevant data is still being analyzed, it appears that acute schizophrenics with an integrating recovery style are more expressive in their art productions than those who "seal-over" the psychotic experience.

Finally, the portrayal of delusions in art productions has indicated the frequent incidence of TV influence in delusion production.

There is little data of a comparative nature on the art productions of any particular population. Most of the writing in this area is directed toward therapeutic benefits rather than diagnosis and evaluation. Where such reports exist, they are primarily speculative and do not report characteristics of a designated population that has been studied systematically, as found in the literature review underway. The purpose of this project is to help counter this lack. In a broader sense, although the outward manifestations of acute schizophrenia are readily studiable (symptoms, progress, etc.), the inner experience of the affected individual is much less accessible. Among the most significant outcomes of this project has been the unexpected material which has surfaced in the art productions. Much of this data has not come to light through other modes of investigation. These findings are of research benefit in increasing understanding of the schizophrenic process, lead to increased diagnostic comprehensiveness, and to greater therapeutic efficacy.

Keyword Descriptors:

Schizophrenia, art, art therapy, hallucinations, delusions, diagnosis, subjective experience, systematic, depression in schizophrenia, pleasurable aspects of psychosis, pictures of brain, universal themes, seclusion room, recovery style, TV, art in mania, art in depression.

Honors and Awards:

"Art Therapy Workshop," Goddard College Colloquium, Aug. 1974.
"Prevalence of Universal Themes and Motifs in Psychotic Delusions," International Congress of Social Psychiatry, Athens, Greece, Sept. 1974.
"Combining Expressive Therapies," American Art Therapy Assoc. Annual Meeting, New York, Oct. 1974.
"The Fluid Family in Multifamily Art Therapy," American Art Therapy Assoc. Annual Meeting, New York, Oct. 1974.
"Conjoint Marital Art Therapy," demonstration, Towson State College, Dec. 1974.
Discussant, American Assoc. of Psychiatric Services for Children, Inc. Annual Meeting, New York, Nov. 1974.
"Art Therapy," River Road Unitarian Church, Maryland, March 1975.
"Art Techniques Used in Marital Therapy," workshop, Chicago Family Institute, March 1975.
"Art Therapy," Washington Hospital Center, April 1975.
"Subjective Experience of Schizophrenia," American Psychiatric Assoc. Annual Meeting, Calif., May 1975.
"Art Expression Workshop," Quest, May 1975.
"Art Psychotherapy in Research and Treatment," Upstate Medical Center, Syracuse, New York, June 1975.
"Art Therapy," Hutchings Medical Center, Syracuse, New York, June 1975.

"The Dynamics of a Normal, Effectively Functioning Family Over Time," American Psychiatric Assoc. Annual Meeting, Calif., May 1975.

Publications:

Wadeson, H. and Carpenter, W.T., Jr.: Pictorial Presentation of Hallucinations and Delusions. Japanese Bulletin of Art Therapy 5: 97-103, 1974.

Wadeson, H. and Carpenter, W.T., Jr.: Prevalence of Universal Themes and Motifs in Psychotic Delusions, Proceedings of International Congress of Social Psychiatry, 1974.

Wadeson, H.: Contribution to Hilgard, Atkinson and Atkinson: Introduction to Psychology. New York, Harcourt Brace Jovanovitch, Inc., 1975.

Wadeson, H.: Suicide: Expression in Images." Am. J. Art Therapy, in press.

Wadeson, H. and Epstein, R.: Intrapsychic Effects of Amphetamine in Hyperkinesis, in Studies on Childhood - Psychiatric and Psychological Problems, PJD Publications, in press.

This project terminates June, 1975.

Project No. Z01 MH 00068-01 AP
1. Adult Psychiatry Branch
2. Section on Neuropsychopharmacology
3. Bethesda, Maryland

PHS-NIMH
Individual Project Report
July 1, 1974 through June 30, 1975

Project Title: Postpsychotic Depression

Previous Serial Number: NONE

Principal Investigators: Thomas H. McGlashan, M.D.
William T. Carpenter, Jr., M.D.

Man Years:
Total: .40
Professional: .38
Other: .02

Project Description:

Postpsychotic depression (PPD) refers to a period of inertia or depression during recovery from a psychotic (usually schizophrenic) break. The following assumptions have emerged from a review of the psychiatric literature: (1) PPD occurs upon remission of other acute psychotic symptoms; (2) depression during the acute psychotic phase predicts the subsequent occurrence of PPD; (3) patients from lower socioeconomic groups develop PPD less frequently; and (4) PPD is a good prognostic sign. The objective of this study is to test these assumptions.

Our data arises from our therapeutic and research interactions with acutely schizophrenic patients from the 4-East Clinical Research Program. Our methodology permits the separation and independence of research variables and clinical judgments, including data collected at one-year follow-up. Twenty-three schizophrenic patients who were recovered by discharge were selected to evaluate the above assumptions. Structured clinical interviews were applied at admission, discharge, and follow-up to identify patients with and without significant depression during recovery. Using an independent data-set consisting of 53 variables (behavioral, social, prognostic, etc.), critical similarities and differences between the PPD and non-PPD groups were determined with a stepwise discriminant function analysis. Follow-up psychopathology and outcome were compared using t-tests.

Twelve of the 23 patients suffered an identifiable depression subsequent to psychosis, setting our incidence at about 50%. Initial depression was not a key predictor of PPD, and our findings on socioeconomic status failed to support its alleged relationship to PPD. No significant differences were found on four reliable measures of outcome at one year, thus refuting with prospective methodology the claims that PPD is a good prognostic sign, at least during the first year. We found depression to be ubiquitous during the initial acutely psychotic phase, and this depression remitted more slowly in patients identified as postpsychotically depressed.

Depression is a common state following psychosis but difficult to predict. Our data imply that PPD is a more complex clinical phenomenon than represented in the literature. Though easily identifiable, PPD is little studied, particularly its psychobiological and treatment aspects. Such investigation of depression which cuts across diagnostic categories could provide important information towards understanding the etiology and phenomenology of different psychotic states.

Keyword Descriptors:

Postpsychotic depression, depression in schizophrenia, prognosis in schizophrenia, acute schizophrenia.

This project will terminate June 1975.

Project No. Z01 MH 00069-02 AP
1. Adult Psychiatry Branch
2. Section on Neuropsychopharmacology
3. Bethesda, Maryland

PHS-NIMH
Individual Project Report
July 1, 1974 through June 30, 1975

Project Title: Integration and Sealing-over As Recovery Styles from Schizophrenia

Previous Serial Number: M-AP(C)-16-17

Principal Investigators: Thomas H. McGlashan, M.D.
Steven T. Levy, M.D.
William T. Carpenter, Jr., M.D.
John P. Docherty, M.D.
Samuel Siris, M.D.
Harriet Wadeson, A.T.R.

Man Years:
Total: 1.00
Professional: .95
Other: .05

Project Description:

This study defines and develops the concepts of integration and sealing-over as distinct recovery styles from acute psychotic episodes through clinical observations of the recovery process in the therapeutic community.

The data arises from our therapeutic and research interactions with acutely schizophrenic patients from the 4-East Clinical Research Program. Judgments dichotomizing patients into integration or sealing-over subgroups are made by the patient's psychiatrist and two research psychiatrists using interviews and medical records. At one-year follow-up interviews patients discuss their psychotic experience and are again rated. Matched patients are selected for group comparisons using independently collected data, such as the patients' art productions.

Patients can be reliably assigned to each group. Operational definitions of integration and sealing-over have been formulated. Integrators are more curious about their symptoms, regard them as part of their life's pattern, and gain information about them, resulting in a more flexible and variable attitude towards illness than patients who seal-over. The latter have fixed views of their illness (generally negative), do not understand their psychotic symptoms, nor do they regard their psychotic experience as a personal expression. These styles of recovery have theoretical continuity with other metapsychological formulations about psychotic states, and they are clinically continuous throughout a patient's hospital course as demonstrated by individual cases. Patients' art productions appear to have special discriminating power between these two styles. Finally, integration and sealing-over can also be identified as group processes within a therapeutic community designed to treat acutely psychotic individuals. These results support the validity of integration and sealing-over as defined and help to refine our understanding of the schizophrenic patient's response to his own psychosis. Specific studies include the following:

Integration and Sealing-over: Clinically Distinct Recovery Styles from Schizophrenia
Integration and Sealing-over: Metapsychologic and Dynamic Concepts
Integration and Sealing-over: Distinguishing Case Studies
Integration and Sealing-over: Validation Through Patient Art
Sealing-over in the Therapeutic Community.

Little research attention has been directed to a patient's recovery style. Integration and sealing-over are important concepts in this context and can be applied to treatment philosophies. For example, the psychiatrist who views psychotic symptoms as the manifestation of organic disease best treated by pharmacotherapy may facilitate sealing-over but impede the integrative process. Likewise, a psychiatrist invested in the psychotherapy of schizophrenia may impede sealing-over in patients so predisposed. Defining and operationalizing these concepts may facilitate matching of treatment philosophy with the patient's style. It may also be important to classify patients according to recovery style in investigations on the differential effects of treatment.

Keyword Descriptors:

Integration, sealing-over, recovery styles, schizophrenia, patient art productions, group process, therapeutic community, metapsychologic formulations of psychosis, response to psychosis.

This project will terminate June 1975.

Publications:

McGlashan, T.H., Levy, S.T. and Carpenter, W.T., Jr.: Integration and Sealing-over: Clinically Distinct Recovery Styles from Schizophrenia, to be published in Arch. Gen. Psychiatry.

Levy, S.T., McGlashan, T.H. and Carpenter, W.T., Jr.: Integration and Sealing-over as Recovery Styles from Acute Psychosis: Metapsychological and Dynamic Concepts, to be published in J. Nerv. Ment. Dis.

Project No. Z01 MH 00028-01 AP
1. Adult Psychiatry Branch
2. Section on Psychogenetics
3. Bethesda, Maryland

PHS-ADAMHA-NIMH
Individual Project Report
July 1, 1974 through June 30, 1975

Project Title: Affect State Dependent Learning

Previous Serial Number: None

Principal Investigators: Herbert Weingartner, Ph.D.; Dennis L. Murphy, M.D.

Other Investigators: None

Cooperating Units: Section on Clinical Neuropharmacology, Laboratory of Clinical Science; University of Maryland (Baltimore)

Man Years:

Total:	2.1
Professional:	1.2
Other:	0.9

Project Description:

Objectives: The purpose of this project is to examine the effects of varying changes in affect, experimentally-induced, as reflected in the affective disturbances and in rhythmical changes of mood (e.g., menstrual cycle) on the manner in which experiences (information) are stored and retrieved in memory. These research efforts have begun with an examination of state dependent learning effects associated with depression and mania in unipolar and bipolar patients. Our initial interest in this research came from both anecdotal and systematic observations of the kinds of learning that are associated with manic-depressed affect states. There appeared an apparent dissociation in the affective switch states in which patients appear to be unable to recall events stored in the disparate affective state. This initial research then expanded in a further definition of affect as a discriminative cue in learning.

Methods Employed: A variety of techniques including self-generated associative patterns, cued versus free recall of words, and the learning and recall of unusual pattern information have all been used in a variety of studies designed to examine some of the affect state specific strategies in which information is stored and retrieved in memory.

Major Findings: We were initially able to demonstrate that patients, observed over long time periods (during which they demonstrated manic, depressed, and normal affective states, as well as switch states), showed affect state dependent storage and retrieval of self-generated information. That is, patients, while manic, were able to retrieve information stored while manic more effectively than when less manic. This observation was particularly striking since previous research had shown that during mania, information is stored less effectively than during periods of more normal affect. We then also found similar effects with information which was presented to subjects for learning, rather than recall of self-generated information. We noted that rated affect change itself is a good predictor of the extent to which information stored is then later dissociated at the time of retrieval. Convergent measures of affective state, other than rating scale data, have also been shown to correlate with the extent to which dissociative effects can be demonstrated in relationship to affect change. Measures such as amount of motor movement correlate well with dissociative effects associated with sharp changes in affect.

Significance to Biomedical Research and the Program of the Institute: There is a growing interest in the affective disturbances in man from both a biological and a behavioral point of view. This research on the state dependent characteristics of depression and mania in bipolar and unipolar patients is felt to be a powerful tool in the examination of the nature of the depressed and manic states, and provides a useful bridge between biological and behavioral approaches to the study of affect in man.

Proposed Course of Project: We are actively pursuing other techniques and methods of exploring the relationship of affective change and its effects on the storage and retrieval of experience. These proposed and continuing studies are being explored in studies using drug manipulations of affect. Concurrently, input and output of stored and retrieved information (in response to the amphetamine and physostigmine treatment) have been studied in state dependent learning studies in which affective change has been one of the major foci of interest. In addition, we are pursuing behavioral manipulations of affect in the psychological laboratory as another way of establishing how affect controls how and what information is stored in memory and then later retrieved. We are also exploring "naturally" occurring changes in mood such as in relationship to the menstrual cycle and its relationship to both affect change and state dependent learning effects. Finally, we are beginning to explore some of the fine structure of information processing, both in terms of storage and retrieval as it relates to affect change. The issue of possible lateralizing effects that are associated with changes in depression and mania may, in fact, be a major determinant in the manner in which information is tagged and encoded and finally stored in memory. Such affect specific lateralizing effect may be a major determinant in the specificity of encoding and retrieval associated with affect.

Key Word Descriptors: State dependent learning; storage and retrieval of information; changes in affect

Honors and Awards: None

Publications: None

Project No. Z01 MH 00029-01
1. Adult Psychiatry Branch
2. Section on Psychogenetics
3. Bethesda, Maryland

PHS-ADAMHA-NIMH
Individual Project Report
July 1, 1974 through June 30, 1975

Project Title: Uncertainty and Organization in Schizophrenic Thinking

Previous Serial Number: None

Principal Investigators: Herbert Weingartner, Ph.D., John Docherty, M.D., Daniel van Kammen, M.D., and Samuel Siris, M.D.

Other Investigators: None

Cooperating Units: Section on Neuropsychopharmacology, APB

Man Years:

Total:	2.7
Professional:	2.5
Other:	0.2

Project Description:

Objectives: The purpose of this research project is to define schizophrenic thinking in the context of contemporary information processing theories and in a manner sensitive to some of the mechanisms which might account for the unique way in which schizophrenic patients think about the world around them. A variety of theories have attempted to account for the kinds of changes that have been noted in schizophrenic thinking as compared to the kinds of cognition and perception associated with more normal behavioral repertories. In this project we have used the methods of uncertainty analysis or information theory to define both the organization and amount of information used by the schizophrenic in dealing with input and informational strategies used at the time of recall of previously experienced information.

Methods Employed: The primary tool that has been used in this project is a method of uncertainty analysis in which input can be described in terms of bits of information, amount and form of organization. This method of analysis is equally useful in describing output of information on recall. In this study, we have examined both schizophrenic patients and normal controls, requiring them to sort, organize, and later remember random and organized words which are then subjected to an uncertainty analysis.

Major Findings: Although schizophrenic subjects are not different from normal controls in their processing of highly organized information (taxonomically organized word sets) - both in their sorting and organizing of that information and on recall - when they are presented with random word sets, the amount of organization imposed in a stimulus situation containing five bits of uncertainty is around three bits for normal controls while only one-and-a-half bits of information are imposed on stimuli by schizophrenic subjects, leaving them with an amount of information or uncertainty in excess of their channel capacity. This greater amount of uncertainty or information which is then to be processed is also reflected in the recall processes in schizophrenic versus normal subjects. Here, again, the total uncertainty that has to be dealt with is far greater in schizophrenics, as compared with normal controls. The data suggest that the schizophrenic subject is unable to ignore irrelevant dimensions of differences between stimuli in their chunking or organizing the sets of words or other kinds of information, thereby leaving them over-stimulated in respect to the amount of information to be stored or recalled. There is almost no overlap at all in the chunking and organizing of information accomplished by normal controls as compared to the schizophrenic subjects. In this sense, these findings are both provocative and robust, and have stimulated further investigation of this population of subjects in response to a number of drugs and also in terms of familial versus state issues.

Significance to Biomedical Research and the Program of the Institute: Much of the research that has attempted to define the cognitive disturbance associated with the schizophrenic process has been difficult to integrate, has been poorly understood, and frequently shows enormous intersubject variability. With the use of an uncertainty analysis tool of approach and a conceptual framework with which to approach schizophrenic cognition, we may have available to us an important view of stable and state-varying characteristics of the schizophrenic thought process. The methods provide us with some potentially important leads to understanding the biological, genetic, and gross behavioral changes associated with schizophrenic processes and its related reflection in the thinking of these patients.

Proposed Course of Project: We plan to examine schizophrenic patients with some procedures similar to those outlined above in studies that involve drug manipulations in these patients. In addition, we plan to look at differences and similarities in how families of these patients deal with known amounts of information (uncertainty) and their methods of organizing, chunking, and clustering pieces of information.

Key Word Descriptors: Schizophrenic thought processes, uncertainty analysis

Honors and Awards: None

Publications: None

Project No. Z01 MH 00030-01 AP
1. Adult Psychiatry Branch
2. Section on Psychogenetics
3. Bethesda, Maryland

PHS-ADAMHA-NIMH
Individual Project Report
July 1, 1974 through June 30, 1975

Project Title: Behavioral Mechanisms of State Dependent Learning

Previous Serial Number: None

Principal Investigators: Herbert Weingartner, Ph.D., Dennis L. Murphy, M.D., Richard Stillman, M.D.,

Other Investigators: James E. Eich, Richard Wurster, and John Martello

Cooperating Units: Section on Clinical Neuropharmacology, Laboratory of Clinical Science, NIMH; University of Maryland (Baltimore)

Man Years:

Total:	1.97
Professional:	1.95
Other:	0.02

Project Description:

Objectives: This project represents an ongoing series of research efforts in the area of state dependent learning where the primary emphasis is an attempt to understand the behavioral mechanisms of state dependent learning, particularly as it relates to basic issues in our understanding of memory storage and retrieval. These studies have emphasized the potential of changes in states induced by drugs or in relation to clinical change as a vehicle for understanding the mechanism by which state dependent effects can be explained and how these relate to viable models of memory.

Methods Employed: Normal controls have been involved in studies in which states have been manipulated using alcohol, marijuana, and the anticholinesterase inhibitor physostigmine as agents to produce state change. The behavioral techniques used to study such effects involved cued versus free recall techniques, part-whole learning techniques (developed by Tulving and others), learning tasks emphasizing encoding specificity, and procedures that allow for the separate manipulation and examination of strategies of storing information and conditions that allow for congruent versus disparate strategies for later retrieval of information under cued or free recall conditions.

Major Findings: Our initial research efforts were able to demonstrate that information that is stored in some disparate state is, in fact, available in memory but temporarily inaccessible; that information recalled in some state different from that which was present at the time of storage is inaccessible because subjects are unable to self-generate retrieval cues necessary to effectively access memory. When these retrieval cues are provided, then subjects recall information previously stored in some disparate state. In another study we were also able to demonstrate that not all information dissociates equally in state dependent learning manipulations. Using alcohol, it was possible to show that high imagery, highly encodable words, are less likely to be dissociated than low imagery, less concrete, less encodable kinds of stimuli. These findings have implications both in terms of potential lateralizing effects of some agents with respect to state dependent information processing mechanisms and also in terms of issues of encodability and its relationship to normal and disrupted memory processes. We have recently also demonstrated that the effect of imagery on relative dissociation of information stored in a disparate state also holds not just for alcohol but also for marijuana. It was possible to show that the imagery dimension is not only an important verbal indicator which can disrupt dissociative effect but imagery can be directly manipulated in a state dependent learning design and, as such, abolishes dissociative effects.In addition, we have been able to show that the mere repetition of information at the time of storage tends to erase some of the state dependent dissociative effects produced by agents such as alcohol and marijuana. Again, this would support the notion of encoding itself being an important issue in the establishment of state dependent dissociative effects in man.

IN a subsequent trial, we have found that strategies by which subjects store information in memory is state specific and are associated with strategies by which subjects access memory in congruent as opposed to disparate storage-retrieval states. These strategies of storage and retrieval predict with accuracy the extent to which information is likely to be dissociated at the time of recall.

Significance to Biomedical Research and the Program of the Institute: The whole area of state dependent learning is of great importance in our understanding of a variety of psychiatric phenomena as well as the action of a variety of drugs that have been shown to alter brain. By pursuing the mechanism of state dependency, we obtain some important pieces of information about the specificity and nature of some key clinical and drug-altered states in man. The research also provides us with new tools with which to examine complex clinical and psychopharmacologically-induced states and, at the same time, provides us with an important new view of "normal" memory processes.

Proposed Course of Project: Research efforts in the direction of the above-described trials will continue.

Key Word Descriptors: State Dependent Learning; Behavioral Mechanisms of SDL; Use of alcohol and marijuana to produce state change.

Honors and Awards: None

PUblications: None

Project No. Z01 MH 00031-01 AP
1. Adult Psychiatry Branch
2. Section on Psychogenetics
3. Bethesda, Maryland

PHS-ADAMHA-NIMH
Individual Project Report
July 1, 1974 through June 30, 1975

Project Title: Cognitive Changes Associated with Huntington's Disease

Previous Serial Number: None

Principal Investigators: Herbert Weingartner, Ph.D., Robert D. Hunt, M.D., and Michael H. Ebert, M.D.

Cooperating Units: Section on Experimental Therapeutics, Laboratory of Clinical Science, NIMH; University of Maryland, Baltimore Campus (Graduate Student Program)

Man Years:

Total:	1.05
Professional:	0.45
Other:	0.60

Project Description:

Objectives: In this study we have attempted to delineate the cognitive deficits and changes that are associated with Huntington's Disease. It has been known for some time that Huntington's patients show clearly discernible cognitive memory deficits. The nature of this deficit and its mechanism has been poorly understood and not seriously investigated to date. We have designed a number of studies which provide us with a vehicle for examining in a systematic way the cognitive changes associated with this disorder, and also contrast these changes with other forms of dementia, for example, in Korsakoff's psychosis, temporal lobe disorder, and senile states.

By investigating some of the cognitive changes in these patients, we hope not only to understand more clearly what may, in fact, be some of the memory changes in Huntington's patients, but also to say something about differences and similarities to other forms of dementia and, in addition, to clarify some important issues in our understanding of normal memory processes.

Methods Employed: A series of Huntington's Disease patients, Parkinsonian patients, and normal controls have been examined to date. Other patient groups will also be examined. The tools used involve a variety of learning-memory procedures which allow for distinctions between attentional, short-term store, long-term store, and retrieval processes. These techniques also provide for a way of looking at the effectiveness of various kinds of cueing devices in retrieving information which may be available in memory but is temporarily inaccessible. Other procedures also examine free recall of stored information and the learning of sequential streams of information, as in paired associates and serial learning.

Major Findings: When Huntington's patients are compared to Parkinsonian patients and normal controls, they show marked deficits in the storage and retrieval of information. These deficits are both striking and of considerable theoretical interest. Although the Huntington's patients show that they are able to store a considerable amount of information in memory (but not as much as control subjects do), they demonstrate a very specific inability to utilize retrieval cues to access information in memory or to recognize previously presented stimuli as in reorganization of memory. It appears, then, that the cognitive deficit is particularly marked in the retrieval end of the memory process. This problem of accessing memory is again most marked in attempting to retrieve sequences of previously learned responses, since the Huntington's patients appear particularly unable to use self-generated information as retrieval cues for eliciting other items stored sequentially.

Significance to Biomedical Research and the Program of the Institute: This research may prove to be a very powerful approach not only in the study of dementia in Huntington's Disease, but in other forms of disturbed cognition associated with changes in the brain. It also provides an unique opportunity for studying some of the neuroanatomical and neurochemical correlates of a variety of stages in the storage and retrieval of information. As such, it represents an important body of research in the study of cognition and memory.

Proposed Course of Project: We plan to study a larger and more diversified group of patients with other forms of dementia as a means of comparing what we have seen to date in patients with Huntington's Disease. In addition, we are looking at changes in the kinds of cognitive deficits associated with Huntington's Disease with respect to a number of drug manipulations presently being investigated. Finally, we are exploring not only the retrieval or accessing problem that appears to be apparent in Huntington's Disease, but also some of the unique ways in which Huntington's patients may be storing informatjon which ultimately makes that information less accessible than it would be in normal subjects.

Key Word Descriptors: Cognitive deficits and changes in Huntington's Disease; storage and retrieval of information.

Honors and Awards: None

Publications: None

Project No. Z01 MH 00032-01 AP
1. Adult Psychiatry Branch
2. Section on Psychogenetics
3. Bethesda, Maryland

PHS-ADAMHA-NIMH
Individual Project Report
July 1, 1974 through June 30, 1975

Project Title: Amphetamine State Dependent Learning in Depressed Patients

Previous Serial Number: None

Principal Investigators: Herbert Weingartner, Ph.D., Daniel van Kammen, M.D., and Dennis L. Murphy, M.D.

Cooperating Units: Section on Neuropsychopharmacology, APB; Section on Clinical Neuropharmacology, LCS

Man Years:

Total:	2.05
Professional:	1.50
Other:	0.55

Project Description:

Objectives: A number of drugs have been shown to produce state dependent learning effects in man. These have included alcohol, marijuana, and the barbiturates. The objectives of this project are to (1) explore possible amphetamine state dependent learning effects (a particularly important issue in that most state dependent learning effects have been demonstrated with depressant-like drugs), (2) to use this drug as a tool in examining some of the behavioral and neurochemical mechanisms that drive this state dependent learning phenomenon, (3) to relate amphetamine-state dependent learning to mood-altering effects of this drug, (4) to explore all these effects in the context of the relative effect of d- versus l-amphetamine in the presence of a drug that might be expected to block amphetamine learning effects (lithium).

Methods Employed: A series of depressed patients have been and will continue to be studied using learning procedures developed by Dr. Weingartner. These are methods particularly useful in examining information processing memory and retrieval. They have been designed to look at discrete storage and retrieval stages in memory and to be sensitive to potential state dependent effects of drug-altered states.

Major Findings: Amphetamines do produce state dependent learning effects in man and this is evident despite any evidence of effects of the drug on the initial learning that takes place on storing information in memory. In addition, the size of the state dependent learning effects produced by amphetamines in depressed patients is directly related to the extent to which the drug produces antidepressant euphoric and activating effects as measured both subjectively and by trained raters. In addition, a number of parameters other than the presence or absence of d- or l-amphetamine with or without lithium predicts some characteristics of the initial storage of information in memory. These effects discriminate between short-term versus long-term memory factors in relationship to the intensity of depression and the response to the amphetamine.

Significance to Biomedical Research and the Program of the Institute: There is a great deal of current interest in the affective disorders. This project provides an important vehicle for understanding not only the response of depressed patients to pertinent pharmacological stimuli, but also provides a means of measuring the kinds of responses (learning, storage, and retrieval) that accompany depressed versus non-depressed states in the presence or absence of some of these drugs.

Proposed Course of Project: The study of amphetamine state dependent learning in depressed patients is continuing at present. Not only are we attempting to enlarge our initial sample of subjects on which these preliminary findings are based, but we are also attempting to bridge the gap between a cognitive and an operant view of state dependent phenomena. In this approach we are attempting to train discretely different sequences of verbal responses in association to stimuli while in the amphetamine versus non-amphetamine state and then to test these potentially separate and discriminable repertories at some point either in the presence or absence of amphetamine. The model for this approach is essentially a cognitive version of a T-base study and allows us to make clear statements about the relative dissociation of the depressed versus non-depressed behavioral repertoire.

Key Word Descriptors: State dependent learning in depression; amphetamine SDL in depression

Honors and Awards: None

Publications: None

Project No. Z01 MH 00081-01 AP
1. Adult Psychiatry Branch
2. Section on Psychogenetics
3. Bethesda, Maryland

PHS-ADAMHA-NIMH
Individual Project Report
July 1, 1974 through June 30, 1975

Project Title: Heritable Characteristics of Cation Transport in Primary Affective Disorders

Previous Serial Number: None

Principal Investigator: James F. Leckman, M.D.

Other Investigators: Elliot S. Gershon, M.D.
Michele R. Van Eerdewegh, M.D.

Cooperating Units: Laboratory of Clinical Science, DCBR, NIMH

Man Years:
Total: 0.5
Professional: 0.25
Other: 0.25

Project Description:

Objective: To determine heritable characteristics of ion transport which distinguish individuals with a primary affective disorder from normal controls.

Methods Employed: The aspect of ion transport currently under investigation is the rate of lithium ion accumulation by erythrocytes during a 24-hour incubation. Converging evidence from two laboratories provide the rationale for focusing on this parameter of ion transport as a possible indicator of liability. Dorus et al., (1974) examined 10 monozygotic and 7 dizygotic twin pairs and calculated a heritability index of 0.85 for the accumulation lithium ions by erythrocytes; indicating that the phenomenon is under substantial genetic control. A second study Hokin-Neaverson, et al. (1974), reports a diminished rate of ^{22}Na efflux from the erythrocytes of individuals with primary affective disorder as compared with controls. If this second report can be replicated, it suggests that some aspects of ion transport can be used successfully to distinguish between the diagnostic groupings of the mood disorders. The speculation that a similar difference may be observable in the lithium ion accumulation is based on the fact that lithium ions are handled by the erythrocyte in a similar way as are sodium ions.

1. Patient Selection: Past and present inpatients of the research wards of NIMH, with an unequivocal diagnosis of a primary affective disorder, will be selected for the study on the basis of past response to lithium treatment. An appropriate set of normal controls will also be selected.

2. Measures of Ion Transport:

a. In vitro incubation of erythrocytes with lithium carbonate will be performed to measure lithium ion accumulation over 24 hours. The three groups of individuals to be studied are unequivocal lithium responders and nonresponders as well as normal controls.

b. Concomitant measures of plasma and intraerythrocyte sodium and potassium will be obtained to monitor changes in these electrolytes during the incubation.

c. Other measures including ^{22}Na efflux and influx in erythrocytes may be obtained if the study of lithium ion accumulation reveals that there indeed exists a heritable membrane characteristic that successfully distinguishes patients from controls.

The technical methodology of the study is presently under development.

Major Findings: None. Study is currently under development.

Significance to Mental Health Research and the Program of the Institute: The basis of lithium carbonate's efficacy in the treatment of primary affective disorders remains largely unknown. Recent speculation has focused on possible membrane abnormalities that are manifest by differences in ion transport. Investigation of this area may be crucial to our understanding of lithium's mode of action in the treatment of mood disorders. In addition, the identification of heritable traits, that are associated with liability to manifest the mood disorders, offers the promise of preclinical diagnosis of high risk individuals and may be the first step in a program of prevention.

Proposed Course: Once the remaining methodologic problems are satisfactorily resolved, the course of investigation will proceed as described above. Present plans call for the participation of approximately 50 probands with a diagnosis of a primary affective disorder (25 lithium responders and 25 lithium nonresponders) as well as an equivalent number of controls. If this heritable measure, erythrocyte lithium ion accumulation, successfully distinguishes individuals with primary affective disorder from normal controls, further work will be necessary to establish the biochemical basis of this erythrocyte characteristic. In addition, a family study would be undertaken to determine if this characteristic is an indicator of liability for affective illness, and to further explore the genetic basis of the characteristic as to mode of transmission, etc.

Alternatively, if this measure fails to distinguish the two groups, it will be necessary to examine other characteristics of ion transport both as to their heritability and their ability to distinguish between diagnostic groups.

Keyword Descriptors:

Primary affective disorders, genetics, lithium incubation, meritable traits , sodium, potassium, lithium, ion transport, manic-depressive illness, ouabain.

Project No. Z01 MH 00082-01 AP
1. Adult Psychiatry Branch
2. Section on Psychogenetics
3. Bethesda, Maryland

PHS-ADAMHA-NIMH
Individual Project Report
July 1, 1974 through June 30, 1975

Project Title: Life Events and Degree of Social Alienation in Affective Disorders

Previous Serial Number: None

Principal Investigator: Eleanor D. Dibble, D.S.W.

Other Investigators: Elliot S. Gershon, M.D.

Cooperating Units: None

Man Years:
Total: 0.5
Professionals: 0.25
Other: 0.25

Project Description:

Objective:

1. To develop a standardized rating scale of life events and social alienation which can be used to collect data about these psychological factors in order to compare them with biological findings.

2. To evaluate the life events in a sample of 100 patients with mood disorders and their relatives and to compare these findings with those from matched controls.

3. To determine (a) whether life events are the same or different in the patient and nonpatient populations, (b) whether there is an accumulation of events for patients vs. nonpatients, (c) whether there is a family culture associated with more life events regardless of whether these were resident or nonresident family members in contrast to the controls, (d) whether nonresident family members have more individual events than events which involve several family members.

4. To correlate the number and stress of life events and alienation with the biochemical levels of DBH, COMT, MAO, etc. which will be obtained under a separate project from this same sample.

Methods Employed: Data on life events and alienation will be collected by a scale adapted from the research of Holmes and Rahe, Paykel, and Brown, events which "common sense" indicates are generally of emotional importance to most people. The scale also includes the statements of alienation from the Srole Anomie Scale in an effort to measure any association between social alienation and mood disorders.

The Life Events and Alienation Scale (LEAS) will be incorporated as part of the family social data interview being conducted with this sample of patients and controls. The scale measures the kind and number of events, the perceived stress of those events, opinions about anomie measures, and the involvement of family members in the events. Assuming the events chosen for the scale may not be exhaustive of those events happening to people, provision is made for the respondents to supply others.

With a sub-sample, those who are successive inpatient admissions, the scale will be administered during their hospitalization and again one year after their discharge for a comparison of findings. This test-retest method may answer questions such as whether patients have a raised rate of events only prior to illness or over their lives, but leading to illness only some of the time; or whether there are different kinds of events which lead to illness.

Factor or cluster analysis and analysis of variance methods will be used to analyze the data.

Significance to Mental Health Research: The meaning of life events in mood disorders has been under investigation for some time. Although this present research will replicate the earlier work, it also provides new features. Data about life events of both patients and their relatives (resident and nonresident) will be gathered to ascertain whether there is a family culture of events in contrast to those of nonpatient controls and their families. It also purports to measure the association between social alienation and mood disorders. This research will analyze the findings on life events and stress with other family data and a number of biological findings. To our knowledge these investigations have not been done before.

Keyword Descriptors:

Life events, social alienation, primary affective illness, stress, anomie, rating scale, mood disorder

Project No. Z01 MH 00083-01 AP
1. Adult Psychiatry Branch
2. Section on Psychogenetics
3. Bethesda, Maryland

PHS-ADAMHA-NIMH
Individual Project Report
July 1, 1974 through June 30, 1975

Project Title: Hypothesis of X-linkage in Bipolar and Unipolar Affective Disorder

Previous Serial Number: None

Principal Investigator: Elliot S. Gershon, M.D.

Collaborating Investigators: William E. Bunney, Jr., M.D.
Michele Van Eerdewegh, M.D.
James F. Leckman, M.D.
Paul Van Eerdewegh
Steven Matthysse, Ph.D.

Cooperating Units: Section on Theoretical Biology, National Cancer Institute
Psychiatric Research Laboratories, Massachusetts General Hospital

Man Years:

Total: 1.0
Professional: 0.75
Other: 0.25

Project Description:

Objectives:

1. To develop new data pertinent to the hypothesis that some affective disorders are transmitted as a single gene on the X-chromosome. This hypothesis was given great impetus by the studies of Mendlewicz, Fieve and Fleiss, in which linkage to both the Xga blood group and protan and deutan color blindness was reported.

2. To develop and test appropriate mathematical models of X-linked inheritance in psychiatric illness, and apply them to existing and newly collected data.

Methods Employed:

1. Patients admitted to NIMH and their first degree relatives (parents, sibs, children) are studied for psychiatric status, color blindness and for Xga blood type. If it is determined that family is genetically informative for Xg or color blindness, more distant relatives are studied until a large pedigree with multiple informative sibships is obtained. Analysis is performed using the method of lod scores and using multigeneration models.

2. Mathematical models are being developed for liability to a psychiatric disorder, with multiple thresholds according to sex and form of disorder found (bipolar, unipolar, or related disorders.) These are then applied for goodness-of-fit to existing and currently collected data.

3. New mathematical methods of analysis of case ascertainment are developed, since previously reported studies use an incorrectly applied method.

4. Careful review and evaluation of previously reported studies is performed.

Major Findings:

1. An association of color blindness with affective illness is present across families in the previously reported data. This precludes linkage between the two characteristics according to the analytic method used (lod scores). Linkage requires that within families there be an association of color blindness or non-color-blindness with affective disorder, but that across families there be no association. Re-analysis of the previously reported linkage of Xg blood group to bipolar illness reveals that the linkage depends on questionable assumptions regarding age of onset and penetrance, and does not reach levels of statistical significance commonly required by geneticists.

2. A multiple threshold mathematical model of transmission through the X-chromosome has been formulated. Testing of the goodness-of-fit to actual data is in progress. Simulation experiments to examine the model are also being performed.

3. An algorithm for ascertainment has been developed which allows more efficient selection of informative families. In a rare X-linked trait such as protanopia, it is much more efficient to find informative families through screening for

color blindness in patients only, than to screen all sibs of all patients. However, the method of analysis of data from such ascertainment has not previously been formulated.

Proposed Course of Project:

Data Collection: 50 patients and their available relatives have been screened to date. Two families informative for linkage to color blindness, and three families informative for linkage to Xg blood group, have been found. It is expected that 100-150 patients will have to be screened before conclusions may be drawn.

Mathematical Models: A multiple threshold model of liability to bipolar and unipolar affective disorder with transmission through the X-chromosome, and with sex-effects on illness thresholds, has been formulated. The mathematical development and computer programming is completed, and application to new and existing data is to be expected shortly.

Significance of These Findings:

The attempt to separate out an X-linked form of affective disorder is a most important and powerful investigative strategy. If the hypothesis were confirmed, it would constitute proof of a genetic factor in the mood disorders. It would also allow more complete definition of the biological and psychological effects of an "affective disorders genotype" than has been possible until now. For these reasons, this hypothesis must be subjected to the most rigorous possible tests and methods of analysis. The development of sophisticated models and analytic methods may allow more accurate conclusions to be drawn. At this time, we can state that linkage to the color blindness locus cannot be considered present. The demonstration of an association of color blindness with manic-depressive illness is more limited in generalizability than demonstration of linkage.

Honors and Awards:

Dr. Bunney presented a paper on X-linkage in affective disorders, co-authored with Dr. Gershon, to the Neurosciences Research Program meeting in Boston, Mass., December 1974. Dr. Gershon was invited to discuss "The question of X-linkage in manic-depressive illness" at the Departmental Seminar of the Division of Medical Genetics, UCLA, in Los Angeles, May 1975. Dr. Gershon is co-editor of an issue in preparation of the Neurosciences Research Program Bulletin, which is partly devoted to the problem of X-linkage.

Project No. Z01 MH 00083-01 AP

Publications:

Gershon, E.S. and Bunney W.E., Jr., The question of X-linkage in bipolar affective illness, Neurosciences Res. Prog. Bulletin, issue in preparation.

Gershon, E.S. and Matthysee S., X-linkage: Ascertainment through doubly ill probands, Neurosciences Res. Prog. Bulletin, issue in preparation.

Keywords:

X-chromosome, genetics, manic-depressive illness, mathematics and statistics, family studies.

Project No. Z01 MH 00084-01 AP
1. Adult Psychiatry Branch
2. Section on Psychogenetics
3. Bethesda, Maryland

PHS-ADAMHA-NIMH
Individual Project Report
July 1, 1974 through June 30, 1975

Project Title: Genetic-Biologic Studies of Psychiatric Disorders

Previous Serial Number: None

Principal Investigator: Elliot S. Gershon, M D.

Other Investigators: William E. Bunney, Jr., M.D., Frederick K. Goodwin, M.D., Leon Cytryn, M.D., Donald McKnew, M.D., Monte Buchsbaum, M.D., James F. Leckman, M.D., Michele Van Eerdewegh, M.D., Eleanor D. Dibble, D.S.W., Nicholas Rogentine, M.D., R. S. Sparkes, M.D., M. Ann Spence, Ph.D. Dennis L. Murphy, M.D.

Cooperating Units: Immunology Branch, DCBD, National Cancer Institute; Laboratory of Clinical Science, DCBR, NIMH; Division of Medical Genetics, UCLA School of Medicine

Man Years:

Total: 3.75
Professional: 2.75
Other: 1.0

Project Description:

Objective:

1. To identify markers of genetically transmitted vulnerability to affective disorders, where the marker is implicated in the pathophysiology of the disorders.

2. To identify chromosomal linkage between affective disorders and known chromosomal linkage markers. Such markers may be physiologically unrelated to mood disorders

3. To develop and apply mathematical models and methods of analysis for genetics of psychiatric disorders and of quantitative variables. Psychiatric disorders present formidable problems for such analyses, because of variable

penetrance and age of onset, and because of multiple nanifestations of single disorders.

Methods Employed: Processes which have been implicated in the pathophysiology of affective disorders, and are being studied in our protocols, include: (1) enzymes active in the synthesis and catabolism of catecholamines, particularly erythrocyte catechol-O-methyl transferase (COMT), and platelet nonoamine oxidase (MAO); (2) cation transport, particularly Li+ transport into erythrocytes, and ouabain dependent active influx of Na+ and efflux of K+ in erythrocytes; (3) cortical evoked potential amplitudes in relation to stimulus intensity. The cation transport studies are under development; the other studies are in data collection phases.

These variables are studied in patients with affective illness admitted to the intramural program, and their available first degree relatives. All are examined for present or past psychiatric disorder and their family history is obtained, using a systematic interview. Previous patients of the program are recalled for examination, and population controls are also studied.

Effects of medication on physiologic measurements are controlled for by studying patients during a drug free period.

Chromosomal linkage markers are also studied in patients nd family members. These include color blindness, Xg blood roup, G6PD (in Black or Mediterranean ancestry families), -P-Gluconate Dehydrogenase, Acid Phosphatase, Haptoglobin and roup Specific Component, and HLA antigens.

Major Findings: We have developed criteria to test if a haracteristic is an independent genetic factor in ulnerability to an episodic psychiatric disorder. To be a arker of vulnerability, a characteristic should (1) istinguish ill persons from normals, (2) be stable and eritable, and (3) not show independent assortment with the llness. The last criterion is satisfied if, within a edigree, the persons who have the psychiatric illness show ifferent measurements on the observed characteristic from heir well relatives.

We have applied these tests to data on erythrocyte COMT nd visual evoked response amplitude-intensity slope, which ere collected in Jerusalem, Israel. The data on COMT activity atisfy all the above criteria, which is compatible with the ypothesis that COMT identifies genetically determined ulnerability to affective disorders. In the case of AER, the well relatives show the same abnormality in AER slope as the ill persons within the pedigrees studied, suggesting that AER augmentation, by itself, is not a genetic factor in the liability to affective disorder.

Mathematical models of genetically transmitted liability to psychiatric illness have been applied to existing family study data. A single genetic diathesis can account for both unipolar and bipolar affective illness, in two studies in which sufficient data to test this hypothesis is present. Neither single major locus or polygenic inheritance can be ruled out in these data. In one study, with different diagnostic criteria, no single diathesis model could be fitted.

Proposed Course of the Project: Data on approximately 50 probands and their first degree relatives has been collected. 100-150 probands and their relatives are needed for testing the hypotheses of linkage of psychiatric illness to specific chromosomal markers, and for testing the hypotheses of linkage of enzymes of monoamine metabolism or cation transport activities to these markers. A similarly large number of probands is needed for studies of enzyme activity or cation transport activity without reference to chromosomal linkage.

Pharmacologic and biological characteristics observed during acute manic or depressive episodes, such as response to lithium carbonate or accumulation of HVA or cAMP in spinal fluid, can be related to morbid risk in relatives. This may serve to reveal genetically distinct subgroups of patients. Again, a larger number of families is required for conclusions to be drawn.

Studies of children and grandchildren of patients with affective illness are ongoing, and are summarized in a separate project report.

Significance of the Findings: The findings on COMT are the first report of non-independent assortment of a biologic characteristic and a psychiatric illness. This is a necessary but not sufficient condition for demonstrating that a biologic factor is of genetic etiologic importance in an illness.

The single diathesis model of unipolar and bipolar affective illness implies that some of the biologic and pharmacologic differences between the two types of patient are quantitative rather than qualitative. One important implication is that many intermediate gradations on the unipolar-bipolar dimension may be found in different patients. These intermediate patients should fall between classical unipolar and bipolar patients in their family morbid risk, pharmacologic responses, and biologic characteristics.

Honors and Awards:

Dr. Bunney presented a paper on "The inheritance of affective illness" at the Behavior Genetics Society meeting in Seattle, Washington in October 1974.

Dr. Gershon presented a paper on "Genetic strategies in schizophrenia" to the Mexican Psychiatric Association meeting and the conference of Latin-American Psychiatrists in Acapulco, Mexico in May 1975.

Dr. Gershon presented a paper entitled "COMT marks genetic liability to affective illness" at the American Psychiatric Association meeting in Anaheim, California in May 1975.

Dr. Gershon has presented lectures at Stanford University, New York State Psychiatric Institute, and University of California at Los Angeles Division of Medical Genetics. He has also been consultant to a television series, "The Thin Edge," and to the extramural program of NIMH as a site visitor.

Publications:

Gershon, E.S., Bunney, W.E. Jr., Leckman, J.F., Van Eerdewegh, M. and DeBauche, B.A.: The inheritance of affective illness: a review of data and hypotheses, in press, Behav. Genet. (1976).

Gershon, E.S. and Jonas, W.Z.: A clinical and genetic study of catechol-O-methyl transferase in primary affective disorders. Accepted for publication, Arch. Gen. Psychiat.

Dunner, D.L., Gershon, E.S. and Goodwin, F.K.: Heritable factors in the severity of affective illness. In press, Biol. Psychiat.

Jonas, W.Z. and Gershon, E.S.: A method for determination catechol-O-methyl transferase in red blood cells. Clin. Chim. Acta, 54: 391-394, 1974.

Keywords:

Genetics, mathematics and statistics, manic-depressive illness, cortical evoked potentials, monoamine oxidase, catechol-O-methyl transferase, family studies, childhood studies, chromosomes, chromosomal linkage markers.

Project No. Z01 MH 00116-01 AP
1. Adult Psychiatry Branch
2. Section on Biochemistry
3. Bethesda, Maryland

PHS-ADAMHA-NIMH
Individual Project Report
July I, 1974 through June 30, 1975

Project Title: Interactions of Neurotransmitters at Bimolecular Membranes

Previous Serial Number: None

Principal Investigator: Marian S. Kafka, Ph.D.

Other Investigator: Ronald W. Holz, M.D., Ph.D.

Cooperating Units: Section on Pharmacology, Laboratory of Clinical Science

Man Years:

Total:	0.7
Professional:	0.6
Other:	0.1

Project Description:

Objectives: To study interactions between neurotransmitters and bimolecular lipid membranes. The bimolecular lipid membrane (bilayer, BLM, black film) separating two aqueous compartments may serve as a model for the cell plasma membrane separating the interstitial fluid from the cell interior. Further, the bimolecular membrane may serve as a model of an intracellular membrane separating the cytoplasm from a vesicle interior, e.g., a secretory vesicle membrane.

Methods Employed: A bimolecular lipid membrane is formed in such a way that it separates two compartments containing buffer, ions, and a water soluble permeant substance. A tracer quantity of isotopically labeled permeant substance (neurotransmitter) in the presence or absence of the ionophore X537A on the ionophore A23187 is added to one compartment and the passage of the permeant across the membrane and into the second compartment measured by counting aliquots removed at successive time intervals in a scintillation counter. From known volumes, measured area, time, and concentrations of labeled and non-labeled permeant, the net flux of the permeant species and the permeability coefficient of the membrane for that permeant can be calculated. A matched pair of calomel-KCE electrodes, one in each compartment, is used to apply a potential difference across the membrane and to conduct the current resulting from the potential difference. The direct current electrical resistance of the membrane and the electrical conductance can be calculated from the measured voltages and known resistances of the electrical circuit.

Major Findings: The ionophore X537A carries (1) dopamine across the phosphatidyl choline:cholesterol or oxidized cholesterol bimolecular membrane. (2) The rate of transport increases linearly with the concentration of X537A. (3) The rate of transport is independent of an applied electrical field across the membrane. (4) This evidence suggests that the permeating species is a 1:1 complex between dopamine and X537A. (5) The ionophore A23187 does not transport dopamine. (6) The permeability of the bimolecular membrane to calcium increases as the square of the X537A concentration. The transport of calcium is also increased by A23187. (7) Calcium is probably transported with X537A and A23187 as an uncharged complex. (8) Neither desmethylimipramine nor cocaine alters the transport rate of dopamine with X537A.

Significance to Biomedical Research and the Program of the Institute: The experiments on bimolecular membranes provide a physical model for the biological actions of X537A and A23187. In agreement with the bimolecular membrane results, the experiments in biological systems suggest that X537A, but not A23187, can act as a catecholamine ionophore in the release of norepinephrine from peripheral nerve endings and dopamine from synaptosomes, and that X537A can release norepinephrine from chromaffin granules. On the other hand, both X537A and A23187 can act as calcium ionophores in peripheral nerve endings and synaptosomes, the neurohypophysis, platelets, mast cells, and many other systems as well. As the transport of catecholamines and calcium through biological membranes may be mediated by naturally occurring ionophores, interactions between X537A and A23187 and lipid bimolecular membranes may also provide physical models for naturally occurring transport systems.

Proposed Course of Project: To study additional actions of neurotransmitters on membranes by examining the interactions between neurotransmitters, ions, and psychoactive drugs with lipid bimolecular membranes.

Honors and Awards:

Chairman, Intersociety Session on Insulin, FASEB, April 1974.
Seminar: Molecular Diseases Branch, NHLI: "The Interaction of Peptide Hormones and Physical Models of Cell Membranes: Monolayers and Bilayers," July 1974.
Seminar: Behavioral Biology Branch, NICHHD, "The Action of Insulin at Model Membranes," July 1974.

Publications:

Kafka, M.S.: The effect of insulin on the permeability of phosphatidyl choline bimolecular membranes to glucose. J. Membrane Biol. 18: 81-94, 1974.

Kafka, M.S. and Holz, R.W.: Ionophores X537A and A23187: Effects on the permeability of lipid bimolecular membranes to dopamine and calcium. Fed. Proc. 34: 609 (Abstract), 1975.

Project No. Z01 MH 00109-08 AP
1. Adult Psychiatry Branch
2. Family Studies Section
3. Bethesda, Maryland

PHS-ADAMHA-NIMH
Individual Project Report
July 1, 1974 through June 30, 1975

Project Title: A Study of the Separation Process in Adolescents and Their Families

Previous Serial Number: M-AP(C)-15-2

Principal Investigator: Helm Stierlin, M.D., Ph.D.

Other Investigators: None

Cooperating Units: None

Man Years:

Total: 0.25
Professional: 0.15
Other: 0.1

Project Description: This project has been reported each year for the last eight years, under the above previous serial number. The objectives, methodology, and major findings have been contained therein.

The project was terminated in September 1974 at the time of departure of the principal investigator.

Honors and Awards: None

Publications:

Stierlin, H., Levi, L.D., and Savard, R.J.: Contrifugal versus centripetal separation in adolescence: Two patterns and some of their implications. In Feinstein, S. and Giovacchini, P. (Eds.): Annals of American Society for Adolescent Psychiatry. Vol. II. Developmental and Clinical Studies. New York, Basic Books, 1973, pp. 211-239.

Stierlin, H.: Separating Parents and Adolescents. A Perspective on Running Away, Schizophrenia, and Waywardness. New York, Quadrangle/The New York Times Book Co., 1974.

Project No. Z01 MH 00110-08 AP
1. Adult Psychiatry Branch
2. Family Studies Section
3. Bethesda, Maryland

PHS-ADAMHA-NIMH
Individual Project Report
July 1, 1974 through June 30, 1975

Project Title: The Conceptualization of Lasting Dyadic Relationships

Previous Serial Number: M-AP(C)-15-6

Principal Investigator: Helm Stierlin, M.D., Ph.D.

Other Investigators: None

Cooperating Units: None

Man Years:

Total:	0.25
Professional:	0.15
Other:	0.1

Project Description:

Objectives:

This project sought to contribute to the theoretical base for the comparative analysis of a wide variety of human relationships. It grew out of conceptualizations which the investigator developed before he joined the Adult Psychiatry Branch eight years ago and which were published in book form (Conflict and Reconciliation, New York: Doubleday-Anchor, 1969; Science House, 1969). The focus continued to be on the ongoing transaction between two persons, considered as subjects - that is, as centers of an individual orientation toward the self, the world, and the other - and who are changed while the relationship unfolds. The phenomenology and dynamics of psychological exploitation are particularly significant. The implications and limits of a dyadic model for the better understanding of family and group relationships were explored. Also, creativity as a response to a binding and conflictual interpersonal field and its relation to self-destruction was a special focus.

Methods Employed: Study, critical evaluation, and integration of a wide range of ideas and findings reported in the literature of human relationships. At the same time, the project drew on the clinical experiences and observations provided through the clinical service of the Adult Psychiatry Branch, and particularly through family therapies. The issues raised and described in Individual Project Report Z01 MH 00109 AP influenced the conceptual efforts.

Major Findings: (1) The concept of psychological exploitation was further developed and clarified and was integrated with the concept of transactional modes. Specifically, it was related to how needs, power, and interpersonal justice evolve and are defined in human relationships. (2) Various themes were pursued within the broad confines of this project. Among these were a study on how creative and self-destructive processes interweave, a comment on the psychogenic theory of history, a study on the psychoanalyst Paul Schilder, a study on Adolf Hitler from a family perspective, and several book reviews on diverse subjects.

Significance to the Program of the Institute: This conceptual work is relevant to the understanding of schizophrenia as a transactional thought disorder. Beyond that, it illuminated various mental disorders as being linked to special types of human relationships. The complexities of human relationships have far outdistanced the conceptualizations so far at our disposal. This project sought to reduce the conceptual lag in this area. The concept of psychological exploitation is relevant to many pressing social issues.

Proposed Course of Project: The project was terminated when the principal investigator left the Branch in September 1974.

Honors and Awards: None

Publications:

Stierlin, H.: Shame and guilt in family relations: Theoretical and clinical aspects. Arch. Gen. Psychiat. 30: 381-389, 1974.

Stierlin, H.: Contribution to Lexikon der Psychiatrie, Muller, C. (Ed.). Berlin-Heidelberg-New York, Springer, 1974.

Stierlin, H.: Konflike og forsoning. Om dynamikken i mellommenneskelige forhold. Oslo, Glydendal Norsk Forlag, 1974.

Stierlin, H.: Psychoanalytic approaches to schizophrenia in the light of a family model. Int. Rev. Psycho-Anal. 1: 169-178, 1974.

Project No. Z01 MH 00126-06 AP
1. Adult Psychiatry Branch
2. Section on Experimental Group and Family Studies
3. Bethesda, Maryland

PHS-ADAMHA-NIMH
Individual Project Report
July 1, 1974 through June 30, 1975

Project Title: Family Views of Its Social Environment: Effects on Family Therapy Process

Previous Serial Number M-AP(C)-18-12

Principal Investigator: David Reiss, M.D.

Other Investigators: Ronald Costell, M.D. and Loann Drake

Cooperating Units: Section on Personality Development (no longer extant); The Psychiatric Institute of the District of Columbia

Man Years:

Total:	.2
Professional:	.1
Other:	.1

Project Description:

Objectives: During the past six years, a series of laboratory studies have revealed that families, functioning as a group, develop shared and vivid concepts of the structure of the larger social community in which they live and work. Some families see their social environment as being patterned and engrossing; others see their social environment as threatening, chaotic, and overwhelming. Evidence suggests that these shared family constructions of their environment are typical and enduring, and dominate a family's response to any novel or stressful challenge in their social environment. We hypothesized that this is particularly true when a family must involve itself in an entirely new social community. Then, their typical reaction patterns play a major role in shaping their adaptations to, and involvement in, the institution's social processes. This kind of encounter between family and the new institution is very well exemplified by a psychiatric hospital that emphasizes family treatment. When the index member is admitted to the hospital, the whole family is actively engaged in the treatment program. Thus, the family, as a group, must orient itself to a set of novel and stressful challenges. This study was designed to test the relationship between family reaction patterns, as measured in the laboratory, and their adaptation during the first six weeks of family-oriented inpatient psychiatric treatment. Laboratory measures have been used to predict the degree to which the family (1) will become involved and engrossed in the treatment program, or (2) withdraw and protect itself from the hospital community and its programs. The interaction between family and hospital also has been viewed as protypical of interactions between families and a variety of institutions in their social environment. We also studied the interaction between families and schools, and families and occupational settings.

Methods Employed: Our independent variable is the family's problem-solving behavior in the laboratory. Based on this, a family can be placed in one of three categories: environment-sensitive, consensus-sensitive, and distance-sensitive. The dependent variables are selected to measure various aspects of the family's adaptation to the hospital community and its treatment program. Two procedures estimate the family's shared experience of the ward.

One procedure is the Ward Perception Q-Sort. Our theory states that a family's typical approach to construing novel social situations will determine its shared experience of the ward community. This shared experience is a variable intervening between family type and adjustment to the treatment program. The Ward Perception Q-Sort is intended as a direct estimate of this shared perception in the family. Specifically, it measures four aspects of the family's shared perceptions: accuracy, stereotypy, coherence, and the similarity between members. The procedure requires family members, each individual in his own booth, to sort a group of 36 cards into seven categories. Each card contains a description that might be applicable to the psychiatric ward and the seven categories are labeled in descending order from "most characteristic" to "least characteristic." The family is urged to discuss together, through an intercom, how to categorize the cards. Objective scores are computed to estimate the four aspects of family perception from their sorts.

A second procedure is the Family Perception Procedure. This procedure is aimed at assessing, from a different perspective, the character of the family's experience of the social community, in this sense supplementing the Ward Perception Q-Sort. Here, a family is tested immediately following a multiple-family group meeting. Members, working together, are asked to make a number of distinctions between different families and between different members of the same family. Following general procedures outlined by George Kelly, an estimate is made of the number, complexity, and character of the dimensions the family uses to discriminate between individuals and families within the group. Here we attempt to distinguish between simple, moralistic, and superficial distinctions and complex, flexible, and psychologically insightful distinctions.

Three other procedures permit a direct assessment of family-hospital interaction; they are utilized on the ward. Both depend on the family's participation in a multiple-family therapy group, a major treatment modality at both the Psychiatric Institute and NIMH.

The first procedure is direct observation and measurement of the family's interaction with other family and psychiatric staff in the group. Over a series of sessions, the family's seating arrangement and the frequency and direction of their speech will be carefully recorded by an observer. The family's engagement and involvement in the ward community will be indexed by its willingness to disperse itself physically in a group rather than stay huddled together in adjoining seats; it will also be indexed by frequent speech directed at many individuals.

The second procedure is the sociometric technique. It, too, is being used as a measure of family engagement and involvement. In particular, we are interested in the experiential boundary the family constructs between itself and the rest of the community. Family members are asked to choose others in the multiple family group whom they like and know well. Impermeable boundaries will be indicated by families who choose few others and where members choose others in the same family. Members in families with impermeable boundaries should also be the object of choice by few others, outside the family, in the multiple family group.

A third procedure is a group cohesiveness questionnaire adapted from studies of outcome and process in therapy groups of unrelated members. This is used to estimate the family's subjective sense of being involved in the multiple family group.

Overall, we have made the following predictions: Environment-sensitive families - who can develop progressively more complex, subtle and accurate solutions to laboratory problems - will show simple kinds of evaluations of the ward social community on the Q-Sort and Family Perception Procedure. They will also show evidence of greater engagement and involvement in the therapeutic process. Consensus-sensitive families - those who force an early agreement among themselves on simple and stereotyped solutions to laboratory puzzles - will show similar characteristics in their conceptions of the social community on the ward and remain isolated and distant from the program.

Progress: Data collection has been completed for the NIMH sample; since complete data collection was obtained on only five families before the inpatient unit was shut down, these data are regarded as useful, though preliminary. The findings show (1) interaction coding in the multiple family group can be done with very high reliability. (2) The Ward Perception and Family Perception tests can be administered without difficulty and are understandable to the families. (3) There are some distinct links between performance of the family in the laboratory and on the ward. On this third point, an example is the near-perfect relationship between the levels of intra-family communication in the laboratory and in the multiple family group.

Proposed Course of Project: Data collection from the Psychiatric Institute sample has been completed. Scoring procedures for both the Family and Ward Perception tests have been developed and computer programs for scoring multiple family group behavior have been completed and applied to the first 13 families. Preliminary analyses have shown that families behave with remarkable consistency in the multiple family group setting. It is this remarkable consistency of family behavior, vis-a-vis other families, that this study is designed to measure and analyze.

Project No. Z01 MH 00127-06 AP
1. Adult Psychiatry Branch
2. Section on Experimental Group and Family Studies
3. Bethesda, Maryland

PHS-ADAMHA-NIMH
Individual Project Report
July 1, 1974 through June 30, 1975

Project Title: Coordinating "Micro-Codes" in Family Consensual Experience: A Study of the Responses to Speech Hesitancy and Fluency in Family Interaction

Previous Serial Number: M-AP(C)-18-2

Principal Investigator: David Reiss, M.D.

Other Investigators: None

Cooperating Units: None

Man Years:

Total: 0
Professional: 0
Other: 0

Project Description:

This project has been reported previously. The Objectives, Methodology, and Major Findings have been contained therein. The project was terminated at the time of departure of the principal investigator on June 30, 1974.

Project No. Z01 MH 00128-06 AP
1. Adult Psychiatry Branch
2. Section on Experimental Group and Family Studies
3. Bethesda, Maryland

PHS-ADAMHA-NIMH
Individual Project Report
July 1, 1974 through June 30, 1975

Project Title: The Effects of Progressive Isolation of an Individual From his Family on his Perceptual Functioning: Use of a Teletype-LINC Apparatus to Study the Reciprocal Relationship of Family Interaction and Individual Thinking

Previous Serial Number: M-AP(C)-18-3

Principal Investigator: David Reiss, M.D.

Other Investigators: None

Cooperating Units: None

Man Years:

Total:	0.1
Professional:	0.0
Other:	0.1

Project Description:

This project has been reported previously (under the previous serial number). The Objectives, Methodology, and Major Findings have been contained therein. The Project was terminated at the time of departure of the principal investigator on June 30, 1974.

Project No. Z01 MH 00129-05 AP
1. Adult Psychiatry Branch
2. Section on Experimental Group and Family Studies
3. Bethesda, Maryland

PHS-ADAMHA-NIMH
Individual Project Report
July 1, 1974 through June 30, 1975

Project Title: Nurse-Doctor-Patient Interaction: An Experimental Study of its Role in Patient Acculturation on Psychiatric Wards

Previous Serial Number: M-AP(C)-18-6

Principal Investigator: David Reiss, M.D.

Other Investigator: Richard Almond, M.D.

Cooperating Units: Department of Psychiatry, Stanford University Medical School, Palo Also, California

Man Years:

Total: 0
Professional: 0
Other: 0

Project Description:

This project has been reported previously (under the previous serial number). The Objectives, Methodology, and Major Findings have been contained therein. The project was terminated at the time of departure of the investigators.

Project No. Z01 MH 00130-06 AP
1. Adult Psychiatry Branch
2. Section on Experimental Group and Family Studies
3. Bethesda, Maryland

PHS-ADAMHA-NIMH
Individual Project Report
July 1, 1974 through June 30, 1975

Project Title: Values and Atmosphere on a Psychiatric Ward: Basic Dimensions and Institution Comparisons

Previous Serial Number: M-AP(C)-18-13

Principal Investigator: Ronald Costell, M.D.

Other Investigator: David Reiss, M.D.

Cooperating Units: NIH Nursing Administration, Nursing Units 3-West, 3-East, 4-West, 4-East, and The Psychiatric Institute of the District of Columbia

Man Years:

Total: 0
Professional: 0
Other: 0

Project Description:

This project has been reported previously (under the previous serial number). The Objectives, Methodology, and Major Findings have been contained therein. The project was terminated at the time of departure of the investigators.

Project No. Z01 MH 00271-06 LCS
1. Laboratory of Clinical Science
2. Office of the Chief
3. Bethesda, Maryland

PHS-ADAMHA-NIMH
Individual Project Report
July 1, 1974 through June 30, 1975

Project Title: Methods for assay of biogenic amine metabolites in human biological fluids

Previous Serial No.: Included in M-CS-OC(C)-21

Principal Investigator: Edna K. Gordon

Other Investigators: Irwin J. Kopin, Sanford Markey, Fredrik Foppen

Cooperating Units: Sections on Experimental Therapeutics, Psychiatry and Clinical Psychopharmacology, Laboratory of Clinical Science

Man Years:		
	Total	3.0
	Professional	2.0
	Other	1.0

Project Description:

Gas chromatography, mass spectroscopy, and fluorimetry are used to assay metabolites of biogenic amines in cerebrospinal fluid, blood, or urine of patients or subjects treated with drugs or isotopically-labelled amines. Appropriately labelled deuterium compounds, synthesized by chemical or enzymatic techniques, are used as internal standards.

The exquisite sensitivity and specificity of these techniques makes possible study of the amine metabolites in the various fluids obtained from the patients. The effects of drugs on these are described in publications from the various clinical units. The interpretation of these finds is facilitated by similar studies in primates which have shown that HVA in CSF is derived mainly from brain but the metabolites of norepinephrine may be formed in the spinal cord.

Keyword Descriptors:

Gas Chromatography	VMA
Mass Spectroscopy	MHPG
Cerebrospinal Fluid	HVA
Probenecid	5HlAA

Honors and Awards:

None.

Publications:

Gordon, E.K., Perlow, M. and Oliver, J.: Origins of catecholamine metabolites in monkey cerebrospinal fluid. J. Neurochemistry (In press).

Gordon, E.K., Oliver, J. and Kopin, I.J.: Mass fragmentographic analysis of vanillyl mandelic acid and other catecholamine metabolites in cerebrospinal fluid and the effect of probenecid. Life Sci. (In press).

Gordon, E.K., Oliver, J., Black, K., and Kopin, I.J.: Simultaneous assay by mass fragmentography of vanillyl mandelic acid, homovanillic acid, and 3-methoxy-4-hydroxy-phenethylene glycol in cerebrospinal fluid and urine. Biochem. Med. 11: 32-40, 1974.

Project No. Z01 MH 00272-04 LCS
1. Laboratory of Clinical Science
2. Office of the Chief
3. Bethesda, Maryland

PHS-ADAMHA-NIMH
Individual Project Report
July 1, 1974 through June 30, 1975

Project Title: Metabolism, Distribution and Biochemical Effects of Psychoactive Drugs

Previous Serial No.: M-CS-OC(C)-19

Principal Investigator: Sanford Markey

Other Investigators: Robert L. Colburn, Fredrik K. Foppen, Edna Gordon, Richard Hawks (Guest Worker) Irwin J. Kopin, Magda Claeys (Guest Worker), Nguyen B. Thoa (Guest Worker)

Cooperating Units: Sections on Experimental Therapeutics, Psychiatry, and Clinical Psychopharmacology, Laboratory of Clinical Science

Man Years:	Total	3.5
	Professional	3.0
	Other	0.5

Project Description:

The metabolism and distribution of drugs in animals and Man are studied to relate the effects of drugs to their biochemical actions and clinical efficacy. Methods for synthesis of isotopically labelled drugs and for detection and assay of cocaine, bromocryptine, amitryptaline, desipramine, etc. and their metabolites have been developed or are in progress. The methods involve primarily gas chromatography and/or mass spectroscopy. The pharmacokinetics and metabolism of cocaine have been described in monkeys and an active metabolite, norcocaine, found in the brain. Other studies are to be done in Man, in collaboration with the clinical units, to relate blood levels and rates of metabolism to clinical efficacy.

Keyword Descriptors:

Gas chromatography	amitryptaline
Mass Spectroscopy	desipramine
Cocaine	plasma levels of drugs
Bromocryptine	drug metabolism

Honors and Awards:

Dr. Markey has been asked by the Acting Director, Regional Resource Program, NIGMS, to serve on a committee to evaluate clinical application of mass spectroscopy.

Publications:

Hawks, R.L., Kopin, I.J., Colburn, R.W. and Thoa, N.B.: Norcocaine: A pharmacologically active metabolite of cocaine found in brain. Life Sci. 15: 2189-2195, 1974.

Project No. Z01 MH 00273-06 LCS
1. Laboratory of Clinical Science
2. Office of the Chief
3. Bethesda, Maryland

PHS-ADAMHA-NIMH
Individual Project Report
July 1, 1974 through June 30, 1975

Project Title: Studies on synaptosomes

Previous Serial No.: M-CS-OC(C)-16

Principal Investigator: Robert W. Colburn

Other Investigators: Irwin J. Kopin and Nguyen B. Thoa

Cooperating Units: Section on Medicine, Laboratory of Clinical Science

Man Years:	Total	0.5
	Professional	0.5
	Other	0.0

Project Description:

A preparation of synaptosomes isolated from rat brain is used as a model of nerve endings to study affects of drugs on uptake and release of biogenic amines. The influence of ionophores, which bind calcium, on the release of norepinephrine from synaptosomes was examined to determine their effect on the release of the amine and their interactions with calcium and magnesium. A 23187 induced release of norepinephrine mainly as the amine and this action was enhanced by calcium and depressed by magnesium. X537A however, releases norepinephrine mostly as deaminated metabolites and acts independently of calcium or magnesium. A 23187, therefore is thought to be associated at least in part, with exocytotic amine release, possibly by enhancing entry of calcium across the plasma membrane. X537A on the other hand may act as a carrier of the amine across the vessicular membrane and expose the amine to intrasynaptosomal monoamine oxidase.

This model system will continue to be used when appropriate to answer questions arising regarding distribution or disposition of putative neurotransmitters or neurohumors.

Honors and Awards: None.

Publications: None.

Project No. Z01 MH 00274-01 LCS
1. Laboratory of Clinical Science
2. Office of the Chief
3. Bethesda, Maryland

Project Title: Methods of ionization suitable for high molecular weight (1000-5000 a.m.u.) mass spectroscopy.

Principal Investigator: Sanford P. Markey
Previous Serial Number: None
Other Investigators: None

Cooperating Units: Technical Development Branch, NIMH/NINDS

Man Years: Total 0.3
Professional 0.2
Other 0.0

Project Description:

Application of Mass Spectroscopy to relatively high molecular weight substances (e.g., peptides) has not been feasible because of the lack of a suitable means for volatilization and ionization without destruction of these compounds. An electrohydrodynamic ion source which can be attached to a double focusing high resolution mass spectrometer has been constructed and is now being tested using various non-aqueous electrolyte fluids suitable for ion spray. It is hoped that this technique can be applied to analysis of physiologically important peptides and other thermally labile compounds of low volatility.

Honors and Awards:

By invitation, Dr. Markey has given three seminars on the "Applications of GC-MS to the Study of Inborne Errors of Metabolism," at the Heart and Lung Institute, NIH, the Washington Area Gas Chromatography Discussion Group, and the Department of Pharmacology, University of Arizona, Tucson, Arizona.

Publications:

None.

Project No. Z01 MH 00421- 13 LCS
1. Laboratory of Clinical Science
2. Section on Pharmacology
3. Bethesda, Maryland

PHS-ADAMHA-NIMH
Individual Project Report
July 1, 1974 through June 30, 1975

Project Title: Biogenic amines and releasing factors in the brain.

Previous Serial Number: M-CS-Ph-6; M-CS-Ph-3; M-CS-Ph-5

Principal Investigators: Michael Brownstein, Juan Saavedra (Visiting Scientist), Miklos Palkovits (Guest Worker), Julius Axelrod

Other Investigators: John Tallman, Adult Psychiatry Branch, Section on Biochemistry; Akira Arimura, Endocrinology Section, Veterans Administration Hospital, New Orleans, La.; Robert Utiger, Department of Medicine, University of Pennsylvania.

Man Years: Total: 4.0
Professional: 3.0
Other: 1.0

Project Description:

Objectives: To develop micromethods for the measurement of normally occurring biogenic amines and enzymes. To localize these amines and enzymes and releasing factors in specific brain nuclei and determine the effects of endocrinological manipulations.

Methods Employed: Biochemical, pharmacological and enzymatic radiochemical techniques.

Major Findings: The following micromethods have been developed: tryptophan hydroxylase, 5-hydroxytryptophan decarboxylase, tyramine, and glutamic acid decarboxylase. These methods and the development of the brain microdissection techniques made it possible to map about 130 nuclei of the brain for their biogenic amines and their enzymes and study the effects of various endocrine manipulations. Tryptophan hydroxylase has been found to be highly localized in serotonergic nerve cell bodies and axons. Dopamine β-hydroxylase and tyrosine hydroxylase have been mapped in the limbic area. There are marked changes in serotonin in raphe nuclei in stress. Lesions in the locus coeruleus affect serotonin metabolism in raphe. Effects of PNMT inhibitors and experimental hypertension on PNMT in discrete areas of the brain are being examined. The distribution of serotonergic terminals were examined after raphe lesions. Serotonergic cell bodies in the raphe project axons into the limbic area as well as the hypothalamus. Combined neurochemical and anatomical studies show that lesions in the locus coeruleus produce degeneration of fibers and disappearance of norepinephrine in cortical and hypothalamic areas. A similar study on the effects of lesions in the substantia nigra was carried out. A cholinergic pathway originating in the habenula and ending in the interpeduncular nucleus was found.

A substantial number of GABA nerve terminals seem to be present in hypothalamic nuclei. Somatostatin (a peptide that inhibits the release of growth hormone) is present in other brain areas in addition to the hypothalamus.

Significance to Biomedical Research and the Program of the Institute: The localization of biogenic amines, enzymes and releasing factors in specific nuclei of the rat brain will enable us to study the effect of drugs, physiological and behavioral manipulations on biogenic amines, enzymes and releasing factors in a more precise manner.

Proposed Course of Project: The effect of endocrinological, pharmacological, physiological and behavioral manipulations on levels of biogenic amines, releasing factors and enzymes in specific brain nuclei will be examined.

Keyword Descriptors:

Noradrenaline, dopamine, serotonin, tyrosine hydroxylase, thyroid releasing factor, LH releasing factor.

Honors and Awards:

Dr. Axelrod received the Paul Hoch Award of the American Psychopathological Society and an honorary Doctor of Science degree from the Medical College of Philadelphia. He was also a Regents' Lecturer at the University of California at Irvine, gave the Gregory Pincus Lecture, was Robbins Lecturer at Pomona College, was Sesquicentennial Lecturer at the Medical University of South Carolina, gave the 15th Anniversary Commemorative Lecture at the Tanabe Amino Acid Research Foundation, Kyoto, Japan, the Henry H. Turner Lecture at the University of Oklahoma and the J. C. Krantz Lecture at the University of Maryland in Baltimore. Dr. Brownstein was an invited visiting scientist at the Department of Anatomy, Semmelweis Medical University, Budapest, Hungary for three months.

Dr. Brownstein was also an invited speaker at Howard University to the Council for the Advancement of Science Writing. Dr. Saavedra gave invitational seminars at the Mayo Medical School, The Massachusetts Institute of Technology and the National Institute of Cardiology in Mexico City, Mexico where he also was an invited discussant and presented a paper at the VI Meeting of the American Society for Neurochemistry. He also was an invited participant in an International Society for Psychoneuro-endocrinology Workshop given by the University of Alabama School of Medicine.

Publications:

ARTICLE PUBLISHED IN A PERIODICAL:

Axelrod, J.: Neurotransmitters. Scientific American 230: 59-71, 1974.

Brownstein, M.J., Saavedra, J.M., Axelrod, J., Zeman, G.H. and Carpenter, D.O.: Coexistence of several putative neurotransmitters in single identified neurons of Aplysia. Proc. Nat. Acad. Sci. 71: 4662-4665, 1974.

Brownstein, M.J., Saavedra, J.M., Palkovits, M. and Axelrod, J.: Histamine content of hypothalamic nuclei of the rat. Brain Research 77: 151-156, 1974.

Brownstein, M., Kobayashi, R., Palkovits, M. and Saavedra, J.M.: Choline acetyltransferase levels in diencephalic nuclei of the rat. J. Neurochem. 24: 35-38, 1975.

Brownstein, M.J., Palkovits, M., Saavedra, J.M., Bassiri, R.M. and Utiger, R.D.: Thyrotropin-releasing hormone in specific nuclei of rat brain. Science 185: 267-269, 1974.

Brownstein, M., Saavedra, J.M. and Palkovits, M.: Norepinephrine and dopamine in the limbic system of the rat. Brain Research 79: 431-436, 1974.

Ciaranello, R.D., Hoffman, H.J., Shire, J.G.M. and Axelrod, J.: Genetic regulation of the catecholamine biosynthetic enzymes. II. Inheritance of tyrosine hydroxylase, dopamine-β-hydroxylase, and phenylethanolamine N-methyltransferase. J. Biol. Chem. 249: 4528-4536, 1974.

Ciaranello, R.D., Lipsky, A. and Axelrod, J.: Association between fighting behavior and catecholamine biosynthetic enzyme activity in two inbred mouse sublines. Proc. Nat. Acad. Sci. USA 71: 3006-3008, 1974.

Coyle, J.T., Wooten, G.F. and Axelrod, J.: Evidence for estranoradrenergic dopamine-β-hydroxylase activity in rat salivary gland. J. Neurochem. 22: 923-929, 1974.

Coyle, J.T. and Kuhar, M.J.: Subcellular localization of dopamine β-hydroxylase and endogenous norepinephrine in the rat hypothalamus. Brain Research 65: 475-487, 1974.

Holz, R.W.: The effects of the polyene antibiotics nystatin and amphotericin α on thin lipid membranes. Annals New York Academy of Sciences 235: 469-479, 1974.

Holz, R.: The release of dopamine from synaptosomes from rat striatum by the ionophores X 537A and A 23187. Biochimica et Biophysica Acta 375: 138-152, 1975.

Holz, R.W. and Coyle, J.T.: The effects of various salts, temperature, and the alkaloids veratridine and batrachotoxin on the uptake of $[^3H]$ dopamine into synaptosomes from rat striatum. Molecular Pharm. 10: 746-758, 1974.

Naftchi, N.E., Wooten, G.F., Lowman, E.W. and Axelrod, J.: Relationship between serum dopamine-β-hydroxylase activity, catecholamine metabolism, and hemodynamic changes during paroxysmal hypertension in quadriplegia. Circ. Res. 35: 850-861, 1974.

Palkovits, M., Brownstein, M., Saavedra, J.M. and Axelrod, J.: Norepinephrine and dopamine content of hypothalamic nuclei of the rat. Brain Research 77: 137-149, 1974.

Palkovits, M., Arimura, A., Brownstein, M., Schally, A.V. and Saavedra, J.M.: Luteinizing hormone-releasing hormone (LH-RH) content of the hypothalamic nuclei in rat. Endocrinology 96: 554-558, 1974.

Palkovits, M., Brownstein, M. and Saavedra, J.M.: Serotonin content of the brain stem nuclei in the rat. Brain Research 80: 237-249, 1974.

Palkovits, M. Saavedra, J.M., Kobayashi, R.M. and Brownstein, M.: Choline acetyltransferase content of limbic nuclei of the rat. Brain Research 79: 443-450, 1974.

Saavedra, J.M. and Axelrod, J.: Brain tryptamine and the effects of drugs. Adv. Biochem. Psychopharmacol. 10: 135-139, 1974.

Saavedra, J.M. and Axelrod, J.: Enzymatic-isotopic micromethods for the measurement of biogenic amines in brain tissue and body fluids. J. Psychiat. Res. 11: 289-291, 1974.

Saavedra, J.M., Brownstein, M.J., Carpenter, D.O. and Axelrod, J.: Octopamine: Presence in single neurons of Aplysia suggests neurotransmitter function. Science 185: 364-365, 1974.

Saavedra, J.M., Brownstein, M., Palkovits, M., Kizer, S. and Axelrod, J.: Tyrosine hydroxylase and dopamine-ß-hydroxylase: distribution in the individual rat hypothalamic nuclei. J. Neurochem. 23: 869-871, 1974.

Saavedra, J.M., Coyle, J.T. and Axelrod, J.: Developmental characteristics of phenylethanolamine and octopamine in the rat brain. J. Neurochem. 23: 511-515, 1974.

Saavedra, J.M., Palkovits, M., Brownstein, J.J. and Axelrod, J.: Localisation of phenylethanolamine N-methyltransferase in the rat brain nuclei. Nature 248: 695-696, 1974.

Saavedra, J.M., Palkovits, M., Brownstein, M.J. and Axelrod, J.: Serotonin distribution in the nuclei of the rat hypothalamus and preoptic region. Brain Research 77: 157-165, 1974.

Saavedra, J.M.: Enzymatic-isotopic method for octopamine at the picogram level. Analytical Biochem. 59: 628-633, 1974.

Saavedra, J.M.: Measurement of biogenic amines at the picogram level. Progress in Analytical Chemistry 7: 33-44, 1974.

Saavedra, J.M., Brownstein, M.J. and Palkovits, M.: Serotonin distribution in the limbic system of the rat. Brain Research 79: 437-441, 1974.

Hoffman, A.R., Ciarnello, R.D. and Axelrod, J.: Substrate and inhibitor kinetics of bovine phenylethanolamine-N-methyltransferase. Biochem. Pharmacol. 24: 544-546, 1975.

Thoa, N.B., Wooten, G.F., Axelrod, J. and Kopin, I.J.: On the mechanism of release of norepinephrine from sympathetic nerves induced by depolarizing agents and sympathomimetic drugs. Molecular Pharm. 11: 10-18, 1975.

Wooten, G.F. and Ciaranello, R.D.: Proportionality between dopamine-β-hydroxylase activity and immunoreactive protein concentration in human serum. Pharmacology 12: 272-282, 1974.

Wooten, G.F. and Saavedra, J.M.: Axonal transport of phenylethanolamine-N-methyltransferase in toad sciatic nerve. J. Neurochem. 22: 1059-1064, 1974.

Ciaranello, R.D. and Axelrod, J.: Effects of dexamethasone on neurotransmitter enzymes in chromaffin tissue of the newborn rat. J. Neurochem. 24: 775-778, 1975.

ARTICLE IN A BOOK, PAMPHLET, OR BULLETIN:

Axelrod, J.: Regulation of the neurotransmitter norepinephrine. In Schmitt, F.O. and Worden, F.G. (Eds.): The Neurosciences. Third Study Program. Cambridge, Mass., MIT Press, 1974, pp. 863-876.

Coyle, J.T.: Biochemical aspects of the catecholaminergic neurons in the brain of the fetal and neonatal rat. In Fuxe, K., Olson, L. and Zotterman, Y. (Eds.) Dynamics of degeneration and growth in neurons. New York, Pergamon Press, 1974, pp. 425-434.

Coyle, J.T.: Development of the central catecholaminergic neurons. In Schmitt, F.O. and Worden, F.G. (Eds.): The Neurosciences. Third Study Program. Cambridge, Mass., MIT Press, 1974, pp. 877-884.

Project No. Z01 MH 00422-04 LCS
1. Laboratory of Clinical Science
2. Section on Pharmacology
3. Bethesda, Maryland

PHS-ADAMHA-NIMH
Individual Project Report
July 1, 1974 through June 30, 1975

Project Title: Biochemical and pharmacological studies on the pineal gland.

Previous Serial Number: M-CS-Ph-7

Principal Investigators: Jorge Romero (Guest Worker), Martin Zatz (Guest Worker), John Kebabian (Guest Worker).

Other Investigators: Julius Axelrod, David O. Carpenter, Armed Forces Radiobiology Research Institute (AFRRI) and William Shain, AFRRI.

Cooperating Units: Armed Forces Radiobiology Research Institute, Neurobiology Department (DNA).

Man Years:	Total:	3.5
	Professional:	2.5
	Others:	1.0

Project Description:

Objectives: To use the pineal as a model to learn how nerves interact with responsive cells.

Methods Employed: Biochemical, pharmacological and radioactive tracer techniques.

Major Findings: Stimulation of the β-adrenergic receptor with catecholamines generates cyclic AMP which in turn acts at two sites to increase pineal N-acetyltransferase. One site involves the stimulation of RNA synthesis (transcription) and the other, protein synthesis (translation). There is an endogenous diurnal rhythm in the synthesis of messenger RNA related to N-acetyltransferase activity. A method for the direct measurement of the β-adrenergic receptor has been developed. The number of available β-adrenergic receptors and the sensitivity of adenylate cyclase are reduced by prior β-adrenergic stimulation.

Venom from Russel's viper has been found to contain a heat labile, non-dialyzable component that selectively antagonizes isoproterenol induced increase in pineal adenylate cyclase, dopamine induced adenylate cyclase from rat caudate and ACTH sensitive adenylate cyclase in the adrenal. Thus, the venom appears to function as an "uncoupler" of the receptor adenylate cyclase complex.

Significance to Biomedical Research and the Program of the Institute: The problems of nerve cell interactions and circadian rhythm are of prime importance to neurobiology and behavior. The pineal has served as a useful model to study these phenomena.

Proposed Course of Project: Further studies of mechanisms as to how neurotransmitters change cell responsiveness will be explored.

Keyword Descriptors:

β-adrenergic receptor, super- and subsensitivity, cyclic ANP

Honors and Awards:

Dr. Romero was an invited participant in a study group at the meeting of the American College of Neuropsychopharmacology in Puerto Rico where he also presented a paper; he also gave an invitational seminar at MIT. Dr. Zatz was an invited seminar speaker at the University of California at San Diego.

Publications:

ARTICLE PUBLISHED IN A PERIODICAL:

Axelrod, J.: The pineal gland: A neurochemical transducer. Science 184: 1341-1348, 1974.

Romero, J.A. and Axelrod, J.: Pineal β-adrenergic receptor: Diurnal variation in sensitivity. Science 184: 1091-1092, 1974.

Project No. Z01 MH 00423-02 LCS
1. Laboratory of Clinical Science
2. Section on Pharmacology
3. Bethesda, Maryland

PHS-ADAMHA-NIMH
Individual Project Report
July 1, 1974 through June 30, 1975

Project Title: Studies on protein carboxymethyltransferase.

Previous Serial Number: M-CS-Ph-8

Principal Investigators: Emanuel Diliberto (Guest Worker), O. Humberto Viveros (Visiting Scientist), Julius Axelrod.

Other Investigators: None

Cooperating Units: None

Man Years:	Total:	2.5
	Professional:	2.5
	Other:	0

Project Description:

Objectives: To study the properties, distribution, and physiological role of protein carboxymethyltransferase.

Methods Employed: Enzymatic and radiometric.

Major Findings: Protein carboxymethyltransferase was found to be highly localized in rat brain and especially in the synaptosomal fraction. It is also high in testis and it is present in most endocrine organs. The enzyme is highly localized in the cytosol of the adrenal medulla. An acceptor protein for this enzyme appears to be concentrated in the membrane of the chromaffin granules. Preliminary evidence for a new methyltransferase in membrane lipids has been found.

Significance to Biomedical Research and the Program of the Institute: This methyltransferase may be involved in nervous function and the exocytotic process.

Proposed Course of Project: The role of this enzyme in exocytosis will be explored.

Keyword Descriptors:

Methanol-forming enzyme, protein-forming enzyme, esodenosyl methyonine.

Honors and Awards:

None.

Publications:

ARTICLE PUBLISHED IN A PERIODICAL:

Diliberto, E. J., Jr. and Axelrod, J.: Characterization and substrate specificity of a protein carboxymethylase in the pituitary gland. Proc. Nat. Acad. Sci. 71: 1701-1704, 1974.

Project No. Z01 MH 00401-10 LCS
1. Laboratory of Clinical Science
2. Section on Medicine
3. Bethesda, Maryland

PHS-ADAMHA-NIMH
Individual Project Report
July 1, 1974 through June 30, 1975

Project Title: Formation, release, disposition and metabolism of biogenic amines in animals.

Previous Serial Number: M-CS-M(C)-08

Principal Investigator: Irwin J. Kopin

Other Investigators: Robert W. Colburn, Gertrude D. Maengwyn-Davies (Guest Worker), Fredrik H. Foppen, Horst Grobecker (Guest Worker), Charles R. Lake, J. Stephen Kizer, Charles W. Popper, John L. Reid, Michael F. Roizen, Nguyen B. Thoa (Guest Worker), Marcel Tappaz (Guest Worker), Yousef Tizabi (Guest Worker), Virginia K. Weise, Michael G. Ziegler, Justin A. Zivin.

Cooperating Units: Sections on Pharmacology, and Histopharmacology, Laboratory of Clinical Science

Man Years:		
	Total	10.5
	Professional	8.5
	Other	2.0

Project Description:

The objectives of this long-term project are to define the mechanisms which control the synthesis, storage, release, action and termination of action of biogenic amines and other putative neurotransmitters, to determine how drugs act through affecting these mechanisms and to establish how genetic or environmental factors may influence these controls of synaptic neurotransmission. The methods used involve study of labelled amines or their precursors to determine the formation and disposition of the compounds, radiometric and fluorimetric assay of the amines and their metabolites in tissues and body fluids, histological techniques to localize the amines and synthetic enzymes in brain areas, and radiometric assays of the enzymes involved in formation or metabolism of the amines. The effects of drugs, toxins, abnormal endocrine states and stress are examined.

Although dopamine-β-hydroxylase (DBH) in plasma is derived from sympathetic nerves, is released in vitro along with norepinephrine, and is transiently elevated in animals subjected to severe stress (cold, immobilization), there is no major alteration of the level of the enzyme in plasma with prolonged changes in sympathetic nerve activity. Drugs which enhance release of catecholamines and elevate plasma levels of the amines do not produce significant alteration in plasma DBH, nor do drugs which inhibit release of norepinephrine from the sympathetic nerves. Reserpine, however, which increases the rate of DBH formation, does increase DBH levels in plasma, but only after a few days. Vinblastin, which interferes with axonal transport, lowers DBH levels. These observations indicate that DBH levels in plasma may reflect the rate of synthesis of DBH in the cell bodies and the transport of the enzymes to the nerve endings rather than the level of sympathetic neuronal activity; the latter is best reflected by plasma levels of catecholamines.

In the rat, levels of epinephrine in plasma are greater than norepinephrine, but epinephrine almost completely disappears after adrenalectomy; presumably epinephrine is derived mainly from the adrenal medulla while norepinephrine is derived from sympathetic nerves. The plasma levels of both catecholamines are markedly depressed during anesthesia with any of a variety of agents and are strikingly sensitive to body temperature, declining as animals became warm and increasing as the temperature falls. DBH levels change only transiently and rapidly returned to normal, presumably because of changes in blood volume. In spontaneously hypertensive rats (SHR) plasma catecholamine levels were higher than appropriate controls, but both SHR and controls have lower levels of plasma DBH than normotensive rats of the same strain (Wistar) derived from a different source. Antihypertensive drugs also influence plasma catecholamine and DBH levels in rats. In mice attacked by other mice (made aggressive by isolation) blood levels of catecholamines are elevated, as are levels of catecholamine synthesizing enzymes and catecholamines in the adrenal glands of these animals. There are genetically controlled differences in this response to attack and isolation may also influence the biochemical changes illicited in the victims.

The isolated guinea pig vas deferens and the perfused bovine adrenal gland have been used to demonstrate that inhalation of anesthetics diminish release of catecholamines by a direct action, as well as by affecting the central nervous systems.

The levels of catecholamines (norepinephrine and dopamine) and of serotonin and the activity of the enzymes responsible for their formation have been studied in regions of brain of animals subjected to treatment with narcotics, anesthetic agents, or brain lesions and in rats with electrodes implanted which allow self-stimulation of the brain. Epinephrine, and PNMT, the biosynthetic enzyme responsible for its formation from norepinephrine, have been found in certain areas of the brain and spinal cord, but the role of this catecholamine has not yet been determined. Spinal cord lesions result in a decrease in catecholamines in the areas damaged and it appears unlikely that the hypothesis that amines contribute to the progression of the lesion can be supported.

Rats treated with amphetamine have altered behavior which varies with dose and age of the animals. There may be a relation of the low-dose effects to the paradoxical sedative effect of amphetamine in hyperactive children.

Biogenic amines are important in mediating the responses of the peripheral sympathetic nervous system and as neurotransmitters in brain. Understanding the mechanisms for control of their synthesis, storage, release, action, and termination of action is essential in exploring how drugs, toxins, hormones, etc. may influence neurotransmission and how these substances may play a role in the pathogenesis of mental and neurological disorders.

Further study of these processes and the influence of genetic, environmental, and endocrine factors and of drugs is planned.

Keyword Descriptors:

Dopamine-β-hydroxylase	Mechanisms of Neurotransmitter Release
Norepinephrine	Biosynthesis of Neurotransmitter Release
Epinephrine	Vinblastin
Rat Plasma	Reserpine
Sympathetic Nervous System	Fighting Behavior of Mice
Anesthetics	Amphetamine
Halothane	Spinal Cord
Body Temperature	
Brain	

Honors and Awards:

By invitation, Dr. Michael Roizen presented a seminar at Georgetown University, Washington, D. C. entitled "Interaction of Anesthetic Agents and Adrenergic Neurones."

Dr. Charles Lake was invited to Shepherd-Pratt Hospital, Baltimore, Maryland to present a seminar on "Catecholamines in Psychiatric Disorders." In addition, Dr. Lake presented two seminars at Georgetown University, Washington, D. C. entitled "Psychopharmacology I" and "Psychopharmacology II."

Dr. Kopin was invited to lecture on "Biochemistry of Catecholamines" at the Department of Pharmacology, University of Arizona, Tucson, Arizona.

By invitation, Dr. Kopin attended and participated at a symposium entitled "Cerebrospinal Fluid and the Brain" at Bar Harbor, Maine. At the University of Alabama, Dr. Kopin participated at a Workshop on Recent Developments in Schizophrenia Research; participated in a symposium on Biological and Clinical Aspects of the Developing Nervous System at Marco Island, Florida; and the Kroc Foundation for the Advancement of Medical Science's International Conference on GABA Research held at Santa Ynez, California.

Publications:

Kopin, I.J.: Regulation of catecholamine-synthesizing enzymes. J. Psychiat. Res. 11: 335-338, 1974.

Reid, J.L. and Kopin, I.J.: Significance of plasma dopamine-β-hydroxylase activity as an index of sympathetic neuronal function. Proc. Nat. Acad. Sci. USA 71: 4392-4394, 1974.

Reid, J.L. and Kopin, I.J.: The effects of ganglionic blockade, reserpine and vinblastine on plasma catecholamines and dopamine-β-hydroxylase in the rat. JPET (in press).

Reid, J.L., Zivin, J.A., Foppen, F.H. and Kopin, I.J.: Catecholamine neurotransmitters and synthetic enzymes in the spinal cord of the rat. Life Sci. 16: 975-984, 1975.

Roizen, M.F., Moss, J., Henry, D.P. and Kopin, I.J.: Effects of halothane on plasma catecholamines. Anesthesiology 41: 432-439, 1974.

Roizen, M.F., Moss, J., Henry, D.P., Weise, V. and Kopin, I.J.: Effect of general anesthetics on arterial plasma catecholamines and blood pressure. JPET (In press).

Roizen, M.F., Thoa, N.B., Moss, J. and Kopin, I.J.: Inhibition by halothane of release of norepinephrine, but not of dopamine-β-hydroxylase, from guinea-pig deferens. Eur. J. of Pharmacol. (In press).

Roizen, M.F., Weise, V., Moss, J. and Kopin, I.J.: Plasma catecholamines: Arterial-venous differences and the influence of body temperature. Life Sci. 16: 1133-1144, 1975.

Thoa, N.B., Wooten, F., Axelrod, J. and Kopin, I.J.: On the mechanism of release of norepinephrine from sympathetic nerves induced by depolarizing agents and sympathomimetic drugs. Mol. Pharmacol. 11: 10-18, 1975.

Webb, J., Berv, K. and Kopin, I.J.: Induction of dopamine-β-hydroxylase in superior cervical ganglia in organ culture. Neuropharmacology (In press).

Webb, J., Moss, J., Kopin, I.J. and Jacobowitz, D.M.: Biochemical and histofluorescence studies of catecholamines in superior cervical ganglia in organ culture. JPET (In press).

Project No. Z01 MH 00402-03 LCS
1. Laboratory of Clinical Science
2. Section on Medicine
3. Bethesda, Maryland

Project Title: Regulatory role of the central nervous system on peripheral autonomic and endocrine function.

Previous Serial No. (Previously included in M-CS-M(C)-08)

Principal Investigator: J. Stephen Kizer

Other Investigators: I.J.Kopin, M.Palkovits, and J. Zivin.

Cooperating Units: Sections on Pharmacology and Histopharmacology, Laboratory of Clinical Science

Man Years:		
	Total	2.5
	Professional	2.0
	Other	0.6

Project Description:

The central nervous system, through the autonomic nervous system and the hypothalamic-mediated control of the endocrine system, influences a wide variety of functions of the body, including the circulatory system, digestive system, adrenal cortical and medullary function, thyroid activity, growth, etc. The object of this project is to identify the neuronal pathways and neurotransmitters which have a role in controlling these functions, and to determine which areas and substances are involved in responding to internal or external stimuli (temperature, internal milieu, stress, etc.) which initiate the homeostatic responses.

Methods for microscopic dissection and micro assay of the neurotransmitters and the enzymes involved in their biosynthesis have been developed by investigators in the Sections on Medicine and Pharmacology and methods for dissection of the small areas of brain developed or adapted in the Section on Histopharmacology. Radioimmunoassays of LH-RH and TRH have been developed.

Changes in endocrine states produce changes in monoamine metabolism in discrete nuclei of the hypothalamus and procedures which injure specific areas or sever connections of the hypothalamus from the remainder of brain produce alterations in the enzymes and neurotransmitters in other areas. Such procedures have been used to map the pathways of neurones of a particular type and to assess their role in response to endocrine manipulations or stress.

The location of the releasing factors and the presence or absence of particular neurotransmitters provides information which is important in assessing the possible role of neurotransmitters in controlling endocrine function of the pituitary by modulating release of hypothalamic peptide hormones. Dopamine appears to be specifically related to TRH in the bovine mediam eminence while acetylcholine is related to LH-RH.

The effects of drugs, hormonal states, stress, lighting, etc. are to be examined. Such studies could provide insight into how psychiatric abnormalities (anxiety, depression, etc.), psychoactive drugs (phenothiazines, lithium, etc.) may influence endocrine function, or alter the responses to stress or environmental stimuli. This could be the basis for understanding or testing neuronal responsivity in neurological or psychiatric disorders and give insights into etiological mechanisms important in the development of the primary or secondary symptoms of these dysfunctions.

Keyword Descriptors:
- Releasing Factors - LHRH - TRH
- Hypothalamus
- Neurotransmitters - norepinephrine, dopamine, histamine, serotonin, GABA, acetylcholine
- Tryptophan Hydroxylase
- Tyrosine Hydroxylase, Dopamine-β-Hydroxylase
- Stress
- Adrenal Cortex
- Adrenal Medulla
- Pituitary - Prolactin

Honors and Awards:

Dr. Kopin participated, by invitation, at the meeting of the Biological Psychiatry Section of the World Psychiatric Association in Munich, W. Germany.

Dr. Kopin lectured on "The Role of Catecholamines in Neuroendocrine Regulation," at the Division of Endocrinology, Mount Sinai School of Medicine, City University of New York.

Publications:

Kizer, J.S.: Endocrine-induced alterations of monoamine metabolism in brain. In Stumpf, W.A. and Grant, L.A. (Eds.): Anatomical Neuroendocrinology Sweden, Kargel-Basel, (In press).

Kizer, J.S., Arimura, A., Schally, A.V. and Brownstein, M.J.: Absence of luteinizing hormone-releasing hormone (LH-RH) from catecholaminergic neurons. Endocrinology 96: 523-525, 1975.

Kizer, J.S., Palkovits, M., Zivin, J., Brownstein, M., Saavedra, J.M. and Kopin, I.J.: The effect of endocrinological manipulations on tyrosine hydroxylase and dopamine-β-hydroxylase activities in individual hypothalamic nuclei of the adult male rat. Endocrinology 95: 799-812, 1974.

Kizer, J.S., Zivin, J.A., Jacobowitz, D.M. and Kopin, I.J.: The nyctohemeral rhythm of plasma prolactin: Effects of ganglionectomy, pinealectomy, constant light, constant darkness or 6-OH-dopamine administration. Endocrinology (In press).

Kizer, J.S., Zivin, J.A., Saavedra, J.M. and Brownstein, M.J.: A sensitive microassay for tryptophan hydroxylase in brain. J. of Neurochemistry 24: 779-785, 1975.

Kobayashi, R.M., Brownstein, M.J., Saavedra, J.M. and Palkovits, M.: Choline acetyltransferase content in discrete regions of the rat brain stem. J. of Neurochemistry (In press).

Kobayashi, R.M., Palkovits, M., Jacobowitz, D.M. and Kopin, I.J.: Biochemical mapping of the noradrenergic projection from the locus coeruleus: A model for studies of brain neuronal pathways. Neurology 25: 223-233, 1975.

Kobayashi, R.M., Palkovits, M., Kopin, I.J. and Jacobowitz, D.M.: Biochemical mapping of noradrenergic nerves arising from the rat locus coeruleus. Brain Res. 77: 269-279, 1974.

Palkovits, M., Kobayashi, R.M., Kizer, J.S., Jacobowitz, D.M., and Kopin, I.J.: Effect of stress on catecholamines and tyrosine hydroxylase activity of individual hypothalamic nuclei. Neuroendocrinology (In press).

Kopin, I.J., Palkovits, M., Kobayashi, R.M. and Jacobowitz, D.M.: Quantitative relationship of catecholamine content and histofluorescence in brain of rats. Brain Res. 80: 229-235, 1974.

Project No. Z01 MH 00403-02 LCS
1. Laboratory of Clinical Science
2. Section on Medicine
3. Bethesda, Maryland

PHS-ADAMHA-NIMH
Individual Project Report
July 1, 1974 through June 30, 1975

Project Title: Factors controlling levels of catecholamines and dopamine-β-hydroxylase in human plasma

Previous Serial Number: Part of M-CS-M(C)-08

Principal Investigator: Irwin J. Kopin

Other Investigators: Michael G. Ziegler, Charles R. Lake, Virginia K. Weise, Ross Eldridge, Michael Coleman, Dennis L. Murphy, Friedhelm Lamprecht, and Ruben Andres

Cooperating Units: Sections on Clinical Psychopharmacology, NINDS, NHLI, Gerantology Research Center

Man Years:		
	Total	3.5
	Professional	2.5
	Other	1.0

Project Description:

Plasma levels of catecholamines are used to assess the activity of the sympathetic nervous system in response to environmental factors (stress, temperature change, posture), treatment with drugs, changes in mental state (anxiety, depression, etc.), alterations of endocrine function, or as a result of neuronal dysfunction. Dopamine-β-hydroxylase in plasma is derived from sympathetic nerves, but its levels appear to reflect the rate of its synthesis and destruction, which appear to be determined mainly by genetic factors. The methods used to assay the catecholamines and dopamine-β-hydroxylase were developed in this laboratory and are based on enzymatic formation of isotopically-labelled methylated derivatives.

Plasma levels of dopamine-β-hydroxylase vary widely among individuals, but in the same person the levels appear to be stable over long intervals (3-5 years). In subjects in whom the blood pressure rises, levels of DBH decline.

Plasma norepinephrine levels increase rapidly in normal subjects when the erect posture is assumed and are further elevated if the subjects perform a relatively mild stressful exercise (maintaining a hand grip for 30 percent maximal force for 5 minutes). Although plasma DBH levels are not elevated significantly by these procedures, there does appear to be a relationship between plasma DBH levels and the increase in plasma catecholamines.

In patients with abnormalities of the autonomic nervous system (Familial Dysautonomia, Shy-Drager syndrome, etc.) levels of DBH tend to be low, and the response of plasma norepinephrine to postural change or stress is clearly abnormal. Patients with familial mediterranean fever who are treated with colchicine show decreased levels of plasma catecholamines, presumably because of a block in release of the amines.

Patients with torsion dystonia of the dominant type tend to have elevated levels of plasma DBH, but subjects with the recessive type of this disorder, and patients with Gilles de la Tourette syndrome appear to have normal levels.

Hypertensive patients treated with reserpine have low levels of plasma norepinephrine, but patients whose blood pressure is decreased by propranolol or hydrochlorothiazide administration have increased levels of the catecholamine.

The investigations in progress include a variety of other psychosomatic, psychiatric, and other disorders. It is hoped that these studies will lead to further understanding of the sympathetic responses during these disease states and the effects of drugs on the activity of the sympathetic nervous system.

In animals, sympatho-adrenal responses occur in a variety of stresses - both physical and psychological, but the degree of these responses in Man has been studied mainly by examining catecholamine excretion. Blood levels provide better and more sensitive indices of the response, particularly over short intervals. Disorders of these responses and the effects of drugs may provide a valuable means for assessing the degree of stress and for determining the role of these responses in perpetuating or alevating psychiatric disorders - e.g., anxiety.

Keyword Descriptors:

Dopamine-β-hydroxylase	Familial Dysautonomia
Norepinephrine	Shy-Drager Syndrome
Epinephrine	Postural Changes
Human Plasma	Stress
Sympathetic Nervous System	Anxiety

Honors and Awards:

Dr. Kopin was invited by the Laboratory of Neuroendocrine Regulation at the Massachusetts Institute of Technology to give a seminar on dopamine-beta-hydroxylase.

Publications:

Lamprecht, F., Ebert, M.H., Turek, I. and Kopin, I.J.: Serum dopamine-β-hydroxylase in depressed patients and the effect of electro-convulsive shock treatment. Psychopharmacologia 40: 241-248, 1974.

Project No. Z01 MH 00404-04 LCS
1. Laboratory of Clinical Science
2. Section on Medicine
3. Bethesda, Maryland

PHS-ADAMHA-NIMH
Individual Project Report
July 1, 1974 through June 30, 1975

Project Title: Growth Characteristics of Aminergic Neurones.

Previous Serial Number: M-CS-M(C)-12

Principal Investigator: Irwin J. Kopin

Other Investigators: Antonia Liuzzi, Fredrik H. Foppen

Cooperating Units: Sections on Pharmacology, Histopharmacology, Laboratory of Clinical Science.

Man Years:		
	Total	1.5
	Professional	1.0
	Other	0.5

Project Description:

To study factors which control the growth and development of adrenergic neurones in the peripheral and central nervous system, both *in vitro* and *in vivo* techniques have been applied in conjunction with radiometric assay of amines and the enzymes concerned with their biosynthesis.

Nerve growth factor (NGF) and dexamethasone increase levels of epinephrine and phenylethonolamine N-methyltransferase in sympathetic ganglia and adrenals of newborn animals. Other treatments of newborn animals are being examined to determine if specific neurological defects can be produced and whether these are attended by abnormalities in biogenic amine formation. Such studies could provide valuable experimental models to examine the effects of drugs, hormones, stress, etc. on brain function.

Honors and Awards:

None.

Publications:

None.

Serial No. Z01 MH-00376-01 LCS
1. Laboratory of Clinical Science
2. Section on Histopharmacology
3. Bethesda, Maryland

PHS-ADAMHA-NIMH
Individual Project Report
July 1, 1974 through June 30, 1975

Project Title: Morphologic studies of central aminergic and cholinergic neurons and pathways

Previous Serial Number: M-CS-HP-1

Principal Investigator: David M. Jacobowitz

Other Investigators: Miklos Palkovits, Paul D. MacLean

Cooperating Units: Laboratory of Brain Evolution and Behavior, NIMH

Man Years:		
	Total	.5
	Professional	.4
	Other	.1

Project Description:

Objectives: (1) Localization of monoaminergic nerves (noradrenergic, dopaminergic, serotonergic) in the brain by histochemical means. (2) Localization of acetylcholinesterase-containing nerves as an initial attempt to identify possible cholinergic nerves or cholinoceptive sites in the brain.

Methods Employed: (1) The morphological procedure involves the use of a specific fluorescence histochemical method (Falck and Hillarp) for the demonstration of catecholamines (norepinephrine, dopamine) and indoleamines (serotonin) within monoaminergic nerves and cells. (2) The histochemical procedure for cholinergic neurons by the use of the acetylcholinesterase-staining technique (Koelle).

Major Findings: A complete brain atlas of the localization of catecholaminergic and acetylcholinesterase-containing neurons was published. A similar atlas of the localization of catecholaminergic neurons and serotonergic cell bodies in the pygmy marmoset monkey brain is currently being prepared. A remarkable similarity between the monkey and rat aminergic neurons is apparent.

To further reveal the course of the final preterminal catecholamine pathways within the forebrain the results of several knife lesions were coupled with the observations of preterminal axons following 6-OHDOPA intraventricular injections. The information obtained from these procedures was plotted on a series of maps (In Press). Lesions of the caudo-lateral part of the commissura supraoptica dorsalis of Meynert (CSDV) and the crus cerebri resulted in the appearance of nonterminal axons coursing with the tractus incertotectalis and tegmentalis. These axons ascend through the lemniscus medialis, zona incerta, internal capsule to the CSDV. These preterminal axons ascend through the retrochiasmatic area and the ansa lenticularis to innervate regions in the hypothalamus, amygdala, septal area, hippocampus and nucleus interstitialis stria terminalis.

Significance to Biomedical Research and the Program of the Institute: Knowledge of central monoaminergic pathways will provide the rationale for placement of neurotoxic drugs to selectively destroy monoaminergic tracts responsible for innervation to various brain regions. The ultimate aim is to locate and destroy, if possible, the final preterminal pathways to discrete brain regions. This should enable experimental ablation of the fine terminal plexuses that are elaborated by the preterminal axons. The aminergic and cholinergic neuronal systems of the brain are of great interest because of evidence of their implication in mental illness.

Proposed Course of the Project: Mapping of monoaminergic and cholinergic terminals in the rat brain has been terminated with publication of an entire brain atlas. The mapping of monoaminergic neurons in the monkey brain will be terminated with publication of an atlas.

Honors and Awards: None.

Publications:

Articles Published in Periodicals:

Jacobowitz, D.M. and Palkovits, M.: Topographic atlas of catecholamine and acetylcholinesterase-containing neurons in the brain. I. Forebrain (Telencephalon, Diencephalon). J. Comp. Neurol. 157:13-28, 1974.

Palkovits, M. and Jacobowitz, D.M.: Topographic atlas of catecholamine and acetylcholinesterase-containing neurons in the brain. II. Hindbrain (Mesencephalon, Rhombencephalon). J. Comp. Neurol. 157:29-42, 1974.

Review Article:

Kostrzewa, R.M. and Jacobowitz, D.M.: Pharmacological Actions of 6-Hydroxydopamine. Pharmacological Reviews 26:199-288, 1974.

Keywords:

Brain Catecholamines
Aminergic neurons
Acetylcholinesterase neurons
Brain nerve atlas
Fluorescence microscopy
Noradrenergic nerves
Dopaminergic nerves
Serotonergic nerves

Serial No. Z01 MH-00377-01 LCS
1. Laboratory of Clinical Science
2. Section on Histopharmacology
3. Bethesda, Maryland

PHS-ADAMHA-NIMH
Individual Project Report
July 1, 1974 through June 30, 1975

Project Title: Development of a method for removal of discrete fresh regions of the rat brain

Previous Serial Number: None

Principle Investigator: David M. Jacobowitz

Other Investigators: None

Cooperating Units: None

Man Years:	Total	.3
	Professional	.2
	Other	.1

Project Description:

Objectives: (1) To develop a method which would enable removal of discrete nuclei and other small regions of fresh unfrozen rat brains.

Methods Employed: (1) Use of the vibratome to cut fresh thin slices of the rat brain. (2) Use of the micropunch method developed by Miklos Palkovits which enables removal of specific nuclei, tracts, and other subdivisions of frozen rat brain sections.

Major Findings: A modification of the micropunch technique for removal of nuclei and other small regions of the rat brain was developed whereby fresh unfrozen discrete regions can be removed by the use of a vibratome which is capable of cutting fresh slices of rat brain.

Significance to Biomedical Research and the Program of the Institute: This method will be useful for isolation of synaptosomal membranes, in tissue culture and for electron microscopy of brain tissue.

Proposed Course of the Project: Terminated with publication of the results. Utilization of this newly developed methodology for isolation of synaptosomal membranes of discrete nuclei which are capable of uptake of radioactive labelled amines is currently underway.

Honors and Awards: None

Serial No. Z01 MH-00377-01 LCS

Publication:

Jacobowitz, D.M.: Removal of discrete fresh regions of the rat brain. Brain Res. 80:111-115, 1974.

Keywords:

Brain nuclei
Micropunch method
Vibratome

Serial No. Z01 MH 00378-01 LCS
1. Laboratory of Clinical Science
2. Section on Histopharmacology
3. Bethesda, Maryland

PHS-ADAMHA-NIMH
Individual Project Report
July 1, 1974 through June 30, 1975

Project Title: Immunofluorescence study of the uptake of the antibody to dopamine-beta-hydroxylase (ADBH)

Previous Serial Number: None

Principle Investigator: David M. Jacobowitz

Other Investigators: Michael G. Ziegler, James A. Thomas, G. Frederick Wooten, Juan M. Saavedra, Julius Axelrod

Cooperating Units: Laboratory of Clinical Science, Sections on Medicine and Pharmacology

Man Years: Total .7
Professional .6
Other .1

Project Description:

Objectives: (1) To study the possible uptake of the antibody to dopamine-beta-hydroxylase (ADBH) into sympathetic neurons and adrenal medulla chromaffin cells following an intravenous injection. (2) Localization of an extraneuronal depot of DBH.

Methods Employed: Histochemical localization of the ADBH by an indirect immunofluorescence technique utilizing a fluorescein-labelled antiserum to the host IgG.

Major Findings: (1) Intravenous injection of the antibody to DBH showed that adrenergic neurons (ganglion cells, nerve terminals) and adrenal medulla cells were capable of taking up the antibody and was observed in these structures 10 days after injection. (2) ADBH was applied directly to frozen sections cut in a cryostat and fixed in alcohol. DBH immunofluorescence in the submaxillary gland is distributed with noradrenergic neurons which is eliminated by superior cervical ganglionectomy. In the sublingual gland DBH immunofluorescence is localized within mucinous acini and small ducts, and the disposition and intensity of staining materials is not affected by noradrenergic denervation for up to 30 days. DBH protein in the sublingual gland had little physiologic activity *in vivo*. Low levels of authentic DBH activity were detected in the rat saliva. Thus, DBH protein is present in the sublingual gland in an extraneuronal location and appears to be a secretory product of the gland.

Serial No. Z01 MH-00378-01 LCS

Significance to Biomedical Research and the Program of the Institute: The ability of the ADBH to be taken up by sympathetic elements poses the question of whether or not DBH itself has the capability of being taken up by these catecholamine-containing structures. This study suggests that reuptake of DBH is feasible. The fact that the ADBH used inhibits DBH enzymatic activity *in vitro* suggests that inhibition of catecholamine synthesis may have occurred. Intravenous ADBH may be useful in the further study of experimental situations characterized by excess sympathetic discharge. Furthermore, the method of intravenous injection of antibodies to components of secretory granules may be applicable to other systems.

The finding of small amounts of DBH activity and DBH protein in the collecting pools within acini and ducts suggests that DBH may be a secretory product of the sublingual gland.

Proposed Course of Project: The initial phase of this study is terminated with publication. Preliminary work concerning the injection of the ADBH in the anterior chamber of the rat eye shows that it is taken up by adrenergic nerves and is transported by an antidromic flow to the nerve cell body. This second phase is currently being pursued.

Honors and Awards: None

Publications:

Jacobowitz, D.M., Ziegler, M.G., and Thomas, J.A.: *In vivo* uptake of antibody to dopamine-beta-hydroxylase into sympathetic elements. Brain Res. 91:165-170, 1975.

Wooten, G.F., Jacobowitz, D.M., Saavedra, J.M. and Axelrod, J.: Localization of extraneuronal dopamine-beta-hydroxylase in rat salivary gland by immunofluorescence histochemistry. J. Neurochem. 24: (In Press), 1975.

Keywords:

Antibody to dopamine-beta hydroxylase
dopamine-beta-hydroxylase
immunofluorescence
adrenergic nerves
salivary gland

Serial No. Z01 MH 00379-01 LCS
1. Laboratory of Clinical Science
2. Section on Histopharmacology
3. Bethesda, Maryland

PHS-ADAMHA-NIMH
Individual Project Report
July 1, 1974 through June 30, 1975

Project Title: Histochemical study of biogenic amines in an isolated perfused rat brain preparation

Previous Serial Number: None

Principle Investigator: David M. Jacobowitz

Other Investigators: Henry A. Sloviter

Cooperating Units: University of Pennsylvania, School of Medicine
Philadelphia, Pennsylaania

Man Years:		
	Total	.4
	Professional	.3
	Other	.1

Project Description:

Objectives: To study the aminergic nerves of the isolated perfused rat brain.

Methods Employed: (1) Perfusion of an isolated rat brain preparation which consists of the skull of a rat and its contents with practically all extra-cranial tissue removed. This isolated brain preparation is made from a rat which is adequately anesthetized by deep hypothermia without the use of a chemical agent for anesthesia. The brain is perfused through catheters in the internal carotid arteries; all other arterial vessels are ligated. The brain is perfused with an 8% solution of BSA in Krebs-Ringer bicarbonate buffer which has suspended a dispersed fluorochemical which acts as an entirely satisfactory substitute for red blood cells. (2) Catecholamine fluorescence microscopy.

Major Findings: The intensity and density of catecholamine fluorescent varicosities in the perfused brain is essentially similar to that observed in the non-perfused brain taken from rats immediately following decapitation. Catecholamine-rich nuclei such as the paraventricular nucleus, periventricular nucleus, nucleus interstitialis stria terminalis, nucleus accumbens, caudate nucleus, anterior ventral nucleus of the thalamus, motor nucleus of the trigeminal nerve, vagal nucleus and nucleus of the tractus solitarius were observed. Other areas such as the retrochiasmatic area, cerebellum and central grey were observed to contain catecholamine-containing fibers. Normal green fluorescent noradrenergic and dopaminergic cell bodies were observed as well as yellow fluorescent serotonergic raphe cells. Nerve terminals of excellent quality were noted around the blood vessels on the base of the brain. The pineal gland contained the relatively quick-fading yellow serotonin fluorescence and green fluorescent noradrenergic nerves.

Significance to Biomedical Research and the Program of the Institute: Studies in vitro with brain tissue preparations (slices, homogenates, or other preparations) yield some information about the direct action of drugs on brain tissue, but such experiments are far from physiological because of the absence of blood circulation and the blood-brain barrier. The isolated perfused brain preparation can provide information about the influence of drugs on neurotransmitters without interference or ambiguity caused by other organs.

Proposed Course of Project: The initial histochemical study has been completed. A manuscript is in preparation. Further use of this method to study the effect of drugs on the aminergic nerves of the brain is anticipated.

Honors and Awards: None

Publications: Manuscript in preparation.

Keywords:

Perfused brain
Fluorescence microscopy
aminergic nerves
serotonergic nerves

Serial No. Z01 MH 00380-01 LCS
1. Laboratory of Clinical Science
2. Section on Histopharmacology
3. Bethesda, Maryland

PHS-ADAMHA-NIMH
Individual Project Report
July 1, 1974 through June 30, 1975

Project Title: Neurochemical study of the dorsal noradrenergic bundle of the rat brain

Previous Serial Number: None

Principle Investigator: David M. Jacobowitz

Other Investigators: Michael F. Roizen
Eric A. Muth

Cooperating Units: Laboratory of Clinical Science, Section on Medicine

Man Years:	Total	.4
	Professional	.3
	Other	.1

Project Description:

Objectives: To measure the catecholamine content and the activity of dopamine-beta-hydroxylase in a segment of the dorsal noradrenergic bundle of the rat brain.

Methods Employed: (1) The micropunch technique (Miklos Palkovits) for isolation of the dorsal noradrenergic bundle of frozen brain sections. (2) Radioisotopic microenzymatic assays for norepinephrine and dopamine (Henry). (3) Assay for dopamine-beta-hydroxylase (Molinoff).

Major Findings: The dorsal noradrenergic bundle of the rat brain was removed by the micropunch technique. The values obtained for catecholamines in the dorsal bundle were 10.51 ± 1.49 and 1.69 ± 0.24 (ng/mg protein ± S.E.M.) for norepinephrine and dopamine, respectively. The average value for DBH was 1.93 ± 0.13 nmol/mg protein/hr ± S.E.M.

Significance to Biomedical Research and the Program of the Institute: These are the first reported values for catecholamines and DBH in a major noradrenergic axonal pathway in the brain. The ability to remove a segment of the noradrenergic axonal pathway in the brain will provide useful models for the study of the synthesis and transport of amines and of enzymes and other specific proteins to their terminal receptor regions in the brain.

Proposed Course of Project: A manuscript was submitted for publication. Studies of the rat of axoplasmic and subcellular localization of norepinephrine and various enzymes following stereotaxic lesions and stressful situations are currently contemplated.

Honors and Awards: None

Publications:

Manuscript submitted for publication.

Keywords:

Dorsal noradrenergic bundle
Brain Catecholamine
norepinephrine
dopamine
dopamine-beta-hydroxylase

Serial No. Z01 MH 00381-01 LCS
1. Laboratory of Clinical Science
2. Section on Histopharmacology
3. Bethesda, Maryland

PHS-ADAMHA-NIMH
Individual Project Report
July 1, 1974 through June 30, 1975

Project Title: Localization of vasopressin in discrete areas of the rat hypothalamus

Previous Serial Number: None

Principle Investigators: Jack M. George and David M. Jacobowitz

Other Investigators: None

Cooperating Units: Department of Medicine
Ohio State University

Man Years:		
	Total	.4
	Professional	.3
	Other	.1

Project Description:

Objectives: To determine the precise localization and quantitation of vasopressin in the brain.

Methods Employed: (1) The microdissection technique of individual hypothalamic nuclei (Palkovits). (2) Radioimmunoassay for arginine vasopressin (George, et al.).

Major Findings: The highest concentration of vasopressin was found in the median eminence (441 ± 15 pg vasopressin/ug protein) with appreciable amounts in the retrochiasmatic area (72 ± 8.0) and supraoptic nucleus (40 ± 2.2). In addition, vasopressin was also found in the paraventricular (24 ± 5.5), suprachiasmatic (23 ± 2.7) and arcuate (4 ± 1.8) nuclei. It is of interest that larger amounts of vasopressin were found in the retrochiasmatic area than in the supraoptic nucleus. The retrochiasmatic area contains much fewer supraoptic cell bodies than the supraoptic nucleus proper. It is probable that the axons of the supraoptic nucleus cells traverse the retrochiasmatic area caudally into the median eminence. Therefore, the higher concentration of immunologically detectable vasopressin in the retrochiasmatic area suggests that vasopressin may undergo a conformational change within the axons in passage to the median eminence, such that more of the hormone becomes recognizable by vasopressin antibody.

Significance to Biomedical Research and the Program of the Institute: Precise localization and quantitation of vasopressin in the brain will enable researchers to study the effects of drugs, experimental brain manipulations and disease states on the content of the antidiuretic hormone vasopressin.

Proposed Course of Project: Terminated with a manuscript accepted for publication. Further studies of the effect of drugs on the vasopressin content of the brain are contemplated.

Honors and Awards: None

Publication:

George, J.M. and Jacobowitz, D.M.: Localization of vasopressin in discrete areas of the rat hypothalamus. Brain Res. (In Press), 1975.

Keywords:

Vasopressin
Radioimmunoassay
Supraoptic nucleus
median eminence

Serial No. Z01 MH 00382-01 LCS
1. Laboratory of Clinical Science
2. Section on Histopharmacology
3. Bethesda, Maryland

PHS-ADAMHA-NIMH
Individual Project Report
July 1, 1974 through June 30, 1975

Project Title: Biochemical mapping of monoaminergic neurons of the rat brain

Previous Serial Number: None

Principle Investigator: David M. Jacobowitz

Other Investigators: Miklos Palkovits, Ronald Kobayashi, Michael Roizen, Steven Kizer, Irwin Kopin

Cooperating Units: Laboratory of Clinical Science, Section on Medicine

Man Years:	Total	.8
	Professional	.7
	Other	.1

Project Description:

Objectives: To study by biochemical means, the sites of innervation of catecholaminergic (noradrenergic, dopaminergic) neurons whose cell bodies are localized in the hindbrain.

Methods Employed: (1) Electrolytic and knife lesions are made by stereotaxic means in the locus coeruleus, dorsal and ventral noradrenergic axonal bundles. (2) After various periods of time specific brain nuclei and discrete regions are removed by a microdissection technique (Palkovits). (3) Changes in amine (NE, DA) content are detected by a sensitive isotopic assay (Henry). (4) Changes in dopamine-beta-hydroxylase (DBH) are made by a sensitive enzyme assay.

Major Findings: (1) The sensitive isotopic assay was capable of detecting relatively small changes in amine in discrete brain regions 9 days following unilateral electrolytic lesion of the rat locus coeruleus. Significant reductions in the NE content were observed ipsilateral to the lesion in all portions of the cerebral cortex (entorhinal, hippocampal cingulate, parietal and occipital areas), rostral half of the cerebellar cortex, hypothalamic periventricular and paraventricular nuclei, anterior ventral thalamic nucleus, ventral thalamic nucleus and habenula. No changes in the NE concentration were observed in the medial preoptic nucleus, nucleus interstitialis stria terminalis (ventralis) and dorso-medial nucleus. NE was reduced bilaterally in the medial geniculate body, inferior colliculus, and posterior half of the cerebellum suggesting a bilateral innervation from the locus coeruleus. The greater content of NE contralateral to the lesion suggests that the locus coeruleus innervation, although bilateral, is predominantly to the ipsilateral side. The site(s) at which axons cross the midline to innervate the colliculus and geniculate body may be at the posterior commissure and the commissure of the superior colliculus. It appears that the cortical noradrenergic nerves are not solely derived from the locus coeruleus cell bodies. (2) Unilateral transection of the dorsal noradrenergic pathway which emanates from the locus coeruleus was made at the caudal mamillary body level. After 38 days a significant reduction, but not complete depletion, of NE was found in the periventricular nucleus of the hypothalamus, anterior ventral nucleus of the thalamus, cingulate cortex and hippocampus. All structures caudal to the level of transection were unchanged. (3) Bilateral lesions were made in the ventral noradrenergic pathway in the medulla. This pathway is thought to emanate from cell bodies (A1-A5) in the hindbrain. DBH was measured in various nuclei. This enzyme is a marker for noradrenergic nerves. A marked decrease in DBH activity was observed in the nucleus preoptic medialis, periventricular nucleus, supraoptic nucleus, posterior median forebrain bundle, paraventricular nucleus, median eminence, arcuate nucleus, ventromedial nucleus. No decrease was observed in the cingulate cortex, hippocampus, superior colliculus or medial geniculate body.

Significance to Biomedical Research and the Program of the Institute: This study represents an investigation of the precise localization of mostly noradrenergic terminals which emanate from either the locus coeruleus-dorsal axonal pathway or the ventral pathway. The anatomical organization of the catecholaminergic pathways and terminal innervation is basic for future work concerning the functional organization of these aminergic neurons in the brain.

Proposed Course of Project: Biochemical mapping of monoaminergic and cholinergic pathways of the brain will continue. Reports of the findings of these studies have been published.

Honors and Awards: Dr. Ronald Kobayashi received the S. Weir Mitchell Award presented at the 26th Annual Meeting of the American Academy of Neurology, San Francisco, 1974 for the paper entitled, "Biochemical mapping of the noradrenergic projection from the locus coeruleus".

Publications:

Kobayashi, R.M., Palkovits, M., Kopin, I.J. and Jacobowitz, D.M.: Biochemical mapping of noradrenergic nerves arising from the rat locus coeruleus. Brain Res. 77:269-279, 1974.

Kobayashi, R.M., Palkovits, Jacobowitz, D.M. and Kopin, I.J.: Biochemical mapping of the noradrenergic projection from the locus coeruleus: A model for studies of brain neuronal pathways. Neurology 25:223-233, 1975.

Serial No. Z01 MH 00382-01 LCS

Palkovits, M., Richardson, J.S. and Jacobowitz, D.M.: A histochemical study of ventral tegmental cholinergic pathways following destructive lesions. Brain Res. 81:183-188, 1974.

Keywords:

Locus Coeruleus
Norepinephrine
noradrenergic neurons
dopamine-beta-hydroxylase
brain noradrenergic pathways

Serial No. Z01 MH 00383-01 LCS
1. Laboratory of Clinical Science
2. Section on Histopharmacology
3. Bethesda, Maryland

PHS-ADAMHA-NIMH
Individual Project Report
July 1, 1974 through June 30, 1975

Project Title: The effects of stress on catecholamine concentration and tyrosine hydroxylase activity in discrete regions of the rat brain

Previous Serial Number: None

Principal Investigators: David M. Jacobowitz, Miklos Palkovits, Ronald Kobayashi, Nguyen B. Thoa, J. Steven Kizer, Irwin J. Kopin

Other Investigators: None

Cooperating Units: Laboratory of Clinical Science, Section on Medicine

Man Years:		
	Total	.8
	Professional	.7
	Other	.1

Project Description:

Objectives: (1) To study the effects of various acute stresses on norepinephrine and dopamine concentration and repeated stress on tyrosine hydroxylase (TH) activity in individual hypothalamic nuclei and other rat brain regions. (2) To study the effect of chronic stress (isolation) on the NE, DA and TH activity in discrete regions of the rat brain.

Methods Employed: (1) Acute and repeated stimuli consisted of formalin injection, exposure to cold, or forced immobilization. Chronic stress consisted of isolation for 3 months. (2) A micro-dissection technique for removal of discrete nuclei and other brain regions (Palkovits). (3) Radioisotopic enzymatic assays for NE and DA (Henry). (4) Tyrosine hydroxylase activity by a sensitive enzyme assay.

Major Findings: (1) NE and DA concentrations were reduced and TH activity increased selectively in the arcuate nucleus. No changes were observed in the median eminence, cortex, paraventricular nucleus.
(2) Three months of isolation resulted in an increased concentration of NE in the cingulate cortex and substantia nigra. No effect of chronic isolation stress was observed in the paraventricular nucleus, median eminence, arcuate nucleus, n. dorsomedialis, olfactory tubercle, n. accumbens,

and caudate putamen. An increase in the tyrosine hydroxylase activity was observed in the periventricular nucleus; no changes occurred in the paraventricular nucleus, median eminence, arcuate nucleus, nucleus dorsomedialis and median forebrain bundle.

Significance to Biomedical Research and the Program of the Institute: These studies indicate that stress can selectively alter catecholamine and TH activity in selective discrete regions of the brain. These results suggest that the arcuate nucleus may be selectively involved in acute stress and support the hypothesis that catecholamines in the medial basal hypothalamus mediate certain of the neuroendocrine changes observed in stress. Reasons for selective differences observed in these studies remain a significant area of study in problems of mental health.

Proposed Course of Project: Studies on stress will be continued. A manuscript has been submitted for publication.

Honors and Awards: None.

Publications: None

Keywords:

Stress
Catecholamines
norepinephrine
dopamine
tyrosine hydroxylase
brain amines
arcuate nucleus

Serial No. Z01 MH 00384-01 LCS
1. Laboratory of Clinical Science
2. Section on Histopharmacology
3. Bethesda, Maryland

PHS-ADAMHA-NIMH
Individual Project Report
July 1, 1974 through June 30, 1975

Project Title: The effects of drugs on the catecholamine and serotonin content of nuclei, fiber tracts and terminal regions of the rat brain. I. Anesthetics.

Previous Serial Number: None

Principal Investigators: Michael F. Roizen and David M. Jacobowitz

Other Investigators: Irwin J. Kopin, Miklos Palkovits, Michael Brownstein, Eric Muth

Cooperating Units: Laboratory of Clinical Science, Sections on Medicine and Pharmacology

Man Years:	Total	.6
	Professional	.5
	Other	.1

Project Description:

Objectives: To study the effects of halothane and cyclopropane on the NE, DA and 5-HT content of discrete nuclei, fiber tracts and terminal regions of the rat brain.

Methods Employed: (1) Micro-dissection technique for removal of specific nuclei, tracts and other subdivisions of frozen rat brain sections (Palkovits). (2) Radioisotopic microenzymatic assays of NE, DA (Henry) and 5-HT (Saavedra, et al.). (3) Halothane anesthesia (1.15%) or cyclopropane (18%) in oxygen for 95-105 minutes.

Major Findings: (1) Significant increase in NE content with both anesthetic agents were observed only in the nucleus accumbens, locus coeruleus and a catecholamine area in the central grey just lateral to the dorsal raphe. Only in the nucleus accumbens and central grey catecholamine areas was the DA level increased by both anesthetics. Cyclopropane also increased the DA content of the substantia nigra and caudate nucleus, while halothane significantly increased the NE level of the anterior portion of the arcuate nucleus. (2) Serotonin levels in the central amygdaloid nucleus, substantia nigra, and nucleus centralis superior (median raphe) were increased following the administration of either anesthetic, while anesthesia with only cyclopropane was associated with an increase in 5-HT levels in the raphe dorsalis.

Significance to Biomedical Research and the Program of the Institute: This study reveals that a drug can effect a few nuclei or regions without significantly affecting other nuclei that contain the same transmitter substance, or arise from contiquous cell bodies, and that during anesthesia with either of these agents, both the serotonergic and adrenergic systems are altered.

Proposed Course of Project: Terminated following publication.

Honors and Awards: None

Publications: Manuscripts in preparation.

Keywords:

Anesthetics
Halothane
Cyclopropane
brain norepinephrine
brain dopamine
brain serotonin

Project No. Z01 MH 00446-06 LCS
1. Laboratory of Clinical Science
2. Section on Psychiatry
3. Bethesda, Maryland

PHS-NIH
Individual Project Report
July 1, 1974 through June 30, 1975

Project Title: Inpatient clinical and psychopharmacological studies of manic-depressive and schizo-affective disorders.

Previous Serial Number: M-CS-Ps(C)-22

Principal Investigator: Frederick K. Goodwin

Other Investigators: Yolande Davenport, Thomas Wehr, Philip Gold, Randi Rubovits, Alina Efron, Giovanni Muscettola (Visiting Scientist), Jacques St.-Laurent (Visiting Scientist)

Collaborating Scientists: Dennis L. Murphy, Robert M. Post, Monte Buchsbaum, Michael Ebert, Edward Donnelly

Psychiatric Consultants: Arnold Meyersbúrg, Marion Richmond, Paul Chodoff, Marvin Adland

Cooperating Units: Nursing Staff and Occupational Therapist on Ward 4-West, Section on Clinical Neuropharmacology, Laboratory of Clinical Science, Section on Cognitive and Perceptual Studies, Adult Psychiatry Branch

Man Years: Total 3.2
Professional 2.0
Other 1.2

Project Description:

This project description encompasses a wide range of research studies, many of which are continuations of ongoing investigations. In this group of studies the overall objective is a more comprehensive understanding of the pathophysiology of manic-depressive and schizo-affective disorders during the acute phase, particularly in relation to specificity of diagnosis, existence of clinically or biologically identifiable subgroups (including subgroups which may predict drug response), the nature of predisposing faccors, and the interrelationship between pharmacological and psychodynamic factors in clinical improvement.

In regard to clinical methodology, this year has seen a major effort towards a more systematic approach to diagnosis. Prior to admission, patients are screened by two psychiatrists and a social worker. Selection is based on meeting criteria for major, primary affective disorder, as defined by the research diagnostic criteria of Spitzer, et al. (1974). Following admission a comprehensive history of the present and past illness is recorded using the newly developed SADS Diagnostic System (schizophrenia and affective disorder system - Spitzer, et al., 1974). The use of this diagnostic instrument (SADS) and diagnostic system (RDC) is especially valuable since it is in use in eight other major psychobiological research centers; this will make meaningful comparisons between different investigative groups possible for the first time, and could provide the basis for major advances in research. The depressed patients admitted to the unit generally show psychomotor retardation and/or agitation, sleep disturbance, loss of appetite with weight loss, excessive tiredness, loss of interest, and thought patterns dominated by feelings of hopelessness, helplessness, and guilt. There is frequently a past history of depressive and/or manic episodes, and often a family history of mood disorders. Manic patients typically evidence increased psychomotor activity with an increased initiation and rate of speech, a labile mood predominated by either euphoria or irritability, and a cognitive state characterized by expansiveness, grandiosity, and over-confidence, more severely manic patients may show extreme dysphoria, with disorganized psychotic features which may be difficult to distinguish from schizophrenia cross-sectionally.

Behavioral data is collected on a longitudinal basis throughout the course of hospitalization utilizing twice daily global ratings by a trained nursing research team; these ratings focus on depression, anxiety, psychosis, anger, and anxiety. Three times a week, a special 34-item Affective Illness Scale is scored for each patient by each member of the nursing staff; this multi-item scale (developed by Dennis Murphy) is capable of generating clusters of behavior which are analyzed by computer. More intensive clinical data is obtained from individual psychotherapy sessions held on a 2-3 time a week basis with behavioral observations recorded systematically. Information regarding the families is obtained through ongoing contact between the social worker and the patient's relatives. This year a new behavioral instrument has been developed in collaboration with Judy Schreiber of the Occupational Therapy Department; this functional rating scale (see below) provides a new dimension to the assessment of the depressed and manic patient.

Sleep is recorded at half-hour intervals throughout the night on all patients. In addition, selected patients are studied for sleep parameters utilizing all night EEG sleep recordings in collaboration with the central sleep facility of the DCBR.

All drug trials are conducted under double-blind conditions with alternating active and placebo periods in a non-random design. The utilization of placebo substitution following active drug increases ones level of confidence in the efficacy of a compound in an individual patient. This strategy is important in the evaluation of drug effects because of the frequency of spontaneous remissions and exacerbations in manic-depressive illness.

The major area of study and major findings during the last year can be divided into ten separate areas:

1. The ongoing effort towards refinement of instruments for behavioral assessment has continued. In collaboration with the Section on Clinical Neuropharmacology (Dr. Murphy), further development of the multi-item computer scored affective disorder rating scale has focused on an evaluation of reliability and on correlations between individual items and/or clusters of items with the global scores for mania, depression and psychosis.

We are actively participating with other units in the development and validation of a brief yet comprehensive instrument for the self-rating of psychopathology (see project reports #Z01 MH 00449-01 LCS and Z01 MH 00450-01 LCS).

In collaboration with Judy Schreiber of the Occupational Therapy Department, a 15-item functional rating scale has been developed. This novel scale (which has been shown to have high interrater reliability) rates the capacity of the patient to complete the structured task assigned as part of the occupational therapy program. The rationale for such a scale in the evaluation of depression is simple; although decreased ability to function is central to the depressive syndrome, it is not readily accessible by the nurse or physician raters since the patients have little opportunity to carry out functions on the ward which outside the hospital would be routine, such as going to work, cooking, child care, planning schedules, etc. Return of functional capacity is a key aspect of recovery from depression (for example, with discharge decisions). The relationship between functional rating scores and the more symptom-oriented global ratings are being explored over time to test the hypothesis that these diverse aspects of depression do not recover at the same rate in response to antidepressant treatments.

2. Evaluation of antidepressant drug treatments has focused on the use of compounds which may potentiate antidepressant response in individuals who have not responded to standard treatments. Work with the thyroid hormone (T_3 - cytomel) has been extended to an additional ten patients who were showing either non-response or incomplete response to imipramine or amitriptyline. As noted in the pilot study, the addition of a small amount of T_3 in females is associated with potentiation of antidepressant response in the majority of patients, in some converting a clear-cut non-responder to a clear-cut responder. On the other hand, the antidepressant response to lithium does not appear to be affected by the addition of T_3. More recently, studies on the use of estrogens in females as potentiators of tricyclic response have been initiated, and are in a preliminary stage.

In a related area, the amino acid precursor of serotonin - L-tryptophan is being tested as a potentiator of response to tricyclic antidepressants, based on the hypothesis that some depressed patients may have a deficit in central serotonin function (particularly those with low serotonin metabolite in the CSF); preliminary results in three patients indicate that L-tryptophan in large doses is not capable of potentiating tricyclic response.

Another area of pharmacological investigation has involved the combined use of lithium and tricyclic antidepressants in bipolar depressed patients who have shown either a partial or minimal response to lithium alone or tricyclic antidepressant alone. To date, 12 patients have been studied with seven showing a very favorable response to this combination.

3. The evaluation of psychotrophic drugs in the treatment of acute mania has continued, focusing on the efficacy of pimozide in comparison with a standard reference neuroleptic (chlorpromazine). Experience in six patients to date suggest that pimozide is an effective antimanic agent but appears to have a slower onset of action, particularly in the acutely excited and hyperactive patient.

4. Attempts at subgrouping depressed patients according to response to specific drugs has continued. Further evidence has been accumulated suggesting that the antidepressant response to lithium is significantly more likely to occur in bipolar than in unipolar patients, whereas the unipolar-bipolar dichotomy in relation to tricyclic response is not as clear, and our initial impressions in this area may require revision. Investigations concerning the unipolar-bipolar dichotomy have focused on delineation of the so-called "bipolar II" group. Our studies involving biological subtypes which may predict drug response are described separately under project reports #Z01 MH 00447-06 LCS and Z01 MH 00448-02 LCS.

5. Psychodynamic studies: these studies, which employ both clinical observation and instruments designed to measure ego-function, have focused on psychodynamic changes associated with drug-induced improvement in depression. In general, successful antidepressant treatment appears to facilitate the reestablishment of more healthy defensive patterns on a more resilient basis.

6. Sleep deprivation studies: in collaboration with 3-West (Adult Psychiatry Branch) the behavioral and biochemical responses of depressed patients to one night sleep deprivation has been evaluated. Results to date indicate dramatic but transient improvement in some depressed patients, particularly those with more endogenous features. Transient improvement with sleep deprivation tends to predict subsequent response to tricyclic antidepressants.

7. Assay of tricyclic antidepressants in plasma, and the associated development of a "plasma bank". In collaboration with the Unit on Clinical Biochemistry, LCS, we have initiated studies of tricyclic levels in patients under treatment with these drugs, utilizing mass fragmentography techniques; pilot studies were conducted in collaboration with the Karolinska Institute. As part of these studies we have instituted a "plasma bank" on the ward, in which 5 ml of fresh frozen plasma is saved each week for each patient. Several hundred plasma samples are already stored and are available for a variety of assays currently under development or proposed. In addition to the once a week sampling routinely, patients on tricyclics have blood samples taken more frequently in order to study kinetic parameters. It is expected

that the availability of tricyclic blood levels will allow patients to be more meaningfully classified as non-responders or responders to a given drug.

8. In collaboration with Edward Donnelly of St. Elizabeths Hospital and Dennis Murphy of the Section on Clinical Neuropharmacology, several studies of psychological functioning in depressed and manic patients are underway. These studies include the Halstead-Retan, a test of associative capacity thought to be a sensitive indicator of organic dysfunction, the Wechsler Adult Intelligence Scale, and the MMPI. Preliminary results suggests that depressed patients show significant deficits on the Halstead-Retan; in the case of the bipolar patients this deficit does not entirely return to normal during the immediate in hospital recovery phase. Studies of IQ have indicated normal ranges for manic-depressive patients, but a striking change (averaging 20 points on the full scale) in the same patient going from depression into hypomania. MMPI studies continue to indicate significant differences between unipolar and bipolar patients in a variety of personality parameters.

9. In collaboration with Monte Buchsbaum of the Section on Cognitive and Perceptual Studies, APB, and Dennis Murphy of the Section on Neuropharmacology, we have continued and extended our studies on the cortical evoked potentials in manic-depressive patients. Attention has focused particularly on the use of differences in the auditory evoked response as a predictor variable in antidepressant drug response. Differences in AER among unipolar and bipolar depressed patients are now well established, and within each of these populations AER has been shown to be associated with age of onset and the presence of a family history of affective disorder. In addition, we have conducted longitudinal studies of AER in two cycling manic-depressive patients (for details of these studies see project report from the Section on Cognitive and Perceptual Studies, Adult Psychiatry Branch).

10. Neuroendocrine studies of affective illness: three measures of hypothalamic function are under investigation. Baseline and L-DOPA stimulated release of growth hormones; baseline and L-DOPA stimulated relase of prolactin; and TRH stimulated release of TSH. It is known that central amine systems are intimately involved in the release of these and other pituitary substances and thus, these techniques represent another approach to the evaluation of central amine function in affective illness. The data to date indicate both age and sex contributions as well as apparent subgroup differences.

We are particularly interested in expanding and improving our clinical descriptive capacities using sophisticated diagnostic and rating instruments to provide reliable data for factor analysis and cluster analysis. It is expected that the application of these more advanced statistical techniques will go far in clarifying the questions about meaningful subgroups in affective disorders.

Our emphasis in drug efficacy evaluation has shifted towards more longitudinal and intensive study of a few drugs, rather than multiple brief trials using large numbers of new drugs.

Honors and Awards:

Dr. Goodwin was elected to Fellowship in the American Psychiatric Association and was appointed to the Peer Review Committee of the Washington Psychiatric Society. He was selected to present a special public lecture on "Depression, Research, Causes, Treatments, and Prevention" as part of the observance of the 25th Anniversary of the NIH.

At the Annual Meeting of the Association for Research in Nervous and Mental Disease, Dr. Goodwin presented an invited lecture on CSF and Urinary Amine Metabolites in Affective Illness and Schizophrenia. He was also invited to Munich, Germany to participate in a special meeting on depression sponsored by the World Psychiatric Association, and there he presented a paper on "Studies of CSF and Urinary Amine Metabolites in Affective Illness - Issues on Specificity". Dr. Goodwin served as moderator for the Taylor Manor Symposium on Rational Psychopharmacotherapy. He participated in a meeting sponsored by the Psychopharmacology Research Branch of the NIMH in order to plan a multi-hospital collaborative study on the maintenance drug treatment of affective disorder, April 1975.

Dr. Goodwin was awarded two special lectureships: the first by the American Psychological Association, Section on Psychopharmacology, where he spoke on recent advances in the treatment of affective disorder, and the second from the Royal College of Physicians of Canada where he lectured on the same subject.

Dr. Goodwin was also an invited lecturer at the University of Minnesota, Department of Psychiatry, the Missouri Institute of Psychiatry, the Ohio Psychiatric Society, the National Capital Medical Education Foundation, and the Missouri Institute of Psychiatry.

At the Annual Meeting of the American Psychiatric Association, May 5-9, 1975, Anaheim, California, Dr. Goodwin presented a paper on "Urinary MHPG in Subtypes of Affective Disorder and Normal Controls", and was a coauthor on five other papers presented at that meeting. He also presented a paper at the Annual Meeting of the Society of Biological Psychiatry on "Stress, AER, and Central Norepinephrine Metabolism in Man" (with Dr. Monte Buchsbaum). Dr. Goodwin coauthored a paper presented at the Annual Meeting of the Early Clinical Drug Evaluation Unit of the Psychopharmacology Research Branch, and on several occasions also served as an Ad Hoc Sight Visitor for grants reviewed by this branch.

Dr. Goodwin served as a special consultant to the Public Broadcasting System for its T.V. production of "The Thin Edge", and was appointed to the committee on Education of the American College of Neuropsychopharmacology.

Dr. Rubovits presented a paper on "The Pharmacology of Tardive Dyskinesia in Man - An Experimental Model" at the Symposium on Side Effects of Long-Term Treatment with Neuroleptics at the IX International Congress of Neuropsychopharmacology in Paris, France, July 1974.

Project No. Z01 MH 00446-06 LCS

Dr. St.-Laurent presented a paper on the "Neurochemical Correlates of Brain Self-Stimulation" at the European Brain and Behavior Society, 1st International Conference on Brain Self-Stimulation Reward, Brugge, Belgium, April 21-24, 1975.

Mrs. Davenport: See Project Report No. Z01 MH 00449-01 LCS.

Dr. Wehr: See Project Report No. Z01 MH 00450-01 LCS.

Dr. Efron: See Project Report No. Z01 MH 00449-01 LCS

Project No. Z01 MH 00446-06 LCS

Publications:

Ablon, S.L., Carlson, G. and Goodwin, F.K.: Ego defense patterns in manic-depressive illness. Am. J. Psychiat., 131:803-807, 1974.

Goodwin, F.K. and Sack, R.L.: Central dopamine function in affective illness: evidence from precursors, enzyme inhibitors and studies of central dopamine turnover. In The Neuropsychopharmacology of Monoamines and Their Regulatory Enzymes, Usdin, E. (Ed.), Raven Press, 1974, pp. 261-280.

Goodwin, F.K.: A summary of the third International Symposium on phenothiazines and structurally related drugs. In The Phenothiazines and Structurally Related Drugs, Forrest, I.S., Carr, C.J. and Usdin, E. (Eds.), Raven Press, New York, 1974, pp. 799-804.

Goodwin, F.K. and Sack, R.L.: Behavioral effects of a new dopamine-beta-hydroxylase inhibitor (fusaric acid) in man. J. Psychiat. Res., 11:211-217, 1974.

Rubovits, R. and Klawans, H.L., Jr.: Effect of cholinergic and anticholinergic agents on tardive dyskinesia. J. Neurol. Neurosurg. Psychiat., 37:941-947, 1974.

Rubovits, R. and Klawans, H.L., Jr.: The pharmacology of tardive dyskinesia in man - an experimental model. Proceedings of the IX International Congress of Neuropsychopharmacology, Paris, France (in press).

Carmen, J., Post, R.M., Teplitz, T.A., and Goodwin, F.K.: Divalent cations in prediction of antidepressant response to lithium. Lancet, ii:1454, 1974.

Belmaker, R., Beckmann, H., Goodwin, F.K., et al.: Relationships between platelet and plasma monoamine oxidase, plasma dopamine-beta-hydroxylase, and urinary 3-methoxy-4-hydroxyphenyl glycol. Life. Sci., 16:273, 1975.

Goodwin, F.K., Wehr, T., and Sack, R.L.: Studies on the mechanism of action of lithium in man: a contribution to neurobiological theories of affective illness. Lithium in Psychiatry: A Synopsis, Les Presses de L'Universite Laval, Quebec, 1975.

Goodwin, F.K. and Sack, R.L.: Behavioral effects of a new dopamine-beta-hydroxylase inhibitor (fusaric acid) in man. In Catecholamines and Their Enzymes in the Neuropathology of Schizophrenia, Matthysee and Kety (Eds.), Pergamon Press, 1975.

Dunner, D.L., Gershon, E.S. and Goodwin, F.K.: Heritable factors in the severity of affective illness. Biol. Psychiat. (in press).

Post, R.M., Kotin, J. and Goodwin, F.K.: Effects of sleep deprivation on mood and central amine metabolism in depressed patients. Arch. Gen. Psychiat., (in press).

Project No. Z01 MH 00446-06 LCS

Rubovits, R.: J. Nerv. Ment. Dis., 160:72-73, 1975. (Book Review on L-DOPA and Parkinsonism: A Psychological Assessment, by Riklan, M.)

Project No. Z01 MH 00447-06 LCS
1. Laboratory of Clinical Science
2. Section on Psychiatry
3. Bethesda, Maryland

PHS-NIH
Individual Project Report
July 1, 1974 through June 30, 1975

Project Title: Brain Amine Function in Mental Illness: Studies of Cerebrospinal Fluid Amine Metabolites

Previous Serial Number: M-CS-Ps(C)-19

Principal Investigator: Frederick K. Goodwin

Other Investigators: Thomas Wehr, Randi Rubovits, Coralyn Jones

Collaborating Scientists: Robert Post, Edna Gordon, Lavonne Brown, David Dunner

Cooperating Units: 4-West and 3-West Clinical Research Units; Unit on Clinical Biochemistry, Laboratory of Clinical Science; Department of Psychiatry, The National Naval Medical Center; New York State Psychiatric Institute

Man Years:		
	Total	2.0
	Professional	1.0
	Other	1.0

Project Description:

This project explores the neurochemistry of various psychiatric conditions using clinical methods previously developed in this section, and lab techniques developed in the Unit on Clinical Biochemistry, LCS.

The purpose of this project is the direct assessment of the functional state of brain neurotransmitter amines in patients by assay of levels and "turnover" (accumulation on probenecid) of the major amine metabolites in the cerebrospinal fluid (CSF). The metabolites under study are 5-hydroxyindoleacetic acid - 5HIAA, the major metabolite of serotonin, homovanillic acid - HVA, the major metabolite of dopamine, and 3-methoxy-4-hydroxyphenylglycol - MHPG, and 3-methoxy-4-hydroxyphenylacetic acid - VMA, the major and the minor metabolite respectively of norepinephrine. Probenecid is included as an adjunct to the baseline studies. This drug inhibits the active transport of acid metabolites of brain amines (5HIAA, HVA and VMA); CSF levels of these acid metabolites are closely related to brain levels and their rate of accumulation during probenecid administration can be used as an indirect index of amine turnover.

A portion of the work involves ongoing efforts to further develop the techniques themselves, including an understanding of the contribution of non-specific variables to the findings. In this regard, some important parameters under study include age, sex, time of day, and position of patient when the lumbar puncture (LP) is done, level of physical activity preceding the tap, diet, non-specific drugs, and CSF probenecid levels. Following up on the previous demonstration of an increase in baseline levels of HVA, 5HIAA and MHPG after experimental hyperactivity ("simulated mania"), we have noted increases in MHPG in patients undergoing normal activity compared to bedrest conditions. In the overall population of depressed patients (the largest patient group under study), age and sex differences have been found for some of the metabolites, but these may not be entirely independent of the illness or its sub-types, and thus, cannot simply be "factored out" of the data. An apparent diurnal variation in 5HIAA has been noted in the depressed patients with higher levels in the morning compared to the afternoon.

In collaboration with Edna Gordon, we have explored the relationship between fluorometrically determined HVA levels and those determined by mass fragmentography. At low levels of metabolite the correlation between the two methods is low, but at levels over 40 ng/ml, the two methods correlate quite well ($r = 0.79$). The relationship between mass fragmentography and gas liquid chromatography is also under investigation for MHPG assays.

Exploration of CSF amine metabolites within and between various diagnostic groups (depression, mania, acute schizophrenia, schizo-affective disorder) has continued, and has expanded to include a study of character disorders in collaboration with the National Naval Medical Center. The major focus continues to be primary affective illness, particularly patients hospitalized for major depressive episodes. In this group (the number is now 85) we continue to find the significantly low level of the norepinephrine metabolite (MHPG) compared to normal individuals, neurological controls, manics, and acute schizophrenics. Studies of CSF VMA, initiated this year, indicate a significantly lower level in depressed patients compared to the other groups.

In the CSF studies of depressed patients utilizing probenecid, HVA accumulation is significantly lower than controls and accumulation tends to be lower in the case of 5HIAA as well. However, the unavailability of a satisfactory control group is a major difficulty. New collaborative studies with the National Naval Medical Center and the New York State Psychiatric Institute are beginning to provide some more satisfactory control data. On the average there are no differences between depressed patients, acute schizophrenics, and manics in 5HIAA or HVA accumulation on probenecid.

Within the population of depressed patients frequency distribution analysis indicates a non-normal, and apparently bimodal distribution for MHPG and 5HIAA after probenecid. When the depressed patients are divided according to the unipolar-bipolar dichotomy (absence or presence respectively of a prior history of mania) there are no differences in 5HIAA or HVA (baseline or probenecid), but there is a tendency for MHPG and VMA to be lower in the bipolar II group (depression with a prior history of hypomania) - a difference which is significant for VMA.

Project No. Z01 MH 00447-06 LCS

Our collaborative study of CSF amine metabolites in acute schizophrenia is detailed in Dr. Post's project report (Adult Psychiatry Branch).

Amine metabolites in character disorders: considerable effort was expended during the last year to establish a collaboration with the National Naval Medical Center. This entailed careful orientation of the medical and nursing staff in a non-research hospital to the potentials and limitations of research procedures. The purpose of this collaborative investment was twofold: first, to provide an opportunity to study other psychiatric diagnostic groups, particularly diagnostic groups without severe illness; and second, to provide a source of patient material which could serve as adequate controls for our studies of the major psychoses. In one phase of the collaborative study, a group of Navy enlisted men with various character diagnoses, and histories of impulse control problems were found to have significant elevated levels of HVA in the CSF compared to normal controls studied in the same laboratory. There were no differences in 5HIAA or MHPG.

Evidence for neurochemical adaptation to psychotrophic drugs has been obtained from studies of the time-dependent effects of some drugs on CSF amine metabolites in depressed, manic and schizophrenic patients. In one study (conducted collaboratively with Robert Post), a large and significant increase in probenecid-induced accumulation of HVA in the CSF was demonstrated after two weeks of treatment with phenothiazines, but was no longer evident after five weeks or more of such treatment. The absence of any continuation of evidence of dopamine receptor blockade (i.e., increased dopamine metabolite levels) is of considerable interest in light of the fact that the full clinical response to these drugs (particularly in schizophrenia) does not really manifest itself until five to six weeks. Also, in relation to the effects of lithium administration on CSF metabolites, we have previously noted a decrease in the probenecid-induced accumulation of 5HIAA following two to three weeks of lithium therapy. This year has seen a major effort to evaluate the more acute effects of lithium on CSF amine metabolites; the data is more variable, but for most patients there was either an increase or no significant change in 5HIAA after acute lithium (3-5 days). Acute versus chronic affects of tricyclics on CSF metabolites are also under investigation. Related to the question of neurochemical adaptation is the somewhat paradoxical finding of decreases in CSF 5HIAA following various antidepressant therapies such as tricyclics, lithium, MAO inhibitors, or ECT. This reduction in serotonin "turnover" following treatment of depression is paradoxical since these patients as a group tend to have a lower mean serotonin "turnover" initially. This finding may provide clinical evidence for the suggestion made on the basis of animal studies that behavioral response to psychotrophic drugs of this type may be related to the neurochemical adaptation to the initial effect of a drug, adaptive responses involving feedback regulatory mechanisms.

Prediction of drug response: another parameter which may define sub-groups of depressed patients is whether they are responders or non-responders to specific drugs. We have found that probenecid-induced accumulation of both 5HIAA and HVA is significantly higher in a group of depressed patients who subsequently showed a response to tricyclic antidepressants compared to a group who were non-responders. Conversely, we have found that lithium responders have low probenecid HVA compared to those who do not respond, and there is a tendency for the same difference to obtain for 5HIAA.

In the coming year, the main thrusts of this project will be in several areas:

1. Further exploration of clinical differences in depressed patients which may correlate with metabolite differences; this involves differential symptom clusters on the 34-item NIMH affective illness rating scale, and specific diagnostic features, particularly the subdivisions of major depressive disorder as outlined in the research diagnostic criteria.

2. Development (with Michael Ebert) of an intravenous probenecid test to allow shorter time studies, and to sharply reduce the incidence of nausea.

3. Further effort will be made to obtain CSF data from various control groups (particularly with probenecid).

4. Studies of CSF amine metabolites in the "well state" to evaluate whether abnormal CSF findings, for example, the low MHPG in depressed patients, return to normal after recovery; preliminary evidence suggests that CSF MHPG may stay low in recovered depressives, representing a state-independent abnormality, perhaps reflecting an aspect of the vulnerability to depression (see description of "well state" studies in project report #Z01 MH 00449-01 LCS).

5. In collaboration with Edna Gordon, the application of mass fragmentography techniques for new compounds will be explored; for example, work is currently underway in Mrs. Gordon's lab to examine levels of dihydroxyphenylacetic acid (DOPAC) in various psychiatric groups with and without drug treatment.

6. More intensive investigation of the time-dependent effects of various drugs on amine metabolites is planned.

7. In collaboration with Robert Post, we will extend studies of CSF calcium, its relationship to depression and recovery, and to amine metabolites.

Honors and Awards:

Dr. Goodwin: See Project Report No. Z01 MH 00446-06 LCS

Dr. Wehr: See Project Report No. Z01 MH 00450-01 LCS

Dr. Rubovits: See Project Report No. Z01 MH 00446-06 LCS

Project No. Z01 MH 00447-06 LCS

Publications:

Post, R.M. and Goodwin, F.K.: Studies of cerebrospinal fluid amine metabolites in depressed patients: conceptual problems and theoretical implications. In Biological Aspects of Depression, Mendels, J. (Ed.), Spectrum Publications, 1974, pp. 47-68.

Goodwin, F.K. and Post, R.M.: Brain serotonin, affective illness, and antidepressant drugs: cerebrospinal fluid studies with probenecid. In Advances in Biochemical Psychopharmacology, Raven Press, New York, Vol. 11, 1974, pp. 341-355.

Goodwin, F.K., Post, R.M. and Sack, R.L.: Clinical evidence for neurotransmitter adaptation to psychotrophic drugs. In Neurobiological Mechanisms of Adaptation and Behavior, Mandell, A. (Ed.), Raven Press, New York, 1975.

Goodwin, F.K. and Post, R.M.: Amine metabolites in cerebrospinal fluid, brain and urine in the major mental illnesses. In The Biology of the Major Psychoses: A Comparative Analysis, Freedman, D. (Ed.), Raven Press, New York, 1975.

Post, R.M. and Goodwin, F.K.: Tolerance to phenothiazine effects on dopamine turnover in psychiatric patients. Science (in press).

Project No. Z01 MH 00448-02 LCS
1. Laboratory of Clinical Science
2. Section on Psychiatry
3. Bethesda, Maryland

PHS-NIH
Individual Project Report
July 1, 1974 through June 30, 1975

Project Title: Studies of Urinary Norepinephrine Metabolites in Affective Disorders and Normal Controls

Previous Serial Number: M-CS-Ps(C)-19

Principal Investigator: Frederick K. Goodwin

Other Investigators: Helmut Beckmann, Giovanni Muscettola, Thomas Wehr, Coralyn Jones

Collaborating Scientists: Dennis Murphy, Monte Buchsbaum

Cooperating Units: 4-West and 3-East Clinical Research Units

Man Years:	Total	1.4
	Professional	0.7
	Other	0.7

Project Description:

The purpose of this project is to study a wide variety of factors which contribute to the urinary excretion of 3-methoxy-4-hydroxyphenylglycol (MHPG) in patients and normal controls. MHPG is the norepinephrine metabolite thought best to reflect brain norepinephrine turnover and studies indicate that the majority of MHPG appearing in the urine has its origin from brain pools of norepinephrine. In conjunction with the study of factors influencing MHPG excretion, we are interested in the usefulness of this important norepinephrine metabolite in evaluating the hypothesis of altered norepinephrine function in depression and mania. Particular attention is given to whether an alteration in MHPG is state-dependent or independent and to what extent the metabolite excretion changes in response to non-specific or secondary factors.

Urine is collected daily on each patient in 24-hour pools which are kept refrigerated with preservative until aliquoted into frozen samples within three days. Conditions which can produce alterations in urinary amines and their metabolites are monitored or controlled to the best of our ability; these include diet, exercise and stress.

The major findings are as follows:

(A) Substantial increases in urinary MHPG are observed following six to 12 hours of moderate exercise in depressed patients. Although it is not yet possible to clarify the relative roles of activity and stress in these changes, the findings do suggest caution in the interpretation of MHPG results in manic-depressive and recovered patients in which large differences in physical activity may be occurring.

(B) In collaboration with Monte Buchsbaum we have been studying MHPG responses to experimentally contrived stressful situations in manic-depressive patients in illness and after recovery. Studies of normal volunteers indicate a modest increase in urinary MHPG following stress, and within the volunteer group, a high correlation between MHPG increase after stress and prestress depressions scores on the MMPI. The findings concerning MHPG responses to stress in depressed patients are more complex, and reflect apparent subgroup differences.

(C) Studies on differential MHPG excretion and the prediction of therapeutic response to specific antidepressant drugs has continued. The clear differential between responders and non-responders to both imipramine and amitriptyline has been shown to apply only to unipolar and not to bipolar patients. Specifically, amitriptyline responders have high pretreatment MHPG, while non-responders have low, with the converse being true for imipramine responders and non-responders.

(D) The effects of drugs on urinary MHPG is under active exploration. We have demonstrated the tricyclic antidepressants uniformly decrease urinary MHPG independent of clinical response or pretreatment MHPG level. Lithium administration per se appears to have no direct effect on urinary MHPG excretion; the changes in MHPG seen in patients on lithium parallel the direction of clinical change, that is, manic patients improving on lithium have decreases in MHPG while depressed patients improving on lithium have increases. In collaboration with Drs. Murphy and Van Kammen we have studied the effects of short-term amphetamine administration on urinary MHPG. The general affect of amphetamine is to decrease MHPG, except in those patients who experienced amphetamine-related hypomania in whom increased MHPG was observed.

(E) Studies of urinary MHPG in subgroups of medication-free depressed patients and normal controls have revealed that depressed patients as a group do not differ significantly from normal controls housed on the same ward and studied under the same conditions of activity, diet, and stress. However, significant subgroup differences in MHPG were found within the depressed population. Thus, bipolar patients excrete significantly less MHPG than unipolar depressed patients ($p < .001$). Compared to the control group the bipolar patients excreted significantly less MHPG, while the unipolars excreted significantly more. Within both the depressed population and the age-matched normal controls, there was a significant positive correlation between systolic blood pressure and urinary MHPG. Correlations between MHPG and anxiety and psychosis ratings were also noted within the depressed population. Multiple discriminate function analysis indicates that urinary MHPG is the most powerful discriminator among the subgroups studied; factoring out anxiety differences does not affect the subgroup differences in MHPG.

In the coming year, studies of MHPG as an indicator of central norepinephrine responses to stress in depressed patients and normal controls will be extended. Of particular interest in the exploration of MHPG stress responses after recovery from the depressive episode. In collaboration with Michael Ebert of the Section on Experimental Therapeutics, isotope techniques will be employed to evaluate the possibility that the relative peripheral versus central contribution to urinary MHPG may differ in the populations we are studying.

Honors and Awards:

Dr. Beckmann presented a paper entitled "Urinary MHPG in Affective Illness: Relationship to Activity, Stress, and Response to Antidepressant Drugs," at the Collegium Internationale Neuropsychopharmacologicum (CINP), IXe Congress, Paris, July 1974.

Dr. Goodwin: See Project Report No. Z01 MH 00446-06 LCS

Dr. Wehr: See Project Report No. Z01 MH 00450-01 LCS

Publications:

Beckmann, H., Jones, C. and Goodwin, F.K.: Unterschiedliche Ausscheidung von 3-Methoxy-4-hydroxyphenylglycol im Urin und Ansprechen auf trizyklische Antidepressiva. Arzneimittel-Forschung, 7:1010-1012, 1974.

Beckmann, H. and Goodwin, F.K.: Urinary MHPG in affective illness: relationship to activity, stress, and response to antidepressant drugs. Journal de Pharmacologie, t.5, Supplement #2, p. 6, 1974.

Beckmann, H and Goodwin, F.K.: Central norepinephrine metabolism and the prediction of antidepressant response to impramine or amitriptyline: studies with urinary MHPG in unipolar depressed patients. Arch. Gen. Psychiat., 32: 17-21, 1975.

Beckmann, H., van Kammen, D.P., Goodwin, F.K., and Murphy, D.L.: MHPG excretion in depressed patients: modifications by amphetamine and lithium. Biol. Psychiat., (in press).

Beckmann, H., St.-Laurent, J. and Goodwin, F.K.: The effect of lithium on urinary MHPG in unipolar and bipolar depressed patients. Psychopharmacologia, (in press).

Project No. Z01 MH 00449-01 LCS
1. Laboratory of Clinical Science
2. Section on Psychiatry
3. Bethesda, Maryland

PHS-NIH
Individual Project Report
July 1, 1974 through June 30, 1975

Project Title: Outpatient followup study of manic-depressive patients and families

Previous Serial Number: None

Principal Investigator: Frederick K. Goodwin

Other Investigators: Yolande Davenport, Alina Efron

Collaborating Scientists: Elliot Gershon, Susan Simmons

Cooperating Units: Unit of Psychogenetics, APB

Man Years: Total 1.4
Professional 0.8
Other 0.6

Project Description:

The establishment of an outpatient clinic for the followup evaluation and treatment of patients with affective illness has been a top priority during the past year. Our primary purpose has been to set up a facility which would be a source of patients for a variety of studies in six key areas: (a) investigations of the "well state,"; (b) the usefulness of couples group therapy in the management of recurrent affective illness; (c) outcome studies; (d) prophylactic efficacy of various drug regimens; (e) the study of the children of patients with affective illness and (f) the evaluation of genetic markers in affective illness.

Patients are admitted to the outpatient department following discharge from the inpatient unit, and may be involved at one of several levels including a full treatment program (maintenance, medication plus individual or group psychotherapy), medication maintenance, or research followup (care provided in the community).

(A) Studies of the "well state": certain biological findings in depressed patients seem to persist in the immediate recovery period while the patient is still hospitalized. The theoretical implications of these findings have underlined the importance of obtaining data at long-term followup, after full recovery can be presumed. For this purpose, patients are restudied at periods ranging from six to 12 months following discharge. A particular interest in these well state studies are the CSF amine metabolites and amine response to stress as measured by urinary 3-methoxy-4-hydroxyphenyl glycol, the metabolite thought best to reflect brain norepinephrine metabolism (described in project reports #Z01 MH 00447-06 LCS and Z01 MH 00448-02 LCS).

(B) Exploration of the usefulness of couples group therapy as an adjunct to the maintenance use of lithium in the prevention of recurrence in affective illness. This project, under the direction of Yolande Davenport, has evaluated outcome in married manic-depressive patients maintained in conjoint couples group therapy compared to manic-depressive patients maintained adequately on lithium but not receiving adjunctive couples therapy. Post-hospital functioning was rated on a multi-item scale developed from a previous followup study of manic-depressive illness done by this group. Significant differences in social functioning, family interaction, and mental status were found between the two groups with a more favorable outcome being associated with the patients receiving both lithium carbonate and couples group therapy.

(C) Followup studies of manic-depressive patients: in this group of studies the relationships between past history, phenomenology of the acute illness and long-term outcome is examined. To date we have demonstrated relationships between outcome and a variety of illness parameters including age of onset, rapidity of cycles, family history, and so forth.

(D) Under the direction of Alina Efron, an evaluation of the prophylactic efficacy of lithium alone versus lithium plus tricyclic antidepressants in unipolar and bipolar affective illness has been undertaken. No results are yet available from this study since the drug codes are still blind.

(E) In collaboration with the Adult Psychiatry Branch (Drs. Cytrin, McNew and Gershon), an intensive study of the children of outpatients with affective illness has been undertaken. Following a two-hour interview the children are rated for depression on multi-item scales by both the interviewer and two independent observers. Interrater reliability in the application of these scales has been demonstrated. Preliminary results suggest a higher than normally expected incidence of diagnosable depression in the children of our affectively ill patients.

(F) In collaboration with Elliot Gershon (Unit on Psychogenetics, APB) data is obtained from the outpatients and their families relevant to questions concerning genetic markers. Thus, plasma and red cell samples are taken for assay of blood types, antigens, and certain proteins which are known to be genetically linked in an effort to explore the question of possible genetic markers for the vulnerability to affective illness.

The further course of the outpatient followup studies depends to a large extent on the availability of additional resources to clinically manage this valuable research asset. The variety of studies dependent upon this resource are all in their initial stages and are focused on areas which are strikingly unexplored in the field of affective illness.

Project No. Z01 MH 00449-01 LCS

Honors and Awards:

Mrs. Davenport is a current member of the EEO Council of NIMH. Mrs. Davenport participated as the NIMH Intramural Program Representative in the Minority and Women's Oppostunity and Resources Conference on April 22-24, 1975, NIMH. At the Annual Meeting of the American Psychiatric Association, May 5-9, 1975, Anaheim, California, she presented a paper entitled "Lithium Prophylaxis: The Married Couples Group".

Dr. Efron participated in a meeting sponsored by the Psychopharmacology Research Branch of the NIMH in order to plan a multi-hospital collaborative study on the maintenance drug treatment of affective disorder, April 1975.

Dr. Goodwin: See Project Report No. Z01 MH 00446-06 LCS

Publications:

Davenport, Y.B.: Depressive illness: some problems of diagnosis in children and blacks. In Integrated Education, Martin, G. (Ed.), (in press).

Ablon, S.L., Davenport, Y.B., Gershon, E.S., and Adland, M.L.: The married manic. Am. J. Orthopsychiat., (in press).

Project No. Z01 MH 00450-01 LCS
1. Laboratory of Clinical Science
2. Section on Psychiatry
3. Bethesda, Maryland

PHS-NIH
Individual Project Report
July 1, 1974 through June 30, 1975

Project Title: Biological rhythms in manic-depressive illness

Previous Serial Number: None

Principal Investigators: Thomas Wehr, Frederick K. Goodwin

Other Investigators: Randi Rubovits, Philip Gold

Collaborating Scientists: Howard Hoffman (NICHD), Monte Buchsbaum, Christian Gillin

Cooperating Units: Division of Computer Resources and Technology, DCRT; APB/LCS Sleep Studies Facility; Section on Cognitive and Perceptual Studies, APB.

Man Years:	Total	1.1
	Professional	0.5
	Other	0.6

Project Description:

Epidemiological evidence has emphasized the essential cyclicity of both unipolar and bipolar affective illness. Since manic-depressive illness is a periodic illness, a study of the role of biological rhythm in its pathophysiology and pathogenesis is important. This project involves longitudinal studies of behavioral, physiological, and biochemical variables in inpatients and outpatients characterized by relatively frequent mood cycles. Focus is on both circadian (i.e., 24-hour) and longer rhythms, requiring both intensive data collection (multiple sampling within the same day) and longitudinal data collection over time (in one patient we have obtained daily measures over 14 months.

Behavioral parameters under study involve both nurses and self-ratings; physiological parameters include evoked response, EEG sleep studies, temperature and heart rate; biochemical variables include urinary 3-methoxy-4-hydroxyphenyl glycol (MHPG - the urinary metabolite thought best to reflect brain norepinephrine metabolism), urinary calcium, magnesium, sodium, potassium (less frequently) CSF amine metabolites. These data are subject to spectral analysis in order to characterize circadian and longer rhythms.

Preliminary findings in these studies can be described under several headings:

1. We have identified a group of bipolar cycling patients who show circadian rhythm desynchronization in temperature and other parameters; that is, these circadian rhythms are not locked into phase with the environmental day-night cycle, but tend to drift gradually in and out of phase. In this respect these patients behave as if they had been cut off from all environmental light and time cues; these findings suggest some disconnectedness in the systems responsible for integretating environmental cues into the regulation of biological rhythms. The systems involved in this integration include the pineal gland and central norepinephrine pathways connecting to it.

2. Diurnal patterns of urinary MHPG excretion are under intensive investigation utilizing 3-hour urine collection periods around the clock both in depressed patients and normal controls. Evidence to date indicates a diurnal pattern for urinary MHPG which appears to change in some patients as they shift from depression into mania.

3. The "basic rest activity cycle," representing an approximately ninety minute rhythm has recently been identified as intrinsic to the human organism. Using special monitoring equipment and information storage systems we are following heart rate continuously in a number of patients in different phases of a manic and depressive cycle. The analysis of this data requires new statistical methods (such as "complex demodulation").

4. The effects of psychoactive drugs on biological rhythms in manic-depressive patients is of special interest. Lithium has been shown to alter the frequency of free-running circadian rhythms in animals and we are currently evaluating the effects of this drug on biological rhythms in manic-depressive patients.

In the future this project will focus on further studies of circadian desynchronization in bipolar patients. One approach to this question involves the use of specific interventions known to alter biological rhythms such as sleep deprivation. We would plan to evaluate the effects of sleep deprivation in phase shifting in various circadian rhythms. An additional approach involves alteration in light-dark cycles and the effects this may have on the biological rhythms under study.

Honors and Awards:

Dr. Wehr participated in the Annual Meeting of the American Psychiatric Association, May 5-9, 1975, Anaheim, California, and presented a paper entitled "Biorhythms and Manic-depressive Illness". Dr. Wehr has also been invited to participate in the XII Biennial Conference of the International Society for Chronobiology, Washington, D.C., August 1975, and will present a paper entitled "Time-structure of the Frequent Mood-Cycles of a Manic-Depressive Patient". Dr. Wehr was the principal speaker on two one-half hour radio shows (WAMU) concerning biological rhythms in medicine and psychiatry, April 1975.

Project No. Z01 MH 00450-01 LCS

Dr. Goodwin: See Project No. Z01 MH 00446-06 LCS

Dr. Rubovits: See Project No. Z01 MH 00446-06 LCS

Publications:

Wehr, T.: Am. J. Psychiat., 131:1418-1419, 1974. (Book review on Depression: Theory and Research, by Becker, Joseph; Washington, D.C., V.H. Winston & Sons, 1974).

Serial No. Z0I MH 00326-02 LCS
1. Laboratory of Clinical Science
2. Section on Clinical Neuro-pharmacology
3. Bethesda, Maryland

PHS-ADAMHA-NIMH
Individual Project Report
July 1, 1974 through June 30, 1975

Project Title: Clinical neuropharmacology and psychobiology of human behavioral disorders, especially mania and depression.

Previous Serial Numbers: M-CS-PS(C)-23

Principal Investigator: Dennis L. Murphy

Other Investigators: Jonathan L. Costa, Carol Hoover, Joseph Tarantolo, Stanley Slater and Eduardo de la Vega (Visiting Fellow).

Collaborating Scientists: Monte S. Buchsbaum, William E. Bunney, Jr., Edward F. Donnelly, Frederick K. Goodwin, Marian Kafka, Donald E. Redmond, Jr., Daniel van Kammen, Herbert Weingartner, Richard J. Wyatt.

Psychiatric Consultants: John Boriello, Donald Boomer, Marion B. Richmond, Leslie Schaffer.

Cooperating Units: Nursing personnel on 3-East; Occupational Therapy (Eleanor A. Stapin), and Art Therapy (Sadie Fishman), personnel on Ward 3-East.

Man Years:		
	Total	9.7
	Professional	6.0
	Other	3.7

Project Description:

Objectives : Individuals with mania, depression and related disorders are studied in attempts to understand the psychological and biological mechanisms involved in therapeutic drug effects in these disorders.

Methods Employed:

1. Behavioral and psychological assessment: Pretreatment evaluation of patients requires information from interviews of the patient and family, from psychometric approaches, and from direct behavioral observation. The elucidation of individual and patient subgroup differences in drug response depends upon this information obtained by the clinical staff, including psychiatrists, psychologists, social workers and nursing personnel. Subsequent evaluation of drug response depends upon objective behavioral assessment as well as self-rated psychological change as obtained from a number of quantitative scales, several of which have been developed on this unit.

2. Biological Assessment: Plasma, platelets, urine, and cerebrospinal fluid are collected for the measurement of enzymes, levels of biogenic amines and their metabolites, other chemical variables, and drug levels. Electrophysiologic measurement of sleep and of cortical evoked potentials are accomplished in collaborative studies with the Adult Psychiatry Branch.

Major Findings:

Behavioral and psychological studies. At the clinical level, the Section has continued to develop and validate behavioral scales for mania, depression and related phenomena. Following the model of our behavioral scale for mania, which is now in routine use here and at some other centers, the Section has developed and examined for reliability and validity a multicomponent affective disorder rating scale. High correlations with other scales for depresssion (the Beck, Hamilton and IMPS sub-scales) and for mania, psychosis and other types of psychopathology have been documented in the last year, and with some final modifications, this optically-scanned, computer-scored scale has now become available for routine clinical use. All of the scale items from the mania scale which were reported in the last year to quantitatively verify some clinical opinions concerning possible subgroups of manic patients and to correlate with therapeutic responses to lithium carbonate are included in the new combined scale.

Quantitative assessment of other phenomena of the depressed and manic patient groups has been carried out in several collaborative projects. Dr. Weingartner, who has worked with our group (especially with Dr. Miller) over the last several years has successfully identified manic state-dependent learning.

Certain information in manic-depressive individuals has been demonstrated to be relatively more readily retrievable in the manic state, and less so in the non-manic states -- a phenomenon paralleling that observed in other studies in our Section with affect-altering drugs, including amphetamine and physostigmine. Whether depression is associated with state-dependent learning also is still under study.

Dr. Donnelly has continued to examine subgroups of patients with affective disorders for psychological test performance differences. In the last year, perceptual tests as well as projective tests have been found to support earlier evidence from the MMPI that bipolar depressed patients differ in many functional ways from unipolar depressed patients. Greater impulsivity and greater social compliance are especially characteristic of the bipolar group.

Clinical pharmacologic studies. In a continuing study of d-and l-amphetamine administration to depressed patients in an attempt to verify suggestions that amphetamine responses might predict tricyclic antidepressant responses, Dr. van Kammen has identified several factors which correlate with the magnitude of antidepressant response to amphetamine, including pretreatment severity of depression, pretreatment diurnal mood variation and amphetamine plasma levels (utilizing a d-amphetamine radioimmunoassay developed by Dr. Ebert). Lithium carbonate co-administration was found to markedly attenuate the activating, euphorogenic and antidepressant effects of amphetamine in a finding which has some implications both for understanding the effects of lithium as an antimanic agent and for the treatment of amphetamine "addiction." Evidence of amphetamine-lithium interactions in EEG-monitored sleep (measured by Dr. Gillin) cortical average evoked responses (measured by Dr. Buchsbaum), and urinary 3-methoxy-4-hydroxy phenylglycol (measured by Drs. Beckman and Goodwin) and learning (measured by Dr. Weingartner) have also been observed in this study.

Clinical and laboratory studies of monoamine oxidase (MAO) and MAO-inhibiting drugs. In a nearly completed study, the MAO-inhibiting antidepressant phenelzine was examined in conjunction with measurements of platelet MAO inhibition in patients receiving the drug in an attempt to determine whether individual differences in platelet MAO inhibition produced by phenelzine might correlate with its therapeutic efficacy. Phenelzine was not found to be a generally effective antidepressant in either unipolar or bipolar depressed patients, and no close relationship with platelet MAO activity reduction (which averaged 75% after 2 weeks of treatment) was observed. However, there was an association between pretreatment platelet MAO levels and some behavioral changes occurring with the drug.

Continuing evidence of associations between some psychiatric patient groups and platelet MAO activity has been demonstrated in studies carried out in chronic schizophrenic patients (with Dr. Wyatt), acute schizophrenic patients (with Dr. Carpenter and Dr. Wyatt) and in patients with affective disorders (with Dr. Brand). A number of factors which influence MAO activity in animals (including sex steroids, thyroid hormone, and iron availability) have been studied in relation to platelet MAO activity, but have not been found to be major variables contributing to the primarily genetically-based differences between individuals. In contrast, additional evidence of an association between platelet MAO activity and behavior and/or personality features has come from studies of natural behavior in non-human primates (by Dr. Redmond and Mr. Jean Baulu) and from studies of psychologic test features in normals (by Drs. Belmaker and Buchsbaum). To further define the biochemical relationship between platelet MAO activity and brain MAO activity, the characteristics of the MAO subtypes A and B have been studied in platelets, sympathetic ganglia, brain and in tissue culture preparations of rat C6 glial cells and mouse neuroblastoma cells (by Mrs. Donnelly and Dr. Richelson). In all characteristics studied thus far, the platelet MAO seems indistinguishable from the brain MAO-B subtype.

The platelet model for neurotransmitter function. Studies of the human platelet as an available model to measure biogenic amine-related cellular processes have been continued by Dr. Costa. He has used the electron microprobe and other techniques to quantitate relationships between calcium, phosphorous and serotonin stored in vesicles. In other studies using the platelet to study reserpine effects, two separable actions of the drug on amine storage vesicle have been identified: (1) an initial uptake-inhibiting action at the vesicle membrane and (2) a separable serotonin-releasing effect. Dr. Costa has also developed a technique to estimate intravesicular versus cytoplasmic amine content on the basis of thrombin-releasable amine and a technique using formaldehyde to interrupt amine transport essentially instantaneously. These procedures are being utilized to study the effects of psychoactive drugs on cellular processes in platelets and other tissue preparations.

In summary, these studies contribute additional information on psychologic and biologic contributions to individual differences in clinical symptomatology and to the drug treatment of psychiatric syndromes. The ability to cross-correlate different behavioral, psychophysiologic and biochemical measures in the investigation of drug responses as exemplified in the d- and l-amphetamine studies provides both greater validity to the conclusions and a more efficient use of resources.

Key word descriptors:

Neuropharmacology	Depression
Memory	Mania
Monoamine Oxidase	Platelet
Amphetamine	Lithium Carbonate

Honors and Awards:

Dr. Murphy was invited to present lectures on the clinical psychopharmacology of the affective disorders at Columbia University, Duke University, the Ohio Psychiatric Society, George Washington University and the University of Pennsylvania. He presented invited papers on monoamine oxidase inhibiting anti-depressants at meetings of the Collegium Internationale Neuro-Psycho-pharmacologium in Paris, the American Association for Research in Nervous and Mental Diseases in New York and the CIBA Foundation in London. He was also invited to present lectures on various aspects of human platelet monoamine oxidase function at the University of Pittsburg, Johns Hopkins University, the Peripatetic Society, Howard University, the International Society for the Study of Psychoneuroendocrinology and the Medical College of Wisconsin. He was invited to participate in and co-chair a meeting on the neurobiology of lithium sponsored by the Neurosciences Research Program, Boston. He was also invited to become a member of the American Psychiatric Association's Program Committee and its Task Force on Research Training, and to become a member of the editorial board of Psychopharmacology Communications.

Dr. Costa was invited to present a paper on uptake and storage of platelet serotonin at Temple University and a paper on platelet secretory responses at the Downstate Medical Center.

Dr. Redmond presented a paper on behavioral correlates of platelet monoamine oxidase activity in non-human primates at the annual meeting of the American Psychosomatic Society.

Publications:

Donnelly, E.F., and Murphy, D.L.: Primary affective disorder: Bender-gestalt sequence of placement as an indicator of impulse control. Percept. Motor Skills 38:1079-1082, 1974.

Murphy, D.L., Beigel, A., Weingartner, H., and Bunney, W.E., Jr.: The quantitation of manic behavior. In Pichot, P. (ed.): Modern Problems in Pharmacopsychiatry, Vol. 7, Basel: S. Karger, 1974, pp. 203-220.

Murphy, D.L., and Donnelly, C.H.: Monoamine oxidase in man: enzyme characteristics in platelets, plasma and other human tissues. In Usdin, E. (ed.): Neuropsychopharmacology of Monoamines and Their Regulatory Enzymes, New York: Raven Press, 1974, pp. 71-85.

Perez-Cruet, J., Chase, T.N., and Murphy, D.L.: Dietary regulation of brain tryptophan metabolism by plasma ratio of free tryptophan and neutral amino acids in humans. Nature 248:693-695, 1974.

Belmaker, R.H., Murphy, D.L., Wyatt, R.J., and Loriaux, D.L.: Human platelet monoamine oxidase changes during the menstrual cycle. Arch. Gen. Psychiat. 31:553-556, 1974.

Murphy, D.L., Donnelly, C.H., and Moskowitz, J.: Catecholamine receptor function in depressed patients. Amer. J. Psychiat. 131:1389-1391, 1974.

Murphy, D.L., and Beigel, A.: Depression, elation, and lithium carbonate responses in manic patient subgroups. Arch. Gen. Psychiat. 31:643-648, 1974.

Murphy, D.L., Belmaker, R., and Wyatt, R.J.: Monoamine oxidase in schizophrenia and other behavioral disorders. J. Psychiat. Res. 11:221-247, 1974.

Belmaker, R., Beckmann, H., Goodwin, F., Murphy, D., Pollin, W., Buchsbaum, M., Wyatt, R., Ciaranello, R., and Lamprecht, F.: Relationships between platelet and plasma monoamine oxidase, plasma dopamine-b-hydroxylase, and urinary 3-methoxy-4-hyhydroxy-phenylglycol. Life Sci. 16:273-280,

77

Murphy, D.L., and Costa, J.L.: Utilization of Cellular Studies of neurotransmitter-related enzymes and transport processes in man for the investigation of biological factors in behavioral disorders. In Mendels, J. (ed.): Recent Biological Studies of Depressive Illness. New York: Spectrum Publications, Inc., 1975, pp. 223-236.

Costa, J.L., Richardson, J.S., and Murphy, D.L.: Comparative evaluation of a platelet serotonin assay utilizing ortho-phthaldialdehyde for fluorophore production. Throm. Diath. Haemor. 33:96-97, 1975.

Project No. Z01 MH 00327-04 LCS
1. Laboratory of Clinical Science
2. Section on Clinical Neuropharmacology
3. Bethesda, Maryland

PHS-ADAMHA-NIMH
Individual Project Report
July 1, 1974 through June 30, 1975

Project Title: Marital Conflict in the Families of Psychotic Patients

Previous Serial Number: M-OD-SW-1

Principal Investigator: Carol F. Hoover, D.S.W. (Social Worker)

Other Investigators: Roy G. Fitzgerald, M.D.; Dr. John Bartko, Theoretical Statistics and Mathematics

Man Years: Total: .5
Professional: .4
Other: .1

Project Description: A 70-item card sort, the Conflict in Marriage Scale (CIMS), is administered to couples on two separate occasions a week apart. This procedure is scored to indicate conflict level and coping mechanisms; item responses are submitted to further analysis.

The objective is to investigate levels of marital conflict, acknowledged anger, and styles of coping with disagreement characteristically reported. Marital dominance, perceived couple interaction, and conflict over children are also studied.

Parents of schizophrenics (S) were compared to the parents of maladjusted (M) and community (C) young people. Same-sexed parental subjects in the original sample of 154 individuals (77 couples) could be divided into the indicated diagnostic groups (S, M, C) based upon responses to the CIMS items. Additional parents of schizophrenics are now being tested to determine how well these new subjects fit the linear function which discriminated S from other parents in the earlier study.

In another segment of the investigation, manic-depressive patients of unipolar, bipolar I, and bipolar II varieties are compared with their spouses, as well as with community husbands and wives. Analysis is currently underway of items and factors, drawn from CIMS responses, which may effectively discriminate among these groups.

Keyword Descriptors: Marital conflict - marital dominance - schizophrenia in families - adolescent maladjustment - parental conflict - Manic-depressive - depression.

Publications: Data from the initial group was reported in a doctoral dissertation, "Conflict Between the Parents of Schizophrenics", Catholic University, 1973. A shorter version is being prepared for publication.

Project No. Z01 MH 00351-01 LCS
1. Laboratory of Clinical Science
2. Section on Experimental Therapeutics
3. Bethesda, Maryland

PHS - ADAMHA - NIMH
July 1, 1974 through June 30, 1975

Project Title: Clinical Pharmacology of the Central Nervous System

Previous Serial Numbers: M-CS-OC(C)-21

Principal Investigator: Michael H. Ebert

Other Investigators: Irwin J. Kopin, Robert D. Hunt, W.W. Havens (guest worker)

Collaborating Scientists: Ronald Kartzinel, S. Harvey Mudd, Herbert Weingartner, Dennis L. Murphy, Edna K. Gordon.

Cooperating Units: Unit on Clinical Biochemistry, Laboratory of General and Comparative Biochemistry, Section on Medicine, Section on Clinical Neuropharmacology, Section on Psychiatry, Adult Psychiatry Branch, Laboratory of Neuropharmacology, (NINDS)

Man Years:	Total	4.5
	Professional	2.5
	Other	2.0

Project Description:

Objectives: 1. To develop metabolic strategies for studying central catecholamine metabolism in man. 2. To carry out pharmacokinetic studies of psychoactive drugs. 3. To utilize these techniques to study patients with neuropsychiatric, psychosomatic, or childhood psychiatric disorders.

Methods Employed:

1. Biochemical methods: Flourometric, gas chromatographic, and mass spectrometric methods are used for assay of endogenous catecholamine metabolites in tissues and body fluids. Mass spectrometric methods are used for assay of deuterium labelled catecholamine metabolites administered exogenously or synthesized endogenously. Gas chromatographic and radioimmunoassay techniques are used for assay of drugs in body fluids (probenecid and d-amphetamine).

2. Behavioral, neurological, and psychometric assessment: Patients admitted this year fall into the diagnostic categories of Huntington's chorea, tardive dyskinesia, anorexia nervosa and minimal brain dysfunction. Objective assessment of the pathology of these patients includes information from the patient and his family; repeated physical examination; self and observer ratings of mood, intellectual function, and movement disorder as appropriate for the study. Of particular interest are the detailed tests of memory function set up on the ward this year with the assistance of Dr. Weingartner.

Major Findings:

Inherited Disorders of Metabolism. Dr. Mudd and Dr. Ebert have conducted a balance study of a 15 year old female with sarcosinemia, a rare inherited disorder of amino acid metabolism. A study of the patient's labile methyl group balance has been carried out on variety of controlled intakes and dietary sources of methyl groups. The study demonstrated that on normal dietary intake, the patient was carrying out some methylneogenesis which was increased by subnormal labile methyl intake, and was turned off by increases in methionine or choline. The results are compatible with a "threshold" hypothesis for methyl group economy in man.

A sensitive gas chromatograph-mass spectrometric assay that measures deuterated and non-deuterated (or endogenous) methionine separately has been developed. This assay will be a useful tool in clinical experiments of methylation in man using stable (or non-radioactive) isotopes as tracers.

Methods for assessing central catecholamine metabolism in man. A modification of the probenecid test for studying central nervous system production of dopamine and serotonin has been accomplished by administering probenecid intravenously to patients. Blood and cerebrospinal fluid levels of probenecid were determined. The plasma levels and half-life of probenecid showed little variance between patients when administered intravenously, and the half-life of probenecid was not affected by the administered dose, as has been claimed in the literature. Both the acidic amine metabolites and probenecid reach peak levels in the lumbar cerebrospinal fluid at 6 hours. Determining cerebrospinal fluid probenecid levels in conjunction with the elevation in acid metabolites of dopamine and serotonin may lead to a more quantitative estimation of central synthesis of these amines.

An approach to central norepinephrine synthesis in man was developed that avoids the necessity of obtaining cerebrospinal fluid from the patient. In this study radioactive dopamine is administered to patients to label peripheral norepinephrine stores. Central norepinephrine stores are not labell because dopamine does not cross the blood brain barrier. The specific activit of two metabolites of norepinephrine, 3-methoxy-4-hydroxymandelic acid (VMA) and 3-methoxy-4-hydroxyphenylglycol (MHPG) are determined in a 24 hour urine. The experiments indicate that there is selective labelling of norepinephrine in sites where VMA is preferentially formed. A substantial portion of MHPG excreted derives from a source which is unlabelled by the radioactive dopamine This source is probably the central nervous system. After further validation, the technique should be capable of estimating central norepinephrine synthesis

Several stable isotope strategies to study brain catecholamine metabo in man are under investigation. Deuterated methionine can be used to label the labile methyl group pool with deuterated methyl groups. Methylated catecholamine metabolites that are three mass units heavier than their endogenous counterparts appear in primate cerebrospinal fluid or in rat brain tissue after incorporating these deuterated methyl groups. The specific activity of deuterated catecholamine metabolites has been studied in relation to specific activity of the precursor deuterated methoinine. The labelled metabolites disappear in a monoexponential curve that parallels the disappearance curve of the precursor, deuterated methionine. Detailed turnover curves and varying amounts of precursor methoinine are under study to optimize the technique for the calculation of catecholamine synthesis rates.

Pharmacokinetics. A radioimmunoassay for d-amphetamine was developed that can be used to measure plasma levels of d-amphetamine after small, single oral doses. The assay clearly distinguishes d-amphetamine from its metabolites and is capable of measureing 200 picograms of amphetamine in 0.1 cc of plasma. The assay is being applied to clinical studies in collaboration with Dr. Murphy and Dr. vanKammen. Initial studies have demonstrated a significant correlation between plasma levels of amphetamine and euphoric response in depressed patients The blocking of euphoric response to amphetamine by pretreatment with lithium was not accounted for by a change in the pharmacokinetics of amphetamine.

Psychometric Studies. Since the dementia of Huntington's disease is as serious a deficit as the choreiform movements, psychometric studies of the dementia were undertaken with Dr. Weingartner. Tests have been set up to rate attention, short and long term memory, and a variety of retrieval strategies including fixed sequence recall, free and cued recall, and recognition memory. The memory deficit can now be followed longitudinally in these patients, and during drug trials. The initial studies pursued this year demonstrate that the dominant abnormality of information processing in Huntington's dementia occurs in the retrieval rather than the storage process. Retrieval is impaired because of the inability to utilize and generate cues to access memory.

Significance to Biomedical Research and Programs of the Institute.

Assessing the rate of amine metabolite formation in animals and inpatients provides information on the rate of amine utilization. The development of more quantitative methods for determining central nervous system amine utilization in man is essential for testing hypotheses regarding the role of amines in psychiatric, medical, and neurological disorders and assessing the effects of drugs on the amines in the brain. Some of the metabolic strategies under development will have broader applications. For example the stable isotope technique for determining the turnover rate of methionine will be a useful tool to study some disorders of amino acid metabolism as well as brain catecholamine metabolism.

Proposed Course of Project.

The techniques described above are now either being applied to studies in man or will be applied during the coming year. They will be further developed and validated during the course of animal and clinical studies. The application of the biochemical techniques in conjunction with psychometric techniques to several neuropsychiatric or psychosomatic diseases has begun and will develop rapidly during the next year.

Publications:

Gordon, E., Perlow, M., Oliver, J., Ebert, M., Kopin, I.: Origins of catecholamine metabolites in monkey cerebrospinal fluid. J. Neurochem. In press, 1975.

Lamprecht, F., Ebert, M., Turek, I., Kopin, I.: Serum dopamine-beta-hydroxylase in depressed patients and the effect of electroconvulsive shock treatment. Psychopharmacologia 40:241-248, 1974.

Ebert, M.H., vanKammen, D.P., Murphy, D.L.: Plasma levels of amphetamine and behavioral response. In Gottschalk, L. and Merlis, S. (eds.): Pharmacokinetics, Psychoactive Drug Blood Levels, and Clinical Response, New York, Spectrum Publications, 1975.

Ebert, M.H., and Kopin, I.J.: Differential labelling of origins of urinary catecholamine metabolites by dopamine-C^{14}. Proceedings of the Association of American Physicians. In press.

Serial No. Z01 MH 00221-15 LDP
1. Developmental Psychology
2.
3. Bethesda, Maryland

PHS-ADAMHA-NIMH
Individual Project Report
July 1, 1974 through June 30, 1975

Project Title: Cognitive, Social and Emotional Behavior in the Preschool Child: Longitudinal and Cross-Sectional Analyses

Previous Serial Number: M-CR-10 (c)

Principal Investigator: Charles F. Halverson, Jr.

Other Investigators: Mary F. Waldrop

Cooperating Units: NONE

Person Years:

Total:	3.75
Professional:	.50
Other:	3.25

Project Description:

This research is directed to the description of individual differences in three-year-old children. Questions to be investigated include: What is the stability over time and across situations of the child's social and play behavior? How situationally and age dependent are the young child's temperamental behaviors? What situational influences affect the expression of positive and negative social interaction (e.g., number of toys in room, age and sex of other children in the group)? What characteristics of the child influence social behavior towards peers and adults (e.g., activity level, cognitive-intellectual maturity, sex of child, attention-span)? How is the child's relationships with adults (mother, teachers) related to peer interaction? How are the cognitive and social behaviors of the child related to coping competently with frustrating situations? How are the child's behaviors observed in the nursery school related to family and social experiences at home? How reliable are individual and sex differences in activity level and how important are they in a child's social and cognitive behavior?

Subjects are 132 children, ages two years four months to three years six months, from middle class white families. The setting was a research nursery school with free-play areas indoors and out, and areas for refreshment and rest. Children attended a 4-week session in mixed-sex groups of 5 where behavioral measures in each of the four settings were based on direct naturalistic observation and teacher ratings. Interest has been focussed on the child's attentional deployment in the various settings of free play, on social behavior towards peers and caretakers, and the nature of assertive and coping behaviors elicited in naturalistic as well as experimental settings.

Times and counts were used for naturalistic observations. Experimental procedures were designed to elicit the child's coping and assertive behaviors when confronted with physical barriers or novel situations. Standardized tests of verbal and cognitive development were administered. Data on current family life were recorded in the home by the mother in a detailed diary (three separate weeks of family life within a three month span were sampled). Interview data were obtained from the mother on her attitudes toward aggression, behavioral control and child rearing in general. Activity level measures were obtained in each of the settings in the nursery school by using activity recorders worn by each child.

The project was designed with many variables similar in content, but coming from different procedures. The total number of variables is large and, to varying degrees, redundant. Therefore, the analysis strategy has been to discard variables of low reliability and/or low stability and to concentrate on forming clusters of variables which have cross-setting and cross-method generality and stability. At the same time, the interrelations of various behavioral dimensions and their contextual determinancs will be examined.

Major analyses are in progress. The following are selected findings from analyses now underway:

1. Observed positive and negative peer behaviors are highly consistent across time and situations for both boys and girls. Situations do, however, affect interaction differently for boys and girls: In free play with a variety of play materials available, boys showed high levels of negative peer interaction relative to girls; whereas in a setting with no play materials available, boys' positive peer interaction was increased and negative interaction decreased while girls' behavior remained about the same. In the setting without play materials boys showed significantly <u>more</u> positive interaction than girls. This interaction of sex and setting for the display of positive and negative interaction indicates the need for caution in making the often quoted generalization that boys are more aggressive and negative than girls.

2. Positive peer interaction increases as children get older while negative interactions remain at relatively stable levels for the ages studied.

3. The sex composition of the play group had significant effects on the expression of negative interactions over possessions: both boys and girls displayed higher levels of conflict over possessions when only <u>one</u> other

same-sexed peer was present in the group and significantly lower levels when two other same-sexed peers were present.

4. Boys are higher in activity level in all settings than girls. There is also rather high temporal and situational stability of activity scores.

The data are yielding basic information concerning the development of social, emotional, and cognitive behavior patterns in the young child. Such data can assist in planning services in the mental health area. The preschool setting could be an important mental health screening opportunity, helping to diagnose possible deviant and exceptional developmental patterns early in life, so interventions could be planned to be maximally effective.

Since the project has just recently finished the data collection, only preliminary analyses have been performed. The methodological focus of the analyses will be to seek measures which are stable. Measures are being summarized in multi-method, multi-setting composites of both observed and rated behavioral characteristics. Additional analyses are planned in the areas of attachment behavior, social behavior, differences between first-born and second-born children, and individual patterns of adult-child interaction.

Keyword Descriptors:

Child Mental Development, Child Behavior
Children, Preschool
Family, (Child Rearing) or (Parent-Offspring)
Population Studies Human, Longitudinal Study
Psychology, Cognition
Psychology, Emotions
Psychology, Social, Group Processes, Peer Groups
Psychology, Social, Interpersonal Relations
Sex, Sex Differences

Honors and Awards:

Group Service Award, NIMH
Principal Investigator selected to Executive Committee Division 7 (Developmental Psychology) 1975-77.

Publications: NONE

Serial No. Z01 MH 00222-01 LDP
1. Developmental Psychology
2.
3. Bethesda, Maryland

PHS-ADAMHA-NIMH
Individual Project Report
July 1, 1974 through June 30, 1975

Project Title: Relations Between Preschool Behavior and Later Cognitive, Social, and Hyperactive Behavior

Previous Serial Number: M-CR-10 (c)

Principal Investigators: Charles F. Halverson, Jr., Mary F. Waldrop

Other Investigators: NONE

Cooperating Units: NONE

Person Years:

Total:	1.85
Professional:	.50
Other:	1.35

Project Description:

The research focus is on the organization of cognitive, social, and play behavior in early preschool years and the relation of these domains of behavior to cognitive, social, and emotional development in the school-age child. Specifically, what are the relations between activity level and attention span at 2½ years and other facets of social and emotional behavior at this age and at 7½ years? How predictive are early assessments of cognitive and social competence of later competence?

The subjects were 27 females and 35 males, from white, middle class families. The children were studied at 2½ and at 7½ years of age. Data on the preschool years are naturalistic observations of children's play and social behavior in groups of five same-sex children. The subjects were observed in a research nursery school setting over a 5-week period. Observations consisted of counts and times of various categories of play and social behavior. In addition there were experimental tests of coping with object blocks which assessed the child's ability to overcome physical blocks to on-going motivated behavior; in this instance, tearing down a barrier to gain access to a set of highly desirable toys. Teacher ratings on social and cognitive competence were also obtained. At 7½, children were observed in a free-play setting, interacting with adults and in a cognitive testing situation. Observations and ratings similar to those in the preschool studies were obtained. Diary accounts kept by the mothers provided information on the child's social behavior with peers.

(1) Experimental assessments of effective coping behavior were related to naturalistic measures of coping, to vigorous play behavior, and to lack of fear at age 2½. Also at age 7½, preschool competence in coping was significantly related to intelligence, coping, and socially effective behaviors.

(2) The children who at age 2½ were assessed as friendly, involved with their peers, and able to cope with aggressive peers were similarly socially involved and competent at 7½: they spent more outside school hours with peers, were socially at ease, and were the ones who made the decisions about what and with whom to play. Peer behavior at 7½ had different characteristics for boys and girls. Highly social boys are more likely than girls to have *extensive* peer relations, that is, playing in groups of children. Highly social girls are more likely to have *intensive* peer relations, that is, playing with only one other child.

(3) The relations between preschool hyperactivity and school-age behavior were explored. Consistent clusters of observed behaviors were associated with teacher ratings of hyperactivity; namely, two independent and replicated factors, Activity Level and Social Participation. These two factors and the hyperactivity ratings were significantly related to behavior at 7½: For both boys and girls, hyperactivity showed considerable stability over five years. Hyperactivity expressed by high activity levels is negatively related to various measures of cognitive and intellective performance at 7½. Hyperactivity as expressed in social participation is positively related to the same measures of intellectual performance. The activity level component is highly related to an index of minor physical anomalies, while the social participation component is not.

The data collected in this project indicate that social and emotional characteristics of the young child have some continuity over a five-year-period. The identification of domains of behavior which have some continuity into middle childhood assists in determining which behaviors may be indicative of adult functioning. With this knowledge it would then be possible to plan intervention programs aimed at the identification and modification of behaviors early in life to modify potentially deviant patterns of social interaction before they became serious and embedded in a matrix of socially pathological behavior. Longitudinal data provide the kind of information which should assist planning services in the area of child mental health.

No further major analyses are now planned. However, these data on early personality functioning will be used in follow-up studies of development in middle childhood.

Serial No. Z01 MH 00222-01 LDP

Keyword Descriptors:

Child Mental Development Disorders, Behavioral, Hyperactivity Syndrome
Children
Population Studies Human, Longitudinal Study
Psychological Adaptation, Coping Behavior
Psychology, Behavior Prediction
Psychology, Social, Group Processes, Peer Groups

Honors and Awards: NONE

Publications:

Halverson, C. F., Jr. and Waldrop, M. F. Relations between preschool barrier behaviors and early school-age measures of coping, imagination, and verbal development. Developmental Psychology, 1974, 10, 716-720.

Waldrop, M. F. and Halverson, C. F., Jr. Intensive and extensive peer behavior: longitudinal and cross-sectional analyses. Child Development, 1975, 46, 19-26.

Serial No. Z01 MH 00223-01 LDP
1. Developmental Psychology
2.
3. Bethesda, Maryland

PHS-ADAMHA-NIMH
Individual Project Report
July 1, 1974 through June 30, 1975

Project Title: The Relation of Problem Behavior and Minor Physical Anomalies in Young Children

Previous Serial Number: M-CR-10(c)

Principal Investigator: Mary F. Waldrop

Other Investigators: Charles F. Halverson, Jr., James B. Victor (non PHS)

Cooperating Units: Department of Educational Psychology, State University of New York at Albany

Person Years:

Total:	.87
Professional:	.70
Other:	.17

Project Description:

To investigate the relation of minor congenital physical anomalies to behaviors that have negative implications for social and cognitive development.

Three samples of children are the bases of this investigation: (1) a cohort of 42 to 103 children studied as newborns, at 3 months, and at 3 years of age; (2) 93 lower middle class girls in one elementary school, ages 5 to 11; 18% were black; and (3) 100 white, middle class children, in a second school, ages 5 to 11.

The presence of one or more of 18 minor physical anomalies (such as low-seated ears, high steepled palate, curved fifth finger, large or small head circumference, etc.) was assessed. The presence of multiple minor physical anomalies is presumed to result from developmental deviations in early pregnancy and/or some form of genetic transmission which mimics such early pregnancy problems. The score for anomalies was the cumulative number of anomalies present. Direct observations, teacher ratings, standard IQ and achievement tests, and peer judgments were the sources of measures of social, emotional, and intellectual development. Assessments of behaviors in the newborns included physiological measures (respiration and heart rate) and various reactivity measures.

In the first elementary school sample of girls: (1) The presence of multiple anomalies is related to teachers' ratings of inhibition, fearfulness, and being socially ill-at-ease. (2) Anomalies were negatively related to IQ and motor coordination and positively related to absenteeism. (3) The mean differences in the anomaly score between the inhibited group and the outgoing group held true over and above those differences that could be expected because of IQ, poor coordination, and number of absences.

In the second elementary school sample: (1) Multiple social problems, and high rankings of hyperactive behavior, were related to the presence of anomalies in boys. (2) A set of judgments by peers of negative social behavior, for both sexes, related to high scores on anomalies. These two samples give consistent evidence of a congenital contributor to the expression of difficult behavior in the early childhood years.

In the longitudinal sample: (1) Anomalies scores have been found to be stable from newborn to 3 months, newborn to nursery school, and 3 months to nursery school. (2) Preliminary analyses show, for the 3 year olds, a replication of relations between anomalies and hyperactive behaviors for boys, and anomalies and inhibited behaviors for girls.

Studies of the relation of "problem" behaviors to the frequency of minor physical anomalies have aided in understanding the interplay between possible constitutional factors and developing cognitive, social and emotional behaviors of young children. The findings of these studies do not indicate constitutional predetermination of early behavioral problems. A more likely hypothesis is that it is the interaction of congenital and experiential factors that lead to the expression of difficult behaviors in early childhood. Other studies will be needed to delineate further these interrelations.

Analyses of the newborn and infant correlates of anomalies have just begun and will continue in the next year. Additional analyses will consist of comparisons across developmental stages to determine the stability of associations between multiple minor anomalies and certain social and affective characteristics.

Keyword Descriptors:

Children
Population Studies, Human, Longitudinal Studies
Child Mental Development Disorders, Behavioral, Hyperactivity Syndrome
Psychology, Abnormal, Cognitive Disorders
Psychology, Abnormal, Social Behavior Disorders (General)
Infant Human
Congenital Abnormalities

Honors and Awards:

None

Publications:

Waldrop, M. F., Bell, R. Q., and Goering, J. D. Minor physical anomalies and inhibited behavior in elementary school girls. Journal of Child Psychology and Psychiatry, 1975, in press.

Victor, J. B. and Halverson, C. F., Jr. Distractibility and hypersensitivity: two behavior factors in elementary school children. Journal of Abnormal Child Psychology, 1975, in press.

Halverson, C. F., Jr. and Victor, J. B. Minor physical anomalies and problem behavior in elementary school children. Child Development, 1975, in press.

Serial No. Z01 MH-00224-01LDP

1. Laboratory of Developmental Psychology
2.
3. Bethesda, Maryland

PHS-ADAMHA-NIMH
July 1, 1974 through June 30, 1975

Project Title: Interrelation of Developmental Data from Preparental, Newborn, Mother-Infant, and Preschool Studies

Previous Serial Number: None

Principal Investigators: Howard A. Moss, Charles Halverson, Raymond Yang, Mary Waldrop

Other Investigators: Richard Bell, Robert Ryder

Cooperating Units: None

Person Years:

Total:	1.94
Professional:	.69
Other:	1.25

Project Description:

The purpose of this research is to interrelate data from four developmental stages: (1) preparental, 2) newborn, 3) mother-infant, and 4) preschool) in order to determine the joint contribution of environmental and congenital influences on development.

Data have been collected by four separate teams of investigators on each of the developmental phases under study. One group has studied early marriage prior to the birth of the infant and thus will provide information on the prospective parents before their attitudes might be shaped by any salient attributes of their infant. Most of these data come from questionnaires and experimental conflict situations. Another team has assessed newborn behavior of infants born to these parents. This assessment focused on psychophysiological and behavioral measures of the newborn between 2-3 days of age in order to determine initial predispositions prior to any direct parental influences. A third group of investigators studied mother-infant interaction through home observations, interviews and questionnaires, and a series of standardized laboratory procedures. Finally, when these children were about three years of age, they participated (in groups of 5) in an experimental nursery school program where they were studied by a fourth team of investigators. Thus the same population was studied at different developmental stages by separate teams of investigators which enabled us to maintain independence of information at each stage. This design allows us to obtain an approximation of the environmental conditions mediated by the parents prior to exposure to the infant; an assessment of the infant's initial response tendencies prior to modification by environmental influences; and therefore enables us better to estimate how these two sources of variance interact in contributing to later behavior.

Each research team is in the process of developing variables that can be used for cross-stage analyses. The total number of variables from all of our procedures is unwieldy, both from a statistical and from a theoretical viewpoint, and thus we are reducing the initial sets of scores into a manageable and optimally functional set of variables. This is being accomplished by discarding variables with inadequate measurement properties (i.e. low reliabilities), selecting the more statistically robust variables from among redundant measures, and utilizing summarizing procedures such as factor analysis. We have just about achieved our final sets of variables for the respective developmental stages. These will consist of both individual variables and summary variables, expressed as factor scores. We are currently in the process of planning cross-stage analyses. These analyses will consist of relating selected measures across stages in terms of specified hypotheses as well as conducting a systematic, overall empirical evaluation of the data from the preparental through the preschool phases.

The first set of hypotheses we are planning to test with these data deals with the antecedents and ontogenesis of early socialization. Some specific hypotheses are:

1. Some newborns appear to be more regulated by internal stimuli whereas others appear to be more under the control of external stimuli. It is predicted that those newborns who appear to be more affected by external stimuli will in turn be more responsive to social stimuli at later stages of development.

2. It is predicted that mothers who are shaped by or are contingent to their infant's signals early in life will acquire greater reinforcement value in regulating and socializing their children's behavior at later stages of development.

3. The energy and activity level of the parents and the degree of stimulation they provide for the infant will be associated with a greater amount of social interaction in the child at the preschool period.

Cross-stage analyses will be initiated within the next few months and will provide us with our initial findings for this project.

The findings from this project will allow us to replace retrospective reconstructions with actual data on the sequence of events by which social, emotional, and cognitive behaviors develop in the young child and should inform us about the respective contributions and interactions between environmental and congenital factors in the development of fundamental behavior patterns. This type of information is important for evaluating developmental theory, and for providing effective guidance to parents and to programs that are aimed at fulfilling the needs of children.

This coming year will be devoted to conducting a series of cross-stage analyses and reporting the findings of this research.

Keyword Descriptors:

Child Mental Development, Child Behavior
Children, Preschool
Family, Maternal Behavior
Family, Parents
Family, Parents-Offspring
Infant Human
Population Studies Human, Longitudinal Studies
Psychology, Learning, Experience, Early Experience
Psychology, Social, Interpersonal Relations
Socialization

Honors and Awards: None

Publications: None

Serial No. Z01 MH 00225-01 LDP
1. Developmental Psychology
2.
3. Bethesda, Maryland

PHS-ADAMHA-NIMH
Individual Project Report
July 1, 1974 through June 30, 1975

Project Title: A Replication Study of the "Inversion of Intensity" Between Newborn and Preschool Age Behavior (An Interpretation Reported by Bell, Weller, and Waldrop, 1971)

Previous Serial Number: M-CR-11 (c)

Principal Investigators: Raymond K. Yang, Charles F. Halverson, Jr.

Other Investigators: NONE

Cooperating Units: NONE

Person Years:

Total:	1.50
Professional:	.65
Other:	.85

Project Description:

To test the longitudinal "inversion of intensity" interpretation describing a negative relationship between newborn intensity and preschool intensity. The "inversion," first reported by Bell, Weller, and Waldrop, (1971) describes a relationship between newborn infants, lethargic in behavioral responses and low in autonomic function, who at 2½ years are active, socially participative, and advanced in speech development in a preschool nursery setting (and vice versa).

The sample of 106 normal children (50 boys, 56 girls) born to middle class, primiparous mothers from intact families residing in the large suburban area of Washington, D. C.

The replication consisted of two parts: (1) An attempt to test on a measure-by-measure basis all specific relations upon which Bell et al. based the inversion interpretation; (2) A conceptual replication, based on the construction of dimensions of intensity at newborn and preschool periods.

At the newborn period, all specific measures contributing to the inversion interpretation were available for replication. These included measures of tactile threshold, respiratory rates, and responses to interruption of sucking. (The measure of tactile threshold did not meet the requirement of reliability and was discarded.) At the preschool period, all major dimensions characterizing the broad areas of behavior contributing to the inversion interpretation were available. This included a dimension of overall intensity of behavior, the specific components of a dimension assessing coping with a physical barrier, and an auditory stimulation dimension. Also included were dimensions of verbal behavior for females, these dimensions being peripherally related to the inversion interpretation. Following the conceptualization of intensity formulated by Bell et al. (high magnitude behavior equals high intensity), two dimensions were constructed at the newborn period representing high reactivity to procedural stimulation and high levels of spontaneous behavior under nonstimulated conditions. At the preschool period three dimensions were constructed, one representing an empirical cluster of behaviors indicating high activity, the other two representing a separation of positively valued high activity, and negatively valued "hyperactivity."

Only one of the numerous specific relations between newborn and preschool behaviors reached statistical significance. Relations between all other specific newborn and preschool measures of intensity failed to reach statistical significance; for these it was concluded that no consistency with the original study was obtained. In summary, on a measure-by-measure basis, the "inversion of intensity" interpretation was not replicated.

In the conceptual replication, a minimal relation was found between the newborn dimension representing reactive intensity and the broad cluster of preschool behaviors representing high activity. This relation existed only for males and represented a minimal replication of the "inversion of intensity" interpretation. A similar relation existed between the newborn dimension of spontaneous intensity and the preschool cluster of behaviors representing high activity for females. This was a new finding. A similarly new finding related newborn reactive and spontaneous intensity to the preschool dimension representing negatively valued "hyperactive" behavior. These relations were much stronger than those between the newborn dimensions and the empirical preschool cluster of active behaviors. On the basis of the relation between the newborn dimension of reactive intensity and the preschool empirical cluster, it was concluded that the dimensional analysis yielded minimal substantive support for the "inversion" interpretation. However, the stronger relation between both newborn dimensions of intensity and preschool negatively valued and "hyperactive" behaviors paradoxically disconfirmed the interpretation of the substantive relationship as an "inversion."

Should other studies also find negatively evaluated, "hyperactive" behavior in preschool settings to be related to neonatal behavior, some justification would be provided for examining potential early "markers" predisposing an infant toward eventual difficulty in preschool. These markers might not only be explored with regard to organismic continuity, but also with regard to distinctive patterns of parent-infant interaction, the latter being of potential value in providing bases from which selective patterns of interaction could be encouraged as "interventive" procedures.

A final report is now in preparation for submission for consideration of publication.

Serial No. Z01 MH 00225-01 LDP

Keyword Descriptors:

Child Mental Development, Child Behavior
Children Preschool
Infant Human Newborn
Methodology
Population Studies Human, Longitudinal Study
Psychology, Behavior Prediction

Honors and Awards: NONE

Publications: NONE

Serial No. Z01 MH 00226-01 LDP
1. Developmental Psychology
2.
3. Bethesda, Maryland

PHS-ADAMHA-NIMH
Individual Project Report
July 1, 1974 through June 30, 1975

Project Title: A Dimensional Description of Neonatal Behavior

Previous Serial Number: M-CR-11 (c)

Principal Investigator: Raymond K. Yang

Other Investigators: Edward J. Federman

Cooperating Units: NONE

Person Years:

Total:	.69
Professional:	.25
Other:	.44

Project Description:

To provide a dimensional (factor analytic) description of neonatal behavior across a broad range of procedures. Also, to examine the potential usefulness of such a description when placed under criteria of test-retest and concurrent reliability.

The sample is 137 clinically normal neonates born of primiparous, middle class mothers from intact families residing in the larger suburban area of Washington, D. C. The neonates averaged 59 hours of age at testing. Testing occurred in the hospitals where the infants were born. Data was obtained in two 2½ hour sessions. Procedures involved samplings of behavior during minimal, moderate, and intense environmental interaction. Twenty-six behavioral and physiological measures were obtained. Factor analyses yielded dimensions which could be compared for stability of factor scores between testing sessions. The components of the factor analyses could also be examined for test-retest stability as single measures.

Generally, the factor analytically derived dimensions were considerably more interpretable and useful than single variables. Three stable factors were obtained, each yielding an orthogonal and interpretable dimension. The first dimension, "Reactivity-Irritability," grouped all variables measuring some aspect of crying. Spanning three separate procedures, this factor described a high scoring neonate as responding rapidly and vocally to the withdrawal of a rubber nipple and other aversive stimuli. The second factor, "Maturity," described a high scoring neonate as large (weight and size), of long gestation, high average respiratory rate and of low autonomic variability in sleep. This factor, combining variables derived from medical records as well as the procedural assessment gave support to the notion that stable measures of individual differences can be constructed that are potentially reflective of intrauterine events. The third factor, "Reflexive and Discriminative Sucking," described a high scoring infant as exhibiting high amounts of reflexive sucking as well as discriminative ability between an appropriate and inappropriate sucking stimulus. Infants scoring high on this factor were also characterized by sleeping patterns frequented by periods of restless (active) sleep.

A broad substantive description of neonatal behavior, based on an empirical approach, provides a base against which standardized developmental assessments (for example, the Brazelton Neonatal Assessment Scale, Rosenblith revision of the Graham Scale) can be evaluated. The description of early behavior is valuable in that it provides potential early "markers" by which later behaviors can be better described; for those later behaviors arousing clinical concern, early "markers" may achieve immediate diagnostic value.

When analyses are completed, a report will be prepared and submitted for consideration of publication.

Keyword Descriptors:

Child Mental Development, Child Behavior
Infant Human
Methodology
Psychological Tests, Behavior Assessment Measurement

Honors and Awards: NONE

Publications: NONE

Serial No. Z01 MH 00227-01 LDP
1. Developmental Psychology
2.
3. Bethesda, Maryland

PHS-ADAMHA-NIMH
Individual Project Report
July 1, 1974 through June 30, 1975

Project Title: Successive Relationships Between Attitudes During Pregnancy, Maternal Analgesic Medication During Labor and Delivery, and Newborn Behavior

Previous Serial Number: M-CR-11 (c)

Principal Investigator: Raymond K. Yang

Other Investigators: Ann R. Zweig, Edward J. Federman, Howard A. Moss

Cooperating Units: NONE

Person Years:

Total:	.75
Professional:	.25
Other:	.50

Project Description:

To determine if sequential or cumulative relationships exist between attitudes during pregnancy, maternal analgesic medication during labor and delivery, and neonatal behavior.

The sample is 85 white primiparous mothers and their newborn infants. The mothers are from middle class, intact families residing in the larger metropolitan area of Washington, D. C. All infants were delivered at area hospitals selected by the mother's private obstetrician. The mother's average age was 23 years. The infant's average age at testing was 58 hours. All infants were judged clinically normal and full term at birth.

Measures: (1) Attitudes during pregnancy -- In the eighth month of pregnancy all mothers responded to a standardized questionnaire assessing fears for self and (as yet unborn) infant, as well as irritability, tension, depression, and withdrawal. (2) Maternal analgesic medication -- Four measures of analgesic medication were obtained assessing total dosage, time of administration of the first and last drugs, and moment of the greatest drug effect. (3) Labor and delivery -- Two measures of duration of labor were obtained. (4) Newborn behavior -- Fourteen measures assessing a broad continuum of behavior ranging from sleep to vigorous crying were obtained.

Included in these measures were percentage and duration of active and quiet sleep, as well as autonomic variability during sleep. During quiet waking periods reflexive as well as discriminative sucking was assessed. Other measures assessed the infant's response to aversive stimulation.

Correlational analyses were used to relate variables between phases. Maternal fears during pregnancy were positively related to the amount of drugs given during labor. Earlier and greater administrations of drugs were, in turn, positively related to increases in length of labor. However, drugs and length of labor were generally unrelated to newborn behavior. In terms of newborn behavior, the critical aspects of drug administration were the moment of greatest drug effect and the time that the last drug was administered. Both measures, however, related to newborn behavior in low magnitudes. These relationships suggest that drugs given earlier in labor were associated with increased homeostatic efficiency; similarly, drugs given later in labor (and closer to birth), were associated with slight decreases in homeostatic efficiency.

Should other studies also find maternal fears during pregnancy to be related to obstetric analgesic medication, and in turn, aspects of analgesic medication to be related to newborn homeostatic efficiency, clear bases would be established for encouraging early psychological preparation of the mother for childbirth. The provision of information as well as increased sensitivity to maternal fears on the part of the obstetrician could contribute to more efficient management of delivery and optimal neonatal outcome.

This study also provides an alternative hypothesis to recent studies demonstrating relationships between maternal obstetric sedation and post-neonatal behavior. These studies have suggested that biochemical mechanisms during critical early periods have been affected by analgesic drugs administered to the mother. This study suggests that maternal fears, to the extent that they characterize enduring maternal traits, may predispose mothers towards certain interactive modes with their infants, and that the effects are recognizable even at this early age and mistakenly attributed to the enduring effects of drugs.

Keyword Descriptors

Infant Human
Family, Maternal Behavior
Pregnancy, Birth
Pregnancy, Perinatal Stress
Psychology, Attitudes to Health
Sensory Depression, Analgesia

Honors and Awards: NONE

Publications:

Yang, R. K., Zweig, A. R., and Douthitt, T. C., in collaboration with Federman, E. J. Successive relationships between attitudes during pregnancy, maternal analgesic medication during labor and delivery, and newborn behavior. Developmental Psychology, in press.

Serial No: Z01 MH 00228-08LDP

1. Developmental Psychology
2.
3. Bethesda, Maryland

PHS-ADAMHA-NIMH
Individual Project Report
July 1, 1974 through June 30, 1975

Project Title: Determinants and Dimensions of Mother-Infant Interaction

Previous Serial Number: M-CR-23 (c)

Principal Investigator: Howard A. Moss

Other Investigators: Sandra J. Jones & Blanche S. Jacobs

Cooperating Units: None

Person Years:

Total:	1.90
Professional:	.40
Other:	1.50

Project Description:

The objectives of this research are to identify primary dimensions of mother-infant interaction and the determinants of these interaction patterns, and to relate these findings to data, provided in a longitudinal program, on earlier infant behavioral and psychophysiological functioning and parental variables. In addition, the present data on mother-infant interaction will be examined in relation to behavior at 3 years of age.

The sample is 121 mother-infant pairs (64 male and 57 female infants) of lower-middle to upper-middle class background. The data include the following:

(1) interviews and questionnaires administered to the expectant mother during the last trimester of pregnancy.

(2) two 6-hour home observations of mother-infant interaction when the infant was 3 months old.

(3) postpartum interviews and questionnaires administered to the mother when the infant was about 3½ months old. Procedures were administered to the mother, the infant was studied in a laboratory situation using procedures that involved vocal conditioning, visual attention, resistance to cuddling, and muscle tonus.

(4) when the child was 11 months old, observations in the home regarding reactions to strangers, separation from the mother, imitation, socialization, exploratory behavior, etc.

Inter-rater reliability coefficients averaged in the .80's for the interview ratings and in the mid .90's for home observations.

Principal component factor analyses were computed for each set of data, and where appropriate, separately for mothers and infants.

Analyses are midway. Summary descriptions of the factors that emerge are as follows (in parentheses is the amount of variance accounted for by that factor prior to rotation):

From the Pregnancy Interview and Questionnaire: Factor I (20.61) - Positive orientation toward infants and toward maternal role; Factor II (10.57) Fearfulness and sense of inadequacy; Factor III (7.64) - Predisposition toward providing and seeking social and physical stimulation; Factor IV (5.44) - Dependency; lack of confidence; establishes close and affectionate ties with family members.

From the Postpartum Interview and Questionnaire: Factor I (22.48) - Depression, sense of inadequacy, irritability; Factor II (10.07) - Positive attitude toward infant and toward maternal role; Factor III (5.06) - Provides social and physical stimulation for infant.

From the Maternal Home Observation at 3 months: Factor I (18.88) - Close affectionate and social interaction with infant; Factor II (7.37) - High activity and noise level in home; Factor III (6.90) - Mother evaluated as skilled and positive toward infant; Factor IV (5.47) - Mother provides social, physical, visual, and auditory stimulation for infant.

From Infant Home Observations at 3 months: Factor I (26.03) - Highly aroused, social infant; Factor II (14.76) - Vigorous, active infant; Factor III (11.44) - Drowsy, flaccid infant.

From Laboratory Procedures at 3½ months: Factor I (11.45) - Infant vocalizes, smiles, vis-à-vis in reinforcement; Factor II (9.73) - Infant vocalizes, smiles, vis-à-vis in baseline; large, heavy infant; Factor III (9.49) Infant protests in reinforcement and extinction; Factor IV (6.59) - Infant smiles in extinction, vocalizes in visual and cuddle procedures; low protest; Factor V (5.58) - Infant vocalizes, smiles, vis-à-vis in extinction; high strength and amount of resistance to cuddle; protests in cuddle procedure.

From the Infant 11-Month Home Assessment: Factor I (12.58) - Infant fearful of strangers; protests; stays by mother; Factor II (7.40) - No negative reactions to mother leaving the house; positive social interaction with Observer; Factor III (6.14) - Infant imitates experimenter, has great deal of experience with adults and children, is left with caretakers, uses and understands words; Factor IV (94.84) - Infant spends long time with mother and with box of toys.

From Maternal 11-Month Home Assessment: Factor I (15.80) - Negative, non-contingent interaction with infant; Factor II (13.39) - Mother responds to infant demands; low social interaction; Factor III (10.05) - Mother provides stimulation and engages in responsive, playful and social interaction with infant; Factor IV (10.77) - Mother leaves child with caretakers; Factor V (9.45) - Mother leaves child overnight; Factor VI (8.91) - Maternal insecurity and concern for infant; responds with and without demands.

Selected findings from analyses based on individual variables and combinations of variables are:

(1) With the sample dichotomized on socio-economic background, mothers in the upper level of the sample were rated significantly higher on interest in affectionate contact and social interaction with the infant, stimulation of the infant, and identification with the father. Mothers in the lower half of the sample were rated higher on variables measuring depression during pregnancy, apprehension over health and well-being of the infant, and degree of generalized apprehension. The female subjects in the upper group had significantly higher scores on both Infant Smiles and Mother Smiles. Furthermore, correlations between the pregnancy ratings and maternal behavior in the home tended to be significantly related only for the upper group of mothers. For example, the pregnancy rating on Interest in Affectionate Contact with Infant was significantly correlated with the frequency with which mothers "kissed" their infants during the 3-month home observations. Correlations that occurred generally replicated for sub-samples of male and female infants.
(2) Previous experimental studies on operant conditioning have shown that infant behaviors (vocalization and smiling) can be increased through contingent reinforcement. The question that remains to be answered is whether contingent reinforcements that occur during the natural course of events are of significance in shaping infant behaviors. To pursue this question, the frequency of naturally-occurring contingent maternal behaviors (at 3 months) was examined in relation to the infants' operant behavior under baseline and reinforcement conditions in the laboratory. The frequency of maternal contingent reinforcement of infant vocalizations in the homes was moderately predictive of differences among infants in their vocalization rates during vocal reinforcement in our laboratory, for females. The tendency to exhibit similar vocalization rates in both the home and the laboratory, irrespective of reinforcement contingencies, was more characteristic of the male infants.

The data from this project will provide information concerning the extent to which early response tendencies in infants, and various parental characteristics, conjointly contribute to early mother-infant interaction patterns. From these data we can begin to determine the variance in the mother-infant interaction that is attributable to infant characteristics, as well as the variance associated with particular maternal predispositions. This kind of information, all too rarely available from past research, is vital to a more solid empirical base for theories of mantal health. From information on the conjoint contribution, we should reach an improved understanding of the mother's and infant's attachment to one another; the emergence of social behavior and responsiveness in the child.

All data has been put on IBM cards except for some factual scores extracted from the pregnancy and postpartum interviews. These remaining data will be processed in the near future. Within-stage analyses have been initiated and some preliminary results have been produced. This coming year largely will be devoted to carrying out and preparing for publication remaining within-stage analyses.

Key Descriptors:

Child Mental Development
Family, Maternal Behavior
Family, Parent-Offspring
Infant Human
Population Studies Human, Longitudinal Studies

Honors and Awards:

None

Publications:

Moss, H. A. Early Sex Differences and Mother-Infant Interaction. In Friedman, R. C., Richart, R. M., & Vande Wiele, R. L. (Eds.), Sex Differences in Behavior. New York: Wiley, 1974.

Moss, H. A., & Jones, S. J. Relations between Maternal Attitudes and Maternal Behavior as a Function of Social Class. In Leiderman, P. H., & Tulkin, S. R. (Eds.), Cultural and Social Influences on Behavior in Infancy and Early Childhood. Stanford: Stanford University Press, In Press.

Moss, H. A. Personality Development: Infancy. In Wolman, B. B. (Ed.) International Encyclopedia of Neurology, Psychiatry, Psychoanalysis and Psychology. New York: In Press.

Serial No. Z01 MH 00229-01LDP

1. Developmental Psychology
2.
3. Bethesda, Maryland

PHS-ADAMHA-NIMH
Individual Project Report
July 1, 1974 through June 30, 1975

Project Title: A Comparison between Maternal-Infant Behavior with First- and Secondborn Offspring

Previous Serial Number: NONE

Principal Investigator: Howard A. Moss and Blanche S. Jacobs

Other Investigators: None

Cooperating Units: None

Man Years:

Total:	1.75
Professional:	.40
Other:	1.35

Project Description:

The objective of this research is to examine differences in maternal treatment of first- and secondborn infants.

The sample is 32 mothers and their first- and secondborn infants selected from a sample of 121 firstborn infants and their mothers that had been observed in their homes as a part of a larger longitudinal project. Cases with second borns were selected on the basis of sex of the infant and sex of the older sibling, to provide four equal size subgroups consisting of same- and opposite-sex siblings, to enable us to study sex by birth order effects.

Two observations, each six hours in length, on non-consecutive days, were conducted when the infants were about 90 days old. A modified time-sampling technique was used. For each of 41 variables, the observer placed a mark in the column following the listed behavior for each minute in which the behavior occurred. Infant variables dealt mainly with the state of the infant (asleep, awake, crying, etc.) while the maternal variables concerned caretaking activities, contact with the infant, stimulation levels, and social-affectional behaviors.

For the main analysis, t's were computed for the total sample as well as the four subgroups of same- and opposite-sex siblings. In addition, to explore the similarity between first- and secondborn infants from the same family and the consistency of mothers with different offspring, correlational analyses were used. To explore whether actions or demands of first borns might account for modifications in maternal attention toward the second born, we correlated a variable which had been added for the secondborn study, First born demands attention with the home observation variables.

Mothers had much less interaction, both social and caretaking, with their second borns than with their first borns. The greatest decrement in maternal treatment toward the second born was for female second borns with older brothers. Male second borns were less affected as a function of their birth order. There was no decrease in maternal attention for male second borns who had firstborn sisters.

The consistency of maternal behavior toward their first- and secondborn offspring, separated in age by an average of 25 months, was examined. This is one way of estimating the mother's contribution to the child-mother interaction, since two infants in the same family often vary greatly. Mothers tended to be highly similar toward both infants in use of physical affection, physical distance maintained from the infant, use of a pacifier, and frequency of imitating infant vocalizations. Correlations ranged from .45 to .74 ($p < .01$). To our knowledge, these are the first systematic data throwing light on maternal consistency in this early age range.

Although it had been assumed that first born demands for attention would be negatively associated with maternal behavior toward the second born, this proved not to be the case; there was a strong positive relation. With male first borns, demands were positively associated with distal caretaking and social behaviors for second borns. With female first borns, demands were associated with close physical contact between the mother and secondborn infant.

In a broad range of studies in the literature there has been an attempt to pinpoint differences in human behavior attributable to birth order. Attempts have been made to relate ordinal position to differences in such diverse areas as achievement, conformity, alcoholism, dependency, intelligence, and schizophrenia. For the most part, such studies have been limited to demonstrating that some of the variance reflected in individual differences is a result of birth order effects and the findings are inconsistent and inconclusive. This study, which is based on direct observation of mothers with both their first and second infants, should enable us to begin to observe processes by which birth order status may mediate differences in behavior.

A manuscript presenting the primary findings from this research is in the process of being prepared and will be submitted for publication in a scientific journal within the next few months.

Serial No. Z01 MH 00229-01LDP

Keyword Descriptors:

Infant Human
Family, Maternal Behavior
Family, Parent-Offspring
Family, Sibling Order

Honors and Awards:

None

Publications:

None

Serial No. Z01 MH 00230-09 LDP
1. Developmental Psychology
2.
3. Bethesda, Maryland

PHS-ADAMHA-NIMH
Individual Project Report
July 1, 1974 through June 30, 1975

Project Title: Discriminative and Conceptual Behavior in Preschool Children

Previous Serial Number: M-P-L-9

Principal Investigator: Albert J. Caron

Other Investigators: None

Cooperating Units: Private and Cooperative Nursery Schools in Montgomery County and the District of Columbia

Person Years: None

This project was temporarily suspended and is being held in abeyance.

Serial No. Z01 MH 00231-01 LDP
1. Developmental Psychology
2.
3. Bethesda, Maryland

PHS-ADAMHA-NIMH
Individual Project Report
July 1, 1974 through June 30, 1975

Project Title: Assessment of Infant Perceptual/Cognitive Capacities

Previous Serial Number: M-P-L-10

Principal Investigator: Albert J. Caron

Other Investigators: V. R. Carlson, Sarah Friedman

Cooperating Units: Laboratory of Psychopathology

Person Years:

Total:	.88
Professional:	.40
Others:	.48

Project Description:

To assess the perceptual/cognitive capacities of human infants at successive periods during the first year of life.

Study A.

The purpose of this study is primarily methodological: To compare different variants of the familiarization-novelty procedure in order to isolate the technique which is most sensitive to infant discriminative capacity. The standard familiarization-novelty method involves exposure of the same stimulus in each of two windows for a fixed familiarization period, following which the stimulus in one of the windows is changed so that both the old and novel stimuli are presented for a brief test interval (a paired comparison presentation). Theoretically, if the infant can discriminate between the two stimuli, he should look longer during the test at the novel one; if not, he should distribute his looking equally between the two. In order to correct for position biases, investigators have modified the procedure in various ways: (1) by giving a second test in which the position of the novel and familiarized stimuli are reversed; (2) by correcting looking on a single test for position biases during familiarization; and (3) by using a successive comparison procedure, presenting the novel stimulus alone on test one and the familiar stimulus on a second test (in either a two-window or a single-window format). Since these variations were producing inconsistent results in assessments for our early experience project, and since none has ever been systematically compared, the present study was designed to calibrate these various approaches.

Four pairs of stimuli varying in discriminative difficulty were presented to infants at two ages (3 and 5 months) in either paired comparison, successive comparison, or control paradigms (involving reversal of the order of novel and familiar test stimuli). Eight males and eight females were tested in each Method X Age sub group, yielding a total of 96 infants. Apparatus specially constructed for the project, which employs a TV photographic procedure for recording infant visual fixation and also permits automatic presentation of stimuli, was used.

Although a few subjects remain to be tested and the data have not been formally analyzed, preliminary inspection of the results indicates that the most sensitive way to assess infant discriminative ability is by means of a single paired comparison test corrected for position bias during familiarization.

Study B:

The general purpose of this study is to provide an assessment of the young infant's sensitivity to the depth dimension and thus to bring evidence to bear on whether infants function from the start in a three-dimensional world or whether detection of depth is acquired as a consequence of later occurring prehensile and locomotor experience. The specific question addressed is whether infants can see a cut-out shape (e.g., a square) as constant despite its being tilted toward or away from them and thereby projecting a different shape (i.e., a trapezoid) on the retina. To the extent that the infant is able to preserve shape constancy under varying slant conditions, he must be taking the orientation of the object in the third dimension into account.

Infants at two ages (3 and 5 months) will be exposed for 90 second familiarization periods to two target areas, each containing the same square in frontal orientation. Immediately following familiarization, one square will be replaced for one group by a large backward-tilted trapezoid (objectively different from the square but which projects on the retina as the identical square), and for a second group, by the same square tilted backward at the same angle as the trapezoid (objectively the same, but retinally different from the square). Apparatus specially designed for this project which also employs a TV photographic procedure for recording infant visual fixation and allows flexible automatic presentation of three-dimensional stimuli, will be used. Comparison of the distribution of visual fixation at test between these groups and appropriate controls will indicate whether infant perception is in accord with an objective, three-dimensional reality (shape constancy) or more primitively dependent upon a single sensory parameter (retinal projection).

The data are about to be collected and the study should be completed during the coming fiscal year.

Study C:

This study also bears on the question of infant depth perception. Its objective is to ascertain whether three-dimensional shapes are more readily discriminated by young infants than two dimensional ones. If the infant's reality is indeed three-dimensional and if two-dimensional projections represent late-developing abstractions from a solid world, then it might be easier for babies to detect and integrate edges in depth rather than those on a flat plane.

Three-dimensional analogues of shapes already determined by us to be non-discriminable at 3 and 5 months of age will be presented to the same-age infants in a comparable familiarization-novelty paradigm. The apparatus used in Study B above will also serve in this experiment.

The findings of this project should contribute to our knowledge of the perceptual and intellective capacities with which the infant is equipped in the early months of life and which enable him to progress to higher levels of competence. Needless to say, this information is basic to the establishment of diagnostic programs for the detection of deficits at an early age or for their ultimate remedial treatment.

This project is an indefinitely continuing one in pursuance of the general objectives stated above.

A manuscript is currently being prepared covering the findings in Study A and additional reports will be forthcoming as data collection is completed for Studies B and C.

Keyword Descriptors:

Infant Human
Methodology
Psychology, Learning, Discrimination
Eye, Vision, Depth Perception Visual

Honors and Awards:

None

Publications:

None

Serial No. Z01 MH 00232-01 LDP
1. Developmental Psychology
2.
3. Bethesda, Maryland

PHS-ADAMHA-NIMH
Individual Project Report
July 1, 1974 through June 30, 1975

Project Title: The Effects of Antecedent Risk Factors on Infant Intellect as Reflected in Habituation and Conditioning

Previous Serial Number: M-P-L-10

Principal Investigator: Albert J. Caron

Other Investigators: Yvonne Brackbill, Rose F. Caron, Sarah Friedman

Cooperating Units: Georgetown University Medical School and George Washington University

Person Years:

Total:	.25
Professional:	.10
Other:	.15

Project Description:

The broad objective of this project is to ascertain whether prenatal or perinatal risk factors may relate to higher-order intellective deficiencies in young infants. Although deficit behaviors appear early in life (and are obviously important to identify), those that have been studied seem to bear no consistent relationship to antecedent risk factors or have had little predictive value for later cognitive functioning. It may be that this equivocal outcome is due in part to the simple sensory-motor character of most of the infant behaviors examined, whereas the effects of the particular risk factors under investigation may be more clearly evidenced in higher-order cognitive performance. In the belief that this might be the case, the purpose of an initial study is to examine the relationship between maternal medication (analgesics, anesthetics, tranquilizers) and rate of habituation to visual stimulation in early infancy. Obstetrical drugs have been shown to depress visual attention in the neonate and to retard rate of habituation to auditory stimulation in the neonate, as well as at 4 weeks, 4 months, and 8 months. Whether these latter effects are confined to the auditory modality is unknown, since there are no studies of the relationship between habituation to visual stimuli and obstetrical medication in infants older than one week.

Reliable data on the visual habituation of over 400 infants at ages 4 and 5 months have already been collected in our laboratory. We are currently in the process of obtaining maternal medication history on sub-samples of extreme cases from this population, and will examine these data for significant medication-behavior relationships.

The medication data are yet to be collected.

Although it is extremely important to be able to detect intellective deficiencies early in life as well as to reveal their possible sources in questionable obstetrical practices, reliable findings have been difficult to come by. Hopefully the present project, in using more sophisticated infant experimental procedures as diagnostic screening devices, will help to remedy this situation.

This project is an indefinitely continuing one in pursuance of the general objectives stated above.

Keyword Descriptors:

Infant Human
Psychology, Learning, Habituation
Psychology, Conditioning
Pregnancy Disorders
Pregnancy, Prenatal Stress

Honors and Awards:

None

Publications:

None

Serial No. Z01 MH 00233-08 LDP
1. Developmental Psychology
2.
3. Bethesda, Maryland

PHS-ADAMHA-NIMH
Individual Project Report
July 1, 1974 through June 30, 1975

Project Title: The Effects of Early Experience on Perceptual/Cognitive Development in Infancy

Previous Serial Number: M-P-L-10

Principal Investigator: Albert J. Caron

Other Investigator: Rose F. Caron

Cooperating Units: George Washington University

Person Years:

Total:	1.73
Professional:	.50
Other:	1.23

Project Description:

This project is designed to provide a fine-grained analysis of the effects of early visual experience on the development of discriminative competence in infancy. Specifically, to examine the respective roles of reinforcement and responding in promoting a particular discriminative ability between three and five months of age. In so doing, the research is intended to resolve competing theoretical views regarding the necessity and sufficiency of differential reinforcement and differential responding in early perceptual learning. A second purpose of the project is methodological: to adopt discriminative operant technology to the special behavioral and sensory requirements of the young human infant.

The project employs both discriminative assessment procedures and discriminative operant training procedures. The former make use of the familiarization-novelty principle, namely that attentional responding to prolonged stimulation tends to decline and then recovers to a novel stimulus or a perceived stimulus change. Recovery of attentional fixation thus can be assumed to reflect the ability to discriminate familiarized from novel stimuli. The technique is being used to identify geometric shapes which are non-discriminable by the average five-month-old and hence which can be used as discriminative training stimuli at three months of age.

The typical discriminative operant training regimen involves the association of one response and one reinforcement schedule with a stimulus (S_1), and a second response and the same schedule, or withholding of response and a different schedule, with a second stimulus (S_2). Thus, there are a number of procedural choices open to the investigator, involving the use of one or two instrumental responses, a variety of schedules of reinforcement (intermittent, continuous, extinction, reinforcing, withholding of behavior -- DRO), and the temporal phasing of S_1 and S_2 components. Much of our recent work has attempted to determine the proper combination of these parameters which would optimize discriminative learning in the young infant. At present we plan to use as a basic paradigm one wherein the infant will be required (1) to close a head-switch in the presence of a circular figure to obtain brief occurrences of music and mobiles on a continuous schedule and (2) to withhold responding for 5 seconds in the presence of an x-shaped figure to obtain comparable reinforcement. Matched groups of three-month-olds will be exposed over a one month period either to this paradigm or to variants of it which differ in terms of (a) the provision of the same or differential reinforcers in association with each stimulus, (b) the necessity for making the same, different responses, or no response at all in the presence of each stimulus, and (c) the exposure of two or three-dimensional versions of the discriminative stimuli. Following training, all infants will be assessed via the familiarization-novelty procedure for their ability to discriminate the shapes seen in training and related stimuli.

Experimentation during this past year has been devoted primarily to the search for the optimal discriminative training paradigm. Some 100 babies were tested under a variety of response, schedule, and S_1 - S_2 phasing conditions. Thus far, we have determined that: (1) The introduction of extinction following the initial conditioning of a response elicits emotional behavior which disrupts stable discriminative performance; (2) responses such as kicking which have extremely high operant rates cannot be inhibited by three-month-olds, and impair discriminative learning. Moreover, excitement and/or frustration elicit increased kicking which is confounded with the conditioned behavior; (3) requiring the infant to respond in the presence of the positive stimulus and to pause during the negative interval (DRO) tends to be more conducive to discriminative performance than requiring two alternative responses (e.g., right versus left head turns); although infants are able to master two responses, the learning process is prolonged and often produces indiscriminate responding; (4) the introduction of the discrimination procedure before the initial response has become too strong tends to be less disruptive of behavior and provides the infant with more exposure to contrasting presentations of S_1 and S_2.

The findings should contribute to (a) our understanding of how early experience promotes perceptual development, (b) the refinement of methodology for studying infant perception and learning, and (c) ultimately to the establishment of a diagnostic, remedial and educational technology which is appropriate and viable in the early months of life.

Serial No. Z01 00233-08 LDP

This project is an indefinitely continuing one in pursuance of the general objectives states above.

A manuscript interpreting our procedural findings is currently being prepared.

Keyword Descriptors:

Infant Human
Methodology
Psychology, Learning, Discrimination
Psychology, Conditioning, Operant
Psychology, Conditioning, Reinforcement
Psychology, Learning, Experience, Early Experience

Honors and Awards:

Consulting Editor, Journal of Developmental Psychology

Publications:

None

Serial No. Z01 MH 00234-02 LDP
1. Developmental Psychology
2.
3. Bethesda, Maryland

PHS-ADAMHA-NIMH
Individual Project Report
July 1, 1974 through June 30, 1975

Project Title: The Infant Conditions His Mother: Experiments on Directions of Influence in Mother-Infant Interaction

Previous Serial Number: M-P-D (c) - 43

Principal Investigator: Jacob L. Gewirtz, Ph.D.

Other Investigators: Elizabeth F. Boyd, Ph.D. (Guest Worker)

Person Years:

Total:	2.00
Professional:	1.00
Other:	1.00

Project Description:

In past years, observed relationships between parent and child behaviors were routinely attributed to the effect of the parent's behaviors on the child's behaviors. Also, experimental learning approaches have been in this same theoretical frame.

There has been increasing concern with the two-way flow of influence between parent and child. This mutual-influence conception has provided the basis for the present studies of sequential mother-infant interchanges. The instrumental-conditioning paradigm has been employed in an experimentally-contrived mother-infant interaction context. The question asked is whether a directed response (e.g., a vocalization) that a mother believes her infant has emitted to her will influence (i.e., reinforce) a response she has been emitting to him, possibly without her even being aware of the process whereby her behavior is being influenced.

<u>Study 1</u>. Four mothers and their normal 3-month-old infants (2 males and 2 females) are the subjects. The mother is seated in a lighted room facing a one-way mirror. She assumes that her infant is in a darkened room on the other side of the mirror. Each mother is asked to say short verbal phrases (from one of two response classes) through a microphone to her infant immediately following a sequence of lights which indicate that her infant has made a (simulated) head-turn in her direction. (The purpose of the procedure was explained as an investigation of whether infants can learn

that their behaviors could have social consequences.) After her verbal response, the mother "listens" for one second for her infant's response. In actuality, she receives output from a recorder, either of nominal vocalizations of her infant or ambient room noise denoting his silence. In this way, vocalizations simulated for each mother's infant were presented immediately following the mother's response. There were 4 response combinations--one verbal class with and without smile and a second verbal class with and without smile. During the initial conditioning phase, the verbal class followed by smiles that was the lower in baseline incidence was followed by a simulated infant vocalization. The other three classes were followed by room noise. A conditioning procedure was continued across 15-trial blocks until, within a reliable number of those trial blocks, the frequency of the reinforced response was greater than the frequency of the nonreinforced responses. Conditions were then reversed: Recorded infant vocalizations followed the theretofore unreinforced verbal and smile response class, and ambient room noise followed the previously reinforced response class. These conditions were in effect until a reliable increase in the earlier nonconditioned verbal response followed by smiles was demonstrated, together with a decrease in the frequency of the previously conditioned response class. Then the response initially conditioned was reconditioned in a second conditioning phase.

Study 2. As in Study 1, each of four mothers was asked to say short verbal phrases, but this time contingent upon the infant's (simulated) vocal rather than head-turn response. Mothers were shown the apparatus in which their infants would be seated. The mothers understood that the accompanying lighting apparatus was something they should ignore. It was part of another investigation to measure the infant's turning toward his mother. A series of red lights denoted head-turning; a single yellow light, non-turning. In actuality, the light sequence denoting head turns toward the mother's face was presented immediately following those of her behaviors that were to be fostered: verbal behaviors, full or partial, smiles, verbal behaviors plus any smiles, or sustained or closed-mouth expressions.

Study 1. The verbal-plus-any-smile responses of three mothers were reliably conditioned, reversed, and reconditioned. The verbal-plus-any-smile response of the fourth mother studied was reliably conditioned and reversed four separate times. Thus, the short vocal responses which the mothers appeared to accept as being those of their own infants, functioned to reinforce the mother's responses to their infants.

Study 2. For one mother, there was reliable conditioning of partial smiles and, under a reversal condition, of full smiles. For a second subject, there was reliable conditioning of one verbal-response class with any smile, and then, under a reversal condition, of the second verbal-response class with any smile, and in a subsequent reversal condition this verbal-response class when not accompanied by a smile. Finally, second verbal response with any smile was reconditioned reliably. For the third mother, there was reliable conditioning of a sustained, open-mouth, facial expression, followed by a reliable reversal during which a closed-mouth expression was conditioned, which in turn was followed by a reliable reconditioning of the sustained open-mouth expression. For the fourth mother, all smiles were reliably conditioned, were reversed with nonsmiles conditioned, and then smiles were reconditioned.

Hence, the infant's assumed looking toward the mother functioned to reinforce the mother's own expressive behaviors to their offspring. Post-experimental interviews and casual comments by the mothers indicated that their expressive behaviors had been conditioned, without the mother's apparent awareness either of the contingency or of the fact that learning had occurred.

As yet very imperfectly understood, the reciprocal-influence process of mother (or other caregiver) and infant upon each other's behavior promises to provide an important key for understanding the end products of mother-infant interaction, and the adaptive learning of child and of caregiver throughout the child's formative years. The principles identified in these experiments are relevant to the understanding of aberrations in learned outcomes and can be of use in developing corrective changes in parent and child interaction. These principles have a bearing on the understanding and remediating of later behavioral anomalies such as learning difficulties and antisocial behaviors that may often stem from maladaptive patterns of adult-child interactions.

The first publications of the results of the project are in press. Given the reliable demonstrations of the efficacy of these two simulated infant behaviors in controlling mothers' interactive behavior, in the next phase of the research the infant will be brought directly into the experimental setting to interact with the mother. The next step will be to approximate more closely the life situation by programming an infant-mother interchange such that a response of the mother (e.g., a facial expression) will be maintained by the actual vocal or orientation response of her infant, for which the mother's response serves as the cue. In order to train the infant to respond discriminatively to the mother's response, the mother would be cued to respond to her infant only after she had smiled. In this way, infant's discriminative vocalization would function to maintain mother's smile behavior, which behavior in turn would serve to cue the infant's vocalization. Hence, a sophisticated discrimination would be learned by the infant and be applied differentially to maintain, indeed to control, some of his mother's expressive behaviors. In these ways, the research program would be moving closer to providing leverage upon the influence that the behavior of one interactor has on the behavior of the other, very much as is assumed to occur in the life situations.

Keyword Descriptors:

Infant Human
Family, Maternal Behavior
Psychology, Conditioning, Reinforcement
Child Mental Development, Child Behavior
Family, Parent-Offspring
Psychology, Cognition, Awareness

Honors and Awards:

None

Publications:

Gewirtz, J. L. Direction of influence in the maternal conditioning of infant crying within the attachment-acquisition process. In Etzel, B. C., LeBlanc, J. J., & Baer, D. M. (Editors), New Developments in Behavioral Research: Theory, Methods, and Applications. Hillsdale, N. J.: L. Erlbaum Associates, in press.

Gewirtz, J. L., & Boyd, E. F. The infant conditions his mother: Experiments on mother-infant interaction underlying mutual attachment. In Alloway, T., Krames, L., & Pliner, P. (Editors), Communication and Affect. Vol. 5. New York: Plenum Press, in press.

Gewirtz, J. L., & Boyd, E. F. Does maternal responding *really* reduce infant crying?: A critique of the 1972 Bell and Ainsworth report. Child Development, in press.

Serial No. Z01 MH 00235-01 LDP
1. Developmental Psychology
2.
3. Bethesda, Maryland

PHS-ADAMHA-NIMH
Individual Project Report
July 1, 1974 through June 30, 1975

Project Title: Early Human Social Learning

Previous Serial Number: None

Principal Investigator: Jacob L. Gewirtz, Ph. D.

Other Investigators: Claire L. Poulson, Ph.D.
Gail Y. Browne, Ph.D. (Guest Worker)

Person Years:

Total:	2.50
Professional:	1.50
Other:	1.00

Project Description:

Our current research centers on two issues that need resolution in order to provide the research methodology for more substantive issues of infant-social interaction. The first issue is: Does the infant more readily learn to respond differentially to two different instrumental learning situations if the situations are alternated frequently over short time periods (concurrent learning), or does he learn more easily if he is allowed to master one set of skills before requiring another (sequential learning)? Alternating experimental conditions during a single session gives more exposure to condition change and thus more opportunities to learn which response pattern is effective under which condition. This procedure, however, could be too complicated for the infant to learn anything. If the infant is exposed to only one condition change per session, on the other hand, he may require longer to differentiate between the two conditions. Experimental analysis of instrumental learning requires that the infant be exposed to each of the experimental conditions within a single session because the state of the growing infant from session to session is so variable that one cannot afford to allow condition change to be confounded with session change. The way to institute condition changes within sessions is, therefore, a critical methodological matter.

The second issue under investigation is: What is the length of time required by the infant to "absorb" the environmental effect of each of his own responses? In instrumental learning research with infants, the duration of the environmental effects of the infant is usually between 5 and 15 seconds, whereas in similar research with older humans or infrahumans the duration has usually been a mere two or three seconds. The issue is of practical as well as theoretical concern. If, for example, it were found that the effect of a response must be present for 10 seconds if it is to maintain responding, such events as parental smiles following infant vocalizations are not likely to maintain those vocalizations unless the smiles last at least 10 seconds. Similarly, if the length of time for "absorption" can be established, refinements in naturalistic observations would be necessary.

Subjects are normal, healthy infants, 2 to 3 months of age. Single-subject experimental designs are used, with group controls for order effects. Each subject is his own control, performing under every condition. Thirty infants will be required for this study series. Each is seen for 6 sessions, which preliminary work has indicated to be the optimal number, under the conditions described, for maintaining the infant's interest and cooperation.

In the investigation of both research issues, the same infant responses and response consequences are measured. The infant response is a head-turn of approximately 15 degrees. Half the infants are required to turn right, half left. The turn is recorded automatically while the infant is seated in an infant carseat facing a screen. In his line of vision in the center of the screen is a window two feet away. A shade covers the window; the mother sits behind the screen. The consequence of the infant's head-turn is the appearance and voice of the mother as she draws up the shade, talks to him for 1 or 2 seconds, and then pulls the shade down again. The duration of her appearance is monitored.

In the comparison of concurrent and sequential condition changes within sessions, two experimental conditions are used with each infant. In Condition A each head-turn immediately produces visual and auditory access to the mother. In Condition B, head-turns never produce the mother within 3 seconds of their occurrence; the mother appears approximately the same number of times as in Condition A, but not within three seconds of a head-turn.

Relevant to the question concerning effects of sequential, as opposed to concurrent, scheduling of experimental conditions, comparisons are made between a group of infants receiving one condition change from A to B per session, and another group of infants receiving many alternations of the A and B conditions per session. Possible different patterns of response a quisition, different latencies of responding at the beginning of the conditions, and different overall frequencies of responding between the two conditions are being analyzed.

Regarding the question of length of time required for infant "absorption", comparisons are made between 2-second and 15-second presentations of the mother following infant head-turning. Two-second and 15-second presentations are distributed evenly across Conditions A and B, and the two conditions occur concurrently within each session. Each infant experiences each condition: the order of presentation of conditions is counterbalanced across infants. Infant head-turning frequencies with the 2-second and the 15-second presentations are examined.

A set of general laboratory procedures has been developed. Data collection is in the early stages.

The orienting-regarding response (represented by head-turning in this investigation) characterizes a considerable portion of the infant's responding in the life setting. It mediates (and hence could also index) much of adaptive and social learning and development in early life. Therefore, the functional relations between an infant's orienting-regarding and such consequences as his mother's reactions to his behavior could serve as a model for understanding human learning. These data could be useful in the development of therapeutic or remedial work with infants.

Other issues in the design of instrumental-learning procedures with infants will continue to be investigated. Data collection will continue on characteristic infant responding under different kinds and patterns of response-produced environmental changes.

Keyword Descriptors;

Infant Human
Methodology
Psychology, Learning, Sequential
Psychology, Learning
Psychology, Conditioning Reinforcement
Psychology Social, Interpersonal Relations, Diadic Interaction
Family, Maternal Behavior
Child Mental Development, Child Behavior
Family, Parent-Offspring

Honors and Awards:

J. L. Gewirtz: Advisory Board Member for the following journals:

Human Development
Journal of Applied Behavioral Analysis
Journal of Autism and Childhood Schizophrenia
Youth and Society

Publications:

None

Serial No. Z01 MH 00236-09 LDP
1. Developmental Psychology
2.
3. Bethesda, Maryland

PHS-ADAMHA-NIMH
Individual Project Report
July 1, 1974 through June 30, 1975

Project Title: Stimulus Conditions, Infant Behaviors, Caretaker-Child Interaction, and Social Learning in Diverse Child-Rearing Environments

Previous Serial Number: M-P-D(C)-30

Principal Investigator: Jacob L. Gewirtz, Ph.D.

Cooperating Units: Department of Psychology, Hebrew University of Jerusalem; Social Science Statistical Center, University of Maryland Baltimore County

Work on this project is temporarily suspended and is being held in abeyance.

Serial No. Z01 MH 00237-07 LDP
1. Developmental Psychology
2.
3. Bethesda, Maryland

PHS-ADAMHA-NIMH
Individual Project Report
July 1, 1974 through June 30, 1975

Project Title: Contextual Determinants of Stimulus Power

Previous Serial Number: M-P-D(C)-34

Principal Investigator: Jacob L. Gewirtz, Ph.D.

Other Investigators: None

Cooperating Units: University of Maryland Baltimore County

Work on this project is temporarily suspended and is being held in abeyance.

Serial No. Z01 MH 00238-05 LDP
1. Developmental Psychology
2.
3. Bethesda, Maryland

PHS-ADAMHA-NIMH
Individual Project Report
July 1, 1974 through June 30, 1975

Project Title: Evaluation of Concepts Employed for Early Learning and Development

Previous Serial Number: M-P-D(C)-42

Principal Investigator: Jacob L. Gewirtz, Ph.D.

Other Investigators: None

Cooperating Units: None

Work on this project is temporarily suspended and is being held in abeyance.

Serial No. Z01 MH 00239-03 LDP
1. Developmental Psychology
2.
3. Bethesda, Maryland

PHS-ADAMHA-NIMH
Individual Project Report
July 1, 1974 through June 30, 1975

Project Title: An Observational Study of Maternal Models

Previous Serial Number: M-S-D-26

Principal Investigators: Carolyn Zahn Waxler and Marian Radke Yarrow

Other Investigators: None

Cooperating Units: National Institute of Child Health and Human Development

Person Years

Total: .56
Professional: .46
Other: .10

Project Description:

The purpose is to investigate, under semi-naturalistic conditions, different aspects of maternal modeling in relation to children's imitative learning. How clearly in evidence are the relations that have been demonstrated under laboratory conditions, regarding reinforcement and the origins of imitation? What are some of the other critical dimensions of mother-child interaction that affect imitation?

Thirty-five Black mothers from middle and lower-middle economic classes were seen with their 20-month-old children. Mother-child interaction was observed in a laboratory trailer in two different contexts--in exploration of a new play environment and in a planned modeling setting. Interactions were recorded, with the mothers' knowledge, from behind a one-way screen. The mother's modeled acts, the child's imitations, and the mother's reinforcements were observed and recorded. Reliabilities on exact matching of sequential behavior units ranged from 68% to 87%.

1. Mothers who rewarded or praised imitation had children who imitated more frequently than children of mothers whose rewards were non-existent or minimal. This relation between reinforcement and imitation was, however, complex, and carried with it no simple explanation. For some children, maternal reinforcement appeared to control the amount of imitation. But equally prominent were patterns in which the frequency of maternal reinforcement was determined by how much imitation was forthcoming from the child. There were cases, too, in which patterns of interactive mother-child

influences were in evidence. Experimental research has characteristically dealt with the mother's effect on the child's imitative learning; the demonstration, under more naturalistic circumstances, that imitation is rewarding to the mother (the child's influence on the mother) highlights the need for expansion of developmental theory to utilize and take into account such reciprocal learning patterns.

2. Other characteristics of mothers as models were associated with children's imitation. Mothers' modeled acts, conceptualized as modes of communication with the child, were coded as "unadorned," highlighted, invitational, attention-demanding. Frequency and variety of modeling were also coded.

Highlighting and variety in modeling, assumed to reflect the mother's interest and eager engagement with the child, were associated with more frequent and more varied imitation by the child. Similarly, invitational modeled acts resulted in more imitation. In contrast, unadorned modeling, and those acts for which the mother demanded attention were not characteristically associated with the imitation; further, they resulted in lower frequencies of imitation. In the planned modeling setting there appeared to be an optimal amount of modeling. Very few and very many presentations by the mother were associated with little imitation. This was interpreted as inappropriate "pacing" by some mothers.

A configuration of an effective model begins to emerge: The adaptive modeling techniques (e.g., highlighting, invitational, variety) are interrelated; i.e., mothers who tend to use one technique, tend to use the others. Similarly, these same mothers also use reinforcement, another adaptive mode of communication, more frequently. Further research is needed to pinpoint how the child is having an input in determining the different ways in which a mother portrays herself and her actions.

Many of the child's enduring behavior patterns, both intellectual habits and emotional styles, are a result of observational learning, i.e., his witnessing and incorporating ways in which significant others (parents, teachers, friends) function in their environments. Identification of the different modes of communication to the child will help to elucidate the process by which such learning occurs. Further, the settings in which imitation is studied are of significance. To date, most of the principles of observational learning have been derived from experimental demonstrations. Before applying these principles to practices in child care, it is necessary to examine them under more nearly natural conditions. Such examinations are needed to validate or modify theoretical formulations and also provide leads for further research.

This project has been completed and a manuscript has been accepted for publication in a scientific journal.

Serial No. Z01 MH 00239-03 LDP

Keyword Descriptors:

Family, Parent-Offspring
Infant, Human
Psychology, Behavior, Imitative
Psychology, Learning, Experience
Psychology, Learning, Reinforcement

Honors and Awards: None

Publications:

Waxler, C. Z., and Yarrow, M. R.: An observational study of maternal models. Developmental Psychology, in press.

Serial No. Z01 MH 00240-10 LDP
1. Developmental Psychology
2.
3. Bethesda, Maryland

PHS-ADAMHA-NIMH
Individual Project Report
July 1, 1974 through June 30, 1975

Project Title: A Comparison of Methods of Obtaining Data on Parent and Child Behavior

Previous Serial Number: M-S-D-28

Principal Investigators: Marian Radke Yarrow and Carolyn Zahn Waxler

Other Investigators: None

Cooperating Units: None

Person Years

Total:	.20
Professional:	.20
Other:	.00

Project Description:

Observational data in behavioral research derive from diverse philosophies, techniques, and degrees of rigor. The resulting raw data are, therefore, highly variable in form, specificity, and reliability. The purpose of this research is to examine some of the influences of observing techniques on the kind of data obtained.

Sample: Approximately 500 pre-nursery school and nursery school aged children were the subjects. About 150 were observed with their mothers; the others were child-teacher and child-child interactions.

Procedures: Eight studies are the basis of these analyses. The designs involve naturalistic observing in homes and nursery schools, observations in quasi-naturalistic settings, and experimental situations involving single pairs and groups of participants. In some of the studies, verbal reports from mothers were another source of data that can be compared with observational records.

Findings were reported in a previous Annual Report on techniques of observing, reporting and coding sequential events and social interactions, on the levels of agreement and the sources of unreliability in various methods. No further work has proceeded on these issues. Attention has been given instead to issues of conceptual levels of observing and to obtaining systematized participant observation records. A procedure has been developed whereby mothers are trained as observers of events otherwise inaccessible to research. Analyses of the outcomes of this approach are in progress.

Improved methods and techniques for obtaining and analyzing observations of interaction are of fundamental importance in the behavioral sciences. The development of standard approaches, with high levels of efficiency and reliability would do much to bring about greater comparability among studies and to reduce variable sources of error in the raw data of research.

Analyses are underway and a theoretical-methodological paper is in preparation.

Keyword Descriptors:

Children, Preschool
Family, Parent-Offspring
Methodology
Observational
Psychology, Social, Interpersonal Relations

Honors and Awards: None

Publications: None

Serial No. Z01 MH 00241-02 LDP
1. Developmental Psychology
2.
3. Bethesda, Maryland

PHS-ADAMHA-NIMH
Individual Project Report
July 1, 1974 through June 30, 1975

Project Title: Dimensions and Correlates of Prosocial Behavior in Young Children

Previous Serial Number: M-S-D-30

Principal Investigators: Marian Radke Yarrow and Carolyn Zahn Waxler

Other Investigators: David Barrett, Jean Darby, Robert King, Marilyn Pickett, Judith Smith

Cooperating Units: None

Person Years:

Total:	2.20
Professional:	1.00
Other:	1.20

Project Description:

Although there is evidence that children as young as 3 to 5 years of age are capable of responding sympathetically to the needs and feelings of others, little is known about the frequency and consistency of prosocial behaviors in young children. Little systematic evidence exists regarding the affective components of prosocial actions or the relation of such behaviors to other kinds of social interchange. The objective of this research is to investigate some of the qualities or correlates of helping, sharing, and comforting behaviors in young children.

The subjects are 108 children, ages 3 to 7. Their families are suburban, largely white, and middle to upper-middle class.

Prosocial behavior was measured in 6 experimental situations: 2 sharing tasks, 2 comforting tasks, and 2 helping tasks. In each instance, the object of intervention was a young adult. The child's prosocial response or its absence was recorded and all actions, expressions, and comments accompanying the intervention or nonintervention.

To assess prosocial acts and also aggressive and non-affective social contacts in the natural setting, each child was observed in 4 10-minute samples of indoor and outdoor play with his peers in the nursery school. An observer noted on a check list the occurrence of specified behaviors in

15-second intervals. Independent observations were used to establish reliability.

With regard to consistency in prosocial responding, experimental measures of comforting and sharing are significantly related to one another, but neither is related to helping. In the natural setting, there are no significant associations among the variables. There is limited consistency in comforting and sharing across situations, no cross-setting consistency for helping behaviors. The results suggest the necessity for conceptualizing and investigating prosocial responses as a complex of distinct behaviors, each of which may develop along independent lines.

Frequencies of prosocial actions are not age or sex related in the sample of children studied.

Observations of children witnessing a person in distress (crying) document a diversity of conditions underlying prosocial intervention and nonintervention by young children. The factors include empathic feelings, perception of adult expectations and prohibitions, indifference, and inhibitory anxiety.

Level of general social involvement is not a good predictor of prosocial behavior.

Kindness and hostility have long been linked in psychological theory. In these young children there is no simple relation between the two behavioral dimensions. Among children who are low to moderate in frequency of aggression directed to peers, increases in sharing and comforting responses are correlated with increases in aggression. However, for children characterized by high absolute levels of aggression, increases in aggression correspond to decreases in sharing and comforting.

Among children who are themselves relatively nonaggressive, sharing and comforting responses increase as experiences of being the target of aggression from others increase. For highly aggressive children, correlations between amount of aggression received and amount of prosocial behavior exhibited are negligible.

Humanitarian ideals and actions are almost without exception positively valued standards. Some of society's formal training is based on the assumption that compassionate behaviors and cooperative efforts can be inculcated as generalized habits of the child. Research which explores the consistency of such responding allows one to test the hypothesis that a generalized train of prosociality exists within the individual. Further, understanding of different kinds of prosocial responses (e.g., sharing, comforting, helping) in relation to each other advances theories of development by providing more refined, precise definitions for conceptualizing prosocial interventions. Data on how prosocial behaviors mesh and interact with other personality characteristics, particularly the anti-social or aggressive tendencies of the child, have implications for theory development, e.g., psychoanalytic theories of reaction formation. These insights into the dynamics of prosocial development and the underlying motivations provide clues regarding whether the compassion is empathically based, a mechanism to alleviate guilt, or sublimation of aggressive impulses into socially acceptable courses of action.

This study has been completed and a report has been submitted to a scientific journal. Out of the analyses have grown a series of issues which will be followed up in further research: The relations between aggressive and prosocial behaviors need further study. Other questions concern the learning histories of children whose responses differ in circumstances calling for sharing, helping, and comforting. Further, an unexplored dimension in investigations of prosociality is the influence of the child himself in determining the prosocial responses that he receives from others.

Keyword Descriptors:

Children
Psychology, Behavior, Aggression
Psychology, Behavior, Altruistic
Psychology, Emotions, Empathy
Psychology, Social, Interpersonal Relations

Honors and Awards: None

Publications:

Yarrow, M. R. Peers and friendship. In Lewis, M., and Rosenblum, L. (eds.): Friendship and peer relations: The origin of behavior. Vol. II. New York, Wiley, in press.

Yarrow, M. R. and Waxler, C. Z. Dimensions and correlates of prosocial behavior in young children. Child Development, in press.

Serial No. Z01 MH 00242-02 LDP
1. Developmental Psychology
2.
3. Bethesda, Maryland

PHS-ADAMHA-NIMH
Individual Project Report
July 1, 1974 through June 30, 1975

Project Title: The Development of Sensitivity to the Feeling States of Others

Previous Serial Number: M-S-D-29

Principal Investigators: Marian Radke Yarrow, Carolyn Zahn Waxler, and Robert A. King

Other Investigators: Judith Smith, C. Jean Darby, Claire Horowitz, Marilyn T. Pickett, Frances L. Polen, and David Eaton

Cooperating Units: None

Person Years:

Total:	4.33
Professional:	1.25
Other:	3.08

Project Description:

The research is a longitudinal study of the development in the second and third years of life of children's sensitivities and responsiveness to emotional states of other persons. How do the psychological states of others enter into the very young child's awareness and into his own feeling states? Are there patterned developmental regularities in responses to the affects of others? How are other aspects of development and differences in rearing related to children's reactions in this sphere?

Three age cohorts of eight mother-infant pairs each were selected at 9-10 months, 15-16 months, and 21-22 months of age, respectively; they were observed over a 9 month period. The volunteer families formed a middle to upper-middle class, suburban sample.

Data were obtained from two sources: (1) The mothers: Given training and provided with a reporting guide, mothers dictated accounts of naturally occurring events in which feelings or emotions were expressed by someone in the presence of the child. Additionally, in semi-standardized fashion, mothers enacted specified feelings (fatigue, pain, affection, sadness, anger, coughing, enjoyment). The circumstances of each event, with the child's reactions, and subsequent responses to the child were reported. (2) The researcher: During home visits at 3-week intervals, mother and researcher reviewed the mother's records. The researcher also carried out semi-standardized "affect" incidents in the home and interviewed the mother on aspects of the child's development and on mother-child interactions. Mothers' and researchers' agreement in reporting was assessed by comparing their accounts of the same standard affect-situations carried out by the researcher during the home visits. There was generally high correspondence.

Analyses of children's reactions to affective situations of others are in beginning stages. Reported findings are, therefore, preliminary and illustrative only.

Sensitivity to affects appears in very young children, younger than heretofore systematically documented. Further, there are sometimes fine discriminations of affect, relating to differences in the persons and kinds of stimuli involved. For example, contagious crying in response to other children's loud crying initially characterized most children in the youngest cohort, but virtually disappeared by 50-60 weeks to be replaced by serious attending, comment, imitation, or comforting.

By 47 to 61 weeks comforting by patting, hugging, or presenting an object occurred in response to observed crying or pain. Similarly, children in the youngest cohort showed distress to parental arguments as early as 60 to 75 weeks. Responses were often marked: crying, imitative yelling, holding hands over ears, comforting a distraught parent, or punitively hitting the parent perceived as the aggressor.

Other feeling states also evoked characteristic reactions from the watching child: observing happiness or affection in others, children frequently attempted to join in. When parents were affectionate toward each other, this enjoyment was sometimes replaced with manifestations of jealousy by the child (hitting, pushing the parents apart).

In response to maternal fatigue (which might be conceptualized as short-term relative maternal deprivation), children often made heightened demands upon the mother, attempting to re-engage her by making body contact, pulling her hair, trying to open her eyes and the like. This situation appeared to be as provocative to the 2½-year-old as to the 9-month-old, though in the middle of this age-span children began also to respond to mother's needs (e.g., by lying down quietly with her or covering her with a blanket).

Self-referential responses to others' pain, sadness, or distress frequently occurred. These included imitation, examination or manipulation of the child's own corresponding body part, or comments such as "I didn't fall down." The child's own concerns sometimes clouded or distorted perceptions of someone else's distress. Yet, even though young children are often described as empathically limited because of their cognitive egocentrism, their self-referential processes also represent active attempts to comprehend others' affects by "trying them on" and to master the feelings which others' emotions stir up in them.

With anger also it was possible to trace the development of the child's imitation and growing stable identification with disapproving and prohibiting aspects of the parents. In the course of disciplinary interchanges, the children echoed parental disapproving words and gestures. Further, in imaginary play and in response to supposed transgressions by others, they minutely replicated the parent's affective style, tone, and attitudes.

Mothers served not only as models and explicit instructors about the interpersonal world; children also frequently used the mother for implicit interpretive guidance in affectually ambiguous situations by glancing at her to check her expression. When observing or confronted with a distraught or angered adult, toddlers in the second year of life often sought to re-establish contact with a part-cajoling, part-exploratory offer of an object or a tentative greeting formula.

Although early interpersonal experience is often regarded as a most important factor in later personality formation, developmental psychology is without a base of empirical data regarding the young child's abilities to comprehend the psychological attributes of those with whom he interacts. The child's social comprehension must powerfully determine what impact parental moods and emotional styles have at any given developmental stage. There are few systematic data on the early indicators of normal development of this comprehension, or on the relation of this ability to the development of self-other differentiation, empathy, or role-taking. Further, psychopathology often involves significant distortions or limitations in the individual's awareness of other people's feelings (e.g., childhood autism, paranoia) and his sense of similarity or difference from others. The genesis of some forms of psychopathology could be better understood by a more thorough knowledge of the phases of the normal child's evolving sensitivity and responsivity to the feeling states of others.

Primary data collection and basic coding have been completed. Analyses are at various stages and will be continued through the next year.

Keyword Descriptors:

Child Mental Development, Child Behavior
Family, Child Rearing
Family, Parent-Offspring
Infant, Human
Population Studies, Human, Longitudinal Study
Psychology, Emotions, Empathy
Psychology, Learning, Experience
Psychology, Social, Social Perception
Socialization

Honors and Awards: None

Publications:

Rixse, R., Powell, N., King, R., Lourie, R.: Attempted suicide in adolescence. Clinical Proceedings (Children's Hospital National Medical Center) 31: 1975.

Serial No. Z01 MH 00243-02 LDP
1. Developmental Psychology
2.
3. Bethesda, Maryland

PHS-ADAMHA-NIMH
Individual Project Report
July 1, 1974 through June 30, 1975

Project Title: Inferential Capabilities and Prosocial Behavior

Previous Serial Number: M-S-D-30

Principal Investigators: Marian Radke Yarrow, Carolyn Zahn Waxler, and Judith Smith

Other Investigators: None

Cooperating Units: None

Person Years

Total:	2.05
Professional:	.75
Other:	1.30

Project Description:

Research on the social and affective growth of young children has neglected to place these developmental patterns in the context of children's expanding cognitive capabilities, their perception of their surroundings and the inferences which they draw about the persons around them. This project relates positive social behavior (helping, sharing, comforting) to the child's apparent understanding of the perspectives and experiences of others. Are children able to infer that the physical and emotional perspectives of others may be different from their own? Is there a relation between inferences about another's physical perspective and inferences about another's preferences and feelings? Are these inferential capabilities related, in turn, to the children's prosocial interventions?

Sample: The subjects are 115 children between the ages of 3 and 7½ years, attending or having previously attended a suburban, largely middle-class nursery school.

Procedures: (1) To assess perspective-taking capabilities a series of 11 "problem-solving" tasks designed to measure the child's ability to understand the social and physical points of view of the other were administered. The tasks included visual and tactile perceptual experiences, and cognitive and emotional experiences that differed for child and "Other." (2) To assess possible prosocial intervention in a standardized manner, experimental situations were created affording the child the opportunity to help, to share, and to comfort. (3) Prosocial interaction with peers was also observed in the natural setting.

Detailed analysis of the cognitive assessments and their relationship to prosocial behavior are just beginning. Preliminary analyses indicate that: (1) Ability to successfully take another's perspective on the administered cognitive tasks increases with age, the most substantial jumps occurring between 4½ and 5 years of age. (2) Ability to take the physical perspective of another does not seem to precede an understanding of another's social perspective. (3) There is no simple relation between perspective-taking abilities on the experimental tasks and prosocial interventions.

Extensive research efforts have been made to assess the cognitive, social, and, to a lesser extent, the affective development of young children, but no one phase of development progresses independently of the others. Little work has been done relating social behavior, particularly prosocial behavior, to the child's cognitive assessments of those persons around him. Understanding the way in which a child perceives others and the inferences he makes about the perceptions of others may shed a qualitatively different light on the motivations behind the child's social interactions.

Analyses will continue through the next year.

Keyword Descriptors:

Child Mental Development, Child Behavior
Children
Psychology, Behavior, Altruistic
Psychology, Cognition, Insight
Psychology, Cognition, Problem Solving
Psychology, Emotions, Empathy
Psychology, Social, Social Perception

Honors and Awards:

Marian Radke Yarrow: Consulting Editor, Journal of Developmental Psychology, APA
Editorial Board, Journal of Child Development, Society for Research in Child Development
Editorial Board, Annual Review of Psychology
Member of American Delegation to the People's Republic of China, Committee on Scholarly Communication
Member, Committee on International Relations, American Psychological Association

Publications: None

Serial No. Z01 MH 00471-20 LPP
1. Laboratory of Psychology and Psychopathology
2. Office of the Chief
3. Bethesda

PHS-ADAMHA-NIMH
Individual Project Report
July 1, 1974 through June 30, 1975

Project Title: Studies of heredity and environment in schizophrenia

Previous Serial Number: M-P-C-(C)-12

Principal Investigator: David Rosenthal

Other Investigators: Paul H. Wender (University of Utah); Seymour S. Kety (Harvard); Shmuel Nagler (Israel); Fini Schulsinger (Denmark); Olive W. Quinn (Goucher College).

Cooperating Units: None

Man Years :

Total 7.0
Professional: 3.0
Others: 4.0

Project Description:

The project is composed of the following studies: (1) A constructively critical, hypothesis-oriented analysis of the worthwhile literature on hereditary and environment in schizophrenia. (2) An intensive multidisciplinary study of a family with MZ quadruplets (daughters) concordant as to schizophrenia but discordant as to severity and outcome. This study was published in book form. We are continuing our contacts with this family to see what happens in the clinical course of these girls and how the course is related to earlier and current life experiences. (3) Studies of adoptees and their biological and adoptive families. (4) A study of children (of schizophrenic and control parents) reared in town or kibbutz in Israel.

The objectives of this project are to understand how hereditary and environmental factors interact to make for schizophrenic outcomes of varying types and degrees.

The analysis of the literature has been reported in a series of papers and in the study of the quadruplets. A textbook which organizes and explicates the literature on the genetics of behavioral disorders, and a modified version of this book have been published. Several papers on our adoption studies are now published. The studies indicate that hereditary factors contribute to the development of schizophrenia, and to other disorders that we include in a group called the schizophrenia spectrum. Several articles are in preparation and eventually a monograph will be written on the adoption studies. Data analysis is continuing. One hundred subjects in the Israel study have been examined, and the research findings are currently being analyzed and evaluated. Preliminary findings indicate that offspring of schizophrenics have more neuropathological signs in childhood than do controls. Four subjects have had a breakdown and all have a schizophrenic parent.

It is significant to bio-medical research and the program of the Institute that we have resolved a chronic, critical problem in psychiatry by demonstrating beyond any reasonable doubt that genetic factors are importantly involved in the etiology of schizophrenia and related mental disorders. Moreover, the evidence thus far suggest that the mode of genetic transmission is polygenic or a dominant single gene with polygenic modifiers.

The proposed course of our project is to examine additional subjects in Denmark with the following goals in mind: 1. to try to discriminate gene carriers and non-gene carriers with respect to personality and test variables; 2. to compare the fate of gene carriers who are reared in the parental home as compared to those reared in adoptive homes; 3. to compare Ss who have a psychotic biological parent but who are reared by nonpsychotics with Ss whose biological parents are not psychotic but who are reared by a psychotic adoptive parent; 4. to find the incidence of schizophrenia spectrum disorder in a random sample of the Danish population. In Israel, our goal is to prepare a volume on our findings and their theoretical implications. During this year we are carrying out reexaminations of this unique sample of subjects.

Keyword Descriptors: adoption studies
environment
heredity
high risk
kibbutz studies
quadruplets
rearing patterns
schizophrenia
schizophrenia spectrum
twins

Honors and Awards: None

Publications:

Rosenthal, D.: Introduction to Manfred Bleuler's, The Offspring of Schizophrenics. Schizophrenia Bulletin, NIMH, No. 8, DHEW Publication No. (HSM) 73-9006, Spring 1974, pp. 91-92.

Wender, P.H., Rosenthal, D., Kety, S.S., Schulsinger, F. and Welner, J.: Crossfostering. Archives of General Psychiatry, 30: 121-128, 1974.

Rosenthal, D.: The genetics of schizophrenia. American Handbook of Psychiatry 3: 588-600, 1974.

Rosenthal, D.: Issues in high-risk studies of schizophrenia. Life History Research in Psychopathology 3: 25-41, 1974.

Rosenthal, D.: The concept of subschizophrenic disorders. In S. A. Mednick, F. Schulsinger, J. Higgins and B. Bell (Eds.): Genetics, Environment and Psychopathology. Amsterdam, North Holland Publishing Company, 1974, pp. 167-176.

Rosenthal, D.: Discussion: the concept of subschizophrenic disorders. In R. R. Fieve, H. Brill and D. Rosenthal (Eds.): Genetics and Psychopathology. Baltimore, Johns Hopkins Press, 1975. In press. Also published in Genetics, Environment and Psychopathology (see above).

Paikin, H., Jacobsen, B., Schulsinger, F., Godtfredsen, K., Rosenthal, D., Wender, P. and Kety, S.S.: Characteristics of people who refused to participate in a social and psychopathological study. In S. A. Mednick, F. Schulsinger, J. Higgins and B. Bell (Eds.): Genetics, Environment and Psychopathology. Amsterdam, North Holland Publishing Company, 1974, pp. 293-322.

Rosenthal, D., Goldberg, I., Jacobsen, B., Wender, P.H., Kety, S.S., Schulsinger, F. and Eldred, C.: Migration, heredity, and schizophrenia. Psychiatry 37: 321-339, 1974.

Van Dyke, J.L., Rosenthal, D. and Rasmussen, P.V.: Electrodermal functioning in adopted-away offspring of schizophrenics. Journal of Psychiatric Research 10: 199-215, 1974.

Rieder, R.O., Rosenthal, D., Wender, P.H., Blumenthal, H.: The offspring of schizophrenics. Fetal and neonatal deaths. Archives of General Psychiatry 32: 200-211, 1975.

Rosenthal, D., Wender, P., Kety, S., Schulsinger, F., Welner, J., Rieder, R.: Parent-child relationships and psychopathology in the child. Archives of General Psychiatry 32: 466-476, 1975.

Rosenthal, D.: Heredity in criminality. Criminal Justice and Behavior 2: 3-21, 1975.

Rosenthal, D., Wender, P.H., Kety, S.S., Schulsinger, F., Welner, J., Lawlor, W.G., Van Dyke, J.L., Rieder, R.O., Saavedra, M.: Assessing degree of psychopathology from diagnostic statements. Canadian Psychiatric Association Journal 20: 35-45, 1975.

Van Dyke, J.L., Rosenthal, D., Rasmussen, P.V.: Schizophrenia: effects of inheritance and rearing on reaction time. Canadian Journal of Behavioral Science. In press.

Fieve, R.R., Brill, H., Rosenthal, D. (Eds.): Genetics and Psychopathology. Baltimore, Johns Hopkins Press. In press.

Kety, S.S., Rosenthal, D., Wender, P.H., Schulsinger, F., Jacobsen, J.: Mental illness in the biological and adoptive families of adopted individuals who have become schizophrenic: a preliminary report based upon psychiatric interviews. In R. R. Fieve, H. Brill and D. Rosenthal (Eds.): Genetics and Psychopathology. Baltimore, Johns Hopkins Press. In press.

Rosenthal, D.: Critique of twin studies. Neurosciences Research Program Bulletin. In press.

Rosenthal, D.: The spectrum concept in schizophrenic and manic-depressive disorders. Association for Research in Nervous and Mental Disease 1974 Symposium on "The Biology of the Major Psychoses: A Comparative Analysis." New York, Raven Press. In press.

Serial No. Z01 MH 00472-12 LPP
1. Laboratory of Psychology and Psychopathology
2. Office of the Chief
3. Bethesda

PHS-ADAMHA-NIMH
Individual Project Report
July 1, 1974 through June 30, 1975

Project Title: The investigation of some formal characteristics of speech

Previous Serial Number: M-P-P-(C)-6

Principal Investigator: Donald S. Boomer, Ph.D.

Other Investigators: Richard Coppola, Monte Buchsbaum, M.D.

Cooperating Units: None

Man Years:

Total:	1.16
Professional:	1.00
Others:	.16

Project Description:

An extended psycholinguistic research program summarized in previous annual reports has contributed to a developing theory of speech production and perception, original in this laboratory. The central hypothesis is that the phonemic clause, a linguistically defined unit of speech averaging about 7 or 8 syllables, is a strategic functional unit in both the production and perception of speech. The major findings from this project, previously reported, include demonstrations that speech non-fluencies such as hesitations, repetitions, and tongue-slips are not random noise but occur lawfully with respect to the structure of the phonemie clause.

During the past year this research program has focused on speech perception. The guiding hypothesis has been that listeners, like speakers, process speech in "chunks," or temporal patterns, the chunks being phonemic clauses. If the decoding process operates with phonemic clause speech units then attention to the incoming speech need not be continuous, even though the speech itself is continuous. Rather than attending to fine detail in the stream of speech, syllable by syllable and word by word, the listener can accumulate a series of 7 or 8 syllables in short-term memory and at its conclusion decode it as a pattern of sound and meaning.

If speech perception operates in this way we would expect that the listener's attention would fluctuate, being maximally occupied at the end of the phonemic clause and minimally occupied while the clause is being accumulated and stored.

In our experimental test of this hypothesis the cortical average evoked response has been employed as a measure of attention. Previous research has shown that the evoked response to an extraneous stimulus, light flash, for example, or a mild electrical stimulus, will be attenuated if the subject's attention is occupied by a cognitive task. By time-locking the experimental stimuli precisely with respect to linguistic units in tape recorded speech we are attempting to test the speech perception hypothesis described above.

Encouraging results have been obtained on an initial group of subjects. These initial trials, however, have also revealed some methodological difficulties, which are now being remedied. This promising line of research will be actively pursued in the coming year. It should be noted that definitive results, if forthcoming, would be extremely significant, in that linguistic processes would be functionally linked to brain processes in an unprecedented way.

Keyword Descriptors: average evoked response
hemispheric differentiation
psycholinguistics
speech perception

Honors and Awards: None

Publications:

Boomer, Donald S.: Speech units in human communication. In A. W. Siegman and S. Feldstein (Eds.): Nonverbal Behavior and Communication. New Jersey, Lawrence Erlbaum Associates. In press.

Serial No. Z01 MH 00473-18 LPP
1. Laboratory of Psychology and Psychopathology
2. Office of the Chief
3. Bethesda

PHS-ADAMHA-NIMH
Individual Project Report
July 1, 1974 through June 30, 1975

Project Title: Individual differences in normal perceptual processes

Previous Serial Number: M-P-L-5

Principal Investigator: V. R. Carlson

Other Investigators: Irwin Feinberg, Eugene Tassone

Cooperating Units: VA Hospital, San Francisco

Man Years:

Total:	2.0
Professional:	.75
Others:	1.25

Project Description:

The general objectives of this project are: (1) To obtain normal control data for standardizing procedures and apparatus in the measurement of perceptual variables, and to obtain comparison data for evaluating the effects of abnormal and other special conditions. (2) To develop a general specification of perceptual response in terms of the parameters of the immediate stimulus-situation, past experience, generalized perceptual-cognitive attitudes, and the subject's motivational reaction to the situation.

Effects on time perception have been implicated in psychiatric disorders on the one hand and related to basic variables of metabolic efficiency and cortical arousal on the other. Just what the relevant behavioral variables are, however, is very much in doubt. Cognitive disorientation, mental alertness, motivation, and other factors are involved in addition to variations in the functional use of time. The specific objective of the present research is to develop a model of the "internal clock" in terms of which biorhythmical variation may be distinguished from cognitive and motivational influences affecting time judgment.

The model postulates a linear relationship between perceived time and presented time intervals and a linear relationship between error variation and presented time intervals. Given these linearities, variations in subjective time rate are reflected in variations in the slope of the time judgment function. A tendency toward indiscriminate responding is reflected in a concomitant variation in the intercept of the function and an inconsistency between time estimation and time production functions. These relationships have proved useful in interpreting time judgments obtained with short presented time intervals under conditions of low subjective arousal. This year longer time intervals and the effects of THC, a drug reported to produce temporal disorganization, were investigated.

Normal subjects were tested on three pre-drug days, six drug days, and three post-drug days. In addition to performing time estimations and time productions of 1 to 60 seconds, the subjects were tested on a perceptual task requiring the functional use of time but not the judgment of time as such.

The postulated linearities were manifested in the time judgment functions. On the average there was an increase in subjective time rate and some improvement in performance under the drug condition. The improvement can probably be attributed to a compensatory motivation for performing the task well, but the change in rate is separable from the improvement in responding. The functional time performance data have not yet been analyzed.

It is necessary in biomedical research to identify those aspects of behavior associated with specific biological variables and those generally affected regardless of the particular experimental condition. Empirically the present model appears to enable the identification of an effect on subjective time rate and a general effect on the subject's motivational approach to the task. It is proposed therefore to formulate the theoretical propositions of the model more rigorously for comparison with other approaches to the measurement of perceptual capacity and response bias and for possible applicability to other behavioral functions.

Keyword Descriptors: arousal
internal clock
motivation
response bias
THC
time estimation
time production

Honors and Awards: None

Publications: None

Serial No. Z01 MH 00474-15 LPP
1. Laboratory of Psychology and Psychopathology
2. Office of the Chief
3. Bethesda

PHS-ADAMHA-NIMH
Individual Project Report
July 1, 1974 through June 30, 1975

Project Title: Perceptual adaptation.

Previous Serial Number: M-P-L-7

Principal Investigator: V. R. Carlson

Other Investigators: Eugene Tassone

Cooperating Units: None

Man Years:

Total:	1.0
Professional:	.25
Others:	.75

Project Description:

The general objective is to investigate the characteristics of perceptual adaptation, both when the adaptation occurs in a single limited period of persistent stimulation and when it is cumulative in a series of stimulations over relatively long periods of time.

The occurrence of visual adaptation to stimulus motion, form, and orientation suggests the operation of specialized receptive units in man of the kind which have been identified in cat and monkey visual cortex. Such adaptation is also similar in some respects to a conditioning or learning process. We have previously found that adaptation established to stimulus motion did not dissipate over a period of neutral stimulation and in that respect resembled a conditioning process more than a strictly sensory one. Specialized receptive units may be differentially sensitive to combinations of motion and color or form, however, and it is necessary to investigate the after-effects and dissipation of adaptation to such combinations of stimuli in order to determine whether conditioning is involved.

Apparatus suitable for presenting the necessary combinations of stimuli has been constructed and is being tested. Subjects will be simultaneously adapted to two different combinations of stimulus motion and color. Then the persistence of aftereffects to both combinations will be measured over increasing periods of exposure to neutral stimulation. If the results indicate that conditioning is involved, it will be pertinent to investigate the kinds of combinations of stimuli to which such adaptation can occur. An understanding of how perception develops and adjusts to altered conditions of stimulation will most probably have to be concerned with conditioning, learning, and memory as well as basic sensory processes.

Keyword Descriptors: aftereffects
conditioning
perceptual adaptation
receptive units
sensory adaptation
stimulus combination

Honors and Awards: None

Publications: None

Serial No. Z01 MH 00475-16 LPP
1. Laboratory of Psychology and Psychopathology
2. Office of the Chief
3. Bethesda

PHS-ADAMHA-NIMH
Individual Project Report
July 1, 1974 through June 30, 1975

Project Title: A study of the means-end thought processes in human subjects

Previous Serial Number: M-P-A-16

Principal Investigator: Edward A. Jerome

Other Investigators: None

Cooperating Units: Technical Development Section, NIMH, Computer Systems Laboratory, DCRT

Man Years:

Total:	3.00
Professional:	1.00
Other:	2.00

Project Description:

The purpose of the project is to investigate those mental processes that are responsible for dealing with the problematic situations of daily life: to supply performance norms on a family of interactive tests of concept identification, to evaluate the performances of various diagnostic groups on tests of heuristic skill, and to develop methods of improving heuristic performance.

From the results of the first experiment it was concluded: (1) People are much more relaxed working at these problem solving tasks by interacting with a machine then they are when they have to interact with an investigator (usual procedure). (2) Performance scores on the various problem forms can be appropriately adjusted for objective complexity by information theoretic indices. (3) These adjustments make it possible to evaluate separately two components of the problem solving process: the gathering of needed information (quality of inquiry) and the ability to interpret information already available. (4) As a result of this analysis two formerly opposed theories of conceptual difficulty appeared complementary; the information theoretic view being more relevant to the quality of inquiry, the hierarchical hypothesis being more relevant to the interpretation of information.

The second experiment tested ability to evaluate the relevance of various aspects of problem situation by interacting with it. A form of the conservative focus strategy determined the presentation sequence via reception method procedure using conditional, alternation, conjunction, bi-conditional and disjunction rules. It was designed to detect performances that were guided by relevance evaluations rather than by guessing and it served this purpose satisfactorily. Although most people initially showed little deviation from "guessing" performances, many learned to use relevance cues with a high degree of competence with little experience. Indeed, positive transfer was found between problem forms that would have led to interference if improvement were accomplished by learning specific aspects of problem forms rather than by mastering general principles of interpretation appropriate to the situation.

As to the relative difficulty of the various problem forms, adjustment having been made for differences in objective complexity, conjunction problems, as expected, were found to be significantly easier than any of the others, which, in turn, did not differ significantly from one another.

Keyword Descriptors: concept formation
concept identification
attribute identification
problem solving
computer controlled experiments
interactive algorithms
selection method
reception method
rule identification
conservative focus
information theoretic
uncertainty
conceptual hierarchies

Honors and Awards: None

Publication: None

Serial No. Z01 MH 00476-04 LPP
1. Laboratory of Psychology and Psychopathology
2. Office of the Chief
3. Bethesda

PHS-ADAMHA-NIMH
Individual Project Report
July 1, 1974 through June 30, 1975

Project Title: The offspring of schizophrenics: markers of a schizophrenic disposition

Previous Serial Number: M-P-C-(C)-45

Principal Investigator: Ronald O. Rieder

Other Investigators: David Rosenthal, Paul Wender (University of Utah); Sarah Broman (NINCDS)

Cooperating Units: NINCDS

Man Years:

Total:	6.0
Professional:	3.2
Other:	2.8

Project Description:

The project is aimed at discovering differences between the offspring of schizophrenics and controls, at an early stage in life, which may represent a predisposition to develop schizophrenia later in life. It is also aimed at evaluating the effect of perinatal complications on the children of schizophrenics. This study has utilized the data previously collected by the National Institute of Neurological and Communicative Disorders and Stroke, Perinatal Research Branch, in their "Collaborative Study on Cerebral Palsy, Mental Retardation and Other Neurological and Sensory Disorders of Infancy and Childhood." In that project, some 55,000 pregnancies and the offspring were studied, with the 7-year follow-up now just completed. About 900 of the mothers or fathers had had a psychiatric hospitalization, and of this group, we took 220 who were studied in the Boston area to use for our study. We gathered the records of their psychiatric hospitalizations, and we proceeded to diagnose these subjects. We diagnosed 150 parents, and assigned a diagnosis of schizophrenia to 67 of these. The 150 families produced a total of 210 children who had been part of the NINCDS study, and 93 of these were the offspring of schizophrenics. Taking the families containing schizophrenic parent, we selected a matched control group, and began comparing the findings for our two groups on the investigations which the NINCDS-PRB had performed.

We have found that there is an increased rate of fetal and neonatal death among the offspring of schizophrenics as compared with controls. Some of these deaths were associated with neurological malformations. Reasons for the deaths were not found at autopsy. The deaths were among the offspring of parents with chronic and severe forms of schizophrenia, as opposed to the acute or borderline forms. The deaths occurred predominately among those offspring who had two schizophrenic parents, or had a schizophrenic mother, rather than among those who had a schizophrenic father only. Two comparison groups, offspring of possible schizophrenics and offspring of non-schizophrenic patients, did not show an increased rate of fetal or neonatal deaths when compared to their matched controls.

There is a lower IQ among the offspring of parents with the more chronic forms of schizophrenia when compared with controls at 4 years. Perinatal factors, such as edema, vaginal bleeding, spinal anesthesia at delivery and mid-forceps delivery are quite highly correlated with IQ in this sample, whereas they are not highly correlated among the control population. These negative correlations were present whether the father or the mother was the schizophrenic parent, and thus the findings might reflect a genetic susceptibility of the infant to perinatal complications.

The significance of this work to bio-medical research and the program of the Institute is that it follows upon other work of this Laboratory on the genetics of schizophrenia. We need to find how the genetic factor underlying schizophrenia clinically manifests itself if we are to effectively intervene or do bio-chemical and physiological investigations of the development of schizophrenia. If a susceptibility to perinatal complications is demonstrated, it would direct research and intervention to the perinatal period.

The proposed course of the project is to further examine the IQ findings listed above. We will also continue to investigate the data which has been collected on these offspring of schizophrenics. This includes serial neurological exams, psychological exams, and language exams.

Keyword Descriptors: schizophrenia
high risk
heredity
genetic susceptibility
perinatal death
perinatal complications
intelligence

Honors and Awards: None

Publications:

Rieder, R. O., Rosenthal, D., Wender, P. H., Blumenthal, H.: The offspring of schizophrenics: fetal and neonatal deaths. Archives of General Psychiatry, 32: 200-211, 1975.

Serial No. Z01 MH 00477-20 LPP
1. Laboratory of Psychology and Psychopathology
2. Section on Neuropsychology
3. Bethesda

PHS-ADAMHA-NIMH
Individual Project Report
July 1, 1974 through June 30, 1975

Project Title: Prefrontal Cortex and Behavior: Biochemical and Pharmacological Studies in the Monkey

Previous Serial Number: M-P-B-2

Principal Investigators: H. Enger Rosvold, Patricia S. Goldman

Other Investigators: Charles Popper (Research Associate, Laboratory of Clinical Sciences); Woodrow Havens (Research Associate, Laboratory of Clinical Sciences); Roger Brown (Grant Foundation Fellow, Laboratory of Psychology and Psychopathology)

Cooperating Units: Laboratory of Clinical Sciences

Man Years:

Total: 4
Professional: 3/5
Other: 3-2/5

Project Description:

As part of a larger program to study the structural and functional organization of the prefrontal cortex in primates, the emphasis of the project this year is to characterize the pharmacological and biochemical properties of prefrontal cortical neurons and to relate these to specific behavioral functions. Accordingly, a combination of behavioral, neurosurgical, pharmacological and biochemical techniques is used. Two studies, currently in progress, will be described.

In one study, normal adult rhesus monkeys are trained to perform a task known to depend upon the integrity of the prefrontal cortex (delayed alternation) concurrently with a task (visual pattern discrimination) that depends instead on nonfrontal mechanisms. These monkeys are subsequently implanted with in-dwelling cannulae over the principal sulcus and orbital prefrontal regions and then tested under a variety of conditions of chemical stimulation. Small quantities of putative neurotransmitters are injected through the cannulae and the animal's performance assessed. The monkeys are also observed for evidence of hyperactivity and stereotypy.

To date, it appears that the injections of putative neurotransmitters (norepinephrine, dopamine, serotonin, acetylcholine, GABA, glycine and histamine) does not consistently alter performance on cognitive tests. However, norepinephrine in microgram quantities elicits hyperactivity and stereotypic movements similar to those observed after systemic injections of amphetamine. The effect of norepinephrine on free behavior is specific and is not elicited by dopamine or any of the other neurotransmitters; further, the effect is produced only by injections into the principal sulcus and not by those into the orbital prefrontal cortex, two regions of the frontal lobe that are known to participate in different functions. Further studies, focusing on the action of norepinephrine, are planned. These studies may lead to identification of a possible physiological role of norepinephrine in the frontal lobe and a possible site of action of amphetamine.

A second study is concerned with neurochemical identification of fiber systems emanating from the frontal cortex to other cortical regions and to subcortical structures. For this purpose, adult rhesus monkeys are given unilateral lesions in particular regions of the frontal lobe and changes in the target structures of norepinephrine, dopamine and serotonin are sought by comparing the levels and synthesis rates of these amines on the lesioned and intact sides of the brain at various intervals of time following surgery. The monoamine neurotransmitters and their metabolites and precursors are assayed spectrofluorimetrically after separation on a Dowex-50 W x 4 cation exchange column. Tyrosine derivatives are assayed by oxidation to a florophor with $K_2Fe(CN)_6$. 5-Hydroxyindoles are assayed by spectrofluorimetric analysis after combining with orthopthaldialdehyde. For estimation of monoamine synthesis rates, animals are treated with NSD 1015 (3-hydroxybenzl hydrazine HCl) 30 minutes before death. This compound inhibits aromatic amino acid decarboxylase and the accumulation of DOPA and 5-HTP during this time gives a reliable synthesis measure as long as measurement is made within 45 minutes of injection. (The results to date indicate that both dopaminergic and serotonergic fibers project from the frontal cortex to the head of the caudate nucleus, while the prefrontal projections to the septum and to the hippocampus appear to be dopaminergic and noradrenergic, respectively.) Other findings include confirmation in primates of adrenaline in the brain stem (5-10% of total assayed adrenaline plus noradrenaline) and the discovery that there may be higher levels in the brain stems of females than males. We have also observed high levels of dopamine in the adrenal medulla, a finding consistent with the idea that this organ is a major source of dopamine. If so, dopamine secretion by the adrenal medulla might well be part of "activation" mechanisms after sympatho-adrenal discharge. Further work is in progress to determine the reproducibility of these findings.

These studies promise to (1) define the biochemical make-up of fiber systems of the frontal lobe; (2) provide important information on the distribution of biogenic amines in discrete regions of the primate brain including, in addition to the structures mentioned above, various other behaviorally-defined sectors of neocortex, the amygdala, the thalamus, the hypothalamus and the brain stem; (3) provide information on synthesis rates in the same areas; (4) increase our understanding of the short and long term consequences of brain injury and possibly provide necessary information for pharmacological treatment of brain disease; (5) serve as a basis for developmental studies, particularly the assessment of sexual dimorphism at a biochemical level; and finally (6) serve as a basis for evaluating molecular mechanisms of behavioral recovery following brain injuries of early origin. Studies such as these are very much needed in an animal phylogenetically close to man for the implications they bear on man's normal mental and emotional life as well as for the understanding and possible treatment of cognitive and emotional disturbances related to cortical dysfunction in mental disease.

Keyword Descriptors: adrenaline
amphetamine
behavior
catecholamines
indolamines
intracerebral chemostimulation
neurotransmitters
prefrontal cortex
primates
subcortical structures

Honors and Awards: None

Publications:

Bowden, D. M. and McKinney, W. Y.: Effects of selective frontal lobe lesions on response to separation in adolescent rhesus monkeys. Brain Res., 75: 167-171, 1974.

In Press:

Bowden, D. M., Galkin, Thelma W., Rosvold, H. E.: Plasticity of the drinking system as defined by electrical stimulation of the brain. Physiol. and Behav.

Lawicka, W., Mishkin, M. and Rosvold, H. E.: Dissociation of deficits on auditory tasks following partial prefrontal lesions in monkeys. Acta Neurobiol. Exp.

Vereczkei, L., Goldman, P. S. and Rosvold, H. E.: The effect of hypothalamic lesions on cognitive behavior in the monkey. Acta Neurobiol. Exp.

Serial No. Z01 MH 00478-19 LPP
1. Laboratory of Psychology and Psychopathology
2. Section on Neuropsychology
3. Bethesda

PHS-ADAMHA-NIMH
Individual Project Report
July 1, 1974 through June 30, 1975

Project Title: Neural mechanisms in vision

Previous Serial No.: M-P-B-5

Principal Investigator: Mortimer Mishkin

Other Investigators: Charlene D. Jarvis (NIMH Staff Fellow)

Cooperating Units: Charles Gross, Princeton University, Princeton, New Jersey; Helen Mahut, Northeastern University, Boston, Massachusetts; Frederick J. Manning, WRAIR, Washington, D. C.; Blair Turner, Howard University, Washington, D. C.

Man Years:
Total: 5
Professional: 1 1/5
Other: 3 4/5

Project Description:

The objective of the five sub-projects described here is to define the role in vision of neural structures outside the primary visual projection system, utilizing behavioral, anatomical, and electrophysiological analyses. (1) Monkeys are prepared at NIMH with various lesions to the visual system and they are then studied electrophysiologically at Princeton by Dr. Charles Gross to determine whether or not the receptive fields of inferior temporal (IT) units have been altered in a manner predicted by our theory of cortico-cortical transmission. In accord with prediction, lesions of the tecto-pulvinar-IT pathway had no effect on the receptive fields, while striate lesions or commissure transection produced corresponding visual field defects. Furthermore, of the IT neurons that receive an input across the commissures, half receive theirs exclusively through the splenium, whereas the other half can obtain their input either through the plenium or anterior commissure. This sub-project will be completed in the next year. (2) Monkeys are prepared at NIMH with bilateral IT lesions combined with an optic-chiasm section and they are trained by Gross at Princeton on a series of visual pattern discriminations, each presented first to one eye and then to the other. Unlike control monkeys (with either IT lesions alone or chiasm sectior alone), the experimental monkeys fail to show interocular transfer, suggesting that stimulus equivalence between the visual half-fields depends on the convergence of their projections onto single IT neurons through the pathways demonstrated in (1) above. Follow-up work will explore possible differences in the kind of information transmitted by the splenium and anterior commissure. (3) We have demonstrated that naive monkeys, shown an object once, will recognize it as familiar when it is shown again a few seconds later. To determine the neural structure on which this ability depends, monkeys trained on the recognition task were prepared with various cerebral lesions and then retested. Only removals of anterior IT cortex impaired recognition ability, suggesting that this is the locus in which the visual trace left by previous viewing is preferentially established. We are now attempting to devise methods to study these newly localized visual traces at the single-unit level. (4) To determine whether visual associative memory depends on a pathway connecting IT cortex with the temporal limbic region, monkeys are prepared with an IT lesion in one hemisphere, a temporal limbic lesion in the other, and either partial or complete forebrain commissurotomies; they are then trained on object reversal learning. Results indicate that cutting the anterior commissure alone in a "crossed-lesion" preparation reproduces the full effect of a bilateral limbic lesion, suggesting that the anterior commissurotomy disconnected the intact limbic region on one side from the intact IT cortex on the other. Further work will investigate which additional output pathways from the visual system must be interrupted to abolish visual learning completely. (5) To test directly whether the temporal limbic system is involved in stimulus-reward learning, single-unit activity is being measured while an animal performs on a visual reversal task. IT neurons, as predicted, discharge selectively to visual patterns, but none appear to code the pattern's reward value. Whether such a code is carried by temporal limbic neurons remains to be determined.

Scientific Significance to Mental Health Research. Vision is perhaps the best understood of the sensory modalities in relation to the functioning of the nervous system. Yet a major problem remains unsolved in vision as it does in all sensory modalities: Delineation of the events which intervene between stimulus reception at the cortex and the observed response. The demonstration that damage to the inferior convexity of the temporal lobes in monkeys produces impairment in visually-guided behavior has opened up the hitherto inaccessible area of the intracerebral processes in vision, i.e., neural activity related to vision but beyond the level of the striate cortex. Unravelling these mechanisms in vision should aid greatly in the solution of a general problem for psychology, viz., accounting for the intervening neural processes (thought and its breakdown) in normal and abnormal behavior.

Keyword descriptors: associative learning
cortex
forebrain commissures
limbic system
receptive fields
stimulus equivalence
temporal lobes
visual perception
visual recognition
visual system

Honors and Awards: None

Publications:

Jarvis, Charlene D.: Visual discrimination and spatial localization deficits after lesions of the tectofugal pathway in pigeons. Brain, Behav. Evol., 9: 195-228, 1974.

Robinson, D. L. and Jarvis, Charlene D.: Superior colliculus neurons studied during head and eye movements of the behaving monkey. J. Neurophysiol., 37: 533-540, 1974.

In Press

Lawicka, Waclawa, Mishkin, M. and Rosvold, H. E.: Dissociation of deficits on auditory tasks following partial prefrontal lesions in monkeys. Acta Neurobiol. Exp.

Mishkin, M. and Delacour, J.: An analysis of short-term visual memory in the monkey. J. Exp. Psychol. (Anim. Behav. Proc.) .

Rocha-Miranda, C. E., Gross, C. G., Bender, D. B. and Mishkin, M.: Visual activation of neurons in inferotemporal cortex depends on striate cortex and the forebrain commissures. J. Neurophysiol.

Serial No. Z01 MH 00479-18 LPP
1. Laboratory of Psychology and Psychopathology
2. Section on Neuropsychology
3. Bethesda

PHS-ADAMHA-NIMH
Individual Project Report
July 1, 1974 through June 30, 1975

Project Title: Histological analysis of cerebral lesions and intracerebral connections in primates.

Previous Serial Number: M-P-B-7

Principal Investigator: H. E. Rosvold, M. Mishkin, Patricia S. Goldman

Other Investigators: T. N. Johnson (Consultant Part-time); Duke Tanaka (Asst. Prof. Department of Anatomy, Howard University); Blair Turner (Asst. Prof. Department of Anatomy, Howard University).

Cooperating Units: None

Man Years:
Total: 2 2/5
Professional: 3/5
Other: 1 4/5

Project Description:

This project has two parts. The first part is concerned with the verification of locus of lesions in the brains of monkeys which have been used in behavioral studies. For this purpose the brains are sectioned, stained for cells and fibers examined microscopically and reconstructed. The data thus obtained are then correlated with behavioral effects. This year 101 brains were processed for this purpose and involved lesions in the hypothalamus, thalamus, parietal lobes, temporal lobes, prefrontal lobes, and head of the caudate nucleus. The second part is concerned with the determination of connections between various parts of the brain. For this purpose the brains are prepared with silver stains, and more recently for histochemical fluorescence and axoplasmic transport. Data this year are available for the silver preparations in which it was determined that the connections between the prefrontal cortex and head of the caudate nucleus increase in density as the animal matures through its first 24 months of development.

The significance of these studies is that they provide an anatomical basis for the understanding of the organization and disorganization of behavior.

These anatomical studies will continue, placing more emphasis on methods of histochemical flurescence and axoplasmic transport.

Keyword Descriptors: anatomical studies
axoplasmic transport
brain development
histochemical fluorescence
prefrontal lobes
temporal lobes

Honors and Awards: None

Publications: None

Serial No. Z01 MH 00480-11 LPP
1. Laboratory of Psychology and Psychopathology
2. Section on Neuropsychology
3. Bethesda

PHS-ADAMHA-NIMH
Individual Project Report
July 1, 1974 through June 30, 1975

Project Title: Development of Brain and Behavior

Previous Serial Number: M-P-B-16

Principal Investigator: Patricia S. Goldman

Other Investigators: H. Enger Rosvold
Roger M. Brown (Grant Foundation Fellow, Laboratory of Psychology and Psychopathology)
Garrett Alexander (Staff Fellow, Laboratory of Behavioral Biology, NICHD)

Cooperating Units: Laboratory of Behavioral Biology, NICHD

Man Years:

Total:	3-3/5
Professional:	1-1/5
Other:	2-2/5

Project Description:

A major goal of this laboratory continues to be the elucidation of neural mechanisms underlying the development of normal behavior and equally to understand the mechanisms responsible for recovery of function or plasticity following central nervous system injuries, particularly those originating in infancy. The approach is broadly multi-disciplinary, involving behavioral, anatomical (to be described in a separate project), electrophysiological, endocrinological, pharmacological and biochemical techniques. The experimental subject is the rhesus monkey, which because of its protracted span of postnatal development and its remarkable capacity for restitution of function following cortical lesions of early onset, is an ideal subject for studies aimed at understanding neurobehavioral specificity and plasticity. Moreover the suitability of the primate as a model of normal and disordered human development is unsurpassed. The focus of these studies is on the prefrontal granular cortex. This slowly maturing neocortical region of the primate brain is particularly appropriate for studies aimed at resolving the sequence, duration, and correlation of structural and functional events in ontogeny.

that this monkey exhibits a clear paradoxical response to relatively high doses of amphetamine (.8 - 1.6 mg/kg). With such doses, the monkey remains alert but sits uncharacteristically still during the 30-60 minute observation sessions, though his activity during control sessions with placebo remains undiminished. These findings increase the probability that this young monkey may provide an animal model of hyperkinetic syndrome. Further behavioral, pharmacological and biochemical studies are planned. Postmortem biochemical and anatomical analysis of this monkey's brain may shed light on the organic nature of hyperkinetic syndrome.

Sexual Dimorphism in Cortical Structure and Function. Previous work in this laboratory has provided evidence that the orbital prefrontal cortex develops function considerably earlier in males than in females. Currently we are studying the behavioral and biochemical consequences of postnatal infections of testosterone in developing female monkeys to determine whether cortical differentiation can be influenced by gonadal hormones at early stages of development. Our post-natal injection regimen has so far produced slight but permanent morphological alterations of the external genitalia in normal genetic females and also modified their ability to learn a task dependent on the orbital prefrontal cortex. These mildly pseudohermaphroditic monkeys exhibited enhanced learning ability compared with nontreated females and performed at level comparable to that of normal males. These findings, obtained months after cessation of hormonal treatment, indicate that neural and nonneural differentiation can still be modified postnatally in primates and that sexual dimorphism extends to cortical as well as to diencephalic mechanisms. Subsequent to further behavioral studies aimed at assessing their psychosexual development, these monkeys will be sacrificed and their brains analyzed for biochemical evidence (distribution and synthesis rates of biogenic amines) of sexual dimorphism.

The possibility that there are neural differences between males and females at the cortical level under the control of gonadal hormones at critical periods in development is of extreme importance for understanding the normal differences in cognitive and social development of the two sexes as well as for understanding disturbances of psychosexual orientation such as adrenogenital syndrome and progestin-induced pseudohermaphroditism, that may occur as a consequence of exposure to an inappropriate hormonal milieu during gestation. Future plans for work in this area include behavioral and biochemical studies of prenatally-androgenized females and prenatally feminized males (chemically gonadectomized with maternal injections of cyproterone acetate, an androgen antagonist). Prenatal studies are warranted because the peak sensitivity of cortical tissue to gonadal hormones in the primate may be expected to coincide with the critical period for corticogenesis in the second trimester of gestation.

Changes in Brain Organization at Different Stages of Development. Our previous work in this laboratory has provided evidence that specific regions of the primate cortex are functionally immature at birth and develop their functions according to widely different time-tables. However, the evidence indicates that developing monkeys differ from adults not only with respect to cortical immaturity but also with respect to cortical regulation of subcortical structures and functions. This year, collaboratively with Dr. Gary Alexander, we have employed cryogenic cooling and electrophysiological recording techniques to further describe the changes in cortical-subcortical organization that take place in ontogeny. Previous studies by Dr. Alexander have shown that the frontal cortex in adult monkeys can be temporarily inactivated by cooling the cortex through stainless steel cryoplates implanted over the dura mater. In the adult monkey, localized cooling of the prefrontal cortex results in behavioral impairments which typically follow ablation of the same cortex but the effects are reversible, i.e., performance returns to criterion level when the cortex is returned to its normal temperature. Furthermore, cooling has been shown to inhibit the firing of neurons in the dorsomedial nucleus of the thalamus in association with behavioral performance. Studies identical to those that have been carried out in mature monkeys are now being conducted in normal monkeys at various stages of postnatal development. Our previous research in this area leads us to expect that frontal cooling will affect behavioral performance and subcortical (striatal and thalamic) neuronal firing patterns less in younger monkeys than in older ones. We have preliminary results indicating that frontal cooling in a 16-month old monkey, unlike cooling in adults, did not alter this young monkey's performance on a cognitive task; electrophysiological data have not been sufficiently analyzed to determine whether striatal or thalamic unit activity was modified by cooling. The results of this study should reveal the extent to which subcortical mechanisms can function more autonomously in the young than the old, a principle of normal brain development suggested by previous research, and one which could help to explain recovery of function after early cortical injuries.

A Possible Animal Model of Hyperkinetic Syndrome. An understanding of the normal changes that take place in brain organization with age may also help to conceptualize certain disorders of human development. For example, the hyperactivity that is an unfailing symptom of frontal cortical damage in the adult monkey is not exhibited by monkeys raised from infancy without their frontal cortex until they reach an age when the cortex would normally mature. Such findings raise the possibility that certain forms of hyperkinesis may be thought of as a consequence of delayed maturation of frontal cortical control over striatal or other subcortical activity. We are now studying an unoperated 6-month old monkey that displays many characteristics of the hyperkinetic syndrome in man. The monkey exhibited incessant locomotor activity and pacing far in excess of that displayed by normal monkeys of this age and was virtually impossible to train on a cognitive task routinely given to monkeys of this age. It has now been shown by Mr. Ken Jurist, a student working with Dr. Brown in our laboratory.

Behavioral and Anatomical Consequences of Prenatally-Induced Brain Damage. Over the past two and one-half years, we have been studying behavioral development of Adam, a rhesus monkey whose dorsolateral prefrontal cortex has been removed during the second trimester of gestation. Subsequent to intrauterine surgery, the fetus had been replaced in utero and delivered successfully at term (168 days) by caesarean section. Over the two and one-half year period, this monkey displayed none of the behavioral deficits exhibited by monkeys sustaining injury to the same area in adulthood and his behavior was indistinguishable from that of normal monkeys at all stages of his development. Postmortem anatomical analysis of his brain will provide information on whether corticogenesis was complete at the time of surgery and whether thalamocortical connections had been formed by the second trimester. The study of prenatal preparations such as this provide a means of determining the precise sequence of events in embryonic brain development and of increasing our understanding of the nature and limits of compensatory neural mechanisms following pre- and post-natal cortical injury.

Keyword Descriptors: behavior
biogenic amines
cryogenic techniques
hyperkinetic syndrome
neurobehavioral plasticity
ontogeny
prefrontal cortex
prenatal brain damage
primates
sexual dimorphism
subcortical unit activity

Honors and Awards: None

Publications:

Goldman, Patricia S.: Recovery of function after CNS lesions in infant monkeys. In E. Eidelberg and D. G. Stein (Eds.): Functional Recovery After Lesions of the Nervous System, Neurosciences Res. Prog. Bull., 12: 217-222, 1974.

Goldman, Patricia S.: An alternative to developmental plasticity: heterology of CNS structures in infants and adults. In D. G. Stein, J. Rosen and N. Butters (Eds.): CNS Plasticity and Recovery of Function. New York, Academic Press, 1974, pp. 149-174.

Goldman, Patricia S., Crawford, H. T., Stokes, L. P., Galkin, T. W., and Rosvold, H. E.: Sex-dependent behavioral effects of cerebral cortical lesions in the developing rhesus monkey. Science, 186: 540-542, 1974.

In Press:

Goldman, Patricia S.: Age, sex, and experience as related to the neural basis of cognitive development. In M. Brazier and N. Buchwald (Eds.): Brain Mechanisms in Mental Retardation. New York, Academic Press.

Goldman, Patricia S.: Neural factors in behavioral development. In R. A. Hinde and J. S. Rosenblatt (Eds.): Advances in the Study Behavior. New York, Academic Press.

Serial No. Z01 MH 00481-04 LPP
1. Laboratory of Psychology and Psychopathology
2. Section on Neuropsychology
3. Bethesda

PHS-ADAMHA-NIMH
Individual Project Report
July 1, 1974 through June 30, 1975

Project Title: Neuroanatomical correlates of development and plasticity.

Previous Serial Number: M-P-B-17

Principal Investigator: Patricia S. Goldman, H. E. Rosvold

Other Investigators: T. N. Johnson, Consultant, Part-time; Duke Tanaka (Asst. Prof. Department of Anatomy, Howard University)

Cooperating Units: Department of Anatomy, Howard University

Man Years:

Total: 1 3/5
Professional: 1 1/5
Other: 2/5

Project Description:

The objectives of this research are twofold: (1) to describe the postnatal development of cortico-cortical and cortico-subcortical connections in the primate; and (2) to search for evidence of anomalous pathways in the brains of monkeys exhibiting behavioral recovery following early brain lesions.

Studies of normal development. Monkeys of various ages extending from birth through adulthood are given discrete unilateral lesions of the dorsolateral or orbital prefrontal cortex or unilateral injections of tritiated amino acids into the same areas and then sacrificed at various intervals of time following surgery. Their brains are subsequently processed for anatomical analysis by silver impregnation (by Dr. Johnson) or autoradiographic techniques (by Dr. Goldman in Dr. W. J. H. Nauta's laboratory) for determining the maturational status of prefrontal connections at different ages. To date, our studies using silver impregnation techniques have extended and confirmed findings obtained with behavioral methods by indicating considerable immaturity in the argyrophilic reactions of pathways emanating from the orbital and dorsolateral prefrontal regions of the cortex to the caudate nucleus and other structures in monkeys under six months of age. The parallel autoradiographic studies now in progress should clarify and extend these findings. To our knowledge there exists no information on the postnatal development of prefrontal connections in the primate nor to our knowledge have autoradiographic methods been applied to the study of corticopetal development in general. The present studies should therefore provide important new information on the development of circuitry, a parameter of neural maturation that is presumptively highly relevant to the development of behavioral capacity.

Studies of Central Nervous System Reorganization. Although central nervous system plasticity is presently an area of active research interest, there has so far been no compelling evidence to indicate that postlesion axonal growth or collateral sprouting is functionally adaptive. Our previous studies of behavioral recovery in monkeys sustaining orbital prefrontal lesions in infancy show that the monkey is an excellent model of behavioral plasticity in development and one highly suitable for studies of neural reorganization. We are therefore employing both the Fink-Heimer silver impregnation technique (in collaboration with Dr. Tanaka) and autoradiographic methods (under the supervision of Dr. W. J. H. Nauta) to examine the brains of monkeys, now adults, that received bilateral orbital prefrontal lesions as infants for evidence of anomalous connections. The brains of these monkeys are to be compared with those of monkeys that received identical lesions and survival times as adults and with normal controls. We have already obtained evidence both in silver-impregnated and autoradiographic material of a previously unknown pathway from the mid-region of the principal sulcus to the septum, a limbic system structure which is interconnected with the hippocampus and hypothalamus and which itself exhibits considerable potential for reorganization after partial deafferentation of its noncortical input in rodents. It is too early to say whether a similar reorganization can take place after cortical deafferentation in primates. These longitudinal studies, which are still in progress, should provide important information on whether behavioral recovery following early brain injury can be attributed to the capacity of the developing nervous system for postlesion axonal growth.

Keyword Descriptors: autoradiography
behavioral recovery
collateral sprouting
early lesions
postlesion axonal growth
postnatal axonal development
prefrontal cortex
primates
silver-impregnation techniques

Honors and Awards: None

Publications: None

Serial No. Z01 MH 00482-14 LPP
1. Laboratory of Psychology and Psychopathology
2. Section on Neuropsychology
3. Bethesda

PHS-ADAMHA-NIMH
Individual Project Report
July 1, 1974 through June 30, 1975

Project Title: Cortical Mechanisms in Somesthesis

Previous Serial Number: M-P-L-12

Principal Investigator: Josephine Semmes, Ph.D.

Other Investigators: Blair Turner, Ph.D., Howard University, Guest Worker

Cooperating Units: None

Man Years

Total:	5 3/5
Professional:	1 2/5
Other:	4 1/5

Project Description:

The general aim is to determine, more precisely than heretofore, the loci of lesion within the sensorimotor cortex that produce deficit on any of a variety of somatosensory discrimination tasks. In addition, the question of what neural circuits are critically involved has been explored further. Of special interest is the issue of whether or not sequential intracortical integration of the incoming somatosensory information is necessary to discrimination. Thus, the effects of lesions of the principal cortical areas to which the primary sensory cortex (the target of the ascending pathways) sends efferents have been evaluated.

Rhesus monkeys are trained to perform somesthetic discrimination tasks requiring them to reach with one hand into an opaque box and select one of two stimulus objects differing in some way and to indicate their choice by pulling the object toward them. For each pair of objects, one (randomly shifted in position) is consistently rewarded whereas the other is never rewarded. Discriminations tested in this situation have involved hardness, shape at different levels of difficulty, size, roughness, and temperature, with each of the last three followed by repeated ascending and descending threshold determinations. A variant of this method, recently introduced, is to require the monkey to palpate the two stimulus objects with one hand and to make a differential response, appropriate to the reward contingency, with the other hand. Tests in which the subject is confined to a primate chair and required to respond to externally-applied stimuli, and tests of competency in motor performances, have also been used.

Ablations of the selected cortical areas are made by gentle aspiration and are, as far as possible, restricted to grey matter. Aseptic techniques, barbiturate anesthesia, and antibiotics (topical and systemic) are routinely employed. The postoperative recovery period is usually four weeks, after which adaptation and training are begun. Following completion of the behavioral observations and formal tests, the animal is given a lethal dose of barbiturate, and his brain is processed for histological examination. The actual limits (and depth) of the cortical lesion, as well as the consequent degeneration of parts of the thalamus, are then determined. Special attention is given to unintended sparing of tissue within the limits of the planned ablation and to unintended damage of grey matter outside these limits or of fibers passing underneath to areas other than that ablated. In some animals, a new histological method has been employed to trace afferent connections. This method does not involve ablation of cortex; instead, selected areas are injected with horseradish peroxidase, a substance which is transported backward along the axon to the cell body. By this method, it can be determined whether or not different areas receive independent projections.

In studies of the postcentral gyrus (areas 3, 1, and 2), we have shown that lesions of the most anterior part, area 3, which receives the densest projection from the thalamus, produce deficits on all the somatosensory discrimination tasks, except those involving temperature or gross size differences. With regard to the two more posterior areas of this gyrus, 1 and 2, removal of the former selectively disrupts discriminations of the textural qualities of objects, whereas removal of the latter disrupts discriminations of shapes or sizes. Thus, the conception of the postcentral gyrus emerging from these findings is that of a focus in area 3 for all submodalities of sensation, behind which are areas in which the cutaneous and proprioceptive aspects are represented more or less separately. From the horseradish peroxidase experiment, it appears that the basis for this functional difference is that there are at least partially independent projections from the thalamus supplying the cortical areas 3, 1, and 2. From the experiment in which one hand palpated the stimuli and the other hand made the response, it appears that only the palpating hand is affected by lesions of the opposite postcentral gyrus, thus indicating that the deficit is in detecting the difference between the stimulus objects rather than in responding correctly to the rewarded one.

Investigation of the effects of removing areas to which the postcentral gyrus sends efferents have revealed that lesions of area 4 or 6 (the cortical motor areas) do not impair any form of somatosensory discrimination that we have tested, although they do produce the expected motor deficits. This finding indicates that the substantial projection from the postcentral gyrus coursing anteriorly to the precentral region is not crucially involved in somatosensory discrimination. Likewise, removal of cortex posterior to the postcentral gyrus (area 5 or 7) fails to impair any of the discrimination tasks except fine roughness discrimination. This one positive finding can probably be discounted, since many lesions entirely outside the sensorimotor cortex produce this kind of impairment, as we have reported in previous years. The effects of removing both anterior and posterior areas in the same animals has also been tried, and so far has yielded negative results, i.e., no impairment.

All these results support the idea that somatosensory discrimination per se is not dependent on interactions of the primary sensory area with the motor or the so-called association cortex of the posterior parietal region. This applies to all the many kinds of discriminations we tested, with the one exception noted above. However, it should be noted that the stimulus objects to be used in the discrimination tasks were deliberately chosen to make it possible for the monkey subject to obtain a differential cue no matter how he palpated them. The justification for this restriction was our observation that even normal monkeys are very poor in examining single objects by touch, although many will palpate (cursorily) the two objects in a discrimination task again and again before making a choice. It is possible, then, that the very feature we sought to avoid, e.g., the necessity for "scanning" the whole of the object, is one which would reveal deficit from lesions of at least some of the areas to which the primary sensory cortex sends efferents.

An understanding of how the afferent inflow to the cortex is processed is the first step toward clarifying the neural basis of higher mental functions, such as complex perception and thought. Such higher functions are often disturbed as a result of cerebral injury or disease or even in certain of the psychoses. The development of rational therapies presupposes detailed knowledge of the workings of the normal brain. If the initial phase in the sequence of cerebral events intervening between stimulus and response is abnormal, later elaborated phases may be disrupted as a direct consequence. It is therefore important to study this initial phase and to find out how it can be disrupted.

Now that we have discovered how the somatosensory projection areas are organized, it would be of value to investigate the functions of its several connections to other parts of the cortex. Considering the anterior connections, what is the significance of the heavy outflow from the postcentral gyrus to the first and second motor areas? And considering its posterior and ventral connections, for what purpose does it relay information to the posterior parietal region (or parts thereof) and to Somatosensory II (in the parietal operculum)? Since we have ruled out a role for these areas in somatosensory discriminations of the types we tested, it is possible that the anterior connections serve to guide motor activity, that the posterior connections function in polysensory integrations (such as spatial orientation), and that the ventral connections to SII are concerned in transmitting information to the other hemisphere. The above guesses tend to be supported in the literature; however, they require empirical confirmation.

Keyword Descriptors: cortical lesions -- postcentral gyrus
somatosensory discrimination behavior
Rhesus monkeys

Honors and Awards: Fellow, 1975, AAAS.

Publications:

Randolph, M.C. and Semmes, J.: Behavioral consequences of selective subtotal ablations of sensory cortex in Macaca mulatta. Brain Res., 70: 55-70, 1974.

Semmes, J., Porter, L., and Randolph, M.C.: Further studies of anterior postcentral lesions in the monkey. Cortex, 10: 55-68, 1974.

In Press:

Deuel, R.K.: Loss of motor habits after cortical lesions. Neuropsychologia.

Serial No. Z01 MH 00483-15 LPP
1. Laboratory of Psychology and Psychopathology
2. Office of the Chief
3. Bethesda

PHS-ADAMHA-NIMH
Individual Project Report
July 1, 1974 through June 30, 1975

Project Title: Reaction time in schizophrenia.

Previous Serial Number: M-P-C(C)-15

Principal Investigator: Theodore P. Zahn

Other Investigator: Paul Fedio

Cooperating Unit: Surgical Neurology Branch, NINDS

Man Years:

Total:	0.1
Professional:	0.0
Other:	0.1

Project Description:

The objectives are to study deficits in attention in schizophrenia, particularly as manifested in difficulties in adopting and maintaining preparatory sets. To study the specificity of such deficits to schizophrenia. To study possible organic and genetic determinants of such deficits. To determine the relation between such deficits and the severity of schizophrenic symptomatology.

The methods employed are as follows: (A) A reaction time (RT) technique which puts severe demands on attention and which discriminates well between schizophrenic and non-schizophrenic subjects is being given to patients before and after unilateral temporal lobectomy for the relief of psychomotor epilepsy. This procedure and a choice technique which compared RT to monaural stimulation in each ear and responses with the same or opposite hand have also been used on postoperative temporal lobe followup cases and normal controls.

(B) Acute schizophrenic and non-schizophrenic patients are being tested with these procedures soon after admission, on discharge from the Clinical Center after 3-4 months and on a followup 6 months to 1 year later. The results will be compared with intensive symptom ratings.

There were no new findings this year.

These studies are designed in part to explore the possibility of a biological basis for schizophrenia. Since patients with lesions in the temporal lobe frequently exhibit a schizophrenic-like personality picture and since patients with other types of brain lesions have been found to exhibit reaction time deficits (but of different types than those shown by schizophrenics) the reaction time performance of these patients might indicate if a temporal lobe disturbance is possibly involved in schizophrenia. The reaction time studies with schizophrenics add to our knowledge of the specific psychological processes involved in the disorders of set and attention that seem to be important aspects of the schizophrenia process.

Analysis of data will begin shortly on completed projects.

Keyword Descriptors: reaction time
attention
schizophrenia
psychomotor epilepsy
temporal lobe
brain damage

Honors and Awards: None

Publications: None

Serial No. Z01 MH 00484-15 LPP
1. Laboratory of Psychology and Psychopathology
2. Office of the Chief
3. Bethesda

PHS-ADAMHA-NIMH
Individual Project Report
July 1, 1974 through June 30, 1975

Project Title: Psychophysiological Responsivity in Schizophrenia

Previous Serial Number: M-P-C(C)-17

Principal Investigator: Theodore P. Zahn

Other Investigators: William Carpenter, Thomas McGlashan
Carmi Schooler

Cooperating Units: Section on Psychiatric Assessment, APB, NIMH; Ward 4E

Man Years:

Total: 1.3
Professional: .7
Other: .6

Project Description:

The general purpose of these studies is to investigate schizophrenic-normal differences in the relative autonomic responsivity to various stimuli, the relationship of autonomic activity to adequacy of performance and to psychiatric condition, and possible genetic determinants.

Peripheral measures of autonomic functioning, namely GSR, heart rate, finger pulse volume, respiration and skin temperature are recorded during several sessions in which stimuli are presented and tasks are performed which vary in the demands placed on the subjects: no stimuli, simple auditory stimuli with no response required, reaction time, and mental arithmetic. Specific and non-specific response frequencies and amplitudes, baseline values and baseline changes are measured. Acute schizophrenic and non-schizophrenic patients have been tested on these procedures soon after admission, at discharge from the Clinical Center (3-4 months later) and at a 6 month to 1 year followup. The patients are all drug free for at least 3 weeks prior to testing and have been diagnosed by sophisticated methods developed in the International Pilot Study of Schizophrenia.

Two new experimental tasks are being used with both schizophrenic patients and normal controls. One is a two flash threshold determination using a forced choice technique. There are data in the literature suggesting that two flash threshold varies with arousal level and that this relationship is different for schizophrenic and normal subjects. The other is a tachistoscopic recognition procedure, also using a forced choice technique, which lends itself to concurrent psychophysiological recording. With this technique we hope to be able to test the differential psychophysiological responsiveness of schizophrenics and normals to such things as task difficulty, success and failure, positive and negative reinforcements, etc., as well as being able to separate sensory reception aspects from response aspects of the stimulus complex.

The major findings so far are as follows: All patients with a diagnosis of acute schizophrenia (N=46) were compared to a group of normal controls drawn from the study of normal twins who were comparable in age, social class, and sex to the patients (N=118). The patients had higher baseline heart rate, produced more spontaneous skin conductance responses (SCRs), and both spontaneous and elicited SCRs had faster recovery times. These differences are all in a direction thought to reflect higher autonomic arousal. However, skin conductance level (SCL) was lower in the patient group, suggesting lower arousal. The latter difference is not as statistically reliable as the high arousal differences. The patients gave fewer phasic SCRs to the meaningless tones as well as to the more "demanding" stimuli in the reaction time (RT) task. Habituation of the orienting response was slower in the patients. Diminished psychophysiological response to the RT task in the patients was also manifested by longer latencies of SCRs and diminished cardiac response in addition to slower reaction time. The arousal response to the word association task was significantly diminished in the patients. In general, these acute patients, like the more chronic groups, we have studied seem highly aroused, autonomically, under quiet conditions and less reactive to environmental stimuli.

On the basis of global psychopathology ratings made at the time of admission and discharge testing we have compared those patients who improved significantly with those whose psychosis remained about the same during their NIH hospitalization. The patients who were to improve, although not differing significantly on pathology ratings were lower in arousal on most variables than not-to-improve patients, but significantly so only for heart rate. In addition, they were more reactive to the RT stimuli in terms of frequency, latency, the cardiac response, and RT itself and had a larger arousal response to the mental arithmetic task on some variables. Thus, the autonomic variables developed here may have some prognostic significance, at least for the short term.

Another set of comparisons has been made of the discharge test data between patients who were relatively free of psychopathology with those who were still actively psychotic. The well group generally did not differ from normal on arousal measures, except for having lower SCL, and gave adequate increases in tonic arousal to the mental arithmetic task. However, they were strikingly lower than normal on phasic SCRs, particularly to the less demanding stimuli. On a measure of the relationship between elicited and spontaneous SCRs the well group was markedly lower than normal in the tones session at discharge as well as at admission, but not in the RT session.

There is a large body of literature on the difference between normals and schizophrenics and between subgroups of schizophrenics in autonomic nervous system functioning. Much of it is conflicting. These studies should help to clarify the effects of hospitalization, drugs and clinical state on these differences. From the analyses done to date it seems as if most of the differences found between acute schizophrenics and controls are due to the presence of an acute schizophrenic state rather than representing permanent "traits", although many seem to have at least short-term prognostic significance. However, some of the variables, reflecting low specific autonomic responsivity are possible indicators of a schizophrenic predisposition. Data from a large sample of monozygotic and dizygotic twins will be analyzed to see if these variables have a genetic basis. If so, they may possibly represent genetic markers for schizophrenia.

Keyword Descriptors: autonomic nervous system
skin conductance
heart rate
reaction time
orienting response
acute schizophrenia
psychophysiology
electrodermal

Honors and Awards: None

Publications:

Zahn, T. P.: Psychophysiological concomitants of task performance in schizophrenics. In M. Keitzman, S. Sutton and J. Zubin (Eds.): Experimental Approaches to Psychopathology. New York, Academic Press, 1975, pp. 109-134.

Serial No. Z01 MH 00485-03 LPP
1. Laboratory of Psychology and Psychopathology
2. Office of the Chief
3. Bethesda

PHS-ADAMHA-NIMH
Individual Project Report
July 1, 1974 through June 30, 1975

Project Title: Psychophysiological Changes During the Menstrual Cycle

Previous Serial Number: M-P-C(C)-46

Principal Investigator: Theodore P. Zahn, Ph.D.

Other Investigators: Betsy Little (Guest Worker); Raymond Matta, Friedhelm Lamprecht

Cooperating Units: Laboratory of Clinical Science

Man Years:

Total: .2
Professional: .1
Other: .1

Project Description:

The major purpose of this project is to elucidate the autonomic nervous system changes occurring throughout the menstrual cycle and to determine the hormonal and biochemical determinants of these changes. Subjects were tested daily in a short procedure which included rest periods, presentation of tones, and performance of time estimation and reaction time tasks. Skin conductance (SC), heart rate (HR), finger pulse volume, skin temperature and respiration were recorded continuously during the session and a mood scale was filled out by both subject and experimenter after each session. Fifteen women were tested over the course of at least one menstrual cycle and seven men were tested 3-4 weeks in a double blind study of the effects of progesterone.

The major findings with respect to the menstrual cycle and effects of progesterone were presented in last year's annual report and have been published. The data have been analyzed in a different way, however, for the purpose of determining the relationships between daily changes in mood and correlated changes in the psychophysiological variables. The design of the studies permits a within-subjects analysis of the covariation between mood and physiology which we feel is a distinct improvement over the usual between-subjects analysis in which many irrelevant variables are confounded. For each S physiological and performance scores (18 variables) were averaged for days with the highest ar lowest (25% plus ties) scores for each of the moods: Aggression, Anxiety, Surgency, Fatigue and combinations of moods called Positive Activation relat to high resting arousal indices for HR and SC. Strong feelings of Surgency and Positive Activation related to increased frequency and amplitudes of SC responses to RT stimuli while Fatigue and Low Activation were associated wit low SC responsivity. Fatigue also produced low SCL but not HR arousal. SC recovery times were longer in low arousal mood states. Respiration was fa and time was overestimated with high Negative Activation. The results show daily changes in mood are associated reliably with autonomic changes, the pattern of which differs for different mood states.

A logical further study would be to test the effects of estrogen and perhaps combined estrogen and progesterone in males. However, our unit has insufficient personnel to attempt this at present.

Analyses of the relationships of the physiological variables with mood and of the adaptation of these variables with repeated testing will continue.

Key Descriptors: autonomic nervous system
skin conductance
heart rate
mood
menstrual cycle
progesterone
endocrines
dopamine-beta-hydroxylase
electrodermal

Honors and Awards: None

Publications:

Little, B. C., and Zahn, T. P.: Changes in mood and autonomic functioni during the menstrual cycle. Psychophysiology, 11: 579-590, 1974.

Little, B., Matte, R. J., and Zahn, T. P.: Physiological and psychologi effects of progesterone in man. J. Nerv. Ment. Dis., 159: 256-262, 197

Lamprecht, F., Matta, R. J., Little, B. C., and Zahn, T. P.: Plasma dopamine-beta-hydroxylase (DBH) activity during the menstrual cycle. Psychosomatic Med., 36: 304-310, 1974.

Serial No. Z01 MH 00486-03 LPP
1. Laboratory of Psychology and Psychopathology
2. Office of the Chief
3. Bethesda

PHS-ADAMHA-NIMH
Individual Project Report
July 1, 1974 through June 30, 1975

Project Title: Psychophysiological Concomitants of Minimal Brain Dysfunction in Children

Previous Serial Number: M-P-C(C)-47

Principal Investigator: Theodore P. Zahn

Other Investigators: Paul H. Wender, Betsy Little

Cooperating Units: None

Man Years:

Total: .1
Professional: .1
Other: 0

Project Description:

Many investigators believe that the autonomic nervous system may be involved in minimal brain dysfunction in children. The objectives of our studies are to investigate differences in autonomic functioning between MBD and normal children by means of peripheral indicators such as skin conductance and heart rate, to predict which MBD children will respond favorably to stimulant drugs and to assess the effects of the drugs in terms of both autonomic activity and task performance.

In our previous studies we did not find lower baseline autonomic activation in the MBD children when off drugs as some (but by no means all) investigators have claimed. In fact, the MBD group had some higher than normal indices of arousal in one session where the amount of environmental stimulation was relatively high. The MBD group, however, showed diminished and "sluggish" responsivity to stimuli on several autonomic measures: skin conductance, heart rate, and pupil size. They also showed deficits in reaction time performance. Drugs improved behavior and increased baseline activation levels but did not clearly affect autonomic responsivity. The hypothesis that autonomic variables might predict clinical response to stimulant drugs was not clearly testable because of the very few subjects that failed to respond clinically. One paper has been published and a second is in preparation on these results.

On the basis of our previous studies, studies in the literature and clinical reports future studies will attempt to assess the effects of increased stimulus intensity, reinforcement for good and poor performance and perhaps changes in arousal level on both performance and autonomic activity in normal and MBD children. We also will test the children's two flash threshold which is purported to be a measure of "cortical arousal". A pilot study is being tested in a variety of situations under the general supervision of the Laboratory of Clinical Science.

Keyword Descriptors: autonomic nervous system
skin conductance
heart rate
minimal brain dysfunction
hyperkinesis
stimulant drugs
reaction time
attention

Honors and Awards: None

Publications:

Zahn, T. P., Abate, F., Little, B. C. and Wender, P. H. Minimal brain dysfunction, stimulant drugs and autonomic nervous system activity. Archives of General Psychiatry, 32: 381-387, 1975.

Serial No. Z01 MH 00487-03 LPP
1. Laboratory of Psychology and Psychopathology
2. Office of the Chief
3. Bethesda

PHS-ADAMHA-NIMH
Individual Project Report
July 1, 1974 through June 30, 1975

Project Title: Autonomic functioning in MZ and DZ twins

Previous Serial Number: M-P-C(C)-48

Principal Investigator: Theodore P. Zahn

Other Investigators: Monte Buchsbaum, APB

Cooperating Units: None

Man Years:

Total:	.3
Professiona:	.1
Other:	.2

Project Description:

The objectives of this project are to determine the relative importance of genetic vs. environmental factors in various aspects of autonomic functioning. To determine the relationships of autonomic nervous system activity to personality, task performance and electrocortical functioning.

Peripheral measures of autonomic functioning, namely skin resistance, heart rate, finger pulse volume, respiration, and skin temperature are recorded during two sessions which include rest periods, a series of mild tones, a reaction time task and mental arithmetic. The subjects are 30 MZ and DZ twin pairs equally male and female. Some opposite sex DZ pairs have also been tested.

Intraclass correlation will be the primary method of analysis. It will be based on base levels, responsivity to non-demanding and demanding stimuli, variability and response specificity.

There are no findings to date.

Data analysis will be continued. Correlation of autonomic data with personality, behavioral and electrocortical data on the same subjects.

Keyword Descriptors: autonomic nervous system
monozygotic twins
dizygotic twins
skin conductance
heart rate
genetics
electrodermal
heredity

Honors and Awards: None

Publications: None

Serial No. Z01 MH 00488-10 LPP
1. Laboratory of Psychology and Psychopathology
2. Office of the Chief
3. Bethesda

PHS-ADAMHA-NIMH
Individual Project Report
July 1, 1974 through June 30, 1975

Project Title: Individual Differences in Survival and Reproduction Among Old Colony Mennonites in Mexico

Previous Serial Number: M-S-SP-4

Principal Investigators: Gordon Allen and Calvin W. Redekop (non-PHS)

Cooperating Unit: Goshen College

Man Years:

Total:	1
Professional:	1
Others:	0

Project Description:

This investigation was undertaken in 1965, mainly to seek evidence of natural selection with respect co human behavioral characteristics. The study of selection in a pre-industrial type of European culture may indicate some of the influences that have produced present genetic tendencies and will draw a base line for future studies of selection under modern conditions. A secondary objective was to define natural patterns of marriage and reproduction that might have a bearing on the growth and regulation of human populations.

The population under study consists of about 13,000 German-speaking Mennonites in a politically integrated cluster of 46 villages in northern Mexico. These people were selected because of their simple and uniform culture insulated from mass communication media and because of their apparently unrestricted fertility. Also important was the fact that, unlike some similar religious isolates, this society supports a considerable degree of economic competition.

Professor Calvin Redekop, of the Department of Sociology and Anthropology at Goshen College, has assisted in the planning and execution of the study. He speaks the Low German dialect of these people and has lived among them.

Information was gathered by means of a combined census and survey that reached a third of the population. This was supplemented with photographs, their holdings, a list of all village and church leaders in the 40-year history of the population, and records of Mennonite births in local hospitals.

Editing of the data for accuracy and consistency was the most time-consuming part of the project, because each set of records, even our own census was collected and recorded by poorly educated farmers. After editing, the main data sets were subjected to cross-tabulation for general descriptive purposes. The survey data were then analyzed by correlational and factoring methods to yield ratings for each farmer in several dimensions of social and economic behavior. These ratings and other data obtained in the census are now being linked to the church records.

The final phase of the study will analyze the relations between vital events and socio-economic variables and will attempt to define family characteristics of people who subsequently have large vs. small families. This should be completed in two years, and another year may be needed for preparation of reports.

Keyword Descriptors: behavior
demography
fertility
mortality statistics
natural selection
population genetics human
simple societies

Honors and Awards: None

Publications: None

Project No. Z01 MH 00671-06 LSES
1. Socio-environmental Studies
2. Bethesda, Maryland

PHS-ADAMHA-NIMH
Individual Project Report
July 1, 1974 through June 30, 1975

Project Title: Social Origins of Stress

Previous Serial Number: M-S-SP-5

Principal Investigator: Leonard I. Pearlin

Other Investigators: None

Cooperating Units: None

Man Years:

Total:	2
Professional:	1
Other:	1

Project Description:

This is a study of social stress. The data for the study were gathered from interviews with a representative cluster sample of 2300 adults in the urbanized area of Chicago. Its ultimate purpose is to understand the daily, recurring problems and strains experienced by people of different social backgrounds, the emotional stresses and psychological disturbance that may result from the strains, and the coping strategies that are used to deal with these difficulties. A guiding perspective of the study is that many important experiences of people are structured around their locations in the society at large, and when these experiences are conflictful, threatening or frustrating, they become sources of inner distress.

The general aims and orientations of the research subsume several subsidiary goals. Much of the work of the past year has centered around three of these: the stresses arising within marriage, sex differences in depression, and the use of alcohol as a coping mechanism.

The inquiry into marital stress, begun in the previous year, was primarily concerned with the emotional consequences of marriage between partners coming from unequal status backgrounds. When status advancement is important to the parties of such marriages, a number of strains are likely to appear in their marital relations that eventuate in stress. People who have married down but to whom status aggrandizement is important are likely to experience disruptions in communications, in the sharing of values and in the exchange of affections. Such disruptions, in turn, are very likely to result in a high level of emotional stress. It should be emphasized that this process is especially likely to occur when marrying down is coupled to a striving for upward movement.

With regard to sex differences in depression, women were found to be considerably more prone than men to symptoms of this state. This finding is consistent with those of many other studies making similar comparisons. However, the present study was able to go beyond existing work by testing some of the possible reasons for the differences. One widely accepted hypothesis is that women are more vulnerable to depression because their role choices are more restricted than those of men. In particular, women who are homemakers do not always have the freedom to choose outside employment. This cannot account for the observed sex differences in depression, however, for women employed outside the home are no less inclined to depression than are homemakers. But though it makes no difference to depression whether women are employed inside or outside the home, the quality of their experiences within the roles is very important. For example, homemakers exposed to the relentless demands of large and young families are more prone to depression than women in the same role but having fewer and older children. Similarly, women employed outside their homes who have difficulty in accommodating their jobs to marital and parental roles are more likely to suffer from depression than women whose work is not in conflict with family obligations. The analysis indicates how a fundamental psychological state is influenced by the organization of experience within social roles.

Turning now to drinking as a coping mechanism, it is apparent that alcohol is consumed by some people as a technique for managing stress. Our analysis was able to establish the presence of a network of conditions leading up to the use of alcohol for this purpose. The analysis particularly emphasized economic factors, showing that limited material resources tend to generate a high level of anxiety which, in turn, leads to drinking as a device to keep the anxiety within manageable bounds. Drinking is especially likely to be used as an anxiety control among people low in self-esteem, with a limited sense of mastery, and who do not have extended educations. The inquiry reveals the intricate connections between the distribution of economic resources, personality factors, psychological distress, and the practices people adopt to deal with their distress.

Two additional analyses are currently underway. One concerns a frequently observed fact: married people display a greater sense of psychological well-being than do either the never married or formerly married. This is not a newly discovered fact and past work, either explicitly or by suggestion, has attempted to explain this difference by presuming that those without mates by their side suffer a psychic deprivation. However, there is a number of circumstances differentially associated with marital status, such as social isolation and economic hardship, and preliminary results indicate that it is these kinds of circumstances that create differences in psychological functioning rather than the sheer presence or absence of a spouse.

The second analysis is broader in scope than any undertaken thus far. It seeks to observe relationships among the entire range of variables included in the data. Thus it will attempt to recreate statistically the process that joins the social characteristics of people, the daily strains they experience in the different role areas of their lives, the stresses they feel and the anxiety and depression they harbor, the coping resources available to them, and their repertoires of coping resources that they employ.

Finally, preliminary plans have been made to reinterview the original sample. This would involve an extensive follow-up study that would attempt to predict how people would respond to new strains in their lives from what is presently known about their existing coping dispositions. The follow-up is being planned in cooperation with senior investigators in the Committee on Human Development of the University of Chicago.

Keyword Descriptors: Social stress
Strains
Psychological disturbance
Coping strategies
Marital stress
Sex differences in depression
Alcohol as a coping mechanism
Mastery
Social isolation
Economic hardship

Honors and Awards: None

Publications:

Pearlin, L. I.: Sex Roles and Depression. In Datan, N. and Ginsberg, L. (Eds.): Life-Span Developmental Psychology Conference: Normative Life Crises, 1974. New York, Academic Press. In press.

Pearlin, L. I.: Status Inequality and Stress in Marriage. American Sociological Review. In press.

Project No. Z01 MH 00672-11 LSES
1. Socio-environmental Studies
2. Bethesda, Maryland

PHS-ADAMHA-NIMH
Individual Project Report
July 1, 1974 through June 30, 1975

Project Title: Social Psychological Correlates of Occupational Position

Previous Serial Number: M-S-C-11

Principal Investigator: Melvin L. Kohn and Carmi Schooler

Other Investigators: None

Cooperating Units: None

Man Years:

Total:	5-5/6
Professional:	1-5/6
Other:	4

Project Description:

The principal goal of this research is to assess the effects of occupational conditions on psychological functioning. The research, until now, has been based on structured interviews with a sample of 3100 men, representative of all men employed in civilian occupations throughout the United States. These interviews were conducted for us and to our specifications by the National Opinion Research Center of the University of Chicago in the spring and summer of 1964. During this past year, the National Opinion Research Center conducted follow-up interviews, again to our specifications, with a randomly-selected one-fourth of the men who had participated in the original survey. Wherever a man was found to be presently married, a nearly identical interview was conducted with his wife. And wherever a man had one or more children in the age-range 13 through 25, a similar interview was conducted with a randomly-selected child. The full rationale for the current study was presented in last year's annual report. Essentially, the follow-up study of the men is designed to provide more definitive data on causal processes than could be provided by a single cross-sectional survey. With these data, we hope to demonstrate that occupational experiences really do affect psychological functioning, that the correlations between the two are not just a statistical artifact. The study of the wives is designed to discover whether occupational conditions affect men and women similarly and to enable us to assess the effects of men's occupational experiences on their wives' psychological functioning and of women's occupational experiences on their husbands' psychological functioning. And the study of the children is designed for exploratory analyses of the effects of parental experiences, values, and practices on their children's psychological development, as well as of the children's own educational and occupational experiences on their own psychological development.

The principal achievements of this past year--and certainly the principal preoccupations of the investigators--have been the successful completion of fieldwork, the development of an elaborate schema for coding the data, the actual coding of the data, and the development of an even more elaborate computer program for checking out the accuracy of the codes. Now, and for an as-yet unpredictable time to come, we shall be using this program to check the accuracy of the codes and to rectify all errors we can find.

Simultaneously with the development of the current study, we have completed two further analyses of the original (1964) data, one on the relationship between occupational structure and alienation, the second on the effects of ethnicity on values and psychological functioning.

1. Occupational structure and alienation.

Before we can even begin to search for the occupational sources of alienation, we must deal with the fact that in social-psychological usage, alienation is an extraordinarily vague and imprecise term. Lacking an adequate general definition, we follow Seeman's example and use the term to refer generally to five distinguishable facets of orientation: powerlessness, self-estrangement, normlessness, cultural estrangement, and meaninglessness. Seeman defines these five types of alienation as follows:

Powerlessness "can be conceived as the expectancy or probability held by the individual that his own behavior cannot determine the occurrence of the outcomes . . . he seeks."

Self-estrangement "refers essentially to the inability of the individual to find self-rewarding--or in Dewey's phrase, self-consummatory--activities that engage him."

Normlessness is the "situation . . . in which there is a high expectancy that socially unapproved behaviors are required to achieve given goals."

Cultural estrangement refers to "assign(ing) low reward value to goals or beliefs that are typically highly valued in the given society."

Meaninglessness refers to the individual's being "unclear as to what he ought to believe when the individual's minimal standards for clarity in decision-making are not met."

Seeman's analysis demonstrated that alienation has such disparate meanings that the term cannot be used analytically without specifying which of its several meanings is intended. We thus attempted to develop indices of all five types of alienation. We actually succeeded in constructing adequate Guttman Scales of four of them, failing only with meaninglessness, which we could not empirically differentiate from the others.

The key to our analysis of how occupational structure affects alienation is our focus on dimensions of occupation, rather than on named occupations; thus, we compare facets of work such as ownership, closeness of supervision, and the substantive complexity of the work, rather than named occupations such as lawyer, plumber, and flight engineer. And we attempt to disentangle the intercorrelated dimensions of occupation by inventorying job conditions of a large, representative sample of men, who necessarily work in many occupations, and then differentiating psychological concomitants of each facet of occupation by statistical analysis.

Essentially, the strategy of analysis is to winnow down a preliminary inventory of more than fifty separable dimensions of occupation to those few that are significantly related to one or another aspect of alienation, even when education and all other pertinent facets of occupation are statistically controlled. We start with such diverse aspects of work experience as relationships with coworkers and with supervisors, pace of work and control thereof, physical and environmental conditions, the substantive complexity of the work, the routinization of the flow of work, job pressures and uncertainties, union membership and participation, bureaucratization, job protections, and fringe benefits. Most of these are statistically related to one or another aspect of alienation, but many only because of their correlation with education (which in most cases precedes and is often a prerequisite for a job) or because of their interconnection with other, more potent, aspects of the job.

To distinguish those occupational conditions that have a non-trivial, non-artifactual, independent effect on alienation, we employ the following procedures: (1) Using analysis of variance, we test each occupational condition to be certain that it is significantly related to at least one of the four types of alienation, even with education statistically controlled; that the effects are preponderantly linear; and that there are no sizeable interactions between the occupational condition and education. (2) Using multiple regression analysis, we test each occupational condition to determine whether or not it is significantly related to at least one of the four types of alienation, even with education and all other pertinent occupational conditions statistically controlled.

Only six of the 50-odd occupational conditions we studied have a significant, independent impact on powerlessness. These six do not include ownership, or even what is often taken to be the modern equivalent of ownership, position in the supervisory hierarchy. Nor would it seem that division of labor is conducive to feelings of powerlessness, for we find that employees of highly bureaucratized firms and organizations--where, presumably, the division of labor is greatest--are somewhat less likely to feel powerless than are employees of non-bureaucratic firms and organizations. Thus, the occupational conditions classically believed to be the source of powerlessness are not, under modern conditions, crucial to this form of alienation. Instead, three types of occupational experience stand out. One is the major extrinsic condition of any job, the salary or wages it provides. The second is the major intrinsic condition of any job, the opportunity it provides to be self-directed in one's work, in particular, to be free of close supervision and to work at substantively complex jobs. And the third is the paramount threat inherent in any job, the risk of losing that job (or failing in that business). In short, the conditions that bear on feelings of powerlessness are sharply focused: low pay; too close supervision and too little substantive complexity to allow the worker to be self-directed in his work; and the threat that he might lose his job or business.

Two of the three principal occupational conditions that bear on powerlessness are important for self-estrangement too. Occupational self-direction appears to have even greater importance for self-estrangement than for powerlessness, the substantive complexity of the job especially so. The risk of losing one's job or business continues to matter, although perhaps not to quite the same degree. To this important extent, then, the occupational conditions that underlie these two types of alienation have a common theme. But there are differences as well. Income is not significantly involved in feelings of self-estrangement. Another threat, that of being held responsible for things outside of one's control, is pertinent for self-estrangement. So one can say that the occupational conditions underlying the two types of alienation that are directly traceable to classical analysis--powerlessness and self-estrangement--are variations on a common theme. Centrally important to both are the conditions that make for occupational self-direction.

Normlessness may come out of a different theoretical tradition, that of Durkheim, but in terms of its underlying occupational conditions, it has one major theme in common with powerlessness and self-estrangement: the conditions that make for occupational self-direction are again centrally involved, perhaps even more for normlessness than for the other types of alienation. In other respects, the occupational conditions are different: Both income and the threat of losing one's job or business have dropped out of the picture. Position in the supervisory hierarchy becomes relevant, although not necessarily as alienation theorists would have predicted: the higher-ups take less personal responsibility for their moral standards than do their subordinates. Mainly, though, the occupational conditions pertinent to normlessness are those that determine whether or not one can be self-directed in one's work: closeness of supervision, routinization, and substantive complexity.

Cultural estrangement presents an altogether different picture from powerlessness, self-estrangement, and normlessness, both in terms of which occupational conditions are involved and how they are involved. For the first time, ownership is significantly involved. Bureaucratization is not. Occupational self-direction is less important than for the other types of alienation. A new uncertainty, that there might be a "dramatic change" in one's income, reputation or position, enters in. So, too, does the time-pressure under which one works. In general, then, the overlap between occupational conditions related to powerlessness, self-estrangement, and normlessness and those related to cultural estrangement is insubstantial. And where there is overlap, the direction of effect is opposite: working at jobs of low substantive complexity, for example, is related to feeling powerless, self-estranged, and normless, but to not feeling culturally estranged. Similarly, competition is oppositely related to powerlessness and to cultural estrangement. One would have to conclude that this type of alienation is not produced by anything like the same occupational conditions as are the other three.

For powerlessness, self-estrangement, and normlessness, though, one can speak of similar underlying conditions, with a lack of opportunity for occupational self-direction being central to all. This is as true for the "Durkheimian" type of alienation, normlessness, as for the two types that stem from the Marxian tradition, powerlessness and self-estrangement. Our conclusion is that the occupational conditions underlying powerlessness, self-estrangement, and even normlessness center on the modern determinants of control over one's essential job conditions. These are no longer ownership and division of labor, but closeness of supervision, routinization, substantive complexity, and a basic sense of job security.

Further analysis, borrowing from the methods of the econometricians, demonstrates that the correlations between occupational conditions and alienation do not result from processes of selective recruitment or from men molding their jobs to match their feelings. It is not, for example, that self-estranged men seek or are selected for jobs of low substantive complexity, or that they perform at the lowest level of complexity the job allows. On the contrary, it appears that jobs of little substantive complexity actually are conducive to self-estrangement. More generally, these analyses indicate that for three of the four types of alienation--powerlessness, self-estrangement, and normlessness--there is substantial evidence that doing work of little substantive complexity is not only associated with, but actually results in, feelings of alienation. Although our data do not permit similar analyses of the other pertinent dimensions of occupation, it seems a fair presumption that other occupational conditions also have a causal impact on alienation. (This we shall be able to test with the data of the follow-up study.)

2. Ethnicity and psychological functioning.

The data gathered for the occupational study were also used to examine the effects of ethnicity on the individuals values and functioning. The analyses asked whether ethnic groups are essentially unorderable or whether they can be conceptualized as existing along a meaningful continuum which reflects social structural conditions known to affect individual functioning. In doing so it also dealt with series of more general questions: Does ethnicity have an effect? If so, which behaviors and attitudes are affected and are its effects independent of those of other social background variables?

The general hypothesis was that Americans belonging to ethnic groups which originated in countries whose mores have been influenced by a relatively recent history of feudal subjugation are different in their intellectual functioning, attitudes toward authority, and moral value systems from Americans belonging to ethnic groups coming from European countries where the institutions of feudal serfdom were terminated in the more distant past.

In line with this hypothesis, the major European ethnic groups were arranged along a continuum reflecting the time of the release of the peasantry from serfdom in the old country. Such an ordering of ethnic groups operates on two levels. On the level of index construction, it objectively orders countries in a manner which insures that findings are not merely the results of arbitrary weighting procedures which capitalize on chance. On a more substantive level, such an index ranks countries according to the degree of self-direction and the number of behavioral options which were available to the agricultural sector of the population, the very segment from which most immigrants to America came.

Although the ethnic continuum is ordered according to the time serfdom was ended, it actually reflects both the degree and recency of a whole series of parallel and interrelated legal, economic, and occupational constraints on the lives of the mass of pre-industrial agricultural workers. Of course, since this complex web of interrelated constraints on the individual's independence occurred in the diverse contexts of different national histories, our present ranking--based as it is on the different times of the ending of legal serfdom--does not perfectly reflect the exact chronology and severity of the various other components of this web of constraints. However, such a ranking does seem to provide us with a reasonable and nonarbitrary way of ordering European countries according to the general magnitude and recency of constraints placed upon the autonomy of the individual peasant.

When we control for age, father's education, religion, rurality, and region of the country in which reared, all of our hypotheses about the effects of ethnicity are generally confirmed. Thus, individuals belonging to ethnic groups originating in countries with a longer history of freedom from serfdom show a higher level of intellectual functioning. The Beta weight for ethnicity and intellectual flexibility is both significant and in the appropriate direction. The Beta weight on ethnicity of intellectually demanding use of leisure time is also in the predicted direction, although its significance is somewhat equivocal.

The predictions about attitudes toward authority also prove to be correct. Members of ethnic groups stemming from countries at the end of the continuum relatively remote from serfdom are less authoritarian and more likely to have self-directed, rather than conforming, parental values.

Proof of the hypothesis that individuals from ethnic groups long free from serfdom value moral autonomy more is found in such individuals' tendency to show more personally responsible morality, to hold themselves more responsible for their own fate, and to have a more self-deprecatory/ self-critical view than do members of ethnic groups more recently emerged from feudalism.

Evidence that the ethnic experience is important in causing these differences can be found in the increased strength of the relevant dependent variables' relationships with ethnicity among respondents who report that their ethnic membership has affected them noticeably.

It is, of course, impossible to confirm each link in the causal chain leading from an ethnic group's past historical circumstances to the present functioning of its descendants, however present day ethnic differences appear congruent with the assumption of an historically determined continuum which reflects the social, legal, economic, and occupational conditions of the European countries from which American ethnic groups emigrated. Furthermore, the apparent effects of these conditions on the culture of the various ethnic groups are remarkably similar to the effects social and occupational conditions have previously been demonstrated to have on the individual in present-day America. Such a similarity raises the possibility that social and occupational conditions prevailing within a society may affect that society's culture in a manner analogous to the way in which an individual's occupational experiences affect his values and functioning.

Underlying the tentative tone and conditional tense of the above conclusions are two lingering doubts: (1) Is ethnicity the actual and nonspurious cause of the differences we have found, and (2) If it is the true cause, are the interrelated legal, economic and occupational correlates of a history of recent serfdom which we have enumerated really centrally involved in the causal processes leading to these differences? The answer to the first question--have we found true ethnic differences--is very probably "yes." The various controls used rule out the possibility that our results are spurious artifacts of differences in rurality, region, age, religion, father's education, present social class and substantive complexity of present occupation. The ethnic differences consistently remain when these variables are controlled. If our ethnic differences are spurious, they would have to be the result of something outside of this wide range of variables.

The answer to the question of the centrality of the conditions related to a history of serfdom to the causal process making for differences among American ethnic groups must remain somewhat tentative. However, here too, certain alternate hypotheses may be ruled out. Thus, although our ethnic continuum reflects the time of the end of serfdom, it does not directly reflect climate, time of industrialization or time of urbanization of the old country, time of major immigration to the United States, and social class and motivation of the immigrants. It would thus seem likely that we are, in fact, dealing with the remnants of cultural patterns originating in the agricultural sectors of the old country, carried over by the immigrants and, carried on to some extent, by their descendants.

To the extent that the ethnic continuum's explanatory power is based on historical differences in occupational conditions, it extends the known range of occupational effects from the individual to the culture to which he belongs. But since the differences in occupational self-direction reflected by the ethnic continuum seem to have been paralleled by legal, economic, and social constraints on the individual's freedom, our model suggests that a whole range of historical circumstances may have combined to determine the differences among American ethnic groups in intellectual functioning, attitudes toward authority, and moral autonomy. Thus, although no longer serfs, Americans from ethnic groups with a long and pervasive history of serfdom appear heirs to the cultural transmission of traditions whose values were molded by the oppressed lives of their ancestors.

Keyword Descriptors: Alienation
Ethnicity
Normlessness
Occupational conditions
Occupational self-direction
Occupational structure
Powerlessness
Psychological functioning
Self-direction
Self-estrangement

Honors and awards: None

Publications: None

Project No. Z01 MH 00673-13 LSES
1. Socio-environmental Studies
2. Bethesda, Maryland

PHS-ADAMHA-NIMH
Individual Project Report
July 1, 1974 through June 30, 1975

Project Title: Parental Care and Child Behavior in Japan and the United States

Previous Serial Number: M-S-P(C)-27

Principal Investigator: Carmi Schooler

Other Investigators: None

Cooperating Units: None

Man Years:

Total: 1-1/10
Professional: 1/10
Other: 1

Project Description:

The objectives of this study, planned and in large part carried out by the late Dr. William Caudill, are twofold: to identify and describe patterns of parental care and child behavior in Japanese and American families, and to determine the relationship of these patterns of behavior to personality development, psychopathology, culture, and social structure in the two countries.

The basic design of the study has been described in detail in previous reports. Briefly, this is a longitudinal observational study of the behavior of parents and children in the home over the first six years of life in Japan and in the United States. During 1961-64, 30 Japanese and 30 American middle-class mother-infant pairs were selected for observation. The infants were first-born, normal babies, and were three-to-four months of age at the time of observation. The first 20 Japanese and the first 20 American cases were selected for follow-up study at 2-1/2 years of age, and observations in the home were completed during 1963-1967. These same children were studied for a third and final time at 6 years of age during 1967-70, and all observations have been completed.

Even with many analyses remaining yet to do, Caudill's achievement is clear. With a sample of only 20 American and 20 Japanese children, he was able to demonstrate conclusively meaningful and consistent cross-cultural differences in the behavior of children and their caretakers which persist from infancy through early childhood. Since the cross-cultural differences in child behavior he found seem to parallel many of those which distinguish Japanese from American adults, and since he was able to show that the genetic contribution to these differences is at most minimal, Caudill's work marks an important step forward in demonstrating the early and persistent effects of culture on personality.

At present our analyses are incomplete. Many other independent variables remain to be investigated. In the analyses of the 2-1/2 and 6-year data we have collapsed the behavior of all of each child's caretakers, disregarded possible effects of different locations in which behaviors occurred, and made no attempt to explore sequential behavior patterns. Most importantly, we have not taken into account all the other information we have available to us in histories, interviews, and observer's notes which could be used to characterize the personal characteristics of the children and their principal caretakers. We are presently attempting to pursue many of the above paths. When these analyses will be completed, the results will be presented to a scientific journal for publication.

Keyword Descriptors: Japan
Child behavior
Parental care

Honors and Awards: None

Publications:

Schooler, C.: A memorial to William Caudill. Transcultural Psychiatric Research Review 11: 149-154, 1974.

Project No. Z01 MH 00674-06 LSES
1. Socio-environmental Studies
2. Bethesda, Maryland

PHS-ADAMHA-NIMH
Individual Project Report
July 1, 1974 through June 30, 1975

Project Title: The Interrelationships between Social Interaction, Psychological Functions, Perceptual Style, Physiological Arousal and Personal History Factors Among Schizophrenics and Normals

Previous Serial Number: M-S-P(C)-38

Principal Investigator: Carmi Schooler

Other Investigators: Theodore Zahn and Monte S. Buchsbaum

Cooperating Units: Laboratory of Psychology, NIMH; Saint Elizabeths Hospital; DCRT

Man Years:

Total:	7/10
Professional:	2/10
Other:	5/10

Project Description:

The objective of this series of studies is to gain understanding of the schizophrenic process by examining the complex interactions between the individual's psychological and physiological systems and between both of these and his social environment. This is done by examining the interrelationships between task performance, physiological arousal, perceptual style, personality characteristics, and everyday behavior patterns in schizophrenics and normals.

Several approaches are presently being followed.

(1) The level of physiological arousal and task performance under different social conditions of both schizophrenics and nonschizophrenics have been measured and related to variations in perceptual style and personal history.

(2) Data has been gathered for a study which involves the interrelating of measures of evoked response, perceptual style, skin temperature (a measure of physiological arousal) and symptomatology. Preliminary analysis of these data carried on this year has revealed several striking

replications of earlier results, particularly in the relationship between augmenting in the evoked response and in the kinesthetic measures. Some of the earlier findings of relationships between kinesthetic measures and symptomatology also seem to have been replicated. However, the picture is complicated by what appear initially to be significant reversals of some of the earlier findings, particularly those involving the behavior and kinesthetic correlates of skin temperature.

(3) In order to facilitate the continuance of both of the above types of study, a generalized computer program has been developed to simplify the analysis of measures of physiological arousal and to relate these measures to each other and to other aspects of the experimental situations. During this year this computer program has been used on the data of a study investigating the psychophysiological reactions of hospitalized schizophrenic and nonschizophrenic psychiatric patients to competitive and cooperative tasks.

(4) A study which examines the exact psychophysiological arousal during the different stages of perceptual task performance is underway. This year, in cooperation with Dr. Theodore Zahn of the Laboratory of Psychology, data were collected on 75 normal subjects and 10 drug-free schizophrenic patients. It is expected that data collection will be completed by July 1975, at which point data analysis will begin.

Although the above experiments may seem somewhat disparate, they have a common underlying theme: The study of the interrelationships among social behavior, psychological functions, perceptual style, physiological arousal, and personal history in schizophrenics and normals. The senior investigator became interested in this line of investigation as a result of his earlier studies of the social psychology of schizophrenia. The findings of interactions between the social situation, the schizophrenic's functioning, and his physiological reactivity pointed to a general weakness in the way this earlier series of studies had been carried out. It had been conducted primarily from one research perspective and was concerned with only a limited area of the individual's functioning. Although the findings were significant, they had not been very powerful, possibly because differences in the nature of physiological reactivity of different subgroups of schizophrenics may have produced contrasting, or at least differing, results.

A review of the literature revealed that the general concentration on one aspect of the individual which had marked these social psychologically oriented studies was at least as pronounced in studies in other areas. It was therefore not at all surprising that the weak results which marked the series of social psychological studies were at least as powerful as the results of studies approaching the problem of schizophrenia from other directions. Thus, for example, years of search for biochemical differences between schizophrenics and others have resulted in no reliably replicable findings. The effects of genetics appear to be less and less powerful, the better controlled the study. Putative social class differences between schizophrenics and others do not seem to exist under all conditions and where they do exist it is far from clear whether such differences are related to the cause of the disease or its effects. Those theoretically based systems of classifying patients into subgroups which have been investigated have not produced consistent findings and, in fact, the most highly touted mode of classification--pre-morbid adjustment--proved totally unable to pass the test of controlled replication.

The lack of findings has certainly not been due to any lack of theories or hypotheses. Hypotheses have been brought forth with the ease of the proverbial blind men describing the elephant, e.g., those studying tails describing the elephant as long, thin, and floppy; those studying problem-solving seeing the essence of schizophrenia in thought disorder.

Two courses seem to be presently open. One can keep on making hypotheses from limited bodies of data, hoping to achieve the flash of insight which will permit us to see from our limited point of view what the elephant is really like, or one can go ahead with the duller task of trying to do studies which attempt to coordinate data from many vantage points in order to get enough information to make meaningful hypotheses possible. The present series of studies represents an attempt to follow the second of these courses with the aid of modern multivariate techniques and computer technology.

Keyword Descriptors: Schizophrenia
Psychophysiological arousal
Perceptual style

Honors and Awards: None

Publications: None

Project No. Z01 MH 00675-01 LSES
1. Socio-environmental Studies
2. Bethesda, Maryland

PHS-ADAMHA-NIMH
Individual Project Report
July 1, 1974 through June 30, 1975

Project Title: Role Values among Japanese Women

Previous Serial Number: None

Principal Investigator: Carmi Schooler

Other Investigators: Karen C. Smith, University of Pittsburgh

Cooperating Units: Mental Health Center, Kobe, Japan

Man Years:

Total: 7/10
Professional: 2/10
Other: 5/10

Project Description:

The study of women's attitudes toward their roles in different cultures is directly relevant to the study of mental illness because the interaction of sex role and culture is an important determinant of the symptoms of mental illness.

Recent cross cultural studies of symptomatology by the present investigator and his colleagues have found that female mental patients not only show more severe symptomatology than do male mental patients, but also that the general pattern of symptom differences found among cultures is reflected more strongly among the women than among the men.

The importance of studying culturally defined sex roles in order to understand mental illness is also emphasized by the results of previous researches by the present investigator among American samples in which experimental, observational, and demographic studies showed that the relationship among symptoms is quite different among women than men. Furthermore, the results of these previous studies strongly indicate that the differences in symptom patterns between the sexes found among American patients may well have been strongly influenced by the effects of cultural definitions of sex roles.

The study of Japanese women's attitudes towards their various roles is particularly germane, not only because Japan was one of the cultures involved in the above-mentioned cross-cultural studies, but also because of almost unique reputations of Japanese wives as exemplars of one type of sex-role definition. Nearly all literary descriptions of Japanese wives view them as paragons of domesticity who selflessly and subserviently meet all of their husbands' domestic needs without circumscribing their freedoms. Needless to say, very few of these descriptions come from the wives themselves.

The present study asks Japanese wives about their own views on the subject. It does so by means of a self-administered questionnaire which addresses itself to a number of relevant areas: (1) The relative importance Japanese women attach to the roles of wife, mother, woman, and person. (2) The relative importance these women believe their husbands attach to the parallel roles of husband, father, and person, and to their occupational roles. (3) The qualities and values the respondents believe important for the fulfillment of the role of wife. (4) The tone of the interpersonal relationship of husband and wife. (5) The division of household responsibilities among family members and the women's satisfaction with this arrangement. (6) The respondents' views of the kinds of problems they see facing themselves and Japanese women in general, and the importance they attach to various dimensions of sexual equality.

The questionnaire also contains a section that deals with the social background of the respondent and her husband. Such questions are important because, despite the pervasiveness of the stereotype presented here, there is a reasonable amount of evidence that the behavior and attitudes of Japanese women have differed substantially throughout the course of Japanese history and within different segments of Japanese society.

In looking at the effects of social structural variables on women's attitudes, the most striking finding is the pervasive effect of social class. This pervasiveness is particularly noticeable in those variables that measure the respondent's ranking of the importance of different roles. Each of the role-ranking variables is affected by social class. Higher social class directly results in a greater emphasis on the role of the individual, both for the respondent and her husband, and greater stress on the other-than-sex roles by the respondent. Thus, middle-class women who may, in comparison to working-class women, maintain some control over their destinies and who may be exposed to relatively complex environments, seem to place a greater emphasis on the role of the individual. The size of the husband's place of work also has an effect on perceived role rankings. Men working in large organizations are seen by their wives as being particularly involved in their work roles, a finding which might be expected from Vogel's discussion of the relatively greater importance of job and firm in the lives of "salarymen" than those working in small businesses.

Social structural variables that increase personal autonomy and environmental complexity also appear to have a tradition-breaking effect on the interpersonal tone of the marriage. Higher present social class and urban upbringing, each independently increase the degree to which husband and wife socialize together and interact with each other as equals. A somewhat similar pattern can be seen in terms of the rejection of the traditional view of the characteristics of a good wife, such rejection being shown by the young, those with fathers employed in high-status occupations, and in relatively large-scale enterprises. Thus, both in terms of behavior and values, social structural conditions that increase environmental complexity and individual autonomy lead to a breakdown of traditional hierarchical marital relationships.

In general, the views of the women in our sample conform to expectations. However, the central question our data cannot definitively answer is how permanent is this state of affairs. There is some evidence that changes may be taking place among Japanese women, even though at present they uncomplainingly accept restrictions on their life space and assume almost all household responsibilities. They do express some desire for greater involvement by their husbands with their children. The traditional values of obedience and patience also now seem to be seen by Japanese women as relatively unimportant qualities for a good wife, and most intriguingly, for many of them the role of person has become very important, being the one chosen second most frequently as most important.

Evidence of potential for change can also be found in the effects of the various social structural variables. Our findings support the hypothesis that social structural variables related to environmental complexity result in an increase in the emphasis on individuality. This seems to be particularly true for social class--middle-class women being more likely to see both themselves and their husbands as concerned with their roles as persons rather than as family members, a tendency that is accompanied by a more egalitarian and close social relationship between husband and wife. Coming from an urban background also independently increases the level of equality and social closeness of the husband-wife relationship. The social closeness of the couple is also significantly correlated with having a father with a high-status occupation, being well-educated, having a husband in a large business, and relatively nontraditional marriage arrangements. Certainly, if these characteristics of the husband-wife relationships are related to environmental complexity, it seems reasonable to expect that both they and the complexity of life will increase in Japan.

In any case, the sterotypical view of the Japanese wife as a paragon of selfless domesticity who is desirous of filling her husband's every wish probably needs revision. Our data can be used to make a relatively strong argument that, although the Japanese wife's behavior may tend in this direction, psychologically she is more a disinterested than a willing servant. At present, her husband frequently does not seem to be a particularly important factor in the wife's social or psychological existence, being nowhere as important to her as are her children. Certainly, when we actually ask Japanese women how important their various roles are to them, the order of the one chosen first is: Mother, person, and then . . . A Japanese Wife.

Present analysis is in the process of completion and the results are being prepared for publication in a scientific journal. The next planned analyses on these data will examine relationships between social structural variables and parental values.

Keyword Descriptors: Role values
Japan

Honors and Awards: None

Publications: None

Project No. Z01 MH 00676-09 LSES
1. Socio-environmental Studies
2. Bethesda, Maryland

PHS-ADAMHA-NIMH
Individual Project Report
July 1, 1974 through June 30, 1975

Project Title: Developmental Study of the Self-Image

Previous Serial Number: M-S-S-12

Principal Investigator: Morris Rosenberg

Other Investigators: Roberta G. Simmons (University of Minnesota)

Cooperating Units: None

Man Years:

Total: 1/6
Professional: 1/6
Other: 0

Project Description:

The main object of this study has been to learn how children's self-images change as they grow older and to gain increased understanding of the social factors that influence self-image formation.

Several major analyses have completed on this study and discussed in previous annual reports. The principal investigator left NIMH for the State University of New York at Buffalo early in this fiscal year. There he has continued the analysis, emphasizing particularly the effects of social structure on children's "committed" and "idealized" self-images.

Keyword Descriptors: Self-image
Self-concept
Self-esteem

Honors and Awards: None

Publications: None

Project No. Z01 MH 00677-13 LSES
1. Socio-environmental Studies
2. Bethesda, Maryland

PHS-ADAMHA-NIMH
Individual Project Report
July 1, 1974 through June 30, 1975

Project Title: Health Orientations of Parents and Children

Previous Serial Number: M-S-PS-1

Principal Investigator: John D. Campbell

Other Investigators: Caren M. Carney

Cooperating Units: None

Man Years:

Total: 2
Professional: 1
Other: 1

Project Description:

The goals of this research on health orientations of family members are, first, to describe variations in children's and mothers' attitudes, values, beliefs, perceptions, and behavior concerning phenomena of illness and health; and second, to examine ways in which selected personal and situational factors relate to these health orientations. Individual perspectives on health, illness, and the sick role are at least in part learned, and to a considerable extent this learning takes place as an aspect of routine family relationships. Systematic research can shed light on the process by which health orientations are acquired and modified.

The data for this study derive from 264 hospitalized children and their mothers. Information was obtained by use of focused interviews, questionnaires, and rating scales. Interviews with children and mothers, and questionnaires completed by mothers provided data on (a) aspects of their definitions of illness, (b) reports of their own and other family members' feelings and actions when ill, (c) their attitudes and beliefs about illness prevention and treatment, (d) their values in selected areas not directly relevant to health, and (e) their views about appropriate standards of behavior (i.e., what should or should not be done in circumstances pertaining to illness and health). Ratings made by nurses in the hospital setting appraised children's emotional dependence and anxiety.

Previously reported analyses have shown that children's age and sex, fathers' socioeconomic status, and mothers' valuation of self-direction were generally associated with variations in children's reports of their own health-relevant role functioning in the following areas: (a) the nature of the child's emotional response to illness and injury, (b) likelihood that the child himself would initiate sick-role identification, (c) the child's inclincation to reject the sick role, and (d) risk taking that might lead to illness or injury. Analyses completed this year have clarified and added to an understanding of the process by which such self-appraisals develop.

Socialization research has conventionally used the father's socioeconomic status as a measure reflecting a class-associated family climate. Though sometimes ignored, the possible independent contributions of similar measures from the mother are also relevant. Maternal and paternal status measures showed some similarities in their impact on children's views of their own behavior. But variations in two aspects of children's self-assessments (their reported emotionality in response to illness and their health-relevant risk taking) indicated that the status of one parent does not invariably serve as an effective "stand-in" for that of the other. Risk taking (the extent to which the child reported taking chances that might result in injury and the extent to which he departed from a number of prescribed hygienic practices) represents an aspect of the child's actions least apt to be subjected to direct maternal scrutiny. Here the father's socioeconomic status played a markedly more important role than did maternal education; the higher his status, the greater the child's reported risk taking. When it was a matter of children's emotional response to circumstances surrounding illness itself, the influence of the mother's status was clearly greater than that of the father; the higher her educational level, the lower the level of emotionality reported by the child. Responsibility for tending the sick child typically devolves on the mother, and status-linked aspects of her functioning as caretaker may contribute to the constellation of factors determining the nature of her child's approach to the sick role.

Parental values provide a subtle, but pervasive, climate for the child's development. Two such values, each statistically independent of the other, have been measured in this study: (a) the importance the mother attached to the child's self-direction, rather than conformity, and (b) maternal valuation of the child's egocentric, rather than sociocentric concerns. These are themselves a function of attributes both of parents and child: Mothers were much more apt to value self-direction for older children, for boys, and if maternal and paternal status were both high (each of these four status dimensions made a highly significant independent contribution to measured importance of self-direction). Sex of child and maternal status were primary contributors to the second of these values: Mothers who were less-well educated and whose child was a boy attached much more importance to egocentric, than to sociocentric concerns; age of child and father's SES had no appreciable impact on this value.

Although both dimensions of maternal values (importance attached to self-direction and to egocentric concerns) were associated with status characteristics of parent and child, children's appraisals appeared to be much more closely related to status than to values. (The relevant canonical correlation between four status attributes and four dimensions of children's role appraisal--emotionality, initiation of sick-role identification, rejection of the sick role, and health-relevant risk taking, was .64. Between maternal values and these same four dimensions of role appraisal, the canonical correlation was .33, and after effects of status were removed, the values-role assessment relationship was reduced to .14.)

In part the lesser contribution of this pair of values might simply suggest that status measures such as age and sex of child, maternal education, and father's SES summarized far more about a family climate than is conveyed by the two values measured. But the situation is more complicated than that. Variations in the importance that mothers attached to self-direction and to egocentric concerns did make a difference. They contributed quite significantly to children's role assessments, but they did so in a conditional manner; their effects were markedly moderated by the age of the child. The older the child, the greater the impact of maternal values. For younger children the canonical correlation between values and self-appraisal was a non-significant .21; for older children, a highly significant .50. After effects of status variables were controlled, the canonical relationship was only .07 for the younger children, but was .34 for the older. (In similar analyses that first controlled for the contribution of parental values, the canonical relationship between status characteristics and younger children's assessments or role functioning was .44, a value nearly identical to the corresponding relationship for the older children.)

Separate multiple-regression analyses showed that value-by-age interactions made significant incremental contributions to each dimension of children's role assessments; both of the orthogonal values measured contributed to these increments. Among older children, those whose mothers attached importance to the child's self-direction characterized themselves as displaying less emotion in illness, making their own decision concerning adoption of the sick role, and taking greater health-relevant risks. Older children whose mothers placed a relatively low value on the child's egocentric concern were also likely to see themselves as risk takers and as the one who made their own decision concerning adoption of the sick role; in addition they characterized themselves as acting in a manner indicating rejection of the sick role.

These associations fit a hypothesis that direction of effect is from maternal values to children's self-assessments (it would be logically less consistent to suggest that the direction be reversed: e.g., that because a child made his own decision to adopt the sick role, his mother subsequently attached importance to the need for self-direction in the child). That maternal values showed relatively little association with younger children's role appraisals may indicate that the process by which parental values impinge on children's role orientations is an indirect one occurring during a relatively long time period. The older child may be more attuned to the subtleties of the communication process involved.

Some exploration of possible antecedents and consequences of attributing to the child responsibility for his own illness has been undertaken. Whether a child should be held accountable for ill health is a more highly subjective matter than are role perceptions. And as one might expect, there is less agreement between mother and child on attribution of responsibility than there is on the presumably more objectively ascertainable matter of whether the mother has scolded the child for becoming ill. Age and sex of child, and maternal status contributed significantly to mothers' assessments: responsibility was more often attributed to older children and to boys, and the less well educated the mother was, the more likely was she to view illness as the child's fault. Sex of child also served to moderate the impact of age and maternal education: their contributions to maternal assessments were considerably greater for mothers of boys.

This research on health orientations provides systematic information on an important area of individual functioning that is currently only inadequately covered. The potential value of the research is not, however, restricted solely to matters of health and reactions to the stressful circumstances surrounding illness. Illness is a universally encountered phenomenon, and there is a recognized role attendant on it. The typically discontinuous, clearly delimited nature of the sick role provides a valuable context in which to consider role learning, attitude formation, and other aspects of the acquisition and change of general social orientations.

One research report has been published in a scientific journal this year and one is in press. Two other reports are currently being prepared. Analysis of data for additional papers continues.

Keyword Descriptors: Attitudes toward health
Child development
Child rearing
Illness
Interpersonal relations
Patient care
Social perception
Social roles
Socialization and social learning
Stress

Publications:

Campbell, J. D.: Illness is a point of view: the development of children's concepts of illness. Child Development, 46: 92-100, 1975.

Campbell, J. D.: Attribution of illness: another double standard. Journal of Health and Social Behavior. In press.

Serial No. Z01 MH 00678-16 LSES
1. Socio-environmental Studies
2. Bethesda, Maryland

PHS-ADAMHA-NIMH
Individual Project Report
July 1, 1974 through June 30, 1975

Project Title: Research on the Processes of Internalization of Rules, Standards, and Values

Previous Serial Number: M-S-D-10

Principal Investigator: Roger V. Burton

Other Investigators: None

Cooperating Units: None

Person Years

Total: .34
Professional: .17
Other: .17

Project Description:

Principal investigator left NIMH 8/30/74; project discontinued.

Serial No. Z01 MH 00851-11 LBEB
1. Laboratory of Brain Evolution and Behavior
2. Section on Comparative Neurophysiology and Behavior
3. Poolesville, Maryland

PHS-ADAMHA-NIMH
Individual Project Report
July 1, 1974 through June 30, 1975

Project Title: Neural substrate of mirror display in squirrel monkey (Saimiri sciureus).

Previous Serial Number: M-LBEB-CN-1

Principal Investigators: Paul D. MacLean

Other Investigators: Robert E. Gelhard, Thalia D. Klosteridis, Levi Waters

Cooperating Units: None

Man Years

Total: 1.7
Professional: 0.3
Other: 1.4

Project Description:

This long-term study utilizes the innate display behavior of the squirrel monkey (1) for investigating forebrain mechanisms underlying species-typical, "prosematic" behavior and (2) identifying structures involved in the integration of the autonomic and somatic components of the display. Prosematic, meaning rudimentary signaling, refers to any kind of nonverbal signal -- vocal, bodily, chemical -- used by animals or human beings in communication. Previous experiments had shown that lesions of certain parts of the globus pallidus (M-LBEB-CN-1, 1973) or its projecting pathways (M-LBEB-CN-1, 1974) resulted in an enduring decline of the display. The present experiments attempt to identify the relative importance in the display of respective pallidal projections to the tegmental area and to n. ventralis anterior (VA) et lateralis (VL) of the thalamus.

The mirror display test for male gothic-type squirrel monkeys has been described in previous project reports (see M-NP-LI-17, 1964). After animals reach criterion in 30 or more trials small electrocoagulations are placed in different parts of the ventral thalamus, subthalamus and tegmentum.

Observations have been made on seven animals. Monkey X-4, in which bilateral lesions destroyed the rostral part of the thalamic fasciculus, as well as the adjacent part of VA, quickly recovered its ability to display. In monkey U-4 the symmetrical lesions involved a longer stretch of the thalamic fasciculus and adjacent parts of VA and VL, as well as the zona incerta and dorsal part of the ansa lenticularis. This animal, which failed to display for 8 months, eventually recovered near-perfect performance in 30 trials.

One animal (U-4) with an extensive lesion in the tegmental area showed greatly reduced general activity and never regained the capacity to maintain a normal body temperature. The medial tegmental area was spared on one side. On one occasion, this animal gave a full, but undirected, display when the rectal temperature was 92°F. (Parenthetically, the findings in this and two other animals indicate that the tegmental area rather than posterior hypothalamus, as traditionally taught, plays a more important role in heat-conserving mechanisms.)

Findings on one animal (T-4) revealed that if the diffuse part of the ansa projections are spared on one side, there may be a full recovery of the ability to display. Another animal (W-4) with bilateral lesions destroying the medial forebrain bundle and ventral diffuse part of the ansa (sparing its dorsal diffuse and compact parts) recovered the somatic manifestations of the display, but was unable to achieve full genital tumescence. On the basis of our previous observations the latter finding can be attributed to destruction of the medial forebrain bundle.

The brains of two animals (Y-4 and Z-4), in which attempts were made to cut, respectively, the thalamic fasciculus and tegmental projections, have not yet been examined.

Although further control experiments must be performed, the present findings, together with preceding observations on the effects of various thalamic lesions, suggest that the pallidal projections to the tegmentum are more important than those to the ventral thalamus for the expression of complex forms of species-typical behavior.

Human communicative behavior can be classified as verbal and nonverbal. Many forms of human nonverbal behavior show parallels to prosematic behavioral patterns of animals. The present experiments provide further evidence that evolutionary derivations of systems of the forebrain found in reptiles and lower mammals are of fundamental importance in the expression of complex forms of species-typical, prosematic behavior.

Key Word Descriptors: Squirrel monkey, Saimiri sciureus, globus pallidus, ansa lenticularis, thalamic fasciculus, N. ventralis anterior, N. ventralis lateralis, tegmental area, species-typical behavior.

Honors and Awards:

1) Invited Speaker: "Three Mentalities of the Brain," Scientific Session of the Washington Psychiatric Society, Georgetown University, Washington, D.C., October 10, 1974.

2) Invited Speaker: "Coping With Our Three Mentalities," Senior Seminar in Foreign Policy, The National Institutes of Health, Stone House, December 17, 1974.

3) Invited Speaker: "The Striopallidal Complex and Species-Typical Behavior," Society for Neuroscience, NIH, Building 36, January 14, 1975.

4) Invited Speaker: "The Brain's Three Mentalities," Woodrow Wilson International Center for Scholars, Smithsonian Institution Building, Washington, D.C., February 11, 1975.

5) Invited Lecturer: "Evolution of the Brain and Behavior," Department of Psychiatry, Rutgers University College of Medicine and Dentistry, New Brunswick, New Jersey, March 12, 1975.

6) Invited Lecturer: "The Human Counterpart of Reptilian Forebrain," Department of Psychiatry, U.S. Naval Medical Center, Bethesda, Maryland, March 26, 1975.

7) Invited Lecturer: "Brain Structures Involved in Species-Typical Displays of Squirrel Monkeys," Behavioral Sciences Seminar, The Rockefeller University, New York, New York, May 22, 1975.

Publications:

MacLean, P.D.: The triune brain. Medical World News/ Psychiatry, October, 1974, 2: 55-60.

MacLean, P.D.: Bases neurologiques du comportement d'imitation chez le singe-ecureuil. In Morin, E. and Piatelli-Palmarini, M. (eds.): L'UNITE DE L'HOMME: Invariants Biologiques et Universaux Culturels, Paris, Editions du Seuil, 1974, pp. 186-212.

MacLean, P.D.: Sensory and perceptive factors in emotional functions of the triune brain. In Levi, L. (ed.): Emotions - Their Parameters and Measurement, New York, Raven Press, 1975, pp. 71-92.

MacLean, P.D.: Brain mechanisms of elemental sexual functions. In Freedman, A.M., Kaplan, H.I. and Sadock, B.J. (eds.): Comprehensive Textbook of Psychiatry. Baltimore, The Williams & Wilkins Company, 1975, Vol. 2, pp. 1386-1392.

MacLean, P.D.: Brain mechanisms of primal sexual functions and related behavior. In Sandler, M. and Gessa, G.L. (eds.): Sexual Behavior: Pharmacology and Biochemistry. New York, Raven Press, 1975, pp. 1-11.

MacLean, P.D.: An ongoing analysis of hippocampal inputs and outputs: Microelectrode and anatomic findings in squirrel monkeys. In Isaacson, R.L. and Pribram, K.H. (eds.): The Hippocampus. New York, Plenum Publishing Corporation, (in press).

MacLean, P.D.: The imitative-creative interplay of our three mentalities. In Harris, H. (ed.): Astride The Two Cultures. London, Hutchinson Publishing Group Ltd., (in press).

MacLean, P.D.: On the evolution of the three mentalities. In Washburn, S.L. and Dolhinow, P. (eds.): Perspectives on Human Evolution. New York, Holt, Rinehart and Winston, Inc., (in press).

MacLean, P.D.: Role of pallidal projections in species-typical display behavior of squirrel monkey. Trans. Amer. Neurol. Assoc., 100, 1975, (in press).

Serial No. Z01 MH 00852-02 LBEB
1. Laboratory of Brain Evolution and Behavior
2. Section on Comparative Neurophysiology and Behavior
3. Poolesville, Maryland

PHS-ADAMHA-NIMH
Individual Project Report
July 1, 1974 through June 30, 1975

Project Title: Seasonal incidence of "fatted state" in caged roman-type squirrel monkeys (Saimiri sciureus)

Previous Serial Number: M-NP-LI-17, 1964

Principal Investigators: Robert E. Gelhard and Paul D. MacLean

Other Investigator: Levi Waters

Cooperating Units: None

Man Years

Total:	0.3
Professional:	0.05
Other:	0.25

Project Description:

Several years ago (see M-NP-LI-17, 1964) it was shown in this laboratory that two varieties of squirrel monkeys could be distinguished on the basis of the arch-shaped circumocular patch. The ones with the peak- and round-shaped patches, respectively, were informally referred to as gothic and roman-type monkeys. In 1967 DuMond and Hutchinson reported that roman-type monkeys developed a "fatted state" associated with the spermatogenic phase during the mating season from December through March. Since 1963 our laboratory has had a colony of roman-type monkeys that have been weighed every one or two weeks. The present report represents a follow-up of a previous analysis of yearly weight variations described in Project Report M-NP-LI 42, 1970.

The findings for the year 1963 to 1972 are based on the weights of five roman-type male squirrel monkeys housed with two or more females in four connecting cages. One male died in late December, 1971. The light cycle approached that of the out-of-doors.

As shown in Figure 1, between 1962 and 1965 the times of highest (H) and lowest (L) average weights shifted to February and August, possibly reflecting the change in the animals' habitat from the southern to the northern hemisphere. Since then the average highest weights have most often occurred in January or February, while the lowest average weights have been recorded either during July or August.

<u>Figure 1</u>

Years	Nov	Dec	Jan	Feb	Mar	Apr	May	Jun	Jul	Aug	Sep	Oct
1. '62-'63									H			L
2. '63-'64				H							L	
3. '64-'65				H						L		
4. '65-'66				H						L		
5. '66-'67		H							L			
6. '67-'68			H						L			
7. '68-'69				H					L			
8. '69-'70	H								L			
9. '70-'71				H						L		
10. '71-'72					H					L		
11. '72-'73					H					L		
12. '73-'74			H						L			
13. '74-'75			H									

Months

DuMond and Hutchinson reported that the "fatted state" and mating season occurred during the dryness of winter, while the birth season coincided with the wet summer months. In a parallel manner the average peak and lowest weights for our animals occurred, respectively, during the months with the lowest and highest humidity.

Since a long-term study on neural mechanisms of display behavior in squirrel monkeys is being conducted in this laboratory, it is important for purposes of control to take into consideration all the various factors that may influence the incidence of display during the course of the year (see Progress Report Z01 MH 00753). The present project will be concluded with the publication of the results for the 13 continuous years of observation.

Keyword Descriptors: Squirrel monkey, <u>Saimiri sciureus</u>, mating season, breeding season, "fatted state".

Serial No. Z01 MH 00853-02 LBEB
1. Laboratory of Brain Evolution and Behavior
2. Section on Comparative Neurophysiology and Behavior
3. Poolesville, Maryland

PHS-ADAMHA-NIMH
Individual Project Report
July 1, 1974 through June 30, 1975

Project Title: Seasonal variation of mirror display in gothic-type squirrel monkeys (*Saimiri sciureus*).

Previous Serial Number: M-NP-LI-43

Principal Investigators: Robert Gelhard and Paul D. MacLean

Other Investigators: Levi Waters

Man Years

Total:	0.3
Professional:	0.05
Other:	0.25

Project Description:

In a long-term investigation on neural mechanisms of species-typical, mirror display behavior of squirrel monkeys we employ animals that display in 80 percent or more of 30 trials. The present report brings up to date an analysis of the seasonal incidence of the display that was described in Project M-NP-LI-43, 1969.

The mirror display test for gothic-type squirrel monkeys was described in Project Report M-NP-LI-17, 1964. Since the previous analysis the number of animals with 30 or more preoperative trials has increased from 75 to 113. The results show that 80 percent or more of the animals (70 percent in the previous analysis) display in 80 percent or more of the trials. Fifty-seven percent of the animals displayed at the 100 percent level, and 73%percent displayed at or above the 90 percent level.

March proved to be the poorest month for display, with 55 percent of the animals failing to reach criterion of 80 percent. A graph showed that from March on there was almost a steady increase in the percentage of animals reaching criterion, with peak performance occurring in January, when 95 percent of the tested animals reached criterion. These results provide an interesting comparison with those in the preceding project (see Z01 MH 00852) pertaining to the seasonal "fatted state" in roman-type monkeys.

Because of the long-term investigation being conducted in this laboratory on neural mechanisms of species-typical display behavior of gothic-type squirrel monkeys, it is important to have as much information as possible about factors other than the surgical intervention that may affect the incidence of the display. A retrospective analysis shows that in most of the few cases in which postoperative testing was conducted during the months of poorest expected performance, there was no statistically significant difference between pre- and postoperative scores.

Keyword Descriptors: Squirrel monkey, Saimiri sciureus, species-typical behavior.

Serial No. Z01 MH 00854-02 LBEB
1. Laboratory of Brain Evolution and Behavior
2. Section on Comparative Neurophysiology and Behavior
3. Poolesville, Maryland

PHS-ADAMHA-NIMH
Individual Project Report
July 1, 1974 through June 30, 1975

Project Title: Reptilian forebrain mechanisms of complex species-typical behavior. II. Ethograms of *Anolis carolinensis* and *Agama agama*.

Previous Serial Number: M-LBEB-CN-30

Principal Investigator: Neil B. Greenberg

Other Investigators: Leland Ferguson, Mary Lee Peter, Michael Mackay, and Pamela Holberton

Cooperating Units: None

Man Years

Total:	2.1
Professional:	0.3
Other:	1.8

Project Description:

Recent histochemical techniques have made it possible to identify corresponding structures of the forebrain in reptiles, birds, and mammals. Of existing reptiles, the behavior of lizards is believed to be most similar to that of mammal-like reptiles which were the forerunners of mammals. The aim of the present project is to obtain a complete behavioral inventory of the behavior of the common green lizard (*Anolis carolinensis*) and the rainbow lizard (*Agama agama*) as a necessary background for brain and behavior studies.

One group of Anolis was maintained in a 55 gallon terrarium providing a substratum, perches, visual barriers like those of a natural habitat, as well as controlled temperature and humidity. For standardizing pre- and postoperative tests of display behavior, 14 double cages divided by removable opaque and clear panels were used for making observations on a dominant male and two subdominant lizards in each compartment (see

Z01 MH 00856). Agama lizards were maintained in a 1 x 3 meter habitat designed to simulate diurnal changes in light and heat. The enclosure was equipped with two devices for automatic dispensing of prey-type food without the intrusion of a human attendant. Observations were made through a one-way mirror and by closed-circuit television. Observations were recorded on television tape, motion picture film, and by means of a computer-facilitated event recorder (see Z01 MH 00858).

About 50 hours of closed-circuit video tapes have been edited. Seventy-two discrete postures and movements have been identified in the Anolis and 69 in the Agama lizard. Some of the behavioral patterns that have not been described in the literature include (1) social grooming and burrowing in the Anolis and (2) the use of the tongue in displays and interactions of the Agama lizards, as well as (3) circling and tail-lashing under conditions of challenge. Social feeding has turned out to be a significant behavioral pattern exhibited by both species. These lists of behaviors will serve as the necessary background for a computer analysis of 40 hours of observations coded by means of the computer-facilitated event recorder.

Complete behavioral inventories are not only of value for comparative studies but also for identifying changes following experimental intervention on the brain that otherwise might be overlooked.

Key Word Descriptors:

Reptile, lizard, Agama agama, Anolis carolinensis, ethogram, behavior.

Honors and Awards: None

Publications: None

Serial No. Z01 MH 00855-01 LBEB
1. Laboratory of Brain Evolution and Behavior
2. Section on Comparative Neurophysiology and Behavior
3. Poolesville, Maryland

PHS-ADAMHA-NIMH
Individual Project Report
July 1, 1974 through June 30, 1975

Project Title: Reptilian forebrain mechanisms of complex species-typical behavior. III. Stereotaxic atlas of the anolis brain (*Anolis carolinensis*).

Previous Serial Number: None

Principal Investigators: Neil B. Greenberg and Paul D. MacLean

Other Investigators: Thalia Klosteridis and Leland Ferguson

Cooperating Units: Technical Development

Man Years

Total:	0.8
Professional:	0.35
Other:	0.45

Project Description:

Observations made in this laboratory indicate that the common green lizard (Anolis carolinensis) would be a suitable type of lizard for brain and behavioral studies (see M-LBEB-CN-30, 1974 and Z01 MH 00854-02 LBEB). For such work it has been necessary to prepare a stereotaxic atlas of the forebrain.

A stereotaxic headholder has been adapted from an instrument used for small mammals. The modification provides a bite plate that establishes the reference horizontal plane along the same line as the roof of the mouth. The centering ear bars are rubber-tipped so as not to injure the tympanic membrane. Since refrigeration is used to obtain anesthesia, the instrument is provided with an adjustable tray for packing the lizard's body in ice. Serial frozen sections of the brain in the three standard planes are obtained after formic acid decalcification of the cranium with the brain *in situ*. Alternate sections are stained for cells and fibers.

It is desirable to have a series of about 30 brains for estimating variations in brain size and location of the commissures used as references. To date, the series includes 7 brains cut either in the frontal or sagittal plane. Twelve brains of other species have been prepared for comparative purposes. The forebrain of the anolis lizard is characterized by a reduction in the lateral (piriform) cortex; a large collection of large and small cells, respectively, in the lateral and medial parts of the dorsal ventricular ridge; and no distinct nucleus sphericus (a structure associated with the vomeronasal nerve) in the amygdala.

In the continuation of this project we hope to prepare an accompanying atlas showing the distribution of cells and terminals of the three known aminergic systems of the brain.

Keyword Descriptors:

Reptile, Anolis carolinensis, lizard, forebrain, paleostriatum, amygdala, stereotaxic atlas.

Honors and Awards: None

Publications: None

Serial No. Z01 MH 00856-01 LBEB
1. Laboratory of Brain Evolution and Behavior
2. Section on Comparative Neurophysiology and Behavior
3. Poolesville, Maryland

PHS-ADAMHA-NIMH
Individual Project Report
July 1, 1974 through June 30, 1975

Project Title: Reptilian forebrain mechanisms of complex, species-typical behavior. IV. The role of the paleostriatum.

Previous Serial Number: None

Principal Investigators: Neil B. Greenberg and Paul D. MacLean

Other Investigators: Leland Ferguson and Thalia Klosteridis

Cooperating Units: None

Man Years

Total: 1.2
Professional: 0.5
Other: 0.7

Project Description:

Previous work in this laboratory has shown that the striatal complex of the forebrain is fundamentally involved in the species-typical display behavior of squirrel monkeys (see Z01 MH 00851). Histochemical studies have been valuable in identifying corresponding parts of the striatal complex in mammals and reptiles. The aim of the present study is to test the effects of lesions of the paleostriatum on the species-typical display behavior of the common green lizard.

Subjects for these experiments live in two-compartment cages divided by removable opaque and clear panels. Each compartment contains one male dominant and two subdominant lizards. When the opaque divider is removed, the dominant males on each side engage in aggressive displays characterized by "head-bobbing," "pushups," elevation of the nuchal crest, lateral compression of the body, and extension of an orange colored throat fan. The incidence of the various components of the display are recorded during 10 minute sessions for several weeks prior to and following surgery. A modified Horsley-Clarke apparatus described in Z01 MH 00855 is used to insert electrodes or micropipettes, respectively, for making electrically or chemically induced lesions.

Twenty-five animals were used for standardizing the operative techniques. Because of the tendency of the small lizard brain to displacement when probed, it was necessary to devise especially fine electrodes and pipettes, as well as a method for vibrating them into the brain without the displacement of tissue. Since application of constant anodal current tends to result in elongated lesions, it has proved preferable to make electrocoagulations by high frequency current. To date control observations have been made on animals with lesions in different parts of the forebrain. No significant changes in behavior have been observed. Unilateral or small asymmetrical lesions in the paleostriatum have resulted in no enduring deficit.

Because of the almost complete crossing of the optic tract in the lizard's brain, we have a promising method which involves placing a lesion on one side of the paleostriatum and then testing the lizard's behavior with and without an eye patch on the same side as the lesion. This method has the potential advantages that (1) it should result in no disturbance of thermoregulation; (2) it circumvents the difficulty of producing absolutely symmetrical lesions; and (3) it allows a normal side for histological comparison both with the routine stains and stains for tracing degeneration. In the one animal that has so far been tested in this manner, there was an absence of display only when the eye on the operated side was covered. It had been shown preoperatively that this animal displayed with equal vigor when wearing an eye patch.

The present investigation, which is to be continued, promises to give important comparative information about the striatal complex, the functions of which have defied analysis for more than 150 years.

Key Word Descriptors:

Reptile, lizard, forebrain, paleostriatum, behavior.

Honors and Awards: None

Publications: None

Serial No. Z01-MH-00857-01 LBEB
1. Laboratory of Brain Evolution and Behavior
2. Section on Comparative Neurophysiology
3. Poolesville, Maryland

PHS-ADAMHA-NIMH
Individual Project Report
July 1, 1974 through June 30, 1975

Project Title: Role of pallidal projections in species-typical behavior of canids.

Previous Serial Number: None

Principal Investigators: Michael R. Murphy and Paul D. MacLean

Other Investigators: Richard J. Radna, Stephen C. Barker, Thalia Klosteridis, and Wayne Fenton

Cooperating Units: Technical Development and Ungulate Unit, Animal Center Section, VRB, NIH

Man Years:

Total:	0.45
Professional:	0.25
Other:	0.2

Project Description:

Investigations conducted in this laboratory have revealed that bilateral lesions of the pallidal portion of the striatal complex or distruction of its main pathways may eliminate the species-typical display of squirrel monkeys (see Z01-MH-00851). Canids may prove valuable in a further analysis of striatal functions because they demonstrate not only species-typical, but also breed-typical behaviors. The purpose of the present experiments is to section the ansa lenticularis in immature canids and then to observe the capacity of members of a particular breed to develop their usual behavioral repertoire.

A stereotaxic device is used for inserting electrodes into structures to be electrocoagulated. Anesthesia is achieved by administering a gas mixture of oxygen, nitrous oxide, and halothane through a tracheal cannula. Cannulation is performed with the animal anesthetized by Surital, a short acting barbiturate. The postoperative administration of ampicillin for 7 to 10 days has proved effective in preventing infection.

Operations have been performed on 6 dogs ranging in age from 4 to 6 months. It became evident from the results in the first 3 animals that one could not depend on available stereotaxic atlases for correct placement of electrodes. The lesions proved to be either too far rostral or too far caudal. It was shown that skull films made it possible to introduce electrodes in the desired frontal plane. Consequently a plastic stereotaxic headholder was constructed for obtaining preoperative cranial measurements by X-Ray and will be used in future experiments.

The animals in which the lesions failed to involve the ansa lenticularis will serve as valuable controls, particularly one animal in which bilaterally symmetrical lesions of the medial forebrain bundle were just ventral to the ansa. None of the animals showed significant behavioral changes.

The striatal complex constitutes a large central mass in the forebrain of all mammals. The traditional clinical view that it serves as a part of the motor systems is not supported by findings that large bilateral lesions may result in no motor deficits. As already mentioned, previous work in this laboratory supports the hypothesis that it plays a fundamental role in species-typical behavior. Its high content of cholinesterase, dopamine, and serotonin, together with its special capacity to bind opiates, make the striatum of unusual interest with respect to psychotropic agents. There is evidence that it may be implicated in amphetamine psychosis.

This project is to be continued.

Keyword Descriptors: Corpus striatum, caudate nucleus, globus pallidus, ansa lenticularis, cholinesterase, dopamine, serotonin, amphetamine, opiate receptors, putamen, biogenic amines.

Serial No. Z01-MH-00858-01 LBEB
1. Laboratory of Brain Evolution and Behavior
2. Section on Comparative Neurophysiology and Behavior
3. Poolesville, Maryland

PHS-ADAMHA-NIMH
Individual Project Report
July 1, 1974 through June 30, 1975

Project Title: The development of a computer assisted behavioral event recorder.

Previous Serial Number: None

Principal Investigators: Richard J. Radna and Neil B. Greenberg

Other Investigators: Michael W. Mackay

Cooperating Units: None

Man Years:

Total:	0.5
Professional:	0.3
Other:	0.2

Project Description:

The aim of this project is to create a behavioral event recording system in which data acquisition and storage are assisted by a high speed digital computer. Heretofore available systems for this purpose are deficient in one or more of the following features which are necessary for broad-based behavioral analysis: recording events as they occur; preserving the sequence and times of their occurrence; transcribing data rapidly into intelligible form; preserving the data in a form amenable to both preliminary and complete data reduction.

The DCRT IBM 370/168 computer was utilized for program development and implementation, through access by a 2741 telecommunication terminal located on site at our laboratory. The event recording system thereby developed uses the resident FORTRAN compiler, assembler and TSO (Time Sharing Option).

The most substantive results of this project reside in the form of the developed system which most efficiently accomplishes the ends noted above. The following is a brief account of our present system:

The main routine is a FORTRAN program which accepts in real time up to twenty-two 2 character codes initiated from the 2741 terminal when carriage return (C/R) is activated. Each 2 character code is unique for an animal's name, behavior or location. Each time C/R is hit, an assembly language routine ascertains the real time to .01 seconds, and all the data with its time and format information is written on a magnetic disk located at the central facility. At the end of the observation session, all data is transferred to a magnetic tape, an index to which is automatically maintained. Most critical, under this system the integrity of all data is guaranteed since it is recorded on a magnetic disk with the input of each new data line. A series of routines have been developed which readily retrieve data on tape. The most recent session's data can be retrieved into a WYLBUR (resident text editor) active area by a straight-forward "use" command.

Thus, behavioral data can be simply entered into a flexible and powerful system, and stored in a form which is readily accessible and thereby convenient for data analysis. This system has wide applicability to behavioral research and will be made available for distribution to interested groups.

It is proposed that this project be continued with the aims of facilitating behavioral research at the LBEB, and of editing the system into a form most suitable for use by other workers.

Keyword Descriptors: Behavioral event recorder, computer.

Serial No. Z01-MH-00859-01 LBEB
1. Laboratory of Brain Evolution and Behavior
2. Section on Comparative Neurophysiology and Behavior
3. Poolesville, Maryland

PHS-ADAMHA-NIMH
Individual Project Report
July 1, 1974 through June 30, 1975

Project Title: A quantum theoretical study of the molecular electronic structure of cholinesterase antagonists.

Previous Serial Number: None

Principal Investigator: Richard J. Radna

Other Investigators: None

Cooperating Units: None

Man Years:

Total: .3
Professional: 0.2
Other: 0.1

Project Description:

The aim of this study is to characterize on quantum theoretical grounds the structural chemical properties of a series of compounds which are active at cholinesterase receptors. These compounds are: physostigmine, edrophonium, neostigmine, pyridine aldoxime methiodide and carbamoyl-beta-methyl-choline. Specifically it is intended to ascertain whether conformational, electronic or stereospecific factors are involved in determining the biological effects of the above compounds.

The conformational stability of each compound is calculated using approximate self-consistent field molecular orbital theory at the INDO (intermediate neglect of differential overlap) level of approximation. For each geometry of a cholinesterase antagonist studied, atomic charge densities, molecular dipole, and molecular volume are also generated. Data reduction is assisted by computer graphics.

None of the compounds considered herein is conformationally excluded from the cholinesterase agonist configuration proposed by Chothia and Pauling. All compounds have analogs of acetylcholine's quaternary nitrogen and carbonyl oxygen separated by a distance close to 4.8 A. Variation in atomic charge densities among compounds in analogous conformations exists, but by itself cannot explain differences in activity. Thus, based on these data, it appears that charge density and stereospecificity govern the activity of the compounds considered.

The present study provides one of the few means by which the structural chemistry of neural receptors may be approached. The quantum theoretical approach to receptors via the study of their substrates is particularly of value since cholinergic receptors have not been purified in a form which is amenable to detailed structural analysis. The understanding of the structural chemistry of cholinergic systems is basic not only to neural receptor theory, but also to clinical pharmacology.

It is proposed that this project be continued with the specific aim of studying the environmental effects of water solvation on conformational stability in the above compounds.

Keyword Descriptors: Cholinesterase antagonists, quantum chemistry, receptor theory.

Serial No. Z01-MH-00860-01 LBEB
1. Laboratory of Brain Evolution and Behavior
2. Section on Comparative Neurophysiology and Behavior
3. Poolesville, Maryland

PHS-ADAMHA-NIMH
Individual Project Report
July 1, 1974 through June 30, 1975

Project Title: Unit analysis of vagal inputs to the amygdala and hippocampus.

Previous Serial Number: None

Principal Investigators: Richard J. Radna and Paul D. MacLean

Other Investigators: Patrick J. Carr and Thalia D. Klosteridis

Cooperating Units: None

Man Years:

Total	2.05
Professional:	0.8
Other:	1.25

Project Description:

The present study is part of a continuing investigation concerned with the nature and mechanism of action of intero- and exteroceptive inputs to the limbic system. In two preceding studies vagal volleys affected the activity of about 20 percent of units in the cingulate cortex (M-LBEB-CN-2) and certain intra- and paralaminar nuclei of the thalamus (M-LBEB-CN-15). The aim of the present study is to test the effects of vagal volleys on unit activity of the hippocampus and amygdala.

Extracellular unit activity is recorded with theta-glass micropipettes (5-15 megaohms) in awake, sitting squirrel monkeys prepared with a chronically fixed stereotaxic platform. A bipolar, concentric, stainless steel stimulating electrode is implanted in the portal of the jugular foramen next to the vagus and glossopharyngeal nerves. The hypoglossal and accessory nerves are sectioned.

As an addition to our other data reduction techniques, a Fortran IV program which accepts digitized unit activity, and generates a surface of unit activity as a function of amplitude and time has been developed. This and related computer graphic routines are presently implemented on the IBM 370/168 in pilot form.

To date, 22 tracks have been explored in three animals. In the one case in which the histological examination has been completed, 30 of the recorded units proved to be in the amygdala and hippocampus. Two hippocampal units were responsive to vagal volleys, one at 20 msec and the other at 600 msec. In some experiments vagal volleys sporadically evoked slow-wave potentials in the amygdala and hippocampus, with latencies ranging from 18 to 27 msec and amplitudes of 0.6 - 3.0 mv.

Clinical and experimental findings have revealed that parts of the amygdala and adjoining hippocampus exert a profound influence on cardiorespiratory and alimentary functions. The present study is designed to provide information now lacking in regard to interoceptive influences on the hippocampus and amygdala. The project is to be continued until a sufficiently large sample of units has been tested.

Keyword Descriptors: Amygdala, hippocampus, unit activity, visceral afferents, vagus nerve.

Serial No. Z01 MH 00861-01 LBEB
1. Laboratory of Brain Evolution and Behavior
2. Section on Comparative Neurophysiology and Behavior
3. Poolesville, Maryland

PHS-ADAMHA-NIMH
Individual Project Report
July 1, 1974 through June 30, 1975

Project Title: Neural basis of olfactory control of sexual behavior in the Syrian hamster (Mesocricetus auratus).

Previous Serial Number: None

Principal Investigator: Michael R. Murphy

Other Investigator: Patricia L. Maykuth

Cooperating Units: None

Man Years

Total:	1.45
Professional:	.40
Other:	1.05

Project Description:

The mating behavior of hamsters is easily elicited and is vigorously displayed in a laboratory setting. Although this genetically constituted behavior pattern is not affected by most experimental manipulations or traumas, it is dependent on olfactory stimuli, being completely eliminated by impairment of the sense of smell. The secondary and tertiary projections of the olfactory bulbs reach many parts of the limbic forebrain and hypothalamus, areas that have been implicated in the regulation of social behavior. The objective of this study is to determine if specific central olfactory pathways are essential for the olfactory control of hamster sexual behavior.

For surgery a special headholder is used that eliminates the need for earbars that may damage the auditory system. Animals are anesthesized with a gas mixture of nitrous oxide, oxygen and halothane. The olfactory bulbs are removed by suction, and nerve tracts are cut with a small knife.

Among the new findings were those showing that (1) normal mating behavior occurs in hamsters with one olfactory bulb removed and destruction of both vomeronasal nerves (7 cases) and (2) normal mating behavior is possible following elimination of the main olfactory bulbs but sparing of the vomeronasal nerve and accessory olfactory bulbs. Most animals described here are still living.

In addition, it has been confirmed that (1) the total elimination of mating behavior follows bilateral olfactory bulb removal in male hamsters (5 cases); (2) unilateral olfactory bulb removal leaves mating behavior intact (9 cases); (3) unilaterally bulbectomized hamsters mating may be eliminated by blocking the nostril contralateral to the bulb removal (7 cases).

The delineation of specific pathways mediating olfactory control of hamster sexual behavior will increase our understanding of the mechanisms by which sensory information elicits genetically constituted behavior patterns. The identification of neural areas involved in the processing or transmission of socially relevant olfactory information should be of significance to behavioral researchers who use macrosmatic animals as experimental models.

This project will be continued.

Keyword Descriptors:

Olfaction, brain lesions, mating behavior, limbic system, vomeronasal system, hamsters.

Honors and Awards: None

Publications:

Murphy, M. R.: Olfactory impairment, olfactory bulb removal and mammalian reproduction. In Doty, R. L. (ed.): Mammalian Olfaction, Reproductive Processes, and Behavior. Academic Press, N. Y., (in press).

Serial No. Z01-MH-00862-01 LBEB
1. Laboratory of Brain Evolution and Behavior
2. Section on Comparative Neurophysiology and Behavior
3. Poolesville, Maryland

PHS-ADAMHA-NIMH
Individual Project Report
July 1, 1974 through June 30, 1975

Project Title: Sensory and possible non-sensory olfactory influences on courtship and copulation in female Syrian golden hamsters (*M. auratus*).

Previous Serial Number: None

Principal Investigator: Michael R. Murphy

Other Investigator: Patricia L. Maykuth

Cooperating Units: None

Man Years:

Total:	0.5
Professional:	0.15
Other:	0.35

Project Description:

In previous work it was found that bilaterally olfactory bulbectomized female hamsters tested 9 weeks following surgery displayed normal copulatory responses with a sexually active male hamster, but failed to show normal courtship behavior with a sexually inactive male. Because of the great importance of olfactory stimuli to hamster social behavior it was at first assumed that this change in behavior was due to the female's inability to perceive olfactory stimuli arising from the male. The first part of this study was designed to test this hypothesis by observing females in which olfactory impairment was produced peripherally.

Peripheral olfactory impairment was produced by removing one olfactory bulb and blocking the contralateral nostril. Courtship behavior was tested by observing a female hamster for 5 minutes in the presence of a non-copulating male hamster (a bilaterally olfactory bulbectomized male). The estrous cycle of experimental females was followed by checking their vaginal discharge.

Contrary to expectation, peripheral anosmia did not have an effect on courtship behavior (5 cases). In addition, a bilaterally bulbectomized female hamster, used as a control, displayed normal courtship during the first 3 weeks postoperatively. In her fourth postoperative week, however, this female stopped displaying courtship; she has continued to be non-courting through her 14th postoperative week. None of the unilaterally bulbectomized females has shown any changes in courtship through at least their 13th postoperative week. One female with bilateral section of the vomeronasal nerves has also shown no postoperative changes in behavior.

The tentative conclusion we reach is that the loss in courtship behavior that was found earlier to follow bilateral olfactory bulb removal was not due to the inability to perceive specific olfactory stimuli. The olfactory bulb, a complex neural structure with many efferent and afferent connections with the forebrain, has long been hypothesized to have modulatory and non-sensory functions. Our results, if confirmed, demonstrate the first unambiguous "non-sensory" effects of olfactory bulbectomy on mammalian reproduction.

This project will be continued.

Keyword Descriptors: Olfaction, olfactory bulbs, brain lesions, courtship, mating behavior, hamsters

Serial No. Z01-MH-00863-01 LBEB
1. Laboratory of Brain Evolution and Behavior
2. Section on Comparative Neurophysiology
3. Poolesville, Maryland

PHS-ADAMHA-NIMH
Individual Project Report
July 1, 1974 through June 30, 1975

Project Title: Sensory control of social preferences in female Turkish hamsters (M. brandti).

Previous Serial Number: None

Principal Investigator: Michael R. Murphy

Other Investigator: Patricia L. Maykuth

Cooperating Units: None

Man Years:

Total:	0.45
Professional:	0.1
Other:	0.35

Project Description:

In previous work it was found that female Turkish hamsters display strong social and sexual preferences of conspecific males over males of a different species. It was also discovered that these preferences could be made on the basis of olfactory stimuli alone. The current phase of this project deals with determining if olfactory stimuli are necessary to elicit such preferences.

Olfactory impairment is produced by removing one olfactory bulb and blocking the contralateral nostril with a surgical wound clip about 1 hour before testing. The control condition involves blocking the nostril ipsilateral to the bulb lesion. Tests are made on the day of estrus for 10 minutes; they consist of the female's free choice behavior between two confined males.

Two females have shown the expected results, displaying a choice for the conspecific when tested under the control condition, but showing little interest or preference when tested under the condition of olfactory impairment. A third female displayed normal preference under both conditions, acting as if she could still smell.

While the mating behavior of male rodents has been extensively studied, the courtship and sexual preferences of females has been neglected. Female Turkish hamsters seem an excellent choice for studies of the hormonal, neural and sensory control of these important behavioral patterns.

This project is to be continued.

Keyword Descriptors: Social preferences, mating behavior, female hamsters, olfaction

Serial No. Z01-MH-00864-01 LBEB
1. Laboratory of Brain Evolution and Behavior
2. Section on Comparative Neurophysiology
3. Poolesville, Maryland

PHS-ADAMHA-NIMH
Individual Project Report
July 1, 1974 through June 30, 1975

Project Title: Effects of apomorphine on the mating behavior of sexually "inactive" male hamsters (Mesocricetus auratus).

Previous Serial Number: None

Principal Investigator: Michael R. Murphy

Other Investigator: Patricia Maykuth

Cooperating Units: None

Man Years:

Total:	0.45
Professional:	0.1
Other:	0.35

Project Description:

Apomorphine, a putative activator of dopamine receptors, has been found to increase intraspecific aggression, mating behavior, and stereotyped activity in male rats. The purpose of the present study was to examine the effect of apomorphine on the sexual behavior of sexually "inactive" male hamsters.

The sexual behavior of male hamsters is tested in 5, 10 or 15 minute sessions. In tests of the action of apomorphine, males are placed with receptive females 15 to 30 minutes following the injection of 0.06 mg of apomorphine in 0.1 of physiological saline intraperitoneally.

Five male hamsters have been tested. Two males (Sy4 and Sy6) had mated before surgical removal of one olfactory bulb, an operation which usually has no effect on mating behavior. After surgery Sy4 mated in only 1 of 5 tests and Sy6 failed to mate in any of 5 tests. Following apomorphine, both males showed the same kind of mating behavior: In the first 5 minutes there was no copulation, but there was an abnormal amount of biting of the female's rump and vaginal area. In the second or third 5 minutes there was a considerable and often exaggerated degree of mating behavior. While a normal number of mounts and intromissions were exhibited, the patterning of these behavioral components seemed grossly irregular. In subsequent tests, given over many weeks after the first administration of apomorphine, both these males have exhibited normal mating behavior. Thus, one administration of apomorphine fully restored mating behavior.

Two other males (Dsl7 and Dsl9) obtained from a commercial breeder failed to show any copulatory responses in 2 - 10 minute mating tests. Such failure is not uncommon for a small percentage of commercially bred hamsters. The behavior of these two males after apomorphine was almost identical to that of Sy4 and Sy6. Also, Dsl7 and Dsl9 have continued to mate normally since the drug treatment.

Finally, a fifth animal (BOBl) which had failed to display any mating behavior in dozens of tests following bilateral olfactory bulbectomy, showed no apparent sexual manifestations after treatment with apomorphine.

The present findings provide further evidence that dopaminergic systems are involved in genetically constituted behavioral patterns. The effects of apomorphine on the mating behavior of hamsters appear to be much greater than those reported for rats. In this respect it should be emphasized that olfaction is required for the mating behavior of hamsters but not for rats. Since Devor's work suggests that olfactory bulb connections with the olfactory tubercle are crucial for sexual arousal in hamsters, it is significant that one component of the mesolimbic dopamine system projects to the olfactory tubercle.

This project will be continued.

Keyword Descriptors: Apomorphine, neuropharmacology, hamsters, mating behavior, olfaction, dopamine systems

Honors and Awards: None

Publications: None

Serial No. Z01-MH-00865-01 LBEB
1. Laboratory of Brain Evolution and Behavior
2. Section on Comparative Neurophysiology
3. Poolesville, Maryland

PHS-ADAMHA-NIMH
Individual Project Report
July 1, 1974 through June 30, 1975

Project Title: Neural substrate of the mating behavior of male hamsters (Mesocricetus auratus)

Previous Serial Number: None

Principal Investigators: Michael R. Murphy, Adeline T. Nunez

Other Investigator: Patricia L. Maykuth

Cooperating Units: None

Man Years:

Total:	0.45
Professional:	0.1
Other:	0.35

Project Description:

The aim of this project is to identify neural mechanisms of reproduction in male Syrian hamsters. As a first approach we are investigating the importance of three major brain tracts. Two of these, the stria terminalis and the stria medullaris, convey olfactory information to the hypothalamus and thalamus; the mating behavior of male hamsters is crucially dependent on olfaction. The third tract, the fornix, has been implicated in control of gonadal function.

The first part of this study involves a simultaneous section of the three tracts in question by chronically implanted blades (3 x 5 mm) 0.2 mm rostral to the bregma.

Two pilot animals have been tested before and after surgery. Except for occasional loss of balance during copulation, the mating behavior of these males appears to be normal. The brains have not yet been examined.

Mating involves components of behavior that are easily

studied and quantified and that can be characterized as genus-typical as well as species-typical. Although mating behavior is in part genetically constituted, it can be modified by experience. The relative importance of hormonal and environmental stimuli to mating can be studied separately. Investigations of the neural substrate of mating behavior will contribute to the knowledge of the role of specific structures of the brain in species-typical behavior.

This project is to be continued.

Keyword Descriptors: Mating behavior, reproduction, hamsters, brain lesions, limbic system, fornix, stria terminalis, stria medullaris.

Project No. Z01 MH 00781-10 LBEB
1. Laboratory of Brain Evolution and Behavior
2. Section on Comparative Bio-psychology
3. Poolesville, Maryland

PHS-ADAMHA-NIMH
Individual Project Report
July 1, 1974 through June 30, 1975

Project Title: Behavioral mathematics and logic of measurement

Previous Serial Number: M-LBEB-CB-8

Principal Investigator: Walter C. Stanley

Other Investigators: None

Cooperating Units: None

Man Years

Total:	.16
Professional:	.10
Other:	.06

Project Description:

The objective is to devise a logic and mathematics uniquely appropriate to the measurement of organismic behavior as it occurs in real space and real time, in natural as well as contrived settings.

Mathematical analyses are applied to the two fundamental issues in the scientific study of behavior: (1) the nature and measurement of behavioral change; and (2) the nature and measurement of the variables controlling behavioral change. Behavior, it is proposed can be measured by its capacity to fill time. The probability of a single behavioral occurrence may then be defined as its relative or proportional time-filling capacity, i.e., filled time divided by available time. The measure of filled time is h, the shortest time required for one occurrence of a member of the behavioral class of interest. Given h, the probability p of overall response occurrence is equal to the product of the number c of occurrences and h, divided by available time t; i.e., $p = ch/t$. As a first approximation and with certain simplifying assumptions, the measure of the strength of a variable controlling behavior is defined as equal to the time rate of change of the probability of behavioral occurrence during time intervals initially unfilled by such behavior.

Project No. Z01 MH 00781-10 LBEB

This conceptual analysis treats behavior directly as a scientific subject matter in its own right. It differs from approaches taken in natural (nontechnical) languages and in nonbehavioristic analyses where behavior is dealt with indirectly as "indexed" by its physical, experiential, and social products. The concepts and measuring techniques resulting from this project should contribute new approaches to the understanding and measurement of individual human behavior as it occurs in natural, therapeutic, and custodial settings. The analytic phase of the project has been terminated; the writing phase is now in progress. The latter will end with the publication of last year's analysis of the use of complex numbers in conflict situations and this year's analysis of the measurable time filling attributes of behavior and behavioral change.

Keyword Descriptors:

Measurement, behavioral measurement, logic of measurement, measurement of control of behavior, behavioral mathematics.

Honors and Awards: None

Publications: None

Project No. Z01 MH 00782-02 LBEB
1. Laboratory of Brain Evolution and Behavior
2. Section on Comparative Biopsychology
3. Poolesville, Maryland

PHS-ADAMHA-NIMH
Individual Project Report
July 1, 1974 through June 30, 1975

Project Title: Ontogeny of adaptive and maladaptive adjunctive behavior

Previous Serial Number: M-LBEB-CB-17

Principal Investigator: Walter C. Stanley

Other Investigators: Rodney M. Sewell, E. Faye Bacon, Stephen N. Lee, Gerson Grosfeld

Cooperating Units: None

Man Years

Total:	2.50
Professional:	.50
Other:	2.00

Project Description:

The aims of this project are to study adjunctive behavior in infant and adult animals. Adjunctive behavior may be defined as repeated behavior in a learning or performance situation other than that specifically required to obtain reinforcement. For example, infant dogs required to lift a key to obtain access to a milk containing nipple develop interfering adjunctive behaviors characterized by the immobilization of the tongue against the roof or the floor of the mouth. Adult dogs may excessively lick metallic parts of the apparatus or consume excessive amounts of water by licking on a water-containing fount. In both infants and adults an intermittent schedule of reinforcement is required for the expression of adjunctive behavior because it occurs only when conditioned behavior is weak. For example, on a fixed interval food reinforcement schedule of two minutes, only the first response emitted two minutes after the immediately previous food-reinforced response, is followed by food. This means that the probability of reinforcement is lowest (most distant) right after a reinforcement has occurred and becomes maximal two minutes later. Accordingly, adjunctive behavior is most likely to begin right after food reinforcement, and least likely to begin two minutes after a reinforcement.

This year four beagle puppies were removed permanently from the dam and bottle fed amounts of milk which were matched with amounts consumed by previously run subjects. Upon reaching nine months of age, each of the four puppies will be run in adult operant key lift conditioning, one session per day for five months. Event recorders will be used to collect data on key lifting and adjunctive water drinking; a time lapse video tape recorder, to collect data on other adjunctive behavior that might occur. Results from previously run dogs are being collated and analyzed. Data already collected are being collated for graphical and tabular presentation and for statistical evaluation.

The manner in which early experience may affect both learned and adjunctive behavior in adulthood should provide new ways of thinking about human behavior disorders. For example, it is possible that some human maladaptive behavior patterns have the functional properties of adjunctive rather than of directly reinforced behavior. If so, the behavior therapist must take this fact into account because only the latter (directly reinforced) behaviors have traditionally been presumed to be sensitive to change by behavior modifying techniques. This project will terminate on or before December, 1975.

Keyword Descriptors:

Adjunctive behavior, maladaptive behavior, operant behavior, early experience and adult behavior, behavioral development, dog.

Honors and Awards: Items pertaining to Dr. Stanley are as follows:

1) Invited Speaker: "Forms of Learning in the Young Dog," Sixth Annual Heart of the South Education Seminar on Dogs, sponsored by the Department of Comparative Medicine, University of Alabama, Birmingham, Alabama, August 10-11, 1974.

2) Attended as Committee Member a meeting of the American Psychological Association "Committee on Precautions and Standards in Animal Experimentation," Washington, D. C., October 5, 1974.

3) Editorial Consultant to Science for submitted article on coyote behavior, December, 1974.

4) Editorial Consultant to Animal Behaviour for submitted articles on the behavior of domestic and wild canids, January, 1975.

5) Invited Speaker: "Neonatal Canine Sucking in the Perspective of Comparative Behavior Analysis," in symposium held at the Biennial Meeting of the Society for Research in Child Development, Denver, Colorado, April 13, 1975.

6) Invited Reviewer of proposed continuation studies of canine behavioral and physiological functioning, Laboratory Animal Sciences Program, Animal Resources Branch, DRR, NIH, April, 1975.

Publications:

Stanley, W. C.: Motor abnormalities in infant dogs induced by intermittent oral stimulation. In Bosma, J. F. (Ed.): Fourth symposium on oral sensation and perception: development in the fetus and infant. U. S. Government Printing Office: Washington, D. C., 353-368, 1973.

Stanley, W. C., Barrett, J. E., and Bacon, W. E.: Conditioning and extinction of avoidance and escape behavior in neonatal dogs. J. of Comparative and Physiological Psychology. 87: 163-172, 1974.

Stanley, W. C., and Bacon, E. F.: Stimuli controlling maladaptive consummatory behavior in infant dogs. J. of Abnormal Psychology, 84: 151-158, 1975.

Project No. Z01 MH 00783-01 LBEB
1. Laboratory of Brain Evolution and Behavior
2. Section on Comparative Biopsychology
3. Poolesville, Maryland

PHS-ADAMHA-NIMH
Individual Project Report
July 1, 1974 through June 30, 1975

Project Title: Adjunctive intake of alcohol in an operant feeding situation

Previous Serial Number: None

Principal Investigator: Walter C. Stanley

Other Investigators: Rodney M. Sewell, E. Faye Bacon, and Stephen N. Lee

Cooperating Units: None

Man Years

Total:	1.93
Professional:	.30
Other:	1.63

Project Description:

This research has two aims. The first is to measure how much ethyl alcohol adult dogs will consume in a situation permitting the drinking of ethyl alcohol as behavior adjunctive to food-reinforced operant key lifting. The second is to assess the effect of this alcohol intake on proficiency in key lifting and other classes of behavior. Two adult beagles were trained in single daily sessions, 7 days per week, to lift a key and thus obtain 3.75 grams of dry food 40-60 times per day. Food delivery was contingent on a fixed interval (FI) 2 minute schedule, wherein, only the first key lift performed 2 minutes or more after the previously reinforced key lift was followed by food. The dogs were allowed water ad libitum in their home pens and received supplementary feedings to maintain their body weight at 75-80% of free feeding weight. Water was also available from a fount alongside the key in the operant chamber. As training progressed, the animals began to take separated drinks from the fount. This discrete drinking behavior was not required, hence it was adjunctive to the required key lifting.

When the adjunctive water drinking stabilized, solutions of successively increasing alcohol concentration (1, 2, 3, 5, 7% v/v etc.) were substituted for the water. The changes in concentration occurred approximately every ten days, until one dog drastically reduced its fluid intake (at 17% alcohol concentration) and the second dog ceased drinking (at 13% alcohol concentration). Aversiveness of taste was presumably the basis for rejection. The dogs were then exposed to alternating 10-day cycles of plain tap water vs. 8% alcohol availability from the fount. Finally, each dog was intragastrically intubated with 2.8 grams of ethyl alcohol per kilogram body weight, using a 16% v/v ethyl alcohol in tap water solution. After 15 minutes had elapsed the dog was placed in the operant chamber for a routine daily session of 40-60 food reinforcements.

Initially, the dogs displayed different amounts of water intake via adjunctive drinking in the operant chamber. The first dog consumed up to a full liter of tap water in a 2-hour session. The second dog confined itself to a modest 200-400 ml.. When alcohol was substituted for the water, the first dog continued to drink heavily and, as the alcoholic concentration increased, consumed up to 41 ml. of alcohol contained in an 11% v/v alcohol in tap water solution in a 2-hour session. It also displayed impaired key lifting performance as well as staggering and circling in the operant chamber. The second dog refused alcohol at weaker concentrations and showed no sustained dramatic reactions to its drinking. During the water-alcohol alternation phase of the study, both dogs key lifted more frequently than necessary during alcohol than during water, indicating a slight disinhibition of the supressed key lifting behavior by the alcohol. During the final (intubation) phase of the study, the heavy alcohol dose produced progressive motor incordination climaxed by relative immobility at about seventeen minutes after intubation (two minutes after placement in the operant chamber). Recovery from the motor deficit was correlated with a relatively high rate of key lifting, distress vocalization, and increased motor activity in both dogs.

In regard to the first aim of the study, which was to determine amount of adjunctive alcohol intake, only one dog clearly overindulged, but its overindulgence was transient. The second dog's adjunctive water and adjunctive alcohol intake remained moderate throughout the study. In regard to the second aim of the research, which was to assess the effect of alcohol on behavior, both dogs reacted to alcohol intake by increasing their operant key lifting, thus demonstrating a disinhibition of behavior suppressed by the fixed interval food reinforcement schedule. Perhaps the most important theoretical implication of the study was the fact that neither dog rejected outright the clearly aversive alcohol solutions and neither maintained excessive drinking. Rather, both dogs eventually exhibited only moderate drinking patterns, with only moderate consequences for their key lifting proficiency. These same consequences became grossly magnified only when the animals were intubated with a massive dose of alcohol. The project will terminate with publication of the data.

Keyword Descriptors:

Alcohol, beagles, dogs, operant conditioning, adjunctive behavior, drinking, reinforcement schedules, intubation.

Honors and Awards: None

Publications: None

Project No. Z01 MH 00784-01 LBEB
1. Laboratory of Brain Evolution and Behavior
2. Section on Comparative Biopsychology
3. Poolesville, Maryland

PHS-ADAMHA-NIMH
Individual Project Report
July 1, 1974 through June 30, 1975

Project Title: Paradoxical resistance to extinction of learned behavior in beagle dogs

Previous Serial Number: None

Principal Investigator: Walter C. Stanley

Other Investigator: Stephen C. Barker

Cooperating Units: None

Man Years

Total:	.18
Professional:	.05
Other:	.13

Project Description:

An instrumental reinforcer is any stimulus that follows behavior and increases the strength of subsequent occurrences of the behavior. When a reinforcer no longer follows the behavior, the behavior extinguishes. Previous findings on a person as a social reinforcer (Serial No. M-LBEB-7, FY 1973) indicated that omission of the person seated in the goal area of an L-alleyway did not generate the theoretically expected loss of learned running behavior in prejuvenile beagles that had occurred in African (barkless) basenjis (Bacon, W. E. & Stanley, W. C. Psychon. Sci. 2: 21-22, 1965). Instead, our research in beagles indicated that a No Person - No Person group ultimately ran to the goal area as fast as the Person - No Person group did. The purpose of the present project was to test the hypothesis that the pattern of behavior found in beagles, so contrary to that usually found, is specific to social reinforcement and thus would not be obtained with another class of reinforcer, such as food.

Ten beagles, eight weeks old at the start of training, were run in the project, half with a preferred moist dog food as the reinforcer in the goal area of the L-alleyway and half with no food in the goal area. After 25 trials (one per day, five days per week) the food was omitted in the Food - No Food Group and all animals were run thereafter with no food in the apparatus. Except for changes necessitated by use of food as a reinforcer, all details of training were the same as they had been in previous Person vs. No Person social reinforcement experiments. Mean reciprocals of running time (in seconds) X 100 averaged over blocks of five trials were as follows in the Food - No Food Group: 36.50, 67.99, 75.43, 75.17, and 75.98 during food; and 82.27, 69.88, 68.20, 74.81, and 59.90 during no food. In the No Food - No Food Group mean scores were: 17.88, 39.55, 53.11, 52.41, 57.16, 74.17, 68.59, 72.29, 68.73, and 63.47. The Food - No Food Group ran faster initially than the No Food Group did, as would be expected from the presence of the food reinforcer. However, the decrease in running speed of the Food - No Food group when the food was omitted was small in magnitude and the running speeds were comparable to those of the No Food - No Food group during the same block of trials. This pattern of data with a food reinforcer and its omission or absence is similar to that previously found for a passive person reinforcer and its omission or absence. Therefore, it is not the class of reinforcer (social vs. nutritional) in the goal area of the L-alleyway that determined the previous results with person reinforcement in beagle dogs. Because basenjis do extinguish when a passive person is omitted, the paradoxical resistance to extinction in beagles is an example of breed-typical behavior in canids. The project will terminate with publication of the data.

Keyword Descriptors:

Reinforcement, conditioning, extinction, breed-typical behavior, dog, alleyway behavior.

Honors and Awards: None

Publications: None

Project No. Z01 MH 00785-01 LBEB
1. Laboratory of Brain Evolution and Behavior
2. Section on Comparative Biopsychology
3. Poolesville, Maryland

PHS-ADAMHA-NIMH
Individual Project Report
July 1, 1974 through June 30, 1975

Project Title: Social responsiveness in young beagle dogs

Previous Serial Number: None

Principal Investigator: Walter C. Stanley

Other Investigator: Brenda Jeffers

Cooperating Units: None

Man Years

Total:	.13
Professional:	.05
Other:	.08

Project Description:

The objective of this project is to determine how much and how rapidly the social responsiveness of beagle puppies beyond the age of normal primary socialization could be changed by differential handling. Eleven 12 1/2 week-old puppies, (five from one litter and six from another) were randomly assigned to a small (20 X 20 ft.) or a large (20 X 80 ft.) outdoor living pen and to a positive or a negative interaction with a person. The interaction was conducted twice daily for 10 days. In the positive condition the experimenter allowed the puppies to approach and contact her. Interaction was gentle, playful, and nonaversive even if it became necessary to move the puppy. In the negative condition, the experimenter raised a rolled up newspaper, verbalized in a threatening manner, "get away," and pushed and prodded the puppy away with the newspaper, the aim being to make the puppy stay at least 20 ft. away from the experimenter. During the first 2 minutes of each session, the experimenter sat quietly and simply noted how soon each puppy first came in contact with her. The three "Small Pen - Positive" subjects needed on the average a total of 300 seconds to reach the experimenter over the 20 sessions; the two "Small Pen -

Negative" subjects, 1250 seconds; the three "Large Pen - Positive" subjects, 595 seconds; and the three Large Pen - Negative subjects, 1805 seconds. These findings are consistent with the expectations that more frequent contact with person would be engendered in small than in large pens, and by positive rather than negative treatment. These treatments, both well within the normal procedures allowed in the caretaking and research usage of experimental dogs, were remarkably effective in generating differential approach-to-person behaviors. These data and those related to the study on paradoxical resistance to extinction in beagle puppies (Z01 MH 00784-01 LBEB) agree in demonstrating again the remarkable sensitivity of young dogs' behavior to control by presence of people, as well as by the nature and conditions of person-dog interactions. The data also indicate that continuous effort must always be exercized when using dogs as subjects in behavioral studies to assure that the large effects of subtle handler variables do not mask the effects of other variables of interest. The project will terminate with the publication of the data.

Keyword Descriptors:

Socialization, social behavior, positive and negative reinforcement, dog, beagle.

Honors and Awards: None

Publications: None

Serial No. Z01 MH 00821-01 LBEB
1. Laboratory of Brain Evolution and Behavior
2. Section on Behavioral Systems
3. Poolesville, Maryland

PHS-ADAMHA-NIMH
Individual Project Report
July 1, 1974 through June 30, 1975

Project Title: Conceptual evolution of the rat

Previous Serial Number: M-LBEB-BS-8

Principle Investigator: John B. Calhoun, Ph. D.

Other Investigators: None

Cooperating Units: None

Man Years:

Total	2.0
Professional:	0.5
Other:	1.5

Project Description:

This study seeks to validate experimentally the central principle of evolution. This principle holds that any assembly of units forming a network of relationships with enhanced capacity to acquire, store, transform, and utilize information has greater probability of surviving.

The entire past year has been devoted to planning this study, including a six-year protocol of day-to-day procedure, and to the design of the habitat and special devices for automatically recording data and influencing behavior. Over the six-year projected length of the study the group size will be allowed to increase in steps from 12 to 24 to 48 to 96 in both a control and an experimental group. As the group size of the experimentals increases, each rat will be induced to assume cooperative roles in several subgroups. Each new subgroup will be composed of representatives of all the other subgroups. Thus the whole group will form a network of overlapping subgroups in which membership in each subgroup demands learning specialized collaborative roles. The total space-time-behavior-association history of every animal will be computer recorded. Visual observations of individual and social behavior will be integrated with the computer recordings for analysis. No opportunity for cooperative activity in social networks will be provided the controls. In situ testing of (a) capacity to cope with increasingly more complex conceptual tasks or situations and (b) ability to exhibit latent creative capacity will be conducted on both control and experimental subjects.

The anticipated results may be summarized as follows: In the designed environment, a group size of 12 will be near optimum for the controls. As the 8-fold increase in group size takes place among the controls, the members will gradually exhibit all the pathologies expected in the octagonal universe mouse study. At the maximum group size of 96, every rat's behavioral capacity will be so impaired as to preclude reproduction. On the basis of capacity to survive through sequential generations, the conceptual capacity of the controls will have been reduced to zero. In contrast, if our theory is correct, the experimentals at an 8-fold increase in density will exhibit no more than the mild pathologies that characterize individuals in an optimum group of 12. Furthermore, at the end of 5-6 years of the study, the conceptual capacity of the average experimental rat should have increased by a factor calculated to be 2.87.

In summary:

		Controls at end state1/	Controls and experimentals at beginning	Experimentals at end state
Group size		96	12	96
Pathology		Maximal	Minimal	Minimal
Conceptual capacity	Individual	0.26	1.0	2.87
	Group total	0.0	12	275

1/ At the end state of extreme crowding, conceptual capacity of control animals is anticipated to become restricted to the simplest basic demands for living related to ingestion and rest. All capacities for social communication and interaction will have been lost.

The term "conceptual capacity" is here used for comparative purposes to represent the total of all means whereby an individual or group becomes aware of surrounding environmental conditions and executes responses to them. The augmented individual conceptual capacity acquired through several generations of guided cultural learning in this study should be equivalent to the 50-60 million years of natural selection intervening between a mid-mammalian stage of evolution represented by the rat and that of the beginning great apes. Furthermore, since the social-brain network of 96 rats is much larger than that attained by any great apes; we can anticipate that the experimental rats in this setting may, as a group, exceed the adaptive capacities of any extant species of great ape despite the actual much less well developed biological brains of the individual rats.

We realize that theory underlying the hypothetical results is built by pyramiding diverse kinds of tested theory into successive stages of untried theory that subsumes the correctness of the intervening stages. If the final results approximate the hypothetical ones, we will have firmly established several principles of behavior, social organization and information processing that may have rather direct applicability to the human condition. These principles should enhance the likelihood that humanity can maneuver successfully through the phase shift in total organization of life that promises to transpire early in the next century as a several millenia trend of increase in human population likely will shift into a similarly long period of decline in numbers.

Anticipated duration: January 1, 1982.

Keyword Descriptors:

rats (Rattus norvegicus)
conceptual evolution
population
cooperation
communication
social organization
group dynamics
behavioral pathology
environmental design

Honors and Awards:

Calhoun gave the ten-minute theme setting presentation in the Public Broadcasting System, December 28, 1974, hour-long program on Human Reality. The other participants were Drs. Jonas Salk and Joel Elkes, and Mr. Roberto Rossellini.

Serial No. Z01 MH 00821-01 LBEB

Publications:

Calhoun, J.B.: The universal city of ideas. In: Richter, Rosemary (Ed.): The Conference Report, The Exploding Cities. London, The Sunday Times-U.N. Population Conference, 1974, pp. 301-306.

Calhoun, J.B.: Metascientific research. In: Human Needs, New Societies, Supportive Technologies, Collected Documents Presented at the Rome Special World Conference on Future Research. Vols. I - V. Rome, Institute of Research and Education in Futures Studies, 1974, Vol. III, pp. 128-157.

Serial No. Z01 MH 00822-01 LBEB
1. Laboratory of Brain Evolution and Behavior
2. Section on Behavioral Systems
3. Poolesville, Maryland

PHS-ADAMHA-NIMH
Individual Project Report
July 1, 1974 through June 30, 1975

Project Title: The ultimate behavioral pathology

Previous Serial Number: M-LBEB-BS-3

Principal Investigator: John B. Calhoun

Other Investigators: None

Cooperating Units: None

Man Years:

Total:	2.0
Professional:	0.5
Others:	1.5

Project Description:

This project seeks to gain an understanding of how the overcrowding that develops in an environment, replete with resources that fulfill physical needs, culminates in a dissolution of social organization in which all individuals are characterized by the ultimate behavioral pathology of inability to integrate complex stimuli or to execute complex behavior required for social communication and group survival.

The entire year has been spent continuing the analysis of the prior study and utilizing these analyses in planning the present study. Particular emphasis has been given to the design and construction of the environment which will house the population of mice from 1975-1979. This habitat is an octagonal universe 15 feet in diameter that will provide optimum space for eight groups of twelve adult mice. The peak population, before cessation of reproduction is anticipated to reach 800-1000. The environment is designed to permit more effective observation of interactions between adults and younger individuals during those critical times when inappropriate communication interferes with the maturation of adequate adult behavior.

Following completion of construction of the habitat,

the population will be initiated by four pairs of Balb C strain mice that have been reared in a comparably complex environment for four generations. One investigator will concentrate on the pre-weaning history to determine the character of change in maternal behavior from normality to infant abuse to rejection. Others will concentrate on the relationship between dissolution of social organization and the fragmentation of individual behavior to the transition to the pandemic state of failure of behavioral development.

This project proposes to establish an experimental model which permits evaluation of individual pathology -- behavioral and physiological -- whose origin is influenced by the degree of stability of social organization, structure of the physical environment, or degree of crowding. This animal model study should provide insight to problems on the human level such as autism, child abuse, behavioral fragmentation and deviance, crowding, group process, environmental design, social influence on tumor origin, and social modification of vitamin A metabolism, which may be anticipated to become more acute with further increase of the human population. Anticipated duration: January 1, 1980.

Keyword Descriptors:

environmental design
population dynamics
mice, Balb C strain
infant abuse
maternal behavior
social organization
behavioral fragmentation
tumor incidence
crowding
behavioral pathology

Serial No. Z01 MH 00881-19
1. Laboratory of Cerebral Metabolism
2. Section on Developmental Neurochemistry
3. Bethesda, Maryland

PHS-ADAMHA-NIMH
Individual Project Report
July 1, 1974 through June 30, 1975

Project Title: The mechanism of action of thyroxine and its relation to cerebral metabolism

Previous Serial Number: M-CM-DN-1

Principal Investigator: Louis Sokoloff, M.D.

Other Investigators: Patricia A. Roberts, Elaine E. Kaufman, Ph.D., Glenna G. Fitzgerald, Ph.D., John E. Kline, J. D. Brown, Esther L. Lewis, and Carolyn S. Cottingham

Cooperating Units: None

Man Years:

Total:	5.5
Professional:	2.25
Other:	3.25

Project Description:

This project is directed at the elucidation of the role of the thyroid hormone in the maturation and development of the brain and the influence of the hormone in the regulation of cerebral metabolic processes. A necessary intermediate objective is the determination of the molecular mechanisms of the physiological and biochemical actions of the thyroid hormone. Previous work in this project demonstrated a stimulating action of thyroid hormones on protein biosynthesis. The mechanism of this effect on protein synthesis and the biochemical basis of the physiological actions of the thyroid hormones is presently the primary focus of this project.

The effects of thyroid hormones on various enzyme activities and on radioactive amino acid incorporation into protein are examined in cell-free systems from various mammalian tissues, such as liver and brain and also in purified enzyme systems. Studies are occasionally carried out in vivo, in which the uptake of amino acids into protein in various tissues is measured in the intact animal or the effects of experimentally induced thyroid disease on various metabolic activities are examined. A wide variety of enzyme purification and assay procedures are employed. Enzymes are purified from brain or liver homogenates by detergent treatment, salt fractionation, gel adsorption and filtration, ion exchange chromatography, etc. Assays of enzyme activities utilize chemical analyses, spectrophotometric techniques, and Geiger-Mueller and liquid scintillation radioactivity measurements.

The major accomplishment of this project thus far has been the demonstration for the first time that thyroxine stimulates protein biosynthesis and that this effect is probably primary to many of the generally recognized physiological actions of the thyroid hormones. Thyroxine, administered in vivo or in vitro, stimulates amino acid incorporation into protein in cell-free rat liver preparations. Conversely, hypothyroidism induced by surgical thyroidectomy, results in a reduction in the rate of amino acid incorporation into protein in similar preparations, indicating that the thyroid effect on protein biosynthesis is tonically active and physiological.

The biochemical mechanism of the thyroxine stimulation of protein biosynthesis has been studied in considerable detail in in vitro systems. These studies have been carried out over a number of years and have demonstrated that the thyroxine stimulation of protein synthesis is exerted by two mechanisms. There is a direct effect on the translational activity of ribosomes leading to accelerated completion and release of newly-synthesized polypeptide chains followed, in vivo only, by an increased synthesis and accumulation of ribosomes, i.e., a transcriptional effect. The transcriptional effect is not a direct action of the hormone but a cellular response or compensation for some earlier effect. The early effect is the one most likely to lead to the elucidation of the primary mechanism of action of the thyroid hormones and is the one which has been of greatest interest to the Section.

The early translational effect on protein synthesis, has, however, also been found to be secondary to an even earlier direct, energy-dependent reaction between thyroxine and the mitochondrial components of the cell. A still unidentified product of this reaction which acts on the ribosomes to stimulate their translational activity has been found. Work has been continuing to isolate, purify, and identify this active factor. It is now known to be a small, dialyzable, heat-stable, acid-labile, anionic, organic, probably non-lipid substance. Continued work on it has increased the knowledge of its properties and narrowed the range of possibilities, but its exact identity remains to be established.

This research has already led to the explanation of the change in sensitivity to thyroid hormones which occurs in brain during development. The brain responds to thyroid hormones in a manner similar to other organs during the period of its development and maturation. Once mature, however, it loses its responsivity to the hormones. This change can be seen in the effects of thyroid hormones on oxidative metabolism, protein synthesis, etc.

One outcome of this project has been to show that the loss of sensitivity of the brain to thyroxine with development is the result of some change in the mitochondria so that they lose the ability to react with thyroxine and form the active factor responsible for the stimulation of protein synthesis.

During the past year attention has been directed at the nature of the reaction between thyroid hormones and the mitochondria and the changes produced in mitochondria in the course of the reaction. It has long been known that thyroid hormones cause swelling and structural changes in mitochondria. An interesting finding resulting from the present studies has been the fact that *in vitro* thyroid hormones cause a very rapid loss of pyridine nucleotides, particularly NAD^+ from the mitochondria of liver. Mitochondria of mature brain, which also fail to react with thyroid hormones in the preliminary reaction leading to stimulation of protein synthesis, fail to exhibit this hormonal effect on their NAD^+ content. The effect *in vitro* is so rapid that it precedes the effect on mitochondrial swelling and cannot, therefore, be a consequence of the structural changes in these organelles. That the effect, which was first observed with mitochondria *in vitro*, may have physiological significance is suggested by experiments in which a single injection of a very small dose of hormone *in vivo* leads to a significant reduction in the mitochondrial NAD^+ content. The time course of the effect *in vivo* is currently being determined, but results thus far indicate that the effect is already apparent by 12 hours after the dose of hormone; its earliest appearance may be much sooner, and it clearly precedes most of the metabolic effects *in vivo* attributable to thyroid hormones. This effect could have very broad implications. Actions of thyroid hormones are observed on very many metabolic processes in sensitive tissues. NAD^+ is a ubiquitous cofactor for many dehydrogenase reactions which are intimately involved at one point or another in most metabolic pathways. This action of thyroid hormones may, therefore, represent the basis for many subsequent effects of the hormone on a variety of processes.

The thyroid hormones promote the structural, functional, and biochemical maturation of the brain. In addition to the studies of the mechanism of action of the thyroid hormones, the Section has also been studying the nature of the biochemical changes which occur in the brain with maturation. A prominent developmental change in the brain is a rise in the level of mitochondrial enzymes involved in oxygen consumption and energy metabolism. One of these, D-β-hydroxybutyric dehydrogenase (BDH), was found in this Laboratory to rise with brain development just like other mitochondrial enzymes but, unlike these others, such as cytochrome oxidase and succinoxidase, to decline again gradually following weaning. Evidence has been obtained that the changes in the level of this enzyme in brain are, at least, in part related to nutritional factors, e.g., the high fat content of maternal milk. Hyperthyroidism shifts the developmental pattern in this enzyme to an earlier age (e.g., it causes a more rapid and earlier rise in the enzyme level in the brain, an earlier achievement of its peak level, and an earlier decline). In the course of these studies an interesting observation was made which might be a valuable model for the elucidation of the mechanism of action of thyroxine in mitochondria. Physiologically active thyroid hormones and their analogues were found in vitro to inhibit BDH activity at extremely low concentrations. The inhibition was found to represent a competitive inhibition by the hormone of the binding of the normal substrates, one of which is NAD^+, to the enzyme. The enzyme is membrane-bound in mitochondria. After considerable effort it has been solubilized and partially purified several-fold from both brain and liver. Efforts are continuing to achieve complete purification. The purified enzyme is to be used to study the mechanisms of the thyroxine-inhibition as well as the mechanisms of the regulation of the enzyme's activity through all its changes during postnatal maturation of the brain. It has already been found with the partially purified enzyme that the enzyme requires a phospholipid cofactor normally present in mitochondria for its activity. This cofactor has been identified as a species of lecithin which can be partially substituted for in vitro by commercial beef heart or egg lecithin. The natural cofactor has been partly purified, and progress has been made to identify the nature of its fatty acid composition. The dioleoyl-lecithin is the most active species examined, but the exact identity is still under investigation.

The Section has recently become interested in the function of this enzyme in the body. D-β-hydroxybutyric acid dehydrogenase catalyzes the reversible interconversion between D-β-hydroxybutyrate and acetoacetate, the two ketone bodies found primarily in the liver when fatty acid utilization is increased, as, for example, in diabetes, starvation, high-fat diet, and various states leading to ketosis. Acetoacetate is the primary ketone body formed from fat catabolism, and it is converted to D-β-hydroxybutyrate by the action of the enzyme. Once formed, however, D-β-hydroxybutyrate cannot be used directly in any of the tissues; it must first be converted back to acetoacetate by the action of the same enzyme. This raises the interesting question of what role the enzyme plays. Why does the body not utilize the directly formed acetoacetate rather than convert it first to D-β-hydroxybutyrate only to oxidize it back to acetoacetate again to utilize it? There is evidence in the literature to suggest that excessive concentrations of acetoacetate in the tissues may be toxic, particularly in brain which has recently been shown to utilize ketone bodies in direct proportion to their levels in the blood. It may be, therefore, that the role of the enzyme is protective to keep the acetoacetate concentrations low by storing it, in a sense, as D-β-hydroxybutyrate. It is noteworthy that there are several metabolic conditions characterized by ketosis and coma. Diabetic coma is one example, and recently Reye's Syndrome has been described. This is a frequently fatal disease of childhood which occasionally follows a viral infection, particularly influenza. It is characterized by fatty degeneration of the liver, ketosis, coma, and a high plasma level of small-chain fatty acids, particularly octanoic acid. It has recently been found in our laboratory that an intraperitoneal injection of octanoic acid causes coma; intravenous doses of the same magnitude have no such effect, suggesting that octanoic acid is not itself directly toxic to the brain but must first enter the liver. Octanoic acid is metabolized in liver at least partially to ketone bodies. It has also been found that octanoic acid strongly inhibits the D-β-hydroxybutyric acid dehydrogenase. This model is being studied further to examine the possibility that the coma is the result of the loss of the ability to convert acetoacetate to D-β-hydroxybutyrate because of octanoic acid inhibition of D-β-hydroxybutyrate dehydrogenase and that ketosis resulting from the oxidation of octanoic acid and other fatty acids is primarily in the form of acetoacetate which then reaches toxic levels in the brain.

A unique feature of the cerebral metabolism is its apparent lack of response to high circulating levels of thyroid hormone. An understanding of the basis of this unique behavior may reveal information concerning the metabolism of the brain in health and disease. Also, the mechanism of action of thyroxine has been under investigation for many decades, but thus far a satisfactory explanation of the mechanism by which it increases metabolic rate, stimulates metamorphosis and growth, or causes the many disturbances in body physiology and biochemistry in thyroid disease has eluded investigators. The solution of this problem could then lead to fundamental advances not only in the understanding of how this important hormone regulates bodily functions but also of the nature of bodily processes on which it acts. The clarification of the relationship between its mechanism of action and its effects on development of the brain might also lead to a better understanding of the many biochemical processes underlying the maturation of the brain and the basis of the mental retardation which occurs in neonatal hypothyroidism; e.g., cretinism. Studies in this project on ketone body metabolism may also lead to an explanation of the coma which occurs in a number of metabolic diseases characterized by ketosis.

The project will be continued essentially on the course already indicated. The major avenues to be pursued are: (1) the attempts to isolate, purify, and identify the product of the thyroxine-mitochondrial reaction responsible for the stimulation of protein biosynthesis; (2) further studies on the elucidation of the mechanism of the stimulation of the protein biosynthetic processes; (3) further study of the mechanism of the thyroxine effects on mitochondrial NAD^+ content and its consequences; (4) further studies of the biochemical differences between mature and immature brain and the role of thyroxine in the biochemical changes leading to maturation and development of the brain; (5) purification of brain D-β-hydroxybutyric dehydrogenase; (6) studies of the mechanism of the inhibition of D-β-hydroxybutyric dehydrogenase by thyroxine; and (7) studies of the possible relationship between ketosis and coma.

Keyword Descriptors:

thyroxine
thyroid hormones
protein synthesis
ketosis

D-β-hydroxybutyric Acid Dehydrogenase
coma
brain maturation
brain metabolism
ketone bodies

Honors and Awards: None

Publications:

1. Sokoloff, L., and Raskin, N. H.: Thyroid Disorders. In Shy, M., Appel, S., and Goldensohn, E. (Eds.): The Cellular and Molecular Basis of Neurological Disease. Philadelphia, Lea and Febiger. (in press)

2. Fitzgerald, G. G., Kaufman, E. E., Sokoloff, L., and Shein, H. M.: D(-)-β-Hydroxybutyrate dehydrogenase activity in cloned cell lines of glial and neuronal origin. J. Neurochem. 22: 1163-1165, 1974.

3. Sokoloff, L.: Possible role of cerebral ketone body metabolism in diabetic coma. Proceedings of Alfred Benzon Symposium VIII on "The Working Brain", Copenhagen, Denmark, 1974. (in press)

4. Sokoloff, L., and Roberts, P. A.: Artifacts in studies of protein synthesis with radioactive amino acids. Invalidity of alleged stimulation of protein synthesis by thyroxine in vitro in absence of mitochondria. J. Biol. Chem. 249: 5520-5527, 1974.

5. Sokoloff, L.: Circulation and energy metabolism of the brain. In Siegel, G. J., Albers, R. W., Katzman, R., and Agranoff, B. W. (Eds.): Basic Neurochemistry, 2nd Edition. Boston, Little, Brown and Company. (in press)

6. Sokoloff, L.: Thyroxine and Brain Development: Approaches to the Problem. Proceedings of conference on Thyroxine and Brain Development, Elkridge, Maryland, April 20-23, 1975. (in press)

Serial No. Z01 MH 00882-08
1. Laboratory of Cerebral Metabolism
2. Section on Developmental Neurochemistry
3. Bethesda, Maryland

PHS-ADAMHA-NIMH
Individual Project Report
July 1, 1974 through June 30, 1975

Project Title:	Studies on regional cerebral circulation and metabolism
Previous Serial Number:	M-CM-DN-2
Principal Investigator:	Louis Sokoloff, M. D.
Other Investigators:	Charles Kennedy, M. D., Michel H. Des Rosiers, M. D., Osamu Sakurada, M. D., Mami I. Shinohara, M. D., Janos Hamar, M. D., Volker Neuser, Ph.D., Carmen Martine, M. D., and Jane W. Jehle
Cooperating Units:	Martin Reivich, M. D. Department of Neurology University of Pennsylvania Philadelphia, Pennsylvania Clifford S. Patlak, Ph.D., and Karen Pettigrew, Theoretical Statistics and Mathematics Branch, NIMH Leslie I. Wolfson, M. D. Department of Neurology Albert Einstein College of Medicine New York, N. Y. E. V. Evarts, M. D., F. Sharp, M. D. Laboratory of Neurophysiology NIMH Bethesda, Maryland

Man Years:

Total:	5.00
Professional:	4.00
Other:	1.00

Project Description:

When the principal investigator first joined the NIMH approximately 20 years ago, his first research activities here were in a research project directed by the then Scientific Director, Seymour S. Kety, M. D., to develop a method for the measurement of the rates of blood flow in the structural and functional units of brain in conscious laboratory animals. This project was successful, and such a method was developed. The method was based on the uptake of a radioactive, chemically inert gas into the tissues of the brain, and a unique quantitative autoradiographic technique was developed which made possible the measurement by densitometric procedures of the concentrations of the radioactive tracer in the individual structures of the brain down to a resolution of a couple of millimeters. The key to the fine resolution of the method was the autoradiographic technique.

Although measurement of local cerebral blood flow is inherently interesting and is useful in studying cerebrovascular disease and disturbances in the circulatory system, it is of limited value in studies of cerebral functional and biochemical activity. The principal investigator, therefore, has sought since that time to devise a method to measure local cerebral energy metabolism with the same degree of structural resolution because energy metabolism could be expected to relate more closely to local cerebral functional activity. It was always anticipated that the quantitative autoradiographic technique designed for the blood flow method would also be at the heart of such a method. It was necessary, however, to choose an appropriately labeled precursor of cerebral energy metabolism. Oxygen could not be used because there are no suitable radioisotopes of oxygen. [^{14}C]Glucose also appeared to be unsuitable because glucose is too rapidly metabolized, and its radioactive products are too quickly removed from brain. It was several years later that the idea occurred to use [^{14}C]deoxyglucose, an analogue of glucose which is handled qualitatively just like glucose by the transport system in the blood-brain barrier and by the initial enzyme, hexokinase, in the pathway of glucose metabolism. Once phosphorylated, however, the deoxyglucose is trapped, unlike glucose which is metabolized further to carbon dioxide and water. Quantitatively, however, deoxyglucose phosphorylation and glucose phosphorylation or utilization could be expected to be different inasmuch as the transport carrier and the enzyme could be expected to discriminate quantitatively between the two substrates. It appeared to be a simple matter to develop a method to measure deoxyglucose phosphorylation, but to relate it to the steady state rate of glucose flux through the phosphorylation step, which would be a measure of the rate of glucose consumption, clearly would require the solution of numerous theoretical and technical problems.

The problem was allowed to incubate for a number of years with occasional thought devoted to it until about three years ago when an intensive effort was launched to develop the method. A theoretical model, which encompassed all that we knew about deoxyglucose and glucose transport between brain and blood and their metabolism in brain tissue, was constructed, and mathematical relationships to describe the model were developed. Experiments were done on one point or another to evaluate and, if necessary, to revise the model and the mathematical relationships to fit the model closer to the real situation.

It was clear that to determine the rate of glucose consumption from the rate of [^{14}C]deoxyglucose phosphorylation would require the determination of the distribution volumes of deoxyglucose and glucose in the cerebral tissues and the hexokinase kinetic constants (V_{max} and K_m) for both deoxyglucose and glucose. By appropriate mathematical manipulations, it was possible to segregate all these separate constants into a single "lumped constant" encompassing all of them. It was now necessary to determine only the single lumped constant rather than the six separate ones. Further mathematical analyses revealed how to design an experiment to determine the "lumped constant". Another equation was developed from the model which showed that if the arterial concentration was maintained constant for a sufficient length of time, e.g., at least 20 minutes, then the ratio of the cerebral extractions of deoxyglucose and glucose would reach a constant level equal to the lumped constant. With the help of the Theoretical Statistics and Mathematics Branch, it was found possible to derive from the analyses of plasma disappearance curves of deoxyglucose an intravenous infusion schedule which results in a constant arterial deoxyglucose concentration for up to 45 minutes or longer. Surgical procedures were developed in the rat and cat to sample arterial and cerebral venous blood from which the extraction ratios are determined. The determination of the lumped constant has been essentially completed in the conscious and anesthetized rat, and preliminary values have also been obtained in the conscious and anesthetized cat.

All the theoretical and technical problems have been solved, and the method is now essentially completely developed. An equation has been derived which relates the rate of glucose consumption to measurable variables and allows the calculation of glucose consumption in the discrete structural and functional units of the brain. The equation prescribes the procedure to be used and the variables to be measured. An intravenous pulse of [^{14}C]deoxyglucose is injected, and arterial plasma concentrations of [^{14}C]deoxyglucose and glucose are measured from the time of injection till about 45 minutes when the animal is decapitated, and the head frozen. Sections of brain are prepared from which local cerebral tissue [^{14}C]deoxyglucose concentrations are determined by the quantitative autoradiographic technique. From these measured variables and the lumped constant local cerebral glucose utilization is calculated by the equation.

The method has been applied to conscious and anesthetized rats. The values obtained cannot be directly compared to any other data in the literature since measurement of local cerebral glucose consumption has never previously been possible, but the average of the local values is very close to the reported values for overall average brain glucose utilization in the rat. Anesthesia has been found to depress cerebral glucose consumption throughout the brain. Carbon dioxide inhalation has been shown to depress local glucose consumption even though it increases cerebral blood flow. Local cerebral blood flow has been found in the normal animal to correlate very closely with local cerebral energy metabolism, a relationship which had been hypothesized but never previously proved. Increased local functional activity produced by electrical stimulation or by experimentally induced focal seizures following local penicillin injection results in increased local glucose consumption in appropriate regions of the CNS. These results established once and for all the often debated but never previously proved fact that energy metabolism in the CNS is closely coupled to functional activity as it is in all other tissues.

Studies have been carried out in the rat on the effects of γ-butyrolactone, a drug alleged to block specifically dopaminergic synapses in the brain. A surprising result was that this agent, which produces a comatose-like state, also depresses local glucose consumption throughout the brain. Indeed, the magnitude of the reduction, which is dose-dependent, can be as great as that seen in profound hypothermia, which is used by cardiac and neurosurgeons to reduce energy metabolism in the brain and thus protect it during surgical procedures necessitating interruption of cerebral blood flow. The effects of the drug are completely reversible. Normal consciousness, EEG, and behavior are recovered approximately 4 hours after the injection, and the animal appears normal. This finding may have enormous practical potentialities It is conceivable that the beneficial effects of hypothermia without its potentially dangerous side-effects and complex technical procedures may be achieved with this drug. These studies will be continued to ascertain whether, in fact, it is safe to try it out in man for surgical procedures.

In the course of the development of the method it became apparent that even without complete quantitation, the autoradiographs represented pictorial displays of the relative rates of energy consumption in all parts of the brain. For example, they demonstrated clearly that the synapse-rich areas, e.g., layer 4 or the neuropile in the cerebral cortex, are the most metabolically active areas of the cortex. It also became apparent that inasmuch as local glucose consumption changed in response to changes in functional activity, regions of the brain which were turned on or off functionally and metabolically in altered physiological states could be mapped simultaneously throughout the brain. The efficacy of this technique of mapping by "evoked metabolic response" has been demonstrated in the visual and auditory systems of the rat and monkey. All the regions involved in visual functions have, for example, been shown to alter activity and be displayed on the autoradiographs after occlusion of vision of one eye and stimulation of the other. By this technique the visual cortical locus of the representation of the blind spots of the visual fields have been demonstrated in the monkey. The resolution of the method is surprisingly good. It has clearly demonstrated the ocular dominance columns described by Hubel and Wiesel, which are believed to represent the structural and functional organization of the visual cortex responsible for the integration of the two images from the two eyes in animals with binocular vision. The method promises to be of enormous usefulness to neuroanatomists and neurophysiologists for the mapping of functional neural pathways in the CNS.

The plan now is to initiate applications of the method to studies of local metabolic changes in the brain associated with subtle neurological and mental functional changes which have thus far defied further understanding. For example, studies will be carried out in deep, slow wave and REM sleep, during severe anxiety induced by epinephrine infusions, in morphine addiction and withdrawal, during the action of psychotomimetic drugs, such as LSD, mescaline, and amphetamine. It will also be used in studies of the normal postnatal maturation of the brain and during experimentally induced cretinism. Indeed, the method opens all sorts of possibilities, and its applications at present are limited only by the availability of animal models. It is almost certain that its power to localize regions of the brain in normal physiological and pathological functional states will help to identify the specific portions of the brain with altered function in at least some of the conditions which mimic human disease.

Keyword Descriptors:

local cerebral glucose utilization
cerebral energy metabolism
neural mapping
deoxyglucose
neuroanatomical techniques
evoked metabolic response

Honors and Awards:

Guest Lecturer, Twelfth Annual Marion Hines Lecture, Emory University, Atlanta, Georgia, March 3, 1975.

Guest Lecturer, Seventh International Symposium on Cerebral Circulation and Metabolism. Aviemore Conference Center, Glasgow, Scotland, June 17-20, 1975.

Publications:

1. Sokoloff, L.: Dementia and old age. In Arbus, L. and Paulson, O. B., (Eds.). Cerebral Blood Flow, Metabolism and Old Age. Symposium, Les Laboratories Dausse, Paris, France, Dec. 10-11, 1973. (in press)

2. Eckman, W. W., Phair, R. D., Fenstermacher, J. D., and Sokoloff, L.: The influence of capillary permeability limitations on the measurement of regional cerebral blood flow. Sixth International Symposium on Cerebral Circulation and Metabolism, Phila., Pa., 1973, Springer-Verlag. (in press)

3. Sokoloff, L.: Influence of functional activity on local cerebral glucose utilization. Proceedings of Alfred Benzon Symposium VIII on "The Working Brain", Copenhagen, Denmark, 1974. (in press)

4. Sokoloff, L.: Effects of epinephrine on cerebral blood flow and metabol in unanesthetized man. Proceedings of Alfred Benzon Symposium VIII on "The Working Brain", Copenhagen, Denmark, 1974. (in press)

5. Reivich, M., Sokoloff, L., Shapiro, H., Des Rosiers, M., and Kennedy, C.: Validation of an autoradiographic method for the determination of the rates of local cerebral glucose utilization. Trans. Am. Neurol. Assoc. 99: 238-240, 1974.

6. Kennedy, C., Des Rosiers, M., Reivich, M., and Sokoloff, L.: Mapping of functional pathways in brain by autoradiographic survey of local cerebral metabolism. Trans. Am. Neurol. Assoc. 99: 143-147, 1974.

7. Sokoloff, L.: Cerebral circulation and metabolism in the aged. Symposium on Geriatric Psychopharmacology: The Scene Today. American College of Psychoneuropharmacology, Puerto Rico, Dec. 10-13, 1974. (in press)

8. Sokoloff, L.: Cerebral circulation and metabolism in the aged. Symposium on Geriatric Psychopharmacology: The Scene Today. American College of Psychoneuropharmacology, Puerto Rico, Dec. 10-13, 1974. To be published in the Psychopharmacology Bulletin. (in press)

9. Eckman, W. W., Phair, R. D., Fenstermacher, J. D., Patlak, C. S., Kennedy, C., and Sokoloff, L.: Permeability limitation in estimation of local brain blood flow with [^{14}C]antipyrine. Am. J. Physiol. (in press

10. Kennedy, C., Des Rosiers, M. H., Reivich, M., Sharp, F., Jehle, J. W., and Sokoloff, L.: Mapping of functional neural pathways by autoradiographic survey of local metabolic rate with [^{14}C]deoxyglucose. Science 187: 850-853, 1975.

11. Kennedy, Charles, Des Rosiers, Michel, Reivich, Martin, Jehle, Jane, and Sokoloff, L.: The ocular dominance columns of the striate cortex as studied by the deoxyglucose method for measurement of local cerebral glucose utilization. Trans. Am. Neurol. Assoc. New York City, June 2-4, 1975. (in press)

Serial No. Z01 MH 00883-09
1. Laboratory of Cerebral Metabolism
2. Section on Developmental Neurochemistry
3. Bethesda, Maryland

PHS-ADAMHA-NIMH
Individual Project Report
July 1, 1974 through June 30, 1975

Project Title: Biochemical bases of alcohol addiction

Previous Serial Numbers: M-CS-CM-11 and M-CM-DN-3

Principal Investigator: Louis Sokoloff, M. D.

Other Investigators: R. J. S. Duncan, Ph.D., and John E. Kline

Cooperating Units: None

Man Years:

Total:	2.00
Professional:	1.25
Other:	0.75

Project Description:

This project is directed at the elucidation of the biochemical changes in brain associated with chronic alcohol ingestion with the ultimate goal of finding the biochemical basis for addiction to alcohol and the symptom-complex which follows its acute withdrawal.

The enzymes associated with ethanol metabolism and that of its products are assayed in brain, liver, and other tissues of normal rats and rats fed various amounts of ethanol for various periods. Classical methods of contemporary enzymology are employed. The results of the assays of enzyme activity in brain are correlated with the results of behavioral tests of alcohol tolerance or alcohol-withdrawal symptoms.

This project was first begun when Dr. Neil H. Raskin was a Research Associate in this Section and continued on a collaborative basis when he left to become an Associate Professor in the Department of Neurology, University of California Medical Center, San Francisco, California. This collaboration was terminated during the last year following publication of our last paper on this problem because our present goals no longer overlap.

Previous work in this project demonstrated by means of a new assay technique the presence of alcohol dehydrogenase, the enzyme responsible for the metabolism of ethanol, in the brain. Previous efforts by other investigators to find the enzyme in brain had been unsuccessful because of inadequately sensitive and specific methods. The kinetic properties and the responsivity to specific inhibitors of the brain enzyme were examined and compared to those of the liver enzyme and found to be almost identical. A tissue survey of the alcohol dehydrogenase has revealed its presence in all ingestion. In studies in rats it was found that the brain enzyme activity rises about 50% with chronic alcohol ingestion. This is in contrast to the liver enzyme which remains unchanged. Behavioral tests of tolerance to alcohol were carried out, and the results showed a very close temporal correlation between the changes in alcohol dehydrogenase activity in brain and in the level of tolerance. Both the tolerance and brain enzyme activity rise very slowly after the beginning of alcohol feeding, reaching their new steady state levels at about two weeks. Both changes, however, fall rapidly to normal within 48 hours after alcohol withdrawal. No symptoms of alcohol withdrawal are seen in the rat model. This is the first evidence of a specific enzyme change in the brain with chronic alcohol intake and suggests a possible relationship to the development of tolerance to ethanol and/or a biochemical basis for the development of CNS symptoms following withdrawal from alcohol after prolonged ingestion.

One of the problems with the interpretation of the results is the fact that the brain alcohol dehydrogenase activity in brain, though present, is very low, approximately 1/4000th that of liver, too low to contribute significantly to the disposition of ethanol in brain. The question arises then what its role in brain may be, and the answer to this requires at the least the determination of the enzyme's distribution within the brain. The possibility that all the enzyme in brain tissue represents only the activity in the blood within the brain has been examined and excluded; blood does contain alcohol dehydrogenase activity which rises with liver damage, but it is too little to account even for the small amount in brain. The possibility has been considered that the activity in brain is not "true" alcohol dehydrogenase but some other enzyme activity that has some small degree of alcohol dehydrogenase-like activity. Dr. Duncan has, therefore, purified rat liver alcohol dehydrogenase by gel filtration, ion exchange, and affinity chromatography and used it to prepare rabbit antibodies to rat liver alcohol dehydrogenase. These antibodies which precipitate liver alcohol dehydrogenase also precipitate brain alcohol dehydrogenase activity, indicating that the brain enzyme is antigenically similar if not the same as the liver enzyme which is unequivocably true alcohol dehydrogenase. It is now planned to attempt to prepare fluorescent antibodies to liver alcohol dehydrogenase and to employ fluorescent microscopic techniques on brain slices to localize the distribution of alcohol dehydrogenase activity in brain at the microscopic level.

This is a project with considerable clinical implications. Numerous drugs and chemical agents cause addiction which results in withdrawal symptoms when their use is discontinued. Alcohol is one of the most common. Although it is clear that some biochemical change must have occurred, none yet has been found which could satisfactorily explain the phenomenon. Elucidation of the biochemical mechanism of alcohol addiction might not only serve as a model for other types of addiction but might also lead to a more rational approach to therapy.

Keyword Descriptors:

Alcohol
Ethanol
Brain
Alcohol dehydrogenase
Alcohol addiction
Alcohol tolerance

Honors and Awards: None

Publications: Raskin, N. and Sokoloff, L., J. Neurochem. 22: 427-434, 1974.

Serial No. Z01 MH 00884-05
1. Laboratory of Cerebral Metabolism
2. Section on Developmental Neurochemistry
3. Bethesda, Maryland

PHS-ADAMHA-NIMH
Individual Project Report
July 1, 1974 through June 30, 1975

Project Title: Regulation of protein synthesis in the brain

Previous Serial Number: M-CM-DN-4

Principal Investigator: Michael J. Schmidt, Ph.D.

Other Investigators: Louis Sokoloff, M. D.: J. D. Brown

Cooperating Units: None

Due to lack of personnel to work on this project, it has been discontinued.

Serial No. Z01 MH 00900-19 LCM
1. Laboratory of Cerebral Metabolism
2. Section on Myelin Chemistry
3. Bethesda, Maryland

PHS-ADAMHA-NIMH
Individual Project Report
July 1, 1974 through June 30, 1975

Project Title: Biochemical studies on myelin and myelin basic protein

Previous Serial Number: M-CM-MyC-1

Principal Investigator: Russell E. Martenson

Other Investigators: Marian W. Kies and Gladys E. Deibler

Cooperating Units: Department of Pathology, New York Medical College Center for Chronic Disease, Bird S. Coler Hospital, Roosevelt Island, New York.

Man Years:

Total:	3.5
Professional:	1.5
Others:	2.0

Project Description:

The objectives of this study are to examine the relationships between chemical structure and biological activities of the myelin basic proteins of several mammalian and submammalian species. The biological activities include the ability to (A) induce delayed hypersensitivity leading to an autoimmune disease, experimental allergic encephalomyelitis (EAE), (B) induce delayed hypersensitivity without necessarily causing EAE, (C) induce the formation of circulating anti-basic protein antibodies without concomitant induction of EAE, and (D) provide structural stability in myelin by its interaction with lipids in the membrane.

The methods used include (1) polyacrylamide gel electrophoresis; (2) amino acid analysis of CNS proteins and their derivatives; (3) chromatographic fractionation of proteins and peptides; (4) paper chromatography; (5) high voltage electrophoresis; (6) thin-layer chromatography; and (6) specific chemical and enzymic cleavage of myelin basic proteins.

A major part of the research has been the continuation of studies on experimental allergic encephalomyelitis in the Lewis rat. The studies have as their goal the definition of the amino acid sequences in the myelin basic protein which are necessary for disease induction. Previously, we had found that Lewis rats recognize two types of regions as being encephalitogenic. One type is present in the guinea pig myelin basic protein and is extremely active, responsible for full-blown disease with 0.02 nmole of basic protein. A second type of determinant, present in the bovine protein, is only mildly active. Up to 12.5 nmole of bovine basic protein is required for this determinant to show full activity.

We had previously found that the extremely encephalitogenic site of the guinea pig protein is present in the sequence of residues 43-88. We are currently trying to define the site more specifically. Studies currently in progress, involving performic acid and N-bromosuccinimide oxidation, have shown that neither the single tyrosine residue nor any of the 4 histidine residues in peptide (43-88) are necessary for activity. Studies involving carboxypeptidase A treatment have shown that the 3 residues at the C-terminus, -Val-His-Phe, are not necessary either.

Regarding the mildly encephalitogenic bovine basic protein, we had previously reported that it contained two encephalitogenic sites, one beginning after residue 19 and extending beyond residue 43 and the other beginning after residue 88 and terminating before residue 153. The presence of two mutually exclusive encephalitogenic sites in the bovine protein of roughly equal activity suggested that the two regions might be similar in their amino acid sequences. Alignment of residues 34-46, a sequence which must include at least part of the major encephalitogenic site, with residues 107-118, which are contained within the second active region, showed a striking sequence similarity. Recent studies have defined the two regions more precisely. The first region must contain the sequence -Asp-Ser-Leu-Gly-Arg-Phe- (residues 37-42) as an essential element, since peptides (1-42) and (37-88) are active, whereas peptides (1-36) and (43-88) are inactive. The second region, present entirely in peptides (89-169) and (89-152), but not in peptides (111-169), has been further localized. Treatment of peptide (89-169) with BNPS-skatole yields fragments (89-115) and (116-169). Fragment (89-115) has activity identical with that of the parent peptide, whereas fragment (116-169) is completely devoid of activity. These latter studies show that the second site lies within residues 89-115 and probably does not include residue 115 (tryptophan) because in the active fragment this residue is oxidized to the dioxindole derivative.

The relationship between microheterogeneity of the basic protein and its *in situ* modification has been studied in more detail. We have found that in addition to loss of C-terminal arginine and phosphorylation, an additional factor must be responsible for producing different electrophoretic or chromatographic forms of the protein. We suspect that this is deamidation.

One of the most significant findings of the past year has been the discovery that the phosphoserine and phosphothreonine residues present in the native myelin basic protein are located in the C-terminal half of the protein. Our studies provide evidence that the protein contains only two sites that are phosphorylated *in vivo*. These two sites appear to be confined to the C-terminal half of the protein.

Myelin basic protein is under intensive investigation in this and a number of other laboratories to determine its role in the structural integrity of the myelin sheath, where it accounts for 30% of the myelin proteins. Closely related to this role is its involvement in an experimental autoimmune disease of the CNS, EAE, where it serves as a potent auto-antigen capable of specifically sensitizing lymphocytes which initiate a delayed-type hypersensitivity reaction in the CNS tissues leading to paralytic lesions. To study the properties of the protein responsible for the induction of the delayed hypersensitivity, both with and without concomitant production of EAE, and those responsible for induction of antibody formation alone, we have examined various areas of the basic protein for the relevant activities. Through these studies we hope to obtain information relevant to molecular events which occur in the afferent part of immune responses in general, and possibly during the early phases of autoimmunity in humans, specifically in multiple sclerosis.

Further studies will be carried out to define more specifically the determinants of the guinea pig and bovine proteins which are encephalitogenic in Lewis rats. The fragments of the basic proteins which have so far enabled us to localize the encephalitogenic determinants to certain, rather large, regions of the basic proteins will be further cleaved by specific chemical and enzymatic means. The resulting fragments, in addition, will be of immense value in locating those regions which are involved in the induction of circulating antibodies in guinea pigs. These latter studies are being carried out by Dr. Driscoll.

The additional fragments obtained from the basic protein will be used to locate the positions in the protein where enzymatic phosphorylation of amino acids takes place, both in vivo and in vitro. These studies should provide us with information relating to the metabolism and function of this protein in the myelin sheath.

Keyword Descriptors:

myelin basic protein
experimental allergic encephalomyelitis
microheterogeneity
phosphoamino acids
encephalitogenic determinants
peptic cleavage
N-bromosuccinimide oxidation
BNPS-skatole cleavage

Honors and Awards:

Dr. Martenson elected to membership, American Society of Biological Chemists; member of Advisory Board, Journal of Neurochemistry.

Publications:

Fishman, M. W., Agrawal, H. C., Alexander, A., Golterman, J., Martenson, R. E. and Mitchell, R. F.: Biochemical maturation of human central nervous system myelin. J. Neurochem. 24: 689-694, 1975.

Gonatas, N. K., Gonatas, J. O., Stieber, A., Lisak, R., Suzuki, J. and Martenson, R. E.: The significance of circulating and cell-bound antibodies in experimental allergic encephalomyelitis. Am. J. Pathol. 76: 529-544, 1974.

Martenson, R. E. and Deibler, G. E.: Partial characterization of basic proteins of chicken, turtle and frog central nervous system myelin. J. Neurochem. 24: 79-88, 1975.

Martenson, R. E., Deibler, G. E. and Kramer, A. J.: The presence of cysteine in frog myelin basic protein. J. Neurochem., in press.

Martenson, R. E., Kramer, A. J. and Deibler, G. E.: Large peptides of bovine and guinea pig myelin basic proteins produced by limited peptic hydrolysis. Biochemistry 14: 1067-1073, 1975.

Martenson, R. E., Levine, S. and Sowinski, R.: The location of regions in guinea pig and bovine myelin basic proteins which induce experimental allergic encephalomyelitis in Lewis rats. J. Immunol. 114: 592-596, 1975.

Martenson, R. E., Deibler, G. E., Kramer, A. J. and Levine, S.: Comparative studies of guinea pig and bovine myelin basic proteins. Partial characterization of chemically derived fragments and their encephalitogenic activities in Lewis rats. J. Neurochem. 24: 173-182, 1975.

Serial No. Z01 MH 00901-20 LCM
1. Laboratory of Cerebral Metabolism
2. Section on Myelin Chemistry
3. Bethesda, Maryland

PHS-ADAMHA-NIMH
Individual Project Report
July 1, 1974 through June 30, 1975

Project Title: Immunologic reactivity of myelin basic protein (BP)

Previous Serial Number: M-CM-MyC-2

Principal Investigator: Marian W. Kies

Other Investigators: Martha L. Bacon, F. J. Seil, L. F. Eng, Henry D. Webster

Cooperating Units: Dept. of Neurology, VA Hospital and Stanford University, Palo Alto, Calif.; Laboratory of Neuropathology and Neuroanatomical Sciences, NINCDS

Man Years

Total: 2
Professional: 1
Others: 1

Project Description:

During the past several years we have maintained a small rabbit colony solely for the production of anti-CNS tissue antibodies. Individual rabbits have been immunized with different CNS antigens for the purpose of studying the immunogenicity of basic protein (BP) and its possible relationship to serum factors (other than specific antibody) involved in experimental demyelination. As long as the rabbits remain healthy, blood samples are drawn at biweekly intervals. Sera are labelled and stored at -25°C and careful records kept of immunization schedules, disease reaction, etc. All sera have been characterized by a qualitative test for precipitating antibody to BP and many have been further analyzed by immunodiffusion for precipitating antibody. A few have been analyzed for soluble antibody complexes and for evidence of anti-cerebroside. The results of the past year's study can best be presented under these 5 major headings:

1) The most effective schedule for production of large quantities of antibody to myelin basic protein (BP).

2) Detection of antigenic impurities in preparations of purified BP.

3) Structural requirements for antibody induction and specific binding.

4) Radioimmunoassay of biologic tissues (CSF, serum, urine, CNS, etc.) for BP or partially degraded BP.

5) The occurrence of anti-myelin factors in antisera.

1. Effective Immunization. It is difficult to specify the most effective immunization schedule. Our goal was to keep rabbits alive as long as possible for antibody production (i.e., by preventing EAE). Within limits of genetic variability (some rabbits never respond to BP-immunization) we have successfully induced antisera by the following schemes:

a. A single injection containing 1 mg BP + 5 mg killed mycobacteria ($H_{37}R_v$).

b. Ten injections, each containing 0.5 mg BP in incomplete Freund's adjuvant (IFA), over a 3-week period, followed by one injection of an emulsion containing 0.5 mg BP + 2.5 mg mycobacteria. (If antibody is not produced within 2-3 weeks by either of the above, the animals are "boosted" with an injection of 5 or 10 mg BP + 2.5 mg mycobacteria).

Other variations of timing and concentration of BP or mycobacteria have been tried but a) and b) appear to be the most effective. EAE is less apt to occur after b) than after a). Some antigens, notably homologous (rabbit) BP and the peptide fragment, 43-89, usually fail to induce antibody and almost invariably induce EAE in rabbits.

2. Detection of Antigenic Impurities. Two rabbits immunized with a partially (95%) purified bovine BP were found serendipitously to be producing antibody to a PNS-specific basic protein (P-2 or BF protein). With these antisera, we have been able to demonstrate the immunologic identity of P-2 with SCP (so-called Spinal Cord Protein which is thought to be a CNS-specific antigen). Studies are now underway to determine the tissue localization of SCP (and/or P-2) and thus establish its CNS- or PNS-specificity.

Anti-BP antibody has been removed from one of these sera by affinity chromatography on BP linked to Sepharose and the resultant anti-SCP (anti-P-2) antibody is being used for localization by fluorescent labelling of the antigen in bovine spinal cord. If present only in spinal nerve roots, the conclusion that SCP is a CNS antigen is not justified. These studies are being carried out in collaboration with Dr. Fritz Fienemann, a German Guest Worker in our laboratory, Dr. C. MacPherson of Canada, and Dr. K. Uyemura of Japan.

3. Studies of Antibody Specificity. We have been able to induce sera which give precipitation reactions with residues 1-89, residues 43-89, and residues 90-169 (all isolated by limited peptic digestion of BP).

Fragments 1-89 and 90-169 contain sites which do not cross-react. Some sera which precipitate with 1-89 also precipitate with 43-89. Both of the larger fragments serve to prime the rabbits (i.e., direct the specificity of antibody binding to their own structure) for antibody production after later sensitization with whole BP. Fragment 1-89 which contains the rabbit encephalitogenic site primes for antibody induction to itself and to 43-89. Priming with 1-89 protects the rabbits against induction of EAE more effectively than priming with fragment 90-169. Fragment 43-89 in our hands has neither primed for nor induced antibody by itself, but occasional sera from rabbits sensitized with whole BP contain antibodies which precipitate on diffusion against this 45-residue fragment.

These studies are preliminary in that the only technique being used for detection of antibody is immunodiffusion. The results of these studies will be combined with the results of further analysis with a better technique (radioimmunoassay) for detecting total antigen-binding capacity.

4. Radioimmunoassay for BP in Biologic Samples. A good stock of highly specific antisera and an adequate supply of well-characterized pure BP are essential for this study. We have provided the purified antigen and good precipitating antisera to Dr. L. F. Eng of Palo Alto, Calif. for use in developing this procedure. Its development is of considerable importance because of its potential application in clinical studies on multiple sclerosis patients. Dr. Eng has already used the method to survey for presence of BP in CSF samples of neurologic patients. Further development is needed to use it in conjunction with BP clearance studies in patients prior to clinical trials on treatment of MS patients with BP.

5. Occurrence of Anti-Myelin Factors in Sera from Rabbits Immunized with BP. These factors are detected by their ability to inhibit myelination or cause demyelination in cerebellar or spinal cord explant cultures, or by their ability to damage Xenopus tadpole optic nerve myelin *in vivo*. Such factors have long been considered to be of major significance in the pathogenesis of demyelination *in vivo*. Unfortunately, many investigators have made unjustified assumptions regarding the immune nature of the serum factors. Use of ambiguous terms such as "EAE serum" and "anti-CNS antibody" have caused other scientists to assume that these factors are indeed antibodies to some encephalitogenic constituent of CNS and are, therefore, involved in pathogenesis of experimentally induced demyelination (i.e., EAE). Such is not the case. EAE is caused by cellular sensitization to BP and no one has ever provided definitive evidence that any serum antibody is required for this reaction.

It appears from our work and that of others that there are multiple factors which interfere with myelin production or maintenance in tissue culture, one of which may be an antibody to the galactolipid, cerebroside, which has demonstrable anti-myelin activity. Cerebroside is a constituent of myelin and it is logical that anti-cerebroside might interfere with the normal metabolic behavior of myelin, but induction of anti-cerebroside has no pathologic effect *in vivo*. Thus some doubt is cast on its role in the pathogenesis of experimental demyelination.

On the other hand, anti-myelin activity can be demonstrated in sera which do not contain anti-cerebroside antibody. Some of these sera contain anti-BP, but not all sera containing antibody to BP contain anti-myelin factor. Our tentative hypothesis is that there are multiple factors (at least two), one of which may not be an antibody. We are currently investigating the nature of this factor.

Keyword Descriptors:

myelin basic protein (BP)
anti-BP antibodies
anti-cerebroside antibodies
antibody specificity
radioimmunoassay of BP in body fluids and tissues
serum anti-myelin factors
CNS tissue culture
demyelination of Xenopus optic nerve

Honors and Awards: None

Publications:

Moore, M. J., Behan, P. O., Kies, M. W. and Matthews, J. M.: Reaginic antibody in experimental allergic encephalomyelitis. I. Characterization of heat-labile skin-fixing antibody. Res. Commun. Chem. Pathol. Pharmacol. 9: 119-132, 1974.

Moore, M. J., Matthews, J. M., Matthews, T. K., Behan, P. O. and Kies, M. W.: Reaginic antibody in experimental allergic encephalomyelitis. II. Histamine and serotonin blockade. Res. Commun. Chem. Pathol. Pharmacol. 9: 133-144, 1974.

Seil, F. J., Kies, M. W. and Bacon, M.: Neural antigens and induction of myelination inhibition factor. J. Immunol. 114: 630-634, 1975.

Serial No. Z01 MH 00902-10 LCM
1. Laboratory of Cerebral Metabolism
2. Section on Myelin Chemistry
3. Bethesda, Maryland

PHS-ADAMHA-NIMH
Individual Project Report
July 1, 1974 through June 30, 1975

Project Title: Studies on immediate and delayed hypersensitivity in experimental allergic encephalomyelitis (EAE)

Previous Serial Number: M-CM-MyC-3

Principal Investigator: Bernard F. Driscoll (Guest Worker)

Other Investigators: Marian W. Kies and Allan J. Kramer (Guest Worker)

Cooperating Units: National Multiple Sclerosis Society

Man Years:

Total:	3.5
Professional:	1.5
Others:	2.0

Project Description:

A study of the relative importance of cellular and humoral responses to myelin basic protein in the development and abrogation of its immunologic reactions: prevention, induction and treatment of experimental allergic encephalomyelitis.

It is well-known that sensitization with a soluble antigen involves at least two types of lymphocytes, thymic dependent (T) cells and thymic independent (B) cells. It is also generally agreed that induction of delayed hypersensitivity involves only T cells whereas antibody production requires both T and B cells. Operationally, those T cells which participate in a delayed hypersensitivity reaction are called "effector" cells; those which cooperate with B cells in the production of antibody are called "helper" cells and those which (theoretically) participate in turning off the immune process are called "suppressor" cells.

The mechanism of antibody production can be dissected into two phases, preparation, or <u>priming</u>, and elicitation or <u>induction</u>. Studies with synthetic antigens have established the fact that the molecular requirements for the two reactions are different--i.e., the B cells and T cells which cooperate in the production of antibody react to different portions of the antigenic molecule.

In the case of natural antigens, such as myelin basic protein (BP), the participation of different parts of the molecule in the induction of T and/or B cells has been assumed but not entirely clarified. Because of the importance of EAE as an experimental tool for studying autoimmune disease, we have examined the structural specificity of BP with regard to these various immune capabilities. Induction of disease in guinea pigs by homologous (guinea pig) BP in complete Freund's adjuvant (CFA) was found to correlate well with the induction of delayed hypersensitivity to the BP molecule. That portion of the molecule responsible for disease induction is a 9-residue peptide (residues 114-122). Its synthetic counterpart has been found to induce disease almost as effectively as the parent molecule. Its ability to induce delayed hypersensitivity is difficult to establish because of its size and diffusibility. Nevertheless, we can conclude tentatively that the structure of this peptide defines the specificity of the effector T-cells responsible for autoimmune damage in the CNS.

Antibody production and specificity is somewhat more complex. It has been known for some time that preimmunization with BP in incomplete Freund's adjuvant (IFA) primes a normal guinea pig for subsequent antibody production when it is sensitized with BP in CFA. Priming also protects the animal from induction of EAE by the BP/CFA injection. We have demonstrated that at least 3 populations of antibodies with mutually exclusive binding specificities are produced when guinea pigs are primed with whole BP. The peptides which bind antibody are located between residues 43 and 89, 90 and 116, and 117 and 169 of the BP molecule. Again, tentatively, these can be designated as B cell sites.

Since priming and induction are two different operations (BP in IFA, followed by BP in CFA) the peptides used to define binding sites can also be used to determine structural requirements for priming and induction and to determine whether the specific requirements for either mechanism are the same as the requirements for prevention and treatment of EAE. The most significant observation made was that no antibody was produced unless the peptide used for induction contained the intact encephalitogenic group. We can conclude tentatively from this that the structural specificity of "helper" T cells is probably the same as that of the "effector" T cells. It is clear that the binding specificity of the antibody is partially determined by the structure of the molecule used for priming. It is also evident that the peptides vary with respect to their ability to prevent and treat EAE. (Some are inactive, some are partially effective, and one was as effective as whole protein.)

Preimmunization with the first 19 or the last 54 residues of the BP molecule provides no protection against sensitization with whole BP in CFA. Only 89-169 confers protection comparable to that provided by the whole BP molecule. Peptide fragments consisting of residues 1-36, 37-88, 43-88 and 1-115 afford partial protection. While their use insures a moderately high incidence of survival compared to sensitized but untreated guinea pigs, they do not prevent the development of clinical signs of EAE as do whole BP or fragment 89-169. The latter two molecules, in contrast to the other peptides, were the only ones which were also encephalitogenic. Thus one conclusion is that the encephalitogenic site itself is required to provide complete protection.

A second mechanism, however, must be responsible for the milder protective effect seen with nonencephalitogenic fragments. When fragment 89-169 was used in place of BP for sensitization, preimmunization with either fragment 1-36 or 37-88 protected animals from fatal EAE. This is surprising because the antigen used for sensitization (89-169) was a completely different antigen from the ones used for preimmunization. The reason for this unexpected "cross-reactivity" is unknown at present.

The same peptides were used in studies on treatment of EAE after disease onset. Again, it was observed that the encephalitogenic fragments were the only ones capable of successful treatment. However, as in protection, some nonencephalitogenic fragments were partially effective. We believe that a direct interaction between sensitized cells and encephalitogenic antigen must account for the rapid and effective reversal of disease onset by whole BP or fragment 89-169. However, a second (unknown) mechanism must be responsible for the slow reversal of the disease state by nonencephalitogenic fragments.

A third subset (suppressor) T cells has been postulated. They presumably would be involved in prevention and treatment of EAE. We have not yet been able to obtain any evidence for their existence by transferring cells from protected to sensitized animals. However, if they did exist, it would be advantageous to stimulate their proliferation in attempts to abrogate an autoimmune disease state. Therefore, the question is of sufficient practical importance to warrant further study.

Since so much of the information regarding participation of T and B cells in immune reactions is derived by inference, we have extended our molecular studies to a parallel investigation in EAE-resistant (Strain 2) guinea pigs. BP sensitization fails to induce EAE in normal Strain 2 guinea pigs and is also incapable of inducing antibody in primed Strain 2 guinea pigs. Tentatively, this failure of the Strain 2 guinea pigs to respond can be explained as a lack of specific T cells which react with the guinea pig encephalitogenic site in myelin BP. However, if the "T cell requirement" is overcome by the use of a large amount of mycobacteria (2.5 mg) in the BP inoculum, both EAE-resistant (Strain 2) and EAE-susceptible (Strain 13) guinea pigs produce anti-BP antibody. Thus both strains possess competent B cells and the "B cell sites" detected by the use of individual peptides for binding specific antibody are identical in both strains. These data are consistent with our hypotheses on the significance of B and T cells in EAE.

Knowledge of the mechanisms involved in the induction, prevention and cessation of immunologic reactions to myelin basic protein as well as the interrelationships between cellular and humoral immunity is a prerequisite to an understanding of autoimmune diseases in general. In particular, they are important for developing a rational plan for immunologic intervention in multiple sclerosis. Even if the precipitating event in this disease does not involve an autoimmune reaction to BP, the repetitive course of the illness suggests an autoimmune reaction to some CNS antigen, and the techniques developed are generally applicable to any immune reaction.

Our data indicate that at least two mechanisms are responsible for both prevention and treatment of EAE. Presence of the encephalitogenic site in the protective molecule accounts for one and some unknown mechanism accounts for the other. Of particular interest are the protective effects seen with regions of the molecule completely separate from and with no apparent immunological sites shared with the inducing molecule (i.e., in the case of fragment 1-36 preventing EAE induction with fragment 89-169). We will continue our attempt to analyze these mechanisms.

Finally, several chronic types of EAE have been observed in our laboratory. These include disease induced by various fragments of the BP in EAE-susceptible guinea pigs and by whole CNS tissue in a resistant strain of guinea pigs. In view of the recent interest expressed in chronic types of EAE as models of human neurological disease, we believe a closer look at these forms of disease is warranted.

Keyword Descriptors:

experimental allergic encephalomyelitis (EAE)
myelin basic protein (BP)
immunologic prevention, induction and treatment of EAE
delayed hypersensitivity
"effector" T cells
"suppressor" T cells
antibody production
B cells
"helper" T cells
Strain 13 guinea pigs (EAE-susceptible)
Strain 2 guinea pigs (EAE-resistant)

Honors and Awards: None

Publications:

Driscoll, B. F., Kies, M. W. and Alvord, E. C., Jr.: Adoptive transfer of experimental allergic encephalomyelitis (EAE): prevention of successful transfer by treatment of donors with myelin basic protein. J. Immunol. 114: 291-292, 1975.

Kies, M. W., Driscoll, B. F., Lisak, R. P. and Alvord, E. C., Jr.: Immunologic activity of myelin basic protein in Strain 2 and Strain 13 guinea pigs. J. Immunol., in press.

Lisak, R. P., Zweiman, B., Kies, M. W. and Driscoll, B.: Experimental allergic encephalomyelitis in resistant and susceptible guinea pigs: in vivo and in vitro correlates. J. Immunol. 114: 546-549, 1975.

Serial No. Z01 MH 00885-14
1. Laboratory of Cerebral Metabolism
2. Section on Membrane Chemistry
3. Bethesda, Maryland

PHS-ADAMHA-NIMH
Individual Project Report
July 1, 1974 through June 30, 1975

Project Title:	Study of the modulation of central nervous system metabolism and function through alterations in membrane permeability and transport
Previous Serial Numbers:	M-CS-Ps(C)-13 and M-CM-MeC-1
Principal Investigator:	William C. Torch, M. S., M. D.
Other Investigators:	James D. Brown, Carolyn S. Cottingham, and Louis Sokoloff, M. D.
Cooperating Unit:	None

Due to lack of personnel to work on it, this project has been discontinued.

Project No. Z01 MH 00931-02 LGCB
1. Laboratory of General and Comparative Biochemistry
2. Section on Proteins
3. Bethesda, Maryland

PHS-ADAMHA-NIMH
Individual Project Report
July 1, 1974 through June 30, 1975

Project Title: Studies on the Characteristics and Regulation of Adenosylhomocysteine

Previous Serial Number: M - LGCB 64

Principal Investigator: Giulio L. Cantoni

Other Investigators: Henry Richards, Peter Chiang

Cooperating Units: None

Man Years:

Total: 1-7/12
Professional: 7/12
Other: 1

Project Description:

S-Adenosylhomocysteine, the product of methyltransfer reaction from S-adenosylmethionine, was discovered and characterized by Cantoni and his collaborators several years ago. The only pathway known for further metabolism of adenosylhomocysteine is the reaction

$$ASR \rightleftharpoons adenosine + homocysteine$$

catalyzed by adenosylhomocysteinase, an enzyme studied in this laboratory several years ago. The reaction is reversible with the equilibrium strongly in the direction of ASR synthesis. ASR is a powerful inhibitor of many of the methyltransfer reactions which utilize adenosylmethionine as the methyl donor, and therefore the tissue levels of ASR become an important regulatory element in the biosynthesis of methylated compounds, such as neurohormone or neurohormone precursors (methylated catecholamines, methylhistamines, methylated indolamines and choline), proteins (myosin, histones, encephalitogenic protein), and nucleic acids (tRNA, mRNA, DNA). ASR hydrolyase has been characterized only very incompletely in the past. Further work on the enzyme, its tissue and intracellular distribution, its regulation and the effect of analogues and/or inhibitors will be of interest. This approach will complement our studies on a series of AMe and ASR analogues that were synthesized for us under Contract #HSM-42-73-8 at the University of Kansas.

A new, very sensitive assay method has been developed. With this assay we have purified extensively the ASR hydrolase from beef liver, and are in the process of determining the molecular weight, amino acid composition and subunit structure of the enzyme. Using the purified enzyme we will be able to prepare antibodies to it and to study by immunochemical methods the tissue and cellular distribution of the enzyme, its half-life and its behavior in a variety of physiological conditions. Also, we can use the enzyme as a general method for the study of methyltransfer reactions from adenosylmethionine; this will enable us to screen rapidly a large number of adenosylmethionine analogues as potential inhibitors of specific and biologically important transmethylation reactions.

This project may be considered a continuation of a project carried out by de la Haba and Cantoni. It complements other studies in progress or being planned and will extend over the next couple of years at least. Adenosylmethionine and its analogues are reported as useful pharmacological agents in the treatment of some human pathological states. While it is too early to assess the validity of these reports, the significance of this and related projects to human disease should not be discounted.

Keyword Descriptors:

S-adenosylmethionine, adenosylhomocysteine, homocysteine adenosine.

Honors and Awards: None

Publications:

Cantoni, G. L.: S-Adenosylmethionine: present status and future prospectives. Presented at Int. Symp. on The Biochemistry of S-Adenosylmethionine. Rome, Italy, May 21-26, 1974 to be published in Proceedings.

Project No. Z01 MH 00932-03 LGCB
1. Laboratory of General and Comparative Biochemistry
2. Section on Proteins
3. Bethesda, Maryland

PHS-ADAMHA-NIMH
Individual Project Report
July 1, 1974 through June 30, 1975

Project Title: Muscle Differentiation in Tissue Culture

Previous Serial Number: M - LGCB 61

Principal Investigator: Giulio L. Cantoni

Other Investigators: B. William Uhlendorf, Sigfrido Scarpa

Cooperating Units: None

Man Years:

Total: 4-1/3
Professional: 2-1/3
Other: 2

Project Description:

Studies of the basic biochemistry of the process of cell differentiation are of fundamental importance for the understanding of the normal development of various cell types. In a highly differentiated organism such as man, it is generally believed that every cell has the same genetic endowment yet different cells express their genome differently. During differentiation, the expression of different genes is finely regulated in a time ordered fashion. The central problem, that completely escapes our understanding, is the nature of the control mechanism that regulates the sequential reading of different portions of the genome.

While differentiation in different cell types such as brain, muscle, liver and kidney cells will exhibit considerable variations there is reason to believe that the overall pattern and mechanism will be very similar in all these cases.

It has been the experience of the last 30 years that basic biochemical phenomena obey the general law on "the unity of biochemistry" formulated originally by O. H. Meyerhof. The tactical consequence of this general law of biochemistry has been of great importance for it has led to the conclusion that the best way to study a particular reaction or sequence of reactions is to select an appropriate model system from any one of the many different biological phyla. Thus, for the elucidation of the genetic code *E. coli* was chosen as the model system and the elucidation of the genetic code in *E. coli* led to its understanding in other bacterial as well as eukaryotic systems. Likewise, pig heart and spinach were selected for studies of oxidative phosphorylation and yeast was selected as the organism best suited to unravel glycolysis.

The differentiation of muscle cells *in vitro* to form muscle fiber appears to offer a potentially advantageous model system for the study of differentiation in general. The advantages that the myoblast system offer are the relative ease with which the differentiative event can be followed cytologically (formation of multinucleated muscle fibers) the stepwise development of differentiated structure (muscle fibers, striated contractile fibers, formation of neuroreceptors); the presence in differentiated muscle cells of specific muscle proteins (myosin, actin, creatine kinase) representing large fractions of total cellular protein and the unidirectional nature of the event (muscle fibers do not revert to undifferentiated structure).

Two cellular systems can be used to study myoblast differentiation *in vitro*: a) muscle cells from chicken or rat embryos; and b) a line of myoblast mutant propagated in culture by serial passage. The myoblast cell line offer certain advantages for biochemical studies, primarily uniform cell types and possibility of selecting mutant clones.

We have made very useful advances in our ability to maintain the competence of the myoblast line in culture to differentiate. Using this system, we have found that cell fusion depend on the cultural medium, more specifically that the cultural medium requirement for cell growth and cell fusion are different and the concentration of fetal calf serum is of critical importance in determining the behavior of myoblast in culture. It has been found that cell fusion does not require DNA synthesis, and is not prevented by a variety of inhibitors of cell replication. We, and others, have determined that cell fusion is accompanied by synthesis of specific muscle proteins such as creatine kinase and myosin. In collaboration with Dr. Robert S. Adelstein of the National Heart and Lung Institute, we have made the interesting observation that the subunit structure of myosin formed before and after fusion is different, a clear indication that there are several different myosin genes and that their expression is related to the stages of differentiation.

Keyword Descriptors:

Cell differentiation, tissue culture, myoblast, myofiber, cell fusion, muscle proteins, myoblast cell line.

Honors and Awards: None

Publications: None

Project No. Z01 MH 00933-01 LGCB
1. Laboratory of General and Comparative Biochemistry
2. Section on Proteins
3. Bethesda, Maryland

PHS-ADAMHA-NIMH
Individual Project Report
July 1, 1974 through June 30, 1975

Project Title: Study of the S-Adenosylmethionine Synthetase of Yeast

Previous Serial Number: None

Principal Investigator: Giulio L. Cantoni

Other Investigators: Peter K. Chiang

Cooperating Units: None

Man Years:

Total:	1-1/12
Professional:	1-1/12
Other:	0

Project Description:

S-Adenosylmethionine (AMe) synthetase is an enzyme found in all living cells. The reaction catalyzed by this enzyme (the adenosylation of methionine at the expense of ATP), has been extensively studied in the past in this laboratory by Cantoni, Durell, Mudd, Jamieson and Mann. It is well established that enzyme bound tripolyphosphate is an obligatory intermediate in the reaction and that this intermediate is cleaved in an oriented manner by a tripolyphosphatase activity that is associated with the synthetase and is stimulated by AMe through a positive allosteric effect. In spite of much work on the reaction mechanism and on the kinetics of the reaction little is known about two aspects of this enzyme: a) its molecular structure; and b) its regulation. With regard to the molecular structure, it is not known at the present time what the molecular weight of the enzyme is nor whether the enzyme, as seems most probable, is composed of subunits. One would indeed anticipate that the enzyme would exhibit a complex structure and studies of the number of subunits, their characteristics and interaction will almost certainly yield very interesting results. With regard to the regulatory properties of the AMe synthetase, very little is known about it in mammals. There are sex differences in the enzyme level in females having higher enzyme levels and androgens lowering the enzyme level in controlled males.

In microorganisms and fungi, on the other hand, there is considerable evidence that links AMe synthetase and/or its product (AMe) to the control of methionine biosynthesis. Mutants have been isolated both in *E. coli* and yeast that have *in vivo* and *in vitro* very low levels of AMe synthetase and in these mutants the control of methionine biosynthesis is dramatically altered.

Based on these considerations, it was decided to return to the study of AMe synthetase and yeast was selected as the source of the enzyme since, for a variety of reasons, yeast might be the organism of choice for studies of the biology and control of AMe synthetase.

In the course of enzyme purification studies, we have made the very interesting observation that the enzyme exists in two forms: AMe synthetase I and II, that differ in their chromatographic behavior. AMe synthetase II has been purified very extensively and purification of AMe synthetase I is currently being perfected. Next, the two purified forms of yeast AMe synthetase will then be compared with regards to their kinetic parameters, molecular weight and subunit structure. The biological significance of these two species of the enzyme will then be studied both in yeast and in other species.

Keyword Descriptors:

S-Adenosylmethionine, S-Adenosylmethionine synthetase, S-Adenosylmethionine biosynthesis control, Molecular weight, Regulatory functions.

Honors and Awards: None

Publications:

Cantoni, G. L.: Biological methylation: selected aspects. *Ann. Rev. Biochem.* 44: 1975, in press.

Project No. Z01 MH 00934-03 LGCB
1. Laboratory of General and Comparative Biochemistry
2. Section on Proteins
3. Bethesda, Maryland

PHS-ADAMHA-NIMH
Individual Project Report
July 1, 1974 through June 30, 1975

Project Title: Studies on the Biochemical Basis of Narcotic Drug Action

Previous Serial Number: M - LGĊB 60

Principal Investigator: Werner A. Klee

Other Investigators: Marshall Nirenberg, Shail Sharma, Everette May, Arthur Jacobson

Cooperating Units: Lab. of Biochemical Genetics, NHLI
Section on Medicinal Chemistry, Lab. of Chemistry, NIAMDD

Man Years:

Total:	2
Professional:	1
Other:	1

Project Description:

Morphine and the very large group of narcotic analgesics related to it have long been believed to interact with specific receptors in the nervous system. Our studies are aimed at the detailed characterization of the receptor-opiate interaction as well as the elucidation of the biochemical consequences of such interactions. The work has as its ultimate goal the arrival at an understanding of the mechanism by which the opiates achieve their analgesic and other specific effects and also of how tolerance and drug dependence develop.

In the past year we have made considerable progress towards both of our major goals. In collaboration with members of the Section of Medicinal Chemistry, NIAMDD, we have been carrying out a systematic investigation of the effect of changes in the structure of opiate analgesics and their antagonists on the interaction with the receptor as studied by binding measurements with partially purified brain receptor preparations. These studies have provided insights into the importance of the several parts of the opiate molecule for recognition by the receptor and have, perhaps, provided some clues as to the nature of the naturally occurring ligand which we believe normally interacts with these receptor sites.

We have also in the past year, in collaboration with members of the Laboratory of Biochemical Genetics, NHLI, obtained data which show that the opiate receptors of neuroblastoma x glioma hybrid cells are coupled to adenylate cyclase in such a way as to inhibit the activity of this master regulatory enzyme when opiates are bound to the receptors. Morphine antagonists are able to reverse its inhibition of adenylate cyclase. Mixed agonist-antagonist narcotics, such as nalorphine, behave as inhibitors when present alone (agonism) and reverse morphine when the two are present simultaneously (antagonism). All of the evidence compiled to date makes it likely that the interaction of opiate receptors with adenylate cyclase is the primary site of action of the narcotics. When the neuroblastoma x glioma hybrid cells are exposed to morphine continuously for one or more days, the cells adapt their adenylate cyclase levels so that they are functionally both tolerant to and dependent upon morphine. These addicted cells have higher than normal levels of adenylate cyclase activity and thus are able to maintain relatively normal cyclic AMP levels even in the presence of morphine, and are therefore tolerant to the drug. They are dependent upon morphine since abrupt withdrawal of the drug causes the production of abnormally high cyclic AMP levels. These effects are being studied in more detail since we have every reason to believe that they may be those responsible for tolerance and dependence in animals and man as well as in cell cultures.

Keyword Descriptors:

Morphine, narcotics, adenylate cyclase, opiate receptors, tissue culture, neuroblastoma x glioma hybrid cells, tolerance, drug dependence.

Honors and Awards: None

Publications:

Klee, W. A. and Nirenberg, M.: A neuroblastoma x glioma cell line with morphine receptors. Proc. Natl. Acad. Sci. USA 71: 3474-3477, 1974.

Sharma, S. K., Nirenberg, M. and Klee, W.A.: Morphine receptors as regulators of adenylate cyclase activity. Proc. Natl. Acad. Sci. USA 72: 590-594, 1975.

Klee, W. A. and Nirenberg, M.: Neuronal cells in tissue culture with narcotic receptor sites. Report of the Committee on Problems of Drug Dependence, 1974, pp. 345-349.

Rogers, M. E., Ong, H. H., May, E. L. and Klee, W. A.: Analgetic activity and *in vitro* binding constants of some N-alkyl-3-benzazocines. J. Med. Chem., in press.

Project No. Z01 MH 00935-08-LGCB
1. Laboratory of General and Comparative Biochemistry
2. Section on Proteins
3. Bethesda, Maryland

PHS-ADAMHA-NIMH
Individual Project Report
July 1, 1974 through June 30, 1975

Project Title: Determination of the Effect of Small Viruses and their Nucleic Acids on the Biochemistry of Living Organisms

Previous Serial Number: M - LGCB 56

Principal Investigator: Carl R. Merril

Other Investigators: M. Geier, R. Yarkin, M. Andrews, R. LaPolla, A. Shankar and M. Gottesman

Cooperating Units: National Cancer Institute

Man Years:

Total: 5
Professional: 1-1/2
Other: 3-1/2

Project Description:

Human cell fibroblasts from galactosemic individuals have been shown to develop UDP-gal transferase enzyme following infection with the bacterial virus, lambda-p-gal. It is clear from extensive studies that there are a number of variables in this system. These variables cause fairly large fluctuations in the enzyme levels that are obtainable in phage infected cells. Methods for separating the E. coli from the mammalian enzyme have been developed. These methods involve differential column chromatography and heat sensitivity of the enzymes.

Preliminary results utilizing these techniques indicate that the enzyme formed following infection with lambda-p-gal virus is "bacterial-like". A further indication that bacterial viruses interact directly with mammalian cells has been the observation that infection with bacterial viruses often protect mammalian cells from destruction by known animal viruses. Collaborative studies with Dr. Kenneth Roozen have shown that this inhibition is not due to interferon production.

The lab has developed two animal diets to simulate genetic disorders. The first diet, a leucine starvation diet for mice, has been developed and has been used to demonstrate that the inability to synthesize leucine, in the mouse, must be due to the lack of at most three enzymes. A bacterial virus containing the genetic information for the enzymes required for leucine synthesis has been constructed and is currently being used on leucine starved mice. The second diet utilizes high levels of galactose. This diet has been shown to be lethal to mice. Studies utilizing a lambda virus carrying the bacterial galactose operon are being conducted to see if infection with such a virus affords protection against this diet. Continued studies on galactose metabolism in both prokaryotes and eukaryotes have led to the development of a new assay for the epimerase enzyme. This assay is essentially 100 times more sensitive than previous assays, and utilizes thin layer chromatography techniques.

Keyword Descriptors:

Bacteriovirus, galactosemia, transferase, epimerase, galactose operon, transducing virus, escape synthesis, genetic disease, intercellular gene transfer, bacteriophage interactions with higher organisms.

Honors and Awards: None

Publications:

Trigg, M.E., Geier, M.R. and Merril, C.R.: Letter to the editor. N. Eng. J. Med. 292: 214, 1974.

Merril, C.R.: Letter to the editor. Science 188: 8, 1975.

Geier, M.R. and Attallah, A.F.M.: Characterization of E. coli bacterial viruses in commercial sera. In Vitro, in press.

Friedman, T.B., Yarkin R.J. and Merril, C.R.: Galactose and glucose metabolism in galactokinase deficient, galactose-1-P-uridyl transferase deficient and normal human fibroblasts. J. Cell Physiol., in press.

Trigg, M.E., Geier, M.R. and Merril, C.R.: Comparative distribution and splenic accumulation of bacteriophage lambda in germfree and conventional mice. IRCS Med. Sci. 3: 261, 1975.

LaPolla, R.J., Geier, M.R., Friedman, T.B. and Merril, C.R.: CO_2 Production from galactose in Gal-deficient E. coli. J. Bacteriol., in press.

Project No. Z01 MH 00936-12 LGCB
1. Laboratory of General and Comparative Biochemistry
2. Section on Alkaloid Biosynthesis
3. Bethesda, Maryland

PHS-ADAMHA-NIMH
Individual Project Report
July 1, 1974 through June 30, 1975

Project Title: Homocystinuria: Methionine Metabolism in Mammals

Previous Serial Number: M-LGCB 43

Principal Investigator: S. Harvey Mudd

Other Investigator: B. William Uhlendorf

Cooperating Units: None

Man Years:

Total: 2
Professional: 1
Other: 1

Project Description:

The objectives of this project are to obtain a detailed knowledge of the biochemistry of sulfur containing compounds in the mammalian body. Inextricably involved also is the biochemistry of transmethylation. Special attention will be focussed upon the regulatory devices which control these areas. We are concerned, too, with the inborn errors of metabolism due to abnormalities in these areas. Definition of the underlying lesions and their pathophysiology may help in the management of these diseases and offers unique help in understanding normal metabolism.

A clear and quantitative understanding of the metabolism of methionine and related compounds has long awaited the answers to a series of interrelated questions: (a) What are the relative demands made by each of the many methyl transfer reactions for which methionine, and its activated derivative, S-adenosylmethionine, are the common precursors? (b) How much methionine is utilized for the mutually exclusive requirements of transmethylation and polyamine (i.e. spermine and spermidine) biosynthesis? (c) What are the relative fluxes of homocysteine at the metabolic branchpoint at which this amino acid must either be condensed with serine to form cystathionine (and subsequently cysteine), or be remethylated back to methionine? (d) What is the relative importance of homocysteine remethylation through preformed ingested methyl groups (i.e. the choline-betaine dependent reactions) compared to remethylation through newly formed methyl groups (the N^5-methyltetrahydrofolate, colabamin (B_{12}) dependent, pathway)?

During the past year we have provided approximate answers to these questions for the intact normal young adult human on several different dietary regimens. The experimental bases for these answers were furnished by measurements of the excretions of the methylated metabolites creatine, creatinine, and sarcosine in normal volunteer subjects on fixed diets containing varying amounts of methionine and choline. The subjects were demonstrated to be in metabolic steady states during these studies, as indicated by maintenance of constant weights, as well as their remaining within the zones of nitrogen and sulfur equilibria. Thus, measurements of intake and output of methyl groups could validly be used for calculation of balances. Young males on "normal" diets containing approximately 9.9 millimole methionine and 4.5 millimole choline daily excreted 15.6 millimole endogenously formed creatinine and 0.4 millimole creatine. Data from the literature indicated that the excretion of all other methylated metabolic end-products combined was only 1.5 millimole. Surprisingly, creatine-creatinine biosynthesis determines to a large extent the demand for labile methyls. Calculations showed, also, that polyamine synthesis consumed less than 0.5 millimole methionine daily. Thus, this pathway does not represent a relatively large drain upon the methionine supply. Under these conditions, the subjects were shown to be absorbing approximately 13.5 millimoles labile methyls, and utilizing 18.6 millimole daily. The difference must be made up by "de novo" labile methyl formation to the extent of 5.1 millimole. These results also permitted the calculation that 8.7 millimoles of homocysteine were being methylated daily, 3.6 by the use of betaine methyl and 5.1 by the use of N^5-methyltetrahydrofolate methyl. Thus, the average homocysteinyl moiety was cycled 1.9 times before being converted to cystathionine. Looked at in another way, the chances were that at any moment 47% of the available homocysteine was being converted to methionine, whereas 53% was being converted to cystathionine.

On diets with the methionine intake limited to 4.7 millimole and choline to 0.4 millimole, or less, the endogenous creatinine-creatine excretions were essentially unchanged. It could then be calculated that methylneogenesis had been greatly enhanced to 13 millimole per day, that the average homocysteine moiety was cycling 3.9 times, and that at any moment 74% of homocysteine was being diverted back to methionine by remethylation using N^5-methyltetrahydrofolate, whereas only 26% was being converted to cystathionine. All these changes are physiologically understandable in terms of conserving the limited available supply of homocysteinyl moieties. Analogous figures were derived for the female subjects.

The significance of these results is that they provide for the first time an approximate quantitative understanding of the metabolism of methionine and related compounds. The methodology developed and the conceptual framework furnish a point of departure for the assessment of the effects of genetic, nutritional, pharmacological, and hormonal factors which may alter the quantitative relationships between the major avenues of methionine metabolism.

At least one area of rather major uncertainty remains in the above analyses: the extent to which oxidation of methyl groups contributes to the consumption of both labile and non-labile methyls. These pathways are difficult to assess in the normal human because the product, formaldehyde, is converted to a variety of other metabolites, and thus is not readily quantitated. To meet this difficulty, we have initiated studies of patients with sarcosine dehydrogenase deficiency. Such subjects have a metabolic block in the major pathway for methyl group oxidation which renders them unable to oxidize the methyl group of sarcosine. As a result, methyls which in the normal human would be converted to formaldehyde and hence be lost to detection are excreted by these patients as the readily measurable amino acid, sarcosine. By studying the sarcosine excretion of such patients in metabolic steady states upon a number of different methionine and choline intakes, we hope to be able to quantitate the extent of oxidation of both the non-labile methyls of choline and the labile methyls of methionine and choline. These studies will be continued during the next year.

Keyword Descriptors:

methionine, homocysteine, methyl balance, sarcosine, choline, betaine, methylneogenesis, cystathionine

Honors and Awards: None

Publications:

Levy, H. L., Mudd, S. H., Uhlendorf, B. W., and Madigan, P. M.: Cystathioninuria and homocystinuria. Clinica Chimica Acta, 58: 51-59, 1975.

Poole, J. R., Mudd, S. H., Conerly, E. B., and Edwards, W. A.: Homocystinuria due to cystathionine synthase deficiency: studies of nitrogen balance and sulfur excretion. J. Clin. Investigation, in press.

Mudd, S. H., Poole, J. R.: Labile methyl balances for normal humans on various dietary regimens. Metabolism, in press.

Freeman, J. M., Finkelstein, J. D., and Mudd, S. H.: Folate responsive homocystinuria and "schizophrenia." A defect in methylation due to deficient 5,10-methylenetetrahydrofolate reductase activity. New Engl. J. Med., 292: 491-496, 1975.

Project No. Z01 MH 00937-10 LGCB
1. Laboratory of General and Comparative Biochemistry
2. Section on Alkaloid Biosynthesis
3. Bethesda, Maryland

PHS-ADAMHA-NIMH
Individual Project Report
July 1, 1974 through June 30, 1975

Project Title: Transsulfuration in Higher Plants

Principal Investigators: John Giovanelli, and Anne H. Datko

Other Investigator: S. Harvey Mudd

Cooperating Units: None

Man Years:

Total: 2-1/12
Professional: 2-1/12
Other: 0

Project Description:

Previous work has shown that plants are potentially capable of synthesizing homocysteine (and methionine) by two main pathways - the direct sulfhydration pathway and the transsulfuration pathway. The long term objective of this project is to determine the relative physiological significance and the mechanism of control of these two pathways. The problem is currently being attacked along the following lines:

(1) A study of the *in vivo* kinetics of incorporation of sulfate-^{35}S into sulfur amino acids, as a means of assessing the relative physiological contribution of the two pathways.

(2) A study of the enzymes involved in the two pathways, and determination of chemical nature and *in vivo* concentrations of the physiologically important substrates for these enzymes.

Most of the results described in this report have been obtained with the green alga *Chlorella*. This is an excellent experimental organism since it grows rapidly in axenic culture under defined conditions. Furthermore, we have demonstrated that this organism can be grown under steady state conditions in which the sizes of the pools of critical sulfur intermediates are such as to allow successful analysis of the kinetics of sulfate assimilation (see below).

Methods were developed for the isolation and quantitation of the important intermediates (cysteine, cystathionine, homocysteine and methionine) and end products (protein methionine, protein cysteine, glutathione and plant sulfolipid) of the incorporation of sulfate-^{35}S by Chlorella grown under steady state conditions with limiting sulfate. Pool sizes of sulfur intermediates and rates of synthesis of end products of sulfur metabolism were determined by allowing Chlorella to grow for many generations in the presence of sulfate-^{35}S of known specific activity. The pool size of each compound was determined from the total radioactivity present in that compound. The rate of synthesis of each end product was calculated from its pool size and the rate of growth of the organism.

These estimates of the pool sizes of sulfur intermediates and rates of synthesis of end products were used to set up two models of homocysteine biosynthesis. In the transsulfuration model, ^{35}S would be incorporated at early times (i.e. less than approximately 1 minute) predominantly into cysteine, next into cystathionine, and then into homocysteine. In the direct sulfhydration model, ^{35}S would appear at early times in cysteine and homocysteine in approximately equal amounts, and cystathionine would be labeled to a small extent. One such kinetic experiment has been carried out. Analyses of the resulting samples have been underway for several months, but are not yet complete. Preliminary indications are that the observed kinetics of ^{35}S incorporation are consistent with transsulfuration being the major pathway. The values for the sample taken at the earliest time (12 seconds) permit the setting of an upper limit of 18% of homocysteine synthesis occurring via direct sulfhydration. In future experiments it is planned to extend this approach to earlier times in hopes of confirming the present findings and obtaining a more accurate estimate of any contribution of the direct sulfhydration pathway.

Optimal conditions were established for assaying in crude extracts of Chlorella and barley seedlings the enzyme(s) (sulfhydrase) that incorporates sulfur in the direct sulfhydration pathway:

$$H_2S + X\cdot(CH_2)_2\cdot CH(NH_2)\cdot COOH \rightarrow HS-(CH_2)_2\cdot CH(NH_2)\cdot COOH + XH$$

α-aminobutyryl donor homocysteine

The sensitivity and specificity of the assay was greatly increased over those of previous methods by coupling the formation of homocysteine to the synthesis of S-adenosylhomocysteine in the presence of added adenosine and rat liver "condensing enzyme". The major product of the sulfhydrase reaction was definitively characterized as homocysteine. Thiothreonine (a structural isomer of homocysteine, $CH_3\cdot CH(SH)\cdot CH(NH_2)\cdot COOH$), which has been reported by other workers to be a major product when extracts of the plants Lemna and peas were incubated under reaction conditions similar to ours, was not formed in detectable amounts in Chlorella extracts. Optimal conditions were determined with O-phosphohomoserine and O-acetylhomoserine as α-aminobutyryl donors. At equimolar concentrations, activity with O-phosphohomoserine is at least 8 fold that with O-acetylhomoserine. Green plants are unique in their capacity to use O-phosphohomoserine as a substrate for the sulfhydrase reaction, since other organisms are specific for either O-acetylhomoserine or O-succinylhomoserine. Crude extracts of Chlorella assayed under optimal conditions in the presence of O-phosphohomoserine were at least as active in the sulfhydrase reaction as in the synthesis of cystathionine. These relative enzyme activities were determined with extracts of Chlorella growing with non-limiting sulfate, and suggest that the direct sulfhydration pathway may play a more important role in Chlorella growing under these conditions than with the limiting concentration of sulfate used for the kinetic labeling experiment described above. The sulfhydrase enzyme system is now being used as a sensitive probe (in the presence of high specific activity $H_2{}^{35}S$) to determine the chemical nature and in vivo concentration of the physiologically important α-aminobutyryl donor(s) in the direct sulfhydration pathway.

Future research will be continued along the following lines:

(a) Efforts to define in more general terms the ratio of homocysteine synthesized by the transsulfuration and direct sulfhydration pathways, and the physiological factors which affect this ratio. Our initial assessment of the importance of the transsulfuration pathway is based on the results of one experiment with Chlorella growing under one set of conditions. It is planned to extend the studies of sulfate-^{35}S incorporation to Chlorella growing under various conditions, and to other members of the plant kingdom. These studies will be corelated with the levels of enzymes and substrates of the two pathways.

(b) Purification and studies of the properties of key enzymes (cystathionine synthase and the sulfhydrase) of the two pathways.

(c) Physiological and biochemical studies with algae (wild type), and algal mutants in which the biosynthesis of homocysteine is affected.

Keyword Descriptors:

transsulfuration, direct sulfhydration, O-phosphohomoserine, cystathionine, homocysteine, chemostat, steady-state kinetics

Honors and Awards: None

Publications:

Giovanelli, J., Mudd, S. H., and Datko, A. H.: Homoserine esterification in green plants. Plant Physiology, 54: 725-736, 1974.

Datko, A. H., Mudd, S. H., and Giovanelli, J.: A sensitive and specific assay for cystathionine: cystathionine content of several plant tissues. Analytical Biochemistry, 62: 531-545, 1974.

Datko, A. H., Giovanelli, J., and Mudd, S. H.: Preparation of cystathionine sulfoxide and sulfone, and some properties relating to their differentiation. Analytical Biochemistry, 64: 80-84, 1975.

Project No. Z01 MH 00981-10 LNB
1. Lab of Neurobiology
2.
3. Bethesda, Maryland, and Woods Hole, Massachusetts

PHS-HSMHA-NIMH
Individual Project Report
July 1, 1974 through June 30, 1975

Project Title: Analysis of the macromolecular structure of nerve membranes during excitation

Previous Serial Number: M-NB-1

Principal Investigators: Ichiji Tasaki, M.D., Akira Warashina, Ph.D. Isao Inoue, Ph.D. and Ronald Sandlin

Cooperating Unit: Marine Biological Laboratory, Woods Hole, Mass.

Man Years
Total: 4.5
Professional: 3.6
Other: 0.9

Project Description:

During the past year the research effort of the group was divided into two directions: (A) elucidation of the behavior of various dye molecules in the nerve membrane during the process of nerve excitation, and (B) analyses of the process of excitation by non-electrical means. Many dye molecules which have finite solubility in both water and lipids can be used to stain the nerve membrane. The optical properties (extinction coefficient, absorption and fluorescence emission spectra, quantum yield of fluorescence, molecular orientation, etc.) of the dye molecules in the membrane are determined by the interaction between the membrane macromolecules and the dye molecules. It was found in this laboratory that the conformational changes in the membrane macromolecules during nerve excitation can be studied by examining the optical properties of the dye molecules. During the summer of 1974, it was found possible to incorporate two kinds of dye molecules in the nerve membrane of squid axons or of crab nerves and to study resonance transfer of electronic energy between the molecules. Furthermore, by measuring the dye absorbance during nerve excitation, it was found that transient changes in the state of aggregation of a certain class of dyes can be examined. The results of these studies of membrane macromolecule-dye interaction are expected to lead us to a better understanding of the physico-chemical properties of the nerve membrane.

Absorption spectra, fluorescence excitation and emission spectra of the dye molecules incorporated in the nerve membrane of squid axons and crab nerves were determined by a special device constructed in this laboratory. (To determine the spectra of the dye in the membrane during action potentials, construction of a special device is required because of the low time-resolution of commercially available spectroscopes.) The reliability of the spectra obtained by the special device has been established by previous studies. In the analyses of the mechanism of nerve excitation by non-electric means, the method of intracellular perfusion invented in this laboratory was employed.

The following results were obtained during the past year:

1. We examined the optical properties of 8 different positional isomers of amino-naphthalene-sulfonate in the nerve membrane. It was shown that the sensitivity of the optical properties to the solvent polarity is essential for production of changes in fluorescence intensity during nerve excitation by a dye molecule.

2. The phenomenon known as resonance transfer of electronic energy was demonstrated by incorporating p-chloro-anilino-naphthalene-sulfonate (donor) and Eastman merocyanin-540 (acceptor) in the nerve membrane. The average distance between these donor and acceptor molecules in the membrane was estimated.

3. Changes in the absorption spectra of a variety of dye molecules in nerve membrane were demonstrated during nerve excitation. These findings indicate that either the state of aggregation or the absorption spectrum of the dye molecules undergo transient changes when the membrane is electrically excited.

4. Under intiacellular perfusion, it was found possible to excite the nerve membrane by various non-electric means. Changes in the internal hydrostatic pressure, osmolarity of the perfusion fluid, internal pH, etc., were found to be effective means of exciting the nerve membrane. The relationship between electrical and non-electrical means of exciting the nerve membrane was found.

To understand the behavior of the nervous system under normal and pathological conditions, it is essential to clarify the process of nerve excitation on the molecular basis. There is little doubt that the effects of many chemicals which affect the function of the nervous system are brought about by binding of the chemicals with the nerve membrane. Since excitable nerve membranes are extremely labile, it is usually very difficult to apply standard biochemical methods to study the mode of non-covalent binding of chemicals to the nerve membrane. The results of the optical and electrophysiological studies described above have already elucidated some important aspects of the labile structure of the nerve membrane and its changes during nerve excitation.

Further experiments using the method of spectral analysis during excitation are required to elucidate the physicochemical basis of nerve excitation. Furthermore, the behavior of various neurotoxic drugs in the nerve membrane will be examined. Dr. Tasaki is planning to publish a monograph summarizing the results of studies carried out in the laboratory during the past ten years.

Keyword Descriptors:

nerve membrane; membrane macromolecules; membrane probes; fluorescence probes; fluorescence signals; absorption signals.

Honors and Awards:

Dr. Tasaki was invited to attend and present papers at a number of symposia, including the multidisciplinary workshop on the inner ear and hearing, chaired by Dr. Jorgen Fex and sponsored by the National Institute of Neurological Diseases and Stroke.

Publications:

Carbone, E., Sisco, K. and Warashina, A.: Physico-chemical properties of 2,6-TNS binding sites in squid giant axons: Involvement of water molecules in the excitation process. J. Membrane Biol. 18: 263-276, 1974.

Inoue, I., Tasaki, I. and Kobatake, Y.: A study of the effects of externally applied sodium-ions and detection of spatial non-uniformity of the squid axon membrane under internal perfusion. Biophys. Chem. 2: 116-126, 1974.

Tasaki, I.: Evidence for phase-transition in nerve membrane. In Mintz, S.L. and Widmayer, S.M. (Eds.): Progress in the Neurosciences and Related Fields. New York, Plenum Publishing Corp., 1974, pp. 59-66.

Tasaki, I.: Nerve excitation. New experimental evidence for the macromolecular hypothesis. In Monnier, A.M. (Ed.): Trends in Neurophysiology. Paris, Masson et Cie, 1974, pp. 79-90.

Tasaki, I. and Carbone, E.: A macromolecular approach to nerve excitation. In Bronner, F. and Kleinzeller, A. (Eds.): Current Topics in Membranes and Transport. New York, Academic Press, 1974, pp. 283-325.

Tasaki, I., Sisco, K. and Warashina, A.: Alignment of anilinonaphthalenesulfonate and related fluorescent probe molecules in squid axon membrane and in synthetic polymers. Biophys. Chem. 2: 316-326, 1974.

Project No. Z01 MH 00982-08 LNB
1. Lab of Neurobiology
2.
3. Bethesda, Maryland

PHS-HSMHA-NIMH
Individual Project Report
July 1, 1974 through June 30, 1975

Project Title: Sensory-motor integration in the primate visual system

Previous Serial Number: M-NB-2

Principal Investigators: Robert H. Wurtz, Ph.D., Charles W. Mohler, M.D.,Ph.D. Joan Baizer, Ph.D. and David L. Robinson, Ph.D.

Man Years

Total:	6.0
Professional:	3.5
Other:	2.5

Project Description:

The visual system in the primate consists primarily of two pathways from the eye to the brain. One pathway traverses the lateral geniculate nucleus in the thalamus to reach the striate cortex of the occipital lobes. The other pathway projects directly from the eye to the superior colliculus which sits at the top of the brain stem. Our immediate goal is to understand the different ways visual information is processed in these two systems and how this information is utilized in producing behavior. By understanding this input to the brain we hope to gain greater understanding of how the brain produces behavior.

As in previous years we have studied the brain in awake monkeys trained to do a number of visual-motor tasks. The discharge of single brain cells has been recorded in awake monkeys (Macaca mulatta) trained to do several visually related tasks. The monkey sat in a chair facing a screen and fixated on a point of light for several seconds in order to obtain a reward. During this fixation period, a second spot of light was projected onto the screen and used to determine the area of the visual field in which the spot modified the discharge of the cell (the visual receptive field of the cell). Rapid eye movements were elicited by turning off one fixation point and turning on another point thereby inducing an eye movement from one spot to the other. An on-line digital computer was used to control the monkey's behavior, display the single cell data while the experiment was in progress, and record the data on film.

We have studied the two visual pathways at the three different anatomical points: the superior colliculus, the lateral geniculate nucleus, and the circumstriate cortex. Since the specific goals of these experiments are different, each one will be presented separately below.

In the first area studied, the superior colliculus, we have previously shown that cells in the top three layers (of a total of seven layers) respond to visual stimuli and that this response is modified when we require the monkey to attend to the stimulus in order to make an eye movement to that stimulus. We had previously found that many of these same cells receive an input from the oculomotor system since their discharge rate is suppressed when the monkey makes an eye movement even in the absence of visual input. The present experiments (done by D.L. Robinson and R.H. Wurtz) determined whether any effect on visual processing resulted from this suppression associated with eye movements. In particular, we were interested to see whether these cells might contribute to the distinction man makes between stimulus movement in the external world and stimulus movement produced by his own eye movements. We found that 60% of the cells in these superficial layers of the colliculus respond to stimulus movement across the stationary receptive field of a cell over a wide variety of range of stimulus velocities -- from stationary up to 900°/sec. This 900°/sec is the peak velocity of a 20° eye movement so that it is clear these cells could discharge to stimuli swept in front of the eye at velocities comparable to those occurring during an eye movement. We then studied such cells to determine their response to stimulus movement produced by the eye movement sweeping the receptive field across a stationary stimulus. About half of these cells did not respond to stimulus movement caused by eye movements; these cells are therefore able to distinguish between stimulus movements resulting from eye movements and those resulting from real world stimulus movements. The ability to distinguish between the two types of stimulus movement is present for all directions of stimulus and eye movements tests.

It seems unlikely that visual factors prevent these cells from responding with eye movements since these cells continue to distinguish eye induced from real stimulus movement when the same experiments are conducted in a very darkened environment where visual factors are greatly reduced. The lack of response with eye movement seems to be caused by the eye movement itself since these cells show a suppression of background firing whenever the monkey makes spontaneous eye movements in total darkness. Thus these cells probably receive a non-visual signal about the occurrence of an eye movement, and it is this signal which prevents them from responding to stimulus movements caused by eye movements. Whether this input is from a corollary discharge of the output to the eye muscles or a proprioceptive input from the eye remains to be determined.

The second area investigated was in the pathway to the striate cortex: the lateral geniculate nucleus. Here the goal (in experiments done by C.W. Mohler) was also to determine the influence of eye movements on visual processing. Previous experiments done in this laboratory indicated that cells in this pathway did not distinguish real stimulus movement from stimulus movement resulting from eye movements. Nor were responses to a visual stimuli better before an eye movement was made to the visual stimulus as was the case in our previous experiments on the superior colliculus. The present experiments were designed to determine whether any influence of the eye movement on visual processing occurred <u>after</u> the eye movement. To do these experiments the visual receptive field was first determined as the monkey fixated. Then the response to a visual stimulus (circular and annular spots centered on the visual field with a duration of 65 msec) was measured during successive fixation trials and compared to the response when the stimulus was presented 0, 100, 200 and 500 msec after completion of saccades from another part of the visual field to the fixation spot. The visual response of 40% of the neurons tested changed when the visual stimulus was presented after a saccade and the effect is usually maximal during the first 200 msec after the saccade. Although the visual stimuli usually elicited a combined excitatory-inhibitory response, the saccade only modifies the excitatory response. On cells which showed a dramatic change in response following a saccade across a lighted background, there is no change in the cell's response following a saccade across a darkened background. This modulation of visual processing therefore results from the sweep of the visual stimulus across the retina rather than from any extra-retinal input. In a few cells there is a consistent change in the visual response following a saccade across a darkened background, suggesting that some modulation of visual processing may result from an extra-retinal source.

The third area studied was the circumstriate area of cerebral cortex just anterior to the termination of the pathway to striate cortex. The elaborate processing carried out in area 17 relating to position, shape, size, color and movement of visual stimuli might be expected to continue in this next anatomical area. The goal of these experiments (done by J. Bazier and D.L. Robinson in collaboration with B.M. Dow of N.E.I.) was to determine what type of processing does occur in this area.

Cells in the buried posterior bank of the lunate sulcus were studied, and about 90% of all cells were visually driven. Most of these cells fall into distinct groups. Each group is concerned with a different feature of the visual stimulus and is relatively insensitive to variations in all other features. Oriented cells are best driven by a properly oriented and positioned slit of light. They respond equally well to different colored slits, and equally well to both directions of movement of the appropriate slit. Their receptive fields are large in relation to the size of the optimal stimulus. Spot-pandirectional cells respond best to small spots of light anywhere over a relatively large area of the visual field. Those that respond to movement respond equally well to all directions of movement of a slit or spot. When tested with slits of light the response is poorer than the response to spots, but it is equal to all orientations. Responses to all colors are equal. Directional cells are especially concerned with moving stimuli. They respond best to a stimulus moving in a certain direction at an optimal velocity. While they may have a preferred size they are insensitive to stimulus contrast, orientation, leading edge configuration, etc. They likewise are not concerned with color. Inhibited-by-light cells have remarkably high spontaneous activity. In our situation, they can only be inhibited by the proper stimulus, which is a large spot filling the receptive field. Some of these cells have antagonistic surrounds, but none sensitive to stimulus orientation have been seen. Color cells likewise do not have much orientation preference, but are, on the whole, concerned with the color of the stimulus falling on their fields. Side-stopped cells have receptive fields that may be mapped with small spots to show an excitatory region. The best response from the cell is achieved with a stimulus that just fills the excitatory region. On one side of the excitatory region is a powerful inhibitory flank; extending the effective stimulus into that flank sharply decreases, then eliminates the response of the cell to light in the excitatory region. These cells, then are sensitive only to stimuli of limited size or extent.

The significance of our experiments in these three areas of the visual system relate to how the brain processes visual information and how it modifies this information. We have extended knowledge of visual processing one step further into the brain through the study of neurons of circumstriate cortex. Experiments confirm the expectation that the visual processing begun in striate cortex proceeds in circumstriate cortex. The processing of different stimulus features is clearly divided between cells, some are more responsible for color some for orientation, etc. Thus a parallel processing of different stimulus features by different cell groups emerges as the apparent mode of operation of this area of cortex.

The modification of visual information is seen most clearly in the ability of cells in the superior colliculus to discriminate real object movement from self-induced movement. No such distinction of stimulus movement is made by striate cortex neurons so that these cells in the colliculus perform a function frequently postulated but never before found in the primate. One hypothesis of the superior colliculus function is that it contributes to the selection of important stimuli from the whole visual field for further examination; these cells might provide the oculomotor system with a signal about the occurrence of external movement -- uncontaminated by inputs from self-induced movements. The visual stimulation produced by the sweep of the visual world across the retina with an eye movement is itself a powerful modifier of visual processing and, in contrast to the colliculus, has powerful effects on striate cortex cells. The experiments on cells in the lateral geniculate nucleus have also shown dramatic effects of the sweep of the visual background during an eye movement on the visual processing. But in addition they suggest that in this pathway there may also be an extra-retinal input.

These findings all emphasize a point stressed in previous reports: while the primate brain has two visual pathways, the type of processing and interactions occurring is strikingly different in the two pathways. This in turn offers some hope that aspects of fairly complex brain function, particularly those closely related to sensory input and motor output, may be localized to a certain set of anatomical structures.

In the future we plan to complete the physiological studies of geniculate nucleus and circumstriate cortex. Dr. Wurtz will spend much of the coming year on a foreign assignment to concentrate on problems related to the visual behavior of man and animals.

Keyword Descriptors:

vision; sensory-motor integration; circumstriate cortex; superior colliculus; lateral geniculate nucleus; corollary discharge; extra-retinal signal; visual processing; receptive field; primate.

Project No. Z01 MH 00983-01 LNB
1. Lab of Neurobiology
2.
3. Bethesda, Maryland, and
Woods Hole, Massachusetts

PHS-HSMHA-NIMH
Individual Project Report
July 1, 1974 through June 30, 1975

Project Title: Isolation and characterization of proteins from nerve membranes

Previous Serial Number: None

Principal Investigator: Harish C. Pant, Ph.D.

Cooperating Unit: Marine Biological Laboratory, Woods Hole, Mass.

Man Years
Total: 1.8
Professional: 1.0
Other: 0.8

Project Description:

It has been suggested that the process of nerve excitation is accompanied by a conformational change in the macromolecules constituting the nerve membrane. This macromolecular involvement in nerve excitation has been pointed out by physicochemical studies of squid axons. The aim of these investigations is to isolate and characterize these membrane macromolecules.

Polyacrylamide gel electrophoresis is being utilized under a variety of salt concentrations and pH to separate and determine the proteins. The radioisotope labeling technique is being used to separate the individual proteins. Radioisotopes which could specifically label the surface proteins of the cells are used to identify the membrane surface proteins. Non-specific labeling is done by using ^{3}H-(leucine). In a few cases double labeling has been used in crab nerves and will be used in squid axons. For surface labeling I^{125}-lactoperoxidase enzymatic labeling is used.

Proteins with molecular weights of 120,000, 68,000, and 14,000 were found to incorporate I^{125} strongly. Some I^{125} incorporation was also found in the peptide with a molecular weight of 46,000. It is known that iodine reacts only with tyrosine and histidine residues of the proteins. There are few labeled compounds available which do not pass the cell surface. At present we are applying these surface labeling compounds to crab nerves and squid axons. Simultaneously lipid components from these nerves are being isolated and examined by thin layer chromatography and DEAE cellulose acetate column chromatography.

We hope these biochemical investigations will make it possible to understand the mechanism of nerve conduction at a molecular level. In order to clarify the process of nerve excitation on a biochemical basis, it is essential to isolate and characterize the macromolecules that constitute the nerve membrane. By combining both biochemical and biophysical techniques, it seems possible to elucidate the nature of the membrane macromolecules that are responsible for the process of nerve excitation.

Further experiments will be carried out in squid as well as crab nerves using double radioisotope labeling techniques and acrylamide gel electrophoresis to isolate and characterize the membrane macromolecules.

Keyword Descriptors:

membrane proteins; squid axon; crab nerve.

Serial No. Z01 MH 01031-07 LNC
1. Neurochemistry
2. Office of the Chief
3. Bethesda, Md.

PHS-ADAMHA-NIMH
Individual Project Report
July 1, 1974 through June 30, 1975

Project Title: The Conversion of Phenylalanine to Tyrosine

Previous Serial Number: M-NC-1

Principal Investigator: Seymour Kaufman

Other Investigators: S. Milstien, J. Donlon

Cooperating Units: None

Man Years:

Total :	3.3
Professional:	2.3
Other :	1.0

Project Description:

The objective of this research project is the detailed description of the complex enzyme system that catalyzes the conversion of phenylalanine to tyrosine. There are two broad goals in our study of this enzyme system.

First, phenylalanine hydroxylase catalyzes an oxidative reaction that is of a different type from most of the oxidative reactions of intermediary metabolism. The latter reactions are dehydrogenations: the substrate is oxidized by removal of electrons and hydrogens, usually in the form of hydride ions. By contrast, phenylalanine hydroxylase is an oxygenase: the substrate is oxidized by addition to it of molecular oxygen. Our understanding of the mechanism of this type of oxidative reaction, which is involved in the biosynthesis of many neurotransmitters and in the metabolism of a wide variety of drugs, is relatively superficial.

A deeper understanding of the mechanism of this type of reaction will probably provide clues to how these enzymes are physiologically regulated, as well as to how they might be pharmacologically controlled. Thus, it is well accepted now that the most potent inhibitors of enzymes are those that bear a structural resemblance to the transition state intermediate of the enzyme-catalyzed reaction. Only through detailed studies of the mechanism of the reaction can insight be gained into the structure of such intermediates.

A second goal of this study is to apply our understanding of the properties of the phenylalanine hydroxylating system to the disease, phenylketonuria (PKU). Basic knowledge of the enzyme system and its individual components can lead to advances in methods of diagnosis of PKU and its variants. Such knowledge can also lead to the development of rational approaches to therapy. For the last goal, knowledge of the manner in which the activities of the components of the hydroxylating system are physiologically regulated is essential.

Using differential absorption spectroscopic methods an unstable intermediate has been detected in the enzymatic conversion of phenylalanine to tyrosine. The intermediate is a pterin derivative. Its conversion to the product, quinonoid dihydropterin, is catalyzed by phenylalanine hydroxylase stimulating protein (PHS), the activator previously isolated from rat liver in this laboratory. The detection and partial characterization of pterin intermediate indicates that the mechanism of pterin-dependent hydroxylases involves the formation of a tetrahydropterin hydroperoxide as the active hydroxylating species. We plan to carry out detailed stability studies on the intermediate to see if it will be feasible to isolate it for the purpose of determining its structure. During the last 15 years, the efforts of this Laboratory have led to the separation and characterization of all of the essential components of the mammalian hepatic phenylalanine hydroxylating system. One of the bonuses of this effort is that the identification of the individual components of the system has provided a logical basis for predicting the occurrence - and, indeed, some of the clinical symptoms - of variants of PKU that might be caused by the lack of a component other than the hydroxylase itself.

Several years ago we predicted that variants lacking either the pterin cofactor or dihydropteridine reductase might be encountered. Since these two factors are also essential components of tyrosine and tryptophan hydroxylases, it could also be predicted that such variants would have defects in neurotransmitter synthesis.

During the last year, in collaboration with a group of neurologists and pediatricians at Johns Hopkins School of Medicine, we have been studying a patient, who is the first example of a PKU variant caused by the lack of dihydropteridine reductase. Using specific enzyme assays developed in this laboratory, we have shown that the patient, a 14 month old boy, lacks the reductase in all tissues examined so far - liver, brain and cultured skin fibroblasts. This enzyme defect has been confirmed by immunological methods. The patient's symptoms - neurological deterioration (seizures) in spite of dietary control of his blood phenylalanine levels - are probably due to defective synthesis of the neurotransmitters, serotonin and dopamine. Several new types of therapy have been tried but so far with limited success. It is possible that this patient's central nervous system has already been irreversibly damaged. For this reason, we are proposing that early assays for dihydropteridine reductase in cultured skin fibroblasts be considered in any patient with PKU in which any neurological disorder persists during treatment with a low phenylalanine diet. We plan to continue our biochemical studies on the patient and to initiate studies on other members of his family (parents and two siblings).

The detection of some phenylalanine hydroxylase activity in a liver biopsy sample from a patient with classical PKU, described in a previous report, has given added impetus to studies of the regulation of the activity of the hydroxylase. During the last year, we have found that the activity of the hydroxylase from rat liver can be doubled by enzymatic phosphorylation. In our experiments, phosphorylation was effected with the use of an exogenous cyclic-AMP-dependent kinase. We also have evidence that an enzyme in liver can activate the hydroxylase by a similiar process. These findings suggest that phosphorylation-dephosphorylation may play an important role in regulating the activity of the hydroxylase. We plan to continue to explore the molecular mechanism for this type of activation. If human liver samples (from both controls and PKU patients) are available, we will also investigate the possibility that the hydroxylase in PKU liver differs from the normal enzyme in its state of phosphorylation.

Keyword Descriptors:
1. phenylalanine hydroxylase
2. phenylketonuria
3. dihydropteridine reductase
4. biological oxidative reactions
5. neurotransmitters
6. regulation of enzyme activities
7. specific enzyme assays
8. neurological deterioration

Honors and Awards: None

Publications:

Milstien, S. and Kaufman, S.: Studies on the Phenylalanine Hydroxylase System in vivo. An in vivo assay based on the formation of HOD from 2,3,4,5,6-pentadeutero-L-phenylalanine. J. Biol. Chem., In Press.

Milstien, S. and Kaufman, S.: Studies on the Phenylalanine Hydroxylase System in Liver Slices. J. Biol. Chem., In Press.

Serial No. Z01 MH 01032-07 LNC
1. Neurochemistry
2. Office of the Chief
3. Bethesda, Md.

PHS-ADAMHA-NIMH
Individual Project Report
July 1, 1974 through June 30, 1975

Project Title: Biosynthesis of Catecholamines

Previous Serial Number: M-NC-2

Principal Investigator: Seymour Kaufman

Other Investigators: Thomas A. Lloyd, Robert Hoeldtke, Ira Katz

Cooperating Units: Laboratory of Biochemical Genetics, National Heart and Lung Institute

Man Years

Total	:	3.4
Professional	:	2.9
Other	:	0.5

Project Description:

These investigations are a continuation of previous studies in this laboratory concerning the biosynthesis and regulation of catecholamines. We have focused our studies on tyrosine hydroxylase, which has been demonstrated to be the rate limiting enzyme in the biosynthesis of catecholamines, and we have explored mechanisms which may be of physiological significance in the regulation of this enzyme.

Production of homogeneous preparations of tyrosine hydroxylase from peripheral and central nervous system tissue has been regarded as a desirable objective in this laboratory since such preparations greatly strengthen the interpretation of <u>in vitro</u> enzyme experiments.

Bovine adrenal tyrosine hydroxylase has been purified to homogenity and some of the physical properties of the enzyme determined. The fundamental purification scheme, worked out several years ago in this laboratory, has now been extended to yield an essentially pure enzyme. Following solubilization with chymotrypsin, the enzyme is subjected to ammonium sulfate fractionation and gel filtration. Further purification is then achieved by ion exchange chromatography with diethylaminoethyl (DEAE) cellulose. The final step in the procedure involves sedimentation in a sucrose density gradient. The resulting enzyme, when analyzed by polyacrylamide gel electrophoresis, appears to be at least eighty-five percent pure. We have determined that the Stokes radius of the protein is 2.58 X 10^{-9} cm, the sedimentation coefficient is 3.25 Svedburg Units, the frictional ratio is 1.1, and the molecular weight is 33,500. The pure enzyme contains approximately

0.5 moles of iron per mole of protein. We are attempting to study the role of the iron in the hydroxylation reaction.

Although the bovine adrenal gland contains a great deal of tyrosine hydroxylase, the enzyme from this source required solubilization by proteolytic digestion before it could be completely purified. It was of interest therefore to attempt to purify tyrosine hydroxylase from the central nervous system without resorting to a digestive procedure. Tyrosine hydroxylase from bovine caudate has been purified to homogeneity from an acetone powder by use of the following steps: chromatography on: (A) 3-iodo-L-tyrosine substituted sepharose 4B, (B) DEAE-cellulose (C) G-25 Sephadex, (D) Hydroxylapatite, and (E) phospho-cellulose The procedure also employs an ammonium sulfate fractionation and a sucrose gradient centrifugation. This native brain tyrosine hydroxylase has been extensively studied with respect to its ability to be activated by phospholipids, polyanions or salts. Kinetic analysis of the stimulation observed with the above agent has demonstrated that the effect is due to an increase of the affinity of the enzyme for the cofactor, with little or no effect upon the maximal reaction velocity. Electrostatic forces have been implicated in this interaction by two criteria. First, the ability to activate does not seem to be sensitive to the chemical nature of the activator, but only to its charge density. Secondl the interaction of polyanions with the enzyme can be screened by salt. Salt, furthermore, can, increase enzyme activity. Each of these effects is reversible and results from a direct interaction of the enzyme with the activators. From these studies certain structural features of the enzyme can be inferred:

a) Tyrosine hydroxylase must be capable of existing in two, or more, states differing in catalytic activity and in eith tertiary or quaternary structure or in the distribution and extent of protonation.
b) The more catalytically active of these states must have, at least, local areas of higher positive charge density and electrostatic potential than the state of lower activity.
c) The differences in charge density between these states must be sufficiently great to give a difference in their electrostatic free energy that is significant, in low salt, relative to thermal energy.

It is clear from this model that polyanions would interact more strongly with the enzyme in its active state and would stab lize it. Similarly, activation by salts probably reflects their ability to decrease the electrostatic free energy of the enzyme in its active form.

Using partially purified bovine caudate tyrosine hydroxylas we have recently observed a marked stimulation of the enzyme aft exposure to enzymatic phosphorylating conditions. The nature of this stimulation appears to be identical to that seen with the polyanions. Since the stimulation persists after subjecting the enzyme to gel filtration or salt fractionation, it appears that the effect is due to a phosphorylated protein, rather than to a small molecule-macromolecule interaction. We are currently engaged in determining whether tyrosine hydroxylase is directly phosphorylated, or whether the stimulation is indirect, i.e., from a secondary protein which has been phosphorylated. Whether the hydroxylase is phosphorylated directly or not, these studies show that protein phosphorylation is a potential mechanism for regulating the activity of tyrosine hydroxylase, and, hence, the rate of synthesis of the catecholamine neurotransmitters.

The adrenergic-like mouse neuroblastoma cells, NIE-115, have high tyrosine hydroxylase activity and can grow in the absence of tyrosine because they can convert sufficient phenylalanine to tyrosine for cell growth. In collaboration with Dr. Xandra Breakfield, in the Labortaory of Biochemical Genetics, NHLI, we have found that when the amount of tyrosine in the medium is increased, there is an increase in the amount of tyrosine hydroxylase activity in the neuroblastoma cells. We determined that an eight-fold increase in tyrosine hydroxylase activity occurred as the medium tyrosine was increased from 0-0.10 mM and the increase required about 24 hours to reach a maximal effect. This increase in activity could have been due to the existance of more enzyme molecules, or to the activation of existing enzyme molecules. We investigated this question by titrating NIE-115 extracts with specific anti-tyrosine hydroxylase α-globulin. Inhibition of higher levels of tyrosine hydroxylase from cells grown in higher media levels of tyrosine required proportionally more antibody. Thus, the increase in tyrosine hydroxylase activity is due to an increase in the number of enzyme molecules. We have not yet determined whether the observed increase in tyrosine hydroxylase protein is due to increased synthesis or decreased degradation of the enzyme. These results show that substrate-induced increases in the number of tyrosine hydroxylase molecules may be a significant factor in the regulation of the activity of this enzyme.

Keyword Descriptors:
1. Tyrosine
2. Tyrosine Hydroxylase
3. Dihydroxyphenylalanine
4. Norepinephrine
5. Sympathetic Nervous System
6. Electrostatic Effects
7. Enzyme Phosphorylation
8. Catecholamine Biosynthesis
9. Neuroblastoma

Honors and Awards: None

Publications:

Lloyd, T., and Kaufman, S.: The Stimulation of Partially Purified Bovine Caudate Tyrosine Hydroxylase by Phosphatidyl-L-Serine. Biochem. Biophys. Res. Comm. 59, 1262-1269, 1974.

Lloyd, T., and Breakfield, X.: Tyrosine-dependent increase of tyrosine hydroxylase in neuroblastoma cells. Nature, 252, 719-720, 1974.

Bachan, L., Storm, C.B., Wheeler, J.W., and Kaufman, S.: Isotope Effects in the Hydroxylation of Phenylethylamine by Dopamine β-Hydroxylase. J. Am. Chem. Soc. 96, 6799-6800, 1974.

Serial No. Z01 MH 01034-07 LNC
1. Neurochemistry
2. Office of the Chief
3. Bethesda, Md.

PHS-ADAMHA-NIMH
Individual Project Report
July 1, 1974 through June 30, 1975

Project Title: The Biochemical Basis of Skeletal Muscle Hypertrophy

Previous Serial Number: M-NC-4

Principal Investigator: Seymour Kaufman

Other Investigator: Philip Fleckman

Cooperating Units: None

Man Years

Total : 1.6
Professional: 1.3
Other : 0.3

Project Description:

The object of this project is the elucidation of the biochemical correlates of skeletal muscle hypertrophy. The animal model involved utilizes compensatory hypertrophy of the synergistic soleus and plantaris muscle effected by tenotomy of the achilles tendon, a procedure which incapacitates the gastrocnemeus. The contralateral sham-operated leg serves as control. Previous work in this laboratory has demonstrated that compensatory skeletal muscle hypertrophy is accompanied by connective tissue cell proliferation and that associated enhanced RNA synthesis is localized to these proliferating elements. Despite this, DNA synthesis and cellular mitotic activity can be almost completely inhibited without significantly affecting muscle hypertrophy. Collagen content, as measured by hydroxyproline, has been shown to be the same in treated and control muscle, strengthening the doubt that collagen metabolism is in some way responsible for initiation of muscle hypertrophy.

Enzymes involved in the activation, transport, and oxidation of fatty acids, enzymes of the citrate cycle, and enzymes of the respiratory chain have been shown to be markedly increased in activity in endurance-trained rats. This results in an increase in the capacity to oxidize fatty acids and pyruvate. To investigate the hypothesis that compensatory skeletal muscle results from work of synergistic muscles following tenotomy, rats have been endurance trained. The animals are trained to run on an animal treadmill, with exercise periods increasing to a maximum of 120 minutes a day for 5 days weekly at 32 meters/minute with one minute sprints of 40 meters/minute every tenth minute. After a twenty week training program, the animals will be studied for differences in muscle hypertrophy as compared to trained but non-running controls.

Other investigators have shown a decrease in protein degradation in addition to an increase in protein synthesis in muscle hypertrophy. Specific rates of degradation of myosin and actin are to be determined in compensatory skeletal muscle hypertrophy.

Work in this laboratory has shown increased incorporation of myoinositol into phospholipid early in muscle hypertrophy. Whether this process is localized to the hypertrophying muscle cell or to the proliferating connective tissue cells is to be answered using autoradiographic techniques.

Plans are being developed for an in vitro model for skeletal muscle hypertrophy using organ culture. An in vitro system, which could be more easily studied than the present animal model, would be of great advantage in investigating the biochemical events in muscle hypertrophy.

Keyword Descriptors:
1. skeletal muscle
2. hypertrophy
3. protein synthesis
4. protein degradation
5. endurance training
6. organ culture
7. phosphoinositides
8. autoradiography
9. collagen
10. fibroblasts

Honors and Awards: None

Publications: None

Serial No. Z01 MH 01035-07 LNC
1. Neurochemistry
2. Office of the Chief
3. Bethesda, Md.

PHS-ADAMHA-NIMH
Individual Project Report
July 1, 1974 through June 30, 1975

Project Title: The Process of Lysogeny

Previous Serial Number: M-NC-5

Principal Investigator: Howard A Nash

Other Investigators: None

Cooperating Units: Molecular Genetics, National Institute of Child Health and Human Development
Molecular Biology, National Institute of Arthritis, Metabolism and Digestive Diseases

Man Years

Total:	2
Professional:	1
Others:	1

Project Description:

In the life history of a cell penetrated by a viral genome, a commonly observed occurrence is the insertion of all or part of the viral genome into the chromosomal material of the host. This event results in a relatively permanent association of viral genes with the host. A subset of the inserted viral genes are usually expressed continuously, leading to subtle alterations in the host cell physiology. In many cases, after many generations of relatively harmonious coexistence, the entire viral genome may be activated by changes in the physical or chemical environment of the host. This phenomenon of viral integration has been demonstrated to occur in many eukaryocytic organisms, most notably in the case of tumor virus interaction with the cells of several mammalian species. From studies in prokaryocytic organisms, it is known that the formation of lysogens, i.e., bacterial cells carrying an integrated virus,is the result of a specific recombination event between the chromosomes of the bacteria and virus.

This project focuses on the biochemical events which lead to the integration of bacteriophage λ DNA into the E coli chromosome; its objective is to elucidate the enzymatic mechanism of the insertion reaction. To accomplish this analysis I have established the first system for production of integrative recombinant DNA *in vitro*. Among the specialized techniques that have been developed for the system are the isolation of a novel bacteriophage strain to serve as substitute for the recombination reaction, analyses of recombinant DNA by spheroplast transfection, and preparation of E. coli extracts containing λ gene products and virtually free of host and viral DNA.

The initial characterization of the reaction has showed that it is indeed the *in vitro* counterpart of the naturally-occurring *in vivo* recombination: 1) the system depends on the presence of the same phage-coded gene products as are required *in vivo* and 2) the product DNA formed *in vitro* has the same genetic makeup and physical length as that formed following infection of whole cells. The cofactor requirements of dialyzed extracts have been determined. Three species of cation-Mg^{++}, K^{+} and the polyamine spermidine are all required for the reaction. In addition, there is an absolute requirement for rATP (and not its non-metabolized analogues). Several protein components of the recombination reaction have been separated. The phage-coded complement has been partially purified. This complement has been shown to include the product of the *int* gene since its enzymatic activity is characterized by increased thermolability when isolated from strains containing either of two temperature sensitive *int* gene mutations. At least two host-coded components have been separated and partially purified. The discovery of these host factors was not predicted by previous genetic evidence and indicates an unsuspected complexity of the reaction.

In this project, the *in vitro* production of integrative recombinant DNA has been analyzed in the most fundamental enzymological terms--identification of cofactors and separation of enzymic components. This represents the most advanced state of understanding of the biochemical basis of any naturally-occurring recombination. This is both a significant contribution to the field of viral integration itself and also provides a basis for the analyses of genetic recombination im many systems of biological and medical interest.

The proposed course of the project includes further purification of enzyme components of the reaction, electron micrographic studies on the structure of the recombinant product, identification of partial reaction products, and extension of the methods developed in the project to other recombination systems.

Keyword Descriptors: genetic recombination
site-specific recombination
viral integration
biochemistry of recombination
spheroplast transfection
bacteriophage DNA
electron microscopy of DNA
gradient centrifugation

Honors and Awards: Guest speaker at University of Ca., Santa Barbara
Guest speaker at Gordon Research Conference, New Hampton, New Hampshire.

Publications:

Nash, H. A.: Integrative Recombination in Bacteriophage Lambda: Analysis of Recombinant DNA. J. Mol. Biol. 91: 501-514, 1975

Nash, H. A.: Integrative Recombination of Bacteriophage Lambda DNA In Vitro. Proc. Nat. Acad. Sci. 72: 1072-1076, 1975.

Serial No. Z01 MH 01036-03 LNC
1. Neurochemistry
2. Office of the Chief
3. Bethesda, Md.

PHS-ADAMHA-NIMH
Individual Project Report
July 1, 1974 through June 30, 1975

Project Title: Molecular Basis For Cell Matrix Formation: Polysacchande - Induced Conformation in Amines and Polypeptides

Previous Serial Number: M-NC-6

Principal Investigator: Audrey Larack Stone

Other Investigator: None

Cooperating Units: None

Woman Years

Total :	0.20
Professional:	0.20
Other :	0

Project Description:

Anionic polysaccharides (glycosaminoglycans, glycolipids) are intimately involved in the biological formation and function of inter- and intra-cellular matrices. Intracellular storage regions, or discrete granules, are well-known in various organs of many species, including the synaptic processes of catecholaminergic neurons. The physicochemical forces which sequester cell solutes from a soluble form to a relatively insoluble, organized structure can be investigated from the standpoint of the molecular conformations of the components and of their interacting species. This was undertaken at the onset of this project in the early 60's.

The histology, chemical composition, and explosive release of the histamme containing granule of the mast cell were well described at that time, therefore, that system was used as a conceptual model for storage and release of small potent biologically active molecules (although the same anion-polyanion/cation would not be obligatory for all systems). Thus, the conformational aspects of heparin (the polyanion):histamine (or cationic aromatic dyes) binding were studied using optical methods of absorption and circular dichroism (CD). The results of those early studies were the first to demonstrate ultraviolet asymmetric absorption bands for heparin and other glycosaminoglycans. Results with the cationic amine dyes led to the first reports of helical structures for these polysaccharides in solution. Direct

X-ray analysis performed in other laboratories now show various helical patterns predicted by the early reports (M-NC-21 1964-67). These results showed clearly that ordered negative charges have profound and specific ordering effects on amine cations.

The current project extends these basic molecular findings to the study of a third component of inter- or intra-cellular matrices, e.g., the polypeptide. As with small amines, acid polysaccarides (PS) play a role in inducing conformational constraints in cationic polypeptides. The major objective of the current project is to quantitatively determine the conformational-directing effect of the various anionic PS and glycolipids, and to determine the degree of specificity of this effect on the basis of PS conformations revealed earlier in this project. These model interactions will be applied directly to studies of enzyme activation and sequentration by heparin and related biopolymers in simulated matrix conditions.

The methods are measurements of molecular asymmetries by extrinsic and intrinsic Cotton effects using the Cary Model 6001 C D apparatus. The metachromatic reaction provides a quantitative measure of the extent of binding to anionic sites. Computer models for determination of the proportion of a α-helical, β- or non-ordered structure in the polypeptide reveal the degree and kind of conformation induced by a given PS.

Results of the current focus of the project are straight forward. A wide variety of purified biopolymers from plant, bacterial and mammalian sources, well-characterized as to the chemical nature of the anionic groups and the charge density, were investigated for their conformation-promoting effects on synthetic poly-L-lysine (PLL) at neutral pH. The non-ordered form of PLL was altered markedly by a strong electrostatic interaction with polysulfates, polyuronates, and mixed polyanionic groups on a homo- or complex polysaccharide backbone. Furthermore, there was little specificity in the interactions since almost all the PS structures promoted a high degree of α-helical conformation in PLL. Specificity dependent upon PS conformation was seen between the λ- and K-carrageenans. λ-carrageenan: PLL interaction induced 30-50 percent β-structure in the polypeptide chain. Some of the results were published in an abstract of an invited report entitled, "Polysaccharide-Polypeptide Interactions." VII International Symposium on Carbohydrate Chemistry, Bratislava, August 1974, p 185.

The significance of molecular conformations of organized multianions (such as the glycoaminoglycans) in brain function and mental health was not apparent to most ten years ago. However, it was clear then that the structure of inter- and intracellular matrices through which neurotransmitters pass, must play a role. The early results demonstrated that small cations were held in specific and highly ordered fashion by various polyanions, described a third parameter of the metachromatic reaction and set down general techniques for measuring the above kinds of interaction. The current findings that such complexes can be held in rigid or flexible polypeptide structures depending upon specific multi-anions: β-structure or α-helix promoting interactions has direct bearing on the biological aspects of amine storage forms in the CNS.

Another visible role for the basic studies of molecular conformations is seen in the activation of certain enzymes by PS; for example, tyrosine hydroxylase, the enzyme responsible for DOPA formation, is known to occur in both soluble and insoluble forms of which the former is markedly stimulated by heparin.

The proposed course of the project is a continuation of the basic studies of PS-polypeptide interactions, investigation of the conformation of purified brain tyrosine hydroxylase and its complex with various multi-anions, including heparin.

Keyword descriptors:
1. Amine Storage Granule Components
2. Bioamines: Multi-anion Conformations
3. Anionic Polysaccharide Conformations
4. Extrinsic and Intrinsic Cotton Effects
5. Glycosaminoglycans
6. Poly-L-Lysine
7. α-helix or β-structure promoting
8. Anionic polysaccharide: Poly-L-Lysine Complexes
9. Heparin
10. Asymmetric Methylene Blue Complexation

Honors and Awards:

Referee for Biopolymers, Biochemistry, Journal of Molecular Biology, Analytical Biochemistry& Thrombosis Research

Invited by Dr. Blackwell to present a symposium paper for the Carbohydrate Division of the ACS on the subject of "Polysaccharide-Polypeptide Conformations," Chicago, 1975.

Publications:

Stone, Audrey L.: "Circular Dichroism and Optical Rotatory Dispersion in Polysaccharide Structural Analysis: Intrinsic and Extrinsic Cotton Effects." Methods in Carbohydrate Chemistry. Eds. Whistler and BeMiller, J.N., Academic Press, New York, 1975, in press.

Serial No. Z01 MH 01037-07 LNC
1. Neurochemistry
2. Biophysical Chemistry
3. Bethesda, Md.

PHS-ADAMHA-NIMH
Individual Project Report
July 1, 1974 through June 30, 1975

Project Title: The Role of the Cell Membrane in Cellular Organization, A Molecular Study

Previous Serial Number: M-NC-7

Principal Investigator: David M. Neville, Jr.

Other Investigators: Ta-Min Chang, Alice Dazord, Ronald Kahn, Karla Megyesi and Jesse Roth, NIAMD

Cooperating Units: National Institute of Arthritis, Metabolism and Digestive Diseases

Man Years

Total : 4.0
Professional: 3.0
Other : 1

Project Description:

The aim of this project is to determine the specific chemical interactions which occur at the surfaces of cells which affect cellular differentiation and cellular organization. Specifically we propose that the recognition which cells have of their solid environment and neighboring cells is mediated by specific proteins on the surface membranes. In addition, the surface of each cell has protein or glycoprotein receptors for a variety of soluble hormones and transmitter substances. Our aim is to study the interaction between the receptor molecules and the soluble and fixed transmitter molecules so that the interaction which leads to altered cell function can be quantitatively defined. Having done this we propose to examine these interactions in pathological states in order to determine if altered receptors or receptor concentration play a role in disease states.

The surface membrane insulin receptor of the insulin resistant obese mouse which was previously found to be reduced 4-fold in concentration has been found to be functionally normal in terms of equilibrium and kinetic constants, biological specificity, and cooperative interactions. This finding strengthens our previous hypothesis that receptor concentration is regulated by control mechanisms which allow the cell to adjust its response to outside signals.

A number of patients suffering from malignancies who exhibit hypoglycemia in the face of normal circulating insulin levels are found to have elevated levels of NSILA-s, a peptide having hypoglycemic actions and liver surface membrane receptors. In several cases removal of the tumor causes NSILA-s levels and blood sugar levels to return to normal. The finding of altered NSILA-s levels in human disease states emphasizes the biological and medical significance of peptides which circulate in the 0.1-1.0 nanomolar range. These peptides, unlike classical peptide hormones, are not stored in glands in high concentrations, hence their detection has been difficult. The use of purified cell surface membranes in radio-receptor assays has made these studies possible. It is likely that there are many such peptides which act as environmental signals and are responsible for changes in cellular behavior.

Key Word Descriptors:
1. plasma membrane
2. receptors
3. hormones
4. peptides
5. obesity
6. insulin resistance
7. radio-receptor assay

Honors and Awards: None

Publications:

Soll, A.H., Kahn, C.R., and Neville, D.M., Jr.: The decreased insulin binding to liver plasma membranes in the obese hyperglycemic mouse (ob/ob): Demonstration of a decreased number of functionally normal receptors. J. Biol. Chem., in press.

Soll, A.H., Kahn, C.R., Neville, D.M., Jr., and Roth, J.: Insulin receptor deficiency in genetic and acquired obesity. J. Clin. Invest., in press.

Neville, D.M., Jr.: Problems in quantitating surface membrane components in normal and pathologic cells and tissues. Fogarty Center Workshop on Cell Surfaces and Malignancy, in press.

Gavin, J.R., III, Kahn, C.R., Gorden, P., Roth, J., and Neville, D.M., Jr.: Radio-receptor assay of insulin: Comparison of plasma and pancreatic insulins and proinsulins. J. Clin. Endocrin. and Metabolism, in press.

Serial No. Z01 MH 01038-04 LNC
1. Neurochemistry
2. Office of the Chief
3. Bethesda, Md.

PHS-ADAMHA-NIMH
Individual Project Report
July 1, 1974 through June 30, 1975

Project Title: Models of Genetic Diseases of Mental Retardation: Murine Phenylketonuria and Dihydropterin-Reductase Insufficiency

Previous Serial Number: M-NC-8

Principal Investigator: Audrey Larack Stone

Other Investigators: None

Cooperating Units: Laboratory of Cerebral Metabolism, Section on Myelin Chemistry, NIMH

Man Years

Total : 1.15
Professional: 0.8
Other : 0.35

Project Description:

Phenylketonuria (PKU) is an inherited biochemical disorder in humans, which, if untreated, causes extreme mental retardation due to an unknown damage in the central nervous system (CNS). Heterozygote carriers are estimated be approximately one in 100 adults; one in 10,000 births are homozygous phenylketonurics. The specific biochemical defect in classical PKU is well understood. The normal hydroxylation of phenylalanine (an essential amino acid, precursor to the catecholamines) to tyrosine is absent due to a genetic lack of the enzyme, phenylalanine hydroxylase (PAH). Detailed studies of the hydroxylation reaction showed the system to require two enzymes, two substrates and a pterin cofactor, and a coenzyme, in the following coupled reactions:

1) phenylalanine + oxygen (O_2) + tetrahydrobiopterin (BH_4)

$$\xrightarrow{\text{phenylalanine hydroxylase}} \text{tyrosine} + H_2O + BH_2$$

2) $$BH_2 \xrightarrow[\text{DPNH} + H^+]{\text{Dihydropteridine reductase (DPR)}} BH_4 + DPN^+$$

The direct cause of the CNS damage and the pathophysiology in PKU have not been elucidated because there has been no suitable animal model for PKU and related diseases. This project is a program of screening offspring of X-irradiated mice to obtain mutants which show deficiency in the phenylalanine hydroxylation system using various criteria. The first objective is the development of a murine model for PKU and/or related diseases. The project naturally falls into three stages. The first is the screening for suspect mutants, followed by the development of the suspect mutant strain. The second stage is the establishment of the precise biochemical lesion and its effect in the given mutant strain, and the suitability of the strain for research on PKU and related disorders. The third part of the project would broadly enter into studies on the role of the biochemical lesion in functional changes in the CNS. Another, related, objective is the elucidation of regulatory mechanisms in the expression of phenylalanine hydroxylation, including the relationships between various components of the reaction.

In the first stage of the program, male mice were irradiated with a double dose of X-ray, 400 R each, at 48 hours apart to induce specific mutations in the surviving spermatogonia. These were used as sires for offspring with normal females. Several criteria for possible deficiency in phenylalanine hydroxylation were established and previously reported (M-NC-8, 1972, 1973). Plasma levels of phenylalanine and the plasma phenylalanine-to-tyrosine (P/T) ratio were determined by fluorometric assays of the amino acids as an indicator of PAH activity. The normal values were computed for 308 female plus male mice since there was no significant sex difference. Values were 80 $\pm$ 23 μM and 0.99 $\pm$ 0.26, respectively. Hepatic levels of dihydropteridine reductase were measured spectrophotometrically on extracts from liver biopsies. Values for 58 biopsy samples gave an average of 223 $\pm$ 45 nmoles of coenzyme oxidized per minute (enzymatic units).

Results using this second criterion moved forward. The early studies indicated that DPR levels in mice were not in great excess in the hydroxylation reaction *in vivo*, contrary to the generally accepted hypothesis. It appeared that dihydropteridine reductase insufficiency at levels of 50-67 percent of normal led to symptoms of deficiency in phenylalanine hydroxylation. Continuation of this study extended to this fiscal year. Two separate lines of investigation were followed. One was the study of pharmacologically induced DPR insufficiency using the anti-folate drug, methotrexate, known to be a competitive inhibitor for DPR. Results showed that chemical interception of DPR also led to symptoms of phenylalanine hydroxylation deficiency in the mouse, and furthermore, that PAH activity in liver and kidney extracts, under fully supplemented assay conditions, was also decreased. These results were presented in part in a paper entitled "Dependence of Expression of Phenylalanine Hydroxylation System on *in vivo* Levels of Dihydropteridine

Reductase" by Audrey L. Stone and Seymour Kaufman (Abstracted in Transactions of the American Society for Neurochemistry 6, No. 1, p. 132, 1975). In order to determine by immunoassays whether the dimunition in measurable PAH activity was due to a decrease in the amount of protein enzyme or to some alteration in the enzyme structure, antibodies to a standard preparation of purified rat liver PAH were raised in inbred guinea pigs. A strong antiserum was obtained with which one ml was equivalent to 30 mg of enzyme. A similar procedure was used to obtain antisera to purified sheep liver DPR.

The second line of investigation was the selection of suspect mutants at the level of impairment indicated by DPR insufficiency (mild elevation of plasma phenylalanine-to-tyrosine ratio) and the subsequent development of several families showing consistent deficiency in phenylalanine hydroxylation. In one suspect strain, for example, the average P/T ratio in an F_2 litter of 7 was 1.69 $\pm$ .12 as compared with 0.99 $\pm$ 0.26 for normal mice. These animals are now in the F_3 generation. A second suspect strain is characterized both high P/T ratios and poor survival rate of the offspring.

The findings from the two separate lines of investigation are of significant importance. First, it was established that the P/T ratio is a sensitive, valid measure of normal and altered in vivo phenylalanine hydroxylation in the mouse. Secondly, the studies of murine dihydropteridine reductase insufficiency are path finding. The variability of this enzyme appears to be relatively high, and furthermore, in some manner determines the level of activity of PAH measurable in vitro in a fully supplemented assay system. Such a relationship may be relevant in certain patients with hyperphenylalaninemia. The development of a murine strain deficient in phenylalanine hydroxylation is of potential importance in:

1. Biochemical studies concerning parameters for correction of the deficiency as well as regulation of PAH;
2. Possible DPR insufficiency with consequent decrease in the BH_4 cofactor for tryptophan and tyrosine hydroxylation; possible abnormality in neurotransmitter levels.
3. Studies on the pathophysiology of PKU or related diseases associated with mental retardation.

Knowledge concerning the specific lesion causing abnormal mental development of the newborn CNS would be attended by a better understanding of the normal parameters required for early imprinting of intellectual capacity.

The project is coming to the second stage as sufficient numbers of mice are produced within the suspect mutant strain. A program for the rapid and automatic determination of plasma phenylalanine and tyrosine, and of the tyrosine formed during assays of PAH activity in tissue extracts, is being set up in the amino acid analyzer model 121 through the generosity of Dr. Marian

Serial No. Z01 MH 01039-04 LNC
1. Neurochemistry
2. Office of the Chief
3. Bethesda, Md.

PHS-ADAMHA-NIMH
Individual Project Report
July 1, 1974 through June 30, 1975

Project Title: The Conversion of Tryptophan to 5-Hydroxytryptophan

Previous Serial Number: M-NC-9

Principal Investigator: Seymour Kaufman

Other Investigators: Norman Chang, Sheldon Milstien

Cooperating Units: None

Man Years

Total	:	1.2
Professional	:	1.2
Other	:	0

Project Description:

The goal of this project is to obtain an understanding of the physiological regulation of tryptophan hydroxylase, the rate-limiting enzyme in the biosynthesis of the neurotransmitter, serotonin, which is thought to play an important role in controlling behavior. The approach to be used is to first obtain purified tryptophan hydroxylase and then fully characterize its properties.

The enzyme has been purified to near homogeneity in this laboratory from rabbit hindbrain using standard methods of protein purification. The use of high concentrations of salt in any of the purification steps had to be avoided to overcome the "aggregation phenomenon". The purification involved treatment with calcium phosphate gel, polyethylene glycol fractionation, Sepharose 6B chromatography, and DEAE cellulose chromatography.

Purified tryptophan hydroxylase was found to be a tetramer of MW 230,000 composed of subunits with MW of approximately 60,000. The resemblance of tryptophan hydroxylase to hepatic phenylalanine hydroxylase is striking since phenylalanine hydroxylase can also exist as a tetramer (MW 210,000) composed of monomers of MW 55,000.

The kinetic properties of the other pterin dependent hydroxylases, phenylalanine hydroxylase and tyrosine hydroxylase vary markedly with the structure of the tetrahydropterin cofactor. Only with the natural cofactor, tetrahydrobiopterin, was purified rabbit hindbrain tryptophan hydroxylase able to catalyze the hydroxylation of both phenylalanine and tryptophan at comparable rates although the K_m values were substantially different (32 μM for tryptophan and 287 μM for phenylalanine). This finding may have relevance to phenylketonuria where there has been found to be a decrease in 5-hydroxytryptophan synthesis. In non-phenylketonuric brains the concentration of phenylalanine and tryptopha are such that the hydroxylation rate of phenylalanine would only be approximately 10% of that of tryptophan. In phenylketonuric patients where brain phenylalanine is increased 5-fold and tryptophan decreased 3-fold, the prediction is that phenylalanine will successfully compete with tryptophan for hydroxylation by tryptophan hydroxylase leading to a decrease in 5-hydroxytryptoph biosynthesis.

Further studies are being carried out on the kinetic properties of the purified tryptophan hydroxylase in order to better understand the physiological regulation of the enzyme. With the availability of relatively large amounts of highly purified enzym structural studies will be undertaken and comparisons made to the other pterin-dependent hydroxylases where more information on structure and properties is available.

Keyword Descriptors:
1. tryptophan hydroxylase
2. serotonin
3. 5-hydroxytryptophan
4. phenylketonuria
5. tetrahydrobiopterin

Honors and Awards: None

Publications:

Tong, J.H., and Kaufman, S.: Tryptophan hydroxylase: Purificati and some properties of the enzyme from rabbit brain. J. Biol. Chem., in press.

Kaufman, S.: Properties of pterin-dependent aromatic amino acid hydroxylases. In Aromatic Amino Acids in Brain, CIBA Foundation Symposium 22. Amsterdam, Elsevier, 1974, pp. 85-108.

Project No. Z01 MH 01081-05
1. Laboratory of Neurophysiology
2.
3. Bethesda, Maryland

PHS-ADAMHA-NIMH
Individual Project Report
July 1, 1974 through June 30, 1975

Project Title: The role of cerebral motor cortex in control of movement

Previous Serial Number: M-NP-63

Principal Investigator: Edward V. Evarts

Other Investigator: Jun Tanji

Cooperating Units: None

Man Years:

Total:	3.94
Professional:	1.42
Other:	2.52

Objectives: The mental disorders of patients with major psychoses are extraordinarily complex, involving a wide range of alterations of thought, perception, and overt behavior. Knowledge of the brain processes underlying psychotic behavior is as yet fragmentary, and in seeking to broaden this knowledge, this project has the objective of discovering the way in which the brain functions in generating movement. It is, after all, movement in its great variety of forms that underlies speech, exploration, and the innumerable additional complex expressions by which the inner workings of the brain make themselves apparent. It is for this reason that a project with the objective of understanding the psychological and neurophysiological factors in cerebral control of movement is being undertaken in a neurophysiology laboratory whose overall goal is to acquire knowledge which will be of value in the understanding, diagnosis, and treatment of mental disease in man.

Project Description: Studies are carried out at two broad levels: animal studies of brain processes in monkeys carrying out learned movements; human studies in normal subjects and patients with psychomotor disorders such as parkinsonism, Huntington's disease and tardive dyskinesia.

Animal Studies. For the animal studies the work utilizes two major procedures:

1. Electrical recording. Microelectrodes are used to record the activity of individual neurons during natural, voluntary movement in the monkey. This use of single unit analysis in relation to voluntary movement is analogous to the long-established use of single unit analysis in determining how the brain receives and elaborates its sensory input, but single unit

analysis has only recently been carried out in animals trained to perform skilled movements during recording.

2. Behavioral training. The current work on this project is concerned with the effects of behavioral set and expectancy on activity of neurons in sensorimotor cortex of the monkey. For this experiment, monkeys were trained to grasp a handle and maintain it in a certain position for 2 to 4 sec. After this 2-4 sec period, an "instruction" was given. This "instruction" told the monkey how he should move in response to a perturbation of the handle which would occur subsequently. The "instruction" was a red or green light which appeared after 2 to 4 sec of correct holding and 0.6 to 1.2 sec prior to the onset of a handle perturbation. The times varied unpredictably within these ranges. The red light informed the monkey that he should pull toward himself when the perturbation occurred and the green light meant that he should push away when the perturbation occurred. There were two different directions of perturbation, one being a movement of the handle toward the monkey and the other a movement of the handle away from the monkey. A given instruction (red or green light) called for a movement synergistic with the tendon jerk and stretch reflex for one direction of perturbation and antagonistic to these reflexes for the other direction of perturbation. According to the hypothesis that modification of the stretch reflex by prior instruction involves a cortical loop, a change of stretch reflexes by prior instruction should be accompanied by a change in the short latency response of sensorimotor cortex neurons. When monkeys had learned to perform this task, recordings from individual sensorimotor cortex neurons were obtained during performance of the movement. Studies have been completed on more than 600 neurons in three monkeys.

Major Findings of Animal Studies. The results of these experiments have shown that both spinal and cerebral responses are modified by prior instruction, and it seems reasonable to conclude that both of these modifications underlie the difference in the later phase of the muscular response, i.e., the phase of muscular response which is responsible for the performance of the movement called for by the instruction. Earlier investigators had proposed that the later phase of muscle activity was a spinal reflex which could be preset by nervous activity from the brain. We have observed changes of pyramidal tract neuron (PTN) discharge which vary depending on the prior instruction, and the ability of motor cortex PTN output to preset spinal reflexes is well documented. Granted that PTNs function in presetting spinal cord reflexes as a result of prior instruction, is it also possible that motor cortex neurons participate in a high-speed loop which actually mediates the later phase of perturbation-evoked muscle activity? Evidence for such cerebral mediation has been provided both by our PTN recordings and by observations in man showing latency measurements compatible with a cortical pathway for the later phase of muscle response in man.

Thus, two components of motor cortex PTN discharge are initiated by a movement of a rod held in an animal's hand. The first component of activity is a short latency response dependent in large measure on the nature of the kinesthetic input. The second component of PTN discharge depends primarily on the intended movement and this discharge occurs at latencies as short as 50 msec. Excitation of PTNs in the course of this second phase of discharge presumably involves very different pathways from those involved in the first phase. The second phase of discharge would seem to be the manifestation of a central program, while the first phase of activity appears to be more automatic and thus akin to a reflex.

Human Studies. Demonstration of the effects of set and expectancy on neural responses in monkeys provides a basis for systematic investigation aimed at understanding the way in which these central states modify motor processes in normal subjects and patients with psychomotor disorders. These studies of motor processes in man have only just begun, and have thus far been confined to normal subjects. However, plans are under way to study patients with disease of the basal ganglia. These patients exhibit a wide variety of intellectual and emotional disturbances as well as motor disorders, and it is hoped that a fuller understanding of the brain mechanisms underlying these disorders will provide an avenue to understanding the intellectual and emotional disorders that occur in Huntington's disease, parkinsonism, and tardive dyskinesia.

Significance to Biomedical Research and to the Program of the Institute: This project seeks to apply basic research results on central control of movement to an understanding of normal and abnormal behavior in man. To the extent that the project succeeds, it will contribute to the research goals of the NIMH.

Proposed Course: As already pointed out, studies of motor function in normal subjects have begun. The major addition to the project in the coming year will be the extension of these studies to patients with psychomotor disorders.

Keyword Descriptors:

Motor Cortex	Attention
Movement	Cerebral Cortex
Reflex	Basal Ganglia

Honors and Awards:

1. President, Society for Neuroscience

2. Chief Editor, Journal of Neurophysiology

3. Invited Lecturer:

    Department of Physiology, University of Western Ontario, August 19, 1974
    Department of Psychiatry, Yale University, May 12, 1975
    Department of Psychology, Massachusetts Institute of Technology, May 23, 1975

4. Participant, Workshop on Huntington's Disease, NIH, May 10-11, 1975

5. Serves on:

Board of Co-Editors, Experimental Brain Research
Advisory Board, International Journal of Neuroscience
Editorial Board, International Review of Neurobiology
Council, Society for Neuroscience
International Research Review Panel, Fogarty International Center, NIH
W. T. Wakeman Award Panel, National Paraplegia Foundation
Scientific Advisory Committee, Whitehead Medical Research Institute
Committee on National Needs for the Rehabilitation of the Physically Handicapped

Publications:

Evarts, E.V.: Relation of motor cortex activity to force exerted during smooth movement and postural fixation. In: Mechanisms of Formation and Inhibition of Conditional Reflex (published in Russian). Moscow, Nauka, USSR Academy of Sciences, 1973, pp. 141-162.

Evarts, E.V.: Brain mechanisms in motor control. Life Sci. 15: 1393-1399, 1974.

Evarts, E.V.: Cerebral mechanisms of movement. Vestnik Leningradskogo Universiteta 21: 88-97, 1974 (published in Russian).

Project No. Z01 MH 01082-10 LNP
1. Laboratory of Neurophysiology
2.
3. Bethesda, Maryland

PHS-ADAMHA-NIMH
Individual Project Report
July 1, 1974 through June, 30, 1975

Project Title: Muscle function and metabolism

Previous Serial Number: M-NP-3

Principal Investigators: S.I. Rapoport and J. Vergara

Other Investigators: K. Matthews, J.V. Passonneau, V. Gentina

Cooperating Units: Laboratory of Neuropathology, NINCDS

Man Years:

Total:	1.20
Professional:	.85
Other:	.35

Project Description:

When a whole striated muscle is stimulated repetitively, its contractile force decreases and it is said to be fatigued. Fatigue does not occur in dystrophic muscles, and is characteristic of fast but not slow mammalian and amphibian muscle fibres. The complexity of the excitation-contraction process in fast muscles makes it difficult to determine where and when fatigue sets in.

Single muscle fibres of the frog semitendinosus muscle were selected to study fatigue and recovery, rather than whole muscle, to avoid rate-limited diffusion and the heterogenous fibre population of whole muscle. A fibre was dissected and mounted in a bath of flowing Ringer at 15°C. Tension was recorded by an RCA 5734 transducer tied to one end of the fibre, and was displayed on an oscilloscope screen and a paper chart recorder. Sarcomere length was measured by a laser diffraction technique. The fibre was stimulated by external platinum electrodes with 0.3 msec condenser discharges. Isometric twitch tension and tetanic tension were measured.

Tetanizing a single fibre in Ringer solution, at 20 cycles per sec for 120 secs, produces an initial and short-lived increase in twitch tension due to post-tetanic potentiation, which reflects calcium redistribution within the muscle. Twitch tension then falls over a period of 5 minutes and may disappear, but it returns in 1 to 2 hours to normal even if glucose is not added to the bathing solution. The fall in twitch tension characterizes fibre fatigue and the recovery shows that fatigue is not due to a total depletion of energy sources within the fibre, an explanation which often is evoked to explain muscle fatigue.

If the muscle fibre is stimulated tetanically in Ringer made hypertonic by the addition of sucrose, contraction is abolished, although the heat of activation and calcium release and uptake are not. When the fibre is returned to isotonic Ringer solution, twitch tension is normal and has not declined. The prevention of fatigue by hypertonic Ringer indicates that repetition of a step in the contraction process causes fatigue, probably by reducing local concentrations of ATP and creatine phosphate which are necessary to support contraction. These high energy metabolites probably are not synthesized rapidly enough from available glycogen or from lactic acid to prevent fatigue in muscles tetanized in normal Ringer solution.

Now that we have defined the parameters of stimulation and the time course of fatigue and recovery in single fibres, we intend to test these suggestions and to correlate individual points in the course with the exact spectrum of metabolites--ATP, creatine phosphate, glycogen--in the fibres. Metabolic analysis of single fibres has not been employed before because measured quantities are at the range of 10^{-12} moles, but in collaboration with Dr. Janet Passonneau we intend to use them for an exact correlation of the fatigue-recovery process and the energy state of the single fibre.

The relation between function (contraction, calcium release and uptake, electrical activity) of a single fibre and the energy state of the muscle is important not only to understanding the basic mechanism of excitation-contraction coupling and fatigue and recovery of muscle, but to see how metabolites are employed generally to support cellular activity. The understanding of these mechanisms in normal muscle should help to comprehend defective relations in diseased muscle.

Key word Descriptors:

Muscle
Contraction
Excitation-Contraction coupling
Fatigue
Muscle metabolism
Neurophysiological responses
Energy utilization

Honors and Awards: None

Publications:

Vergara, J.L. and Rapoport, S.I.: Fatigue in single muscle fibres. Nature 252: 727-728, 1974.

Project No. Z01 MH 01083-09 LNP
1. Laboratory of Neurophysiology
2.
3. Bethesda, Maryland

PHS-ADAMHA-NIMH
Individual Project Report
July 1, 1974 through June 30, 1975

Project Title: Transport mechanisms across membranes and the blood-brain barrier

Previous Serial Number: M-NP-8

Principal Investigator: S.I. Rapoport

Other Investigators: K. Matthews, H. Thompson, M.W. Brightman, H. Levitan, T. Kuwabara, and J.S. Robinson

Cooperating Units: (a) Laboratory of Neuropathology and Neuroanatomical Sciences, NINCDS

(b) Department of Zoology, University of Maryland, College Park, Maryland

(c) Laboratory of Vision Research, National Eye Institute

Man Years:

Total:	3.55
Professional:	0.90
Other:	2.65

Project Description:

The blood-brain barrier at the cerebral vasculature, choroid plexus and arachnoid membrane covering the brain regulates the ionic environment of the nervous system, has specific mechanisms for the delivery of amino acids and glucose to support brain metabolism, and prevents access of blood-borne proteins to the brain, as well as of water soluble drugs like penicillin and methotrexate.

Research on the brain and pharmacotherapy of the brain and meninges often are hindered by the restrictive influence of the barrier in preventing drugs from entering the brain. It would be useful, therefore, to be able to modify barrier permeability, reversibly and without affecting neuronal function, in order to overcome these restrictions.

The aim of this project is (a) to understand the basic morphological and physiological properties leading to and protecting barrier function and integrity; (b) to develop a method to open the barrier, based on these properties, that may prove useful in brain pharmacotherapy; and (c) to understand how the barrier responds to different stresses to the brain, including the loss of autoregulation of cerebral blood flow.

Different methods are employed in these studies. Surgical procedures are used to open the skull and dura of rabbit, rat or Rhesus monkey, and to isolate and perfuse the internal carotid artery. Neurological examinations are performed to evaluate function, and methods of perfusion and fixation are used for brain and eye histology. Quantitative chemical techniques are employed for analysis of wet and dry weights of brain tissue, and atomic absorption spectrophotometry employed for studying brain electrolytes.

Statistical methods and theory of irreversible thermodynamics are used to consider results quantitatively and to formulate and test models for osmotic barrier opening and the effect of capillary hydrostatic pressure in the brain. Computers are used for data analysis and development of models. Electron microscopy is used to determine passage of horseradish peroxidase from blood to brain, and to evaluate cellular morphology.

The major findings of the project are as follows:

(a) Theory and physiological and morphological demonstration of osmotic opening of the blood-brain barrier. The blood-brain barrier in the rabbit or monkey can be osmotically opened in a reversible manner by injecting hypertonic solutions of relatively lipid insoluble nonelectrolytes--e.g., urea, lactamide or arabinose--into the internal carotid artery for 20 seconds. The barrier to proteins, which is due to tight junctions that connect the cerebrovascular endothelium, is opened by osmotic shrinkage of the endothelial cells and widening of the tight junctions without grossly affecting neuronal function. The theory of osmotic opening, which I had proposed on the basis of previous experiments, and extended and confirmed in collaborative efforts by means of electron microscopy, was elaborated in detail and interpreted in terms of general clinical observations on the barrier. It is to be included in a book which I am currently writing and which is entitled "The Blood-Brain Barrier in Physiology and Medicine."

(b) Application of osmotic blood-brain barrier opening to pharmacotherapy of the brain. It is pointed out in the publication entitled "Target organ modification in pharmacology: reversible osmotic opening of the blood-brain barrier by opening of tight junctions" (See Publications) that osmotic barrier opening provides a means to grant access to the brain of agents normally excluded by the barrier. These include drugs like methotrexate, but also blood-borne antibodies that may be of use in the treatment of viral encephalitis. Before the method can be successfully employed, however, it is necessary to be sure that barrier opening can be accomplished without measurable changes in brain electrolytes or the production of cerebral edema. We therefore are conducting experiments to determine brain Na, K and water, and initial evidence indicates that if barrier opening is done without compromising cerebral blood flow, brain electrolytes and water are unaffected by the procedure. This work is being done in collaboration with K. Matthews and H.K. Thompson.

(c) Equi-osmolal opening of the blood-brain barrier by X-ray contrast media used in carotid arteriography. This work was done in collaboration with J. Bidinger and H.K. Thompson. We demonstrated that solutions of X-ray contrast agents, which are used in the clinical procedure of cerebral angiography, are concentrated enough to open the blood-brain barrier osmotically and do so at equi-osmolal concentrations. In all probability, they shrink cerebrovascular endothelial cells and widen tight junctions. Their repeated injection under clinical conditions leads to additive barrier effects and contributes to the morbidity and mortality associated with the angiographic procedure. These agents should be used over short periods of time and, if possible, repeated doses should be avoided within a period of 3 hours, which is the approximate time necessary for the osmotically opened barrier to close again.

(d) Dependence of neurotoxicity of X-ray contrast media on lipid solubility. This work is theoretical and is being done in collaboration with H. Levitan. When I recognized that the X-ray contrast media opened up the barrier osmotically at equi-osmolal concentrations, it became obvious that a factor other than osmotic barrier opening determined differences in neurotoxicity, which are marked from one medium to another. We rank ordered clinical neurotoxicity of 8 X-ray contrast media and calculated their olive oil/water partition coefficients, which are classical parameters of lipid solubility. The correlation between lipid solubility and neurotoxicity was significant at the P = 0.05 level. We proposed that the more lipid soluble the agent, the faster it enters the brain across the blood-brain barrier. We are now able to design series of X-ray contrast agents which are less lipid soluble than any in current use. We hope that they can be synthesized and tested, since they also should be less neurotoxic and should reduce the incidence of neurological sequelae following carotid and spinal cord angiography.

(e) Opening of the blood-brain barrier by acute hypertension and other conditions that modify autoregulation of cerebral blood flow. The demonstration that cerebrovascular tight junctions could be made more permeable by physical stresses produced by osmotic barrier opening, suggested to me that the junctions might also be made more permeable by conditions which produce vasodilatation of the cerebral vessels and increase vascular pressure. Such conditions occur when autoregulation of cerebral blood flow becomes defective, as in acute hypertension, electroconvulsions, brain trauma and other insults to the brain and cerebral vasculature. I elaborated a theory that autoregulation normally protects the barrier against excessive physical stresses associated with increased blood flow (see Honors below). In order to test whether tight junctions are opened when autoregulation is lost, we developed an acute hypertension model for barrier opening (Rapoport, S.I. and H.K. Thompson, Opening of the blood-brain barrier by a pulse of hydrostatic pressure, Biophysical Journal, 15: 326a, 1975). Perfusion of isotonic saline into the common carotid artery of the rat for 10 seconds was shown to open the blood-brain barrier to Evans blue-albumin. We currently are using the model to see, with electron microscopy, whether tight junctions are opened up by acute hypertension. This work is being done in collaboration with J.S. Robinson and M.W. Brightman.

(f) Selective damage of ciliary epithelium of the eye by concentrated solutions, and breakdown of blood-acqueous barrier. We showed quite early that perfusion of hypertonic solutions into the internal carotid artery of monkeys led to breakdown of the blood-aqueous and blood-vitreous barriers to protein tracers in the blood (Rapoport, S.I., D.S. Bachman and H.K. Thompson, Science, 176: 1243-1245, 1972). In order to determine the mechanism for these effects, Dr. T. Kuwabara, S. Okisaka and I studied the electron microscopy of the eye of the monkey in response to hypertonic perfusion, and related morphological changes there to changes in intraocular pressure. We found that hypertonic solutions damage the pigmented layer of the epithelium of the ciliary body, reduce the blood-aqueous barrier to proteins, and dramatically decrease intraocular pressure. Several months following hypertonic perfusion, the blood-aqueous barrier is restored and intraocular pressure has returned to its normal level.

The results are significant for the following reasons:

(a) Osmotic barrier opening is the first method that has been developed that can reversibly allow the entry of normally excluded drugs into the central nervous system, and should be useful as a technique in clinical and experimental pharmacotherapy of the brain.

(b) The demonstrated mechanism of osmotic barrier opening, namely the widening and increased permeability of cerebrovascular tight junctions, shows that the junctions are labile and suggests that the barrier is modified by conditions which alter autoregulation of cerebral blood flow. This hypothesis, put forth by me, must be tested in the future, but if it is correct, the effects on cerebral function of clinical hypertension, convulsive activity, trauma and other conditions which alter autoregulation should be reevaluated in terms of the influence of altered barrier function.

(c) Osmotic barrier opening probably plays a role in producing toxic sequelae following repeated injections of X-ray contrast media in cerebral angiography. This suggests that agents must be designed with lower osmolalities, so as to reduce their effects in modifying the barrier. Even if osmolality is reduced, however, X-ray contrast media enter the brain as a function of lipid solubility, since the barrier is selectively permeable for lipid soluble drugs. This is the first time that neurotoxicity of the media is considered in terms of simple physical chemical laws of membrane permeation, and it is hoped that new media can be synthesized with lower lipid solubilities and, as predicted by theory, reduced neurotoxic effects.

(d) We have for the first time distinguished the role of the pigmented and nonpigmented epithelial layers of the ciliary body of the eye in regulating aqueous secretion. We have shown that the pigmented layer alone can control secretion and maintain normal intraocular pressure. The mechanism controlling pressure must be understood before successful therapy of glaucoma can be accomplished. Our findings that intraocular pressure can be reduced below normal over a period of months suggest that hypertonic infusion of the eye might be of eventual use in the treatment of acute glaucoma. It remains to demonstrate whether perfusion produces important irreversible changes in eye function.

In the next year, we shall continue to study brain electrolytes and water content following osmotic barrier opening. These tests provide an objective means to evaluate the sequelae of the method, to refine the method, and to determine which agent is best suited for osmotic barrier opening.

We are designing X-ray contrast agents which should be less neurotoxic than those currently employed, by taking into account the role of lipid solubility, osmolality and dissociation coefficients in regulating their diffusion across the blood-brain barrier.

We shall try to evaluate the mechanism by which acute hypertension, and in all probability other conditions which alter autoregulation, open the barrier. We shall use electron microscopy and the intravascular tracer, horseradish peroxidase, to accomplish this.

We shall evaluate data and write up the experiments on the effect of hypertonic perfusion on the blood-aqueous and blood-vitreous barriers.

Finally, I believe that the major part of my book on the blood-brain barrier will be completed in the next year.

Key Word Descriptors:

blood-brain barrier, osmosis, cerebral blood vessels, autoregulation, hypertension, tight junctions, cell connections, brain, eye, blood-aqueous barrier, blood-vitreous barrier, ciliary epithelium, transport, permeability, electron microscopy, brain pharmacotherapy, X-ray contrast agents, cerebral angiography, membrane transport, neurotoxicity.

Honors and Awards:

Invited participant: Symposium on the Fluid Environment of the Brain, Bar Harbor, Maine, September, 1974: "Experimental modification of blood-brain barrier permeability by hypertonic solutions, convulsions, hypercapnia and acute hypertension."

Invited participant: Erwin Riesch-Symposium on the Cerebral Vessel Wall, March 14 and 15, 1975. Klinikum Steiglitz, Freie Universität Berlin: "Modification of cerebrovascular permeability by hypertonic solutions and conditions which alter autoregulation of cerebral blood flow."

Invited participant: Chicago Conference on Neural Trauma, March 21-23, 1975, NINDS: "Blood-brain barrier permeability, autoregulation of cerebral blood flow and brain edema."

Publications:

Okisaka, S., Kuwabara, T. and Rapoport, S.I. Selective destruction of the pigmented epithelium in the ciliary body of the eye. Science 184: 1298-1299, 1974.

Rapoport, S.I. and Levitan, H. Neurotoxicity of X-ray contrast media. Relation to lipid solubility and blood-brain barrier permeability. American J of Roentgenology, Radium Therapy and Nuclear Medicine 122: 186-193, 1974. (Award paper of the American Society of Neuroradiology)

Rapoport, S.I., Thompson, H.K. and Bidinger, J.M. Equiosmolal opening of the blood-brain barrier in the rabbit by different contrast media. Acta Radiologica (Diagnosis) 15: 21-32, 1974.

Rapoport, S.I. Target organ modification in pharmacology. Reversible osmotic opening of the blood-brain barrier by opening of tight junctions. In: Pharmacology and Pharmacokinetics: Problems and Perspectives, Fogarty International Center, Proceedings No. 20, T. Teorell, R.L. Dedrick and P. Condliffe, Eds. Plenum Publishing Company, New York, 1974. pp. 241-251.

Project No. Z01 MH 01084-04 LNP
1. Laboratory of Neurophysiology
2.
3. Bethesda, Maryland

PHS-ADAMHA-NIMH
Individual Project Report
July 1, 1974 through June 30, 1975

Project Title: Eye-head coordination in the primate: neural substrate and plasticity

Previous Serial Number: M-NP-66

Principal Investigator: F. A. Miles

Other Investigator: James Fuller

Cooperating Units: None

Man Years:

Total:	4.27
Professional:	2.00
Other:	2.27

Project Description:

Objectives: Experimental objectives were two-fold: 1. Chronic brain recording techniques were used to study the interactions between the various sub-systems controlling oculomotor behavior at the single cell level in the vestibular nuclei and so-called vestibular cerebellum. We extended this analysis to include neurons involved in the generation of head movements, about which much less is known. 2. Behavioral studies have attempted to define some of the factors involved in the calibration of the vestibulo-ocular reflex (VOR)--a classic open-loop control system--by observing the effects of wearing telescopic spectacles on the compensatory eye movements linked to head rotations.

Methods: Single unit recordings were made in the vestibular nuclei, vestibular nerve, oculomotor nuclei and flocculus of the awake rhesus monkey working on a previously learned visual fixation task. By shifting the fixation point, the monkey could be induced to make rapid saccadic eye movements of any desired magnitude and direction, or alternatively to track more slowly moving targets. The monkey was seated in a special chair which could be oscillated about a vertical axis by a servo-controlled torque motor. Since the animal's head was secured to the chair through implanted bolts, the chair rotation provided controlled vestibular stimulation, and unit firing patterns were examined in a variety of situations, which involved the animal tracking fixation targets which were either stationary or moving, in or out of phase with the chair rotation. In this way we obtained a general description of each unit's firing pattern in a variety of visuo-vestibular conditions. On-line data analysis is essential for the efficient organization of such complex unit analysis and we used both raster dot displays of unit activity triggered on saccadic eye movements, and simultaneous polygraph recordings of chair position, eye position, gaze (obtained by summing eye and head position signals), head torque (an index of attempted head movements) and instantaneous frequency of unit firing. With such on-line data displays, it was possible to identify salient firing characteristics and adopt experimental protocols best suited to reveal the major determinants of firing for each neuron.

In the behavioral project, monkeys were fitted with telescopic spectacles to magnify or diminish their view of the world. Initially, animals wearing such spectacles must rely heavily on visual stabilization during head rotations because the compensatory eye movements generated by the non-visual VOR are now too small (or too large, depending on the power of the lenses) to keep the retinal image stationary. The animal must therefore at first suffer some increased slippage of the retinal image during head turns because the frequency response of the visual feedback system is considerably less than that of the vestibulo-ocular system. However, if the latter is plastic and subject to some visually-mediated optimization process, then one might expect magnifying lenses to bring about increase in the VOR gain and diminishing lenses a reduction. We recorded the monkey's compensatory eye movements during chair oscillations in total darkness and defined the gain of the VOR as the ratio eye velocity/chair velocity. These measurements were made twice daily before, during and after exposure to telescopic lenses. We also measured the monkey's normal self-generated head and eye movements, allowing us to estimate the magnitude of the animal's compensatory eye movements during normal head turns.

Major Findings:

1. The recordings in the vestibular nuclei revealed that signals concerning saccadic, vestibular and tracking oculomotor functions converge on this area, but individual neurons usually receive only some and not all of these inputs; thus, their activity is dissociated from the overt output (eye movement) whenever the system is being influenced by any of the inputs that the given unit does not receive. The "total" oculomotor message is only found in relatively few neurons in this area, and their behavior, like that of oculomotor motoneurons, correlates with eye movements under all conditions.

2. The activity of a large proportion of the units in the vestibular nuclei is related to the generation of head movements. Even though such efforts are always thwarted by head mountings in these experiments, they are still attempted by the animal. Clear evidence for this comes from neck electromyograms and strain gauges attached to the head mount. Such attempted head movements are often coupled to eye movements, but not always, and, at such times we can see that some units are related to a head, rather than an eye movement function. Such units often receive a semicircular canal input,

modulating in phase with chair velocity during oscillations in darkness when the monkey is quiescent. If a unit increased firing as the chair was passively moved towards one particular side, then it would also invariably fire whenever the monkey attempted to turn its head towards the opposite side. Such neurons may fulfill a comparator function in the servo-stabilization of the head in space.

3. The finding that neurons in the vestibular nuclei often fired in association with eye movements or attempted head movements as well as labyrinthine inputs raised the possibility that vestibular efferents were involved. To examine this question, we recorded primary afferents in the eighth nerve and recorded the effects of various fixation paradigms on their activity. We never saw any activity in the primary afferents which could be attributed to non-labyrinthine sources and hence convincingly demonstrated that the neural interactions which we have described above must occur in the brainstem and not out in the labyrinth.

4. Preliminary single unit recordings in the monkey's flocculus have revealed that the Purkinje cell output from this area discharges specifically in relation to visual tracking towards the ipsilateral side. These cells generate a velocity profile of the pursuit target which, within limits, is largely independent of any passively superimposed head rotations during tracking. Most of the mossy fiber input elements discharge in relation to saccadic eye movements or labyrinthine inputs, but we have identified a class of visual units responding to retinal image slip in the region of the fovea with strong preferences for ipsilateral motion. Such units may provide the basic visual information from which the Purkinje cell fashions a velocity construct of the track target.

5. Animals that had worn telescopic spectacles showed adaptive changes in the gain of their VOR. The normal rhesus monkey has a VOR gain of close to unity and after x2.0 lenses values up to 1.85 were recorded, while after x0.5 lenses values as low as 0.6 were found. These changes took 2-3 days to reach asymptote and recovery following removal of the spectacles took a similar period of time. There was no "learning effect", i.e., with subsequent repetitions of the spectacle experience the time required to adapt did not shorten. Prolonged head immobilization after prior adaptation considerably delayed recovery back to normal. The compensatory eye movements following these various exposures were always of very similar gain for both active and passive head movements. In addition, gain changes could be brought about by spectacle experience even when all of the head movements were passively imposed, though the recalibration under these circumstances seems to be restricted to the experienced frequency range.

Significance to Biomedical Research and the Program of the Institute:

1. The recordings in the vestibular nuclei clearly establish that this area has a central role in the coordination of head and eye movements, bringing together both the basic motor programs and the feedback adjustments which

result from movements of either the head or the fixation target.

2. From recordings in the vestibular nerve, it is also clear that vestibular efferents do not play any significant role in the visuomotor processes which we have been concerned with.

3. The recordings in the flocculus suggest that, in the primate at least, this structure is involved in smooth pursuit eye movements and may indeed provide oculomotor centers with the target velocity information needed to support such tracking. These ideas are in line with very recent clinical findings which point to deficits in smooth pursuit eye movements when this part of the cerebellum is compromised.

4. The effects of telescopic spectacle experience on the compensatory eye movements coupled to head turns clearly indicate that the primate vestibulo-ocular system is both plastic and adaptive, seeking always to optimize retinal image stability. The relative simplicity of this system, its easy quantification, and our ability to induce modifications in its performance without apparent pathological side effects, make it a powerful new substrate for studying plastic mechanisms in brain function.

Proposed Course:

1. The single unit studies will follow up the preliminary findings in the flocculus, concentrating on the following questions: (a) What are the quantitative relations between target velocity, eye velocity and Purkinje cell firing? (b) Is Purkinje cell firing obligatorily related to tracking *per se*, to the slip of the track target's retinal image, or some other co-variant? (c) Do these Purkinje cells encode the ipsilateral horizontal vector during oblique tracking? (d) What are the receptive field characteristics of the visual input units--binocularity? field size? directional selectivity? stimulus shape preferences? velocity characteristics? spatial interactions between center (fovea) and surround? etc.

2. The plasticity studies will continue to examine fundamental properties, e.g., stability of the VOR in prolonged darkness? Can the VOR have asymmetrical directional gains, i.e., greater in one direction than another? Is the VOR gain for each eye calibrated separately, i.e., can we simultaneously increase the VOR gain for one eye and decrease it for the other?

Keyword Descriptors:

Eye-head coordination
Vestibulo-ocular reflex
Vestibular nuclei
Flocculus
Oculomotor
Visual tracking
Plasticity

Honors and Awards:

Invited Lecturer:

Department of Psychology, Massachusetts Institute of Technology, December 12, 1974

Department of Anatomy, Case Western University, March 12, 1975

Department of Neurology, Johns Hopkins University, April 7, 1975

Invited to present a paper at an International Symposium entitled "Eye Movements and Visual Motion Perception" in Rochester, New York, May 29-31, 1975.

Publications:

Miles, F.A. and Fuller, J.H.: Adaptive plasticity in the vestibular-ocular responses of the rhesus monkey. Brain Research 80: 512-516, 1974.

Project No. Z01 MH 01085-02 LNP
1. Laboratory of Neurophysiology
2.
3. Bethesda, Maryland

PHS-ADAMHA-NIMH
Individual Project Report
July 1, 1974 through June 30, 1975

Project Title: Neurochemical and neuroanatomical correlates of behavior

Previous Serial Number: M-NP-70

Principal Investigator: Frank R. Sharp

Other Investigators: None

Cooperating Units: Laboratory of Cerebral Metabolism, NIMH

Man Years:

Total:	2.00
Professional:	1.00
Other:	1.00

Project Description:

Objectives: This project is aimed at developing neurochemical and neuroanatomical correlates of central nervous system activity and applying these to the study of normal and abnormal behavior. Chemical changes or neuronal perikarya, neuropil, and glia should eventually be related to some aspect of CNS activity. Chemical changes of discrete brain areas related to behavior may be of great benefit in studying those areas where there is little electrical activity or the activity is difficult to record or interpret. It should be possible to map functional areas of the brain.

Methods Employed:

The major method used to date involves mapping of cerebral glucose consumption. A tracer dose of radioactive 2-deoxyglucose is administered to an animal. The animal is sacrificed after 45 minutes, and the brain frozen. Frozen sections are then cut and either autoradiographed on X-ray film or on frozen emulsion covered slides. Optical density readings or grain counts are done to quantitate the results.

Another method which is currently being developed in this laboratory involves administration of radioactive glucose followed 45 minutes later by intra-aortic perfusion of formalin or glutaraldehyde-formaldehyde mixtures. The brains are then frozen, cut, and autoradiographed.

Major Findings:

A series of rather basic discoveries have been made over the last two years in the Laboratory of Neurophysiology and the Laboratory of Cerebral Metabolism.

Stimulation of the sciatic nerve in the anesthetized rat increased the glucose consumption in the ipsilateral dorsal horn of the spinal cord several times the control side. This was the first demonstration that CNS activity could be related to glucose consumption.

Enucleation of the eye of a rat resulted in decreases of metabolism in the structures related to vision.

Swimming rats showed large but rather generalized increases of metabolism compared to resting rats. This was the first demonstration that a physiological change could result in an increase of metabolism.

Improved resolution with ^3H 2-deoxyglucose showed that the glucose consumption of neuronal perikarya was only slightly greater than the surrounding neuropil and that the bulk of gray matter glucose consumption is accounted for by neuropil. This indicated 2-deoxyglucose may be useful in mapping changes of neuropil metabolism related to function.

Rotation of rats results in increased metabolism in the vestibular nuclei and vestibulocerebellum. This demonstrated localized changes of metabolism related to a physiological stimulus.

Exposure of rats to specific odors results in characteristic localized increases of metabolism in the olfactory bulb. This demonstrates a spatial representation of odor in the olfactory bulb which will undoubtedly provide the basis for a long series of studies.

A monkey trained to rapidly squeeze a bulb with the right hand and to hold the left hand quiet showed increases of metabolism in the hemisphere of the cerebellum ipsilateral to the left hand and increases of metabolism in the hemisphere of the cerebellum ipsilateral to the right hand. There were other changes of metabolism in the frontal lobe and sensory-motor areas of the brain.

Preliminary experiments indicate that the incorporation of glucose into glutaraldehyde-fixed radioactivity may be related to activity. The distribution of this radioactivity is similar to that of 2-deoxyglucose, however. It is not known yet whether the incorporation of glucose into protein (formaldehyde-fixed radioactivity) is related to activity. This is of importance since protein is only made in neuronal perikarya.

Significance to Biomedical Research and the Program of the Institute: This project is already opening new areas of investigation and providing new information concerning the brain. The methods used will be adopted widely to redefine and continue to explore the function and anatomy of the nervous system. It is hoped that the techniques being developed could provide additional tools to study behavioral, pathological, and pharmacological states of the central nervous system. The project has already benefited greatly from the collaboration of the Laboratories of Neurophysiology and Cerebral Metabolism and should provide eventual ties with Neuropharmacology and Neuropathology within the Institute.

Proposed Course of Project: Current plans include several avenues of investigation. The effects of odor stimulation on olfactory bulb metabolism will be explored further. The effect of rotation, stimulation of the sciatic nerve, and eye enucleation on the incorporation of radioactive glucose into protein in neuronal cell bodies will be investigated. Studies of brain metabolism related to the abnormal movement produced with 6-hydroxydopamine lesions of the substantia nigra will be conducted in a line of work aimed at understanding the pathophysiology of Parkinsonism. Changes of brain metabolism during normal movement in the behaving monkey will be used to define the spatial representation of parameters of movement in the cerebellum as well as other areas. Other experiments may include study of the CNS control of blood pressure, thermoregulation, and studies of CNS plasticity.

Keyword Descriptors:

Cerebral metabolism related to function
Neurochemical correlates of behavior
Deoxyglucose
Autoradiography
Glucose

Honors and Awards: None

Publications:

Kennedy, C., DesRosiers, M., Reivich, M., Sharp, F. and Sokoloff, L.: Mapping of functional neural pathways by autoradiographic survey of local metabolic rate with (^{14}C) deoxyglucose. Science 187: 850-853, 1975.

Project No. Z01 MH 01086-03 LNP
1. Laboratory of Neurophysiology
2.
3. Bethesda, Maryland

PHS-ADAMHA-NIMH
Individual Project Report
July 1, 1974 through June 30, 1975

Project Title: Red Nucleus Neurons During Learned Movements

Previous Serial Number: M-NP-69

Principal Investigator: Jesus B. Otero

Other Investigators: None

Cooperating Units: None

Man Years:

Total:	2.52
Professional:	1.00
Other:	1.52

Project Description:

Objectives:

The overall goal of this research is to understand the role played by different cerebral structures in the initiation and during the performance of voluntary movements. Previous work has investigated the effect of secobarbital and chlorpromazine on precentral motor cortex neurons in behaving animals during the performance of a discrimination task (J.B. Otero and A.F. Mirsky: "Influence of secobarbital and chlorpromazine on precentral neuron activity during attentive behavior in monkeys," submitted to J. Neurophysiol). The results of this investigation as well as findings from different authors (Bucher and Burgui, 1952; Kuypers, 1966; Myers, 1964; Delgado, 1965; Kadobayashi, 1973; Barkay and Mirsky, unpublished data) strongly suggested to extend our research to the red nucleus. This structure has been thought to be concerned with control of body equilibrium and gait (Armstrong, 1974; Orlowsky, 1972) and with skilled distal movements (Lawrence and Kuypers, 1968; Hongo et al, 1969). The present study was designed as an attempt to determine more precisely the function of the red nucleus in movements of intact primates.

Methods Employed:

Monkey subjects are trained to depress a "hold" key for a period of 2 seconds, following which either a red or a green cue lamp comes on. The red lamp requires the hand to be moved from the hold key to a target button within 1 second of the cue presentation, whereas the green lamp requires continued depression of the hold key for 1 second following presentation of the green cue. Correct performance is reinforced with fruit juice. Extracellular activity is recorded from precentral motor cortex and red nucleus, and EMG from distal and proximal muscles of the contralateral upper limb.

Major Findings:

Data collection for the first stage of the experimental project has been completed and is the subject of a manuscript recently submitted for publication to Brain Research (J.B. Otero: "Comparison between red nucleus and precentral neurons during learned movements in the monkey"). Analysis of 48 red nucleus and 46 precentral neurons shows that:

1. Red nucleus neurons discharge in a clear and consistent relation to the occurrence of motor activity suggesting a close relation to the output or feedback pathways directly associated with the movement.

2. Most red nucleus neurons discharge later than most precentral neurons.

3. The initial response of red nucleus neurons is usually an increase in activity, whereas the initial response of precentral neurons could be either an increase or a decrease.

4. Analysis of timing relations between neuronal and EMG activity shows that, as previously reported (Evarts, 1972), precentral neurons discharge earlier than the onset of muscular activity, but red nucleus neurons discharge later.

5. Timing and firing characteristics of red nucleus neurons suggest that their activity is dependent on sensory feedback inputs from movement.

Significance to Biomedical Research and the Program of the Institute:

The pathophysiology of the motor system diseases (Parkinsonism, Chorea, Athetosis, Cerebellar Syndromes, different kinds of tremor, etc.) is largely unknown. Information concerning the physiology of the motor system should aid in the understanding of the brain pathology which is associated with these clinical problems.

Proposed Course of Project:

On the bases of the findings reported, it was decided to study in detail the possible sensory feedback in which the red nucleus is involved. A new task, in which the animal's hand movement is triggered by kinesthetic rather than by visual stimulation has been designed. In this task the animal grasps a handle which must be maintained in a determined initial position for a period which varies between 4 and 12 seconds. In a moment that the animal can't anticipate, an external force acts on the handle in the extension or flexion direction of the wrist, in a random sequence. The response--replacement of the handle in the initial position--is performed against a force which goes off after the initial position has been maintained for at least 1.5 seconds.

Two animals have been trained in this task and unitary recording from red nucleus and sensory motor cortex is in progress at present.

Keyword Descriptors:

Physiology of motor system
Voluntary movements
Red nucleus
Sensory motor cortex

Honors: None

Publications: None

Project No. Z01 MH 01087-02 LNP
1. Laboratory of Neurophysiology
2.
3. Bethesda, Maryland

PHS-ADAMHA-NIMH
Individual Project Report
July 1, 1974 through June 30, 1975

Project Title: Anatomical and physiological analysis of inputs to the primate motor cortex

Previous Serial Numbers: M-NP-65 and M-NP-71

Principal Investigator: P. L. Strick

Other Investigators: None

Cooperating Units: None

Man Years:

Total:	4.60
Professional:	1.83
Other:	2.77

Project Description:

Objectives: The anatomical phase of this project is aimed at determining the origin of thalamic and cortical inputs to the arm area of the primate motor cortex.

The physiological studies are directed towards learning how these inputs control movement and posture through regulating motor cortex output.

Methods Employed: The anatomical studies utilize the phenomenon of "retrograde axonal transport" to label the origin of inputs to the motor cortex. Low molecular weight proteins injected into the motor cortex are "taken up" (through a relatively unknown process) by synaptic terminals in the motor cortex. These proteins are then transported from the terminals, through the axon, back to their cell body (i.e., retrograde axonal transport). When the tissue is processed by the appropriate histochemical methods, the protein is visualized in the somas and proximal dendrites of neurons which send their axons to the motor cortex.

In the physiological studies, microelectrodes are used to record the activity of individual neurons in awake monkeys, a technique developed in this laboratory over the past years. Monkeys are trained to perform skilled movements and cell activity is correlated with various aspects of the movements.

Major Findings:

Anatomical. The anatomical experiments have demonstrated the existence of a previously unknown pathway from the thalamus to the motor cortex. The pathway originates from the thalamic intralaminar nuclei, and is quite substantial. Prior studies have shown that the intralaminar nuclei receive input from the basal ganglia and the cerebellum. Therefore the intralaminar input may establish an important link between subcortical motor centers and the motor cortex.

The bulk of the thalamic input to the motor cortex originates from the ventrolateral thalamic nuclei (VL). VL input to the motor cortex was also demonstrated in the present experiments; however, this study demonstrated VL input to be much more extensive than previously imagined. In addition, the protein transport experiments have provided important new details on the functional organization of VL. For example, an "arm area" was discovered in VL. This arm area was organized in the following manner: VL neurons which influence regions of the motor cortex that control distal arm musculature were situated ventrally in caudal VL. VL neurons which influence regions of the motor cortex that control more proximal arm musculature were situated more dorsally in caudal VL. No such dorso-ventral organization was found in the rostral VL arm area, which indicates that important differences exist in the way rostral and caudal VL control the motor cortex. The largest portion of the VL arm area was allotted to the control of those regions of motor cortex which influence distal musculature. Thus VL, like the motor cortex, is most concerned with the control of skilled distal extremity movements.

Physiological. The activity of thalamic neurons was recorded in awake monkeys trained to maintain the handle of a manipulandum within a small zone, despite perturbations to the handle, and to perform slow and rapid arm movement triggered by a visual stimulus.

The physiological experiments supported the concept of a VL arm area developed from the anatomical studies. Neurons related to largely active arm movements were found within the same ventral thalamic region which the anatomical studies identified as the VL arm area. Units related to jaw, tongue and neck activity associated with the juice reward occurred only medial to the VL arm area. Units related to spontaneous leg movements occurred only lateral to the VL arm area.

Microstimulation through the recording electrode in the VL arm area evoked contractions of arm musculature. Contractions of proximal musculature were evoked from dorsal regions of VL, while contractions of more distal arm musculature were evoked more ventrally.

A comparison of VL neuron and muscle activity indicates that some VL neurons modify their activity as much as 60 msec before any change in muscle activity. This finding is consistent with the hypothesis that some VL neurons play a role in movement initiation.

Significance to Biomedical Research and the Program of the Institute:

The outputs of the basal ganglia and the cerebellum converge on the ventrolateral nucleus of the thalamus (VL) which is the major source of subcortical input to the motor cortex. Thus, the thalamus can play an important role in the initiation and control of movement by processing and relaying the outputs of the major subcortical motor nuclei to the motor cortex. Analyses of the function of the thalamus in movement control have previously relied largely on the techniques of stimulation and ablation, or cell recording in anesthetized animals. This project applies both anatomical and physiological techniques to discover the origin of thalamic inputs to the motor cortex, and to learn more about the function of the thalamus during normal movement.

Experimental and clinico-pathologic studies in both animals and man have long indicated that the basal ganglia and cerebellum play an important role in the control of movement and posture. Abnormalities in movement, posture and involuntary movements frequently result from damage to these structures produced either experimentally or through disease.

It has been suggested that in a number of movement disorders the thalamus plays a prominent role in propagating the abnormal signals of diseased subcortical structures to the motor cortex. For this and other reasons, VL thalamic lesions have been made in human patients for a number of years (e.g., to reduce the tremor and rigidity accompanying Parkinson's disease). The discovery, in this project, of a previously unknown source of thalamic input to the motor cortex (from the intralaminar nuclei) should cause many of the theories on the anatomical basis of movement disorders to be modified. Thus, the present project should provide a firmer basis for the treatment of brain disorders causing abnormal movements by furthering our understanding of the role of the thalamus in the control of normal and abnormal movement.

Proposed Course of Project: Physiological experiments now in progress are concerned with further defining the type of information the thalamus provides the motor cortex. The questions which will receive the most attention will be: 1) Do thalamic neurons provide the motor cortex with information on what events have transpired in the periphery (sensory role)? or 2) Do thalamic neurons provide the cortex with motor commands generated in subcortical structures (motor role)? 3) Or both, possibly gating information which is made available to motor cortex.

In addition, experiments will test the contribution of the thalamus to different types of movement by lesioning it and recording the changes in the animal's ability to perform motor tasks.

Anatomical experiments will concentrate on determining the origin of cortical inputs to the motor cortex arm area, particularly those from the premotor and supplementary motor areas.

Keyword Descriptors:

Thalamus
Movement
Motor cortex
Retrograde axonal protein transport
Motor control

Honors and Awards: None

Publication:

Strick, P.L.: Multiple sources of thalamic input to the primate motor cortex. Brain Res. 88: 372-377, 1975.

Project No. Z01-MH-01131-02-SMRD
1. Division of Special Mental Health Research
2. Section on Neurochemistry
3. Saint Elizabeths Hospital

PHS-ADAMHA-NIMH
Individual Project Report
July 1, 1974 through June 30, 1975

Project Title: Ammonia Formation in Brain Slices

Previous Serial Number: M-SMR-DN-1

Principal Investigator: H. Weil-Malherbe

Other Investigator: None

Cooperating Units: None

Man Years:
Total: 0.3
Professional: 0.3
Other: 0

Project Description:

The effect of specific enzyme inhibitors on the ammonia formation of brain slices was investigated. Three such inhibitors were used: 5-bromofuroate, an inhibitor of glutamate dehydrogenase, hadacidin, an inhibitor of adenylosuccinate synthetase, and cycloheximide, an inhibitor of electron transport. Particular attention was paid to the kinetic analysis of the effects produced by the inhibitors singly or in combination, in the hope of elucidating the mechanism of ammonia formation and identifying the terminal deaminating enzyme.

It was found that, at relatively low concentrations, the effects of 5-bromofuroate and hadacidin in combination were strictly additive whereas the combination of either of these agents with cycloheximide resulted in effects which fell short of the sum of the single effects. These results are compatible with the function of two independent deaminating systems acting side by side, one, inhibited by 5-bromofuroate, with glutamate dehydrogenase as terminal enzyme, the other, inhibited by hadacidin, with adenylic deaminase as terminal enzyme. The action of cycloheximide occurs at a point of the metabolic pathway common to both deamination mechanisms. The conclusion that there are two independent deamination mechanisms is however valid only if the action of the two inhibitors is strictly specific. In that case, additivity should be maintained at inhibitor concentrations approaching saturation levels. Experiments designed to study this problem were inconclusive owing to the fact that, at least in the case of 5-bromofuroate, no true saturation could be obtained. In fact, kinetic analysis indicated an inhibition of 100% at infinite concentration of the inhibitor.

It is intended to pursue the problem further by studying the changes in free endogenous amino acids during the incubation of brain slices, in the presence and absence of inhibitors.

Keyword Descriptors:

Ammonia formation, brain slices, 5-bromofuroate, hadacidin, cycloheximide, deaminating enzymes

Honors and Awards:

None

Publications:

Weil-Malherbe, H.: Ammonia formation in brain slices. Molecular and Cellular Biochemistry, 4, 31-44, 1974.

Weil-Malherbe, H.: Further studies on ammonia formation in brain slices: the effect of Hadacidin. Neuropharmacol., 14, 175-180, 1975.

Project No. Z01-MH-01132-01-SMRD
1. Division of Special Mental Health Research
2. Section on Neurochemistry
3. Saint Elizabeths Hospital

PHS-ADAMHA-NIMH
Individual Project Report
July 1, 1974 through June 30, 1975

Project Title: The Subcellular Distribution of Rat Brain Adenylate Deaminase and Its Association with Neurostenin

Previous Serial Number: None

Principal Investigator: H. Weil-Malherbe

Other Investigator: None

Cooperating Units: None

Man Years:
Total: 0.3
Professional: 0.3
Other: 0

Project Description:

Adenylate deaminase, an enzyme possibly involved in the ammonia formation of brain slices, is known to be closely associated with myosin in muscle. Since an actomyosin-like protein (neurostenin) has recently been discovered in brain and credited with an important function during the process of transmitter discharge, it seemed of interest to find out whether a similar association exists in brain. The experiments also provided an opportunity to study the subcellular distribution of brain adenylate deaminase, a subject of which many conflicting opinions have been published.

It was indeed found that twice precipitated neurostenin had adenylate deaminase activity which was 3-4 times as high as that of any of the other subcellular protein fractions. Of the total activity in homogenized rat brain 34% was present in the cytoplasmic fraction, 42% in the mitochondrial fraction, 17% in the synaptosomal fraction and 7% in the microsomal fraction. The project has been terminated.

Keyword Descriptors:

Adenylate deaminase, subcellular distribution in rat brain, neurostenin

Publications:

Weil-Malherbe, H.: The subcellular distribution of rat brain adenylate deaminase and its association with neurostenin: J. Neurochem. 24, 801-803, 1975.

Project No. Z01-MH-01133-01-SMRD
1. Division of Special Mental Health Research
2. Section on Neurochemistry
3. Saint Elizabeths Hospital

PHS-ADAMHA-NIMH
Individual Project Report
July 1, 1974 through June 30, 1975

Project Title: Formation of Tryptamine and Serotonin from Tryptophan by Brain Slices

Previous Serial Number: None

Principal Investigator: H. Weil-Malherbe

Other Investigator: None

Cooperating Units: None

Man Years:
Total: .3
Professional: 0.3
Other: 0

Project Description:

Although tryptamine has been detected in brain in minute amounts, it is not clear from previous work whether it is actually synthesized by brain cells or merely deposited there after having been formed elsewhere. The question is important in view of the hypothetical role of tryptamine as a neurotransmitter and, moreover, as the parent compound of hallucinogenic compounds supposed to arise in the brain of schizophrenics.

Slices from four areas of guinea pig brain, hypothalamus, corpus striatum, the median part of pons and medulla and cerebral cortex, were incubated with ^{14}C-L-tryptophan in the presence of 5×10^{-5} M pargyline, an inhibitor of monoamine oxidase. The amines formed were isolated by cation exchange chromatography and separated by thin layer chromatography.

Tryptamine formation was detected in all four areas tested at a tryptophan concentration, 2×10^{-5} M, within the physiological range. It was of the order of 0.2 nmol/g/h in slices of corpus striatum, pons and cortex, but was about three times as strong in slices of hypothalamus. Serotonin was formed at a much higher rate: about 1 nmol/g/h in slices from c. striatum and cortex and about 3 nmol/g/h in slices from hypothalamus and pons.

Kinetic analysis of tryptophan metabolism by cortical slices has shown an apparent K_m value of $4\text{-}5 \times 10^{-5}$ M L-tryptophan for serotonin formation. The formation of tryptamine however increased in approximately linear fashion with increasing tryptophan concentration within the range studied (up to 3×10^{-4} M). It was therefore not possible t compute a value for K_m but it may be assumed that $K_m > 10^{-4}$ M. Th difference in the kinetic parameters for the two reactions results a decrease of the ratio of serotonin formation to tryptamine forma with increasing concentrations of tryptophan. The different ratio observed at a constant tryptophan concentration in different brain areas may be due to differences of K_m. This point is under invest

Keyword Descriptors:

Tryptophan decarboxylation, brain slices, serotonin synthesis tryptamine

Honors and Awards: None

Publications: None

Project No. Z01-MH-01134-02-SMRD
1. Division of Special Mental Health Research
2. Section on Neurochemistry
3. Saint Elizabeths Hospital

PHS-ADAMHA-NIMH
Individual Project Report
July 1, 1974 through June 30, 1975

Project Title: Serotonin Metabolism in Brain Slices

Previous Serial Number: M-SMR-DN-4

Principal Investigator: J. W. Gordon

Other Investigator: H. Weil-Malherbe

Cooperating Units: None

Man Years:
Total: 1.1
Professional: 0.1
Other: 1.0

Project Description:

Methods have been developed for the separation of the labeled serotonin metabolites, 5-hydroxyindoleacetic acid (5-HIAA), 5-hydroxytryptophol (5-HTOL) and 5-hydroxyindoleacetaldehyde (5-HIALD). These three metabolites were found to be formed in the same proportion by slices of four different areas of guinea pig brain upon their incubation in the presence of ^{14}C-labeled serotonin, namely in the ratio of 100 (5-HIAA) : 10 (5-HTOL) : 2 (5-HIALD). Activities were similar in slices from cortex, pons and corpus striatum, but the rate of metabolism was about doubled in hypothalamus slices.

In brain slices depleted of oxidizable substrates the overall rate of serotonin metabolism was reduced by about 50% but the ratio of the three metabolites was not affected.

So far no unknown or minor metabolites besides those mentioned have been detected. An unidentified radioactive derivative of serotonin, at first thought to be a new metabolite eventually turned out to be the methyl ester of 5-HIAA, formed when the mixture of metabolites was passed over a column of Dowex 50 and eluted at pH2.5 with 60% methanol. This artifact could be avoided by switching to a more weakly acidic cation exchange resin which did not require elution by methanol.

Keyword Descriptors:

Serotonin metabolites, brain slices, 5-hydroxyindoleacetic acid, 5-hydroxytryptophol, 5-hydroxyindoleacetaldehyde, methyl ester of 5-hydroxyindoleacetic acid

Honors and Awards: None

Publications: None

Project No. Z01-MH-01135-03-SMRD
1. Division of Special Mental Health Research
2. Section on Neurochemistry
3. Saint Elizabeth Hospital

PHS-ADAMHA-NIMH
Individual Project Report
July 1, 1974 through June 30, 1975

Project Title: Formation of L-α-hydroxyglutarate from α-ketoglutarate in tissues

Previous Serial Number: M-SMR-DN-3

Principal Investigator: Margaret Martin

Other Investigator: H. Weil-Malherbe

Cooperating Units: None

Man Years:
Total: 1.0
Professional: 1.0
Other: 0

Project Description:

In spite of numerous modifications in the methods used it has not been possible to obtain statistically significant results, largely due to the instability of the starting material and the absence of a suitable method for monitoring the very low concentrations of di-and tricarboxylic acids.

The project has been terminated.

Keyword Descriptors:

α-Hydroxyglutarate, tissue slices

Honors and Awards: None

Publications: None

Project No. Z01 MH 01181-05 SMRN
1. Division of Special Mental Health Research
2. Laboratory of Neuropharmacology
3. Saint Elizabeths Hospital

PHS-ADAMHA-NIMH
Individual Project Report
July 1, 1974 through June 30, 1975

Project Title: Investigation of chemical transmitters and mechanisms responsible for neuromotor control of peripheral blood vessels

Previous Serial Number: M-SMR-N-C-10

Principal Investigators: G. R. Siggins, D. Forman and F. E. Bloom

Other Investigator: None

Cooperating Unit: None

Man Years

Total: 0.1
Professional: 0.1
Others: 0

Project Description:

Keyword Descriptors:
Nervous system, ganglia postganglionic fibers, neurohormones, vasomotion, neurotoxins.

Objectives:
The identification of peripheral autonomic neurotransmitters requires several pieces of data beyond the simple correlation between the effects of nerve stimulation and the response to a putative transmitter. The smooth muscle of blood vessels, for example, responds to a variety of locally elaborated and circulating vasoactive agents in addition to the specific response to the neurotransmitters. The objectives of the present study are to develop micro-cytochemical methods for the study of the smooth muscle "receptors" and innervation of small blood vessels, which are combined with previously developed microphysiological and pharmacological techniques. Study of this peripheral innervation will provide a convenient nerve-effector model for central adrenergic systems.

Methods Employed:
Small arterioles of the retrolingual membrane of the frog and cheek pouch of the hamster are exposed for viewing in a light microscope. The nerves and the arterioles are electrically stimulated by microelectrodes and the responses recorded visually, physiologically and photographically. Various types of pharmacological agents are applied topically and the

physiological effect recorded. The preparation is then fixed for examination by cytochemical, fluorescence histochemical and electron microscopical techniques. Arterioles known to respond by constriction and dilation to peripheral nerve stimulation exhibit profuse innervation. Membrane arterioles examined after treatment with 6-hydroxydopamine (6-OHDA) exhibit physiologically a progressive loss of constrictor responses to nerve stimulation and by electron microscopy demonstrate abundant degenerating adrenergic, sympathetic nerve profiles. Concomitantly, uptake of exogenously applied norepinephrine by the nerves is blocked, as shown by fluorescence histochemistry. However, no inhibition of nerve-induced vasodilation is apparent after 6-OHDA treatment, and those nerve profiles specifically containing small clear synaptic vesicles do not degenerate. The latter nerves are thought to be cholinergic vasodilator nerves, resistant to 6-OHDA treatment. This hypothesis is supported by recent studies showing abundant peri-arteriolar nerves which stain positively for the enzyme acetylcholinesterase, even in preparations chronically treated with 6-OHDA to produce degeneration of adrenergic nerves. In the electron microscope these acetylcholine-stained nerves appear distinct from adrenergic nerve profiles marked with 6-OHDA or potassium permanganate.

More recently, the physiology of the postsynaptic receptors has been evaluated by topical application to the arterioles of various agents such as prostaglandins.

Major Findings:

These findings support the existence of a profuse adrenergic and cholinergic innervation of small muscular arterioles and show that the capability of coordinated vasomotion depends upon the activity of these nerves. In addition to the basic physiological knowledge of the control of arterioles, the techniques permit a simple model for studying the more complex adrenergic and cholinergic systems of the central nervous system and the effects of drugs upon such systems.

The use of 6-OHDA and surgical denervation is now being used to evaluate the effect of several agents on a totally denervated preparation, allowing discrimination between pre- and post-synaptic effects. Thus, prostaglandins E_1, E_2, $F_{1\alpha}$, $F_{2\alpha}$ and A_2 are seen to be potent direct vasodilating agents when applied topically to either normal or denervated preparations. However, only prostaglandins E_1, E_2 and $F_{2\alpha}$ were capable of blocking the sympathetic vasoconstrictor response to topically applied catecholamines in denervated preparations, or, in normal arterioles, to stimulation by microelectrode of the adrenergic vasomotor nerves. This blockade of sympathetic responses was very dramatic, lasting up to an hour and requiring as little as 10^{-10}gm/ml of PGE_1 or PGE_2. It appears, therefore, that these prostaglandins have two potent postsynaptic effects, blocking the effects of catecholamines, and producing marked vasodilation.

An example of the use this preparation as a model adrenergic system is a study just completed, in which 6-aminodopamine, a close structural analogue of 6-hydroxydopamine, was applied to the arteriolar nerve plexus. Since 6-aminodopamine was also found to produce rapid fluorescence histochemical and electron microscopic signs of selective degeneration of the periarteriolar adrenergic nerves, it was then administered intracisternally to rat brains, where it again produced ultrastructural evidence of degenerating terminals and reduced levels of norepinephrine. This finding of equivalence of action of 6-amino- and 6-hydroxydopamine has allowed some speculation as to a potentially common oxidative by-product which actually elicites the intra-neuronal degeneration.

This research has also been applied to establish the existence of cholinergic nerves which can control vascular diameter, specifically by electron microscopic histochemical techniques. The adrenergic vasomotor nerve terminals are being studied after potassium permanganate, acetylcholinesterase and other treatments to determine if the 'marking' techniques are truly specific for brain adrenergic nerves. These techniques may now be applied to other types of small arteriole preparations in mammals, such as the hamster check pouch, and to central adrenergic and cholinergic pathways.

Significance to Bio-medical Research and the Program of the Institute:
This project has temporarily been deferred. However, the studies with analogues of 6-hydroxydopamine may permit further meaningful modification of the molecule to provide even more potent and selective capabilities for lesioning the central adrenergic systems. Furthermore, all of the studies with other drugs, neurotransmitters and histochemical staining techniques can now be applied to central neurons with greater understanding of basic adrenergic and cholinergic properties.

Publications:

Siggins, G. R., and Bloom, F. E.: Structure-function relationships of neurovascular control after 6-hydroxydopamine. Pharmacologist 11: 263, 1969.

Weitsen, H. A., Siggins, G. R., and Bloom, F. E.: Cytochemical and neuropharmacological differentiation of periarteriolar nerves. Pharmacologist 12: 262, 1970.

Siggins, G. R.: Some aspects of humoral and neuromotor control of the microvascular system. In Malinin, T. I. (Ed.): Microcirculation, Perfusion and Transplantation of Organs. New York, N.Y., Academic Press, 1970.

Siggins, G. R. and Bloom, F. E.: Cytochemical and physiological effects of 6-hydroxydopamine on peri-arteriolar nerves of frogs. Circulation Res. 27: 23-38, 1970.

Siggins, G. R., and Weitsen, H. A.: Cytochemical and physiological evidence for cholinergic, neurogenic vasodilation of amphibian arterioles and precapillary sphincters. I. Light microscopy. Microvascular Res. 3: 308-322, 1971.

Siggins, G. R.: Prostaglandins and the microvascular system: Physiologic and histochemical correlation. In Ramwell, P. W., and Pharris, B. B. (Eds.): Prostaglandins in Cellular Biology and the Inflammatory Process. Plenum Press, New York, p. 451-478, 1972.

Siggins, G. R., and Forman, D. S.: Degenerative effects of 6-aminodopamine and 6-hydroxydopamine on peripheral adrenergic nerves. Z. Zellforsch. 146: 339-349, 1973.

Bloom, F. E. and Siggins, G. R.: Techniques for the localization of parasympathetic nerves to smooth muscle. In Daniel, E. E. and Paton, D. M. (Eds.): Methods in Pharmacology. New York, Plenum Press, in press.

Project No. Z01 MH 01182-03 SMRN
1. Division of Special Mental Health Research
2. Laboratory of Neuropharmacology
3. Saint Elizabeths Hospital

PHS-ADAMHA-NIMH
Individual Project Report
July 1, 1974 through June 30, 1975

Project Title: Studies of Axonal Transport

Previous Serial Number: M-SMR-N-C-11

Principal Investigator: David S. Forman

Other Investigators: G. R. Siggins, Ante Padjen

Cooperating Units: Dr. R. S. Lasher, Dept. of Anatomy, Univ. of Colorado School of Medicine, Denver, Colorado.

Man Years

Total:	1.0
Professional:	1.0
Others:	0

Project Description:

Keyword Descriptors:
Nervous system, neurons axoplasmic flow, optics (microscopy), optics (photography), optics (image processing and display).

Objectives:
These studies are designed to analyze basic properties of axonal transport (the intracellular movements of materials in axons), to identify the nature of transported materials, and to study the mechanism of transport. A subsidiary goal is to develop the use of axonal transport as a tool for tracing neuroanatomical pathways, for studies of the metabolism of synaptic macromolecules, and for studies of neuronal regeneration.

Methods Employed:
Analysis of intracellular particle movements in cultured neurons with time-lapse cinemicrography and computer analysis.

Major Findings:
A promising new way to study axonal transport is the direct observation of the movements of subcellular particles by optical methods. Intra-axonal organelles can be visualized using phase, darkfield, and Nomarski differential interference contrast optics. We have examined

movements in carefully dissected single axons from bullfrog sciatic nerve and in neurites of frog dorsal root ganglia in tissue culture. In collaboration with Dr. Robert Lasher of the University of Colorado Medical School, we are also studying particle transport in cultured rat cerebellar neurons. The organelle movements were recorded by time-lapse cinemicrography, and the films of the movements were analyzed with an L-W analyzer system. Frame-by-frame measurements of the positions of particles were analyzed with the aid of a PDP-12 computer. This project represents the most extensive quantitative study which has ever been made of optically detectable axonal particle movements. The data which has been gathered has been used to characterize the basic features of axonal organelle movement: The movements are saltatory and bidirectional. The velocities of individual particles vary from moment to moment, and net speeds vary. However, the velocity distributions of the entire population of particles in a fiber are similar from axon to axon. An important result is that most of the particles (90% in the frog sciatic axons) move toward the cell body. Thus, microscopic observation of intra-axonal organelles (which can only show the larger organelles that are above the limit of resolution of the light microscope) is a selective tool for studying the retrograde component of axonal transport.

Significance to Bio-medical Research and the Program of the Institute:
Axonal transport is a fundamental process in neuronal metabolism which is still poorly understood. The optical study of movements of subcellular particles in single nerve fibers provides a wealth of information which cannot be obtained by the more popular radiotracer and enzyme accumulation methods. This approach should yield information on such basic questions as the mechanism of transport and the relation between anterograde and retrograde movements. As well as shedding light on numerous physiological and pathological phenomena to which axonal transport is relevant, basic knowledge may also help improve our ability to use transport as a tool for studying other neurobiological problems (such as neuroanatomical tracing).

Proposed Course:
The PI will transfer to DOD, Navy Laboratories, on nerve regeneration and the study of intra-axonal particle movement will continue there and be extended to include studies of the effects of drugs on axonal transport. The present project is terminated.

Project No. Z01 MH 01183-03 SMRN
1. Division of Special Mental Health Research
2. Laboratory of Neuropharmacology
3. Saint Elizabeths Hospital

PHS-ADAMHA-NIMH
Individual Project Report
July 1, 1974 through June 30, 1975

Project Title: Interdisciplinary studies on neurons in vitro

Previous Serial Number: M-SMR-N-C-12

Principal Investigators: W. J. Shoemaker, D. Forman, M. Schlumpf, G. R. Siggins and A. Padjen

Other Investigators: F. E. Bloom, C. Chen

Man Years

Total: 2.5
Professional: 2.0
Others: 0.5

Project Description:

Keyword Descriptors:
Nervous system, central tissue culture, mixed neurohormones, nervous system, nerve terminals.

Objectives:
The objective of this project is to examine the molecular mechanism of action of neurotransmitters on neurons maintained in vitro under controlled conditions of ionic and metabolic environment. Additional objectives are to determine the time-course of synapse formation of different types of neurons under different environmental conditions.

Methods Employed:
Regions of brain or peripheral nervous system from rats and frogs are removed aseptically and either placed by themselves in culture or co-cultured with other tissues. Isolated explants are placed under culture conditions with specified pH and gas composition. Cells are observed microscopically by a variety of methods including inverted phase, Nomarski, and fluorescence microscopy. Specific neurons are impaled with intracellular microelectrodes and studies during the application of transmitters and surface receptor probes. Membrane physical parameters and surface receptor migration are examined. The movement of intracellular particles is recorded by time-lapse cinematography and analyzed by computer methods. The biosynthesis of catecholamine neurotransmitters is measured by radioenzyme assay techniques sensitive in the picogram level.

Major Findings:

The optimum culture conditions for rat CNS neurons have been determined by microscopic and electrophysiologic criteria. Parametric studies of age of tissue, state of separation of cells, plating surface conditions, plating density, media composition, source of additional serum, pharmacological agents to inhibit glial growth, osmolarity and viscosity of media, frequency of media changes, use of antibiotics, incubating temperature and humidity, media pH buffer, change in media constituents with time and ionic concentration of media have been carried out.

Presently, rat brain locus coeruleus, substantia nigra, cerebellum, cerebral cortex, rat sympathetic ganglia and frog ganglia have all been successfully cultured as determined by neuronal morphology, process outgrowth, membrane resting potentials, and spontaneous and evoked action potentials. Brain stem neurons, in addition, are capable of synthesizing catecholamines up to 3 weeks after culturing.

Significance to Bio-medical Research and the Program of the Institute:

These studies reflect upon the fundamental biology of central neurons and the mechanisms by which cells recognize each other, react to drugs and endogenous chemicals and supply essential organelles and nutrients to the synaptic terminals.

Proposed Course:

This project will continue to expand as experiments now in progress reveal how best to culture cells for physiological and pharmacological experiments.

Project No. Z01 MH 01184-05 SMRN
1. Division of Special Mental Health Research
2. Laboratory of Neuropharmacology
3. Saint Elizabeths Hospital

PHS-ADAMHA-NIMH
Individual Project Report
July 1, 1974 through June 30, 1975

Project Title: Comparative neuropharmacology of the vertebrate cerebellum

Previous Serial Number: M-SMR-N-C-13

Principal Investigators: G. R. Siggins, B. J. Hoffer and S. J. Henriksen

Other Investigator: None

Cooperating Units: D. J. Woodward, Univ. of Rochester, Rochester, N.Y.; S. C. Landis, Children's Hospital Med. Center, Boston, Mass.

Man Years

Total:	0.75
Professional:	0.75
Others:	0.0

Project Description:

Keyword Descriptors:
Brain, cerebellum, neurophysiology, impulse inhibition, neuropharmacology.

Objectives:
The primary objective of this study is to determine whether the neuropharmacological properties of Purkinje cells in the cerebella of the different vertebrates show any similarity. Anatomical and electrophysiological studies have shown that the cerebella of the lower vertebrates (elasmobranchs, amphibia) resemble those of mammals. We also wish to determine at which point in phylogenetic development the pharmacological receptivity to various putative neurohumors develops. Finally, the cerebellum of the mouse is being explored because of the availability of several mutations of this structure in the mouse. Cerebella of lower vetebrates may provide model systems for analysis of neurotransmitters of the excitatory and inhibitory cerebellar pathways.

Methods Employed:
The discharge of single Purkinje cells in cerebella of various species are recorded by the central barrel of a 5-barreled micropipette. Drugs are applied by microelectrophoresis from the peripheral barrels. Various excitatory and inhibitory pathways to Purkinje cells are stimulated electrically. The cerebella are also studied histochemically, and sometimes biochemically.

Major Findings:
Purkinje cells of frog, pigeon, cat, mouse and rabbit have been studied. Responses to norepinephrine, serotonin, gamma-amino-butyric acid, acetylcholine, glutamate, glycine and cyclic adenine and guanine nucleotides have been found. In the frog, picrotoxin and bicuculline, but not strychnine, block the depressant action of gamma-amino-butyric acid. The inhibitory effects of glycine are antagonized by strychnine but not picrotoxin or bicuculline. When the interneurons of the frog cerebellum are electrically stimulated, their inhibitory actions on Purkinje cells are also blocked by picrotoxin and bicuculline but not strychnine. This evidence suggests that gamma-amino-butyric acid mediates the inhibitory action of cerebellar interneurons. In addition, interneurons in the frog molecular layer actively take up H^3GABA, as seen with light microscopic autoradiography.

Most cerebellar Purkinje cells of virtually all the species studied respond to cyclic adenine nucleotides predominantly by inhibition of firing rates as in the rat cerebellum. Also like rat, nearly 100% of Purkinje cells of all the species except pigeon exhibit marked inhibitory responses to norepinephrine. Responses to other agonists (5-HT, acetylcholine, cyclic GMP) tend to be more mixed although mouse Purkinje cells are always inhibited by 5-HT. In general, however, responses to putative transmitters are fairly uniform across the species.

Only one mouse mutant has so far been studied: Weaver, which is characterized by a lack of granule cells and parallel fibers in the cerebellar cortex. In spite of this loss of the major excitatory input to the Purkinje cell, the neurons still discharge spontaneously and respond like normal mouse Purkinje cells to most iontophoretically applied neurotransmitters and cyclic nucleotides. Only responses to acetylcholine are different in that more excitatory effects are seen.

Significance to Bio-medical Research and the Program of the Institute:
This study will yield basic information about the evolution and phylogenetic development of neuropharmacological mechanisms and provide information about possible transmitters mediating excitation and inhibition in the vertebrate cerebellum. Studies of animals with cerebellar mutations may provide valuable data on trophic interactions, plasticity and receptor sensitivity in complex neuronal arrays.

Proposed Course:
We plan to examine cerebella of elasmobranchs, reptiles and other species and eventually to define those neuropharmacological alterations which have accompanied evolution of the cerebella. The cerebelli of some species will be explored to determine their viability in vitro for studies of ionic mechanisms in synaptic function. The cerebella will also be studied histochemically to localize pathways utilizing GABA and

catecholamines as inhibitory transmitters. Other mouse mutants will be investigated to examine possible trophic effects of pathway degeneration on neuronal responsiveness to neurotransmitters.

Publications:

Woodward, D. J., Hoffer, B. J., Siggins, G. R., and Oliver, A. P.: Inhibition of Purkinje cells in the frog cerebellum. II. Evidence for GABA as the inhibitory transmitter. Brain Res. 33: 91-100, 1971.

Bloom, F. E., Hoffer, B. J., Siggins, G. R., Barker, J. L. and Nicoll, R. A.: Effects of serotonin on central neurons: Microiontophoretic administration. Fed. Proc. 31: 97-106, 1972.

Bloom, F. E., Hoffer, B. J., Nelson, C., Sheu, Y-s and Siggins, G. R.: The physiology and pharmacology of serotonin mediated synapses. In Usdin, E. and Barchas, J. D. (Eds.): Serotonin and Behavior. New York, Academic Press, 1973, pp. 249-261.

Bloom, F. E., Siggins, G. R. and Hoffer, B. J.: Interpreting the failures to confirm the depression of cerebellar Purkinje cells by cyclic AMP. Science 185: 627-629, 1974.

Project No. Z01 MH 01219-07 SMRN
1. Division of Special Mental Health Research
2. Laboratory of Neuropharmacology
3. Saint Elizabeths Hospital

PHS-ADAMHA-NIMH
Individual Project Report
July 1, 1974 through June 30, 1975

Project Title: Computer based electronic visual scanning devices for quantitating and qualitating the central nervous synapses

Previous Serial Number: M-SMR-N-Y-6

Principal Investigators: F. E. Bloom and W. J. Shoemaker

Other Investigator: E. Battenberg

Cooperating Unit: Dr. J. Prewitt and Ms A. Barber, DCRT, NIH

Man Years

Total:	0.75
Professional:	0.50
Others:	0.25

Project Description:

Keyword Descriptors:
Nervous system, nerve endings, neuronogenesis, optics, microscopy (electron), computer diagnosis.

Objectives:
A specific stain was developed by which the synaptic specialization can be selectively visualized in the electron microscope. By using this staining technique, different qualitative types of synaptic contacts can be estimated as well as quantitating their total number in a given sample of nervous tissue. The objectives of these studies were to evaluate the relative changes in synaptic contacts during behavioral phenomenological challenges, and to quantitate the rate of development of synaptic contact formation in various areas of the rat brain during neonatal and postnatal development.

A computerized system is now being developed that will allow us to observe the changes of the central synaptic junctions both quantitatively and qualitatively during the normal growth of brain during experimental degeneration and after drug administration. This computerized method will allow us to process the experimental tissue more rapidly and objectively.

Method Employed:
Animals were obtained which had been exposed to different types of behavioral stimulation (such as the environmental enrichment procedure);

other animals were obtained at various stages of postnatal development between 0 and 14 days after birth. Tissues were fixed with glutaraldehyde, and stained with the ethanolic phosphotungstic stain in the block. Thin sections were cut and the total number of synapses quantitated for the regions desired.

The electron microscopic picture of the nervous tissue (stained by phosphotungstic acid) were digitized by using the optical scanner (FIDAC) at the Georgetown University National Biomedical Foundation. The programs for quantitating the size of the synapses and recognizing the shape of the object, as well as quantifying the number of junctions are now operational.

Major Findings:

Synaptic formation within the molecular layer of the cerebral cortex appears to have an extremely constant value. After performing large numbers of quantitations on various stages of behavioral stimulation, there appears to be no reproducible relationship between the behavioral stimulation, maze performance and the quantitation of synaptic contacts in the molecular layer. In the cerebellar cortex, the onset of synapse formation within the outer molecular layer occurs between days 5 and 6; the synapse formation on Purkinje cell dendrites appears to become most rapid between days 6-9. At the same stage of development, synaptic formation is well under way in the ventral and medial hypothalamus.

In animals raised for one week in utero and 4 weeks post-partum on maternally derived protein deficient diets, the number of synaptic contacts which are visualized in the hippocampus and cerebellar cortex are reduced by more than 30%. Upon prompt re-feeding, the number of contacts returns toward normal. A computerized detection system is still required in order to maximize the sample sizes and reduce sampling variations.

Significance to Bio-medical Research and the Program of the Institute:

The main site of interneuronal communication is at the synapse. The ability to quantitate synaptic formation and to describe qualitatively different states of synapses would seem the most pertinent cellular information to obtain in studies directed at the learning process and neuronal plasticity.

Proposed Course:

This project will be terminated during 1976 and transferred with the PI; methods of rapid processing of electron microscopic data are under development. In FY 1975 a new attempt at collaboration has been initiated through the NIH, DCRT. Micrographs will be processed through an optical analyzer system supported by DCRT through the Jet Propulsion Laboratory in Pasadena, California and data tapes of these scans will be analyzed by DCRT in Bethesda.

Publications:

Bloom, F. E.: The ultrastructure of synapses: Correlating structure and function. In Schmitt, F. O., Quarton, G. C., and Melnechuk, T. (Eds.): The Neurosciences - A Study Program. New York, N.Y., Rockefeller University Press, 1970, pp. 749-766.

Bloom, F. E.: The formation of synaptic junctions in developing rat brain. In Pappas, G. D. (Ed.): Structure and Function of Synapses. New York, N.Y., Appleton-Century-Crofts, 1972.

Woodward, D. J., Hoffer, B. J., Siggins, G. R., and Bloom, F. E.: The ontogenetic development of synaptic junctions, synaptic activation, and responsiveness to neurotransmitter substances in rat cerebellar cortex. Brain Res. 34: 73-79, 1971.

Bloom, F. E.: The gains in brain are mainly in the stain. In Worden, F., Adelman, G. and Swazey, J. (Eds.): The Neurosciences: Paths of Discovery. Cambridge, MIT Press (in press).

Lauder, J. M. and Bloom, F. E.: Ontogeny of monoamine neurons in the locus coeruleus, raphe nuclei and substantia nigra of the rat. II. Synaptogenesis. Brain Res. (in press).

Project No. Z01 MH 01220-07 SMRN
1. Division of Special Mental Health Research
2. Laboratory of Neuropharmacology
3. Saint Elizabeths Hospital

PHS-ADAMHA-NIMH
Individual Project Report
July 1, 1974 through June 30, 1975

Project Title: Cytochemistry of monoamine-containing nerve fibers in cerebellum and brainstem

Previous Serial Number: M-SMR-N-Y-8

Principal Investigator: F. E. Bloom

Other Investigator: E. Battenberg

Cooperating Units: None

Man Years

Total:	0.5
Professional:	0.3
Others:	0.2

Project Description:

Keyword Descriptors:
Optics, microscopy (electron), histochemistry, neurohormones.

Objectives:
This project is intended to bring cytochemical methods to bear upon the problem of identifying specific types of nerve fibers in various regions of the brain by using electron microscopic cytochemical techniques and fluorescence histochemical techniques. This type of methodology has been used successfully in examining the hypothalamus. The overall objective of this project is to develop new techniques for light and electron microscopic demonstration of specific synaptic transmitters.

Methods Employed:
Animals are injected either intraventricularly or intracisternally with radioactive neurotransmitter or neurotransmitter precursors. After variable periods of time animals are perfused with glutaraldehyde and tissues processed for light and electron microscopy. Autoradiography is performed on 1μ thick sections and on 800 Angstrom thin sections. The relationship between autoradiographic grains and tissue elements is determined. Fluorescence microscopy is performed by standard methods of formaldehyde coupling on freeze-dried tissues or by a newly developed

procedure for demonstration of glyoxylic acid induced fluorescence.

Major Findings:

Using the methods, norepinephrine and serotonin-containing nerve endings can be localized to particular regions along the Purkinje cell dendrite and soma. Serotonin terminals appear to be particularly dense in the internal granule cell layer. These methods appear to be confirmed by fluorescence histochemistry. In the brainstem of the cat and the rat, the raphe neurons (normally serotonin containing) receive afferent nerve endings containing both norepinephrine and serotonin. Blocking sulfhydryl reagents by conversion to disulfide bonds, greatly reduces the osmiophilia of small and large granular vesicles. Exposure of sulfhydryl groups gives a moderate increase in the osmiophilia of the same vesicle.

The locus coeruleus (LC) projects norepinephrine-containing fibers to the telencephalon and cerebellum. The cell bodies of the locus coeruleus, raphe nuclei and substantia nigra were examined at various ages using formaldehyde-induced fluorescence and H^3-thymidine autoradiography. The cells of the locus coeruleus (as studied by autoradiography) differentiate on days 11-13 of gestation with peak at 12 days, whereas the cells of the raphe nuclei and substantia nigra differentiate on days 11-15 of gestation with peaks on day 13. At birth, the cells have already migrated to the adult position. After the first week of life, NE fluorescence shows no further increase. Cell discharge during the first week of life is slow and regular at 1-2/sec. In older animals faster rates (up to 25/sec) are found. Iontophoresis of NE appears to produce an inhibitory action.

Synaptogenesis begins in all 3 structures as early as 20 days of gestation and continues throughout adulthood, indicating that monoamine circuitry is present before birth and continues to be formed throughout postnatal development.

Significance to Bio-medical Research and the Program of the Institute:

These cytochemical methods are used to support the significance of the electrophysiological data obtained by microelectrophoretic experiments on the identical animals from the same experimental source. This type of information is necessary in order to determine a) that the pharmacological responsiveness has some relationship to the types of neurotransmitters in the area being tested; b) that the same type of method can be used to imply that a particular type of neurotransmitter does innervate an area to be studied in future experiments.

Proposed Course:

This project is being terminated with resignation of the PI. The results of experiments combining the injection of radioactive transmitter substances with previous injections of 6-OHDA or other drugs which will affect the binding of neurotransmitter substances is being prepared for publication.

Publications:

Bloom, F. E.: The ultrastructure of synapses: Correlating structure and function. In Schmitt, F.O., Quarton, G. C. and Melnechuk, T. (Eds.): The Neurosciences - A Study Program. New York, Rockefeller Univ. Press. 1970, pp. 729-746.

Bloom, F. E.: The fine structural localization of biogenic monoamines in nervous tissue. Int. Rev. Neurobiol. 13: 27-66, 1970.

Bloom, F. E., and Crayton, J. M.: Electron microscopic localization of biogenic amines. In Berson, S., Yalow, R., Dorfman, R., Rall, E. and Kopin, I. (Eds.): Methods in Investigative and Diagnostic Endocrinology. Amsterdam, North-Holland Publishing Co., 1972, pp. 369-397.

Bloom, F. E.: Electron microscopy of catecholamine-containing structures. In Blaschko, and Muscholl, B. (Eds.): Handbook of Experimental Pharmacology. Berlin, Springer Verlag, 1972, pp. 45-78.

Bloom, F. E., Hoffer, B. J., and Siggins, G. R.: Studies on norepinephrine-containing afferents to Purkinje cells of rat cerebellum. I. Localization of the fibers and their synapses. Brain Res. 25: 501-521, 1971.

Bloom, F. E.: Localization of neurotransmitters by electron microscopy. In Kopin, I. J. (Ed.): Proc. Association for Research in Nervous and Mental Diseases. Baltimore, Md., Williams and Wilkins, 1972, Vol. 50, pp. 25-57.

Hoffer, B. J., Siggins, G. R., and Bloom, F. E.: The role of cyclic AMP in the effects of norepinephrine on cerebellar Purkinje cells. In Costa, E. and Greengard, P. (Eds.): Role of Cyclic AMP in Neuronal Function. New York, Raven Press, 1970.

Hoffer, B. J., Chu, N-s., and Oliver, A. P.: Cytochemical and electrophysiological studies on central catecholamine-containing neurons. Proc. Vth Int'l. Pharmacol. Congr., 1972.

Hoffer, B. J., Siggins, G. R., Oliver, A. P., and Bloom, F. E.: Activation of the pathway from locus coeruleus to rat cerebellar Purkinje neurons: Pharmacological evidence of noradrenergic central inhibition. J. Pharmacol. Exp. Therap. 184: 553-569, 1973.

Hoffer, B. J., Chu, N-s., and Oliver, A. P.: Cytochemical and electrophysiological studies on central catecholamine-containing neurons. Proc. Vth Int'l. Pharmacol. Congr., 1972.

Nicholson, J. L., and Bloom, F. E.: Cell differentiation and synaptogenesis in the locus coeruleus, raphe nuclei and substantia nigra of the rat. Anat. Rec. 175: 398, 1973.

Bloom, F. E., Krebs, H., Nicholson, J., and Pickel, V.: The noradrenergic innervation of cerebellar Purkinje cells: Localization, function, synaptogenesis, and axonal sprouting of locus coeruleus. In Fuxe, K. (Ed.): Wenner-Gren Symposium on "Dynamics of Degeneration and Growth in Neurons". England, Pergamon Press, pp. 413-423, 1974.

Nelson, C. N., Hoffer, B. J., Chu, N-s. and Bloom, F. E.: Cytochemical and pharmacological studies on polysensory neurons in the primate frontal cortex. Brain Res. 62: 115-133, 1973.

Segal, M., Pickel, V. M. and Bloom, F. E.: The projection of the nucleus locus coeruleus, an autoradiographic study. Life Sci. 13: 817-821, 1973.

Chu, N-s. and Bloom, F. E.: The catecholamine-containing neurons in the cat dorso-lateral pontine tegmentum: Distribution of the cell bodies and some axonal projections. Brain Res. 66: 1-21, 1974.

Pickel, V. M., Segal, M. and Bloom, F. E.: A radioautographic study of the efferent pathways of the nucleus locus coeruleus. J. Comp. Neurol. 155: 15-42, 1974.

Pickel, V. M., Segal, M. and Bloom, F. E.: Axonal proliferation following lesions of cerebellar peduncles. A combined fluorescence microscopic and radioautographic study. J. Comp. Neurol. 155: 43-60, 1974.

Segal, M. and Bloom, F. E.: The action of norepinephrine in the rat hippocampus: II. Activation of the input pathway. Brain Res. 72: 99-114, 1974.

Bloom, F. E. and Siggins, G. R.: Techniques for the Localization of parasympathetic nerves to smooth muscle. Methods in Pharmacol. (in press).

Bloom, F. E.: The gains in brain are mainly in the stain. In Worden, F., Adelman, G. and Swazey, J. (Eds.): The Neurosciences: Paths of Discovery. Cambridge, MIT Press (in press).

Nicholson, J. L. and Bloom, F. E.: Ontogeny of monoamine neurons in the locus coeruleus, raphe nuclei and substantia nigra of the rat. I. Cell differentiation. J. Comp. Neurol. 155: 469-482, 1974.

Bloom, F. E. and Landis, S. C.: Correlated histochemical, electron microscopical, pharmacological and physiological observation on aminergic mechanisms in the central nervous system. In Eranko, O. (Ed.): Symposium on SIF Cells. Washington, D.C., GPO (in press).

Lauder, J. M. and Bloom, F. E.: Ontogeny of monoamine neurons in the locus coeruleus, raphe nuclei and substantia nigra of the rat. II. Synaptogenesis. Brain Res. (in press).

Freedman, R., Foote, S. L. and Bloom, F. E.: Histochemical characterization of the neocortical projection of the nucleus locus coeruleus in the squirrel monkey. J. Comp. Neurol. (in press).

Landis, S., Shoemaker, W. J., Bloom, F. E. and Schlumpf, M.: Catecholamines in mutant mouse cerebella: Histochemical fluorescence and neurochemical studies. Brain Res. (in press).

Battenberg, E. L. F. and Bloom, F. E.: A rapid, simple and more sensitive method for the demonstration of central catecholamine-containing neurons and axons by glyoxylic acid induced fluorescence. I. Specificity. Psychopharmacol. Commun. 1: 3-13 (1975).

Project No. Z01 MH 01221-07 SMRN
1. Division of Special Mental Health Research
2. Laboratory of Neuropharmacology
3. Saint Elizabeths Hospital

PHS-ADAMHA-NIMH
Individual Project Report
July 1, 1974 through June 30, 1975

Project Title: Experimental studies on the fine structure and content of brain monoamine-containing nerve fibers

Previous Serial Number: M-SMR-N-Y-9

Principal Investigators: F. E. Bloom and W. J. Shoemaker

Other Investigators: S. Landis, E. Battenberg, M. Schlumpf, S. Henriksen and L. Koda

Cooperating Unit: L. Neckers (SMRP)

Man Years

Total:	2.3
Professional:	1.8
Others:	0.5

Project Description:

Keyword Descriptors:
Nervous system (central), optics electron (microscopy), histochemistry, neurohormones, neurotoxins.

Objectives:
The objectives of this project are to determine the changes in the distribution and morphology of nerve fibers containing norepinephrine, dopamine, and serotonin by various experimental manipulations including: surgical or chemical lesions in regions containing cell bodies thought to give rise to these axons, genetic mutations, undernutrition or chemical toxins such as 6-hydroxydopamine, a substance which is taken up into catecholamine containing nerve endings and which causes toxic degeneration of these nerve endings.

Methods Employed:
Small electrolytic lesions were placed within nuclei of cats and rats, or monkeys using stereotaxic approaches. Six-hydroxydopamine was injected intracisternally for 1 or 3 days. At various times after the acute degenerating process, brains were either prepared for electron microscopy or removed, dissected into regions and prepared for formaldehyde induced fluorescence histochemistry. In separate experiments at various times after the acute treatment with 6-hydroxydopamine

(6-OHDA), radioactive H^3-5HT and H^3-NE were injected intracisternally and the brains prepared for light microscopic autoradiography. At the light microscopic level, monoaminergic fibers and cell bodies are examined either with formaldehyde- or glyoxylic acid-induced for catecholamine histofluorescence or with autoradiography following administration of radioactive neurotransmitter or neurotransmitter precursors. In FY-1974, four of the genetic mutations which affect cerebellar development in the mouse were used. Also, rats which were undernourished by feeding low protein diets during the last week of gestation and the first 3 weeks of post-natal development were studied by these morphological indices.

Major Findings:

The treatment with 6-OHDA produces a severe and prolonged degeneration of the norepinephrine-containing nerve endings as reflected by the persistent lack of norepinephrine content in the nerve ending rich regions of these brains. Serotonin levels in these brains are not affected. By electron microscopy, those regions of the brain rich in norepinephrine-containing nerve endings are found to have evidence of a toxic degenerative process in which the synaptic vesicles become broken and the axoplasm becomes extremely electron-dense. In later stages profound glial lamellations occur around these nerve endings. By fluorescence histochemistry the degeneration can be seen as greatly reduced numbers of catecholamine fluorescing nerve terminals. Those which survive appeared to be dilated and dystrophic. Examination of brain stem regions rich in catecholamine fluorescing cell bodies in normal animals show a persistence of such cell bodies in the treated animals although the number and size appears to be affected. Within 5 days after treatment with 6-hydroxydopamine the hypothalamus, caudate nucleus and cerebellar cortex all show greatly reduced ability to take up and bind tritiated NE but show no impairment of the ability to take up H^3-5HT.

The three cerebellar mutants (staggerer, weaver and reeler) with hypoplastic cerebella all manifest greatly increased catecholamine fluorescence per unit area. Abundant varicosities are present in each of the three but the patterns of fluorescent fibers were distinctive. The large number of terminals in the mutant cerebella offers the opportunity to identify them ultrastructurally. Following permanganate fixation, with and without 5-OHDA administration, axonal boutons containing small granular vesicles were present and opposed to Purkinje cell dendritic spines. After 6-OHDA treatment, degenerating boutons are also present near Purkinje cell spines. In undernourished rats, norepinephrine and dopamine levels are reduced, but the number and fluorescence intensity of the catecholamine neurons are at best as good as normal.

In FY 1975, a new and improved method was devised with which to perform fluorescence histochemical identification of the brain catecholamine pathways and this new method has greatly simplified the ease of accomplishing the identification with the light microscope. The modified method requires that brains be perfused with paraformaldehyde and glyoxylic acid. Fixed brain slabs are frozen onto cryostat chucks by immersion in powered dry ice. Sections are cut in a cryostat at 18-20°C, immersed in glyoxylic acid solution, then air dried and heated at 100°C for 10 min. all known perikaryonal and axonal elements containing fluorescent catecholamine are visible by this method. Brain sections can be examined within minutes after sacrifice of the experimental animal and no freeze-drying or other machinery is required. The method does not reveal serotonin fluorescence in either neurons or axons. Cortical norepinephrine projection systems can be clearly mapped.

Also in FY 1975, attempts were made to determine whether p-Cl-amphetamine or fenfluramine lower brain 5-HT levels and synthetic capacities through destruction of brain 5-HT neurons analogous to the type of toxic effects produced by 6-OHDA on the catecholamine systems. Light and electron microscopy have been used to analyze these possibilities in the dorsal and pontine raphe nuclei and in the hippocampus where the pontine raphe neurons send terminals. Analyses obtained this far have revealed no clear-cut patho-toxicological effects.

Significance to Bio-medical Research and the Program of the Institute:
The efficacy of psychotherapeutic drugs is based on their presumed specific effects on certain types of nerve fibers. In order to determine the circuitry involved in these fibers, methods must be found for detailed analysis of the pathways involved. The methods being developed in this project will be useful in ascertaining the relative distribution of particular types of catecholamine and indole amine containing nerve fibers throughout the brain. This information can then lead to studies on functions of these nerve fibers in the various portions of the central nervous system.

Proposed Course:
This project will be terminated during FY 1976 with the departure of the PI. Subsequent behavioral studies utilizing these methods will be performed to determine the functional importance to the brain of the missing or underdeveloped catecholamine pathways.

Honors and Awards:
Invited participant in International Conference on 6-hydroxydopamine, Lucerne, Switzerland, October, 1970.
Invited participant at the Conference on Neurotransmitters (ARNMD), New York, New York, December, 1970.
Invited participant at the ASPET Symposium on Serotonin, FASEB, 1971.
Invited participant in the Histochemical Society Meeting, October, 1972.
Invited participant in the IIIrd Neurosciences Intensity Study Program, 1972.

Arthur S. Flemming Award, 1972.
Mathilde Solowey Award, 1973.
Biological Sciences Award for 1974, Washington Academy of Sciences

Publications:

Bloom, F. E., Algeri, S., Groppetti, A., Revuelta, A., and Costa, E.: Lesions of central norepinephrine terminals with 6-OH-dopamine: Biochemistry and fine structure. Science 166: 1284-1286, 1969.

Bloom, F. E.: The fine structural localization of biogenic monoamines in nervous tissue. Int. Rev. Neurobiol. 13: 27-66, 1970.

Hoffer, B. J., Siggins, G. R., and Bloom, F. E.: Possible cyclic AMP mediated adrenergic synapses to rat cerebellar Purkinje cells: Combined structural, physiological and pharmacologic analyses. In Costa, E., and Greengard, P. (Eds.): Advances in Biochemical Psychopharmacology. New York, Raven Press, 1970, pp. 349-370.

Bloom, F. E.: Fine structural changes in rat brain after intracisternal injection of 6-hydroxydopamine. In Malmfors, T., and Thoenen, H. (Eds.): 6-Hydroxydopamine and Catecholamine Neurons. Amsterdam, North-Holland Publ., 1971, pp. 135-150.

Bloom, F. E., Hoffer, B. J., Siggins, G. R., Barker, J. L., and Nicoll, R. A.: Effects of serotonin on central neurons: Microiontophoretic administration. Fed. Proc. 31: 97-106, 1972.

Bloom, F. E.: Ultrastructural identification of catecholamine-containing central synaptic terminals. J. Histochem. and Cytochem. 21: 333-348, 1973.

Landis, S. C.: Changes in neuronal mitochondrial shape in brains of nervous mutant mice. J. Heredity 64: 193-196, 1973.

Bloom, F. E., Krebs, H., Nicholson, J. and Pickel, V.: The noradrenergic innervation, of cerebellar Purkinje cells: Localization, function, synaptogenesis, and axonal sprouting of locus coeruleus. In Fuxe, K., Olson, L. and Zotterman, Y. (Eds.). Dynamics of Degeneration and Growth in Neurons. England, Pergamon Press, 1974, pp. 413-423.

Bloom, F. E. and Hoffer, B. J.: Norepinephrine as a central synaptic transmitter. In Usdin, E. and Snyder, S. (Eds.). Frontiers in Catecholamine Research. England, Pergamon Press, 1973, pp. 637-642.

Chu, N-s. and Bloom, F. E.: The catecholamine-containing neurons in the cat dorso-lateral pontine tegmentum: Distribution of the cell bodies and some axonal projections. Brain Res. 66: 1-21, 1974.

Pickel, V. M., Segal, M. and Bloom, F. E.: A radioautographic study of the efferent pathways of the nucleus locus coeruleus. J. Comp. Neurol. 155: 15-42, 1974.

Pickel, V. M., Segal, M. and Bloom, F. E.: Axonal proliferation following lesions of cerebellar peduncles. A combined fluorescence microscopic and radioautographic study. J. Comp. Neurol. 155: 43-60, 1974.

Bloom, F. E. and Siggins, G. R.: Techniques for the localization of parasympathetic nerves to smooth muscle. Methods in Pharmacol. (in press).

Robinson, R. G., Shoemaker, W. J., Schlumpf, M., Valk, T. and Bloom, F. E.: Experimental cerebral infarction in rat brain: Effect on catecholamines and behavior. Nature (in press).

Bloom, F. E. and Landis, S. C.: Correlated histochemical, electron microscopical, pharmacological and physiological observation on aminergic mechanisms in the central nervous system. In Eranko, O. (Ed.). Symposium on SIF Cells. Washington, D. C., GPO (in press).

Landis, S., Shoemaker, W. J., Bloom, F. E. and Schlumpf, M.: Catecholamine in mutant mouse cerebella: Histochemical fluorescence and neurochemical studies. Brain Res. (in press).

Battenberg, E. F. and Bloom, F. E.: A rapid, simple and more sensitive method for the demonstration of central catecholamine-containing neurons and axons by glyoxylic acid induced fluorescence: I. Specificity. Psychopharmacol. Commun. 1: 3-13, 1975.

Bloom, F. E.: Monoaminergic neurotoxins: Are they selective? J. Neural Transmission (in press).

Project No. Z01 MH 01222-01 SMRN
1. Division of Special Mental Health Research
2. Laboratory of Neuropharmacology
3. Saint Elizabeths Hospital

PHS-ADAMHA-NIMH
Individual Project Report
July 1, 1974 through June 30, 1975

Project Title: Cytochemical and functional studies of the raphe nuclei

Previous Serial Number: M-SMR-N-Y-11

Principal Investigators: F. E. Bloom, S. Henriksen, L. Koda

Other Investigator: F. E. Bloom

Cooperating Units: None

Man Years

Total:	0.5
Professional:	0.5
Others:	.0

Project Description:

Keyword Descriptors:
Nervous system, central neuroanatomy, neurohormones, optics, microscopy, electron.

Objectives:
The objectives of this project have been to characterize the raphe neurons of the rat with respect to cytochemical and neurochemical correlations with the pituitary-adrenal axis.

Methods Employed:
In rats, the terminal fields of specific raphe nuclei were mapped with fluorescence histochemistry and axoplasmic transport autoradiography; high resolution, dry-mount autoradiography was used to determine whether the raphe neurons or their postsynaptic target cells would accumulate glucocorticoids when given in physiologic amounts.

Major Findings:
By fluorescence histochemistry, 5-HT containing terminals have been observed in brain regions thought to be important in the regulation of the

pituitary adrenal axis such as the nucleus suprachiasmatics, medial septal nucleus and in the hippocampus. Cytochemical estimation of intermediary oxidative metabolic enzyme activity has shown that raphe nuclei contain substantial amounts of NAD and NADP diaphorases.

Significance to Bio-medical Research and the Program of the Institute:

Alterations in 5-HT metabolism, implying altered function with the 5-HT raphe neurons, have been linked to many affective disorders including depression. These same mental syndromes are also associated with endocrine imbalances, particularly when sleep imbalance is pronounced. Definition of the role of 5-HT neurons in regulation of sleep and in the temporal sequences controlling central endocrine regulation and diurnal rhythmicity is essential to an understanding of the possible dysfunctions in these systems which may be pathogenic in the affectively disordered states.

Proposed Course:

This project will be merged with Z01 MH 01220.

Publications:

Sheu, Y., Chu, N., Nelson, J. P., and Bloom, F. E.: Recording single neurons in cat brain during chronic unrestrained behavior freedom. Proc. Western Pharm. Soc. 14: 133-134, 1971.

Bloom, F. E., Hoffer, B. J., Nelson, C., Sheu, Y-s., and Siggins, G.R.: The physiology and pharmacology of serotonin mediated synapses. In Usdin, E. and Barchas, J. D. (Eds.) Serotonin and Behavior. Academic Press, New York, 1973, pp. 249-261.

Sheu, Y., Nelson, J. P., and Bloom, F. E.: Discharge patterns of cat raphe neurons during sleep and waking. Brain Res. 73: 263-276, 1974.

Project No. Z01 MH 01223-04 SMRN
1. Division of Special Mental Health Research
2. Laboratory of Neuropharmacology
3. Saint Elizabeths Hospital

PHS-ADAMHA-NIMH
Individual Project Report
July 1, 1974 through June 30, 1975

Project Title: Effects of stimulation of the locus coeruleus on Purkinje cells of rat cerebelli

Previous Serial Number: M-SMR-N-Y-16

Principal Investigators: G. R. Siggins, B. J. Hoffer, R. Freedman, F. E. Bloom, and S. J. Henriksen

Other Investigator: A. P. Oliver

Cooperating Unit: S. Landis, Children's Hospital Medical Center, Boston, Mass.

Man Years

Total: 1.0
Professional: 1.0
Others:

Project Description:

Keyword Descriptors:
Neurophysiology, nerve impulse inhibition, neurohormones, neuropharmacology, brain, cerebellum.

Objectives:
The objective of this project is to characterize the physiological and pharmacological properties of the pathway from locus coeruleus to the cerebellum. The locus coeruleus, a discrete nucleus of norepinephrine-containing cell bodies in the brainstem, is believed to be the source of the catecholamine afferent projection to Purkinje cells of rat cerebellum.

Methods Employed:
Adult albino rats and, as a control, normal and mutant Balb C57 mice are anesthetized with halothane. Extracellular action potentials and transmembrane potentials from Purkinje cells are recorded with single and multibarrel micropipettes. Drugs are administered at the site of recording by microiontophoresis, and by other systemic routes. The locus coeruleus, juxtafastigial region, cerebral cortex, and brainstem loci are electrically stimulated with small concentric bipolar electrodes.

Major Findings:
Repetitive stimulation of the locus coeruleus, but not adjacent

brain-stem structures, produces a prolonged inhibition of Purkinje cell discharge, thus mimicking the effects of iontophoreti norepinephrine. As with directly applied NE, this inhibition is blocked by PGE_1 and E_2, and the phenothiazines, fluxphenazine and flupenthixol, and potentiated by papaverine. It cannot be elicited after destruction of cerebellar catecholamine-containing afferents by 6-OHDA. Intracellular recording has shown that the Purkinje cell inhibition is accompanied by a hyper-polarization and an increased resistance. The pharmacological and physiological changes produced by locus coeruleus stimulation are thus similar to the changes produced by microiontophoresis of NE and cyclic AMP (see project Z01 MH 01298). Activation of the locus coeruleus has also been found to selectively elevate intra-Purkinje cell levels of cyclic AMP, as shown by a new histochemical method for cyclic AMP developed in our laboratory (see project Z01 MH 01224). When applied topically to the cerebellum, only norepinephrine, and not other putative neurotransmitters such as serotonin, GABA, histamine and acetylcholine, had the potential to elevate Purkinje cell cyclic AMP. This finding further strengthens the view that the inhibitory locus coeruleus projection to Purkinje cells releases norepinephrine as a transmitter, and that the postsynaptic effect of this transmitter is mediated by cyclic AMP.

Recently, research on the locus coeruleus projection has centered on the cerebellum of normal mice and those with the weaver cerebellar mutation, characterized by a lack of parallel fiber synapses from granule cells to Purkinje cells. Purkinje cells of the weaver are also inhibited by stimulation of the locus coeruleus, thus providing a negative control for the possibility that stimulation of the locus coeruleus could inhibit Purkinje cells by dysfacilitation of tonically active input from nearby brain stem structures via the mossy fiber-granule cell-Purkinje cell excitatory input. Histochemical studies confirm an abundant norepinephrine input from locus coeruleus to cerebellum in weaver.

Significance to Bio-medical Research And the Program of the Institute:
The study will permit, for the first time, evaluation of a central nervous norepinephrine-containing afferent pathway. Such a pathway provides an ideal in vivo test system for many of the psychoactive drugs believed to act by changing CNS catecholamine metabolism. A study of one such commonly used neuroleptic fluphenazine has shown it to be a potent selective antagonist of the effects of stimulating this pathway and of norepinephrine. Since branches of this same pathway project to the limbic system and cerebral cortex, study of this projection will also furnish information about the function of catecholamine regions of the brain which subserve behavior and motivation.

Proposed Course:
Studies are now underway to evaluate the effects of such psychoactive agents as desmethylimipramine, lithium, tetrahydrocannibinol, and

mescaline on this pathway. Additional experiments on the histochemical, anatomical and electrophysiological properties of the pathway are also planned. Particular attention will be paid to interaction with other known cerebellar afferents. Studies are also now underway to evaluate the effect of activation of a collateral pathway from locus coeruleus to the cerebral cortex, and to determine possible effects of psychotropic drugs on this pathway.

Honors and Awards:

This work won the A. E. Bennett Prize for Basic Research in Biological Psychiatry for 1971, and the A. Cressy Morrison Award of the New York Academy of Sciences, 1971 for best paper in a natural science.

Publications:

Siggins, G. R., Bloom, F. E., Hoffer, B. J., and Oliver, A. P.: Inhibition of rat Purkinje neurons by norepinephrine, cyclic AMP and locus coeruleus stimulation. Proc. Internat. Union Physiol. Sci. 9: 514, 1971.

Bloom, F. E., Siggins, G. R., Hoffer, B. J., Oliver, A. P., and Woodward, D. J.: Mechanisms of inhibition of cerebellar Purkinje cells in rat and frog. Experientia 27: 3, 1971.

Siggins, G. R., Hoffer, B. J., Oliver, A. P., and Bloom, F. E.: Activation of a central noradrenergic projection to cerebellum. Nature 233: 481-483, 1971.

Bloom, F. E., Hoffer, B. J., and Siggins, G. R.: Norepinephrine mediated synapses: A model system for neuropsychopharmacology. Biol. Psychiatry 4: 157-177, 1972.

Hoffer, B. J., Siggins, G. R., Oliver, A. P., and Bloom, F. E.: Cyclic adenosine monophosphate mediated adrenergic synapses to cerebellar Purkinje cells. Adv. Cyclic Nucleotide Res. 1: 411-423 1972.

Hoffer, B. J., Siggins, G. R., Oliver, A. P., and Bloom, F. E.: Activation of the pathway from locus coeruleus to rat cerebellar Purkinje neurons: Pharmacological evidence of noradrenergic central inhibition. J. Pharmacol. Exp. Therap. 184: 553-569, 1973.

Siggins, G. R., Battenberg, E. F., Hoffer, B. J., Bloom, F. E., and Steiner, A. L.: Noradrenergic stimulation of cyclic adenosine monophosphate in rat Purkinje neurons: An immuno-cytochemical study. Science 179: 585-588, 1973.

Bloom, F. E.: Dynamics of synaptic communication: Finding the vocabulary. Brain Res. 62: 299-305, 1973.

Bloom, F. E.: Dynamics of synaptic modulation: Perspectives for the future. In Schmitt, F. O. (ed.). The Neurosciences: Third Study Program. Cambridge, Mass., MIT Press, 1974, pp. 989-999.

Bloom, F. E.: To spritz or not to spritz: The doubtful value of aimless iontophoresis. Life Sci. 14: 1819-1834, 1974.

Bloom, F. E., Chu, N-s., Hoffer, B. J., Nelson, C. N. and Siggins, G. R.: Studies on the function of central noradrenergic neurons. Neurosci. Res. 5: 53-71, 1973.

Project No. Z01 MH 01224-07 SMRN
1. Division of Special Mental Health Research
2. Laboratory of Neuropharmacology
3. Saint Elizabeths Hospital

PHS-ADAMHA-NIMH
Individual Project Report
July 1, 1974 through June 30, 1975

Project Title: Histochemical localization of cyclic 3'5' adenosine phosphate in brain

Previous Serial Number: M-SMR-N-Y-17

Principal Investigators: F. E. Bloom and J. Nathanson

Other Investigator: E. Battenberg

Cooperating Units: Dr. A. Steiner, Dept. of Medicine, Albany Medical College, Albany, New York; Drs. H. J. Wedner and C. W. Parker, Dept. of Medicine, Washington Univ. School of Med., St. Louis, Missouri; Drs. P. Greengard and J. Kebabian, Dept. of Pharmacology, Yale University; Dr. H. Goodman, Dept. of Biochemistry, Univ. of Pennsylvania.

Man Years

Total:	.1
Professional:	.05
Others:	.05

Project Description:

Keyword Descriptors:
Purine nucleotides, cyclic AMP, brain, cerebellum, histochemistry and cytochemistry, general optics, microscopy (electron).

Objectives:
The object of this study is to develop a histochemical technique to localize cyclic 3'5' adenosine monophosphate (C-AMP) in the central nervous system and to test the specificity and selectivity of the method by analysis of the effects of hormones on cyclic nucleotide levels in other tissues. Enzymes pertinent to the formation, catalysis and expression of cyclic nucleotides formed in neurons will be localized histochemically through the development of enzyme cytochemical methods.

Methods Employed:
Thin frozen sections of rat brain are treated with a specific anti-C-AMP antibody obtained from rabbits or goats. Following this, fluorocein-labelled anti-rabbit or anti-goat antibody is placed on the sections. The tissues are then examined by fluorescence microscopy.

Major Findings:

Nervous cells in various brain regions, such as cerebellar Purkinje cells, show a specific fluorescence after treatment with the two antibodies. This fluorescence is not seen after treatment with control rabbit antiserum, from animals not sensitized with the cyclic AMP antigen. Control experiments show only cyclic AMP is stained by this method. The number of reactive cerebellar Purkinje neurons increases after local application of norepinephrine or selective stimulation of norepinephrine synapses. Improved resolution for the immunocytochemical localization of bound cyclic nucleotides is being sought through the use of di-aminobenzidine coupled peroxidase labeled antibody markers, obtained from Dr. L. Sternberger at Edgewood Arsenal, Md. Use of the present standard immunocytochemical method indicates that in bovine sympathetic ganglia, incubation with dopamine results in elevation of cyclic AMP content in post-ganglionic macroneurons, while cyclic GMP levels in these cells do not change. When the slices are exposed under similar conditions to acetylcholine, the cyclic GMP immunoreactivity of the same class of post-ganglionic macroneurons increases without changes in cyclic AMP. In epithelial epithelial cells of the toad bladder exposed to anti-diuretic hormone in vitro, the content and immuno-reactivity of the cuboidal cells exhibits an immediate rise. Lead, an essential cytochemical ingredient for the available published methods localizing adenylate cyclase activity, has been found to be a very potent inhibitor of brain adenylate cyclase. The sensitivity of the enzyme to lead is so profound that this inhibitory action could underlie the neurotoxic actions of lead in human beings.

Significance to Bio-medical Research and the Program of the Institute:

This technique may permit localization of cyclic AMP in nerve cell bodies and processes and, thus, furnish information about which neuronal circuits use cyclic AMP physiologically as a second messenger. In addition, by using microspectrophotometer, this method may eventually be used to measure the cyclic AMP content of single neurons.

Proposed Course:

Further experiments are planned to test the specificity of the antibody reaction and to determine which experimental conditions will optimize the histochemical reactions. An attempt will also be made to correlate the degree of fluoroscein in various brain regions with the amount of biochemically detectable cyclic AMP.

Honors and Awards

Invited participant in the IIIrd Neurosciences Intensity Study Program, 1972.

Invited participant in the New York Heart Association Meeting, 1973.

Recipient of the Mathilde Solowey Award, 1973.

Recipient of the Biological Sciences Award, 1974.

Publications:

Wedner, H. J., Hoffer, B. J., Steiner, A. L., Parker, C. W., and

Bloom, F. E.: Localizing cyclic AMP intracellularly by immunofluorescence. Fed. Proc. 31: (2), 513, 1972.

Wedner, H. J., Hoffer, B. J., Battenberg, E., Steiner, A. L., Parker, C. W., and Bloom, F. E.: A method for detecting intracellular cyclic adenosine monophosphate by imunofluorescence. J. Histochem. Cytochem. 20: 293-295, 1972.

Bloom, F. E., Hoffer, B. J., Battenberg, E. F., Siggins, G. R., Steiner, A. L., Parker, C. W., and Wedner, H. J.: Adenosine 3'5'-monophoaphate is localized in cerebellar neurons: Immunofluorescence evidence. Science 177: 436-438, 1972.

Bloom, F. E., Chu, N-s., Hoffer, B. J., Nelson, C. N., and Siggins, G. R.: Studies on the function of central noradrenergic neurons. Neurosciences Res. 5: 53-71, 1973.

Siggins, G. R., Battenberg, E. R., Hoffer, B. J., Bloom, F. E., and Steiner, A. L.: Noradrenergic stimulation of cyclic adenosine monophosphate in rat Purkinje neurons: A immuno-cytochemical study. Science 179: 585-588, 1973.

Bloom, F. E., Wedner, H. J., and Parker, C. W.: The use of antibodies to study cell structure and metabolism. Pharmacol. Rev. 25: 343-358, 1973.

Bloom, F. E.: Dynamics of synaptic communication: Finding the vocabulary. Brain Res. 62: 299-305, 1973.

Bloom, F. E.: Dynamics of synaptic modulation: Perspectives for the future. In Schmitt, F. O. (Ed.). The Neurosciences: Third Study Program. Cambridge, Mass., MIT Press, 1974, pp. 989-999.

Bloom, F. E.: The gains in brain are mainly in the stain. In Worden, F., Adelman, G., and Swazey, J. (Eds.): The Neurosciences: Paths of Discovery. Cambridge, Mass., MIT Press (in press).

Wedner, H. J., Bloom, F. E. and Parker, C. W.: The role of cyclic nucleotides in lymphocyte activation. Proc. 9th Ann. Leukocyte Culture Conf. (in press).

Bloom, F. E., Siggins, G. R., Hoffer, B. J., Segal, M. and Oliver, A. P.: The role of cyclic nucleotides in the central synaptic actions of catecholamines. In Greengard, P. and Robinson, G. A. (Eds.): Advances in Cyclic Nucleotide Research. New York, Raven Press (in press).

Goodman, D. B. P., Bloom, F. E., Battenberg, E. R., Rasmussen, H. and Davis, W. D.: Immunofluorescent localization of cyclic AMP in toad urinary bladder: Possible intercellular transfer. Science (in press).

Nathanson, J. A. and Bloom, F. E.: Lead-induced inhibition of brain adenylate cyclase activity. Nature (in press).

Shoemaker, W. J., Balentine, L. T., Siggins, G. R., Hoffer, B. J., Henriksen, S. J. and Bloom, F. E.: Characteristics of the release of adenosine 3':5'-monophosphate from micropipets by microiontophoresis. J. Cyclic Nucleotide Res. 1: 97-106, 1975.

Bloom, F. E.: The adenylate cyclase system in brain. In Schmitt, F. O., Schneider, D. M. and Crothers, D. M. (Eds.): Functional Linkage in Biomolecular Systems. New York, Raven Press, 1975, pp. 209-213.

Kebabian, J., Bloom, F. E., Steiner, A. L. and Greengard, P.: Neurotransmitter induced increases in cyclic nucleotide and post-ganglionic neurons in mammalian sympathetic ganglia: Immunocytochemical demonstration. Science (in press).

Project No. Z01 MH 01225-07 SMRN
1. Division of Special Mental Health Research
2. Laboratory of Neuropharmacology
3. Saint Elizabeths Hospital

PHS-ADAMHA-NIMH
Individual Project Report
July 1, 1974 through June 30, 1975

Project Title: Localization of non-monoaminergic synaptic transmitters in CNS

Previous Serial Number: M-SMR-N-Y-18

Principal Investigator: F. E. Bloom

Other Investigator: E. F. Battenberg

Cooperating Unit: None

Man Years

Total:	0.0
Professional:	0.0
Others:	0.0

Project Description:

Keyword Descriptors:
Nervous system, nerve endings (central), neurohormones, histochemistry and cytochemistry, optics, electron microscopy.

Objectives:
The objectives of this study were to develop methods for localizing those neurotransmitter substances for which there are currently no cytochemical methodologies available.

Methods Employed:
With Dr. Iversen, methods have been developed for the autoradiographic localization of radioactive amino acids which may act has transmitters based upon the sites which accumulate these amino acids in tissue slices incubated in vitro. With Dr. Hanker, methods are being developed for specific localization of oxidative enzymes related to the catabolism of putative neurotransmitters and for the enhancement of the localization of enzymes previously not feasible to study histochemically because of their low specific activity.

Major Findings:
Slices and synaptosome fractions of rat cerebral cortex actively accumulate H^3GABA. Since H^3GABA undergoes minimal catabolism while entering endogenous GABA storage sites, localization of the labeled compound by ultrastructural autoradiography offers a possible method of demonstrating

GABA-containing processes. Small slices of rat cortex or cortical homogenates were incubated with 5 μM H^3GABA as previously described (Iversen and Neal, J. Neurochem. 15: 1141, 1968). More than 95% of the tissue radioactivity after incubations of 10-30 min, was unchanged GABA and more than 2/3 of this was retained during fixation with glutaraldehyde. Electron-microscopic autoradiographs prepared from these samples were examined after exposures to 9, 15 or 21 days and grains distributions analyzed quantitatively. In slices, more than 82% of the grains were found over nerve terminals or unmyelinated preterminal axons. In pellets of cortical homogenates, grains were found exclusively over nerve terminals. In each type sample, approximately 27-30% of the terminals were labeled. Longer exposure periods resulted in more grains per labeled terminals but no greater proportion of labeled terminals. These results indicate H^3GABA is selectively accumulated by discrete populations of nerve terminals after in vitro labeling.

Significance to Bio-medical Research and the Program of the Institute:
These methods will permit the localizations needed to identify and analyze the possible influence of specific nerve circuits in the maintenance of normal brain and behavioral functioning.

Proposed Course:
This project has been terminated.

Honors and Awards:
Invited participant in Neurosciences Research Program Work Session on Natural Amino Acids and Polypeptides in Synaptic Function.

Publications:

Bloom, F. E., and Iversen, L. D.: Localizing ^{3}H-GABA in nerve terminals of rat cerebral cortex by electron microscopic autoradiography. Nature 229: 628-630, 1971.

Iversen, L. L. and Bloom, F. E.: Localizing H^3-GABA in rat cerebral cortex by electron microscope autoradiography. Fed. Proc. 30: 318, 1971.

Iversen, L. L. and Bloom, F. E.: Studies of the uptake of H^3-GABA and H^3-Glycine in slices and homogenates of rat brain and spinal cord by electron microscopic autoradiography. Brain Res. 41: 131-143, 1972.

Bloom, F. E.: Amino Acids and Polypeptides in Neuronal Function. Neurosci. Res. Bull., 1972.

Project No. Z01 MH 01226-02 SMRN
1. Division of Special Mental Health Research
2. Laboratory of Neuropharmacology
3. Saint Elizabeths Hospital

PHS-ADAMHA-NIMH
Individual Project Report
July 1, 1974 through June 30, 1975

Project Title: Effect of chlorpromazine on feeding behavior

Previous Serial Number: M-SMR-N-Y-23

Principal Investigator: R. G. Robinson

Other Investigators: F. E. Bloom and B. J. Hoffer

Cooperating Units: None

Man Years

Total: 75
Professional: 0:75
Others: 0

Project Description:

Keyword Descriptors:
Nervous system, control psychopharmacology, nutrient intake activity.

Objectives:
This project was designed to document the phenomenon of chlorpromazine induced hyperphagia and investigate its time course, dose - response, behavioral and motivational correlates, and neural mechanisms.

Methods Employed:
Parenteral injections of chlorpromazine were given to rats and subsequent food intake was measured. Classical conditioning cage was used to measure bar presses as a measure of motivation, sedative effect was measured by photocell counts in activity cages. Parenteral injections of phentolamine and propranalol and surgical hypophysectomy were used to investigate the neural mechanisms of chlorpromazine induced hyperphagia.

Major Findings:
1) Hyperphagia elicited by chlorpromazine is a one day phenomenon. That is, on the first day of treatment the treated animals eat more than controls, but with continued daily treatment the treated animals eat the same or less than controls. 2) Chlorpromazine has a maximum effect on feeding

behavior at a dose of about 8 mg/kg body weight. Further increases in dose up to 50 mg/kg have no further effect. 3) Chlorpromazine has a pronounced sedative effect altering the animals eating pattern. But other sedatives such as chloral hydrate do not induce hyperphagia. 4) Animals required to press a bar for food at any reinforcement schedule up to 20:1 eat more. 5) The hyperphagia is partially blocked by treatment with either phentolamine or propranalol but hypophysectomy completely blocks the hyperhagia.

Significance to Bio-medical Research and the Program of the Institute:
Finding a behavioral system on which chlorpromazine works and finding the neural circuits involved may give some insight into the mechanism of action of chlorpromazine in treating psychotic disorders and elucidating the neural basis of feeding behavior.

Proposed Course:
Further motivational studies are planned to determine how strong is the increased desire for food following chlorpromazine treatment. The neural mechanisms involved will be investigated by looking at whether pharmacological agents can block the phenomenon and by measuring the effect of chlorpromazine on extracellular unit cell recordings. The project as originally proposed has been completed and no further work is presently planned.

Publications:
Robinson, R. G., McHugh, P. R. and Bloom, F. E.: Chlorpromazine induced hyperphagia in the rat. Psychopharm. Comm. 1: 37-50, 1975.

Project No. Z01 MH 01257-03 SMRN
1. Division of Special Mental Health Research
2. Laboratory of Neuropharmacology
3. Saint Elizabeths Hospital

PHS-ADAMHA-NIMH
Individual Project Report
July 1, 1974 through June 30, 1975

Project Title: The projections from the brain stem to the hippocampus of the rat.

Previous Serial Number: M-SMR-N-P-10

Principal Investigator: P. Oliver

Other Investigators: F. E. Bloom, M. Segal, S. Landis

Cooperating Units: None

Man Years

Total:	1.5
Professional:	1.0
Others:	.5

Project Description:

Keyword Descriptors:

Brain, Cerebrum, Hippocampal Formation, Brain Mapping, Neuropharmacology, Neurophysiology, Neural Transmission.

Objectives:

The objective of this project was to characterize the anatomical, physiological, pharmacological, and functional properties of the monoamine afferent projections from the brain stem, the locus coeruleus (LC) and the raphe nuclei, to the hippocampus.

Methods Employed:

Adult albino rats were used. In the anatomical localization studies, the methods of fluorescence histochemistry, electron and light microscopic autoradiography following the injection of H-Proline into the n. locus coeruleus (LC) for tracing the pathway, or alternately retrograde of transport of horseradish peroxidase after injection into the terminal area to label cells which project to the studied area were employed. The physiological and pharmacological studies were performed on halothane anesthetized rats. Extracellular action potentials of hippocampal pyramidal cells were monitored with single and multibarrel pipettes. Membrane potential and resistance were measured with intracellular electrodes. Drugs were iontophoresed at the site of recording. The n. locus coeruleus or the raphe nuclei were electrically stimulated. Behavioral studies were performed with freely moving rats previously implanted with stimulating and unit recording electrodes.

Major Findings:

1. There is a direct pathway between the nucleus locus coeruleus and the hippocampus. a) Labelled amino acids injected into LC was transported into the hippocampus; b) Horseradish peroxidase injected into the hippocampus was transported from the terminals to cell bodies in LC; c) The responses of hippocampal cells to locus coeruleus stimulation mimic their responses to iontophoretically applied NE: i) the response to both is mainly inhibition of spontaneous firing rates; ii) both responses are blocked by PGE and MJ-1999, and potentiated by DMI and papaverine. d) Responses to locus coeruleus stimulation are absent in 6-OHDA or reserpine treated rats. e) the responses of hippocampal cells to c-AMP, dibutyl c-AMP, papaverine, aminophylline, and prostaglandins indicate the possibility that the responses to NE are mediated by c-AMP. f) Stimulation of locus coeruleus, extracellular application of norepinephrine, and c-AMP as well as intracellular application of c-AMP, cause hyperpolarization and increase of membrane resistance of hippocampal pyramidal cells. 2) There is a direct pathway from the raphe nuclei to the hippocampus. a) horseradish peroxidase injected into the hippocampus is transported to cells in the raphe nuclei; b) radioactive amino acids injected into the raphe nuclei are transported to the hippocampus; c) the responses of hippocampal cells to raphe stimulation mimic their responses to iontophoretically applied serotonin. i) the response to both is mainly inhibition of spontaneous firing rates; ii) both responses are blocked by serotonin antagonists; methysergide and cyproheptadine. 3. Stimulation of LC in an awake rats inhibits spontaneous activity of hippocampal cells; a) Rats like to electrically stimulate electrodes placed in LC; b) Both the behavioral self stimulation and the associated inhibition of spontaneous hippocampal cellular activity are potentiated by amphetamine and blocked by AMT. c) LC stimulation facilitates the generation and retrieval of learned cellular responses in the hippocampus and thus may affect memory functions in the hippocampus. 4. With intracellular recordings, stimulation of the locus coeruleus produces hyperpolarization and increased membrane resistance. Iontophoresis of norepinephrine and cyclic AMP produce similar changes in membrane potential and resistance. When cyclic AMO, but not GABA, norepinephrine or 5'AMP are ionotophoretically applied intracellularly during intracellular recordings, the same hyperpolarizing response is observed. This result suggest that the cyclic AMP can act to produce the membrane changes from within the cell, while typical first transmitter substances seem to act only externally. 5. In preliminary studies, it is possible to record small amounts of spontaneous activity in slices of guines pig hippocampus in vitro; this system may provide a means to examine the ionic components of the cyclic AMP induced changes in membrane properties of pyramidal cell.

Significance to Bio-medical Research and the Program of the Institute:

This research will permit the analysis of a defined norepinephrine and serotonin pathway in the limbic forebrain system. This system, with the hippocampus as its main component is involved in motivation, emotion, memory, and control of behavior. It is, perhaps, the main target area of most psychoactive drugs, many of which are known to act by modifying NE and serotonin metabolism. The understanding of the monoamine role in this system is the key to our understanding of normal as well as abnormal neural mechanisms subserving basic behavioral functions.

Proposed Course:

The behavioral and in vivo studies have been completed and the results are being readied for publication. In the future, work will be restricted to the analysis of hippocampal unit and synaptic activities in vitro.

Publications:

Segal, M., Pickel, V. M., and Bloom, F. E.: The projections of the nucleus locus coeruleus: An autoradiographic study. Life Sci. 13: 817-820, 1973.

Segal, M., Sims, K., Maggiora, L., and Smissman, E.: Microiontophoretic studies of conformationally restricted analogues of GABA on rat hippocampus. Nature, 295: 88-89, 1973.

Segal, M. and Bloom, F. E.: Norepinephrine in the rat hippocampus: I. Iontophoresis study. Brain Res. 72: 79-99, 1974.

Segal, M. and Bloom, F. E.: The action of norepinephrine in the rat hippocampus: II. Activation of the input pathway. Brain Res. 72: 100-114, 1974.

Pickel, V., Segal, M., and Bloom, F. E.: Axon proliferation following lesions of cerebellar peduncles. A combined fluorescence microscopic and radioautographic study. J. Comp. Neurol., 155: 43-60, 1974.

Pickel, V., Segal, M., and Bloom, F. E.: A radioautographic study of efferent pathways of the nucleus locus coeruleus. J. Comp. Neurol., 155: 15-43, 1974.

Segal, M.: Responses of septal nuclei neurons to microiontophoretically administered putative neurotransmitters. Life Sci., 14: 1345-1351, 1974.

Segal, M.: Lithium and the monoamine neurotransmitters in the rat hippocampus. Nature, 250 No. 5461: 71-73, 1974.

Segal, M. and Landis, S.: Afferents to the hippocampus of the rat studied with the retrograde transport of horseradish peroxidase. Brain Res. 78: 1-15, 1974.

Project No. Z01 MH 01258-03 SMRN
1. Division of Special Mental Health Research
2. Laboratory of Neuropharmacology
3. Saint Elizabeths Hospital

PHS-ADAMHA-NIMH
Individual Project Report
July 1, 1974 through June 30, 1975

Project Title: Changes in catecholamine containing neurons and behavioral correlates following injury

Previous Serial Number: M-SMR-N-P-11

Principal Investigator: R. G. Robinson

Other Investigators: F. E. Bloom, W. Shoemaker, M. Schlumpf, and L. Battenberg

Cooperating Units:

Man Years

Total: 3.4
Professional: 3.2
Others: 0.2

Project Description:

Keyword Descriptors:
Brain, cerebral cortex, brain lesions, surgical, nervous system regeneration.

Objectives:
The objectives of this project were to study the responses of adrenergic neurons to injury including axonal sprouting and dynamic fluctuations of catecholamines concentrations. Other objectives were to investigate the effects of nerve injury on spontaneous activity, shock induced agression, feeding behavior and intracranial self-stimulation.

Methods Employed:
Fluorescence histochemistry and autoradiography were used to study the cytology of the pathways and cell bodies. Biochemical assay were measured by levels of dopamine and norepinephrine. Extracellular recording of spontaneous Purkinje cell activity and analyses of feeding, emotional reactivity and motor behavior were determined before and after injury. Bilateral median forebrain bundle electrodes were used for studies of self-stimulation.

Major Findings:

1. The projections from each locus coeruleus (LC) to the cerebellar cortex through the superior cerebellar peduncle (SP) can be demonstrated not only by catecholamine fluorescence, but also by autoradiography following local injections of labeled amino acids. The labeled fibers entered the SP from the injection site in the locus and terminated around Purkinje soma and proximal dendrites as previously indicated for fluorescent fibers and axon terminals in the cerebellum. LC neurons in the posterior-lateral pole of the nucleus give rise to axons which ascend to cerebellum in a posterior-lateral segment of the superior peduncle (SP), whereas LC neurons of the anterior-lateral pole send axon-collaterals which course in an anterior-medial segment of the SP. Approximately half the LC neurons appear to participate in the noradrenergic pathway to the cerebellum.

Under visual inspection both the medial and the lateral branches of this pathway are directly accessible to discrete surgical manipulation. Appropriate partial SP cuts eliminate a significant proportion of NE-containing preterminal axons and/or axon collaterals.

2. After reduction of cerebellar NE-containing terminal axons (unilaterally or bilaterally), the remaining, intact NE-containing terminals proliferate in about four weeks, presumably through collateral axon sprouting. Following the initial post lesion reduction, a spectacular increase in terminals ("overshoot" or hyperinnervation) ensued. At the time of this maximum fiber proliferation (30 days) as determined by catecholamine fluorescence, the number of labeled terminals observed in H^3-Proline autoradiographs of cerebellar cortex also appeared to be greater than in controls. Terminal density reached control levels within ten weeks, however.

3. Analysis of mean firing rates and discharge patterns (interspike interval histogram) indicates that LC stimulation and NE administration slows Purkinje cell discharge rate by prolonging pauses (Z01 MH 01223). During maximum proliferation mean spontaneous firing rate was significantly below normal mean rate (14/sec. compared to 34/sec.), while pauses were prolonged. Further, thresholds for LC stimulation and for NE iontophoretic administration were consistently lower for experimental rats. In general, LC inhibition lasted longer (30-150 sec. compared to 10-60 sec.) following stimulation at minimal threshold.

4. Following experimental vascular occlusion, a discrete lesion involving only neocortex is obtained.

5. Norepinephrine in the lesioned parietal cortex, ipsilateral occipetal cortex and both sides of the brainstem decreased by 5 days after vascular

occlusion and then returned partially or completely to control levels by 20 or 40 days. Dopamine in the ipsilateral brainstem continues to drop throughout the postoperative period.

6. Spontaneous horizontal activity increases during the period from 2-20 days after operation and then returns to control levels. Shock induced aggression increase at 2 days after operation and then drops below control levels for the remainder of the 40 day post-operative period. There is no change in feeding behavior.

7. The increased spontaneous activity following vascular occlusion can be blocked by daily treatment with desmethylimipramine.

8. Cortical fluorescence decreases by 5 days after vascular lesioning and returns by 20 days with evidence of sprouting around the lesion site. The fluorescent cell bodies in the locus coeruleus ipsilateral to the lesion have decreased cytoplasmic fluorescence at 5 and 20 days after lesioning. At 40 days, the processes which project from the cell bodies have increased in length.

9. Intracranial self-stimulation changes by 2 days after operation in rate, right-left preference and the amount of current needed to sustain half maximal self-stimulation rate. Determination of the magnitude and direction of these changes has not been completed.

Significance to Bio-medical Research and the Program of the Institute:
An experimental animal model of a "CVA" has biomedical significance for the study of biochemical and structural changes which follow a common human injury and for the comparison of changes in animal behavior with those clinically observed in humans. Blocking these behavioral effects by pharmacological agents may provide a model for testing drugs useful in post-stroke patients or hyperactive child syndrome. Additionally this research will help to clarify concepts such as synaptic reorganization or plasticity in the adult mammalian central nervous system, regeneration and collateral axon sprouting of injured or intact catecholamine-containing neurons, "triggers" for growth and the functional significance of compensatory growth of adrenergic neurons. Intracranial self-stimulation experiments may give indication of the functional nature of adrenergic neurons which are depleted of catecholamines.

Proposed Course:
1. Investigate the relationship of increased spontaneous activity after vascular occlusion to catecholamine neurons by testing other pharmacological agents including 6 hydroxydopamine.

2. Further delineate the anatomical changes after vascular lesioning by fluorescence histochemistry and electromicroscopy.

3. Continue to study the self-stimulation changes after vascular occlusion. Additionally unit cell recordings will be done in the awake animal during self-stimulation behavior.

Publication:

Pickel, V. M., Krebs, H., and Bloom, F. E.: Proliferation of norepinephrine-containing axons in rat cerebellar cortex after peduncle lesions. Brain Res. 59: 169-179, 1973.

Pickel, V. M., Segal, M., and Bloom, F. E.: Axonal proliferation following lesions of cerebellar peduncles. A combined fluorescence microscopic and radioautographic study. J. Comp. Neurol. 155: 43-60, 1974.

Pickel, V. M., Segal, M., and Bloom, F. E.: A radioautographic study of the efferent pathways of the nucleus locus coeruleus. J. Comp. Neurol. 155: 15-43, 1974.

Robinson, R. G., Shoemaker, W. J., Schlumpf, M., Valk, T., and Bloom, F. E.: Effect of experimental cerebral infarction in rat brain on catecholamines and behavior. Nature (in press).

Project No. Z01 MH 01259-03 SMRN
1. Division of Special Mental Health Research
2. Laboratory of Neuropharmacology
3. Saint Elizabeths Hospital

PHS-ADAMHA-NIMH
Individual Project Report
July 1, 1974 through June 30, 1975

Project Title: Organization and functional properties of monoamine pathways in the squirrel monkey cerebral cortex

Previous Serial Numbers: M-SMR-N-P-12

Principal Investigators: S. L. Foote, R. Freedman, and A. Schwartz

Other Investigators: F. E. Bloom, and A. P. Oliver

Man Years

Total: 2.1
Professional: 1.8
Others: 0.3

Project Description:

Keyword Descriptors:
Brain, cerebral auditory cortex, neurohormones, phenylalicylamines, norepinephrine, neuropharmacology.

Objectives:
These studies are designed to determine the anatomical characteristics of monoamine pathways within primate neocortex, where these pathways originate, and what their physiological and behavioral functions might be.

Methods Employed:
Squirrel monkeys were studied using electrophysiological and histochemical techniques. Microiontophoresis was used to determine the pharmacological sensitivity of cortical neurons in the awake animal. Formaldehyde induced fluorescence, autoradiography, and peroxidase transport were used to localize monoamine innervation of the neocortex.

Major Findings:
Neurons of the monkey auditory cortex are uniformly inhibited by local application of small doses of norepinephrine and GABA and excited by glutamate and acetylcholine. This is true for both spontaneous and stimulus-evoked activity. Histochemical observations indicate that there are a substantial number of NE and serotonin-containing fibers within neocortex. These fibers make axosomatic

and axodendritic synapses on auditory cortex neurons. The locus coeruleus was identified as the putative source of the NE fibers by ortho- and retrograde-transport histochemical techniques.

Significance to Bio-medical Research and the Program of the Institute:

These studies provide initial evidence for a role of monoamine inputs in the function of "higher cortical centers". Drugs with known efficacy in clinical psychiatry, such as chlorpromazine and desmethylimipramine, can now be studied with respect to interaction with specific cortical pathways. Elucidation of the mechanism of action of these drugs is one of the major programs of our laboratory.

Proposed Course:

The detailed anatomy of monoamine pathways will be assessed using histochemical techniques. The effects on cortical neurons of electrically stimulating these pathways will be determined. Experiments have been begun for studying the effects of psychotherapeutic and/or abusable drugs on operant behavior and neuronal activity in aawake monkeys.

Publications:

Chu, N-s. and Bloom, F. E.: Norepinephrine-containing neurons: Changes in spontaneous discharge patterns during sleeping and waking. Science 179: 908-909, 1973.

Nelson, C. N., Hoffer, B. J., Chu, N-s., and Bloom, F. E.: Cytochemical and pharmacological studies on polysensory neurons in the primate frontal cortex. Brain Res. 62: 115-133, 1973.

Bloom, F. E., Hoffer, B. J., Nelson, C., Sheu, Y-s., and Siggins, G. R.: The physiology and pharmacology of serotonin mediated synapses. In Usdin, E. and Barchas, J. D. (Eds.) Serotonin and Behavior. Academic Press, New York, pp. 249-261, 1973.

Bloom, F. E., Chu, N-s., Hoffer, B. J., Nelson, C. N., and Siggins, G. R.: Studies on the function of central noradrenergic neurons. Neurosciences Res. 5: 53-71, 1973.

Chu, N-s. and Bloom, F. E.: The catecholamine-containing neurons in the cat dorso-lateral pontine tegmentum: Distribution of the cell bodies and some axonal projections. Brain Res. 66: 1-21, 1974.

Chu, N-s. and Bloom, F. E.: Activity patterns of catecholamine-containing pontine neurons in the dorsolateral tegmentum of unrestrained cats. J. Neurobiol., 5: 527-544, 1974.

Foote, S. L., Freedman, R. and Oliver, A. P.: Effects of putative neurotransmitters on neuronal activity in monkey auditory cortes. Brain Res. 86(2): 229-242, 1975.

Sheu, Y-s., Nelson, J. P. and Bloom, F. E.: Discharge patterns of cat raphe neurons during sleep and waking. Brain Res., 73: 263-276, 1974.

Project No. Z01 MH 01295-02 SMRN
1. Division of Special Mental Health Research
2. Laboratory of Neuropharmacology
3. Saint Elizabeths Hospital

PHS-ADAMHA-NIMH
Individual Project Report
July 1, 1974 through June 30, 1975

Project Title: Technical methods for investigating the physiology and pharmacology of synaptic transmission

Previous Serial Number: M-SMR-N-S-1

Principal Investigator: A. P. Oliver

Other Investigators: None

Cooperating Units: None

Man Years

Total: 1
Professional: 0
Others: 1

Project Description:

Keyword Descriptors:
Electrodes, microelectrodes, brain, spinal cord, neuropharmacology.

Objectives:
The objective of this study is to develop and improve technical methods and older ones used for the study of synaptic transmitters at the level of the single nerve cells. This is primarily accomplished by comparing the response of the cell to activation of a synaptic pathway with local application of the suspected transmitter substance by iontophoresis. Additionally, the pharmacology of the natural system may be tested with pharmacological agonists and antagonists at the single neuron level.

Methods Employed:
Several kinds of glass micropipette electrodes have been developed to study the activity of single nerve cells while either stimulating their natural synaptic input or applying pharmacological substances to them or to study the interactions of natural versus applied substances. More recently, techniques have been developed in which one electrode is glued to another in such fashion that one may be used to measure intracellular responses to applied substances. (Mr. Oliver received a Superior Performance Award for technical development achieved at this

stage). To avoid the difficulties encountered with the gluing techniques a newer method has been developed and proven in which a diamond knife blade is used to cut holes at varying distances from the tip in some of the side barrels of pipettes with three or more barrels. One intact barrel is then used to record transmembrane potentials during extracellular drug applications from the others.

In addition to improvements in the micropipettes other equipment used to stabilize the tissue has been developed.

Major Findings:
The electrodes have been developed to the point where extra and intracellular measurement of synaptic activity and applied substances has become a routine laboratory procedure.

Significance to Bio-medical Research and the Program of the Institute:
Understanding the physiology and pharmacology of CNS depends on identification and characterization of transmitter action. The development of reliable technical methods is of considerable importance in obtaining this information.

Proposed Course:
The project is continuing to develop and improve the technical methods of single neuron studies.

Publication:
Oliver, A. P.: A simple rapid method for preparing parallel micropipette electrodes. Electroenceph. clin. Neurophysiol. 31: 284-286, 1971.

Project No. Z01 MH 01296-07 SMRN
1. Division of Special Mental Health Research
2. Laboratory of Neuropharmacology
3. Saint Elizabeths Hospital

PHS-ADAMHA-NIMH
Individual Project Report
July 1, 1974 through June 30, 1975

Project Title: Development of neuropharmacological receptivity in Purkinje cells of the neonatal cerebellum

Previous Serial Number: M-SMR-N-S-8

Principal Investigators: B. J. Hoffer, G. R. Siggins and R. Freedman

Other Investigator: F. E. Bloom

Cooperating Units: D. J. Woodward, Univ. of Rochester, Rochester, N.Y.; L. Olson and A. Seiger, Karolinska Inst., Stockholm, Sweden

Man Years

Total:	0.2
Professional:	0.2
Others:	0.0

Project Description:

Keyword Descriptors:
Brain, cerebellum, neuronogenesis, neurophysiology, impulse inhibition, neurohormones, nervous system, synapses, transplantation.

Objectives:
The objective of the present study is to determine in the neonatal rat cerebellum the time of onset of neuropharmacological receptivity, the development of morphological synapses, and the development of specific monoamine containing pathways, and the effect on receptivity of altering or preventing certain synaptic inputs.

Methods Employed:
Single Purkinje cell discharge is recorded with the central barrel of a 5-barreled micropipette. Neurohumoral agents are applied microelectrophoretically from the peripheral barrel. Rats from 0 to 30 days of age have been studied. Littermates of these animals are also fixed for routine electron microscopy, for electron microscopy with specific synaptic staining (see project Z01 MH 01220) or for formaldehyde-induced fluorescence histochemistry. The cerebella of rats X-irradiated shortly after birth to prevent the growth of granule cells and their synapses with Purkinje cells have been analyzed in a similar fashion, as have cerebella which have been transplanted from fetuses to the anterior eye chamber of adult female

recipients.

Major Findings:

Purkinje cells in 1-2 day old rats increase their discharge in response to glutamic acid and decrease their discharge in response to norepinephrine, serotonin, and gamma-amino-butyric acid. The responses to these neurohumors are present far earlier than the onset of synaptic development either morphologically or electrophysiologically. Thus, pharmacological receptivity appears to be an intrinsic property of the postsynaptic neuronal membrane itself. Cyclic AMP mimics the action of norepinephrine in these neonatal animals. Norepinephrine responses are blocked by microelectrophoresis of prostaglandins. Uncoupling oxidative phosphorylation with dinitrophenol results in increased discharge rate and eventually hyperdepolarization block of all discharge. Fluorescent nerve terminals indicating the presence of norepinephrine have been detected as early as day 3. Synaptic contacts on the Purkinje cell do not appear to develop until day 3 and increase rapidly in number from days 3 through 9, and again from days 12 through 26, Electrophysiological evidence of transynaptic activation of Purkinje cells has been detected as early as day 3, correlating well with the ultrastructural evidence.

The elimination of the granule cell to Purkinje cell pathway by X-irradiation appears to have little effect on the responses of Purkinje cells to norepinephrine, cyclic AMP, serotonin or acetylcholine. Moreover, the overall spontaneous activity of such Purkinje cells does not change. There is, however, a reorganization of excitatory and inhibitory input such that multiple climbing fibers excite a single Purkinje cell and inhibitory recurrent collaterals project to neighboring Purkinje neurons.

A similar maturation pattern appears in cerebellar transplants in oculo, suggesting a marked autonomy in development. Spontaneous Purkinje cell activity is in the normal range (20-40 action potentials/sec.). Local excitatory and inhibitory circuits are established. The responses to Purkinje neurons in the transplants to iontophoresis of norepinephrine, amphetamine, acetylcholine and GABA are also similar to those in situ. Interestingly, peripheral adrenergic fibers from the iris may establish functional connections with neurons in the transplant.

Significance to Bio-medical Research and the Program of the Institute:

This project will yield basic information about mechanisms of neuronal maturation and the factors governing the establishment of synaptic connection in the developing nervous system.

Proposed Course:

After the initial characterization of the normal developmental milestones of the rat Purkinje cell, electrophysiologically, neuropharmacologicall and anatomically, we plan to examine the effects of physical, chemical and biological agents upon maturation of this cell and to use genetic mutations with known anomalies of cerebellar development. The electrophysiological and morphological characteristics of cerebella of rats raised under various conditions of malnutrition and altered hormonal titers will also be explored. These preparations will aid in the analysis of causal relationships during neuronal maturation, our long-term goal. Study of the maturation of cerebellar transplants in the eye after exposure to various drugs, injected into the anterior chamber, will also be carried out.

Publications:

Woodward, D. J., Hoffer, B. J., and Lapham, L. W.: Correlative survey of electrophysiological, neuropharmacological, and histochemical aspects of cerebellar maturation in rat. In Llinas, R. (Ed.): Neurobiology of Cerebellar Evolution and Development. Chicago, Ill., American Medical Association, 1969, pp. 725-741.

Woodward, D. J., Hoffer, B. J., Siggins, G. R., and Bloom, F. E.: The ontogenetic development of synaptic junctions, synaptic activation and responsiveness to neurotransmitter substances in rat cerebellar Purkinje Cells. Brain Res. 34: 73-97, 1971.

Siggins, G. R., Woodward, D. J., Hoffer, B. J., and Bloom, F. E.: Responsiveness of cerebellar Purkinje cells to norepinephrine, cyclic AMP, and prostaglandin E_1 during synaptic morphogenesis in neonatal rat. Pharmacologist 12: 198, 1970.

Hoffer, B. J., Bloom, F. E., Siggins, G. R., and Woodward, D. J.: The development of synapses in the rat cerebellar cortex. In Mayer, F. (Ed.): Maturation of Brain Mechanisms Related to Sleep Behavior. Springfield, Charles Thomas, pp. 33-48, 1972.

Woodward, D. J., Hoffer, B. J., and Altman, J.: Physiological and pharmacological properties of Purkinje cells in rat cerebellum degranulated by postnatal X-irradiation. J. Neurobiol. 5: 283-304, 1974.

Hoffer, B., Seiger, A., Ljungberg, T. and Olson, L.: Electrophysiological and cytological studies of brain homografts in the anterior chamber of the eye: Maturation of cerebellar cortex in oculo. Brain Res. 79: 165-184, 1974.

Hoffer, B., Olson, L., Seiger, A. and Bloom, F.: Formation of a functional adrenergic input to intraocular cerebellar grafts: Ingrowth of sympathetic fibers and inhibition of Purkinje cell activity by adrenergic input. J. Neurobiol. (in press).

Project No. Z01 MH 01297-03 SMRN
1. Division of Special Mental Health Research
2. Laboratory of Neuropharmacology
3. Saint Elizabeths Hospital

PHS-ADAMHA-NIMH
Individual Project Report
July 1, 1974 through June 30, 1975

Project Title: Role of amino acids and peptides in synaptic transmission in the frog spinal cord.

Previous Serial Number: M-SMR-N-S-10

Principal Investigator: A. Padjen

Other Investigator: R. A. Nicoll

Cooperating Unit: Lab. of Neurobiology, SUNY at Buffalo, Amherst, N.Y.

Man Years

Total:	1.0
Professional:	1.0
Others:	0

Project Description:

Keyword Descriptors:
Nervous system central, spinal cord lumbosacral, neurophysiology, nerve impulse inhibition, neuropharmacology.

Objectives:
The objectives of these experiments were: a) identification of chemical transmitters released at primary afferent terminals, and onto them, with special focus on the role of amino acids and peptides; characterization of the receptors for amino acids in the spinal cord; analysis of the (ionic) mechanism of action of amino acids (a.a.) on primary afferents and motoneurons.

Methods Employed:
The frog spinal cord was removed from the frog, hemisected and placed in a chamber which permitted recording of the membrane potentials of the primary afferent terminals and motoneurons (by sucrose gap technique). Standard technique of intracellular recording and measurement of membrane characteristics as well as recording of extracellular field potential.

Major Findings:
Role of amino acids in presynaptic inhibition: Presynaptic inhibition occurs via axo-axonic synapses which depolarize primary afferent terminals.

In frog spinal cord this action is recorded as the dorsal root potential (DRP), elicited either by stimulating an adjacent dorsal root (DR-DRP pathway) or by stimulating the ventral root (VR-DRP pathway).

Our studies, using interaction of convulsants picrotoxin, bicuculline and strychnine, with synaptically and a.a. evoked potentials on primary afferents, identified GABA and taurine (or close compounds) as chemical transmitters involved in DR-DRP and VR-DRP, respectively. These findings were used to analyze the action of several other convulsants. It was found that morphine acts as a strychnine-like compound effectively blocking VR-DRP and the action of taurine. This effect, however, does not seem to be related to opiate (analgesic) receptor /for morphine/ since several inactive derivatives of morphine (e.g. dextrorphane) show similar action. b) d-tubocurarine, pentylenetetrazole and mephenesine (in decreasing order of potency) exert a picrotoxin-like effect while bemegride shows a weak strychnine-like effect. These observations may explain their common (convulsive) pharmacological action.

Studies of the role of acidic amino acids in neurotransmission: In contrast to the neutral a.a., the action of acidic a.a. (glutamate, aspartate, D, L-homocysteate, etc.) seems to be lacking specific antagonists. It is obvious that such substances would be of great importance in analysis of the part of acidic a.a. in the synaptic transmission. In the course of the studies of different glutamate analogs it was discovered that two natural cyclic amino acids of plant origin, kainic acid (KA) and quisqualic acid (QA) posses 200-500 times stronger depolarizing action than glutamate on both motoneurons and primary afferents. Their depolarizations characteristically differed: KA showed slow onset and recovery that outlasted period of application; QA depolarizations resembled that of glutamate, both in speed and characteristic after hyperpolarization (activation of Na pump?). This difference is explained by the lack of inactivating mechanism for KA.

Recently, several compounds were proposed as possible blocking agents of acidic a.a. receptors. Only two compounds showed positive results in our system. Glutamate diethyl esther (GDEE) in high conc (10^{-2}M) attenuated glutamate and aspartate responses and insignificantly DR-VRP but it also directly depolarized the neurons. On the other hand, hydroxy-aminopyrolidone (HA-966) markedly antagonized DR-VRP but only slightly glutamate and aspartate responses. It also directly hyperpolarized both motoneurons and primary afferents.

By analogy to GDEE, kainic acid diethyl esther was synthesized. Although this compound also manifested a direct depolarizing action, it showed selective and significant antagonism of aspartate and glutamate responses as well as a marked antagonism of DR-VRP. Since KDEE was effective in low concentration (10^{-5} -$5x10^{-5}$ M) it appears to be the most potent antagonist of acidic amino acid receptors so far.

Role of peptides: Several observations were recently published on the high potency of peptides (substance P, physalemin, eleidoisine) in depolarizing frog motoneurons. These findings have reinstated the possibility that primary afferent fibers in the spinal cord contain and release certain peptides as neurotransmitters of sensory input. Experiments were repeated in our lab, but the observed potency of different peptides was less than originally claimed (perhaps as a result of different experimental conditions or different sources of drugs). The action of substance P (and other peptides tested) was characterized with slow onset and prolonged depolarization, up to thirty minutes after the cessation of application. It did not significantly interfere with the depolarizations evoked by glutamate, but preliminary experiments indicate it may potentiate hyperpolarizing action of neutral amino acids. This action of substance P makes it unlikely to be a neurotransmitter substance at primary afferents but it does not exclude a possible modulatory action.

Ionic mechanism of presynaptic inhibition: Since the amino acid responses were abolished in zero sodium Ringer solution, it was initially concluded that the drug responses were due to a sodium mechanism. However, extensive studies involving changes in the concentration of sodium, chloride and calcium suggests that although glutamate responses on primary afferent terminals involve a sodium mechanism, the GABA and beta-alanine responses are probably due to chloride ions.

Technical difficulties did not allow a definitive statement to be made on the ionic mechanism of synaptically and a.a. evoked depolarization on primary afferent terminals. However, GABA also depolarizes proximal part of primary afferents including spinal ganglia and this phenomenon was used for detailed analysis of GABA action using intracellular recording and intrabath application of GABA. Depolarization was associated with decrease in membrane resistance and it was dependent on membrane potential with extrapolated reversal point around -40 mV. Since spinal ganglion membrane rectifies on depolarization it was impossible to visualize the reversal potential in normal conditions. However, using Ba^{++} ions to block the rectification, the reversal of GABA depolarization (=hyperpolarization) was recorded. Furthermore, prolonged bathing of ganglia in Cl free medium reduced GABA depolarization. These findings stongly suggest GABA increases permeability of spinal ganglion membrane for chloride ions, and increases the possibility that the same mechanism operates on the p.a. terminals.

Significance to Bio-medical Research and the Program of the Institute:
The frog spinal cord provides an ideal model for analyzing the mechanisms involved in synaptic transmission in the vertebrate nervous system. It satisfies several requirements for such studies: drugs could be applied in known concentration and responses measured from identified structures (i.e., motoneurones and/or primary afferent terminals, providing that indirect responses were blocked by high levels of Mg^{++} ions or TTX) with minimal interference from diffusional barriers; ionic medium bathing

the preparation could be changed, an approach that in conjunction with intracellular recording and use of bridge circuit for polarization allows determination of ionic mechanism of drug or/and synaptic action. In particular we have been able to identify two transmitters involved in the presynaptic inhibition on primary afferents, namely GABA and taurine. Furthermore, we have provided the first demonstration that a transmitter (GABA) in the vertebrate CNS can act both as an excitatory and an inhibitory transmitter at different synapses. This dual synaptic action is accomplished by the same basic ionic mechanism but the gradient for the ion involved is opposite at the two sites, resulting in opposite effects.

Discovery of the potent glutamate and antagonist and analogs is expected to have an important part in clarification of the role of acidic amino acids in neurotransmission.

Our results do not identify, as yet, any peptide as a candidate for neurotransmitters in the spinal cord. On the other hand, these substances could play a role in synaptic transmission by modifying action of other transmitters.

Proposed Course:

Further work is planned in several directions: 1) Radiochemical labelling of glutamate analogs will provide an useful tool for analysis of glutamate receptor in CNS. Antagonistic action of KDEE will be used to analyze different monosynaptic inputs to frog motorneurons, one of which (primary afferents) is believed to be operated by glutamate; Analysis will also be extended into studies on mammalian CNS. 2) A prerequisite of GABA depolarization on primary afferents through a Cl mechanism is high levels of internal chloride ions. This has not been ascertained experimentally, as yet, because of the difficulties encountered in measuring intracellular ionic content of myelinated fibers. Many of these problems will be circumvented by using Cl ion sensitive microelectrodes which are relatively easy to insert into spinal ganglion cell. Other ion sensitive electrodes (K+, Ca++) will be used to analyze DRP as well as dual action of neutral amino acids on the motoneurones. 3) Studies of the role of peptides in synaptic transmission will be continued on the same model (f.s.c.) as well as on the other sites where it is known that they exert a powerful action (e.g., sympathetic ganglia). Special attention will be done to the possible modulatory action of peptides as well as the relation of their action to other cellular functions.

Publications:

Barker, J. L., Nicoll, R. A.: GABA: Role in primary afferent depolarization. Science 176: 1043-1045, 1972.

Barker, J. L., Nicoll, R. A.: The pharmacology and ionic dependancy of amino acid responses in the frog spinal cord. J. Physiol. 228: 259-277, 1973.

Padjen, A., Nicoll, R. A., and Barker, J. L.: Hyperpolarizing and depolarizing receptors to glycine on frog motoneurones. Proc. 3rd Ann. Meeting of Soc. for Neurosci., 1973.

Barker, J. L., Nicoll, R. A. and Padjen, A.: Studies on convulsants in the isolated frog spinal cord. I. Antagonism of amino acid responses. J. Physiol. 245: 521-536, 1975.

Barker, J. L., Nicoll, R. A. and Padjen, A.: Studies on convulsants in the isolated frog spinal cord. II. Effects on root potentials. J. Physiol. 245: 537-548, 1975.

Nicoll, R. A., Padjen, A. and Barker, J. L.: Analysis of amino acid responses of frog motoneurons. Neuropharmacol., (in press).

Nicoll, R. A., and Padjen, A.: Pentylenetetrazole: An antagonist of GABA et primary afferents of the isolated frog spinal cord. Neuropharmacol., (in press).

Nicoll, R. A. and Padjen, A.: The distribution and ionic requirements of primary afferent amino-acid responses in the frog spinal cord. J. Physiol., (in press).

Barker, J. L., Nicoll, R. A. and Padjen, A.: Factors underlying the genesis of dorsal root potentials in the frog spinal cord. J. Physiol., (in press).

Project No. Z01 MH 01298-07 SMRN
1. Division of Special Mental Health Research
2. Laboratory of Neuropharmacology
3. Saint Elizabeths Hospital

PHS-ADAMHA-NIMH
Individual Project Report
July 1, 1974 through June 30, 1975

Project Title: The rat cerebellum: Potential neurotransmitters to Purkinje cells and their "receptors"

Previous Serial Number: M-SMR-N-S-11

Principal Investigators: B. J. Hoffer, R. Freedman, G. R. Siggins, S. Henriksen, F. E. Bloom and D. Taylor

Other Investigator: A. P. Oliver

Cooperating Unit: T. Stone, University of Aberdeen, Aberdeen, Scotland

Man Years

Total:	1.5
Professional:	1.3
Others:	0.2

Project Description:

Keyword Descriptors:
Brain, cerebellum, cerebral cortex, neurophysiology, impulse inhibition, neurohormones, purine nucleotides, cyclic AMP, cyclic GMP, phosphotransferases, ATP:AMP.

Objectives:

The objectives of the current studies are to identify the excitatory and inhibitory transmitters in the cerebellar cortex, and to determine the mechanism of action of these substances. Although the major synaptic pathways within the cerebellar cortex appear to be well characterized, little is known of the neurotransmitters in this region.

Methods Employed:

Adult rats were anesthetized with chloral hydrate, urethane or halothane. Standard methods for using 5-barrel glass micropipettes to record from single neurons and to administer drugs at the site of recording by microelectrophoresis were used. Changes in electrical activity of single cells during or after application of the drugs were analyzed by frequency analysis. In addition, a PDP-12 computer was programmed to sum the drug responses as poststimulus time histograms in order to minimize variability and quantitate the magnitude of the effect. This novel type of analysis has proven of great value in distinguishing between specific and non-specific drug interactions.

Major Findings:

We have previously demonstrated a remarkably reproducible response of Purkinje cells to the microelectrophoresis of norepinephrine (NE); see below. In addition, Purkinje cells respond to microelectrophoresis of gamma amino butyric acid by a slowing of discharge, and to microelectrophoresis of glutamic acid by increasing discharge. Serotonin and acetylcholine produce increases in the discharge rate of some cells and decreases in the discharge rate of others. Although serotonin produces variable effects in normal adult rats, recent evidence has led to the hypothesis of a direct depressant effect on Purkinje cells. In neonatal rats, or in rats whose cerebellar interneurons were destroyed by neonatal X-irradiation, serotonin almost always inhibits Purkinje cells. Purkinje cells in both types of preparation are devoid of most excitatory and inhibitory synaptic input. The excitatory effects of serotonin, then, may be indirect due to influences on cerebellar interneurons. This theory is supported by experiments which sh an excitatory influence of serotonin on cerebellar granule cell interneurons. Indeed, histochemical studies with formal-fluorescence and H^3-serotonin autoradiography indicate a serotonergic pathway to the granule cells.

Norepinephrine was found to inhibit spontaneous Purkinje cell discharge by specifically augmenting the population of normally occurring pauses. This effect of NE is mimicked by 3'5'cyclic adenosine monophosphate (C-AMP) and responses to both agents were potentiated by drugs which blocked C-AMP catabolism. NE responses are blocked by beta sympatholytic agents and the E series of prostaglandins, and are potentiated by drugs which block reuptake of this monoamine, such as desmethylimipramine. It appears likely, in view of the above data, that NE action is mediated by activation of adenyl cyclase and the subsequent increased synthesis of C-AMP. Studies in which the proposed origin of NE-containing nerves to Purkinje cells was stimulated electrically and C-AMP levels in cerebellum were localized histochemically support this theory (see project Z01 MH 01222 and 23).

Our recent studies have centered around the effects of clinically important neuroleptic agents on the adrenergic input to Purkinje cells and the responses to cyclic AMP derivatives. Clinically active phenothiazine neuroleptics such as fluphenazine and alpha fluphenthixol specifically antagonize the noradrenergic input to Purkinje neurons. Responses to other putative neurotransmitters (GABA) and stimulation of other pathways (climbing fibers, parallel fibers, basket cells) are not affected. Clinically inactive phenothiazine derivatives (such as beta flupenthixol and promethazine) do not affect the noradrenergic input. Our recent evidence also suggests that activation of a protein kinase may be involved in responses to noradrenalin. The inhibitory effects of a series of cyclic AMP derivatives correlate markedly with their ability to activate protein kinase.

In the cerebral cortex, identified pyramidal tract neurons respond to acetylcholine by excitation, and to norepinephrine by inhibition. On these cells, cyclic AMP inhibits, but cyclic GMP excites. These data suggest that the cyclic nucleotides could mediate opposing cellular functions.

Significance to Bio-medical Research and the Program of the Institute:

These investigations have provided an initial characterization of potential neurotransmitters to the cerebellar cortex of the rat. Norepinephrine, serotonin, gamma amino butyric acid, glutamate and acetylcholine all thus appear to be possible neurotransmitters to the Purkinje cell.

These investigations on the response to NE and C-AMP provide the first evidence for trans-synaptic activation of an enzyme system in the central nervous system, and provide a possible link between rapid presynaptic electrical activity and macromolecular changes in the postsynaptic cell. This type of synapse is uniquely different from those in which classical neurotransmitters merely produce a conductance change in the postsynaptic membrane. It is possible that higher functions of the central nervous system, such as memory and learning may be related to such "metabolic" synapses. The data on specific interactions with phenothiazine neuroleptics offer the promise that dysfunction of catecholamine input may be related to human mental illness. These physiological responses become more significant in light of the findings obtained by histochemical and fine structural studies.

Proposed Course:

Initially, other neuroleptics and cyclic nucleotide compounds will be studied to further test the hypothesis that behaviorally active neuroleptics block noradrenergic input and that norepinephrine effects involve cyclic nucleotide-dependent protein kinase. Subsequently, noradrenergic drug interactions will be studied in animals chronically treated with phenothiazine (see Project Z01 MH 01225) to more closely approximate the therapeutic regimen in human mental illness. Finally, to help delineate the mechanism of these drug interactions, phenothiazines and cyclic nucleotides will be studied by superfusion on brain pieces transplanted to the anterior eye chamber of the eye (see Project Z01 MH 01296). This will eliminate remote effects via afferent pathways from other brain regions.

Honors and Awards:

This work won the A. Cressy Morrison Award of the New York Academy of Science, for 1971.

Publications:

Hoffer, B. J., Siggins, G. R., and Bloom, F. E.: Cyclic 3',5'-adenosine monophosphate mediation of the response of rat cerebellar Purkinje cells to norepinephrine: Blockade with prostaglandins. Pharmacologist 11: 238, 1969.

Hoffer, B. J., Siggins, G. R., and Bloom, F. E.: Response of single cerebellar Purkinje cells to microelectrophoresis of norepinephrine and serotonin. Fed. Proc. 28: 443, 1969.

Siggins, G. R., Hoffer, B. J., and Bloom, F. E.: Cyclic adenosine monophosphate: Possible mediator for norepinephrine effects on cerebellar Purkinje cells. Science 165: 1018-1020, 1969.

Hoffer, B. J., Siggins, G. R., and Bloom, F. E.: Prostaglandins E_1 and E_2 antagonize norepinephrine effects on cerebellar Purkinje cells: Microelectrophoretic study. Science 166: 1418-1420, 1969.

Oliver, A. P., Siggins, G. R., Hoffer, B. J., and Bloom, F. E.: Changes in transmembrane potential of Purkinje cells of rat cerebellum during microelectrophoretic administration of norepinephrine. Fed. Proc. 29: #2, 1970.

Siggins, G. R., Woodward, D. J., Hoffer, B. J., and Bloom, F. E.: Responsiveness of cerebellar Purkinje cells to norepinephrine, cyclic AMP, and prostaglandin E_1 during synaptic morphogenesis in neonatal rat. Pharmacologist 12: 262, 1970.

Hoffer, B. J., Siggins, G. R., and Bloom, F. E.: Possible cyclic AMP mediated adrenergic synapses to rat cerebellar Purkinje cells: Combined structural, physiological and pharmacologic analyses. In Costa, E., and Greengard, P. (Eds.). Advances in Biochemical Psychopharmacology. New York, Raven Press, 1970, pp. 349-370.

Bloom, F. E., Hoffer, B. J., and Siggins, G. R.: Studies on norepinephrine-containing afferents to Purkinje cells of rat cerebellum. I. Localization of the fibers and their synapses. Brain Res. 25: 501-521, 1971.

Hoffer, B. J., Siggins, G. R., and Bloom, F. E.: Studies on norepinephrine-containing afferents to Purkinje cells of rat cerebellum. II. Sensitivity of Purkinje cells to NE and related substances administered by microiontophoresis. Brain Res. 25: 523-534, 1971.

Siggins, G. R., Hoffer, B. J., and Bloom, F. E.: Studies on norepinephrine-containing afferents to Purkinje cells of rat cerebellum. III. Evidence for mediation of NE effects by cyclic 3'5'-adenosine monophosphate. Brain Res. 25: 535-553, 1971.

Siggins, G. R., Hoffer, B. J., and Bloom, F. E.: Prostaglandin-norepinephrine interactions in brain: Microelectrophoretic and histochemical correlates. Ann. N. Y. Acad. Sci. 180: 302-323, 1971.

Hoffer, B. J., Siggins, G. R., Oliver, A. P., and Bloom, F. E.: Cyclic AMP mediation of norepinephrine synaptic inhibition in rat cerebellar cortex: A unique class of synaptic responses. Ann. N. Y. Acad. Sci. 185: 531-549, 1971.

Bloom, F. E., Hoffer, B. J., and Siggins, G. R.: Norepinephrine mediated synapses: A model system for neuropsychopharmacology. Biol. Psychiatry 4: 157-177, 1972.

Bloom, F. E., Hoffer, B. J., Siggins, G. R., Barker, J. L., and Nicoll, R. A.: Effects of serotonin on central neurons: Microiontophoretic administration. Fed. Proc. 31: 97-106, 1972.

Woodward, D. J., Hoffer, B. J., Siggins, G. R., and Oliver, A. P.: Inhibition of Purkinje cells in the frog cerebellum: II. Evidence for GABA as the inhibitory transmitter. Brain Res. 33: 91-100, 1971.

Siggins, G. R., Oliver, A. P., Hoffer, B. J. and Bloom, F. E.: Cyclic adenosine monophosphate and norepinephrine: Effects on transmembrane properties of cerebellar Purkinje cells. Science 171: 192, 1971.

Hoffer, B. J., Siggins, G. R., Woodward, D. J. and Bloom, F. E.: Spontaneous discharge of Purkinje neurons after destruction of catecholamine-containing afferents by 6-hydroxydopamine. Brain Res. 30: 425-430, 1971.

Wedner, H. J., Hoffer, B. J., Battenberg, E., Steiner, A. L., Parker, C. W. and Bloom, F. E.: A method for detecting intracellular cyclic adenosine monophosphate by immunofluorescence. J. Histochem. Cytochem. 20: 293-295, 1972.

Bloom, F. E., Hoffer, B. J., Battenberg, E. F., Siggins, G. R., Steiner, A. L., Parker, C. W. and Wedner, H. J.: Adenosine 3',5'-monophosphate is localized in cerebellar neurons: Immunofluorescent evidence. Science 177: 436-438, 1972.

Siggins, G. R., Battenberg, E. F., Hoffer, B. J., Bloom, F. E. and Steiner, A. L.: Noradrenergic stimulation of cyclic adenosine monophosphate in rat Purkinje neurons: An immuno-cytochemical study. Science 179: 585-588, 1973

Hoffer, B. J., Siggins, G. R., Oliver, A. P. and Bloom, F. E.: Activation of the pathway from locus coeruleus to rat cerebellar Purkinje neurons: Pharmacological evidence of noradrenergic central inhibition. J. Pharmacol. Exp. Therap. 184: 553-569, 1973.

Hoffer, B. J., Siggins, G. R., Oliver, A. P., and Bloom, F. E.: Cyclic adenosine monophosphate mediated adrenergic synapses to cerebellar Purkinje cells. Adv. Cyclic Nucleotide Res. 1: 411-423, 1972.

Freedman, R., Hoffer, B. J. and Woodward, D. J.: A quantitative microiontophoretic analysis of the responses of central neurons to norepinephrine: Interactions with cobalt, manganese, verapamil, and dichloroisoproterenol. Brit. J. Pharmacol. (in press).

Freedman, R. and Hoffer, B. J.: Phenothiazine antagonism of the noradrenergic inhibition of cerebellar Purkinje neurons. J. Neurobiol. (in press).

Siggins, G. R. and Henriksen, S. J.: Analogues of cyclic adenosine monophosphate: Correlation of inhibition of Purkinje neurons with protein kinase activation. Science (in press).

Stone, T. W., Taylor, D. A. and Bloom, F. E.: Cyclic AMP and cyclic GMP may mediate opposite neuronal responses in the rat cerebral cortex. Science 187: 845-847, 1974.

Bloom, F. E.: The role of cyclic nucleotides in central synaptic function. Ergebnisse Physiologie (in press).

Project No. Z01 MH 01299-05 SMRN
1. Division of Special Mental Health Research
2. Laboratory of Neuropharmacology
3. Saint Elizabeths Hospital

PHS-ADAMHA-NIMH
Individual Project Report
July 1, 1974 through June 30, 1975

Project Title: Sympathetic ganglia: Synaptic mechanisms

Previous Serial Number: M-SMR-N-S-14

Principal Investigator: F. F. Weight

Other Investigators: G. Petzold, P. Greengard, P. Smith, J. Schulman, N. Busis

Cooperating Unit: Department of Pharmacology, Yale University

Man Years

Total:	2.7
Professional:	2.5
Others:	0.2

Project Description:

Keyword Descriptors:
Nervous system, antonomic sympathetic ganglia, neurohormones, neurophysiology, purine nucleotides, cyclic AMP, cyclic GMP.

Objectives:
Slow synaptic potentials have recently been found in sympathetic ganglia with mechanisms that appear to be different than other synaptic potentials in the central and peripheral nervous system. The objective of this study is to investigate the mechanisms of these slow synaptic potentials.

Methods Employed:
The lumbar sympathetic ganglia, IX and X, of bullfrogs were investigated in vitro in a chamber with continuous perfusion of oxygenated Ringer's solution. Suction electrodes were used to stimulate preganglionic axons and postganglionic axons antidromically. Gross potential changes were recorded from the postganglionic ramus communicantes near the ganglion with a suction electrode. Ganglion cells were recorded intracellularly using standard electrophysiological techniques, a bridge circuit being used to inject current intracellularly. The ionic composition of the bathing solution was varied by changing the perfusion solution. Drugs were administered either by microelectrophoresis or added to the bath. Ganglia have also been analyzed chemically by radioimmunoassay for cyclic adenosine monophosphate (cyclic AMP) and cyclic guanosine monophosphate (cyclic GMP) content.

Major Findings:

Synaptic excitation results from an increased ion conductance of postsynaptic membrane at virtually all chemically transmitting synapses that have been investigated. This has also been found to be true for the fast EPSP in sympathetic ganglion cells, where the transmitter acetylcholine (ACh) acting on nicotinic membrane receptors increases the postsynaptic conductance to sodium and potassium. During the fast EPSP, therefore, a decrease in membrane resistance is measured. The equilibrium potential for the increased ion conductances involved is in the depolarizing direction so that electrical hyperpolarization of the membrane increases the size of the EPSP, whereas progressive depolarization decreases and then reverses the EPSP to a hyperpolarizing potential.

In addition to the fast EPSP, repetitive preganglionic B fiber stimulation generates in B ganglion cells a muscarinic slow EPSP with unique properties. In contrast to the increased conductance associated with other known EPSP's, membrane conductance (measured by a constant current pulse) decreases significantly during the slow EPSP. Furthermore, contrary to the effect of electrical membrane polarization on other EPSP's, depolarizing current increases the size of the slow EPSP, whereas hyperpolarizing current decreases the slow EPSP. Further hyperpolarization reverses the slow EPSP to a hyperpolarizing potential. The reversal potential of the slow EPSP is close to the potassium equilibrium potential. This data suggests that slow EPSP is generated by a decrease in potassium conductance. Removal of extracellular chloride from the Ringer bath had no significant effect on the slow EPSP, excluding the possibility that an inactivation of chloride conductance plays a significant role in the generation of the slow EPSP. Changing extracellular potassium shifted the ACh reversal potential in a manner consistent with a change in potassium conductance. On the basis of these data, we have proposed that the slow EPSP is generated by an inactivation of resting potassium conductance.

In addition to the slow EPSP in B cells, repetitive stimulation of C fibers generates a slow IPSP in C cells. The slow IPSP also has unique properties compared to other known IPSPs. In contrast to the increased conductance associated with other IPSPs, membrane conductance decreased significantly during the slow IPSP. In addition, contrary to the effect of electrical membrane polarization on other IPSPs, depolarizing current decreased the size of the slow IPSP, whereas hyperpolarizing current increased its size. These data suggest that the slow IPSP is generated by an inactivation of resting sodium conductance. Further evidence for this hypothesis is provided by the observation that removal of extracellular sodium abolished the slow IPSP. Additional studies indicate that acetylcholine has a direct hyperpolarizing action on C cells with properties identical to the slow IPSP. This data coupled with the morphological evidence (Project No. Z01 MH 01300) that chromaffin cells are sparsely distributed and do not receive or make synaptic connections in the Xth ganglion suggests that the slow IPSP is generated by a direct cholinergic mechanism.

In an attempt to determine whether these slow synaptic potentials might be associated with the activation of intracellular metabolic systems, we have investigated the effect of synaptic stimulation on cyclic nucleotides in the ganglion. Brief stimulation of the cholinergic preganglionic nerve fibers resulted in a rapid increase in cyclic guanosine monophosphate (cyclic GMP). When the release of ACh was blocked by high-magnesium/low calcium Ringer solution or when muscarinic post-synaptic receptors were blocked by atropine, cyclic GMP was not increased by stimulation of the preganglionic nerves. These data indicate that the increase in cyclic GMP is associated with synaptic transmission and support the possibility that cyclic GMP may act as an intracellular second messenger mediating the post-synaptic action of ACh. In addition, cyclic adenosine monophosphate (cyclic AMP) was also increased in the ganglion. We are currently investigating whether the increase in cyclic AMP might be associated with possible adrenergic synapses in the ganglion (Project No. Z01 MH 01300-03).

Significance to Bio-medical Research and the Program of the Institute:

In order to understand how the nervous system functions, it is necessary to determine the mechanisms of synaptic transmission. With present techniques, it is often difficult or impossible to investigate in detail such mechanisms in the central nervous system because: (1) the transmitters are not known at most central synapses; (2) in general, central pathways cannot be selectively stimulated, and (3) it is not possible to change extracellular ion concentrations over a wide range or to administer certain chemical substances. The sympathetic ganglion, however, is well suited for studying the mechanisms of synaptic transmission. First, because the synaptic transmitter is known to be acetylcholine. Second, because the ganglion can be investigated in vitro permitting changes in the ionic and chemical composition of the bath. Third, because it is possible to record electrical changes in the ganglion both grossly and intracellularly.

Using the advantages of this preparation, it has been possible to determine that the slow excitatory action of acetylcholine on postsynaptic muscarinic membrane receptors appears to be an inactivation of resting potassium conductance. Since similar ACh responses have been reported in the mammalian central nervous system, synaptic inactivation of potassium conductance may be a mechanism of general significance in the synaptic regulation of neuronal activity. The data also indicate that the slow inhibitory action of acetylcholine on postsynaptic muscarinic membrane receptors appears to be generated by an inactivation of resting sodium conductance. Since the conductance change in B and C cells involve different ions but both appear to be due to cholinergic activation of muscarinic receptors, the data imply that there may be different intermediate steps between receptor activation and membrane conductance change in different cell types. The increase in cyclic nucleotides produced by synaptic stimulation raises the question of whether cyclic nucleotides may serve as intracellular mediators of slow synaptic responses.

One of the important current questions in neurobiology is how the discrete rapid events of nerve cells, such as action potentials or synaptic potentials, lasting only a few milliseconds are transferred into the longer term changes in neurons. The investigation of slow synaptic responses may provide an understanding of at least some mechanisms of long-term changes in neurons resulting from synaptic activity.

Proposed Course:
The continuation of the project will be directed toward a further elucidation of how the action of a synaptic transmitter on postsynaptic receptors leads to an inactivation of different membrane conductances. Attempts will be made to determine whether these membrane changes are initiated by the synaptic activation of metabolic systems and, if so, we will attempt to determine the mechanisms involved.

Honors:
Editorial Advisory Board, Neuropharmacology (Journal)

Invited Lectures

Weight, F. F.: Symposium on Synaptic Mechanisms in the Vertebrate Nervous System, Neurophysiology Group, American Physiological Society, Chicago, 1971.

Weight, F. F.: Chairman, Session on Neuropharmacology. XXV International Congress of Physiological Science, Munich, 1971.

Weight, F. F.: Symposium on the Physiology and Pharmacology of Synapses, Basel, 1971.

Weight, F. F.: Chairman, Session on Synaptic Integration in the Vertebrate Nerous System. Winter Brain Research Conference, Colorado, 1972.

Weight, F. F.: Symposium on Dynamic Aspects of Synaptic Modulation, NRP Intensive Study Program, Boulder, 1972.

Weight, F. F.: Symposium on Synaptic Transmission and Interneuronal Communication, Society of General Physiology, Woods Hole, 1972.

Weight, F. F.: Chairman, Session on Synaptic Transmission. Society for Neuroscience, St. Louis, 1974.

Publications:

Weight, F. F. and Votava, J.: Slow synaptic excitation in sympathetic ganglion cells: Evidence for synaptic inactivation of potassium conductance. Science 170: 755-758, 1970.

Weight, F. F.: Mechanisms of synaptic transmission. Neuroscience. Res. 4: 1-27, 1971.

Weight, F. F. and Votava, J.: Inactivation of potassium conductance in slow postsynaptic excitation. Science 172: 504, 1971.

Weight, F. F.: Mechanisms of synaptic excitation in sympathetic ganglion cells. Experientia 27: 14, 1971.

Weight, F. F., and Padjen, A.: Slow synaptic inhibition: Evidence for synaptic inactivation of sodium conductance in sympathetic ganglion cells. Brain Res. 55: 219-224, 1973.

Weight, F. F., and Padjen, A.: Acetylcholine and slow synaptic inhibition in frog sympathetic ganglion. Brain Res. 55: 225-228, 1973.

Weight, F. F.: Synaptic potentials resulting from conductance decreases. In Bennett, M.V.L. (Ed.): Synaptic Transmission and Neuronal Interaction, New York, Raven Press, 1974, pp. 141-152.

Weight, F. F.: Physiological mechanisms of synaptic modulation. In Schmidt, F.O. (Ed.): The Neurosciences, Third Study Program, Cambridge, MIT Press, 1974, pp. 929-941.

Weight, F. F., G. Petzold and P. Greengard: Guanosine 3',5'-Monophosphate in Sympathetic Ganglia: Increase Associated with Synaptic Transmission. Science. 186: 942-944, 1974.

Project No. Z01 MH 01300-03 SMRN
1. Division of Special Mental Health Research
2. Laboratory of Neuropharmacology
3. Saint Elizabeths Hospital

PHS-ADAMHA-NIMH
Individual Project Report
July 1, 1974 through June 30, 1975

Project Title: Sympathetic ganglia: Functional organization

Previous Serial Number: M-SMR-N-S-15

Principal Investigator: F. F. Weight

Other Investigator: H. Weitsen

Cooperating Unit: Dept. of Anatomy, LSU Med. Center, New Orleans, Louisiana

Man Years

Total:	.2
Professional:	0.2
Others:	0

Project Description:

Keyword Descriptors:
Nervous system, antonomic ganglia optics, microscopy, electron neuroanatomy, histochemistry, general.

Objectives:
The objective of this study is to correlate the structural and functional organization of the IX and X sympathetic ganglia of the bullfrog in order to study the mechanisms of synaptic transmission in sympathetic ganglia (cf. project No. Z01 MH 01299-05).

Methods Employed:
In this study both physiological and anatomical methods were employed. For the physiological investigation, the ganglia were studied in vitro in a perfusion chamber; preganglionic nerve roots were stimulated using suction electrodes. The effect of stimulation on the ganglion cells was recorded grossly by a suction electrode on the postganglionic ramus communicantes near the ganglion and intracellularly with standard electrophysiological techniques. The ganglia were studied anatomically using a variety of different techniques including fluorescence histochemistry, acetylcholinesterase staining, methylene blue staining and electron microscopy. Preganglionic nerves were also transsected to study the degeneration of preganglionic fibers innervating various ganglion cells.

Major Findings:
The lumbar ganglia IX and X of the bullfrog have two types of ganglion cells, B. and C, classified by the conduction velocity of their postganglionic axon. The B cells receive preganglionic B fiber innervation and the C cells receive preganglionic C fiber innervation. The major preganglionic B fiber contribution to the lumbar IXth and Xth ganglia is from the sympathetic chain rostral to the VIIth lumbar ganglion. On the other hand, preganglionic C fibers are contributed by the VIIIth lumbar nerve. A single preganglionic B fiber innervates each B ganglion cell. With acetylcholinesterase staining, the single preganglionic axon can be seen to form a unique spiral arrangement around the axon hillock region of the ganglion cell. The fine structure of this synaptic innervation studied in the electron microscope shows that the spiral gives off numerous synapses to the proximal soma and adjacent axon hillock region of the ganglion cell. We are currently investigating the functional significance of this spiral arrangement and also whether C cells also receive such spiral innervation.

Repetitive stimulation of preganglionic B fibers generates a slow EPSP in B ganglion cells which is due to the transmitter acetylcholine acting on muscarinic receptors (cf Project No. Z01 MH 01299-05). On the other hand, repetitive stimulation of C fibers generates a slow IPSP in C cells, and we have studied whether this opposite response is due to a special anatòmical arrangement, such as an inhibitory interneuron, or some other synaptic mechanism. In addition, although the cholinergic C fibers do no connect directly with B cells, a repetitive (2 sec) stimulation of preganglionic C fibers (VIIIth nerve) generates a long latency, very slow depolarization of B cells ("heterosynaptic excitation") lasting 5 or 6 minutes. We are attempting to determine the integrative significance, anatomical basis and transmitter responsible for generating this heterosynaptic excitation.

The slow IPSP has previously been proposed to be generated by cholinergic innervation and activation of chromaffin cells which in turn are supposed to release a catecholamine that inhibits ganglion cells. Using a combination of fluoresence histochemistry and toluidine blue staining, we have been able to identify and characterize chromaffin cells in the electron microscope. We find that there are few chromaffin cells in the Xth sympathetic ganglion of frog and those present do not appear to either receive or make synaptic connections. This morphological data is not consistent with the so-called catecholamine hypothesis for the generation of slow synaptic inhibition. On the other hand, physiological data (Project No. Z01 MH 01299-05) indicate that acetylcholine has a direct hyperpolarizing action on C cells in frog sympathetic ganglion. This morphological data is consistent with the idea that slow synaptic inhibition in the sympathetic ganglion of frog is generated by a direct cholinergic mechanism.

In addition to the slow synaptic potentials produced by repetitive preganglion stimulation, a slow hyperpolarization has recently been found following repetitive antidromic stimulation. This antidromic hyperpolarization is currently being investigated to determine if the transmitter is a catecholamine.

Significance to Bio-medical Research and the Program of the Institute:
Since the different preganglionic fibers are in separate nerves, the transmitter is known to be acetylcholine and the fibers stain for acetylcholinesterase, and the transmitter of the postganglionic cells is epinephrine and the cells can be visualized with fluorescence histochemistry; the sympathetic ganglion is an ideal structure for correlating structural and functional synaptic organization, thus furthering our knowledge of synaptic organization and function in the vertebrate. nervous system.

Proposed Course:
The continuation of the project will be directed toward further elucidation of the organization of the ganglia in relation to the generation of different types of synaptic potentials. A manuscript is in preparation.

Project No. Z01 MH 01301-02 SMRN
1. Division of Special Mental Health Research
2. Laboratory of Neuropharmacology
3. Saint Elizabeths Hospital

PHS-ADAMHA-NIMH
Individual Project Report
July 1, 1974 through June 30, 1975

Project Title: Determination of the effects of norepinephrine and other putative neurotransmitters on identifiable brain stem neurons.

Previous Serial Number: M-SMR-N-S-26

Principal Investigator: A. P. Oliver

Other Investigator: None

Cooperating Units: None

Man Years

Total: 0.3
Professional: 0.3
Others: 0

Project Description:

Keyword Descriptors:
Nervous system, cranial nerves, trigeminal, facid, hypoglossal, neuropharmacology, neurohormones.

Objectives:
To test the effect of norepinephrine and other substances on neurons in brain stem nuclei which are known to receive norepinephrine containing terminals.

Methods Employed:
Albino rats (200-300 gm) are anesthetized with halothane and mounted in a stereotactic head-holder. Various cranial nerves (facial, hypoglossal) are stimulated to drive the neurons antidromically or synaptically either to identify them or to test effects of norepinephrine and other substances of interest on driven action potentials. In addition these substances are tested against spontaneous activity. Standard microelectrophoretic techniques are used to test and record activity. Further identification of the cells tested is provided by histological examination of electrode tracts.

Major Findings:

All identifiable cells tested with norepinephrine responded with a reduction in firing rate. This is true of both spontaneous and driven firing. The same phenomena were observed following application of gamma-aminobutyric acid. Cells in sensory trigeminal nucleus, respond with a reduction in spontaneous and driven firing rates to local application of norepinephrine, serotonin, and gamma-aminobutyric acid.

Hypoglossal motoneurons driven by synaptic and antidromic stimuli respond identically as above to the same applied substances.

Responses of unidentified, randomly encountered cells in reticular formation are unpredictable.

In all cells which showed a response to serotonin the response was "inhibitory", but some cells (about 10%) showed no response.

Excitation was not observed in any test with these substances.

Proposed Course:

To continue with a systematic investigation of cranial nerve nuclei.

Project No. Z01 MH 01302-03 SMRN
1. Division of Special Mental Health Research
2. Laboratory of Neuropharmacology
3. Saint Elizabeths Hospital

PHS-ADAMHA-NIMH
Individual Project Report
July 1, 1974 through June 30, 1975

Project Title: Function of the dopamine projection to rat caudate nucleus; possible involvement of cyclic AMP

Previous Serial Number: M-SMR-N-S-28

Principal Investigators: G. R. Siggins, B. J. Hoffer, and S. Henriksen

Other Investigator: F. E. Bloom

Cooperating Units: U. Ungerstedt, Karolinska Institute, Stockholm, Sweden

Man Years

Total:	0.2
Professional:	0.2
Others:	0

Project Description:

Keyword Descriptors:

Brain, basal ganglia, caudate nucleus, brain mesencephalon, substantia nigra, neurophysiology, nerve impulse inhibition, neuropharmacology, purine nucleotides, cyclic AMP.

Objectives:

The objective of the study is to determine the effect on caudate neurons of iontophoretically applied dopamine, cyclic AMP, apomorphine, acetylcholine and adenosine derivatives, and of activation or removal of the nigro-striatal dopamine-containing pathway. Recent studies indicate that dopamine and apomorphine increase cyclic AMP levels in homogenates of caudate. Caudate nucleus is one of the few brain areas in which the mechanisms of a dopaminergic system can be studied directly in vivo, as already described by us for the noradrenergic synapses in rat cerebellum (see Z01 MH 01223).

Methods Employed:

Adult rats are anesthetized and placed in a rigid frame where single neurons of the caudate nucleus and fibers of the nigral caudate pathway can be electrophysiologically identified by a stereotaxic approach. A bipolar stimulating electrode is used to stimulate the nigral pathway while 5-barrel micropipettes are used to record the unit electrical activity of caudate neurons while applying various drugs locally by microiontophoresis. Unit spontaneous discharge rate is determined before and after lesioning of the nigral dopamine pathway by 6-hydroxydopamine, and after electrical stimulation of the intact nigral-striatal fibers. Computer techniques are used to construct histograms of spontaneous activity and to determine the effects of nigral stimulation by post-stimulus time histograms.

Major Findings:

Caudate neurons respond reproducibly to the microiontophoresis of dopamine, which inhibits the spontaneous or excitant amino acid induced firing of most caudate neurons. Removal of the dopamine pathway by 6-hydroxydopamine causes a significant increase in spontaneous firing rate and an increased responsiveness to dopamine and apomorphine, indicating that the dopamine fibers probably supply a tonic inhibitory input to caudate cells; removal of the input causes supersensitivity to locally applied dopamine. Furthermore, both iontophoretically applied apomorphine, proposed by biochemists to stimulate dopamine receptors in vitro, and cyclic AMP reproducibly mimic the effects of dopamine by inhibiting spontaneous or drug-evoked firing. Caudate neurons respond to cyclic AMP, to cyclic AMP derivatives and to ATP and 5'AMP in the same qualitative manner as they respond to dopamine. Phosphodiesterase inhibitors (papaverine, isobutyl methyl xanthine) potentiate these responses to dopamine, as do prostaglandins of the E series. Neuroleptic phenothiazines such as chlorpromazine, flupenthixol and fluphenazine inhibit the response to dopamine selectively, but MJ-1999 does not. These results suggest that DA-mediated synapses have different pharmacological sensitivity from NE-mediated synapses such as those in cerebellum and hippocampus.

Significance to Bio-medical Research and the Program of the Institute:

These investigations have already provided fundamental knowledge of the cellular function of the vast numbers of dopamine-containing nerve terminals in the caudate. In addition, evidence is accumulating that cyclic AMP may be the second messenger inside caudate neurons which actually intermediates the dopamine response. These studies are highly significant from a clinical point of view, since knowledge of the dopamine pathway to caudate will probably provide the best means of ultimately controlling the sequelae of Parkinson's Syndrome, known to result from an effective reduction in caudate dopamine. Moreover, many of the behavioral sequelae of psychotropic drugs which interact with central monoamines have recently been related to effects on the nigra-striatal pathway. Furthermore, only these kinds of studies will currently verify if apomorphine and other opiates do indeed stimulate dopamine receptors in brain, and determine if the analgesic and addicting properties of the opiates arise from an interaction with the dopamine system.

Proposed Course:

In the future, emphasis will be placed on applying methods for the reproducible and selective stimulation of the rat nigral-striatal dopamine pathway. The ontogenetic development of the nigrostriatal and cortico-striatal projection will also be studied in relation to behavioral maturation. Furthermore, the significance of the potent inhibitors of caudate firing produced by ATP and 5'AMP will be probed. It is thought that these inhibitions result from degradation of these nucleotides to adenosine, which is known to generate cyclic AMP in caudate in vitro. The possible mediation by cyclic AMP of ATP, AMP and potential adenosine responses will be tested by iontophoresing potent analogues of adenosine and methyl xanthines, known to block the cyclic AMP generating effect of adenosine. Finally, studies identical to those applied to caudate will be used in areas of mesolimbic forebrain and cortex known to receive a dopamine input and thought to be involved in behavioral abnormalities.

Publications:

Siggins, G. R., Hoffer, B. J. and Ungerstedt, U.: Electrophysiological evidence for involvement of cyclic adenosine monophosphate in dopamine responses of caudate neurons. Life Sci. 15: 779-792, 1974.

Ungerstedt, U., Ljungberg, T., Hoffer, B. and Siggins, G.: Dopaminergic supersensitivity in the striatum. In Calne, D., Chase, T. N. and Barbeau, A. (Eds.): Advances in Neurology, Vol. 9. New York, Raven Press, 1975, 425 pp.

Project No. Z01 MH 01303-02 SMRN
1. Division of Special Mental Health Research
2. Laboratory of Neuropharmacology
3. Saint Elizabeths Hospital

PHS-ADAMHA-NIMH
Individual Project Report
July 1, 1974 through June 30, 1975

Project Title: Transmitter release: Mechanisms of modulation

Previous Serial Number: M-SMR-N-S-29

Principal Investigator: F. F. Weight

Other Investigator: S. D. Erulkar

Cooperating Units: Dept. Pharmacology, University of Pennsylvania, and Marine Biology Laboratory, Woods Hole, Massachusetts.

Man Years

Total:	0.4
Professional:	0.4
Others:	0

Project Description:

Keyword Descriptors:
Neurophysiology, neural transmission, neurohormones, calcium, magnesium potassium.

Objectives:
The objective of this study was to investigate the mechanisms of the phenomena which can modulate the release of transmitter from synaptic terminals. The role of extracellular potassium in controlling the release of transmitter and the effect of potassium accumulation, resulting from trains of impulses, on transmitter release were investigated.

Methods Employed:
The giant synapse in the stellate ganglion of the squid (Loligo) was investigated in vitro. Synaptic transmission was studied by intracellular recording in the presynaptic terminal and postsynaptic axon. The ionic composition of the artificial sea water was varied to study the effect on transmitter release.

Major Findings:
Repetitive stimulation of the presynaptic axon of the giant synapse results in a reduction in EPSP amplitude. During the train of impulses,

a depolarization of the presynaptic membrane potential and a reduction in the presynaptic spike after-hyperpolarization was observed, indicating an accumulation of extracellular potassium (K) ions (Frankenhaeuser and Hodgkin, J. Physiol. 131, 343, 1956). This observation raised the question of whether the accumulation of extracellular K contributed to the depression of EPSP amplitude. Changing the concentration of K was found to control the release of synaptic transmitter; increasing extracellular K, decreased the amplitude of the EPSP, and decreasing extracellular K, increased the amplitude of the EPSP. This effect was due to changes in presynaptic spike height produced by the extracellular K. Kinetic and quantitative analysis revealed that the accumulation of extracellular K contributed approximately 13% of the depression EPSP amplitude produced by a presynaptic train of impulses; the remainder being due to depletion of transmitter readily available for release.

In view of the observation that extracellular K depresses transmitter release, we investigated the possibility that the accumulation of K resulting from a train of impulses in the post-synaptic axon might affect the release of transmitter. It was found that repetitive antidromic stimulation of the postsynaptic axon resulted in the signs of K accumulation, not only around the postsynaptic axon, but also around the presynaptic terminal. The K accumulated around the terminal was 60-80% of that around the postsynaptic axon. Associated with the accumulation of K around the terminal was a reduction in the amplitude of the EPSP. There was good quantitative agreement between the magnitude of K accumulation around the terminal and the reduction in EPSP amplitude. The depression in transmitter release can therefore be ascribed to the accumulation of K. Thus, repetitive impulses in the postsynaptic axon has a negative feedback effect on the release of transmitter from the presynaptic terminal.

Significance to Bio-medical Research and the Program of the Institute:
In the central nervous system there are many limitations to the study of the modulation of transmitter release, particularly because it is not possible to record the electrical activity of presynaptic terminals. Extracellular recordings from terminals have been obtained at the neuromuscular junction; however, the size of the potential is so small that it is difficult to detect small changes. The squid giant synapse is the only synaptic junction known with a presynaptic terminal sufficiently large to permit intracellular recording. It is thus possible to study the factors that affect the electrical potentials in the terminal to modulate the release of synaptic transmitter.

The data obtained indicate that the accumulation of extracellular potassium ions resulting from physiological activity can modulate the release of synaptic transmitter. This may be an important physiological mechanism for modulating transmitter release.

Proposed Course:

The continuation of the project will be directed toward an understanding of other mechanisms of modulating transmitter release. In addition, the influence of varying the ionic composition, as well as the effects of drugs which affect transmitter release, will be studied. A manuscript is in preparation.

Project No. Z01 MH 01332-02 SMRC
1. Division of Special Mental Health Research
2. Laboratory of Clinical Psychopharmacology
3. Saint Elizabeths Hospital

PHS-ADAMHA-NIMH
Individual Project Report
July 1, 1974 through June 30, 1975

Project Title: Coronary Prone Behavior Pattern in the NHLI Type II Study

Previous Serial Number: M-AP(C) 19-3

Principal Investigator: Richard J. Wyatt, M.D.

Other Investigators: none

Cooperating Units: NHLI Type II Coronary Intervention Study
NHLI, Molecular Diseases Branch
NHLI, Cardiology Branch
Dr. Ray Rosenman, Harold Brunn Institute for Cardiovascular Research, San Francisco, Calif.

Man Years: none

Project Description: This project has been temporarily suspended. A two-year follow-up study is planned.

Honors and Awards: none

Publications: none

Project No. Z01 MH 01333-07 SMRC
1. Division of Special Mental Health Research
2. Laboratory of Clinical Psychopharmacology
3. Saint Elizabeths Hospital

PHS-ADAMHA-NIMH
Individual Project Report
July 1, 1974 through June 30, 1975

Project Title: The Distribution and Concomitants of Schizophrenia, and Other Psychopathologies, in a Systematic Sample of 15,909 Twin Pairs

Previous Serial Number: M-AP(C) 19-5

Principal Investigator: Richard J. Wyatt, M.D.

Other Investigators: none

Man Years: none

Project Description: This project has been temporarily suspended and is being held in abeyance.

Honor and Awards: none

Publications: none

Project No. Z01 MH 01334-03 SMRC
1. Division of Special Mental Health Research
2. Laboratory of Clinical Psychopharmacology
3. Saint Elizabeths Hospital

PHS-ADAMHA-NIMH
Individual Project Report
July 1, 1974 through June 30, 1975

Project Title: The Twin Intrapair-Comparative Technique in the Study of the Determinants of Early Personality Development

Previous Serial Number: M-AP(C) 19-6

Principal Investigator: Eleanor Dibble, DSW

Other Investigator: Richard J. Wyatt, M.D.

Cooperating Units:

Yale University Child Study Center, New Haven, Conn., Dr. Donald J. Cohen

Man Years (computed for the 12 month period)

Total:	.5
Professional:	.5
Other:	0

Project Description:

Objectives:

1. To develop methodologies for the study of the antecedents of personality in children, based especially on the comparative study of pairs of twins. To study differences between children in relation to a) non-genetic biological differences between the twins, i.e. differences in the congenital endowment of the children and early differences during the first weeks of life; b) parental personalities and behaviors, specifically, differences in relationship and perceptions of parents to Twin A versus Twin B; c) the impact of such differences in parent-child relationship, and of traumatic experiences such as illness or surgery, on the child; and d) the origins of, and differences between the children in relation to behavior problems.

Methods Employed:

(1) Longitudinal Study. Families of ten sets of twins who had been referred by local obstetricians have been followed since the twin pregnancy was diagnosed. The children's current ages in this cohort range from 5 to 9 years. During the years the children and their families have been followed, a protocol of testing has been accomplished: developmental evaluation and Bayley testing; neurological evaluation; psychiatric diagnostic evaluations of the twins and parents; periodic family interviews; information from the Experimental Nursery School of the NIMH in which the children were studied for a half-day at age 3; evoked cortical potentials; projective psychological testing; and social work evaluations. Dr. Martin Allen has interviewed the parents and Dr. Stanley Greenspan, child psychiatrist, interviewed the children at age five to six years to study the increasingly complex structuralization of their behavior as they develop more complex coping and defense systems and the fantasies. Special psychological testing including: a Rorschach test, a specially devised twin TAT, the "World Test" for children, the Stanford-Binet (IQ) test and the Bender-Gestalt test in order to gain information about the twins' psychic development (both conscious and unconscious).

(2) Epidemiological Study. On the basis of our studies on psychopathology and on the longitudinal study of normal twin development data, the study titled "Childhood Personality Development: Twins and the Antecedents of Personality," approved by the Technical Review Committee on March 31, 1972, was completed. This epidemiological investigation aims at exploring the hypotheses and conclusions from the previous studies and extends the size of the sample, explicates and operationally defines particular variables that have emerged from clinical observations, and uses newly devised psychological instruments. These instruments have been described elsewhere (1972 Annual Report).

The sample includes 377 families recruited to participate in this study by personal appearance at local Mothers of Twins Clubs and at the Annual Convention of the National Organization of Mothers of Twins Clubs.

Patient Material:

The Longitudinal Study consists of a cohort of 10 sets of twins, 8 monozygotic and 2 dizygotic. The cohort of the epidemiological study consists of 377 sets of twins.

Major Findings:

A. Longitudinal Study: During fiscal year 1975 the following has been accomplished: 1) all parents completed a newly devised form, Behavior Problems, on the children for a retest; and 2) the younger five sets of children were seen and tested according to the new procedure described above. The use of this sample has been completed and the results are being prepared for publication.

B. Epidemiological Study: During fiscal year 1975 data from 377 families has been analyzed and written up. The analysis of all the forms has not, however, been completed.

Intraclass correlations of The Childhood Personality Scale show a high degree of intrapair similarity in attention, behavior modulation, and sociability among monozygotic twins and a lower degree among dizygotic twins. For the dimensions of zestfulness and verbal expressiveness, monozygotic and dizygotic twinships were quite similar; they had high intrapair similarity. These findings indicate that general familial experiences play a relatively larger role in shaping children's verbal interests and general affective style (ebullience and positive mood), or parental perceptions of these than in shaping attention, activity level, and introversion-extroversion. The analyses also indicate the difference in parental expectations of boys and girls -- the mixed-sex fraternal twins pointing this up vividly.

The Childhood Personality Scale, after factor analysis, has been reduced from a 48-item scale to a 20-item Factor Scale which can be validly used to measure the same behavior.

Similar analysis is being done with The Parents Report and The Pregnancy Delivery First Month of Life questionnaire. Mothers (44) of a singleton child as well as twins have completed this latter form on the single child. Comparisons between the twin and singleton pregnancies are being made, and comparison between infant constitutional factors in single versus twin pregnancies.

Responsibility for the work on the Epidemiological Study is carried jointly with Dr. Donald Cohen, Yale University Child Study Center. Future reports will give details of the analyses.

Both the Longitudinal Study and the Epidemiological Study of twins are providing a testing ground for our hypotheses about genetic and non-genetic antecedents of personality. The psychological instruments which have been developed for the epidemiological study will have broad applicability in other studies which aim at understanding the social and emotional development of children during the first years of life.

Proposed Course of the Study:

This study is being terminated.

Keyword Descriptors:

development, child
child behavior
pregnancy, multiple
behavior, paternal
behavior, maternal
parent-child
child-rearing

Publications:

Dibble, E., Cohen, D.J.: Companion instruments for measuring children's competence and parental style. Arch. Gen. Psychiat. 30: 805-815, 1974.

Project No. Z01 MH 01335-05 SMRC
1. Division of Special Mental Health Research
2. Laboratory of Clinical Psychopharmacology
3. Saint Elizabeths Hospital

PHS-ADAMHA-NIMH
Individual Project Reports
July 1, 1974 through June 30, 1975

Project Title: Studies of Schizophrenia

Previous Serial Number: M-SMR-C-2,4,25,26; M-SMR-C-P-1,2,5,6,7,8,9,10,15,17; M-SMR-C-C-13

Principal Investigators: Richard Jed Wyatt, M.D., J. Christian Gillin, M.D., Llewellyn B. Bigelow, M.D., and Farouk Karoum, Ph.D.

Other Investigators: Jack Barchas, M.D., Richard Green, M.S., Dennis Murphy, M.D., Lewis Mandel, Ph.D., Robert Belmaker, M.D., Michael Schwartz, M.D., William Carpenter, M.D., Norton Neff, Ph.D. David M. Stoff, Ph.D.

Cooperating Units: Laboratory of Clinical Science, Laboratory of Preclinical Pharmacology, Adult Psychiatry Branch, NIMH, Merck Institute for Therapeutic Research, and Stanford University

Man Years:

Total: 7.2
Professional: 3.2
Other: 4.0

Project Description:

Objectives:

To test existing and create new hypothesis relating to the possible organic basis of schizophrenia. This project attempts to synthesize psychological, physiological, and biochemical disciplines around the subject of schizophrenia.

Methods Employed:

All studies have been carried out in phenothiazine refractory chronic schizophrenics. The drugs were given and measurements made in a double blind fashion.

Major Findings:

I. The Rating Scale

Experience gained with the rating scale we had been using on the research wards to record clinical status indicated that it had many shortcomings. We, therefore, undertook to design a more useful nursing scale that could yield quantitative estimates of the level of psychopathology of chronic schizophrenics. To be useful, the scale had to be objective as possible and be comprehensible to nursing staff trained to the level of nursing assistant.

Numerous conferences were held with the nursing staff to determine which psychiatric concepts were comprehended and could be inquired about on a rating form. Sample forms were devised and tested in the following manner. Every staff member on each shift would complete the rating on two patients. The results of this exercise were then subjected to statistical analysis in order to determine reliability and to find if, in fact, any meaningful consensus had been found as to the meaning of the questions. Different pairs of patients were used and the same patients were tested again to determine if reliability was consistent over time.

We have evolved a rating scale that appears usable by nursing staff trained at the nursing assistant level which will accurately reflect the daily clinical status of the patient. The new nurses' rating scale was tested extensively and various ambiguities eliminated. In an effort to shorten the scale correlations were run between 26 items. Although in a given patient there were various high correlations between specific questions, these correlations did not hold consistently in each patient. Thus, no questions could be demonstrated to be expendable. Computor programs for processing the scales have been devised and a new optical scanning machine activated so that quick feedback can be gained from each patient.

II. Serotonin and Its Precursors

Behavioral: The study has now been underway for 54 months. The first three patients were given alpha-methyl-5-hydroxytryptophan for one month preceded and followed by one month placebo periods. The active drug made these patients worse.

The subsequent 18 patients were given L-5-hydroxytryptophan together with a peripheral decarboxylase inhibitor (MK-486). MK-486 blocks the conversion of 5HTP to serotonin outside the brain and because MK-486 does not enter the brain makes more 5HTP available for conversion to serotonin within the brain parenchyma. In addition, it is thought that MK-486 reduces 5HTP's side effects.

The patients were given placebo for one month, the active drugs for up to three months, and then a second placebo for one month. Behavioral ratings were done by nurses four times daily. The last 7 days of the highest active drug period were compared to the last 7 days of both placebo periods. For a change to have taken place, we required that the active drug period had to be higher or lower than both placebo periods ($p<0.05$, 2 tailed "t" test).

By the criteria indicated, 12 patients have improved, 2 have become worse, and for 4 there was no change. It must be emphasized that these comparisons were made against placebo only and as yet, we have not determined how 5HTP compares to conventional drugs. What is clear is that these drug combinations chemically differentiate at least two kinds of schizophrenic patients; those who became better and those that became worse. Further efforts to determine if these chemical differentiations correlate with any behavioral distinctions are being made.

Two patients have been given the 5HTP-MK-486 combination on a chronic basis. Both patients who had improved on 5HTP in the shorter study, did once again. Unfortunately with time, they became tolerant to the 5HTP.

In order to determine if there are any additive effects of 5HTP and neuroleptics, we are now treating our patients with a constant dose of a neuroleptic, MK-486, and 5HTP (3-6 gm/day). The first three patients were given chlorpromazine as the neuroleptic and appeared to do well. The neuroleptic was then changed to haloperidol. Five male and two female chronic schizophrenics received a combination of haloperidol, L-5HTP, and MK-486 in a double blind, crossover study.

Patients were stabilized for at least one month on an optimal dose of haloperidol and an antiparkinson agent when necessary. After a month on haloperidol and placebo L-5HTP, patients began L-5HTP, 100 mg/24 hours, along with MK-486, 200 mg/24 hours. The intent was to follow a program of stepwise increments of L-5HTP dosage to achieve levels of 3 or more grams/24 hours as in the previous study, but this turned out to be impossible. Of the 7 patients, 3 became so activated on 100 mg/24 hours of L-5HTP that they had to be removed from the protocol. All 7 patients showed some activation of illness in terms of their underlying pathology or character traits, but in 4 of the 7, these particular reactions subsided quickly, and permitted increased dosage of L-5HTP.

Preliminary data suggest that with each increment of L-5HTP, there was an increment of agitation or an exaggeration of existing pathology. There then followed in some patients an improved clinical status with better integration of thinking and more social interaction. This kind of improvement was vividly reported by 3 patients' families, who were, of course, unaware of the timing of the medication changes.

These measurable clinical changes are striking, considering that such low doses of L-5HTP were used. We found earlier that without haloperidol, activation of symptoms occurred only when doses of L-5HTP of 2 to 3 grams per 24 hours were reached. Tolerance to some side effects of L-5HTP developed in the patients during both studies. Transient parkinsonian side effects occurred in this study, whereas they did not at the much higher levels of 5HTP given in absence of haloperidol. It is clear that haloperidol in some way sensitized the central nervous system to exogenous L-5HTP.

B. <u>Sleep Studies</u>: Previously we found that chronic schizophrenic patients had a decreased number of rapid eye movements during REM sleep (REM density) and an increased number during NREM sleep. This situation is similar to one seen after the administration of parachlorophenylalanine (PCPA). PCPA decreases serotonin by inhibiting tryptophan hydroxylase. 5HTP reverses the sleep effects of PCPA-treated patients.

The sleep of 18 male, chronically hospitalized, schizophrenic patients was studied during prolonged 5HTP administration. This was compared to sleep studies of various lengths during the month-long placebo periods and immediately preceding and following 5HTP ingestion. During active drug administration, the peripheral decarboxylase inhibitor, MK-486, was also given. Seven of the 18 patients were studied at intermediate doses, 11 at high doses, and 7 during withdrawal from 5HTP.

Effect of 5HTP Administration and Withdrawal on Mean Sleep Parameters

	P_1	5HTP (3600-5500mg)	P_1	5HTP (5600-6000mg)	P_1	Withdrawal
No. Subjects		7		11		7
Total Sleep	318	274	335	273***	297	213
Stage II	223	209	219	18*	190	195**
Delta	6	0.04**	19	6***	28	11**
REM Latency	71	192	70	175***	91	19*
REM Time	78	52	86	69***	71	77
REM Density (Index)	1.4	1.6	1.5	1.6	1.5	1.7
REM %	23.2	19.4	24.3	25.2	21.9	36.2**

P_1 - sleep during the month placebo period immediately preceding drug
Withdrawal - sleep during the first week following last drug administration
*p<.05 (Wilcoxin matched-paired signed rank test)
**p<.02
***p<.01
Values are in minutes/night except for REM % and REM Density

At low dosages of 5HTP (<2000 mg) there was a significant increase in REM Latency (190 vs. 65), but no other changes in sleep. Total REM Sleep and Delta were significantly reduced on intermediate dosages (3500-5500 mg/day) and high dosages (4500-6000 gm/day). Total Sleep time and Stage II were also significantly reduced on high dosages. Patients were agitated and sleep was poor during the first week of withdrawal; however, there was a significant increase in REM % and a decrease in REM Latency. During the second week of 5HTP withdrawal, all sleep measurements returned to baseline.

In addition, at the high dosages, the number of REM periods decreased compared to placebo (2.1 vs. 3.7, p<.01). Although the length of the first REM period was increased on high 5HTP dosages (43 vs. 18 min, p<.02), the time from onset of the first REM period to the second was unaltered.

The interpretation of the effects of 5HTP on sleep are complicated by such factors as dose, tolerance, and patient's behavioral response. Contrary to the hypothesis relating serotonin to sleep maintenance, total sleep decreased on 5HTP and contrary to the phasic-event suppression hypothesis, the REM density was not affected; however, REM density may not be the appropriate measurement of PGO spike density.

C. DMT

N,N-Dimethyltryptamine (DMT) is a short-acting hallucinogen and our laboratory has determined critera by which it and other agents could be tested as the possible endogenous producer of schizophrenia. Following an intramuscular injection of 0.7 mg/kg of DMT to normal subjects who had previously used DMT, the blood levels increase in pulse rates, increase in blood pressure, increase in pupillary diameter, and changes on a brief questionnaire followed a similar time course rising to a peak within 12 minutes and gradually decreasing until effects disappeared within 70 minutes.

An agent responsible for chronic schizophrenia would not render the subject tolerant to its effects. We attempted to see if tolerance would develop to repeated IM injections. No tolerance developed to DMT's effects during 5 consecutive DMT days in four subjects to whom a standardized 0.7 mg/kg DMT injection was given twice a day.

There was no difference in the blood concentration of DMT between normals, acute or chronic schizophrenics using a combined gas liquid mass spectrometric method.

We have developed a reliable, consistent animal behavior assay for DMT which allows us to study the interactions between DMT, the neuroleptics and drugs which influence biogenic amines. The paradigm uses a shuttlebox escape/avoidance test during different phases of performance training (e.g., acquisition of continual avoidance response [CAR] performance on an on-going, well-established CAR).

DMT in doses ranging from 0.5 mg to 4 mg/kg and 5-methoxy-N,N-Dimethyltryptamine (5-MeO-DMT) in doses ranging from 0.25 to 2 mg/kg do not share excitatory effects with LSD and Mescaline: (1) on acquisition of shuttlebox avoidance; and (2) on experienced poor shuttlebox performers, in Long-Evans hooded rats. If anything, DMT and 5-MeO-DMT show a suggestion of inhibition in these situations.

DMT, 0.5-4 mg/kg, shares inhibitory effects with LSD and Mescaline on good shuttlebox performers in Fisher 344's and hooded rats.

DMT, 8 to 16 mg/kg, and 5-MeO-DMT, 4 to 16 mg/kg produce extremely potent behavioral effects with rapid onset in hooded rats. These effects include: (1) forelimb tremors; (2) hyperthermia and body shivering; (3) clonic convulsions; (4) gait and postural dysfunction; and (5) aggressivity.

Parachlorophenylalanine (PCPA) which depletes brain 5HT by inhibiting tryptophan hydroxylase at a dose which is alone without behavioral effect, potentiates both excitatory effects of mescaline. A single injection of 150 mg/kg PCPA produced significant depletion in both serotonin (40%) and norepinephrine (25%); PCPA plus Mescaline produced the same amount of depletion as PCPA in both cases and there were no effects on brain dopamine.

III. Physostigmine

It has long been known that the neuroleptic porperties of the commonly used anti-psychotic phenothiazines appear to co-vary with the cholinergic potential exerted by this series of compounds. In fact, some have suggested that the beneficial effect of phenothiazines is directly related to their potential for generating what are taken to be central cholinergic side effects. We are attempting to induce central cholinergic activity by inhibiting the activity of cholinesterase and thereby clarify to what extent the symptoms of schizophrenia might be related to central cholinergic function.

Our original findings in a completed non-blind study with physostigmine were that remission could be induced in chronic schizophrenics for a brief period (about 2 days) by giving physostigmine orally in divided doses four times a day. The onset of remission was about 2 days after beginning the medication and it lasted about 1 or 2 days before the patients became refractory (2 patients). In a further five patients, the physostigmine was given as a single daily dose at noon. In these patients, remission appeared in 7 to 14 days and lasted a further 7 to 21 days before relapse occurred. We then gave the physostigmine to 6 patients for one week on a t.i.d. divided schedule. Anecdotal evidence from nursing staff suggested that there had been significant reduction in psychopathology in 4 patients, but the formal rating scales employed did not reflect any significant change. A further 5 patients received b.i.d. administration of physostigmine and two of these were drug-free during the experimental period. None of these five patients showed significant clinical change.

IV. Pineal Extract

Dr. Altschule reported in 1957 that injections of an aqueous extract of bovine pineal substance exerted a beneficial effect in chronic schizophrenia. A subsequent blind study on eight elderly, extremely chronic lobotomized schizophrenic women failed to show major therapeutic potential of the extract. We are testing the extract on a less chronically ill population to see if there might be any merit to Altschule's earlier observations.

When the patients are clinically stabile they are started blind on either a course of placebo or pineal extract. After 4-6 weeks on this medication, there is a crossover to the type material not already received. If the findings warrant, there is another shift of medication.

From the previous study done here using younger patients, it appears that there is a statistically significant but generally slight beneficial effect exerted by the extract on some patients. Only one patient can be said to have achieved a major remission associated with extract treatment. This finding has been confirmed in numerous crossover experiments.

A further three patients have been tried on pineal extract. Of the three one responded with significant clinical improvement. Six months after completing the protocol, this patient was given a second trial of pineal extract vs. placebo injections and again showed significant clinical improvement coincident with extract administration.

The most pronounced responder had been tried on enteric coated pineal tablets. Although an open study, the results were sufficiently encouraging to justify having more of these tablets made for further clinical trials, again in selected patients. The advantage of administering the pineal substance in this form is that dosage can be increased. The earlier studies with intramuscular preparations was handicapped by the inherent volume limitations imposed by that route of administration.

It has been confirmed in two laboratories that the extract contains inhibitory activity against the DMT-forming enzyme, indoleethylamine-N-methyltransferase. In collaboration with other workers, the fraction responsible for the inhibitory activity is being isolated. We plan to give to selected patients, a preparation with a theoretical increase of potency of a factor of 10.

V. Lithium Carbonate With Other Neuroleptic Drugs

There is good documentation in the literature indicating that chlorpromazine is superior to lithium in acute schizophrenic illness. The superiority of chlorpromazine in controlling extreme mania also appears to be established. Publications bearing on the use of lithium in schizo-affective illness are less unanimous in their conclusions. All of the studies so far reported do not indicate a superiority for the use of lithium in over-chlorpromazine in patients diagnosed as schizo-affective. There are no studies of the merits of using both medicatons simultaneously. It is our personal experience that many clinicians are using lithium carbonate in combination with major tranquilizers in the treatment of schizophrenic and schizo-affective patients, despite the fact that there are no controlledexperiments in the literature bearing on the efficacy of this combination.

Two patients, one bearing a diagnosis of chronic undifferentiated schizophrenia and the other a diagnosis of schizo-affective schizophrenia, manic type, had been stabilized on haloperidol, 36 mg a day, and sufficient lithium carbonate to give a plasma level of 0.8 - 1.0 mEq/l. After several months on this regimen, placebo was substituted for lithium for a four-week period, at the end of which lithium carbonate was reintroduced. Neither the patients nor the clinical nursing staff completing the ratings was aware of the changes in medication.

Analysis of the ratings revealed that there was overall exacerbation of both patients' illnesses. Significant elevations of symptom ratings were found for both patients in hyperactivity, anxiety, social incompetence, and uncooperativeness. Bizarre behavior and paranoid distrust also showed significant worsening with placebo substitution. All of these items reverted to their pre-placebo levels after lithium was reintroduced. Individual questions relating to the specific changes indicating that lithium had a beneficial effect on these symptoms also.

VI. Formation of Tryptolines (Tetrahydro-β-Carbolines) By Human Brain and Platelets

We have examined the products formed from tryptamine, N-methyltryptamine, and 5-hydroxytryptamine by an enzymatic preparation from either human brain or platelets, using 5-MTHF as a cofactor. In each case, we have demonstrated by TLC, co-crystallation, and gas chromatrography/mass spectrometry that the reaction involves the addition of a carbon unit to the side-chain nitrogen, with subsequent cyclization to yield a tricyclic, tryptoline derivative. These compounds have been found in plants, but have not previously been associated with mammallian systems. For both enzymatic preparations, the optimal pH is 6.5 and phosphate buffers of increasing strength enhance the reaction. For the brain enzyme, methylcobalamine, flavin adenine dinucleotide, and ascorbic acid each enhance the reaction, while cupric ion inhibits it. We have also done preliminary investigations on platelet enzyme activities in normal volunteers. We found marked diurnal changes and wide variability among individuals; however, male enzymatic activities were significantly lower than those for females. These studies demonstrate that 5-MTHF does not act as a methyl donor, as previously believed.

VII. Sleep

The sleep of 13 drug-free chronic male schizophrenics was studied during a one-month trial on chlorpromazine (CPZ) and compared with one-month placebo periods. Recordings were made only after subjects had been on the drug or placebo at least 3 weeks. Sleep Latency and awake time was significantly less on CPZ while Stage II, delta sleep, delta %, non-REM sleep, REM activity, and REM density were significantly increased. There were no significant changes in REM latency, REM time, REM %, Stage II %, and non-REM %.

We investigated whether schizophrenics have a normal REM rebound following REM deprivation. In addition, since Cartwright, et al. previously suggested that "good REM compensators" tend to be field independent, we related a measure of field independence (the portable rod and frame test) to degree of compensation.

Eight actively ill schizophrenic patients (E) (5F, 3M, mean age = 25) and 8 non-psychotic control patients (C) (5F, 3M, mean age = 26) were partially REM deprived by the awakening method for two nights. Sleep on each of 5 Recovery nights (R_{1-5}) was compared with that of Baseline Sleep. All patients were unmedicated except for a single control patient who received chlorpromazine.

Mean Baseline Sleep Patterns (min) were Similar in E and C Patient Groups:

	Total Sleep	REM Sleep	REM Latency	REM %	Stage III+IV
E	378	93	72	25.0	37
C	390	99	78	25.5	32

Mean loss of REM was 71.8% for E and 72.8% for C. Controls had to be awakened significantly more frequently than E (35 awakenings compared with 28, $p<.05$).

On R_1 mean change in REM compared with Baseline was +38 min for C and -2 min for E ($p<.01$); on R_2 it was +17 for C and -10 for E ($p<.05$). Mean change in REM during all Five Recovery nights was +14.5 min for C and +1 for E ($p<.05$).

A two-way multivariate analysis of variance--one factor being patient groups, the other being a repeated measure, linear trend analysis--revealed that C had significantly different sleep patterns than did E during Recovery ($p<.03$, $F = 2.45$). The major source of difference was in REM sleep recovery ($p<.006$, $F = 8.06$) but, suprisingly, Stage III+IV was also a significant contributor ($p<.02$, $F = 6.13$). E tended to have elevated Stage III+IV on the first two Recovery nights and low and normal amounts on the last two except on the last Recovery night when Stage III+IV tended to be elevated, though not significantly.

REM rebounds during Recovery were correlated with increased Total Sleep ($r = .52$, $p<.01$). Nevertheless, after removing the effect of change in Total Sleep during Recovery by analysis of co-variance, the controls still had the normal pattern of REM rebound and the actively ill schizophrenic patients did not, i.e., the two groups differed in rate of REM decline over the 5 Recovery nights ($p<.03$).

Amoung 4 E and 4 C patients tested, there was a significant correlation between degree of REM rebound and field independence ($p<.05$, rho = .79). Mean change in REM during Recovery was 27 min for 3 field independent patients and -1.5 min among 5 field dependent subjects ($p = .036$, Mann-Whitney U-test).

These results suggest that actively ill schizophrenics differ from other psychiatric patients in failing to have a normal REM rebound. This difference was not attributable to differences in age, sex, baseline sleep, anxiety, or change in Total Sleep time during Recovery. REM compensation may also be correlated with field independence, though further research needs to be done to substantiate this finding before any conclusions may be drawn.

VIII. Activity

An F.M. telemetry package has been developed with the assistance of the NIMH Technical Development Unit. This package consists of wrist transmitters that are activated by the patient's body motion. The F.M. signal is received through an anatomical switching system and fed through amplifiers and pre-amplifiers to a triggered printer that pulse prints every 15 minutes around the clock.

The system will be used to determine longitudinal as well as any diagnostic differences based on activity.

IX. Evoked Potentials

We studied the evoked potentials of 21 schizophrenics and 21 controls. They were matched for age and exposed to a 10-minute sequence of frequent and infrequent auditory stimuli. The amplitude of P_3, a response component of the evoked responses to infrequent stimuli, was much larger in the control group ($p < .0003$). Using a P_3 amplitude of 3.20 μV in the first 2.5 minutes as a dividing point, only 7 of the 42 subjects were misclassified. This amplitude had a significant correlation of 0.48 with the patient's age at first hospitalization. The group P_2 amplitude to frequent stimuli was also much larger in the control group ($p < .003$). This amplitude has a significant correlation of -.41 with medication dosage in terms of equivalent amounts of chlorpromazine. Behavioral scales failed to correlate significantly with evoked response measures. Evoked response latencies did not distinguish the two groups.

X. Brain Dopamine β-Hydroxylase

Stein and Wise (1971) postulated that there might be a deficit in dopamine-β-hydroxylase (DBH), the enzyme that converts dopamine to norepinephrine, in schizophrenic patients.

Wise, Baden and Stein (1974) tested their hypothesis by collecting the brains of 18 chronic schizophrenics dying in a state hospital and 12 persons without a history of psychiatric illness dying suddenly of heart attacks or accidents. The schizophrenics had decreased DBH activity ranging from 49 in the hippocampus, 58 in the diencephalon and 70 percent in pons-medulla. All these differences were statistically significant at $p < .05$. Because of these dramatic differences in the predicted direction, Wise, et al. (in press) made a number of attempts to control for artifacts. After considering all these sources of artifacts, the large differences between schizophrenic and normal DBH activity remained.

We attempted to replicate their study. Specimens of autopsied brains from five chronic schizophrenic patients were obtained with the aid of the neuropathologist at Saint Elizabeths Hospital. Brain specimens from four chronic schizophrenics and nine controls were obtained by a similar arrangement with the D.C. Medical Examiners Office. Information about the subjects was obtained by interviews with family members, and hospital and police records. The control brains were obtained from persons without evidence of a psychiatric history, although one was from an individual with a police record and two were from heavy drinkers. The schizophrenics (7 males; 2 females) had a mean age of 49.2 ± 6.3. Four died suddenly after traumatic suicides (in our experience suicide is common amongst chronic schizophrenics), 3 from cardiac arrests, 1 from pulmonary aspiration, and 1 suddenly from pulmonary edema. The controls (all male) had a mean age of 42.3 ± 4.5. Six died suddenly of trauma and 3 from cardiac arrests.

The periaqueductal pons-mesencephalon, hypothalamus and hippocampus were dissected out at autopsy and immediately placed on dry ice and subsequently stored at -80°C for up to one year (Wise, et al., 1974) found DBH activity stable for one year at -15°C. There was no difference in mean storage time for the schizophrenics and controls. All DBH assays were performed by a staff member unaware of whether the samples were from schizophrenics or controls.

There was no significant difference in DBH activity in any area between the two groups. While the differences were not statistically different, DBH activity mean for the schizophrenic groups ranged between 77 and 89 percent of controls. Although 7 of 9 of our patients were taking phenothiazines at the time of death, Wise, et al. (1974) indicate that this is probably not a cause of their DBH differences. Rats who had been given chlorpromazine (20 mg/kg 24 hour) for 12 weeks had a small increase in DBH activity. Although the patients in our study were taking a number of non-neuroleptic drugs, there were significant (p 0.05) negative correlations between the daily dosage of chlorpromazine or chlorpromazine equivalent and the DBH activity in the hypothalamus (r = -.60) and pons (r = -.65). This could mean that in the brains of schizophrenics, neuroleptics do decrease DBH activity, or possibly that there is a negative correlation between clinical pathology (as determined by the need for higher dosages) and DBH activity.

Wise, et al. (1974) also attempted to determine the effects of postmortem intervals on brain DBH activity (after a person dies, it may take several hours for that person to reach the morgue). Simulating this situation rats that were killed and allowed to remain three hours at room temperature prior to assay had DBH activity reduced by 27%. In a similar experiment performed in our laboratory over a six-hour period, there was 15% decrease in activity. Since Wise, et al. (1974) human brain postmortem intervals were "several hours" and ours a mean of 4.2 for the controls and 3.0 hours for the schizophrenics, this does not seem to be an important factor, except possibly for one control who was not brought to the morgue for 27 hours. Since he had the lowest DBH activity of any of the subjects, the DBH activities were examined for the controls with and without this subject's values. The exclusion of this value did not change the failure to reach statistical significance. Two subjects with death-to-morgue times of 7 and 11 hours had DBH activities about their group means. One subject with 3.5 hour time lag was low. All other subjects had intervals of about 1 hour.

Wise, et al. (1974) also compared the effects on brain DBH activity of the time from which the subject reached the morgue to the time of autopsy. They did this by storage of rat brains at 4°C for up to 3 days and found a decrease in DBH activity of 18%. Their subjects' brains, however, ranged from 1 day to 8 days at this temperature. Because of this, they matched time intervals for controls and schizophrenics and still found the DBH activity of the schizophrenics lower. Our controls were in the morgue for a mean of 9.7 ± 1.9 hours, while the patients were there for 35.6 ± 7.9 hours, which is statistically significant ($t = 2.73$ $p<.02$). Furthermore, there are significant negative correlations between time in the morgue to autopsy and DBH activity in the hippocampus ($r = -.53$ $p<.05$) and hypothalamus ($r = -.49$ $p<.05$) while that for the pons ($r = -.46$) was not significant. This suggests that the uneven distribution between the two groups in morgue time may be responsible for the small non-significant differences in DBH activity in our samples. Since the Wise, Baden and Stein brains came from two sources, it is possible some of their group differences may be due to different storage techniques.

XI. Dopamine Sensitive Adenylyl Cyclase

Striatal adenylyl cyclase activity from autopsied human brain is selectively stimulated by low concentrations of dopamine. Under the experimental conditions used, dopamine was about three times more potent than norepinephrine. Histamine and serotonin were ineffective. This stimulation by dopamine was competitively inhibited by haloperidol. There was no difference between the basal adenylyl cyclase activity or its activation after dopamine stimulation between nine of the autopsied brains (head of caudate) of the control subjects without a psychiatric history and seven patients with chronic schizophrenia.

XII. Platelet Monoamine Oxidase

Since monoamine oxidase (MAO) is a crucial enzyme in the metabolism of biogenic amines, our initial finding that MAO was low in the platelets of schizophrenics started us (together with Dr. Dennis Murphy) on an extensive exploration to determine which patients had the deficit, whether the deficit was in some way a secondary process to being schizophrenic, the chemical nature of the deficit, and whether the deficit was present elsewhere in the body.

A. MAO Assay in Blood Platelets

Venous blood was collected in Becton-Dickinson Co. Vacutainer tubes containing ACD (acid-citrate-dextrose), NIH formula A, the platelets separated and stored. MAO activity was determined using tryptamine-2-^{14}C HCl (8×10^{-5}m, 8.9mCi/mM) as substrate and is expressed as nM of tryptamine converted per mg of platelet protein. The product is indoleacetaldehyde, whose formation is linear with time and enzyme concentration. Tyramine and benzylamine were also used as substrates for a limited number of subjects.

B. Reliability of Assay

Because the studies require considerable assay reliability, we have endeavored to determine what variability to expect with our method. It is clear after using and improving upon the assay during the last four years that the variation between separate runs can be moderately high and that each run must contain its own controls. Our means for normal controls over that period of time have run from 6.4 to 5.2, with lower values occurring during the last year. On the same run, however, the average sample variation -- $\bar{X}$ of $\frac{(a - b)}{(a + b)}$ x 100% for the same individual having blood drawn twice during a day is ±9 percent while that for the same individual drawn a week apart is ±17 percent.

C. Subjects

The normal bloods were drawn from hospital personnel and normal volunteers at both the Clinical Center in Bethesda and the William A. White Building (WAW). The bloods from the acute schizophrenics largely came from a research ward at the Clinical Center while those from the chronic schizophrenic patients came from special research wards at the WAW Building.

D. Age and Sex

In our samples, males and females between the age range of 18 to 50 are not statistically different. Females under 20 and over 50 years may have higher platelet MAO activity than males.

E. Drugs

Although early experiments with chlorpromazine in intact systems indicated that chlorpromazine had some effects on amine degradation, this seemed to be due to poor amine accessibility to the enzyme because of alteration in the cell membrane. Tricyclic drugs like impramine, and phenothiazines like chlorpromazine, have effects on MAO activity in homogenized systems only in very very high concentrations. To test in vivo activity in the presence of chlorpromazine, 17 chronic schizophrenics on our research wards were taken off all drugs for at least one month and their platelets sampled for MAO activity. The same patients were placed on chlorpromazine (400 mg/24 hr) for three weeks and again their platelets were sampled. The mean ± s.e.m. for the drug-free patients was 2.8 ± 0.60 while that for the patients on chlorpromazine was 2.8 ± 0.43. Nevertheless, for reasons that are not clear (perhaps multiple batches) the average sample variation across individuals from the first to the second assay was high (45%). Six depressed patients were studied prior to and during treatment (18 to 76 days) with thioridazine (100 to 600 mg/24 hr). The means were 5.24 ± 0.69 and 5.47 ± 0.82 respectively.

F. Hormones

Samples were collected three times a week for menstrual cycle studies. There were small (23%) peak to troug variations in activity in the majority of women. The peak MAO activity occurred during the preovulatory interval and the nadir occurred five to 11 days later. A small number of patients taking prednisone have been seen and have normal MAO activities.

G. Chronic Schizophrenics

To date we have studied platelet MAO activity in 68 chronic schizophrenic patients. Their mean MAO activity was 2.86 ± 0.25 while the values for 181 normals (ages 18-40) were 5.24 ± 0.20. This difference, using a two-tailed "t" test, is significant at p<.001. The mean for the 53 male chronic schizophrenics was 2.91 ± 0.30 while that for 79 normal males was 5.12 ± 0.32 (p<.001). The mean for the 15 female chronic schizophrenics was 2.72 ± 0.49 while that for 102 normals was 5.34 ± 0.26 (p<.001). To date, we have not been able to find systematic differences related to length of illness or hospitalization. By our definition, the chronic schizophrenic patients have a minimum hospitalization period of at least one year and have been ill for at least two years. Furthermore, there are no clear differences in platelet MAO activity between schizophrenic subtypes.

H. Acute vs. Chronic Schizophrenics

To determine whether acute schizophrenics have a reduction in platelet MAO as did the chronic schizophrenics, platelet MAO's of 27 acute schizophrenics free from all drugs for at least two weeks were studied. These patients were housed on a special NIMH research ward in Bethesda, supervised by Dr. William Carpenter. The acute schizophrenics (ages 16-30) had a mean platelet MAO activity of 5.48 ± 0.44 which was no different from that for 181 age-matched normals (5.24 ± 0.70). The 11 male acute patients had a mean of 4.56 ± 0.45 which was no different from that for 79 normal males (5.12 0.30). The 16 female acute schizophrenics had a mean of 6.11 ± 0.64 which was no different from that of 102 normal females (5.34 ± 0.27).

I. Specificity with Regard to Other Illness

A usual strategy in psychiatric research once a given effect is established is one patient group is to look at other diagnostic groups for the same alteration. Since the various diagnostic classifications are thought to represent different entities, a defect in one should not be seen in the other. The depressive illnesses are the group we most diligently contrasted with the schizophrenias.

Forty-three unipolar depressed patients were found to have platelet MAO activity that was no different from our controls while 34 bipolar I depressed patients had reduced activity (3.6 ± .32 p<.001). The bipolar patients had a negative skew which was not as large as that of the chronic schizophrenics. If two units of MAO are used as a point of cut-off, a point under which 40 percent (X^2 = 33.46, df = 1; p>0.001) of the chronic schizophrenic fit we find seven of 34 bipolar patients. This is about 20 percent which is not significantly different (X^2 = 2.69, df = 1; p>0.1) than that for controls. There was no significant difference (X^2 = 2.47, df = 1; p>0.1) between the chronic schizophrenics and the bipolar I patients. Thus even though the bipolar I patients using the arbitrary cut-off of two MAO units have a mean MAO which is low, it is not yet clear whether they represent a separate group. It is possible therefore that the factors which lower platelet MAO in the chronic schizophrenic and bipolar patients are different.

J. Twins Discordant for Schizophrenia

To exlude the possibility that the low platelet MAO activity seen in the chronic schizophrenics was caused by nongenetic factors as opposed to genetic ones, we studied monozygotic twins discordant for schizophrenia. If the low platelet MAO activity is due to some aspect of being schizophrenic, low platelet MAO should only be present in the schizophrenic twin. Thirteen schizophrenic index twins, all of whom had been hospitalized at least once for schizophrenia and had been extensively studied by Dr. William Pollin and his associates, were examined along with their nonschizophrenic co-twins. At the time of the study, one patient resided within a hospital while five were in remission. Four of the patients had had acute forms of schizophrenia and six patients were not receiving any antipsychotic medication. The nonschizophrenic co-twins had never been hospitalized for a behavioral disorder and were functioning well within their families and communities, except for one individual with boderline psychosocial adjustment.

Only two twin pairs were living in the same household and nine of the co-twins were living in different cities. It was, therefore, necessary to obtain and prepare the blood samples at various facilities throughout the country. Because of this, normal control samples were obtained at the same time as those from the twins. They were coded and shipped to the laboratory. All samples were batched together before assay. (In all studies samples are run in a manner so that their origins are unknown to all investigators until the final calculations are made.)

The MAO activity of the 23 normal controls was the same as that obtained for previous controls (6.4 ± .562 s.e.m.). The schizophrenic twins (3.9 ±.638 s.e.m., p<.005) and nonschizophrenic twins (4.7 ± .804 s.e.m., p<.05) were significantly lower than the normals, but there was no difference between the twin groups. There was a significant Pearson correlation (r = .67, p<.01) between the MAO activities in the schizophrenic and nonschizophrenic twins.

K. Family Studies

In order to study further the relationship of low platelet MAO to schizophrenia the blood of first degree relatives of index schizophrenics (N=10) was collected. Using schizophrenic indexes (N=7) with low MAO (mean

1.99) the mean MAO activity for the first degree relatives (N=27) was 3.22. The mean activity for first degree relatives (N=15) of patients with high MAO activity (N=3, mean 5.55) was 5.19. The Pearson correlation between indexes (N=12 including two psychologically normal families) and first degree relatives (N=44) was 0.73.

L. Physical-Chemical Studies

To date we have found no physical differences between the low and normal platelet MAO. The Km's from six schizophrenic patients (all below 3.1 units) and from eight normals were nearly identical (4.1×10^{-5} and 4.3×10^{-5}M). The heat inactivation curves for both groups showed reductions in activity at 50°C which were not different for the two groups. The platelet MAO is not easily solubilized, which has, to date, prevented reliable electrophoretic studies. Dialysis of platelet sonicates from 10 schizophrenic patients and seven controls did not reveal any post-dialysis differences in activity between schizophrenic patients and controls.

M. Relationship of Platelet MAO to Brain MAO

One approach to this problem has come from the finding that selective inhibition of MAO can be used to identify multiple forms of MAO. Clorgyline was the first MAO inhibitor employed in this manner. It was found that tissue homogenates pretreated with increasing concentrations of clorgyline produced stepwise inhibition to the substrate tyramine, suggesting the presence of an enzyme sensitive to the inhibitor and one relatively resistent to it.

The preferred substrates for the Type A MAO are norepinephrine, serotonin, and normetanephrine, while the Type B they are benzylamine and B-phenylamine. Dopamine, tyramine and tryptamine are common substrates. Clorgyline, Lilly 51641, and harmaline are specific inhibitors of Type A while deprenyl inhibits Type B. Most of the other MAO inhibitors used in clinical medicine, however, are nonspecific. Platelet MAO, forming a single band on electrophoresis, appears to be one enzyme and is more like the Type B enzyme than Type A, but a full comparison has not yet been made.

N. MAO in the Brain and Liver of Schizophrenic Patients

We collected 15 regions of autopsied brain from nine chronic schizophrenics and nine persons without history of psychiatric illness. Using tryptamine as a substrate, there was no difference in mean MAO activity in any region examined with Dr. Norton Neff. The brains were subsequently examined using serotonin and clorgyline to test for MAO A and B-phenylethylamine and deprenyl for MAO B. Again, there were no differences in the mean MAO activity between the schizophrenics and controls.

O. Function

To determine whether or not the low platelet MAO activity might have a functional significance, platelet-rich plasma was obtained from 20 normal controls (age 29.6 ± 1.1) and 16 chronic schizophrenic patients (27 ± 1.4). Since plasma serotonin is almost entirely contained in the platelet the values are expressed in platelet units (ng/10^8 platelets). The platelet counts for the normals and schizophrenics were the same. When the patients had been off phenothiazines (N=12) for 30 days or longer the serotonin concentration was higher ($p<0.01$) in the schizophrenics (127 ± 12) than in the normals (80 ± 4), while when the patients were taking phenothiazines (N=12) their platelet serotonin concentration was normal (90 ± 9). The reason for the discrepancy between patients taking and not taking phenothiazines may be due to the latter's ability to block serotonin uptake into platelets.

XIII. Biogenic Amines, Their Precursor Amino Acids and Their Metabolites

The role of biogenic amines in mental illness may include amines other than serotonin and catecholamines. In the present state of our understanding, little information is available on these amines. To bridge this gap, we have undertaken the task to develop comprehensive and sensitive mass fragmentographic methods to measure almost all known biogenic amines, their amino acid precursors and their metabolites.

Our initial goal is to apply the method developed to measure the concentrations of the various amines and their derivatives in plasma, cerebrospinal fluid (CSF) and brain tissues. After establishing the normal ranges of these substances in biological materials, we hope to carry out several clinical and pharmacological studies in order to probe further the possible role of biogenic amines in mental illness.

The principal technique employed is mass fragemntography. To enhance the specificity of the method, selective gas chromatographic columns are used. These columns were chosen after extensive preliminary trials with various stationary phases and with different lengths of columns.

The biogenic amines, their amino acid precursors and their metabolites are partially separated and concentrated by either extraction into organic solvents or by thin layer or column chromatography. They are next dried down derivatized to their appropriate pentafluoropropionate or trifluoroacetate derivatives and then injected into the GC column.

To correct for variations in processing the samples, internal deuterated isomers of the compounds of interest are run through the whole procedure and then used to correct for any inconsistency.

The metabolites derived from tyramine, octopamine, dopamine and norepinephrine were extensively studied in the rat brain, lumbar and ventricular CSF.

In the rat brain, all the expected metabolites were found to be present in concentrations low enough to suggest their neuronal origin. Some of these metabolites were not reported before. Of particular interest, is the detection of vanilmandelic acid (VMA) in concentrations about 5% that of 3-methoxy-4-hydroxyphenylglycol (MHPG).

In the CSF, the concentrations of the acidic metabolites were found to be higher in the ventricular region than in the lumbar space.

The detection and quantification of the metabolites mentioned above will considerably aid our understanding on the role of tyramine and octopamine in the central nervous system (CNS). It will also enable us to design future clinical and pharmacological experiments to study the interaction between the above four amines in normals and mentally ill persons.

XIV. Measurement of Norepinephrine (NE) Turnover Rate in the CNS

The overall procedure is still under investigation. The following summarizes some of our exploratory findings on the way the human body handles H^3-NE and of the effect of debrisoquine on urine excretion of 3-methoxy-4-hydroxyphenylglycol (MHPG) excretion.

a) The time course of H^3-NE deaminated metabolites excretion after i.v. injection of 10 μci H^3-NE follows an exponential curve.

b) The amount of radioactivity detected in the urine 3 days after 10 μci H^3-NE is less than 5% of the total urine count after 10 hrs from the time of injection.

c) Single doses of 20 mg debrisoquine increased both the urinary output of MHPG and N^3-NE deaminated metabolites.

d) Nine hours following three repetitive doses of 10 mg debrisoquine 1 hr, DA and NE metabolites excretion started to show a definite trend towards declining.

Publications:

Wyatt, R. J. and Gillin, J. C.: Development of tolerance to and dependence on endogenous neurotransmitters. In Mandell, A. J.(Ed.): Neurobiological Mechanisms of Adaptation and Behavior. New York, Raven Press, 1975, pp. 47-59.

Garelis, E., Gillin, J. C., Wyatt, R. J., and Neff, N.: Elevated blood serotonin concentrations in chronic, unmedicated schizophrenics: a preliminary study. Am. J Psychiatr. 132:184-186, 1975.

Kaplan, J., Dawson, S., Vaughan, T., Green, R., and Wyatt, R. J.: Effects of prolonged chlorpromazine administration on the sleep of chronic schizophrenics. Arch Gen Psychiatr. 31: 62-66, 1974.

Gillin, J. C., Buchsbaum, M. S., Jacobs, L. S., Fram, D. H., Williams, R. B., Jr.,Vaughan, T. B., Mellon, E., Snyder, F. and Wyatt, R. J.: Partial REM sleep deprivation, schizophrenia and field articulation. Arch.Gen.Psychiatr. 30: 653-662, 1974.

Post, R. M., Gillin, J. C., Goodwin, F. K., Wyatt, R. J., Snyder, F.: The effect of orally administered cocaine on sleep of depressed patients. Psychopharmacologia 37: 59-66, 1974.

Mendelson, W., Guthrie, R. D., Guynn, R., Harris, R. L., and Wyatt, R. J.: Rapid eye movement (REM) sleep deprivation, stress and intermediary metabolism. J.Neurochem. 22: 1157-1159, 1974.

Frankel, D., Patten, B. and Gillin, J. C.: Restless legs syndrome: sleep EEG and neurological findings. JAMA 230: 1302-1303, 1974.

Gillin, J. C., Jacobs, L. S., Snyder, F. and Henkin, R. I.: Effects of ACTH on the sleep of normal subjects and patients with Addison's Disease. Neuroendocrinology 15: 21-31, 1974.

Gillin, J. C., Fram, D. H., Wyatt, R. J., Henkin, R. I., and Snyder, F.: L-histidine: failure to affect the sleep-waking cycle in man. Psychopharmacologia 40: 305-311, 1974.

Wyatt, R. J., Neff, N., Vaughan, T., Franz, J., and Omaya, A.: Ventricular fluid 5-HIAA concentrations during human sleep. In Costa, E., Gessa, G. L., and Sandler, M. (Eds.): Serotonin-New Vistas. New York, Raven Press, 1974, pp. 193-198.

Wyatt, R. J., Gillin, J. C., Kaplan, J., Stillman, R., Mandel, L. Ahn, H. S., VandenHeuval, W. J. A. and Walker, R. W.: N,N-dimethyltryptamine--a possible relationship to schizophrenia? In Costa, E., Gessa, G. L. and Sandler, M. (Eds.): Serotonin-New Vistas, New York, Raven Press, 1974, pp. 299-315.

Kaplan, J., Mandel, L. R., Stillman, R., Walker, R. W., VandenHeuval, W. J. A., Gillin, J. C. and Wyatt, R. J.: Blood and urine levels of N,N-dimethyltryptamine following administration of pscyhoactive dosages to human subjects. Psychopharmacologia 38: 239-245, 1974.

Barchas, J. D., Elliott, G. R., DoAmaral, H., O'Connor, S., Bowden, M., Brodie, H. K. H., Berger, P. A., Renson, J. and Wyatt, R. J.: Tryptolines: formation by a preparation from brain with 5-methyltetrahydrofolic by human platelets. Arch.Gen.Psychiatr. 31: 862-867, 1975.

Wyatt, R. J., Erdelyi, E., DoAmaral, J. R., Elliott, G. R., Renson, J., and Barchas, J. D.: Tryptoline formation by a preparation from brain with 5-methyltetrahydrofolic acid and tryptamine. Science 187: 853-855, 1975.

Wyatt, R. J., Schwartz, M. A., Erdelyi, E., and Barchas, J.: Dopamine-beta-hydroxylase activity in the brains of chronic schizophrenic patients. Science 187: 368-370, 1975.

Schwartz, M., Aikens, A. M. and Wyatt, R. J.: Monoamine oxidase activity in brains from schizophrenic and mentally normal individuals. Psychopharmacologia 38: 319-328, 1974.

Belmaker, R., Murphy, D., Wyatt, R. J. and Lorieux, D. L.: Human platelet monoamine oxidase changes during the menstural cycle. Arch.Gen.Psychiatr. 31: 537-541, 1974.

Murphy, D. L., Belmaker, R., and Wyatt, R. J.: Monoamine oxidase in schizophrenia. J.Psychiatr.Res. 2: 221-247, 1974.

Schwartz, M. A., Wyatt, R. J., Yang, H. and Neff, N.: Multiple forms of monoamine oxidase in brains: a comparison of enzymatic activity in mentally normal and chronic schizophrenic individuals. Arch.Gen.Psychiatr. 31:557-560, 1974.

Wyatt, R. J.: The multiple monoamine oxidases. In Usdin, E. (Ed.): Neuropsychopharmacology of Monoamines and Their Regulatory Enzymes. New York, Raven Press, 1974, pp. 1-2.

Belmaker, R., Beckman, H., Goodwin, F., Murphy, D., Pollin, W., Buchsbaum, M., Wyatt, R. J., Ciaranello, R., and Lamprecht, F.: Relationships between platelet and plasma monoamine oxidase, plasma dopamine-beta-hydroxylase and urinary 3-methoxy-4-hydroxy phenylglycol. Life Sciences 16: 273-280, 1975.

Murphy, D. L. and Wyatt, R. J.: Neurotransmitter-Related Enzymes in the Major Psychiatric Disorders: I. Catechol-O-Methyl transferase, monoamine oxidase in the affective disorders, and factors affecting some behaviorally-correlated enzyme activities. In Freedman, D. X. (Ed.): The Biology of the Major Psychoses: A Comparative Analysis. New York, Raven Press, (in press).

Wyatt, R. J., and Murphy, D. L.: Neurotransmitter-Related Enzymes in the Major Psychiatric Disorders: II. MAO and DBH in schizophrenia. In Freedman, D. X. (Ed.): The Biology of the Major Psychoses: A Comparative Analysis. Raven Press, (in press).

Wyatt, R. J.: Platelet Monoamine oxidase. Neuroscience Bulletin (in press).

Wyatt, R. J., and Gillin, J. C.: The transmethylation hypothesis--25 years later. Psychiatric Annals (in press).

Cohen, S. M., Nichols, A., Wyatt, R. J., and Pollin, W.: The administration of methionine to chronic schizophrenic patients: a review of ten studies. Biol.Psychiatr. 8: 209-225, 1974.

Gillin, J. C. and Wyatt, R. J.: Schizophrenia--Perchance a dream? In Pfeiffer, C. C. and Smythies, J. R. (Eds.) International Review of Neurobiology, New York Academic Press, 1975, 297-342.

Wyatt, R. J. and Gillin, J. C.: Biochemistry of Human Sleep. In Karacan, I. (Ed.): Pharmacology of Sleep. New York, Academic Press (in press).

Authors: Slaby, A. E. and Wyatt, R. J.: Dementia in the Presenium. Springfield, Illinois, Charles C. Thomas, 1974, 227 pp.

Guthrie, R. D. and Wyatt, R. J.: Biochemistry and schizophrenia III: a review of childhood psychosis. Schizophrenia Bulletin (in press).

Donnelly, E. F. and Murphy, D. L.: Primary affective disorder: Bender-Gestalt Sequence of placement as an indicator of impulse control. Perceptual and Motor Skills, 38: 1079-1082, 1974.

Donnelly, E. F., Murphy, D. L. and Scott, W. H.: Perception and Cognition in patients with bipolar and unipolar depressive disorders: A study in Rorschach Responding. Arch.Gen.Psychiatr. (in press).

Stoff, D. M., Mandel, I. J., Gorelick, D. A., Bridger, W. H.: Acute and Chronic effects of LSD and 3,4-Dimethoxyphenylethylamine on shuttlebox escape/avoidance in rats. Psychopharmacologia 36: 301-312, 1974.

Karoum, F. and Costa, E.: Excretion of norepinephrine and dopamine alcoholic metabolites after 6-hydroxydopamine. Biochem.Parmacol. 23: 533-538, 1974.

Karoum, F., Wyatt, R. J., Costa, E.: Estimation of the contribution of peripheral and central noradrenergic neurones to urinary 3-methoxy-4-hydroxyphenylglycol in the rat. Neuropharmacology 13: 165-176, 1974.

Bigelow, L. B.: Effects of aqueous pineal extract in chronic schizophrenia. Biol.Psychiatr. 8: 5- , 1974.

Bigelow, L. B.: Some effects of aqueous pineal extract administration on the symptoms of chronic schizophrenia. In Altschule, M.D.(Ed.) Frontiers of Pineal Physiology, Massachusetts Institute of Technology Press, 1975, 225-263.

Walls, P. D., Walls, L. H. and Langsley, D. G.: Psychiatric training and practice in the People's Republic of China. Am.J.Psychiatr. 132: 121-128, 1975.

Mendelson, W., Guthrie, R. D., Frederick, G., and Wyatt, R. J.: The "flowerpot technique" of rapid eye movement (REM) sleep deprivation. Pharmacology Biochem. and Behavior 2: 553-556, 1974.

Karoum, F., Gillin, J. C., McCullough, and Wyatt, R. J.: Vanillymandelic acid (VMA), Free and conjugated 3-methoxy-4-hydroxyphenylglycol (MHPG) in human ventricular fluid. Clin.Clim.Acta. (in press).

Karoum, F., Gillin, J. C., and Wyatt, R. J.: Mass fragmentographic determination of some acidic and alcoholic metabolites of biogenic amines in the rat brain. J Neurochem. (in press).

Woodrow, K. M.: Gilles de la Tourette's disease--a review. Am. J. Psychiatr. 131: 1000-1003, 1974.

Murphy, D. L. and Wyatt: R. J.: Platelet monoamine oxidase in schizophrenics. Nature (in press).

Karoum, F. Ruthven, C. R. J., and Sandler, M.: Urinary Phenolic acid and alcohol excretion in the newborn. Arch. of Disease in Childhood (in press).

Keyword Descriptors:

schizophrenia
serotonin
sleep
dopamine-beta-hydroxylas
monoamine oxidase
biogenic amines
hallucinogenic agents
neuroloptic drugs

Project No. Z01 MH 01336-04 SMRC
1. Division of Special Mental Health Research
2. Laboratory of Clinical Psychopharmacology
3. Saint Elizabeths Hospital

PHS-ADAMHA-NIMH
Individual Project Report
July 1, 1974 through June 30, 1975

Project Title: Longitudinal Studies of Schizophrenic Behavior

Previous Serial Number: M-SMR-C-S-2, 3

Principal Investigator: Thomas D. Reynolds, M.D.

Cooperating Units: William A. White Building - Ward 4

Man Years:

Total: 1.6
Professional: .6
Other: 1.0

Project Description:

Objectives:

To obtain a quantitative description of behavior which permits empirical construction of predictive models. It is hoped that such models can be used as the units of an input-output theory of behavior, with particular reference to the problem of behavioral stability.

Methods Employed:

Behavioral notes are made 30 times daily on each of 14 chronic patients (12 schizophrenics, 2 organics for comparison purposes) on Ward 4 of the William A. White Service of Saint Elizabeths Hospital. The unit datum is a percentage of daily (or weekly) check-times positive for a given behavior (e.g., pacing, finger movement, talking, etc.). The resulting time-series is examined in a variety of ways for evidence of non-random components. The models developed from the data are used to predict into new data, and progressively refined. When a model has been shown to be consistently superior to others, it is regarded as a better or more valid representation of the process being studied.

Major Findings:

Work previously reported involved a variety of successful predictors for the time-series studied, but no uniform computational approach has been successful for all of the time-series. It became desirable, therefore, to develop an algorithm which would compete successfully with all previous individual predictors, so that each time-series could be meaningfully compared to another, for the purpose of stronger statements about comparisons across patient type. An additional stimulus to this arose from the fact that a single computer simulation experiment, involving differential equations rather than time-series analysis, suggested a characteristic lag time in the data from excitatory input to output response. This suggested the working hypothesis that in some schizophrenia, such lag times might be characteristic, and the data suggested that the lag time was shortened by chlorpromazine. To explore these ideas, it seemed necessary to handle more time-series than could be dealt with by this very laborious method. Accordingly, an algorithm was sought which was not only uniformly applicable to the different time-series, but which would display in a reliable way any lag time present in the data, so that once again meaningful comparisons could be made, and the effect of psychotropic drugs examined. Most of the work to date this year is concerned about developing such algorithm. Its form can be stated as follows: One forms a predictor into, say, a given week's rate for some piece of behavior, constructed by any three previous weekly rates, up to a lag of 13 weeks, the lags being determined by iterative computation to best fit. A polynomial expression up to quadratic terms, is constructed from these three values, which the polynomial terms weighted in such a way as to guarantee an asymptotic expression. Gaussian weights have been most useful here. The resulting expression is relatively straightforward, and its parameters can be determined by mixed normal equations and iterative computation. After much trial and error, it has been established that this approach is better or statistically equivalent in power to all previous modeling techniques. It will be applied to data subsequent to the 100 weeks used up in modeling. It cannot be said at this point whether the model will be verified by further predictive trials.

Data collection has been refined somewhat; not in basic principle, but by more strict definition of check times, and more consistent conditions during the observation period. This is for the purpose of obtaining more reliable daily rates, for daily rates fluctuate in highly suggestive ways, which for some patients at least, appear more germane to their homeostatic difficulties than the slower weekly rates which up to now have only been reliable estimates. The approach described above will be applied to sequences of daily rates, under different conditions of drug administration. General strategy will be to obtain optimal drug dosages empirically with the entire patient group, in some cases including the use of tricyclic antidepressants. After a period of stability sufficient to do the later computational studies, the various drugs used will be removed one at a time for a comparable period, or reduced by an appreciable amount, in order to estimate the type of effect on the parameters of the model. It is hoped thereby to either verify or refute the ideas presented above about lag times and drug response, and to seek to refine a method which can be applied extensively to the different classes of patients in a fairly efficient fashion.

Significance to Bio-Medical Research and the Program of the Institute:

While the basic purpose of the study continues to be the ultimate development of input-output modeling of human behavior in specific environments, with particular reference to a study of disturbances of regulation in the major psychoses, it would appear that the overall methodology may be applicable to the study of response to psychotropic drugs, and perhaps yield some clues as to their mode of action in functional as opposed to biochemical terms.

Proposed Course:

The course for the next few years is fully determined by the above remarks. With the recent shift in data collection methods, we would expect to proceed in an uniform fashion over an extended period of time, in order to seek reliable modeling data. Duration cannot be well estimated, because we are going to be focusing on daily rates, which up to now have not been carefully studied.

This project includes a separate project entitled "Drug Treatment of Labile Schizophrenia" included in last year's report, which now should be considered fully unified with the longitudinal studies project.

Keyword Descriptors:

predictive models
input-output theory
time-series
algorithm
schizophrenia

Project No. Z01 MH 01337-04 SMRC
1. Division of Special Mental Health Research
2. Laboratory of Clinical Psychopharmacology
3. Saint Elizabeths Hospital

PHS-ADAMHA-NIMH
Individual Project Reports
July 1, 1974 through June 30, 1975

Project Title: Studies of Drugs of Abuse

Previous Serial Number: M-SMRC-C-P-17, 18, 19

Principal Investigators: Richard Jed Wyatt, M.D., Richard Stillman, M.D. and J. Christian Gillin, M.D.

Other Investigators: James Eich, B.A. and Herbert Weingartner, Ph.D.

Cooperating Units: National Institute of Drug Abuse
University of Maryland

Man Years:
Total: 2.85
Professional: 1.5
Other: 1.35

Project Description:

Objectives:

To learn more about the mechanism of action and the reason why these drugs are abused.

Methods Employed:

Subjects were chronic marijuana users, usually administered 7.5 mg THC (assayed) or a placebo cigarette prior to the biochemical or psychological testing.

Major Findings:

A. State-Dependent Effects on Memory

Several recent studies have shown that certain psychoactive drugs, particularly the so-called "drugs of abuse," have distinct state-dependent properties when used by human subjects. These properties include the production of a partial amnesia for material which is learned in one drug state but recalled in another. This results in a surprising, but well-replicated phenomenon that material learned when intoxicated is in fact better recalled by the subject when he is again intoxicated than when he is sober. This phenomenon of state-dependence may be relevant to explaining the habitual use of drugs. Little is known, however, about the fundamental mechanisms of state-dependence.

Our research demonstrated for the first time that it is possible for subjects to use verbal cues to overcome the pharmacological state-dependent effects of marijuana on memory. State-dependent deficits in disparate drug states (e.g., learn under marijuana, recall when sober) disappeared for subjects who were prompted with category names. When so prompted, disparate-state subjects recall essentially equalled congruent-state recall (e.g., learn and recall under marijuana). This data strongly suggests that subjects trying to remember material learned in a different drug state from that at recall simply are unable to produce the appropriate retrieval cues to access what was learned in the different drug state. Thus, they fail to access material which they do, in fact, have stored in memory. This work shows that access can be provided by appropriate verbal cueing as well as by a return to the original drug state.

An additional study of self-generated imagery provided additional clues containing the mechanism in which learned material succeeds or fails to cross disparate drug states.

B. Subjective Effects of Marijuana

Several aspects of the subjective effects of marijuana have not received the attention they deserve. One is the extent to which the euphoriant properties of a drug are correlated with its ability to produce a "high" i.e., to alter the user's state of consciousness. A related question is, "Do people smoke to get high or to be happy?" A final question concerns the rapidity and sequences of onset of the earliest effects.

In a group of 36 subjects smoking marijuana under controlled conditions, attained "high" and degree of euphoria reported were poorly correlated across sessions. Overall enjoyment of the session was strongly correlated with subjective "high" ($r=.71$, $p<.01$) but not with experienced euphoria. This suggests that marijuana users prize their subjective high more than any euphoriant effect of the drug, which may distinguish marijuana from opiate use. Eight individuals were able to identify subjective effects within 45 seconds following a single inhalation of marijuana (corrected by substracting their placebo response). A rapid transport of the active ingredient of smoked marijuana is thus indicated.

C. Attention and Slow Brain Electrical Potentials

Marijuana users consistently report difficulty remembering the thread of a conversation or maintaining focus on a task. The phenomenon has been called impairment of "short-term memory" or "temporal disintegration;" it could also be called impairment of attention. The contingent negative variation (CNV) is a slow potential that develops over central and frontal scalp during the foreperiod of a reaction time task, and has been described as a correlate of attentional processes. We expected that if attention were impaired by marijuana then CNV amplitudes should decrease.

There was no significant difference in CNV amplitude with drug. There was, however, a clear relationship between CNV change in marijuana and the subject's rating of his "high" on marijuana. Subjects reporting an "average" high had larger CNV's than on placebo; those with more intense highs had smaller CNV's than on placebo. Change in CNV with drug did not correlate significantly with change in reaction time.

Our results call into question the widespread assumption that CNV amplitude is a correlate of attentional performance. Possible alternative explanations are that the CNV reflects either effort of concentration of interest in a task.

We have found in a subsequent study that the response of the CNV to THC is an inverted-u, apparently of much shorter duration than the u-shaped pulse and subjective symptom measures. It seems that homeostatic mechanisms return the CNV (attention) to baseline well before the homeostatic mechanisms of pulse regulation do.

D. Marijuana and Pain

Pain threshold and tolerance were measured in a group of normal volunteers using a blunt-caliper compression device over the Achilles tendon. After smoking marijuana, pain thresholds were moderately raised. The effect, although statistically significant, was not impressive compared with conventional analgesics (indeed, alcohol was found to have analgesic properties equivalent to those of morephine).

Proposed Course:

This coming year we will continue our investigations into the effects of certain drugs of abuse (THC, alcohol, amphetamines) on memory, cognition, and perception.

We will initiate and continue studies designed to show precisely which memory functions are affected by these agents. Our experiments will incorporate tests specifically focusing on generation versus recognition of memory components, and will examine the differential effects of these drugs on various levels of abstraction in the encoding and retrieval of memories.

The effect of drugs of abuse in short-term memory will be tested using the well-known Sperling paradigm, in which visually presented material is followed by probes which provide an unusually sensitive measure of immediate recall. Similarly, we will use the Sternberg reaction time paradigm, in cooperation with a group at Stanford University, to measure the effects of drugs on preparatory set and serial-processing speed. Computer programs are being developed here and at Stanford for acquisition and analysis of this data. Further modification will include the effects of ipsimodal and cross-modal abstraction on drug-intoxicated subjects, and a signal/noise analysis of errors committed. These will enlarge our knowledge of the extent to which these drugs increase user's vulnerability to endogenous and external distraction or irrelevant stimuli.

We have just received an automated apparatus for recording eye-movements, and will attempt to establish quantitative differences in the visual scanning patterns of subjects in various drug states, relating these to cognitive changes induced by the drugs.

Inter-hemispheric differences in information storage and information processing have received considerable attention recently. Many of the differences in function of the right and left hemispheres of normal subjects seem to parallel differences between the sober and intoxicated states associated with psychedelic drug use. For example, marijuana and other psychedelic drugs produce increased awareness of patterns and "primary process" thinking together with a decreased ability to plan and think rationally. This shift parallels quite closely the differences being discovered in non-drug subjects between right and left hemisphere function; the psychedelic change might be described as a shift from left to right hemisphere dominance in information processing. Such differences have been established in non-drugged subjects recently using reaction time paradigms in which material is presented tachistoscopically to alternate visual fields. We will use these tested paradigms to see whether certain abusable drugs (THC, hallucinogens) cause a suppression of left-hemisphere function and whether this is related to their hallucinogenic potential and appeal as mind-altering agents.

Publications:

Stillman, R. C., Weingartner, H., Wyatt, R. J., Eich, J.: State-dependent (dissociative) effects of marijuana on human memory. Arch.Gen.Psychiatr. 31: 81-85, 1974.

Galanter, M., Stillman, R. C., Wyatt, R. J.: Effects of marijuana on contingent negative variation and reaction time. Arch.Gen.Psychiatr. 31: 553-556, 1974.

Kaplan, J., Mandel, L. R., Stillman, R., Walerk, R. W., VandenHeuval, W. J. A., Gillin, J. C., and Wyatt, R. J.: Blood and urine levels of N,N-dimethyltryptamine following administration of psychoactive dosages to human subjects. Psychopharmacologia 38: 239-245, 1974.

Stillman, R. C., Eich, J., Weingartner, H. and Wyatt, R. J.: Cannabis-induced amnesia and its non-pharmacologic reversal. In Braude, M. and Szara, S.: Pharmacology of Marijuana. University Park Press Maryland, 1975 (in press).

Stillman, R. C., Weingartner, H., Eich, J., Merriam, M. S. and Wyatt, R. J.: Marijuana and memory: recent research and an overview. Addictive Behaviors (in press).

Eich, J., Weingartner, H., Stillman, R. C., and Gillin, J. C.: State-dependent accessibility of retrieval cues in the retention of a categorized list. J. Verbal Learning and Verbal Behavior (in press).

Keyword Descriptors:

drugs of abuse
state-dependence
THC
marijuana
short-term memory
mind-altering agents

Project No. Z01 MH 01338-06 SMRC
1. Division of Special Mental Health Research
2. Laboratory of Clinical Psychopharmacology
3. Saint Elizabeths Hospital

PHS-ADAMHA-NIMH
Individual Project Report
July 1, 1974 through June 30, 1975

Project Title: Assessing the "Focus" of N Independent Events Within Nominal, Ordinal, and Circular Sets of K Categories

Previous Serial Number: M-SMR-C-4

Principal Investigator: Wilson L. Taylor, Ph.D.

Man Years:

Total: .90
Professional: .90
Other: .00

Project Description:

Objectives:

To develop nonparametric methods of quantifying, and assessing the significance of, the degree to which N independent events (occurrences, observations, ratings, etc.) fall into one category (perfect focus or interagreement), or a few, or a few closely related categories, instead of being equally distributed among all possible of K categories which form any of three kinds of "scales" -- nominal (no scale at all); ordinal (linearly ranked like the common rating or "intensity" scale); or circular (like hues around a color wheel, the hours of a day, days of a week, etc.).

Methods Employed:

Construction, for each kind of scale and each combination of N and K values, of the exact probability distributions of all possible focus values from perfect to the opposite. It begins with the computation of the focus values -- by formulas developed by this investigator -- and the permutations of all possible sizes and arrangements of K sets of frequencies which total to N. This is a tedious and exacting task involving hand tabulation, desk calculators, and many cross-checks on accuracy, and most of this work has been done by math-inclined patients in occupational therapy. Then all focus values are combined, and the frequencies are cumulated from one end of the distribution to the other. The cumulated frequencies are then divided by their total to obtain proportionate probabilities from which "critical values at conventional levels -- $p \leq .05$, .01, .001, etc. -- can be extracted for publication as reference tables.

Major Findings:

In this project, the focus methods (formulas) and the exact distributions of the focus values they yield are themselves the findings, i.e., they are the results of statistical research aimed at developing rational and expedient ways for quantifying and assessing certain kinds of observed distributions of frequencies for which no adequate methodology was already available. These findings (methods) are "major" in that they appear potentially applicable to at least some problems in virtually all fields of quantitative research.

In Fiscal Year 1975 a number of important additional formulas (mathematical relationships) were derived and tested. Such formulas are not as much for the use of Focus methods by applied statisticians as for persuading editors and referees of the reliability and theoretical soundness of the methods, and those formulas are discussed under the heading, "Proposed Course."

Significance to Bio-Medical Research and the Program of the Institute:

These three different but conceptually related focus methods apply to the analysis of frequency data in situations where samples are too small to permit the use of any kind of conventional probability assessment. Instead, the significance of any result can be found only by tedious exact computation, and the essence of thousands of such computations already performed is what this project will contribute to research methodology along with three widely applicable formulas.

Particularly applicable to investigating how well different subjects interagree in their verbal responses is the nominal case formula for focus. It is a special form of that chi-square method which compares an observed allocation of frequencies to K categories with an "expected" equal distribution. The focus method, however, is not restricted by the chi-square rule that no expected cell entry can be smaller than 5, e.g., that if K = 4, then N must be at least 20. The corresponding focus method allows for K's $\geq$ N; thus if N = 4 and K = 20, computed focus and probability values would show that a distribution like 2,2,0,0,0...(18 zero frequencies altogether), though far from perfect focus like 4,0,0,0...(19 zeroes), is significantly focused, i.e., $p \leq .05$.

The ordinal case method bears a constant relationship to the familiar variance formula, and provides the only way this investigator knows to assess the significance of the degree of interagreement among, say, five raters (N=5) using a seven-point (K = 7) intensity scale to judge the same object, e.g., a patient's behavioral response to a drug.

The circular focus method seems uniquely applicable to the distribution of events around a cycle. It can assess the relative interagreement of judgments about color hues and whether a class of events is significantly focused on a certain part of a day or week or month (or season of year); it could be used in a clinical study of diurnal changes in a patient or ward.

Proposed Course:

The number of exact probability distributions for various combinations of K and N values has, in 12 years, grown to include 409, more than half of which are for the nominal case, for which computation is the easiest. The rest are split about equally between the ordinal and circular cases, and by now the computation has become so tedious that it has approached a limit which can be exceeded only if all construction operations can be effectively automated. Attempts to "computer-program" them are underway.

This investigator had concluded that the volume of work already accomplished was more than sufficient to make focus methods applicable to many kinds of research, so publication should not be delayed any longer. In FY 1973, a preliminary manuscript -- Taylor, W. L., and Waldman, I. N.: Assessing the "focus" of N independent events within nominal, ordinal, and circular sets of K categories -- was completed and submitted for clearance. In FY 1974, after clearance was obtained, the manuscript was revised, somewhat improved and enlarged, and submitted in late December, 1973, to the Journal of the American Statistical Association (JASA), in which the author published two separate articles -- both accepted in their first drafts -- more than a decade ago. To my surprise, the Focus article (which is far more original and widely applicable than the first two) was rejected late in May 1974 on the advice of two anonymous referees whose comments showed that they had not read it thoroughly enough to understand it. Their real objectives seemed to be stylistic rather than substantive, i.e., I had not written in the arcane advanced mathematical symbolism that a "real" mathematical statistician would use. In search of helpful advice, the authors turned to Prof. Jerome Cornfield of George Washington University and current president of the American Statistical Association, and he agreed that JASA had changed editorial policy in recent years and published no more articles by authors, or for readers, who were mere applied statisticians. He gave the authors a two-hour interview, expressed great interest in Focus, supplied us with two relevant references we had not known about, suggested we shorten it where possible, and resubmit it to some such applied statistic journal as Psychometrika, or Psychological Bulletin. We left him a copy, sent him further supporting materials, and tried our best to enlist his aid in reading the manuscript carefully and making a specific suggestions for revision, but he said he was too busy. So, FY 1974 ended without an acceptance for publication and with the beginning of an intensive hunt for someone competent and willing to advise us...Also, with regard to FY 1974, I note that I was incapacitated (on "sick leave") for half of it while I underwent and recovered from two separate cataract operations.

About 90% of all my duty time in FY 1975 will have been devoted entirely to Focus. That divides into four general categories: (1) continuing the accuracy check of all the more than 400 exact frequency distributions which should be preserved in toto for future researchers; (2) devising and testing out new formulas for accuracy testing and for demonstrating exact mathematical relationships among the three cases -- nominal, ordinal, and circular -- and with already well established statistics, null-case chi-square, the variance of ranks, and circular variance, respectively; (3) seeking and finally finding competent and willing consultants; and (4) re-revising the Focus manuscript for submission to some applied statistics journal, probably either Psychometrika or Educational and Psychological Measurement.

The accuracy check of exact frequency distributions is being done almost wholly by a talented part-time volunteer statistical clerk, and that operation will continue into FY 1976. I have devised and tried out several new and very useful formulas for our purposes, some of which will become part of the new manuscript. Competent and willing consultants were hard to find: a few of them went so far as to scan the manuscript and give us offhand impressions, but many of them refused to receive a copy of it, and some of those who did accept a copy never found time to look at it. In October, 1974, we found two mathematical statisticians, Robert R. Rawlings, M.S., and Darryl Bertolucci, M.S., who spent 10 hours with Mr. Waldman and myself, and many more hours between themselves, studying the mathematical aspects of our formulas. They, both of the Division of Computer Systems, OAM, ADAMHA, at Parklawn, showed us that all three of our cases are based on ranks and are tests of the symmetric multinomial (our "zero focus" where all N events are equally divided among K categories). And they showed our circular formula was a function of a more general formula for circular variance. Finally I reached Dr. George A. Miller of Rockefeller University. He is a past president of the American Psychological Association, and he knew and admired my work on "cloze procedure." He read the paper closely and on January 21, 1975, wrote a letter which praised Focus as an original and valuable statistic, and he made specific recommendations about how to proceed in preparing what we hope will be the final (successful) version. He remains available for further help if needed.

This project has been terminated effective April 30, 1975.

Keyword Descriptors:

Focus

Project No. Z01 MH 01481-01 SMRP
1. Division of Special Mental Health Research
2. Laboratory of Preclinical Pharmacology
3. Saint Elizabeths Hospital

PHS-ADAMHA-NIMH
Individual Project Report
July 1, 1974 through June 30, 1975

Project Title: Short and Long Term Regulation of Tryptophan Hydroxylase in Brain Nuclei

Previous Serial Number: None

Principal Investigator: L. Neckers

Other Investigators: J. Meek and E. Costa

Cooperating Units: None

Man Years:

Total:	1.5
Professional:	1.5
Others:	0

Project Description:

Until recently, little information has been available on the short term modulation of neurotransmitter synthesis and on the molecular nature of the events that modulate changes in enzyme activity. Recent work by Dr. Zivkovic (see MH 01511-03 FY 1975) has shown that the Km of tyrosine hydroxylase for the pteridine cofactor is decreased in striatum and N. accumbens following a single dose of various antipsychotics. The mechanisms whereby short-term changes of serotonin synthesis is mediated has not been elucidated; moreover it is not known whether tryptophan hydroxylase participates in the regulation of such short term changes. We have developed a new technique which permits us to assess changes in the kinetic state of tryptophan hydroxylase in a single brain nucleus. Our aim is to understand the short term regulation of this enzyme, and how it is triggered. We have also examined the long term changes in tryptophan hydroxylase seen after p-chloroamphetamine, a drug which was used clinically as an antidepressive and causes a very extensive decrease of serotonin content in brain nuclei innervated by serotonergic axon terminals.

To measure tryptophan hydroxylase with the necessary sensitivity and selectivity, a new technique had to be developed. High pressure liquid chromatography has recently been shown to allow the rapid separation for certain types of compounds. When separation by high pressure chromatography was combined with - detection by known fluorometric methods, 5hydroxytryptophan (5HTP), the product of tryptophan hydroxylase could be detected with a sensitivity 100 times greater than that of conventional techniques. This breakthrough allows the measurement of tryptophan hydroxylase activity in discrete brain nuclei (about 100 μg protein).

We have examined the effects of p-chloroamphetamine, a drug that causes a long lasting depletion of 5HT in terminals and selectively damages a midbrain area turned B9 which contain serotonergic cell bodies, but not the raphe nuclei that also contail such cell bodies. We also studied the acute effects of two psychoactive drugs, which act on 5HT dynamics by mimicking 5HT effects on receptors (LSD) and by blocking 5HT uptake (chlorimpramine).

Our major findings are:

1. p-chloroamphetamine (PCA) produces a rapid and long lasting loss of enzyme activity in 10 brain areas that contain abundant 5HT terminals.

2. The loss of enzyme activity was slower in onset and in recovery in the brain areas containing cell bodies than in those containing terminals.

3. The loss of activity was greater in area B9 than in the raphe nuclei.

4. Electrolytic lesions of B9 did not cause a loss of tryptophan hydroxylase activity in those brain areas where the enzyme activity was almost completely absent as a result of PCA treatment.

5. Chlorimipramine, but not desmethylimipramine increases the apparent Vmax of tryptophan hydroxylase without changing the Km for the pterine cofactor. This increase excludes the participation of a negative feed back activated by an increased availability of transmitter at specific receptor sites.

6. The increase of the apparent Vmax of tryptophan hydroxylase after chlorimipramine is rapid in onset, $\underline{<}$ 15 min.

7. Preliminary experiments indicated that LSD does not cause a rapid change in the kinetic properties of tryptophan

hydroxylase.

Alterations in the function of the serotonergic pathways may be involved in mental depression. Destruction of cell bodies in area B9 by PCA was suggested as a model for studying one of these pathways. Our data show that the function of terminals originating from B9 can not be studied using PCA depletion as a model. However PCA may be a tool to study the role of retrograde axonal transport in the control of the synthesis of specific proteins involved in transmitter biosynthesis.

The change in the kinetic properties of tryptophan hydroxylase helps to settle the question of whether the enzyme activity is modulated by changes in nerve firing rate, and suggests that blockade of uptake may control enzyme activity in some unknown manner. Our subsequent experiments may clarify the molecular nature of the processes that control the kinetic properties of tryptophan hydroxylase.

1) The effects of chlorimipramine will be examined in various brain nuclei to establish whether this drug has any regional selectivity in the regulation of tryptophan hydroxylase. Moreover the molecular mechanisms involved in the changes of the kinetic regulation of tryptophan hydroxylase will be studied. Particular emphasis will be given to the possibility that phosphorylation of the enzyme participates in this regulation.

2) Steroids such as progesterone have been reported to acutely increase tryptophan hydroxylase activity. We will determine whether they might be involved in the changes of the kinetic properties of tryptophan hydroxylase seen after psychotropic drugs.

Keyword Descriptors:

Brain, serotonin, high atmospheric pressure chromatography, tryptophan 5-hydroxylase, and phenylalkylamines.

Project No. Z01 MH 01482-02 SMRP
1. Division of Special Mental Health Research
2. Laboratory of Preclinical Pharmacology
3. Saint Elizabeths Hospital

PHS-ADAMHA-NIMH
Individual Project Report
July 1, 1974 through June 30, 1975

Project Title: Synaptic dynamics of serotonergic neurons

Previous Serial Number: M-SMR-P-19

Principal Investigator: A. Foldes

Other Investigators: None

Cooperating Units: None

Man Years:

Total:	0.3
Professional:	0.3
Others:	0

Project Description:

It is important to know whether the turnover of 5HT directly reflects the activation of serotonergic receptors. Workers in England have proposed a model in which the increase in motor activity elicited by tryptophan injections in animals pretreated with a monoamine oxidase inhibitor directly parallels 5HT turnover. Preliminary studies in this lab (see M-SMR-P-19, FY 1974) suggested that this model was inaccurate. The present study is aimed at clearly establishing which alternative explanations must be considered to account for the motor activation after tryptophan loading.

The change in motor activity following tryptophan injection was studied as a function of: 1) the actual monoamine oxidase inhibitor given, (tranylcyptomine vs pargyline), 2) the isomer of tryptophan given (D vs L), 3) time of onset of hyperactivity after tryptophan, 4) effects of pretreatment with drugs affecting other aminergic systems and, 5) the effects of tryptophan metabolites.

There was no correlation between the increase in motor activity and 5HT turnover. For example, D and L tryptophan have similar effects on brain 5HT dynamics, but cause hyperactivity with different onset times. Additionally, tranylcypromine and pargyline that cause a similar increase in brain 5HT content have different effects on motility.

Tryptamine, a tryptophan metabolite occurring in significant concentrations after a MAO inhibitor and tryptophan injection, also causes hyperactivity. The effect of tryptophan or tryptamine injection was blocked by reserpine, 6 hydroxydopamine or α-methyl tyrosine. These data strongly suggest that tryptamine not 5HT might be the activating substance formed after trytophan loads. Moreover the possibility that the increased motility depends from a release of brain dopamine is also supported.

The data do not favor the possibility that tryptophan loads act via stimulation of 5HT receptors as claimed by the English workers. Instead, these experiments indicate that an indole metabolite, other than perhaps tryptamine, could trigger the motor activation, perhaps by releasing dopamine from dopaminergi neurons.

The present results underline the importance of avoiding simplistic interpretations of brain function based on a model in which a load of a neurotransmitter precursor has an effect only on that transmitter. Instead it is important for pharmacologists and clinicians alike to note the multiple actions of such an amino acid precursor load, both via effects elicited by possible metabolites, and via the actions of transmitters itself when present in huge excesses, in sites where the transmitter is devoid of physiological effects.

This project is terminated. A paper has been accepted for publication in Biochemical Pharmacology.

Keyword Descriptors:

Serotonin, brain, tryptophan, monoamine oxidase inhibitors as antidepressants.

Project No. Z01 MH 01483-01 SMRP
1. Division of Special Mental Health Research
2. Laboratory of Preclinical Pharmacology
3. Saint Elizabeths Hospital

PHS-ADAMHA-NIMH
Individual Project Report
July 1, 1974 through June 30, 1975

Project Title: Studies of Taurine in discrete brain nuclei and in cerebrospinal fluid

Previous Serial Number: None

Principal Investigator: J. L. Meek

Other Investigators: None

Cooperating Units: None

Man Years:

Total: 0.1
Professional: 0.1
Others: 0

Project Description:

Although the occurrence of taurine in brain and its pattern of preferential location in brain areas are well known, its functional significance has not yet been clarified. Recently, taurine administration has been reported to be useful in the control of convulsions, and a genetically transmitted form of depression has been described which has low levels of taurine in brain and CSF. Work in this laboratory (see MH 01515-03 SMRP) suggests that taurine may regulate the afferent stimulatory input to cerebellar purkinje cells. Perhaps this action of taurine is independent from an activation of GABAergic receptors. With the development of a highly sensitive assay for taurine, it will be possible to determine which brain nuclei are characterized by high concentrations of taurine. Thus we can begin to understand which neuronal pathway are rich in taurine. Moreover we can study whether the taurine steady state changes in brain nuclei of rats receiving lithium and other drugs shown to be able to control mental depressions.

A rapid, sensitive and selective method for taurine assay was developed based on high pressure liquid chromatography, with flurescence detection. For this method the experience gained in the assay of 5-hydroxytryptophan in brain nuclei was of great assistance (see M-SMR-P FY 1975). Brain tissue is homogenized in perchloric acid and centrifuged; the extract is injected into the liquid chromatograph. After separation on an ion exchange column, taurine is reacted with o-phtaldehyde, and the fluoresence of the resulting compound is measured.

Taurine can be detected at 20 times blank level in 0.5 mg cerebellum, in just 3 minutes. Since this amount of tissue is equivalent to 0.5 mm^3, it will be easily possible to examine th concentration of taurine in discrete brain nuclei in small volumes of CSF and in plasma.

Since the administration of taurine has been reported to be useful in the treatment of convulsions, an inexpensive and ultr rapid assay of this compound will be useful for the concurrent pharmacokinetic studies of taurine in these patients. Furthermore, if taurine is found to be present in an unusually high concentration in certain nuclei, the physiological role of this compound and the clinical implications deriving from this findi will become apparent. Moreover the taurine content in plasma and cerebral spinal fluid of mental patients may be studied to assess its value in characterizing the biochemical profile o certain forms of mental depression.

The distribution of taurine in brain nuclei will be examine both in normal rats, and in rats receiving psychoactive drugs. Nuclei such as in inferior olivary nucleus whose projections (climbing fibers) to the cerebellum are apparently influenced by intraventricular injections of taurine will be an immediate target of this study. The concentration of taurine will be measured after injections of harmaline which selectively activates the olivary nucleus causing an increase of climbing fibe activity. Lesions of the olivary nucleus will be used and the taurine concentration of cerebellar cortex or deep cerebellar nuclei will be determined in normal and lesioned rats.

Keyword Descriptors:

Taurine, high atmospheric pressure chromatography, cerebrospinal fluid, brain, and amino acids.

Project No. Z01 MH 01484-02 SMRP
1. Division of Special Mental Health Research
2. Laboratory of Preclinical Pharmacology
3. Saint Elizabeths Hospital

PHS-ADAMHA-NIMH
Individual Project Report
July 1, 1974 through June 30, 1975

Project Title: Fundamental Biochemical and Pharmacological Characteristics of a Suggested Neurotransmitter

Previous Serial Number: M-SMR-P-24

Principal Investigator: J. L. Meek

Other Investigators: None

Cooperating Units: None

Man Years:

Total:	0.1
Professional:	0.1
Other:	0

Project Description:

Workers in Japan and the United States have recently reported occurence of piperidine in brain and suggested that it may be a neurotransmitter. Since little is known of the fundamental biochemical characteristics of this compound, it is difficult to assess the pathways importance. Earlier work in this laboratory (see M-SMR-P-24, FY 1974) using labelled piperidine suggested that the piperidine in brain was probably in equilibrium with peripheral piperidine stores although the metabolic compartmentation of brain stores distinct from that of peripheral stores is a normal method for localizing transmitter action to brain tissues. However, for a better understanding of piperidines pharmacodynamics, a simple inequivocal method for the measurement of brain piperidine was needed. This project was aimed at measuring piperidine in brain by high pressure liquid chromatography.

The technique of high pressure liquid chromatography, which has been successfully developed in this laboratory for the measurements of 5-hydroxytryptophan and taurine (see MH 01483-01 and MH 01481-01) was applied to piperidine. The approaches taken were: 1) the separation of the dansyl derivatives of the brain amines, followed by determination of the fluoresence, and 2) separation of the amines followed by reaction of the amines with fluorescamine or o-phthalaldehyde.

The available liquid chromatography technology was not adequate for the assay of brain piperidine. Approach number 1 was unsuccessful since currently available columns do not have sufficient resolving power to separate piperidine from interfering compounds. The second approach, which was successful when applied to the primary amines 5-hydroxytryptophan and taurine, could not be successfully adapted to the secondary amine piperidine.

This project is terminated.

Keyword Descriptors:

Piperidines, neural transmitters, biogenic amines and brain.

Project No. Z01 MH 01485-01 SMRP
1. Division of Special Mental Health Research
2. Laboratory of Preclinical Pharmacology
3. Saint Elizabeths Hospital

PHS-ADAMHA-NIMH
Individual Project Report
July 1, 1974 through June 30, 1975

Project Title: Mode of Action of Neuroleptics and Antidepressants on the regulation of synaptic mechanisms

Previous Serial Number: None

Principal Investigator: E. Moja

Other Investigators: P. D. Uzunov, E. Costa and R. Wyatt

Cooperating Units: Laboratory of Clinical Psychopharmacology, DSMHR

Man Years:

Total: 0.9
Professional: 0.9
Others: 0

Project Description:

Numberous studies (Uzunov and Weiss, 1971; 1974, Palmer et al., 1971; 1972; Clement-Cormier et al., 1973; Karobath and Leitsch, 1974) have indicated that the supramolecular organization of some postsynaptic receptors in brain includes an adenylate cyclase which is specifically stimulated by certain transmitters. The clinical efficacy of antipsychotics has been related to their ability to block the stimulation of adenylate cyclase by dopamine. In contrast, some antidepressants may interfere with the inactivation of norepinephrine or serotonin by the uptake mechanisms. However, this action cannot account for their clinical efficacy. The endogenous protein activator plays a leading role in regulating the activity of cyclic 3',5'-AMP phosphodiesterase, and controls the time course of the increase of cAMP concentrations when they are increased by transsynaptic activation of adenylate cyclase. Therefore it was noteworthy to study the effect of both major tranquilizers and antidepressants on the activity of the endogenous phosphodiesterase activator as measured in stereomicroscopically isolated nuclei of brains of rats injected with major tranquilizers and antidepressants.

antidepressants.

The objective of this work is to explore the in vivo changes of phosphodiesterase activator in some rat hypothalamic nuclei after treatment with either major tranquilizers (chlorpromazine, haloperidol) or antidepressants (desmethylimipramine, chlorimipramine, iprindol).

Rats were injected i.p. with the drugs, dissolved in saline. The limbic and hypothalamic nuclei were stereomicroscopically dissected from 400 μ brain slices prepared with a cryostat microtome. The endogenous protein activator of PDE was isolated and measured in these samples according to the procedure of Uzunov et al. (1975). An activator deficient cyclic 3',5'-AMP phosphodiesterase isolated from brain was used to measure the endogenous activator. The enzyme activity was measured by the isotopic method of Filburn and Karn (1973).

The drugs used produced in vivo changes of the activity of endogenous protein activator of PDE in some hypothalamic nuclei; the direction of the effects was different in the two classes of drugs studied.

The two major tranquilizers (chlorpromazine and haloperidol) increased in a dose-dependent manner the activity of PDE activator in n. hypothalami anterior, n. accumbens, n. paraventricularis and nuclei septi medialis and lateralis. This effect was seen 30 min after i.p. injection of chlorpromazine, reached maximum at 60 min and persisted for at least 2 hr. The increase of activator was measurable after injection of a dose as small as 1.25 μmoles/kg. A dose of 10 μmoles/kg produced at least double increase of activator in n. hypothalami anterior at 60 min after the injection. The same dose of haloperidol produced three fold increase of activator in n. accumbens.

In contrast to the major tranquilizers, the antidepressants studied decreased the activity of the endogenous protein activator of PDE in some hypothalamic nuclei. This effect was seen after DMI (5 mg/kg) in n. accumbens, n. hypothalami anterior and in n. paraventricularis, after chlorimipramine (5 mg/kg) in n. paraventricularis and nuclei septi medialis et lateralis, and after iprindole (5 mg/kg) in n. hypothalami anterior and n. paraventricularis. The time-course study showed that the effect of DMI was maximal 1 hr after i.p. treatment. Although all of the antidepressants studied decrease the PDE activator in the above mentioned nuclei, in some nuclei examined, the antidepressants either failed to change the activity of PDE activator or produced a slight increase. Thus DMI (5 mg/kg) increased the activator in N. septi medialis et lateralis by about 25% whereas chlorimipramine (5 mg/kg) elicited a similar increase in N. accumbens and hypothalami anterior.

Preliminary studies showed that DMI and chlorimipramine inhibited in vitro the activation of an activator-deficient PDE by the endogenous protein activator. Quantitative studies in this direction are in progress.

The preliminary evidence that antidepressants and tranquilizers change the in vivo activity of the endogenous protein activator of PDE in opposite directions opens a new vista in the profile of the pharmacological studies that may be relevant to explain mechanisms that participate in their therapeutic action. Since the content of cAMP in postsynaptic cells can be regulated trans-synaptically, drugs that interfere with the specific protein that regulates phosphodiesterase can enlarge or restrict the extent and duration of the transsynaptic response. This mode of action is presently being assessed as an approach to locate sites of therapeutic action at specific synapses.

It remains to be elucidated whether the changes in the activity of endogenous protein activator of PDE in various brain nuclei are results of the direct effect of the drugs or they are rather a compensatory mechanism. Previous studies showed that the cellular concentration of cyclic 3,5-AMP regulates the activity of endogenous protein activator. The quantitative in vitro studies of the effect of these drugs on the activation of phosphodiesterase by the endogenous protein activator might help in answering this question. The effect of these drugs on the phosphorylation of PDE activator also deserves attention, because it is possible that cAMP regulates its activity by phosphorylation and dephosphorylation of this protein.

Keyword Descriptors:

Psychopharmacological agents, antidepressants, 3':5' cyclic AMP phosphodiesterase, phosphodiesterases.

Project No. Z01 MH 01486-01 SMRP
1. Division of Special Mental Health Research
2. Laboratory of Preclinical Pharmacology
3. Saint Elizabeths Hospital

PHS-ADAMHA-NIMH
Individual Project Report
July 1, 1974 through June 30, 1975

Project Title: In vivo regulation of the endogenous activator of cyclic 3',5'-nucleotide phosphodiesterase.

Previous Serial Number: None

Principal Investigator: P. D. Uzunov

Other Investigators: A. Revuelta and E. Costa

Cooperating Units: None

Man Years:

Total:	1.2
Professional:	1.2
Others:	0

Project Description:

To explore the regulation of the endogenous protein activator by the intracellular concentration of cyclic 3',5' AMP. This regulation was studied by measurement of the dynamic changes of the endogenous activator during the course of changes in cyclic 3',5' AMP concentrations in several rat tissues induced either by drug treatment or environmental factors.

In order to detect the activator of PDE in discrete brain areas, a sensitive and versatile method was developed, which allows measurement of the activity of this protein isolated from samples as small as 10 μg of tissue. The activator was separated from PDE by taking advantage of its relative thermostability. Its activity was measured by the degree of activation of an activator-deficient phosphodiesterase, isolated from rat brain. The activator-deficient enzyme was isolated according to procedure developed in this laboratory.

Cyclic 3',5'-adenosine monophosphate and cyclic 3',5'-guanosine monophosphate phosphodiesterase activities were measured by the method of Filburn and Karn (1973) and Weiss et al. (1970).

The data support the idea that the increase of cyclic 3',5' AMP concentration in the cell can regulate the activity of the endogenous protein activator of PDE. It seems that this is a physiological mechanism for regulation of the duration of the response elicited by the elevated concentrations of cyclic 3', 5-AMP.

In different rat tissues and in numerous experimental conditions the activity of the endogenous protein activator increases by several fold. This increase was preceeded in all studies by an elevation of the intracellular concentration of cyclic 3',5-AMP. The activity of the endogenous protein activator reaches a peak when cyclic 3,5 -AMP content begins to decline. The increase of phosphodiesterase activator persisted for at least 30 min after the concentration of cyclic 3,5-AMP goes back to the control values. Such pattern of changes in both cyclic 3,5-AMP and the activity of endogenous protein activator was seen in rat pineal gland after treatment with isoproterenol (5 mg/kg), pituitary gland after reserpine (10 mg/kg) and adrenal medulla after carbamylcholine (5.9 μmoles/ug) and cold exposure at 4°C. (IN VIVO REGULATION OF cAMP CONTENT BY CHANGES IN THE ENDOGENOUS PHOSPHODIESTERASE ACTIVATOR. P. Uzunov, A. Revuelta and E. Costa, Fed. Proc. 34, 261, 1975; A ROLE FOR THE ENDOGENOUS ACTIVATOR OF 3',5'-NUCLEOTIDE PHOSPHODIESTERASE IN RAT ADRENAL MEDULLA, P. Uzunov, A. Revuelta, and E. Costa, Mol. Pharmacol., 1975, in press).

The idea that the increase of cyclic 3,5 AMP concentration is the treager for an increase of endogenous protein activator also stems from the fact that agents which are known to block the increase of cyclic 3,5-AMP also prevent the increase in the activator activity. Thus, hexamethonium (45 μmoles/kg) but not atropine (5 mg/kg) prevented both the increase of cyclic 3,5-AMP and endogenous protein activator of PDE in adrenal medulla of rats exposed to cold at 4°C.

A mechanism regulating the duration of the second messenger response elicited by hormones and neurotransmitters was described. When the content of cyclic 3,5 AMP exceeds a certain limit it can activate its own metabolism by increasing either the activity or the content of phosphodiesterase activator.

Exploring the possibility for selective inhibition the activity of phosphodiesterase
for monitoring the hormonal and neurohormonal effect. It is conceivable that both genetic and environmental induced changes of the activator of PDE in brain may participate in the pathogenesis of some psychosis.

It is important to study whether the in vivo increase of the activity of PDE activator reflect a change in the activity state of a protein present in constant amounts in the cell or represents an increment in the rate of synthesis or a decrease in the rate of degradation of this protein. The turnover of the endogenous activator and the factors regulating its activity will be explored. This avenue of research can be followed by producing specific antibodies against highly purified samples of PDE activator. Such efforts are in progress.

Measurement of activator in the blood and spinal fluid of patients could be another promising way of extending this work and an attempt to clarify the role of activator in psychopathology.

Keyword Descriptors:

Phosphodiesterases, cyclic GMP, 3';5' cyclic AMP phosphodiesterase, pineal body, pituitary gland, adrenal glands, isoproterenol, reserpine, carbamylcholine and cold stress.

Publications:

Uzunov, P., A. Revuelta, and E. Costa: A role for the endogenous activator of 3',5'-nucleotide phosphodiesterase in rat adrenal medulla. Mol. Pharmacol., 1975 (in press).

Project No. Z01 MH 01487-01 SMRP
1. Division of Special Mental Health Research
2. Laboratory of Preclinical Pharmacology
3. Saint Elizabeths Hospital

PHS-ADAMHA-NIMH
Individual Project Report
July 1, 1974 through June 30, 1975

Project Title: Regulation of the cyclic 3,5-mononucleotide phosphodiesterase by the endogenous protein activator.

Previous Serial Number: None

Principal Investigator: P. D. Uzunov

Other Investigators: R. Lehne, P. Gnegy, A. Revuelta and E. Costa

Cooperating Units: None

Man Years:

Total: 1.1
Professional: 0.9
Others: 0.2

Project Description:

To characterize the mechanism of activation of brain cyclic 3,5-nucleotide phosphodiesterase by the endogenous protein activator. Such study is important for understanding the role of PDE activator on the regulation of cyclic nucleotides metabolism and in the control of concentrations of cyclic 3,5-AMP and cyclic 3,5-GMP when they increase in postsynaptic cells as results of the transsynaptic activation of adenylyl and guanylyl cyclases.

The activator sensitive phosphodiesterase (PDE peak II) was one of five molecular form of phosphodiesterase isolated from rat brain by polyacrylamide column electrophoresis according to the method of Uzunov and Weiss (1972). PDE peak II represerts the major bulk of phosphodiesterase activity in brain has high Km for cyclic 3,5-AMP (350 μM) and a low Km for cyclic 3,5-GMP (Km=6 μM).

Cyclic 3,5-AMP and cyclic 3,5-GMP phosphodiesterase were measured by the isotopic method of Filburn and Karn (1973).

The activator of phosphodiesterase was isolated from rat brain by the modified method of Lin et al. (1974) and from bullfrog sympathetic ganglia by the method of Uzunov et al. (1975).

The endogenous protein activator increases the activity of only those molecular forms of cyclic 3',5'-AMP phosphodiesterase, which have high Km for cyclic 3,5-AMP. The molecular forms of this enzyme which have a low Km for cyclic 3,5-AMP were activator independent.

The activator added at subsaturating and saturating concentrations decreased the Km of PDE peak II, an activator deficient cyclic 3,5-AMP phosphodiesterase without changing its Vmax. Saturating concentrations (20 μg protein) of the activator decreased the Km from 350 μM to 80 μM.

Since the activator deficient peak II PDE hydrolyses cyclic 3,5-GMP we also studied the effect of the endogenous activator on the hydrolysis of this mononucleotide. We found that the activator did not change the Km of this enzyme when cyclic 3,5-GMP was the substrate of peak II phosphodiesterase, however the Vmax was moderately increased. The PDE activator isolated from bullfrog sympathetic ganglia decreases the Km of the peak II PDE for cyclic 3,5-AMP and increases the Vmax when cyclic 3,5-GMP is the substrate.

It was of major importance to study the effect of cyclic 3, 5-GMP on the activation of cyclic 3,5-AMP phosphodiesterase by the endogenous activator because both mononucleotides are naturally occurring substrates for peak II PDE.

It was found that cyclic GMP was a potent competitive inhibitor of the activation of peak II PDE using cyclic 3',5' AMP as a substrate. The Ki (1.8 μM) is in the range of the Km of this enzyme for cyclic 3',5' GMP (5-9 μM). Cyclic AMP, however, is a very poor inhibitor of the hydrolysis of cyclic GMP by this enzyme (Ki-155 μM).

A purified activator deficient cyclic nucleotide phosphodiesterase (PDE peak II) isolated from rat brain follows classical Michaelis Menten kinetics (has one Km for cAMP=350 μM) and represents a great proportion of the enzyme present in brain. The endogenous protein activator increases the affinity of the enzyme for cAMP by about 5-fold thus converting a high Km enzyme into a low Km enzyme. It deserves to be mentioned that the PDE peak II has the highest turnover number among all the enzymes separated from rat brain. It appears that the decrease of Km of cyclic nucleotide phosphodiesterase by the activator might be a way of turning on the PDE. Probably this regulation of the Km of PDE expresses the function of the endogenous activator of PDE. When the activator from bullfrog sympathetic ganglia is added to the peak II PDE from rat brain it produces the same changes as the activator isolated from rat brain indicating that this regulatory protein lacks both tissue and species specificity. Therefore, this might be a general regulatory mechanism for PDE.

We shall proceed in the investigation of the mechanism whereby the endogenous activator increases the affinity of PDE for cAMP. Previous studies have shown that an increase in intracellular concentration of cAMP triggers an increase in the activity of this protein. Since protein kinase is an unusual receptor for cAMP the effects elicited by this cyclic nucleotides are mediated by phosphorylation. It would be at variance from this general principal if phosphorylation were not participating in the activation of the endogenous protein activator elicited by cAMP. Therefore, we shall study whether phosphorylation and dephosphorylation of the activator change the intrinsic activity of this protein. To facilitate these studies and that of the cellular location of the PDE activator we are preparing an antibody to the PDE activator.

Keyword Descriptors:

3',5' Cyclic-AMP phosphodiesterase, cyclic-GMP, phosphodiesterases, and enzyme mechanisms.

Project No. Z01 MH 01488-01 SMRP
1. Division of Special Mental Health Research
2. Laboratory of Preclinical Pharmacology
3. Saint Elizabeths Hospital

PHS-ADAMHA-NIMH
Individual Project Report
July 1, 1974 through June 30, 1975

Project Title: Studies on the phosphorylation of tyrosine hydroxylase *in vitro* and *in vivo*.

Previous Serial Number: None

Principle Investigator: D. Chuang

Other Investigators: E. Costa

Cooperating Units: None

Man Years:

Total: 0.6
Professional: 0.6
Other: 0

Project Description:

In nerve endings, the tyrosine hydroxylase affinity for the pteridine cofactor is increased as a part of short term regulation of the catecholamine synthesis during brief periods of increase in nerve impulse flow (Molecular Pharmacol. (1974) 10, 727; Proc. Nat. Acad. Sci. (1974) 71: 4283). This decrease in the Km for the pteridine cofactor occurs without changes in the Vmax. Recently it has been demonstrated that tyrosine hydroxylase in the high speed supernatant of mammalian brains can be activated by the addition of adenosine 3':5'-monophosphate (cAMP) or protein kinase to the incubation medium (J. Biol. Chem. (1975) 250, 1946). These results suggest that cAMP-dependent protein kinase may mediate the activation of tyrosine hydroxylase *in vitro*, however fail to provide evidence that phosphorylation of either tyrosine hydroxylase or other proteins indeed controls the hydroxylase activity. Moreover whether protein kinase is involved in the activation of tyrosine hydroxylase by neuronal activity *in vivo* remains unanswered. In fact, others have suggested that a change in the environmental ionic strength may induce conformational changes of tyrosine hydroxylase which in turn regulate the affinity of this enzyme for its cofactor.

This project is addressed to answer these questions using

the antibody specific to tyrosine hydroxylase to isolate the enzyme molecules. We have obtained antibody specific to highly purified tyrosine hydroxylase (Chuang and Costa (1974) Proc. Nat. Acad. Sci. 71: 4570). To initiate the study on phosphorylation of tyrosine hydroxylase we have set up an affinity column conjugated with the antibody to tyrosine hydroxylase. The immunoglobulin purified from tyrosine hydroxylase antiserum was coupled to Sepharose using cyanogen bromide linkage according to the procedures of Cuatrecasas and Anfinsen (Methods in Enzymology (1971) 23, 345). We have been able to demonstrate by the mobility on polyacrylamide gel electrophoresis that the radioactive proteins from adrenal glands adsorbed by this affinity Sepharose indeed represent only tyrosine hydroxylase.

In the immediate future, it will be feasible to perform the experiment in which the tissue homogenates containing tyrosine hydroxylase are incubated with gamma-^{32}P-ATP in the presence and the absence of cAMP and then the ^{32}P incorporated into tyro sine hydroxylase will be examined by our affinity chromatography. Moreover using the technique of immunoassay it will be possible to examine whether phosphorylation of tyrosine hydroxylase occurs _in vivo_. Thus, rats will be administered with ^{32}P and then the tyrosine hydroxylase in various regions of the brain and peripheral nerve system will be examined for the ^{32}P content before and after a change in the nerve activity. The final goal of this project will be to correlate the storichiometry of phosphorylation with the activity of tyrosine hydroxylase. We believe that this study will be of value to understand the mechanisms of the short term regulation of the activity of tyrosine hydroxylase. Since tyrosine hydroxylase catalyzes the rate limiting step of the synthesis of the neurotransmitter dopamine and norepinephrine, an understanding of the molecular nature of these control mechanisms will aid the knowledge of a novel set of receptors to be used in devising new drugs that may help in correcting defects in the synthesis of brain neurotransmitters involved in psychopathology.

Keyword Descriptors:

Tyrosine 3-hydroxylase, protein kinase, phosphorylation, immunoassay, and affinity chromatography.

Project No. Z01 MH 01489-02 SMRP
1. Division of Special Mental Health Research
2. Laboratory of Preclinical Pharmacology
3. Saint Elizabeths Hospital

PHS-ADAMHA-NIMH
Individual Project Report
July 1, 1974 through June 30, 1975

Project Title: Mechanisms of trans-synaptic control of protein synthesis in neurons.

Previous Serial Number: M-SMR-P-4

Principle Investigator: D. Chuang

Other Investigators: E. Costa and G. Zsilla

Cooperating Units: None

Man Years:

Total: 1.2
Professional: 1.2
Others: 0

Project Description:

The aim of this study is to obtain a better understanding of the long term control of tyrosine hydroxylase in peripheral sympathetic nerve systems of rats through changes in the synthesis rate of the enzyme mediated transsynaptically.

Tyrosine hydroxylase can be induced trans-synaptically in adrenal medulla and cervical sympathetic ganglia. Using cold exposure as the stimulus, we have previously demonstrated an increased rate of amino acid incorporation into tyrosine hydroxylase in adrenals beginning 6 hours following an exposure to 4°C for 4 hrs. This project is addressed to investigate whether a decreased degradation rate of this enzyme plays any role in the induction of tyrosine hydroxylase. Moreover we are extending our previous investigation to provide additional evidence for the association of the increased synthesis with induction of tyrosine hydroxylase. Finally we are attempting to study the mechanism of the trans-synaptic regulation of messenger RNA synthesis in neuronal tissues as it relates to tyrosine hydroxylase biosynthesis.

The rate of synthesis and degradation of tyrosine hydroxylase were measured by prelabelling the proteins *in vivo* followed by precipitation of the enzyme molecules using the antibody specific to tyrosine hydroxylase. The activity of tyrosine hydroxylase was assayed by measuring the formation of $^{14}CO_2$ from ^{14}C-dopa produced. Cellular nuclei were purified by washing through a 2.0 M sucrose cushion and the synthesis of RN in isolated nuclei was assayed by the method of cold trichloro-acetic acid precipitation.

The specificity of our antibody has been demonstrated by affinity chromatography using a sepharose conjugated with the antibody to tyrosine hydroxylase. When the ^{3}H-adrenal proteins adsorbed by this affinity column were eluted and examined on disc gel electrophoresis, only one distinct protein peak was ob served. Moreover the mobility of peak is identical to that of the tyrosine hydroxylase activity in adrenal medulla.

Using the technique of radioimmunoprecipitation we have bee able to confirm our previous finding that cold exposure enhance the incorporation rate into adrenal tyrosine hydroxylase. Furthermore, we found that the enhanced rate of synthesis preceded the increment of the enzymatic activity. Thus, the increased synthesis was evident in about 10 hrs after the beginni of cold exposure (4 hrs at 4°C) and was even more at 16 hrs af exposure. However the synthesis returned to the basal values in about 48 hrs after stimulus application. The activity of tyrosine hydroxylase began to increase between 10 and 16 hrs after stress, reaching a maximum and new steady state in 30 to 50 hrs. The enzyme level then declined with a half life of about 3 days and was back to normal in about 10 days. The increases of the rate of synthesis and the activity of tyrosine hydroxylase elicited by cold could be blocked by adrenal denervation. Moreover 4 hrs of cold exposure increased neither the activity nore the synthesis rate of tyrosine hydroxylase in superior cervical sympathetic ganglia. Thus the increased synthesis of tyrosine hydroxylase is closely associated with the enhancement of the enzymatic activity. The degradation rate of tyrosine hydroxylase was measured at 48 hrs after cold exposure at this time the enzyme was in a new steady state. The results obtained from the radioimmunoprecipitation indicate that the first order degradation constant of tyrosine hydroxylase was no altered by cold exposure. From the exponential decay cf the radioactive tyrosine hydroxylase, a half life of 68 hrs has bee obtained. These values agree with the half life obtained by th decay of the enzymatic activity.

It was shown that trans-synaptic induction of tyrosine hydroxylase can be prevented by treatment of rats with actinomyci D (Otten, U. et al. N-S" Arch. Pharmacol. 280: 117, 1973).

Furthermore, Guidotti et al. (Proc. Nat. Acad. Sci., 72: 1152, 1975) have demonstrated that activation of cAMP-dependent protein kinase is an obligatory event for the trans-synaptic induction of this enzyme. It thus seems to be most likely that the increased synthesis of tyrosine hydroxylase is due to the transcription of new messenger RNA which is brought about by phosphorylation of some nuclear proteins through a nuclear translocation of the activated protein kinase. We have initiated this study by developing an in vitro system capable of synthesizing RNA at high rate in isolated medullary nuclei of rats. Furthermore, using the specific inhibitor alpha-amanitin, we can now examine whether the stress elicited by cold exposure enhances the activity of nuclear RNA polymerase II-the enzyme responsible for the synthesis of messenger RNA in vivo.

It is currently believed that a defect in the synthesis of brain noradrenaline is the cause of several mental diseases. Because of the homogenity in cell population and a relatively simple nerve innervation in adrenal medulla, our system offers an ideal model for the study of the biosynthesis regulation of tyrosine hydroxylase-the enzyme catalyzing the initial and rate limiting step for adrenaline synthesis. The understanding of the control mechanisms of the induction of tyrosine hydroxylase will undoubtly aid the new basis for the therapy of mental diseases. Moreover, the transsynaptic induction in adrenal medulla appears to be mediated by the increased amounts of cholinergic transmitter released from axon terminals that innervate adrenal medulla. The regulation of protein synthesis by the amounts of neurotransmitter transacting exchange of information at synapses is not unique to medullary chromaffin cells. Several lines of independent evidence support the idea that neuronal activity directs the synthesis of a variety of specific proteins in various postsynaptic cells. Thus, our model system will be of value to understand how a change in synaptic transmission can cause a permanent alteration of behaviour responses such as biological memory.

Keyword Descriptors:

Tyrosine 3-hydroxylase, adrenal glands, cold stress, immunoassay, chromatography, disc electrophoresis, RNA biosynthesis and protein biosynthesis.

Publications:

Chaung, D. and Costa, E.: Biosynthesis of tyrosine hydroxylase in rat adrenal medulla after exposure to cold. Proc. Nat. Acad. Sci. U.S.A. 71: 4570-4574, 1974.

Guidotti, A., Kurosawa, A., Chuang, D. M. and Costa, E.: Protein kinase activation as an early event in the trans-synaptic induction of tyrosine 3-monooxygenase in adrenal medulla. Proc. Nat. Acad. Sci. U.S.A. 72: 1152-1156, 1975.

Project No. Z01 MH 01490-01 SMRP
1. Division of Special Mental Health Research
2. Laboratory of Preclinical Pharmacology
3. Saint Elizabeths Hospital

PHS-ADAMHA-NIMH
Individual Project Report
July 1, 1974 through June 30, 1975

Project Title: Treatment of Tardive Dyskinesia: A Biochemical Study of the possible mechanism of action of 2-Dimethylaminoethanol (Deanol).

Previous Serial Number:

Principal Investigator: C. K. Garrison

Other Investigators: N. H. Neff

Cooperating Units: None

Man Years:

Total:	0.6
Professional:	0.6
Others:	0

Project Description:

Tardive dyskinesia, a disease apparently induced in man by treatment with neuroleptic drugs, is now of major concern to the mental health profession. Our objective is to provide information about the pharmacology of 2-dimethylaminoethanol, a drug used successfully in the treatment of tardive dyskinesia. Because of the structural similarity between choline and 2-dimethylaminoethanol, our working hypothesis was that the drug might be acetylated by choline acetyltransferase and the ester might serve as a substitute transmitter for acetylcholine in cholinergic neurons. Reduced cholinergic activity might explain the effectiveness of 2-dimethylaminoethanol in tardive dyskinesia.

Choline acetyltransferase was purified from rat brain by a procedure involving gel filtration, ion exchange chromatography, affinity chromatography and isoelectric focussing. The acetylation of various amines was evaluated by incubation with purified enzyme and radiolabelled acetyl CoA. Products of the reaction were separated from acetyl CoA by anion exchange column chromatography.

Only 2-dimethylaminoethanol, of seven structurally related compounds, was a substrate for purified choline acetyltransferase of rat brain. None of the 2-dimethylaminoethanol related compounds were good inhibitors of the enzyme.

Tardive dyskinesia is becoming a common side effect of treatment with neuroleptic drugs. It is imperative that the symptoms of the disease be recognized and treated. Our studies are an attempt to provide a biochemical bases for the treatment of this disease.

A kinetic analysis of the acetylation of 2-dimethylaminoethanol and related compounds by choline acetyltransferase will be undertaken. We will also attempt to demonstrate that the drug can be converted to 2-dimethylaminoethylacetate in brain slices and when injected into brain.

Keyword Descriptors:

Tardive dyskinesia, 2-ethanolamines, choline acetyltransferase.

Project No. Z01 MH 01491-01 SMRP
1. Division of Special Mental Health Research
2. Laboratory of Preclinical Pharmacology
3. Saint Elizabeths Hospital

PHS-ADAMHA-NIMH
Individual Project Report
July 1, 1974 through June 30, 1975

Project Title: Rat Pineal Cyclic Adenosine 3',5'-monophosphate Phosphodiesterase Activity: In Vivo Modulation by a Beta-Adrenergic Receptor.

Previous Serial Number: M-SMR-P-18 (Project Title Updated)

Principal Investigator: M. A. Oleshansky

Other Investigators: N. H. Neff

Cooperating Units: None

Man Years:

Total:	1.0
Professional:	1.0
Others:	0

Project Description:

Adenosine 3',5'-monophosphate (cAMP) phosphodiesterase activity of serveral cell lines has been noted to increase under conditions that increase cAMP concentrations (Science, 180: 304, 1973). cAMP is hydrolyzed by the enzyme implying that cAMP may modulate its own inactivation. Treatment with beta-adrenergic receptor agonists results in activation of adenylate cyclase of rat pineal gland with the subsequent accumulation of cAMP (Science 156: 1750, 1967). Our objective was to determine whether cAMP phosphodiesterase activity of pineal gland would increase *in vivo* following treatment with l-isoproterenol. Such studies may lead to a better understanding of the tolerance that develops to repeated administration of beta-receptor agonist.

Double reciprocal plots of the cAMP phosphodiesterase activity in various tissues are not linear. These data have been interpreted as indicating the existence of various forms of the enzyme with characteristic high and low Km values. Our studies were performed under conditions suitable for measuring the low Km enzyme activity as it is probable the enzyme important for the *in vivo* inactivation of cAMP. Enzyme activity was assayed by the enzymatic hydrolysis of radiolabelled cAMP.

We found that l-isoproterenol (5 mg/kg, i.p.) treatment increased the activity of the low Km phosphodiesterase of pineal by 40% within 1 hr and the activity returned to normal within 5 hr. The gain of enzyme activity was accompanied by an increase of Vmax. dl-Propranolol blocked the increase of enzyme activity elicited by l-isoproterenol, while phentolamine did not, suggesting that the enzyme activity is modulated through beta-adrenergic receptor activation. The increase of enzyme activity occurred at postsynaptic sites as phosphodiesterase activity could still be increased by l-isoproterenol treatment after bilateral superior cervical ganglionectomy. Pretreatment of rats with cycloheximide prevented the response indicating that protein synthesis was required for this activation. Treatment with aminophylline, a phosphodiesterase inhibitor, produced a small but significant increase of enzyme activity. Aminophylline in combination with a dose of l-isoproterenol below the threshold for enzyme activation resulted in greater activity than with aminophylline. These results suggest a direct relationship between the increase of pineal cAMP concentrations and the increase of enzyme activity.

Repeated administration of drugs to patients often leads to decreased responsiveness to the drugs. Our studies are providing biochemical information that might, in part, explain the tolerance that develops to continual use of some drugs.

Our studies will be extended to include cAMP phosphodiesterase of brain and the possible increase of enzyme activity following drugs that are thought to activate receptors for the catecholamines.

Keyword Descriptors:

3';5' Cyclic-AMP phosphodiesterases, pineal body, Isoproterenol, and adrenergic beta receptor blocking agents.

Project No. Z01 MH 01492-03 SMRP
1. Division of Special Mental Health Research
2. Laboratory of Preclinical Pharmacology
3. Saint Elizabeths Hospital

PHS-ADAMHA-NIMH
Individual Project Report
July 1, 1974 through June 30, 1975

Project Title: Properties of the Monoamine oxidases

Previous Serial Number: M-SMR-P-12

Principal Investigator: J. Fuentes

Other Investigators: N. H. Neff

Cooperating Units: None

Man Years:

Total: 1.0
Professional: 1.0
Others: 0

Project Description:

Drugs that block monoamine oxidase (EC 1.4.3.4.; MAO) have been used to treat depression, however a variety of side effects have limited their clinical usefulness. The side effect of major concern is hypertensive episodes following the ingestion of foods containing amines. The identification of types A and B MAO (See M-SMR-P-12, 1972-1974) has prompted studies to define the role of these enzymes. Our objectives were: 1) to identify drugs that could be used to block one form of the enzyme and not the other; 2) to use these drugs to define body functions that are apparently modulated by a participation of these enzymes; and 3) to investigate the actions of MAO inhibitor drugs on blood pressure in order to prevent the hypertensive episodes that have limited the clinical usefulness of this class of antidepressants.

MAO activity was determined in various tissues of the rat using several amine substrates in the presence and absence of inhibitor drugs. In some studies rats were treated with the drugs before they were killed. Motor activity was measured with an infrared electronic motility meter. Blood pressure was measured with a rat tail electro-sphygmomanometer.

<u>Identification of drugs that selectively block type A and B enzyme in vitro and in vivo.</u>

Six drugs with different chemical structures suspected of being selective inhibitors of MAO were evaluated for their ability to prevent the deamination of serotonin (substrate for type A MAO) and 2-phenylethylamine (substrate for type B MAO). When evaluated *in vitro* and *in vivo* (Table 1), clorgyline, harmaline and Lilly 51641 were more active in blocking serotonin deamination than 2-phenylethylamine deamination. The opposite was true for (-) deprenyl and pargyline. The selectivity of enzyme blockade was greater *in vitro* than *in vivo*. Apparently the disposition of the drugs or the accessibility of the enzymes *in vivo* reduces the selectivity of the drugs. These drugs, in the doses shown on Table 1, were used to study some functions that are apparently modulated by amines that are destroyed by the MAO enzymes.

Pharmacological effects that can be reversed by selective MAO inhibitor drugs.

Reserpine releases transmitter amines from their storage sites in nerve endings and causes a rapid metabolism of the amines by MAO. By administering selective MAO inhibitor drugs to reserpine treated animals, thus sparing some amines from destruction and not others, we attempted to evaluate the functions that are modulated by the different forms of the enzyme.

Reserpine treatment depresses motor activity. Only type A MAO inhibitor drugs (clorgyline, lilly 51641 and harmaline) prevented motor depression induced by reserpine. The above procedure is often used as a laboratory test for potential antidepressant drugs. Our results suggest that drugs that block type A enzyme might be better antidepressants than the non-selective inhibitor drugs that are currently used in the clinic.

Reserpine treatment induces hyperthermia in rats. Type A drugs were capable of preventing the elevation of body temperature but not type B drugs. Following destruction of serotonergic neurons with 5,6 dihydroxytryptamine, type A drugs were unable to prevent the hyperthermia induced by reserpine, indicating that the stabilization of endogenous serotonin tissue levels prevents the rise of body temperature after reserpine treatment.

In addition to the action of the drugs on brain mechanisms, we study palpebral ptosis induced by reserpine, a pharmacologic response mediated by peripheral sympathetic neurons. Only type A inhibitor drugs were capable of reversing ptosis.

A Study of the Action of Pargyline on Blood Pressure.

The MAO inhibitor drugs are thought to lower blood pressure by acting directly on the circulatory system. Therefore our initial studies attempted to differentiate the type of MAO that is found in small blood vessels and heart. We observed that the mesenteric artery of the rat contains type A enzyme, a connective tissue MAO but not type B MAO. Apparently type B enzyme is not involved in regulating blood pressure in small vessels. Heart, in contrast, contains type A and B enzyme and a connective tissue MAO. Pargyline, which is often used to treat hypertension, was administered in increasing doses to spontaneous hypertensive rats and blood pressure was recorded. We observed that blood pressure decreased at doses that did not inhibit MAO in the mesenteric artery or the heart. These results are consistent with the notion that the inhibition of MAO in small vessels and heart does not induce the hypotension elicited by pargyline.

MAO inhibitor drugs are useful in the treatment of some forms of mental depression. Our studies are providing new information about the type of MAO enzymes as well as about the selectivity of the drugs that block the various MAO enzymes. Moreover, our studies are providing the basis for developing new and more specific drugs which potentially may be less toxic than the drugs that are currently used in the clinic.

We will continue our investigation of the biochemical basis for type A and type B MAO and their possible role in body functions. With pargyline we will attempt to determine whether the antihypertensive activity is due to blockade of MAO or to another action of the drug.

Keyword Descriptors:

Monoamine oxidase inhibitors as antidepressants, serotonin, phenylethylamines and hypertension.

Publications:

Neff, N. H., Yang, H.-Y. T., Garelis, E. and Sampath, S. S.: Biogenic amines containing neurons: Biochemical mechanisms of synaptic transmission. Psychother. Psychosom. 23: 159-168 (1974).

Neff, N. H. and Yang, H.-Y. T.: Another Look at the Monoamine Oxidases and the Monoamine Oxidase Inhibitor Drugs. Life Sciences, 14: 2061-2071 (1974).

Yang, H.-Y. T. and Neff, N. H.: The Monoamine Oxidases of Brain: Selective Inhibition with Drugs and the consequenc for the Metabolism of the Biogenic Amines, J. Pharmacol. Exptl. Therap., 189: 733-740 (1974).

Neff, N. H., Yang, H.-Y. T. and Fuentes, J. A.: The Use of selective MAO Inhibitor Drugs to Modify Amine Metabolism in Brain, Advan. in Biochem. Psychopharmacology, 12: 49-58 (1974).

Goridis, C. and Neff, N. H.: Selective Localization of Monoami Oxidase in Rat Mesenteric Artery, In: Frontiers in Catecholamine Research, 157-160 (1973) Pergamon Press, London.

Schwartz, M. A., Wyatt, R. J., Yang, H.-Y. T. and Neff, N. H.: Multiple Forms of Brain Monoamine Oxidase in Schizophrenic and Normal Individuals., Arch. Gen. Psychiat. 31: 557-560 (1974).

TABLE 1

A COMPARISON OF THE ABILITY OF SIX MONOAMINE OXIDASE INHIBITORS TO PREVENT THE DEAMINATION OF SEROTONIN (5HT) AND 2-PHENYLETHYLAMINE (PEA) IN VITRO AND IN VIVO

	In vitro		In vivo		
	EC_{50} (μM)[a]		% Inhibition of Monoamine Oxidase[b]		
	5HT	PEA	Dose (mg/kg)	5HT	PEA
Clorgyline	0.07	>1000	1.0	99	10
Harmaline	0.57	1000	0.1	91	27
Lilly 51641	0.63	47	1.0	64	20
(-)-deprenyl	560	0.50	1.0	10	83
Pargyline	100	0.75	0.5	21	82

[a] EC_{50} is the effective concentration of drug which inhibited enzyme activity by 50%

[b] Drugs were administered intravenously and the animals were killed 2 hr later.

Project No. Z01 MH 01493-01 SMRP
1. Division of Special Mental Health Research
2. Laboratory of Preclinical Pharmacology
3. Saint Elizabeths Hospital

PHS-ADAMHA-NIMH
Individual Project Report
July 1, 1974 through June 30, 1975

Project Title: A Comparison of the Antidepressant Activity of (-) and (+) tranylcypromine

Previous Serial Number: None

Principal Investigator: J. Fuentes and M. A. Oleshansky

Other Investigators: N. H. Neff

Cooperating Units: None

Man Years:

Total: 0.7
Professional: 0.7
Others: 0

Project Description:

Tranylcypromine, a monoamine oxidase inhibitor endowed with antidepressant properties, is a mixture of (-) and (+) trans-2-phenylcyclopropylamine. The (+) isomer is a more potent monoamine oxidase inhibitor, while the (-) isomer is reported to be more potent than the (+) isomer in inhibiting uptake of catecholamines by nerve endings. Our objective was to evaluate whether the antidepressant activity of tranylcypromine was associated with the inhibition of monoamine oxidase (+ isomer) or with inhibition of amine reuptake (- isomer).

Antidepressant drugs that inhibit monoamine oxidase as well as those that block amine reuptake will antagonize reserpine-induced depression in the rat. We evaluated the antidepressant activity of the two isomers of tranylcypromine, using as a model the antagonism of reserpine-induced depression. The level of the drug in brain necessary to counteract reserpine depression was compared with that necessary to block monoamine oxidase. The concentrations of the isomers of tranylcypromine in rat brain were measured from the enzymatic transfer of ^{14}C-methyl from S-adenosyl-l-methionine-^{14}C to the isomers. Monoamine oxidase activity was measured from the oxidative deamination of radiolabelled amines.

The isomers of tranylcypromine readily entered the rat brain after intraperitoneal administration and reached peak concentrations within 15 minutes. Levo-tranylcypromine, however, entered the brain more rapidly and reached somewhat higher concentrations than the (+) isomer. After a dose of 2.5 mg/kg (-) or (+) tranylcypromine there was significantly more drug in brain than has been reported necessary to block the reuptake of amines by synaptosomes. Both drugs blocked monoamine oxidase *in vivo* and *in vitro*. The (+) isomer was between 10-60 times more active in preventing reserpine-induced depression in the rat than the (-) isomer. The ability to prevent the reserpine syndrome was apparently related to the ability of the drugs to block monoamine oxidase activity rather than their ability to block amine reuptake.

Tranylcypromine is a clinically useful antidepressant drug. By studying its mechanism of action we might learn about the cause of depression as well as provide information for the development of new drugs for treating depression.

The results of the study will be prepared for publication.

Keyword Descriptors:

Monoamine oxidase inhibitors as antidepressants.

Project No. Z01 MH 01494-02 SMRP
1. Division of Special Mental Health Research
2. Laboratory of Preclinical Pharmacology
3. Saint Elizabeths Hospital

PHS-ADAMHA-NIMH
Individual Project Report
July 1, 1974 through June 30, 1975

Project Title: Regulation of Hydroxyindole-0-methyltransferase Biosynthesis by Sympathetic Nerve Activity

Previous Serial Number: M-SMR-P-27·

Principal Investigator: H.-Y. T. Yang

Other Investigators: N. H. Neff and E. Costa

Cooperating Units: None

Man Years:

Total:	0.6
Professional:	0.6
Others:	0

Project Description:

Environmental lighting and sympathetic nerve activity influence hydroxyindole-0-methyltransferase (HIOMT) activity of rat pineal. Our objective is to study whether HIOMT is regulated by changing the rates of enzyme biosynthesis or degradation or by changing the kinetic properties of the enzyme. Immunochemical titration with a HIOMT specific antiserum is used to assess the participation of enzyme synthesis in the regulation of HIOMT. The reversal by exogenous norepinephrine of the decrease in HIOMT activity elicited by ganglionectomy is used as a model to study the short term regulation of the enzyme.

Highly purified HIOMT was prepared from bovine pineal, and with this preparation a specific antiserum to the enzyme was produced in the rabbit. To estimate the quantity of HIOMT enzyme protein that was present in samples of pineal, increasing amounts of the antiserum were added to a series of tubes containing a fixed quantity of pineal extract. The amount of antiserum which is required to precipitate total enzyme activity was taken as the indication of the enzyme protein level.

Pineal glands from animals kept in continuous darkness contained about three times more enzyme protein than those from animals kept in continuous light. With a fixed concentration of S-adenosyl-l-methionine, a similar Km value, for the substrate about (20 μM), was obtained for the pineals of both groups of animals; however in the animals exposed to continuous darkness the Vmax increased from about 0.66 to 2.0 nmol melatonin/min/mg protein.

Superior cervical ganglionectomy decreased the HIOMT activity in rat pineal. This decrease was not observed until 7 days after the ganglionectomy and the lowest value which is about half of control value was obtained 10 days after the surgery. By immunochemical titration, we have shown that the reduced enzyme activity is the result of decreased enzyme protein. Exogenous norepinephrine restored about 50% of ganglionectomy induced decreased in pineal HIOMT activity in 4 hours.

By immunochemical titration we have demonstrated that changes in sympathetic nerve activity regulate the accumulation of HIOMT enzyme protein in rat pineal gland. It was reported that the sympathetic nerves which innervate the rat pineal form norepinephrine at a faster rate in darkness than in the light. Thus the increased sympathetic nerve activity may also be responsible, in part, for the increased HIOMT protein in rats kept in continuous darkness. With the enzyme specific antibody, it is now also possible to study whether the changes in HIOMT enzyme protein is due to altered enzyme protein synthesis or degradation.

Our proposed course is as follows:

1) To study the effect of sympathetic nerve activity on the rates of HIOMT enzyme protein synthesis and degradation.

2) To study the mechanism of the short term regulation of the HIOMT activities such as the circadian rhythm and the effect of exogenous norepinephrine on the ganglionectomized animal.

Keyword Descriptors:

Hydroxyindole-O-methyltransferase, protein biosynthesis, lighting, immunological tests and immunoassay, and nerve impulse facilitation.

Project No. Z01 MH 01495-02 SMRP
1. Division of Special Mental Health Research
2. Laboratory of Preclinical Pharmacology
3. Saint Elizabeths Hospital

PHS-ADAMHA-NIMH
Individual Project Report
July 1, 1974 through June 30, 1975

Project Title: N-Acetyltransferase Activity of Brain

Previous Serial Number: M-SMR-P-16

Principal Investigator: H.-Y. T. Yang

Other Investigators: N. H. Neff

Cooperating Units: None

Man Years:

Total: 0.6
Professional: 0.6
Others: 0

Project Description:

N-Acetyltransferase of brain acetylates a wide variety of naturally occurring biogenic amines as well as amphetamine. Our objective is to explore the physiological role of the enzyme in the brain by: 1) searching for drugs which will inhibit the enzyme, 2) comparing the brain enzyme with pineal and liver N-acetyltransferases, and 3) determining the Km of the enzyme for some naturally occuring amines in searching for the endogenous product of the enzyme in brain.

Enzyme activity was assayed by measuring the radioactive products formed from the enzymic acetylation of amines by acetyl-1-^{14}C coenzyme A. A partially purified enzyme preparation from pooled rat brain and liver was used for this study.

We found β-carboline derivatives, harmane, harmol and 5-methoxyharman to be good competitive inhibitors of the enzyme (Table 1). Brain N-acetyltransferase is different from pineal N-acetyltransferase in substrate specificity and inhibitory properties (Table 2). On the other hand, the brain enzyme is identical to liver-N-acetyltransferase in inhibitory properties. The enzyme of brain was found to have a higher affinity for indolethylamines (Table 3) suggesting that serotonin and methoxytryptamine may function as endogenous substrates.

Melatonin and 5-methoxytryptamine are normally present in hypothalamus of rat. Recently, the presence of an acetylindolethylamine in cerebellum of rats has been suggested. Moreover, brain N-acetyltransferase has a relatively low Km for 5-methoxytryptamine. Thus it is possible that one of the function of the enzyme is to catalyze the formation of melatonin in brain.

By using the inhibitors, it is now possible to study whether the N-acetyltransferase of brain plays any role in amine metabolism. N-acetyltransferase of liver plays an important role in drug detoxication and is genetically determined. In view of the similarity between the brain and liver enzymes, the N-acetyltrans ferase of brain may be a physiological detoxication mechanism similar to that of liver.

We will attempt to purify the N-acetyltransferase of brain and establish its identity with the enzyme activity of other tissues.

TABLE 1

INHIBITION OF N-ACETYLTRANSFERASE OF RAT BRAIN BY

β-CARBOLINE DERIVATIVES

INHIBITOR	% of Control Activity
Harmaline	73
Harmine	50
Harmane	30
Harmol	28
6-Methoxyharmalan	51
Yohimbine	99
Melatonin	33
6-Hydroxymelatonin	62
6-Methoxyharman	32
Harminic Acid	84

* 1 mM Tryptamine was used as substrate
* 0.01 mM Inhibitor was preincubated at room temperature for 30 min.

TABLE 2

INHIBITION OF N-ACETYLTRANSFERASE OF BRAIN AND PINEAL

TISSUE	INHIBITOR	% OF INHIBITION
Brain	Harmane	88%
	Harmaline	75%
Pineal	Harmane	9%
	Harmaline	0

0.1 mM inhibitor was used.

TABLE 3

SUBSTRATE SPECIFICITY OF N-ACETYLTRANSFERASE

Substrate	Km M
Tryptamine	6.8×10^{-5}
Methoxytryptamine	4.1×10^{-5}
Serotonin	6.0×10^{-5}
2-Phenylethylamine	5.7×10^{-4}
3,4-Dimethoxy-phenylethylamine	$1.x \times 10^{-4}$
3-Methoxy, 4-hydroxy phenylethylamine	5.2×10^{-5}

Keyword Descriptors:

Acetyltransferases, biogenic amines, carbolines and coenzyme A.

Project No. Z01 MH 01496-05 SMRP
1. Division of Special Mental Health Research
2. Laboratory of Preclinical Pharmacology
3. Saint Elizabeths Hospital

PHS-ADAMHA-NIMH
Individual Project Report
July 1, 1974 through June 30, 1975

Project Title: Mechanisms for the removal of the acidic metabolites of the biogenic amines from cerebrospinal fluid.

Previous Serial Number: M-SMR-P-5

Principal Investigator: S. S. Sampath

Other Investigators: N. H. Neff

Cooperating Units: None

Man Years:

Total:	0.5
Professional:	0.5
Others:	0

Project Description:

This project has been terminated and a manuscript is being prepared for publication.

Project No. Z01 MH 01497-02 SMRP
1. Division of Special Mental Health Research
2. Laboratory of Preclinical Pharmacology
3. Saint Elizabeths Hospital

PHS-ADAMHA-NIMH
Individual Project Report
July 1, 1974 through June 30, 1975

Project Title: The use of stable isotopes and mass fragmentography to measure the in vivo biosynthesis of monoamines in brain nuclei of rats.

Previous Serial Number: M-SMR-P-32

Principle Investigator: H. F. LeFevre

Other Investigators: S. H. Koslow and E. Costa

Cooperating Units: None

Man Years:

Total:	2.0
Professional:	2.0
Others:	0

Project Description:

Our objectives are:

1) To obtain an in vivo method for the determination of the metabolic state of putative neurotransmitters in rat brain nuclei.

2) To establish a method, utilizing the stable isotope Oxygen-18, for determining the turnover rate of biogenic amines and their metabolites at the synaptic level in animal studies. Thereby allowing the accurate study of psychoactive agents at their site of action.

Methods employed were:

1) Use of $D_2\,^{18}O$ electrolysis system and high vacuum gas transfering apparatus.

2) Use of a closed homeostatic system for the administration and monitoring (gas phase) of $^{18}O_2$ to unrestrained animals.

3) Mass Fragmentography:

a) Direct inlet (variable leak) for the continuous monitoring of atmospheric gases during the administration of $^{18}O_2$ to animals.

b) Utilizing Gas-Chromatography-Mass Spectrometry (GC-MS). The amines and acid metabolites, following suitable derivatization, are identified and quantified by their GC retention time, fragmentation pattern, and intensity relative to suitable internal standards. The ^{16}O and ^{18}O labeled variant compound concentrations are simultaneously determined by methods developed in this laboratory.

Major Findings were:

1) The closed system for the electrolytic production and high vacuum gas handling of the $^{18}O_2$ produced has been modified to enable gas mixing thus permitting control of the gas composition to be administered to animals. This allowed the protocol described below for a more efficient use of $^{18}O_2$ to obtain the desired degree of label.

2) The homeostatic closed system for the administration of $^{18}O_2$ to animals has been modified in accord with experimental findings to provide minimal stress to the animals. This involved designing individual animal compartments as well as multiple-vent and increased flow positive ventilation to provide moisture, heat, and CO_2 control. A manifold with electrically operated valves was added to permit the option of 97% $^{18}O_2$ or lower percentage label mixtures to be supplied to the atmosphere respired by the animals.

3) Utilizing the newly developed methods, the major metabolites of dopamine: Homovanillic Acid (HVA) and 3,4-dihydroxyphenyl acetic acid (DOPAC) were identified and quantified together with DA in the same animals. The rate of metabolite labeling with ^{18}O led to a revised protocol for the administration of $^{18}O_2$. Presently, the atmosphere respired consists initially of room air. As the O_2 is consumed it is replaced with $^{18}O_2$ (97%) until $^{18}O_2$ constitutes 35% of total oxygen. This enrichment is then maintained for 30 minutes. Following this reproducible labeling period, the animals are returned to room air (kinetic time zero, t_0) and sacrificed after various time intervals to observe the decay of labeling and thereby obtain kinetic data of synthesis and destruction.

4) ^{18}O incorporation at t_0 into dopamine in seven discrete areas of rat brain is shown in the following table.

TABLE 1

CONCENTRATION OF DOPAMINE IN RAT BRAIN NUCLEI AND REGIONS CONTAINING EITHER DOPAMINERGIC TERMINALS OR CELL BODIES AND THE INCORPORATION OF ^{18}O INTO DOPAMINE*

Nucleus or Region	Sample Size (µg protein)	Dopamine pmol/mg protein	% ^{18}O Incorporated
Caudatus	62 ± 3.3	473 ± 46	6.5
Caudatus/Putamen	63 ± 2.2	364 ± 34	5.5
Accumbens	61 ± 2.4	610 ± 46	8.5
Amygdaloideus			
Centralis	55 ± 2.2	238 ± 13	8.8
Tuberculus Olfactorius	61 ± 2.9	251 ± 41	8.9
Substantia Nigra			
Zona Compacta (A9)	61 ± 1.9	105 ± 29	23
Interpeduncularis (A10)	41 ± 3.9	151 ± 21	16

* Values for ^{18}O are from animals which have been maintained in an $^{18}O_2$ enriched environment (35%) for 30 min, and sacrificed at that point.

5) Decay of DA-^{18}O concentrations in these same regions at later times following the labeling period yields the following DA turnover rate data:

Area	DA-Turnover Rate (pmol mg prot^{-1} min^{-1})
N. Caudatus	2.6
N. Caudatus-Putamen	3.0
N. Accumbens	4.2
N. Amygalaloideus Centralis	2.7
Olfactorium tuberculum	5.4

6) Preliminary data show that ^{18}O labeling is relatively uniform in terminal regions. Also, cell body area (A9 and A10) appear to have a faster turnover rate, 2 to 3 times that of terminal regions.

7) Our preliminary data also demonstrate that ^{18}O labeling is greater in DA than in either HVA or DOPAC for a given region. Should this finding be corroborated by further experimentation one might suggest that DA is stored in a single metabolic pool.

Our results thus far indicate that this is a suitable approach to the in vivo labeling of the 5HT and DA present in various brain nuclei. Since the pool of O_2 in the body is quite generalized this technique should facilitate the estimation of monoamine turnover rate. From all points of view this technique should be applicable to man. $^{18}O_2$ has been shown to be nontoxic and its administration to man is simple. The measurement of either the biogenic amines and/or their metabolites from CSF is feasible by using the specific technique of GC-MS. The biomedic significance has no bounds, since if this proves to be a method of analyzing the dynamics of neurotransmitters in human brain, we could establish whether or not the turnover of NE, DA and 5HT is affected in mental diseases. In addition, we could study the alteration in these neurotransmitters as produced by various psychoactive agents.

Keyword Descriptors:

Stable isotope labeled, mass fragmentometry, and biogenic amines.

Publications:

Costa, E.: Multiple ion detection: A new tool for Neurochemistry and Biological Psychiatry. J. Psychiat. Res., 1974, pp 295.

Project No. Z01 MH 01498-03 SMRP
1. Division of Special Mental Health Research
2. Laboratory of Preclinical Pharmacology
3. Saint Elizabeths Hospital

PHS-ADAMHA-NIMH
Individual Project Report
July 1, 1974 through June 30, 1975

Project Title: Post tetanic potentiation: A phenomenon employed to assess anxiolytic and anticonvulsant drug actions.

Previous Serial Number: M-SMR-P-9

Principal Investigator: Amin Suria

Other Investigators: E. Costa

Cooperating Units: None

Man Years:

Total: 0.8
Professional: 0.8
Others: 0

Project Description:

To investigate the mechanism by which anxiolytic and non-sedative anticonvulsant drugs inhibit post-tetanic potentiation in sympathetic ganglia.

Preganglionic stimulation of a curarized sympathetic ganglion elicits a fast excitatory postsynaptic potential (EPSP), a slow inhibitory post-synaptic potential (IPSP) and a slow EPSP. The intensity of these potentials elicited by a single shock is increased when a single shock is preceded by an appropriate train of conditioning stimuli. This phenomenon is usually termed post-tetanic potentiation (PTP). These post-synaptic potentials as well as their PTP were recorded in the sympathetic ganglion of the bullfrog using extracellular as well as sucrose gap recording techniques. The effects of various anxiolytics on this phenomenon were then studied. The drug action on the resting membrane potential recorded from the preganglionic nerve terminals was also measured.

We found that benzodiazepine derivatives, eg., diazepam

(1 x 10^{-8}), chlordiazepoxide (1 x 10^{-6}M) and RO 5-5807 (1 x 10^{8}M) produced an inhibition of PTP of EPSP in a dose dependent, reproducible, and reversible fashion. Structurally related compounds, such as N-desmethyldiazepam and 3-OH-diazepam, reported metabolites of diazepam in various animal species including man, did not affect the PTP of EPSP. This observation was further substantiated by the fact that other classes of antiepileptic drugs, e.g., diphenylhydantoin (1 x 10^{-6}M), N-phenylbarbital (1 x 10^{-8}M) also suppress the PTP. A nonsedative barbiturate, hexobarbital (up to 1 x 10^{-4}M) has no effect on this response. None of these compounds altered the potential change evoked by single shock. Also the sedative properties of these agents were unrelated to their action on the PTP.

We also found that dibutyryl guanosine 3',5'-monophosphate (cGMP) and PGE_1 and PGE_2 (1 x 10^{-8}M) mimicked the action of diazepam on the PTP. Adenosine 3',5'-monophosphate (up to 1 x 10^{-4}M) had no effect on this response.

The inhibition obtained with diazepam could be potentiated in the presence of cGMP, PGE_1 or arachidonic acid, a precursor for prostaglandin synthesis. When the prostaglandin synthetase activity was blocked with 5, 8, 11, 14 eicosatetraynoic acid (ETA, 1 x 10^{-7}M), inhibition of PTP by diazepam and cGMP could be reversed but not that by PGE_1. When the receptors for prostaglandins were blocked with SC 19220 (1 x 10^{-8}M) the inhibition of PTP by diazepam, diB cGMP, PGE_1 and arachidonic acid could be abolished.

In curarized ganglia, these compounds neither inhibited the ganglionic EPSP elicited by a single shock, nor changed the membrane potential. In addition, diazepam does not change the time period required for curare to block the spike generation in sympathetic ganglia. PGs, diazepam and diB cGMP failed to reduce the membrane depolarization elicited by acetylcholine suggesting that these drugs may act presynaptically, perhaps by limiting the transmitter release. However, the drug effects described thus far were evaluated by recording the potential changes from the postganglionic sites. Since these observations led us to believe that drug effects may be limited to preganglionic sites, we decided to probe into the mechanism by which these compounds may modify the resting membrane potential of preganglionic nerve terminals per se.

Employing the sucrose-gap technique we found that cyclic adenosine 3',5'-monophosphate, its dibutyryl derivative or cGMP (10^{-5}M) failed to change the membrane potential recorded from the preganglionic nerve endings or from the interganglionic nerve

nerve axons. However, diBcGMP (10^{-6}M) depolarized the preganglionic nerve terminals without affecting the interganglionic nerve trunk membrane potential. Similarly, GABA (10^{-4}M) and diazepam (10^{-6}M) depolarize preganglionic nerve terminals. Glycine or glutamic acid (upto 10^{-5}M) had no effect. When the preganglionic nerve terminals were depolarized by diB cGMP, diazepam or GABA the amplitude of the action potential elicited by antidromic supramaximal stimulation was decreased. Furthermore, the depolarization exerted by these compounds could be blocked by picrotoxin (10^{-5}M). When the synthesis of GABA was inhibited by isoniazid or thiosemicarbazide (10^{-5}M) the presynaptic membrane depolarization elicited by diazepam and diB cGMP was abolished, however GABA retained its action.

In the presence of GABA synthesis inhibitors, nicotine could still depolarize the terminals of preganglionic nerves. The nicotine induced depolarization was blocked by d-tubocurarine (2×10^{-4}M). Picrotoxin did not abolish the depolarization elicited by nicotine.

From these data it was inferred that the depolarization of nerve terminals elicited by diazepam may depend on the release of GABA located in the glial cells in this ganglion. Reports by Bowery and Brown (Nature (New Biol) 238: 89-91, 1972) have indicated that a high affinity uptake for GABA may be present in glial cells of sympathetic ganglia. Assuming this to be true we studied the uptake of ^{3}H-GABA in the rat superior cervical ganglia and found the tissue/medium ratio to be 10:1 within 30 minutes. Benzodiazepines did not change the uptake of GABA in this ganglion. However, preliminary investigation have shown that diazepam and related compounds were able to release ^{3}H GABA taken up presumably by glial cells located in this ganglion preparation.

In view of the data we have obtained we suggest that in sympathetic ganglia, the depolarization of nerve terminals elicited by GABA that is released by diazepam from the glial cells storage sites may decrease the amount of transmitter released from the preganglionic nerves by incoming stimuli. This inhibition may explain the inhibition of PTP elicited by diazepam and diB cGMP. Since a short-term stimulation of preganglionic nerves of bullfrog sympathetic ganglia has been reported to increase the levels of cyclic GMP (Weight, F., Petzold, G., and Greengard, P.: Science, 186: 942-944, 1974) it is possible that endogenous cGMP accumulating in the ganglia after stimulation may have a role in limiting the PTP through the release of endogenous GABA. This working hypothesis presumes that the cGMP increase occurs in glial cells, because only in these cells has been shown a high affinity uptake for GABA. If anxiety is related to increased release of transmitters diazepam may cause the anxiolytic effect by stabilizing the amount of transmitter released by nerve impulses.

Although these drugs are the most widely used agents in clinical psychiatry, we do not yet understand why they exert an anxiolytic and antiepileptic action. This study helps to gain some insight into the mode of action of benzodiazepines. These studies are also directed to establish a biochemical and electrophysiological parameters to define antiepileptic and anxiolytic actions.

At present, studies are being conducted to investigate the effects of anticonvulsants after altering the metabolism of GABA and also the transmitter, acetylcholine. Studies are also underway to investigate the changes in prostaglandins effects after interfering with its metabolism. Experiments are being designed to define the sequence of events that may take place in altered synaptic transmission for compounds such as diazepam to act. In addition, studies are also being conducted to look at the role of IPSP and its PTP, that may contribute to the action of anticonvulsants.

Keyword Descriptors:

Sympathetic ganglia, nerve thresholds, azepines, gamma-aminobutyric acid, and brain cells.

Publications:

Suria, A. and Costa, E.: Diazepam inhibition of post-tetanic potentiation in bullfrog sympathetic ganglion: Possible role of prostaglandins. J. Pharmacol. Exp. Ther., 189: 690-696, 1974.

Suria, A. and Costa, E.: Benzodiazepines and post-tetanic potentiation in sympathetic ganglia of the bullfrog. Brain Res., 50: 235-239, 1973.

Suria, A. and Costa, E.: Action of diazepam, diBcGMP and GABA in the presynaptic terminals in bullfrog sympathetic ganglia. Brain Res., 87: 102-106, 1975.

Project No. Z01 MH 01499-01 SMRP
1. Division of Special Mental Health Research
2. Laboratory of Preclinical Pharmacology
3. Saint Elizabeths Hospital

PHS-ADAMHA-NIMH
Individual Project Report
July 1, 1974 through June 30, 1975

Project Title: Action of benzodiazepines on the second messengers of bullfrog sympathetic ganglia

Previous Serial Number: none

Principal Investigator: Richard Lehne and Amin Suria

Other Investigators: Petko Uzunov and E. Costa

Cooperating Units: None

Man Years:

Total:	1.4
Professional:	1.4
Others:	0

Project Description:

We have recently shown that benzodiazepines endowed of anxiolytic activity, limit the increment in the release of transmitter from presynaptic terminals of bullfrog sympathetic ganglia, observed at various times after a conditioning stimulus (see Serial No. M-SMR-P-9, 1974). We explored the mechanisms by which anxiolytic drugs may modify the release of presynaptically located acetylcholine by electrical stimuli delivered at various times after a conditioning stimulus. Moreover, we investigated whether this modification involves the participation of cyclic nculeotides. This possibility was enhanced by the finding that diBcGMP can mimic the inhibition of posttetanic potentiation elicited by diazepam in bullfrog sympathetic ganglia. Our objective is to investigate the possibility that anxiolytics exert their action by reducing ACh release and hence decrease synaptic transmission by a mechanism involving modulation of cyclic nucleotide metabolism.

Cyclic AMP and cyclic GMP contents were determined in the IXth and Xth paravertebral sympathetic ganglia of the bullfrog (Rana Catesbiana) following electrical stimulation (40Hz for 4 seconds) at a voltage capable of eliciting a half maximal action potential as observed by oscilloscope monitoring. The cAMP and cGMP present in tissues were separated by the method of Mao et al. (Analytical Biochem. 59, 63-68, 1974), and quantitated by their ability to activate protein kinase.

Cyclic AMP phosphodiesterase (cAMP-PDE) and cyclic GMP phosphodiesterase (cGMP-PDE) activities were measured by the method of Filburn and Karn (Anal. Biochem. 52, 505-516, 1973).

Phosphodiesterase activities were assayed using either crude homogenates of bullfrog sympathetic ganglia or a purified, activator-deficient phosphodiesterase (peak II) isolated from rat cerebral cortex by the method of Uzunov and Weiss (Biochem. Biophys. Acta 284: 220-226, 1972). The endogenous PDE activator protein was purified from rat brain homogenate by modified procedures of Lin et al. (J. Biol. Chem. 249: 4943-4954, 1974).

We have found that electrical stimulation of bullfrog sympathetic ganglia in the presence of 10 μM Diazepam produces a 4 to 6 fold increase in endogenous cAMP levels as compared to nonstimulated controls. Stimulation in the absence of diazepam produces only a 2 fold increase in cAMP levels. The stimulation induced increase occurs within 10 seconds after stimulation for 4 seconds at 40 Hz and 3.5V. The elevated cAMP persists for at least one minute after stimulation. This increase in cAMP is not blocked by cholinergic receptor antagonists (d-tubocurarine or atropine). We have failed to observe significant changes in cGMP levels under the stimulation conditions employed.

To investigate the mechanism by which diazepam potentiates the stimulation induced increase of cAMP content in bullfrog ganglia, we determined the inhibitory kinetics of this drug on cAMP-PDE and cGMP-PDE in crude homogenates of bullfrog ganglia. The Km of the enzyme for cGMP-PDE is 2.4 μM and the Ki of diazepam for cGMP is 40 μM. The Km values for cAMP-PDE in the ganglion are 20 μM and 4 μM. The Ki of diazepam for cAMP-PDE is 20 μM.

An endogenous protein activator can regulate Km of the activator deficient PDE; moreover conditions that cause the cAMP and cGMP tissue content to increase can also cause an increase of the PDE activator. There is a coincidence between the increase of the PDE activator and the decline of the cyclic nucleotide content. We decided to investigate the inhibitory action of the benzodiazepines on a purified PDE system using activator deficient PDE ± the purified endogenous activator protein. These experiments were designed to determine the effects of the benzodiazepines in the regulation of the PDE kinetic constants by the protein activator.

The kinetic effects of the protein activator on both cAMP and cGMP hydrolyzing activity by PDE in the absence of inhibitors are described in Project No.
The benzodiazepines inhibit the activator deficient PDE. The activator protein produces both a qualitative and a quantitative change on the inhibitory action of benzodiazepines using both cAMP and cGMP as substrates. Some benzodiazepines (medazepam, diazepam, desmesmethyldiazepam) are more effective inhibitors of the activated PDE than of the activator deficient enzyme, using either cAMP or cGMP as substrates. Nitrazepam, flunitrazepam, and oxazepam became less effective inhibitors in the presence of activator. The Ki of chlordiazepoxide remains unchanged in the presence of activator.

When cGMP is the substrate, the type of inhibition of PDE seen using benzodiazepines is always competitive, whether the enzyme is activated or not. With cAMP as substrate, however, addition of activator changes the inhibition from non-competitive to competitive for medazepam, chlordiazepoxide, oxazepam, desmethyl-diazepam and RO-5-5807.

The purified PDE has a Km for cAMP by about 450 μM which drops to 170 μM in the presence of 6 μgm of the activator protein. The Ki values of the benzodiazepines for the activator deficient cAMP-PDE range from 243 μM (Medazepam) to 2116 μM (RO-11-3624). The Ki's of various benzodiazepines for the activated cAMP-PDE range from 28 μM (Medazepam) to 218 μM (RO-11-3624).

The Km for cGMP-PDE is about 9 μM. The Ki values for the activator deficient cGMP-PDE range from 27 μM (Medazepam) to 237 μM (RO-5-5807). In the presence of 6 μgm of activator protein the Ki range is from 12 μM (medazepam) to 619 μM (Oxazepam).

We have also determined that the benzodiazepines do not interfere with the interaction between the PDE and the activator, and hence presumably they interact with the substrate at the active site of the enzyme. This has been concluded from the inability of increased activator to overcome inhibition by medazepam. Preincubation with activator ± diazepam fails to effect the degree of inhibition observed also indicating that the drug does not interfere with the PDE-activator interactions.

We have determined the PDE inhibitory constants for dilantin and phenetharbital, compounds capable of producing electrophysiological changes in bullfrog sympathetic ganglia similar to those elicited by diazepam, but known to be similar to those elicited by diazepam, but known to be non-anxiolytics. The Ki values of these drugs are 10 to 1,000 times greater than those of the benzodiazepines, indicating that they have different mechanisms of action.

Benzodiazepines are useful in treating clinical conditions characterized by neuronal hyperactivity. If inhibition of cAMP-PDE is involved in the therapeutic actions of the benzodiazepines, we must conclude that the elevated cAMP levels induced by this PDE inhibition must somehow exert an inhibitory influence on neuronal firing or synaptic transmission. The possibility that benzodiazepines work through a cAMP mechanism is substantiated by the observation that both diazepam and diBcAMP exert the same potentiating action on the post tetanic potentiation of the inhibitory post synaptic potential recorded from bullfrog sympathetic ganglia. We have shown the benzodiazepines to have Ki values 10 to 40 times below the Km of cAMP-PDE. The Ki values for cGMP-PDE, however, are from 2 to 60 times above the Km. These values would indicate a greater in vivo capacity to inhibit cAMP-PDE than the cGMP hydrolyzing enzyme, and hence increase cAMP levels but not those of cGMP. This is consistent with our observation that diazepam increases cAMP levels in electrically stimulated bullfrog ganglia. We have also shown that certain benzodiazepines have increased potency as cAMP-PDE inhibitors in the presence of the PDE activator protein. This body of evidence allows the hypothesis that interference with cAMP metabolism may be involved in benzodiazepine action.

The mechanism by which anxiolytics exert their action remains unknown. Knowledge of the biochemical mechanism by which these drugs modify synaptic transmission may lead to a better understanding of the disease states for which they are used and aid in the development of more specific drugs to treat them.

We plan to measure the effects of benzodiazepines on cGMP levels in electrically stimulated and non-stimulated bullfrog sympathetic ganglia to see if these drugs can also interfere with cGMP metabolism in the intact ganglion.

Studies are planned to evaluate the effects of dilantin and phenetharbital on cAMP and cGMP levels in stimulated and control ganglia. These drugs produce electrophysiological effects similar to diazepam, but lack the ability to effectively inhibit cyclic nucleotide PDE. An absence of an effect on cAMP or cGMP levels would suggest that these compounds produce their electrophysiological responses by different biochemical mechanisms from the benzodiazepines.

We plan to measure the effects of electrical stimulation on the level of protein activator of PDE in bullfrog ganglia in the presence and absence of diazepam. This would allow us to evaluate the contribution of this PDE regulatory mechanism to the observed effects of the benzodiazepines. We will also determine if diazepam interferes with activator metabolism.

Studies are planned to measure PTP of the IPSP in bullfrog ganglia in the presence of those benzodiazepines whose PDE inhibitory kinetics we have established. This will allow a correlation between the electrophysiological and biochemical properties of these drugs.

Keyword Descriptors:

Sympathetic ganglia, azepines, nucleases, nucleotides, nucleoside monophosphates cyclic

Project No. Z01 MH 01500-04 SMRP
1. Division of Special Mental Health Research
2. Laboratory of Preclinical Pharmacology
3. Saint Elizabeths Hospital

PHS-ADAMHA-NIMH
Individual Project Report
July 1, 1974 through June 30, 1975

Project Title: Mass fragmentographic studies on the metabolism and function of indolealkylamines in discrete areas of the central nervous system.

Previous Serial Number: M-SMR-P-8

Principal Investigator: L. Bertilsson

Other Investigators: E. Costa and S. H. Koslow

Cooperating Units: None

Man Years:

Total:	1.0
Professional:	1.0
Others:	0

Project Description:

Our objectives are:

(1) To identify and quantitate known and novel indolealkylamines in various tissues of animals and man, with the primary emphasis being on neuronal tissue.

(2) To understand the function of these putative transmitters at the synapse and the effect of various pharmacological agents on these compounds.

The methods used were gas chromatography-mass spectrometry and microdissection. In order to study the integration of various neurotransmitter function at synaptic level, we have developed a technique for the reproducible removal of discrete brain nuclei (40-400 μg protein) containing specific nerve terminals and cell bodies.

Influence of p-chloroamphetamine (PCA) on 5-hydroxytryptamine (5-HT) in rat brain nuclei: PCA has been used in man as an antidepressant drug. It has recently been reported that PCA causes cytopathological changes in brains of rats (Harvey et al.,

Science 187: 841-843, 1975). This neurotoxic effect was localized primarily to an area of the ventral midbrain tegmentum corresponding to the B9 serotonergic group of cell bodies. Using a microdissection technique and mass fragmentography, we have measured the concentration of 5-HT in the nuclei called B7, B8 and B9. The level of 5-HT in these nuclei was 173 ± 8, 208 ± 10 and 105 ± 4 picomoles/mg protein, respectively. When rats were injected with PCA (25 μmoles/kg; i.p.) the level of 5-HT in B7 or B8 did not significantly change 0.67, 6, 14 and 21 days after injection. On the other hand, the concentration decreased significantly in the B9 cell body group 6 and 14 days postinjection. At a higher dose of PCA (100 μmoles/kg), the concentration of 5-HT and the activity of tryptophan hydroxylase (measured by higher-pressure liquid chromatography in collaboration with Drs. Meek and Neckers in this laboratory) were both significantly decreased in the B9 area, but not in B7 or B8 3 weeks after treatment. It may be concluded that the selective cytopathological changes observed in the B9 area after administration of PCA are probably correlated to decreased serotonergic function.

5-Methoxytryptamine (5-MT):

To improve the mass fragmentographic determination of 5-MT, this compound labelled with three deuterium atoms has been synthesized. This will be used as an internal standard for the precise quantitation of small amounts of the parent compound.

The pathology associated with effective disorders may include serotonergic brain mechanisms. It is therefore of importance to study the influence of drugs on this transmitter system at a basic level. Our studies have revealed a specific neurotoxicity elicited by PCA, and have focused our attention on possible influences exerted by drugs on the control of protein synthesis.

Methylated indoles (e.g. 5-MT and melatonin) have beem implicated in the pathogenesis of various mental disorders. As such compounds now have been shown to occur in man, it seems possible that an alteration in their metabolism may be considered as a cause of mental disorders. The measurement of indoleamines at specific brain nuclei allows for studies to understand basic molecular mechanisms that control neuronal trophism and function. An understanding of such mechanism may open new vistas in our knowledge of how the integration and regulation of various neurotransmitters at synapses.

Our proposed course is:

(1) The effect of the anorexogenic drug fenfluramine on serotonergic cell bodies and nerve terminals will be studied.

(2) 5-MT will be measured in human cerebrospinal fluid to evaluate its possible correlation to various psychiatric disorders.

(3) In the rat brain the regional distribution of 5-MT will be determined. The influence of different drugs on the concentration of 5-MT in rat brain nuclei will also be studied.

Keyword Descriptors:

Microdissection, phenylethylamines, serotonin, and mass fragmentometry.

Publications:

Koslow, S. H., Racagni, G. and Costa, E.: Mass fragmentographic measurement of norepinephrine, dopamine, serotonin and acetylcholine in seven discrete nuclei of the rat teldiencephalon. Neuropharmacol. 13: 1123-1130, 1974.

Project No. Z01 MH 01501-04 SMRP
1. Division of Special Mental Health Research
2. Laboratory of Preclinical Pharmacology
3. Saint Elizabeths Hospital

PHS-ADAMHA-NIMH
Individual Project Report
July 1, 1974 through June 30, 1975

Project Title: Biochemical and morphological characterization of sympathetic ganglia and neuronal chemoreceptors.

Previous Serial Number: M-SMR-P-34

Principal Investigator: S. H. Koslow

Other Investigators: E. Costa

Cooperating Units: Department of Anatomy, University of Umea, Sweden

Man Years:

Total: 0.2
Professional: 0.2
Others: 0

Project Description:

To ascertain the neurochemicals involved in the neurotransmitter or neurohumoral role in the different cellular elements within the superior cervical ganglion and the carotid body.

Gas Chromatography-Mass Spectrometry (Koslow, Cattabeni and Costa, Science, 176: 177-180, 1972); Microdissection (Koslow, Third Int. Catecholamine Sŷmp., Pergamon Press, 1085-1090, 1973); Light and Electron Microscopy. Morphometric analysis (Hellstrom, J. Neurocytology 4; 77-86, 1975).

Rat superior cervical ganglion contains a finite amount of epinephrine all of which is of ganglionic origin. Treatment of newborn rats with dexamethasone results in a 112 fold increase in the epinephrine concentration whereas the norepinephrine and dopamine are increased by only 1.4 and 1.9-fold respectively. This epinephrine increase in newborn rats is reversible if treatment is discontinued, and it fails to occur in adult animals. The epinephrine store of normal and dexamethasone treated animals is resistant to the depletion by reserpine. There is no increase in the epinephrine content in organs innervated by axon emanating from the ganglion.

The normal levels of the biogenic amines were measured in both the adult and infant carotid body. This grouping of chemoreceptors is extremely small (dry weight adult = 8.3 ug infant 5.6 ug) and thus the measurements were possible on individual carotid bodies by using the technique of GC-MS. In adult carotid body high concentration of dopamine (1950 pmol/mg protein) and norepinephrine (1140 pmol/mg protein) were found together with a comparatively low concentration of serotonin (505 pmol/mg protein). The carotid body of infant rats contain 1065 pmol dopamine/mg protein and 410 pmol norepinephrine/mg protein. Epinephrine could not be detected. Surgical sympathetic denervation and chemical sympathectomy (6-hydroxydopamine) did not significantly change the catecholamine content of the adult carotid body. Reserpine, L-DOPA, and pargyline each produced their predictable effect. Reserpine depleted the catecholamines in a dose dependent fashion, while L-DOPA and pargyline drastically increased the catecholamine concentration in the carotid body. Following inhibition of dopamine-β-hydroxylase by diethyldithiocarbonate there was the expected decrease in norepinephrine however, there was not a reciprocal increase in the dopamine concentrations.

Treatment of adult rats with dexamethasone for 10 days results in both biochemical and morphological alteration of the rat carotid body. Norepinephrine and dopamine concentrations more than doubled after dexamethasone treatment. The increase in NE was relatively greater than that of DA, 2.5 and 2.0 times, respectively. No epinephrine was detected even though the sensitivity of the method is greater than 0.1 pmol. Quantitative electron microscopic studies showed that the dense core vesicles of both subclasses of Type I cells (small vesicle cells (SVC) and large vesicle cells, LVC) increased in volume densities and diameter. These increase were more pronounced for SVC than for LVC.

Using the highly sensitive and specific technique of gas chromatography-mass spectrometry the catecholamine content of different cell types of the rat superior cervical ganglion and carotid body has been determined. In the ganglion our previous studies have shown the existence of dopaminergic, small intensity fluorescent (SIF) cells. The current results suggest that there is a second population of SIF cells which contain epinephrine. This conclusion is based on the correlation of our biochemical findings with histochemical and enzymatic data.

It is apparent that the Glomus, Type I cells are similar to

ganglion cells in that there are at least two types of these chemoreceptors. One type contains LVC and probably stores DA as supported by the more pronounced change in dopamine concentrations and morphometric results following DOPA treatment. The other types contains LVC and store NE since following dexamethasone there is a correlation in NE concentration and SVC morphology.

These peripheral neuronal grouping, (1) the superior cervical ganglion (a relay station) and (2) the carotid body (chemoreceptor) are relatively simple models to study the interactions and function of catecholamines. Similar types of neuronal mechanisms may operate in the brain and will therefore be easier to comprehend if there is a simple model to build from.

Further studies will be done on both the ganglion and carotid body to expand on the relationship of these neurotransmitter to function. The approach will be pharmacological, using the parameter of chemical, morphological and enzymatic changes as end points.

Keyword Descriptors:

Mass fragmentometry, catecholamines, superior cervical ganglion, carotid body, receptors, morphogenesis, electron microscopy.

Publications:

Suria, A., Koslow, S. H.: Heterogenerous reinnervation of sympathetic lumbar ganglia with sympathetic postganglionic nerves. In: Dynamics of Degeneration and Growth in Neurons. ed. Fuxe, Olson and Zotterman. Pergamon Press, Oxford and N. Y. pp 469-477, 1974.

Koslow, S. H., Bjegovic, M. and Costa, E.: Catecholamines in sympathetic ganglia of rat effects of Dexamethasone and Reserpine. J. Neurochem. 24: 277-281, 1975.

Costa, E., Bjegovic and Koslow, S. H.: Mass Fragmentography: A method to study monoamine neurotransmitters in Brain Nuclei. Psychoneuroendocrinology, 304-312, 1974.

Project No. Z01 MH 01502-04 SMRP
1. Division of Special Mental Health Research
2. Laboratory of Preclinical Pharmacology
3. Saint Elizabeths Hospital

PHS-ADAMHA-NIMH
Individual Project Report
July 1, 1974 through June 30, 1975

Project Title: Mass Fragmentographic studies on the metabolism and function of catecholamines in discrete brain nuclei of the central nervous system.

Previous Serial Number: M-SMR-P-21

Principal Investigator: S. H. Koslow

Other Investigators: E. Costa

Cooperating Units: SMRN-IR-MH
Department of Neurology and Pediatrics, Johns Hopkins Hospital, Lab. Neurochemistry, NIMH, Bethesda, Md.

Man Years:

Total:	0.2
Professional:	0.2
Other:	0

Project Description:

Our objective is to study the functional interactions between catecholaminergic and other neuronal systems in relation to the action of pharmacological agents and the changes elicited by disease states.

Gas Chromatography-Mass Spectrometry (Koslow, Cattabeni and Costa, Science: 176, 177-180, 1972). Microdissection of specific brain nuclei (Koslow, Racagni and Costa; Neuropharmacology: 13; 1123-1130, 1974).

Norepinephrine, dopamine, and epinephrine are measured in discrete nuclei of the rat brain, containing .050-.100 mg protein. The mass fragmentographic results substantiate the location of norepinephrine and dopamine described in histochemical reports but add quantitation to the mapping of the transmitter. In single nuclei these measurements show that the precursor pool of dopamine in noradrenergic terminals is approximately 6 percent of the norepinephrine pool. In the N. Caudatus/putamen the distribution of dopamine varies along the major axis of the nucleus, suggesting a biomodal distribution of the dopaminergic terminals.

Epinephrine has been localized in specific nuclei of the rat brain of 15 regions studied 5 contained epinephrine. The highest epinephrine concentrations is found in the periventricular area, 6.5 and 2.6 percent respectively. Using a specific inhibitor of PNMT, the enzyme responsible for the synthesis of epinephrine from NE, it is possible to selectively decrease the epinephrine concentration.

Catecholamines and their metabolites were measured in human brain biopsy and CSF of a patient with dihydropteridine reductase deficiency were done. The CSF concentration of HVA were low and minimally increased after probenocid treatment. The brain biopsy showed apparently normal values for norepinephrine, while the dopamine values were apparently deficient.

The measurement of neurotransmitter at their site of action is paramount to the study of neuronal function. The dissection of very discrete regions and nuclei allows us to study the effect of drugs and the consequences of disease states at synaptic level, with almost absolute specificity in the transmitter measurements.

The finding that dopamine in noradrenergic neurons is only 6 percent of the norepinephrine concentration, gives an index to test if various "noreadrenergic" nerve terminals impinging upon a given brain nucleus are pure or are also intermixed with dopaminergic neurons. The biomodal distribution of nigrostriatal dopamine neurons, which one neuronal population confined to the N. Caudatus and the other to the N. Caudatus/Putamen has multiple implications. Sampling of this region must be done with care for a study should entertain the possibility of different afferent connection as well as some different functions.

The presence of epinephrine in discrete regions supports the idea of an adrenergic neuronal system within the mammalian CNS. Some of the areas which contain epinephrine coincide with regions whose neurons give a positive reaction for PNMT (Hckfelt, 1974). It is now important to completely map this adrenergic system and establish its functional significance.

Dihydropteridine reductase is responsible for regeneration of tetrahydrobiopterine, an essential cofactor for hydroxylation of phenylalanine, tyrosine in the synthesis of dopamine and norepinephrine. The normal levels of norepinephrine with impaired dopamine synthesis in brain suggest the participation of alternative pathways or the preferential formation of norepinephrine which do not relay on hydroxylation of tyrosine to dihydroxyphenylalanine. These impaired biosynthetic functions may be causal to undefined degenerative neurological disorder this patient has.

Extensive pharmacological studies will be done to ascertain the effects of specific agents of different amine systems at both the cell body and terminal sites.

The mapping of the epinephrine system will be continued and the effects of specific drugs or this system studied.

Analysis of the CSF from the patient with dihydropteridine reductase deficiency will be done following various treatments to restore a neurotransmitter balance.

Keyword Descriptors:

Mass fragmentometry, catecholamines, microdissection, homovaillic acid, and pteridines.

Publications:

Koslow, S. H. and Schlumpf, M.: Quantitation of epinephrine in rat brain nuclei and areas by mass fragmentography. Nature, Vol. 251, 530-531, 1974.

Koslow, S. H., Racagni, G., and Costa, E.: Mass Fragmentographic measurement of norepinephrine, dopamine, serotonin and acetylcholine in seven discrete nuclei of the rat tel-diencephalic. Neuropharmacology, 13: 1123-1130, 1974.

Project No. Z01 MH 01503-02 SMRP
1. Division of Special Mental Health Research
2. Laboratory of Preclinical Pharmacology
3. Saint Elizabeths Hospital

PHS-ADAMHA-NIMH
Individual Project Report
July 1, 1974 through June 30, 1975

Project Title: Application of gas chromatography-mass spectrometry to the study of choline and acetylcholine metabolism in nuclei of rat brain

Previous Serial Number: M-SMR-P-13

Principal Investigator: G. Racagni

Other Investigators: D. L. Cheney, G. Zsilla, H. LeFevre, and E. Costa

Cooperating Units: None

Man Years:

Total: 0.3
Professional: 0.3
Others: 0

Project Description:

To label endogenous brain stores of choline and acetylcholine in order to establish a basis for measuring turnover rate of neuronal acetylcholine and choline at the synaptic level.

Concentrations of acetylcholine and choline have been measured using gas chromatography/mass spectrometry (Finnigan 3000). D-9 choline and D-9 acetylcholine were used as internal standards. The gas chromatographic method described by Hanin, Cheney, Trabucchi, Massarelli, Wang and Costa, JPET 187: 68-77 (1973) was used for the separation of the demethylated products of choline and acetylcholine. Fragments with m/e of 58 and 64 were selected for mass fragmentographic determination of choline and acetylcholine. The measurement by mass fragmentography allows for quantitation of extremely low levels of acetylcholine (10^{-13} moles) with a high degree of specificity. By this approach concentrations of both acetylcholine and choline could be measured in microgram quantities of protein. Application of focused microwaves (75 W/cm^2) to the skull which instantaneously inactivates brain enzymes has added reliability to the estimations of acetyl holine in stereomicroscopically isolated discrete brain nuclei. tained 400 micron thick sections were examined by light micro-copy in order to measure the distance to the nuclei from other andmarks within a given section, using the atlas of Konig and .lippel. These approaches made it possible to localize and :issect the nuclei reproducibly. The nuclei were punched out 'ith stainless steel tubing (0.8-1.2 mm i.d.), were transferred .o ground glass homogenizers (-70°C) and prepared for analysis. ιcetylcholine and choline stores in brain nuclei were labelled ›y a constant rate intravenous infusion with D-4 choline. By :ocusing the mass anlayzer on three characteristic ions (i.e. m/e ›8, 60 and 64) and measuring the intensity of the ion current at ;pecific gas chromatographic retention time the enrichment of leuteriated cholıne and acetylcholine in brain nuclei was ιeasured at various times of infusion.

In order to measure turnover rates of ACh in individual ıuclei of rat brain, the concentrations of acetylcholine were neasured, these results are summarized in Table 1. From these lata it was postulated that when the ACh/CAT x 100 is greater :han 0.7 and the ACh content is 0.30 nmoles/mg protein or greater :he transmitter may be located in nerve terminals. When this ratıo is smaller than 0.4 and the CAT activity is greater than 5.0 nmoles/mg protein/hr, the ACh measured may be located in :holinergic cell bodies or small cholinergic interneurons. This postulate is supported by measurement of the ACh content and CAT activity in brain nuclei containing a large number of cholinergic cell bodies (e.g., motor nucleus of the vagus) or small cholinergic interneurons (n. caudatus and n. accumbens) or cholinergic nerve terminals (n. locus coeruleus, dorsal raphes).

An intravenous infusion of deuterated choline (5 or 25 μmoles/kg/min) increases the concentration of acetylcholine in cortex but only 25 μmoles/kg/min increases the acetylcholine content in striatum. When constant infusion of deuterated choline is used to measure acetylcholine turnover rate, a dose of 1 μmole/kg/min appears to be a maximal infusion rate. The enrichment was sufficient to allow determination of the turnover rate of acetylcholine.

It has been postulated that alteration in the dynamics that regulates transmitter function at synaptic level may be involved in ghe genesis of various forms of psychopathology. The role of acetylcholine in mental diseases is still unknown. Since neuronal activity is regulated by the rates of release and enzymatic inactivation of transmitters including acetylcholine, the study of the turnover rate of acetylcholine is a good tool to better understand the functional involvement of the cholinergic system.

Drugs that change cholinergic function in selected brain nuclei of normal animals are used successfully in the therapy of mental diseases. The in vivo study of acetylcholine turnover rate in specific brain nuclei may yield an understanding of the processes involved in the control of acetylcholine steady state at the synaptic level.

We propose to use a combination of two techniques: (1) Rapid and permanent inactivation of the enzymes involves in the synthesis and degradation of acetylcholine through the use of focused microwave irradiation and (2) measurement of acetylcholine turnover in discrete nuclei of rat brain using gas chromatography-mass spectrometry. First we will determine the acetylcholine turnover in different nuclei of the rat brain. Then we can determine the effect of cholinergic drugs on these nuclei. Moreover we will study the interrelationships between the cholinergic and monoaminergic functions in these specific nuclei.

Keyword Descriptors:

Acetylcholine and choline.

Publications:

Cheney, D. L., LeFevre, H. F. and G. Racagni: Choline acetyltransferase activity and mass fragmentographic measurement of acetylcholine in specific nuclei and tracts of rat brain Neuropharmacology, in press, 1975.

TABLE 1

ACh CONCENTRATION AND CHOLINE ACETYLTRANSFERASE (CAT) ACTIVITY IN NUCLEI OF RAT BRAIN.

	ACh nmoles / mg Protein	CAT nmoles / mg Protein hr.	ACh / CAT x 100
White matter			
genu corporis callosi	0.07 ± 0.014	2.3 ± 0.77	3.04
anterior commissura	0.14 ± 0.029	3.0 ± 0.92	4.6
capsula interna	0.19 ± 0.051	2.4 ± 0.70	7.9
Rostral limbic nuclei			
tractus olfactorius	0.20 ± 0.09	1.6 ± 0.43	12.5
tuberculum olfactorium	0.20 ± 0.017	7.4 ± 0.50	2.70
N. accumbens	0.60 ± 0.061	240 ± 22	0.25
Nuclei septi			
N. Septi medialis	0.20 ± 0.04	50 ± 9.1	0.40
N. Septi triangularis	0.27 ± 0.027	90 ± 1.7	0.30
Nuclei Amygdalae			
Area Amygdalodea anterior	0.37 ± 0.052	180 ± 36	0.20
N. amygdaloideus basalis	0.31 ± 0.044	53 ± 7.0	0.58
N. amygdaloideus medialis	0.33 ± 0.043	80 ± 7.7	0.41
N. amygdaloideus corticalis	0.49 ± 0.097	70 ± 7.8	0.70
N. amydgaloideus lateralis pars posterior	0.16 ± 0.011	70 ± 16	0.22
Preoptic area			
N. preopticus medialis	0.06 ± 0.021	4 ± 1.5	1.5
N. preopticus lateralis	0.21 ± 0.037	170 ± 17	0.12
Basal ganglia			
N. Caudatus	0.60 ± 0.032	200 ± 35	0.30
Globus pallidus	0.16 ± 0.023	80 ± 13	0.20
Hypothalamic and thalamic nuclei			
N. anterior (hypothalamus)	0.20 ± 0.050	30 ± 1.2	0.60
N. thalamus ventralis	0.23 ± 0.016	20 ± 2.5	1.2
N. thalamus lateralis	0.18 ± 0.016	20 ± 2.8	0.90
N. thalamus anterior	0.29 ± 0.061	40 ± 5.2	0.70
N. thalamus medialis pars medialis	0.40 ± 0.041	50 ± 3.1	0.80
Habenula			
N. habenula lateralis	0.43 ± 0.12	50 ± 8.1	0.86

	ACh nmoles / mg Protein	CAT nmoles / mg Protein hr.	ACh / CAT x 100
Corpus Mamillaris			
N. mamillaris lateralis	0.26 ± 0.051	10 ± 0.81	2.6
Midbrain nuclei			
N. dorsalis raphes	0.72 ± 0.17	40 ± 3.4	1.8
N. medialis raphes	0.13 ± 0.024	40 ± 3.4	0.32
N. linearis pars caudalis	0.53 ± 0.18	50 ± 0.16	1.1
Formatio Reticularis	0.27 ± 0.051	30 ± 3.6	0.90
N. ruber	0.43 ± 0.10	40 ± 2.1	1.1
Substantia nigra	0.11 ± 0.018	5.0 ± 0.6	2.2
N. geniculatus medialis	0.17 ± 0.040	20 ± 1.7	0.85
N. interpeduncularis	1.27 ± 0.11	576 ± 63	0.22
Nuclei Pontis			
N. locus coeruleus	0.34 ± 0.050	12 ± 2.1	2.8
N. tegmenti dorsalis	0.38 ± 0.020	61 ± 14	0.62
N. dorsalis Vagi	0.36 ± 0.070	132 ± 33	0.27
Nuclei cerebelli			
N. dentatus	0.17 ± 0.0010	25 ± 3.9	0.68
N. interpositus	0.19 ± 0.040	17 ± 2.8	1.1

Project No. Z01 MH 01504-02 SMRP
1. Division of Special Mental Health Research
2. Laboratory of Preclinical Pharmacology
3. Saint Elizabeths Hospital

PHS-ADAMHA-NIMH
Individual Project Report
July 1, 1974 through June 30, 1975

Project Title: Interactions of cholinergic and monoaminergic neuronal systems: Effect of neuroleptics

Previous Serial Number: M-SMR-P-15

Principal Investigator: G. Racagni

Other Investigators: D. Cheney, G. Zsilla and E. Costa

Cooperating Units: None

Man Years:

Total: 0.5
Professional: 0.5
Others: 0

Project Description:

To study the interactions between various neuronal systems by measuring turnover rate of ACh in nuclei known to contain cholinergic cells and monoaminergic efferent innervation.

The methodology and techniques used in these studies have been described in detail in annual report M-SMR-P-14.

Clozapine and Haloperidol

Since small cholinergic interneurones participate in the regulation of corpus striatal function, we have measured acetylcholine content and turnover rate in striatum and cortex of rats receiving haloperidol and clozapine. Clozapine (30 μmoles/kg i.p.) and haloperidol (10 μmoles/kg i.p.) reverse the decrease of striatal acetylcholine turnover rate elicited by apomorphine (11 μmoles/kg i.p.). Haloperidol, per se, fails to change the striatal acetylcholine content but increases the acetylcholine turnover from 1.09 ± 0.092 μmoles/g/hr to 1.90 ± 0.11 μmoles/g/hr (15 and 30 μmoles/kg i.p.) rate. Clozapine fails to decrease the striatal content of either acetylcholine or choline nor does it affect the turnover rate of striatal acetylcholine. Moreover 60 and 90 μmoles/kg i.p. of clozapine causes a 40% decrease of acetylcholine content without affectin the turnover rate. These results suggest that both haloperidol and clozapine inhibit the activation of dopamine receptors in striatum. The lack of effect of clozapine on the striatal acetylcholine turnover rate suggests the possibility of a regulation within the cholinergic interneurons. Studies on behavio have demonstrated that clozapine (30 μmoles/kg i.p.) blocks the increase of locomotor activity elicited by apomorphine (11 μmoles/kg i.p.) without modifying the stereotypic behavior of this dopaminergic receptor stimulant.

We hope that these findings will help to elucidate how various synapses are interconnected in their function in a given brain nucleus. These studies suggest that in striatum there is a relationship between cholinergic and dopaminergic systems. The lack of effect of clozapine on the turnover of striatal acetylcholine suggests that an increase of striatal acetylcholine turnover elicited by neurolytics may be important in the genesis of extrapyramidal side effects. The introductio of neuropharmacology of the study of drug effects on regulatory interactions between cholinergic and dopaminergic neurons has widened the level of our understanding of the mode of action of antipsychotics. These studies may also help to design new criteria to evaluate the potential extrapyramidal side effects of novel neuroleptics.

We are currently investigating the effect of other pharmacological agents on the turnover rate of acetylcholine in accumbens and other nuclei of the mesolimbic system where similar interactions between cholinergic and monoaminergic neurons may occur.

Keyword Descriptors:

Acetylcholine, choline, haloperidol, apomorphine, and psychopharmacological agents.

Publications:

Trabucchi, M., Cheney, D., Racagni, G. and Costa, E.: Involvement of brain cholinergic mechanisms in the action of chlorpromazine. Nature, 249: 664-666, 1974.

Trabucchi, M., Cheney, D. L., Racagni, G. and Costa, E.: In vivo inhibition of striatal acetylcholine turnover by l-dopa apomorphine and (+)-amphetamine. Br. Res. 85: 130-134, 1975

Project No. Z01 MH 01505-02 SMRP
1. Division of Special Mental Health Research
2. Laboratory of Preclinical Pharmacology
3. Saint Elizabeths Hospital

PHS-ADAMHA-NIMH
Individual Project Report
July 1, 1974 through June 30, 1975

Project Title: Pharmacological investigation of factors controlling acetylcholine turnover rate in rat brain *in vivo*.

Previous Serial Number: M-SMR-P-3

Principal Investigator: G. Racagni

Other Investigators: D. L. Cheney, G. Zsilla, and E. Costa

Cooperating Units: None

Man Years:

Total:	0.2
Professional:	0.2
Others:	0

Project Description:

Little is known concerning the mechanisms that regulate the function of cholinergic neurons in the central nervous system.

The methodology and techniques used in this study were described in annual report M-SMR-P-14. Striatal concentrations of choline and acetylcholine were stabilized by focusing a beam of microwave radiation to the skull (1.5 sec for mice and 2 sec for rats).

Oxotremorine (5 µmol/kg, i.p.) increased acetylcholine but not choline content in striatum of rats.

Studies of acetylcholine turnover at the new steady state demonstrated that oxotremorine decreased the acetylcholine turnover rate in rat striatum. Clozapine but not haloperidol, antagonized the increased acetylcholine content and the decreased turnover rate of rat striatal acetylcholine elicited by oxotremorine.

Physostigmine (22 µmol/kg i.p.) increased the brain concentrations of choline and acetylcholine in total brain of mouse while in rats only the acetylcholine content in striatum was enhanced by physostigmine. In mice, physostigmine decreased the turnover rate of striatal acetylcholine. This drug was injected 30 min before killing and phosphoryl (Me-^{14}C)choline was given as a pulse label at various times before killing. From the changes in brain acetylcholine and choline radioactivities it was found that the turnover rate of brain acetylcholine had decreased from 0.34 μmole/g/hr to 0.061 μmole/g/hr in total brain of mice.

Pentobarbital: The in vivo turnover rate of acetylcholine was measured in total brain of mice and brain parts of rats after treatment with pentobarbital (161 μmoles/kg i.p.). Pentobarbital decreased the turnover rate of acetylcholine both in total brain of mice and in cortex of rats, but no significant changes were detected in the striatum. Subcronic treatment with parachlorophenylalanine decreased the cortical content of acetylcholine and choline and partially reversed the decrease of turnover rate of acetylcholine elicited by pentobarbital.

A clarification of the influences exerted by stimulation of synaptic receptors on the regulation of acetylcholine turnover helps to understand the basic regulation of cholinergic neurons. Once this is accomplished then the possible sites where cholinergic neurons are altered in disease can be determined and specific models to test new drugs can be instituted.

We are extending these studies to other brain nuclei that contain acetylcholine terminals only or cell bodies only. The turnover rate of acetylcholine in these nuclei is measured by using the technique described in the annual report M-SMR-P-13. We are investigating the effect of cholinomimetic and cholinolytic drugs on ACh turnover to verify whether the general principles regulating ACh turnover reflect synaptic mechanisms or regulation of acetylcholine synthesis in cell bodies.

Keyword Descriptors:

Oxotremorine, physostigmine, acetylcholine, choline, and pentobarbital.

Publications:

Trabucchi, M., Cheney, D. L., Hanin, I., and Costa, E.: Application of principles of steady state kinetics to the estimation of brain acetylcholine turnover rate: Effects of oxotremorine and physostigmine, JPET, In press, 1975.

Trabucchi, M., Cheney, D. L., Racagni, G., and Costa, E.: Pentobarbital and in vivo turnover rate of acetylcholine in mouse brain and in regions of rat brain. Pharm. Res. Comm. 7: 81-94, 1975.

Project No. Z01 MH 01506-02 SMRP
1. Division of Special Mental Health Research
2. Laboratory of Preclinical Pharmacology
3. Saint Elizabeths Hospital

PHS-ADAMHA-NIMH
Individual Project Report
July 1, 1974 through June 30, 1975

Project Title: Narcotic analgesics and the regulation of dopaminergic pathways of rat brain.

Previous Serial Number: M-SMR-P-6

Principal Investigator: G. Racagni and G. Zsilla

Other Investigators: E. Costa, A. Guidotti, and D. L. Cheney

Cooperating Units: None

Man Years:

Total:	1.2
Professional:	1.2
Others:	0

Project Description:

To study the action of narcotic analgesics administered acutely and chronically on the function of catecholaminergic system.

To establish if narcotic analgesics interact with dopaminergic striatal system at the pre or post synaptic receptor site we compared changes of catecholamine turnover rate and changes of tyrosine hydroxylase activity elicited by morphine and viminol with the changes obtained injecting amphetamine, haloperidol, and apomorphine. Moreover, as the drugs we used may also stimulate the dopamine dependent adenylyl cyclase system located in striatum at postsynaptic sites, we tried to correlate the changes in the activity of dopaminergic neurons with changes of cAMP and cGMP concentrations in striatum. Analgesic doses of morphine and viminol R_2 increase the turnover rate of dopamine (DA) in rat striatum but fail to increase the striatal concentration of 3',5' cyclic adenosine monophosphate (cAMP) or the affinity of tyrosine hydroxylase (TH) for the pteridine cofactor. When morphine is added to striatal homogenates it changes neither the basal activity of adenylate cyclase nor the enzyme activation by DA. Haloperidol enhances the turnover rate of striatal DA and the TH affinity for the pteridine cofactor.

However, it blocks the DA activation of adenylate cyclase in striatal homogenates and fails to increase striatal cAMP concentrations. (+) amphetamine increases DA turnover rate and the striatal cAMP content, but changes neither striatal adenylate cyclase activity nor the affinity of TH for the pteridine cofactor. The increase of striatal cAMP by amphetamine is blocked by pretreatment with large doses of reserpine or small doses of haloperidol. However morphine is ineffective in blocking the effect of amphetamine. Moreover morphine and no amphetamine produce a pronounced increase of cGMP in striatum. This study shows that (+) amphetamine, haloperidol and morphine increase the turnover rate of striatal DA by different molecular mechanisms. An attempt is made to relate the biochemical effects to the pharmacological action of these drugs.

The mechanism of narcotic dependence is relevent to the mission of NIMH in many ways. Our results show that analgesia is associated with an increase of striatal dopamine turnover but this increase of dopamine metabolism does not appear to be related to either an increase in the firing rate of dopaminergic axons or to the stimulation of postsynaptic dopaminergic receptors. This effect evinces tolerance. Thus a better understanding of the mechanisms involved may elucidate on one hand basic mechanisms that control dopaminergic functions and on the other hand it may clarify the molecular basis of morphine tolerance and dependence.

It has been established that the function of the nigrastriatal dopaminergic neuronal system is integrated with that of cholinergic, serotonergic and gabaminergic neurons in a complex feedback loop of neuronal regulation. We plan to study this functional integration as it relates to the action of analgesics by measuring:

a) The effect of morphine on the dopaminergic system and striatal cGMP concentrations after treatment with drugs that alter the function of serotonergic, cholinergic and gabaminergic systems.

b) The effect of morphine and that of other analgesics in telecephalic nuclei which receive a strong dopaminergic imput and are involved with emotional and goal directed behavior (i. e., amygdala nuclei, N. accumbens, and limbic cortex).

c) The action of chronically administered morphine on the sensitivity of postsynaptic receptors. The response of adenylate and guanylate cyclase of striatum and pineal homogenates to different neurotransmitters will be used as a model.

Keyword Descriptors:

Morphines, opium, analgesics, drug abuse, tyrosine 3-mono-oxygenase, adeny cyclase, d-amphetamine, haloperidol, dopamine, catecholamines.

Publications:

Gerhards, H. J., Carenzi, A., Costa, E.: Effect of nonifensive on motor activity, dopamine turnover rate, and cyclic 3'5' adenosine monosphosphate concentrations of rat striatum. Naunyn Schiedberg's Arch. Pharmcol. 286, 49-63, 1974.

Costa, E., Carenzi, A., Cheney, D., Guidotti, A., Racagni, G., and B. Zivkovic: Compartmentation of striatal DA: Problems in assessing the dynamics of functional storage pools of transmitters. Proc. Symp. Metab. Compt. 1975, in press.

Carenzi, A., Guidotti, A., Revuelta, A., and E. Costa: Molecular mechanisms in the action of morphine and viminol (R_2) on rat striatum, JPET, in press.

Project No. Z01 MH 01507-06 SMRP
1. Division of Special Mental Health Research
2. Laboratory of Preclinical Pharmacology
3. Saint Elizabeths Hospital

PHS-ADAMHA-NIMH
Individual Project Report
July 1, 1974 through June 30, 1975

Project Title: Possible neuronal alterations in muscular dystrophy.

Previous Serial Number: M-SMR-P-25

Principal Investigator: D. L. Cheney

Other Investigators: G. Racagni, G. Zsilla, A. Guidotti and E. Costa

Cooperating Units: None

Man Years:

Total: 0.2
Professional: 0.2
Others: 0

Project Description:

To study the possible neuronal alterations in muscular dystrophic mice by evaluating differences in enzyme activity in various tissues and in the dynamic state of the putative neurotransmitters.

Bar Harbor 129 ReJ strain dystrophic mice (dy/dy) and healthy littermates (dy/+) were used for these experiments. Acetylcholine turnover was measured according to the method described by Cheney et al. (JPET 192: 288-296, 1975). Norepinephrine and dopamine turnover rates were measured using the procedures described by Neff et al. (JPET 176: 701-709, 1971). Enzyme assays were conducted using standard published procedures.

Choline acetyltransferase activity (CAT) in diaphragm of Bar Harbor strain (129 ReJ dy/dy) with muscular dystrophy was significantly lower than that of phenotypically normal littermates (129 ReJ dy/+). CAT, tyrosine hydroxylase (TH) and dopamine-β-hydroxylase (DβH) activities were identical in adrenal gland and in brain homogenates of normal and dystrophic mice. Brain concentrations of dopamine, norepinephrine, serotonin GABA, tyrosine, tryptophan, and choline were unaltered. The brain content of acetylcholine was significantly lower in the dystrophic mice. Furthermore the turnover of acetylcholine in total brain was lower in muscular dystrophic mice than in phenotypically normal littermates. The turnover rates of brain dopamine and norepinephrine in these two groups were similar.

The studies suggest the possibility of a neuronal dysfunction underlying the muscular alteration in muscular dystrophy. Localization of the dysfunction in the cholinergic system might suggest possible therapy in human muscular dystrophy.

We propose to:

1) Study choline uptake in brain synaptosomal preparations.
2) Study adenyl cyclase and guanylcyclase systems in brain and diaphragm.
3) Study choline acetyltransferase in biopsy samples from muscular dystrophic patients.

Keyword Descriptors:

Muscular dystrophy, acetylcholine, choline acetyltransferase.

Publications:

Costa, E., Cheney, D. L., Hanbauer, I. and Trabucchi, M.: Murine muscular dystrophy: a defect in brain cholinergic mechanisms. In: Seeman, P. and Brown, G. (eds.): Frontiers in Neurology and Neuroscience Research; Toronto, Canada, Toronto University Press, P. 36-39, 1974.

Trabucchi, M., Cheney, D. L., Susheela, A. K., and Costa, E.: Possible defect in cholinergic neurons of muscular dystrophic mice. J. Neurochem. 24: 417-423, 1975.

Project No. Z01 MH 01508-06 SMRP
1. Division of Special Mental Health Research
2. Laboratory of Preclinical Pharmacology
3. Saint Elizabeths Hospital

PHS-ADAMHA-NIMH
Individual Project Report
July 1, 1974 through June 30, 1975

Project Title: Turnover of acetylcholine and opiate action, dependence and tolerance.

Previous Serial Number: M-SMR-P-7

Principle Investigator: D. L. Cheney

Other Investigators: G. Racagni, G. Zsilla and E. Costa

Cooperating Units: None

Man Years:

Total: 0.3
Professional: 0.3
Others: 0

Project Description:

To measure acetylcholine turnover rate in various cholinergic nuclei during the action of opiates and at various stages of morphine dependence and withdrawal.

Male Zivic-Miller rats were injected with various doses of morphine each administered as a single injection (35-140 μmoles/kg, i.p. 45 min). Other rats were made dependent by implantation of morphine pellets subcutaneously (250 μmoles 3.5 and 2.5 days before killing). Dependence was determined and withdrawal was precipitated by injection of naloxone (24 μmoles/kg; i.p., 15 min). Rats were also injected with the opiate viminol R_2 (5 mg/kg, i.p. 20 min).

Rats were killed using a beam of microwave radiation focused to the skull. Acetylcholine turnover was measured in rat brain parts following constant rate infusion of radiolabelled phosphorylcholine using a method described in SMR-P-14 and published (Life Sciences, 15: 1961-1975, 1974).

Rats were implanted with pellets of morphine (250 μmoles each) on day 1 and day 2. On day 4 they were infused with radiolabelled phosphorylcholine for 2, 4, 6, and 8 min. The steady state striatal acetylcholine content was unchanged by the phosphorylcholine or by the chronic morphine treatment. It was found that the change with time of the specific radioactivity of choline in striatum of morphine implanted and sham implanted rats was identical. However the specific radioactivity of acetylcholine in striatum of morphine implanted rats at the various times studied was smaller than that same value in sham implanted rats. The fractional rate constant for the efflux of ACh was calculated by finite difference method and as published (Life Sciences, 15: 1961, 1974). The values obtained with the two methods were in good agreement.

A single injection of morphine reduced the synthesis of acetylcholine in cortex but not in striatum. Morphine pellets decreased striatal turnover rate of acetylcholine in striatum but failed to alter the turnover rate in occipital cortex. Naloxone reversed both changes of acetylcholine turnover rate elicited by morphine although it was devoid of any effect on the synthesis of acetylcholine in rat brain parts.

Viminol R_2 did not affect the concentrations of acetylcholine or choline in caudate, accumbens, habenula, substantia nigra, interpeduncularis or locus coerulus.

We plan to study the turnover rate of acetylcholine in brain nuclei at various times after morphine, viminol R_2 or other opiates. The changes in ACh turnover rate elicited by the opiates in various nuclei will be analyzed in conjunction with drugs which affect various putative transmitter system which are known to participate in the regulation of ACh in various cholinergic nuclei. By this study we hope to understand the molecular nature of morphine action on cholinergic mechanism as it relates to actions of morphine on other neuronal systems that impinge on cholinergic neurons.

If the mechanisms involved in opiate action were unde[illegible]od at synaptic levels the possibility of an opiate receptor [illegible]onsible for morphine action could be discussed in terms of synaptic mechanisms involved.

Keyword Descriptors:

Morphines, drugs addiction, drugs withdrawal, acetylcholine, and choline.

Publications:

Cheney, D. L., Costa, E., Hanin, I., Racagni, G. and Trabucchi,

M.: Acetylcholine turnover rate in brain of rats and mice: effects of various dose regimens of morphine. In: Cholinergic Mechanisms. Waser, P. (ed.) New York, Raven Press, pp, 217-228, 1975.

Cheney, D. L., Trabucchi, M., Racagni, G., Wang, C. and Costa, E.: Effects of acute and chronic morphine on regional rat brain acetylcholine turnover rate. Life Sciences 15: 1977-1990, 1974.

Project No. Z01 MH 01509-06 SMRP
1. Division of Special Mental Health Research
2. Laboratory of Preclinical Pharmacology
3. Saint Elizabeths Hospital

PHS-ADAMHA-NIMH
Individual Project Report
July 1, 1974 through June 30, 1975

Project Title: Application of steady state kinetics to the estimation of in vivo turnover rates of choline and acetylcholine in rat brain.

Previous Serial Number: M-SMR-P-14

Principal Investigator: D. L. Cheney

Other Investigators: G. Racagni, G. Zsilla, and E. Costa

Cooperating Units: None

Man Years:

Total:	0.3
Professional:	0.3
Others:	0

Project Description:

Our objective is to estimate in vivo turnover rates of neuronal acetylcholine and choline stores by applying principles of steady-state kinetics.

A constant rate intravenous infusion of phosphoryl(Me-^{14}C) choline (25 μCi/kg/min) was administered to rats and the specific radioactivities of choline and acetylcholine were measured in various areas of rat brains at different times. Principles of steady-state kinetics were employed to derive equations whereby the fractional rate constant for the choline compartment could be calculated from the curve generated by infusing phosphorylcholine for different times. Using the specific radioactivities of acetylcholine and choline and the fractional rate constant for choline the fractional rate constant for acetylcholine could be calculated. By multiplying the fractional rate constant for acetylcholine by the acetylcholine content of a brain area the turnover rate could be determined.

An efficient labelling of brain choline at steady state can be determined only by infusing phosphorylcholine. Rats were infused for 2, 4, 6 and 8 minutes and then killed by focussed microwave irradiation. The specific radioactivities were measured in the following brain areas: Brainstem, occipital cortex, limbic cortex and striatum. Specific radioactivities of acetylcholine and choline increase during the 8 min infusion time in each of the brain areas. The fractional rate constant for the choline compartment was calculated using the derived equations and the data from each brain region at 4 and 6 min of infusion. Using the fractional rate constant for the efflux of choline from the brain compartment and the ratio of the choline specific radioactivities to the acetylcholine radioactivity at 6 min of infusion time, the fractional rate constant for the efflux of acetylcholine from the brain compartment was determined (Table 1). Then the turnover rate was obtained by multiplying the fractional rate constant for the efflux of acetylcholine by the acetylcholine content.

This method was compared to the method of finite differences (Neff et al., JPET 176: 701, 1971). It was found that the fractional rate constant for acetylcholine of each one min segment calculated for each of the brain areas by the finite difference method was not significantly different from that obtained by the procedure outlined briefly in this report and described in detail elsewhere (Racagni et al., Life Sciences 15: 1961-1975, 1974).

	Method Reported here		Finite Difference Method	
	kACh[1] (hr^{-1})	TR_{ACh}[2] (nmoles/g/hr)	kACh (hr^{-1})	TR_{ACh} (nmoles/g/hr)
Brain Stem	2.5±0.20	0.092±0.0074	2.3±0.60	0.086±0.014
Occipital cortex	13.0±0.91	0.20 ±0.010	9.6±0.8	0.15 ±0.016
Limbic cortex	8.8±1.6	0.20 ±0.035	9.0±1.8	0.20 ±0.030
Striatum	25.0±1.2	1.3 ±0.063	26 ±2.4	1.3 ±0.12

1. Fractional rate constant for acetylcholine

2. Turnover rate of acetylcholine

The new method offers the possibility of measuring the turnover rate of acetylcholine in brain parts with a single infusion time. Thus it is more convenient than the finite different method. Moreover, with the new method the fractional rate constant for choline can be estimated.

The role that brain acetylcholine plays in mental diseases is still unknown. However, acetylcholine is involved in the mediation of extrapyramidal side effects elicited by drugs. The measurement of brain acetylcholine turnover rates may be an expression of neuronal activity and therefore it is an important tool to understand the transmitter involvement in neuronal function.

By measuring acetylcholine turnover we can gain further insight into the mechanisms regulating neurotransmitter function in the central nervous system.

Keyword Descriptors:

Acetylcholine, choline, phosphorylcholine.

Publications:

Cheney, D. L., Costa, E., Hanin, I., Trabucchi, M., and Wang, C. T.: Application of principles of steady state kinetics to the in vivo estimation of acetylcholine turnover rate in mouse brain. J. Pharmacol. Exp. Therap. 192: 288-296, 1975.

Racagni, G., Cheney, D. L., Trabucchi, M., Wang, C. T. and Costa, E.: Measurement of acetylcholine turnover rate in discrete areas of rat brain. Life Sciences 15: 1961-1975, 1974.

Project No. Z01 MH 01510-01 SMRP
1. Division of Special Mental Health Research
2. Laboratory of Preclinical Pharmacology
3. Saint Elizabeths Hospital

PHS-ADAMHA-NIMH
Individual Project Report
July 1, 1974 through June 30, 1975

Project Title: Effect of gaba-minergic drugs on the cholinergic system.

Previous Serial Number: None

Principal Investigator: G. Zsilla

Other Investigators: D. L. Cheney, G. Racagni, and E. Costa

Cooperating Units: None

Man Years:

Total: 0.3
Professional: 0.3
Others: 0

Project Description:

To study the effects of GABA drugs (picrotoxin, bicuculline, isoniazid, strichnine) on the cholinergic system in rat brain areas.

Acetylcholine and choline content of rat brain caudate and cortex was measured by the gas chromatographic method originally described by Hanin and Jenden (Biochem. Pharmac. 18, 837 (1969) and further modified by Hanin, Massarelli and Costa (J. Pharmac. exp. Ther. 181, 10 (1972).

Preliminary experiments suggested that the gabaminergic drugs failed to change the acetylcholine content, but did alter the concentration of choline in cortex and caudate. Isoniazid (450 mg/kg; s.c.) increased and picrotoxin (2 mg/kg; s.c.) decreased the choline level in caudate. Bicuculline (0.2 mg/kg i. v.) increased the choline content in cortex. It appears that strichnine does not affect the acetylcholine or the choline levels in either cortex or caudate significantly.

The study of the relationship between cholinergic and gabaminergic systems may be useful to elucidate physiopathological situations. Striatum contains high concentrations of acetylcholine and GABA, both transmitters are stored in small interneurons. Acetylcholine in striatum is involved in the genesis of the extrapyramidal side effects observed during the administration of antipsychotics (see Annual Report No. M-SMR-P-15, 1974). The role of GABA in striatum and the interactions of this inhibitory transmitter with the cholinergic neurons has not been established. From this study, focused mainly on the effect of drugs known to affect the gabaminergic neurons on the turnover of acetylcholine, one would acquire greater understanding concerning the complex regulation of the extrapyramidal system.

We propose to study:

1. The turnover rate of choline and acetylcholine after injection of GABA receptor inhibitors and blockers of GABA synthesis.
2. Rate of GABA decline in striatum after injection of 3-mercaptopropionic acids to assess turnover rate of GABA.
3. Action of cholinomimetics and cholinolytics on the turnover rate of striatal GABA.

Keyword Descriptors:

Gamma-aminobutyric acid, acetylcholine, choline.

Project No. Z01 MH 01511-03 SMRP
1. Division of Special Mental Health Research
2. Laboratory of Preclinical Pharmacology
3. Saint Elizabeths Hospital

PHS-ADAMHA-NIMH
Individual Project Report
July 1, 1974 through June 30, 1975

Project Title: Neuronal monoamines --- A study of their integration and regulation

Previous Serial Number: M-SMR-P-22

Principal Investigator: B. Zivkovic

Other Investigators: A. Guidotti and E. Costa

Cooperating Units: None

Man Years:

Total: 0.8
Professional: 0.8
Others: 0

Project Description:

Catecholaminergic nerve function is associated with the metabolic status of the amine which the neurons uses as a transmitter. In noradrenergic nerves, regulation of this metabolism involves the biosynthesis or activation of the enzyme molecules which catalyze the rate limiting processes in the norepinephrine formation. Since the regulation of the synthesis of brain dopamine is poorly understood, we attempt to study the mechanisms involved in the regulation of tyrosine hydroxylase in dopaminergic nerve terminals. Our immediate objectives were:

1) To measure short-term changes in the activity of tyrosine hydroxylase in striatum and nucleus accumbens after treatment with drugs that specifically impair dopaminergic transmission.

2) To characterize the changes of tyrosine hydroxylase activity induced by drugs.

3) To investigate other brain neuronal systems that might be involved in the regulation of tyrosine hydroxylase in dopaminergic neurons.

The assay of tyrosine hydroxylase activity was performed by radiometric method. Rate of synthesis of dopamine and norepinephrine were measured by pulse labelling of the precursor's pool. The amines and aminoacids were measured by fluorimetric methods. All the parameters were measured with procedures developed in our laboratory.

1) A single intraperitoneal injection of antipsychotic drugs (Methiothepin, haloperidol, pimozide, chlorpromazine, clozapine and thioridazine) produces a decrease of the apparent Km of tyrosine hydroxylase for pteridine cofactor in striatum and nucleus accumbens. The doses of methiothepin, pimozide and haloperidol required to change the kinetic state of tyrosine hydroxylase in striatum were lower than those required to produce similar changes in nucleus accumbens. In contrast, clozapin and thioridazine were more effective in nucleus accumbens. Chlorpromazine was equally potent in these two brain regions. Haloperidol increased the turnover rate of dopamine in striatum with doses that are relatively lower than those required for nucleus accumbens. In contrast, clozapine was more active in increasing turnover rate of dopamine in nucleus accumbens, while chlorpromazine was equally potent in both regions.

Thus, antipsychotics with high incidence of extrapyramidal side effects preferentially increase dopamine turnover and chang tyrosine hydroxylase in striatum.

2) (+) but not (-) enantiomer of the antipsychotic butaclamol changes the kinetic state of tyrosine hydroxylase in striatum and nucleus accumbens. Similarly, only (+) enantiomer possesses neuroleptic activity and blocks dopamine sensitive adenylyl cyclase, indicating high stereospecificity of dopaminergic receptors involved in the regulation of certain behavioral patterns and kinetic state of tyrosine hydroxylase. Within 30 min after cutting of nigro-striatal dopaminergic pathway by means of cerebral hemisection the Km of striatal tyrosine hydroxlase for pteridine cofactor was decreased. This decrease can not be blocked by apomorphine, although this drug blocked the decrease of the Km of tyrosine hydroxylase for pteridine cofactor induced by antipsychotic drugs. Moreover haloperidol given 30 min after cerebral hemisection did not affect the kinetic state of tyrosine hydroxylase suggesting that the receptors involved in the regulation of tyrosine hydroxylase in striatum are located postsynaptically.

3) Physostigmine and arecoline (Cholinomimetic drugs) increase tyrosine hydroxylase preferentially in striatum than in accumbus, while benztropine, an anticholinergic drug, block the change of tyrosine hydroxylase kinetics induced by antipsy-

chotic drugs in striatum to a greater extent than in nucleus accumbens. Flunitrazepam and γ-hydroxybutyric acid, (these drugs believed to exert their action through GABA-ergic mechanisms) produce a dose-related antagonism on the effect of antipsychotic drugs, being equally potent in both striatum and nucleus accumbens.

An increasing body of evidence has been accumulated suggesting that brain monoaminergic function may be altered in mental disorders. The beneficial effects of antipsychotic drugs in the treatment of schizophrenia indicate that brain dopaminergic neurons might be involved in the etiology or at least in the manifestation of some symptoms of this disease. An understanding of the mechanisms whereby antipsychotic drugs affect synaptic function of central dopaminergic neurons appears to be a reasonable approach to study the biochemical basis of schizophrenia. Moreover, the study of the effects of antipsychotic drugs on dopaminergic mechanisms may offer a better understanding of the regulation of such neuronal systems. The findings reported here may have a practical application in designing new antipsychotics which would cause less incidence of dopaminergic mechanism in brain may open a new avenue in therapy of schizophrenia by employing drugs which would affect specifically neuronal systems that regulate dopaminergic function.

Our experiments offer the possibility of developing experimental models to predict occurrence of extrapyramidal side effects in drugs that exert a neuroleptic action by blocking postsynaptic dopaminc receptors. By measuring the effects of drugs on the enzyme activities of brain nuclei, we hope to find specific sites where these drugs are acting, to understand the integrated role of other neurotransmitters in the regulation of dopaminergic function. One of the points that remain open at the present state of the research is the understanding of the molecular mechanisms involved in the activation of tyrosine hydroxylase.

Recently it has been proposed that phosphorylation of tyrasine hydroxylase can activate the conversion of tyrosine to dopamine. If this mechanism of activation is operative in vivo than neuroleptics drugs, should be able to work directly in the phosphorylation or dephosphorylation processes in dopaminergic neurones. Therefore we plan to investigate the role of antipsychotic drugs on the protein kinases and phosphoprotein phosphatases activities in discrete brain nuclei. We have accumulated substantial evidence that activation of tyrosine hydroxylase can be obtained by manipulating in vitro the ionic composition of the buffers. Therefore we intend to study whether in these conditions the enzyme is subjected to some changes of its physical state: release of subunit, removal of inhibitors, etc.

Finally since the enzymatic hydroxylation of tyrosine requires an absolute presence of pteridine cofactors. We plan to develop methods to measure the steady state level and the synthesis rate of the pteridine cofactor to find drugs that may change the concentration of this important step in the regulation of tyrosine hydroxylase.

Keyword Descriptors:

Tyrosine 3-monooxygenase, pteridines, dopamine, psychopharmacological agents, antidepressant, ganglionic blocking agents, gamma amino butyric acid and parasympatholeptic.

Publications:

Costa, E., Guidotti, A. and Zivkovic, B.: Short and long term regulation of tyrosine hydroxylase. In: Usdin, E. (ed.): Advances in Biochemical Psychopharmacology, 12: 161-175, 1974.

Zivkovic, B. and Guidotti, A.: Changes of kinetic constnat of striatal tyrosine hydroxylase elicited by neuroleptic drugs that impair the function of dopamine receptors. Brain Res., 79: 505-509, 1974.

Zivkovic, B., Guidotti, A. and Costa, E.: Effect of neuroleptics on striatal tyrosine hydroxylase: changes in affinity for the pteridine cofactor. Molec. Pharmacol. 10: 727-735, 1974.

Zivkovic, B., Guidotti, A., Revuelta, A. and Costa, E.: Effect of thioridazine, clozapine and other antipsychotics on the kinetic state of tyrosine hydroxylase and on the turnover rate of dopamine in striatum and nucleus accumbens. J. Pharmacol. Exp. Ther., in press.

Zivkovic, B., Guidotti, A. and Costa, E.: The regulation of the kinetic state of striatal tyrosine hydroxylase and the role of postsynaptic dopamine receptors. Brain Res., in press.

Zivkovic, B., Guidotti, A. and Costa, E.: Stereospecificity of dopamine receptors involved in the regulation of the kinetic state of tyrosine hydroxylase in striatum and nucleus accumbens. J. Pharm. Pharmacol., in press.

Project No. Z01 MH 01512-03 SMRP

1. Divison of Special Mental Health Research
2. Laboratory of Preclinical Pharmacology
3. Saint Elizabeths Hospital

PHS-ADAMHA-NIMH
Individual Project Report
July 1, 1974 through June 30, 1975

Project Title: The role of cyclic nucleotides in the regulation of pituitary function.

Previous Serial Number: M-SMR-P-17

Principal Investigator: A. Guidotti

Other Investigators: P. Uzunov and E. Costa

Cooperating Units: None

Man Years:

Total: 0.6
Professional: 0.6
Others: 0

Project Description:

To study the role of cyclic nucleotides in the regulation of pituitary and hypothalamic function.

cAMP, cGMP content, the activator of phosphodiesterase and the protein kinase activity were measured with procedures developed in our laboratory. Hypothalamic nuclei in frozen sections from fresh brain and from brain of rats exposed to a beam of microwave focussed to the head were dissected, with a stereomicroscopic technique developed in our laboratory.

The purpose of these studies is to investigate the role of various neuronal structures in the rat hypothalamus for the neuroendocrine regulation of pituitary. In order to perform these studies we need sensitive measurements that reflect the activation of specific postsynaptic receptors from various structures. Since cAMP and cGMP function as a second messenger in neuroendocrine responses of pituitary we have measured factors that express their activity at molecular levels (activation of protein kinase) or control their concentration at the site of action (phosphodiesterase activator). We have shown that the increase of cAMP in pituitary following reserpine injection or exposure of the rat to cold is controlled in its duration and extension by the activity of a phosphodiesterase activator (mW 15000). The concentration of this activator can be measured in different hypothalamic nuclei and can be used as a parameter to detect activation of receptor, at the synaptic level. Another parameter which can be measured in hypothalamic nuclei and other brain nuclei with great precision and sensitivity is the activity of the cAMP independent and cAMP dependent protein kinase. As shown in the table , protein kinase activity can be measured in all the studied nuclei.

Reserpine, chlorpromazine and cold exposure activate the protein kinase in pituitary. The time course of this activation lasts longer than the increase of pituitary cAMP content. In fact 2 hours after the injection of reserpine and the termination of cold exposure the levels of cAMP are approached normal values but the protein kinases are still fully activated.

Neuronal mechanisms regulate transsynaptically the synthesis and release of hormones from the hypothalamus, which in turn regulate pituitary function.

Since we could establish that drugs environmental stimuli which change the activity of pituitary activate protein kinases and increase the phosphodiesterase activator activity in discrete nuclei of hypothalamus these changes can be used to locate the neuronal pathways involved. The activation of protein kinases offer an additional tool to detect phosphorylation of nuclear protein that mediate transsynaptically induced changes in the synthesis of macromolecules in the cells involved. Our attention will be focused mainly on the study of the action of antipsychoti to understand their action in neuroendocrine functions. This specific profile of these drugs is important for the understanding of their long term side effects on hypothalamic functions.

Keyword Descriptors:

Protein kinase, phosphodiesterases, cyclic AMP, cyclic GMP, pituitary gland, and hypothalamus.

Publications:

Guidotti, A., Zivkovic, B., and E. Costa: Possible involvement of cyclic nucleotides in the stimulation of pituitary function elicited by reserpine. Psychoneuroendocrinology, Ed. by N. Hatotani, page 259-266, 1974. Karger, Basel

Costa, E., Guidotti, A., Uzunov, P., and B. Zivkovic: (Symposium on neuroendocrine regulation of fertility. Simla, India,

1974) Methods to study the in vivo regulation of cyclic nucleotides in pituitary.

TABLE 3

cAMP DEPENDENT AND INDEPENDENT PROTEIN KINASE ACTIVITY IN HYPOTHALAMIC NUCLEI DISSECTED STEREOMICROSCOPICALLY, IN PINEAL AND IN PARTS OF PITUITARY GLAND

	^{32}P Incorporated into Histone (cpm x 10^{-3}/min/mg protein)		$\frac{-cAMP}{+cAMP}$
TISSUE	+ cAMP	- cAMP	
Anterior pituitary	10	5.5	0.54
Posterior pituitary	13	5.7	0.44
Preoptic nucleus	12	6.9	0.56
Anterior hypothalamus	18	9.9	0.56
Paraventricular nucleus	10	4.1	0.41
Arcuate Nucleus	12	6.3	0.53
Median eminence	15	11	0.69
Pineal	17	11	0.63

Tissue was homogenized in 10 mM K phosphate buffer containing 10 mM EDTA and 5 mM aminophylline. The protein kinase activity of the supernatant (20.000 g x 20 min at 4°C) was measured in the presence or in the absence of cAMP (0.7 μM) at 30°C for 5 minutes. The substrate was calf histone mixture (2 mg/ml) and 500 μM ^{32}P ATP (S.A. 100 μCi/μmole)

Project No. Z01 MH 01513-01 SMRP
1. Division of Special Mental Health Research
2. Laboratory of Preclinical Pharmacology
3. Saint Elizabeths Hospital

PHS-ADAMHA-NIMH
Individual Project Report
July 1, 1974 through June 30, 1975

Project Title: First and Second messenger involvement in the synthesis of enzymes that are regulating rate-limiting processes in neuronal tissue.

Previous Serial Number: None

Principal Investigator: I. Hanbauer

Other Investigators: E. Costa and A. Guidotti

Cooperating Units: Section of Biochemical Pharmacology, Hypertension Endocrine Branch, National Heart and Lung Institute

Man Years:

Total: 0.5
Professional: 0.5
Others: 0

Project Description:

The goal of these studies is to understand the participation of transmitters and hormones in the regulation of tyrosine hydroxylase (TH) biosynthesis in sympathetic ganglia and adrenal medulla.

cAMP, cGMP, tyrosine hydroxylase activity were assayed with procedure developed in this laboratory.

We have accumulated substantial evidence that cAMP in adrenal medullary cells is involved in the biochemical processes mediating the increase of TH biosynthesis elicited transsynaptically. In a tentative to acquire more information on mechanisms involved in the transfer of the synaptic information from post-synaptic sites to the structures that control protein synthesis we have directed our attention to the superior cervical ganglion of the rat. When demedullated rats were placed for four hours at 4°C we observed an immediate increase in the cAMP content of superior cervical ganglia. The increase of cAMP content peaked at 3 to 5 fold normal values and lasted for about four hrs which is the threshold time for the induction of ganglion TH by cold exposure. The increase of cAMP is paralleled by a marked and prolonged decrease of cGMP concentration. The cAMP/cGMP ratio i SCG increased from a basal level of five to approximately 40. Since the increased cAMP/cGMP ratio elicited by cold in the superior cervical ganglion of adrenal demedullated rats is block by propranolol and decentralization of the ganglion, we tested whether isoproterenol epinephrine, dopamine, norepinephrine, and carbamylcholine could change the cAMP and cGMP content and induc TH in superior cervical ganglion of intact animals. Repeated injections of isoproterenol or a single injection of a large dos of epinephrine injected s.c. with phenoxybenzamine produces a prompt and 3 to 5 fold increase of ganglionic cAMP content lasti about 2 hr. This increase is associated with a delayed modulati of TH. No change in ganglionic cGMP content was observed.

Also large doses of dopamine and norepinephrine injected with phenoxybenzamine produce an increase in ganglionic cAMP content. This increase, however, lasts less than 30 min and is not followed by TH induction. Carbamylcholine (8.2 μmoles/kg i.p.) failed to cause an immediate change of cAMP or cGMP conten and a delayed induction of TH in ganglia. Since propranolol (34 μmoles/kg, i.p.) antagonizes the increase of cAMP and the i duction of TH produced by isoproterenol and epinephrine and sin decentralization fails to block the cAMP increase and the TH induction elicited by isoproterenol in ganglia, it was conclude that β adrenergic receptors can mediate the TH induction in ganglia.

It has been reported that enzyme induction, in several tissues, is under the control of corticosteroids. To test this possibility we studied the action of dexamethasone on TH activi in ganglia and adrenal medulla. Dexamethasone (3.8 μmoles/kg i.p.) induces TH in sympathetic ganglia but not in adrenal medulla. Unlike the β-adrenergic agonists, dexamethasone fails to induce TH in decentralized sympathetic ganglia. Dexamethaso produces a sharp decrease in ganglionic cGMP content and enhanc the cAMP/cGMP ratio from five to approximately 20. The increas of TH by dexamethasone is antagonized by pretreatment with cortexolone: a metabolite of corticosterone with high affinity for the corticosteroids receptor protein but devoid of intrinsic glucocorticosteroid activity. The action of cortexolone is specific, it does not block the induction of TH elicited by epinephrine. While carbamylcholine fails to induce TH in gangl nicotine can induce TH in sympathetic ganglia. The dose respon relationship is typcial for nicotinic receptor activation: hig doses inhibit the induction, low doses are active. The simultaneous injection of atropine facilitates the TH induction by nicotine which is blocked by hexamethonium or methacholine. Nicotine induces TH in decentralized ganglia, also in this tissue the affects of nicotine are antagonized by the activation of muscarinic receptors. These results indicate that nicotinic and muscarinic receptors can control the induction of TH in ganglia. This interaction can explain why carbamylcholine which has a small differential activity for nicotinic and muscarinic receptor fails to induce ganglionic TH. It should be noted that in adrenal medulla there is no interaction between muscarinic and nicotinic receptor.

These findings suggest that three factors can induce TH in ganglia: β adrenergic receptor agonists, nicotinic receptor agonists and corticosteroids. It remains to be clarified how these three factors interact in the "transsynaptic induction of TH" in SCG.

Several lines of evidence indicate that corticosteroids can have a "permissive role" in the synthesis or degradation rate of enzymes. It is now widely accepted that most if not all, glucocorticosteroid responses in target tissue are mediated by specific steroid receptors present in cytosol. The association between the steroid and its receptor, protein appears to be required to transport steroids from the cytoplasm to the nucleus where steroids by interacting with repressor proteins in the nucleus, stimulate RNA transcription.

Our findings demonstrate that corticosteroids reduce the cGMP levels in adrenal medulla and superior cervical ganglion. Considering the antagonistic role that cGMP exerts on the cAMP-dependent gene expression in several cellular systems, we can propose that an interaction between corticosteroids and cAMP system may be important in elucidating the mechanism whereby the adrenergic cells increase the synthesis of specific macromoleculer to adapt to persistent environmental stimuli.

We intend to elucidate in superior cervical ganglion the:

1) Role of glucocorticosteroids on guanylate cyclase system.
2) The role of cGMP in the regulation of the phosphorylated state of non-histone nuclear proteins.

Keyword Descriptors:

Enzyme induction, repression and derepression, tyrosine 3-monooxygenase, protein biosynthesis, superior cervical ganglion, adrenal medulla, corticosteroids, parasympathomimetic, ganglionic blocking agents, parasympatholytic, sympatholytic, sympathothomin

Publications:

Hanbauer, I., Kopin, I. J., Guidotti, A., and E. Costa: Inducti of tyrosine hydroxylase by β adrenergic receptor agonists in normal and decentralized sympathetic ganglia. Role of 3',5' cyclic adenosine monophosphate, JPET, in press.

Hanbauer, I., Guidotti, A., and E. Costa: Involvement of cyclic nucleotides in the long term induction of tyrosine hydroxylase. Collegium International Congress of Neuropsychopharmacology. Paris, France, 1974.

Guidotti, A., Hanbauer, I., and E. Costa: Role of cyclic Nucleotides in the induction of tyrosine hydroxylase. Advances in Cyclic Nucleotides Res., Vol. 5, 619-640, 1975.

Hanbauer, I., and A. Guidotti: cAMP dependent regulation of tyrosine 3-monoxygenase in adrenal medulla: Effect of Denervation. Arch. N-S Pharmacol., in press.

Hanbauer, I., Guidotti, A., and E. Costa: Dexamethasone induces tyrosine hydroxylase in sympathetic ganglia but not in adrenal medulla, Brain Res., 85: 527-531, 1975.

Costa, E., Guidotti, A., and Hanbauer, I.: Do cyclic nucleotide promote the transsynaptic induction of tyrosine hydroxylas Life Sciences, 14: 1160-1188, 1974.

Project No. Z01 MH 01514-04 SMRP
1. Division of Special Mental Health Research
2. Laboratory of Preclinical Pharmacology
3. Saint Elizabeths Hospital

PHS-ADAMHA-NIMH
Individual Project Report
July 1, 1974 through June 30, 1975

Project Title: Transsynaptic control of protein synthesis

Previous Serial Number: M-SMR-P-20

Principal Investigator: A. Kurosawa

Other Investigators: A. Guidotti and E. Costa

Cooperating Units: Laboratory of Clinical Sciences, IRP-NIMH

Man Years:

Total:	0.9
Professional:	0.7
Others:	0.2

Project Description:

To study the regulation of the synthesis of specific proteins by transsynaptic mechanisms or by the injections of cholinergic receptor agonists.

1. Cyclic 3',5'-AMP (cAMP), phosphodiesterase, and adenylate cyclase activity was assayed according to the procedures developed in this laboratory.

2. Cyclic 3',5'-GMP (cGMP) and guanylate cyclase activity was assayed according to the procedures developed in this laboratory (see ref.).

3. Tyrosine hydroxylase activity was measured according to the method of Waymire et al. (Anal. Biochem. 43: 558, 1971).

4. Protein kinase activity was measured with a procedure developed in this lab (see ref.).

An increase of cAMP/cGMP concentration ratio is the earliest biochemical event that has been measured in the trans-synaptic induction of adrenal TH. In rats receiving reserpine alone

(16 μmoles/kg i.p.) reserpine and propranolol (40 μmoles/kg i.p. 30 minutes before reserpine) or exposed to 4°C for 4 hrs, the increase of cAMP/cGMP concentration ratio exceeds the critical extent and duration which is required to activate the protein kinases. This activation of protein kinases is characterized by an increase in the activity of the cAMP independent protein kinases (low molecular weight enzymes). This activation lasts longer than the increase in cAMP/cGMP concentration ratio and appears to be an obligatory early event that mediates the increase of TH synthesis. In adrenal medulla of rats reserpine and carbamylcholine elicit an early activation of protein kinase and a delayed induction of TH which were dose related. With both drugs the threshold doses for both responses were quite similar. When protein kinases were activated and the cAMP independent activity in adrenal medulla increased the total amount of enzymes (cAMP dependent + cAMP independent) activity in the 2 10^4xg supernatant was reduced of about 40%. The activity lost from the supernatant could be recovered in the pellets. This translocation of protein kinase activity from the soluble to the particulate fraction of the cells may indicate that the protein kinase catalytic activity has migrated from the cytoplasm to the nucleus. Perhaps through phosphorylation of nuclear proteins, this translocation mediates the gene directed induction of TH in adrenal medulla.

In mammalian cells the role of cAMP in specialized protein synthesis is not yet well defined. However, the concept that cAMP may be involved in regulating RNA transcription and protein synthesis (Langan, Raven Press, N. Y., p. 307, 1970) received in the past years some experimental support. For example, changes in the concentration of cAMP and cGMP in thymocytes, lymphocytes, and bacteria can affect rates of DNA synthesis and cell replication. In neuroblastoma tissue cultures, cyclic 3',5'-AMP promotes differentiation and axonal elongation. In vivo cAMP or its dibutyryl derivatives are involved in the induction of specific enzymes (for references, see Robison, A., Butcher, R. W. and Sutherland, E. W., Cyclic AMP, Academic Press, N. Y., 1971). Since in adrenal medulla the availability of catecholamines and the adrenergic function are regulated by tyrosine hydroxylase and since adrenergic mechanisms have been implicated in the etiology of affective disorders, an understanding of the molecular nature of the regulation of catecholaminergic biosynthesis may open new avenues in the therapy of mental diseases.

The goal of our future research is to study the molecular mechanism that in the chromatine structure of neuronal cells regulates the transcription of individual genes. Phosphorilation of histones and non histone proteins may somehow be involved in the mechanisms by which these molecules regulate gene transcription.

While nuclear histones are quite similar in nuclei of different cells and in cell nuclei of various animal species, acidic nuclear proteins exhibits a tremendous hetergenity both structurally and functionally. These proteins may control gene transcription.

We plan to study:

1. The mechanisms regulating translocation of protein kinase from the cytosol to the nucleus of chromaffine cells.

2. The nature of the chromasomal proteins that are selectively phosphorylated or dephosphorylated.

3. The role of nerve impulses in the phosphorylation and dephosphorylation of selective nuclear proteins.

4. To purify and characterize nuclear nonhistone proteins that are phosphorylated during transsynaptic induction. To use these proteins in chromatine reconstitution experiments to determine their participation in the regulation of tyrosine hydroxylase induction.

Keyword Descriptors:

Adrenal medulla, enzyme induction, repression and derepression, protein biosynthesis, tyrosine 3-monooxygenase, cyclic AMP, cGMP, ATP: protein phosphotransferase, parasympathomimetics, and parasympatholytics.

Publications:

Guidotti, A., Hanbauer, I. and E. Costa: Role of cyclic nucleotides in the induction of tyrosine hydroxylase. Adv. in Cyclic Nucleotide Research, Vol. 5, 619-640, 1975.

Guidotti, A., Kurosawa, A., Chuang, D. M., and E. Costa: Protein kinase activation as an early event in the transsynaptic induction of tyrosine 3-mono-oxygenase in adrenal medulla. Proc. Nat. Acad. Sci., 1975, in press.

Guidotti, A., Mao, C. C., and E. Costa: Delayed increase of tyrosine hydroxylase activity induced by transsynaptic stimulation in chromaffin cells: Role of cyclic nucleotides as second messengers. Adv. in Cytopharmacology, Vol. 2 Page 39-46, Ed. F. Cicarelli, F. Clements, J. Meldolesi.

Raven Press, N. Y., 1974

Costa, E., Guidotti, A., and B. Zivkovic: Short and long term regulation of tyrosine hydroxylase. Neuropsychopharmacology of monoamines and their regulatory enzymes. Page 161-175, E. Usdin, Raven Press, N. Y. 1974.

Project No. Z01 MH 01515-03 SMRP
1. Division of Special Mental Health Research
2. Laboratory of Preclinical Pharmacology
3. Saint Elizabeths Hospital

PHS-ADAMHA-NIMH
Individual Project Report
July 1, 1974 through June 30, 1975

Project Title: Regulation of cerebellar guanosine 3',5' cyclic monophosphate and adenosine 3',5' cyclic monophosphate by excitatory or inhibitory transmitters.

Previous Serial Number: M-SMR-P-10

Principal Investigator: G. Biggio

Other Investigators: C. C. Mao, S. Naik, A. Guidotti and E. Costa

Cooperating Units: None

Man Years:

Total:	0.8
Professional:	0.8
Others:	0.3

Project Description:

The cerebellum is the brain region where the functional synaptology of various neurones has been determined with the greatest detail and precision. The project is designed to relate changes in the two second messengers due to transmitter release in the molecular layer of cerebellar cortex and in deep cerebellar nuclei. Such a study is possible in cerebellum because: 1) the climbing fibers and the mossy fibers are the two major excitatory inputs to this structure; 2) Harmaline selectively activates the olivary cell bodies of the afferent climbing fibers; 3) the deep cerebellar nuclei receive all the terminals of the cerebellar Purkinje cells.

Tissue cGMP and cAMP concentrations were determined after isolation of the two cyclic nucleotides by the activation of a cAMP and a cGMP dependent protein kinase (Mao, Guidotti, 1974).

Gamma-aminobutyric acid and glutamic acid in brain were measured enzymatically as reported by Okada et al. (Exp. Brain

Res. 13: 514, 1971) and Graham and Aprison (Anal. Biochem. 15: 487, 1966) respectively. All techniques mentioned above have been modified in order to determine the four compounds simultaneously in a single small tissue sample. Taurine was measured as previously reported (Guidotti et al., J. Neurochem.). cAMP phosphodiesterase was assayed with the method of Weiss et al. (Anal. Biochem. 45: 222, 1972); cGMP phosphodiesterase with that of Thompson and Appleman (Biochemistry 10: 311, 1971). Adenyl cyclase and guanyl cyclase activities were assayed by techniques developed in our laboratory.

The cGMP content in cerebella of rats increased by several folds in about 5 minutes of cold exposure. Although the rats were kept at 4°C the cerebellar cGMP content slowly declined and approached basal values in about 30 minutes. The cAMP content failed to change. No changes of cGMP or cAMP content were observed in striatum, hyppocampus or cerebral cortex. The increase of cerebellar cGMP by cold was not influenced by pretreatment with drugs capable of either blocking the function of cholinergic, catecholaminergic and serotonergic receptors inhibiting the metabolism of these transmitters. Moreover injection of thyroxine or that of glucocorticosteroids was ineffective on cerebellar cyclinucleotide concentrations. In searching for a possible transmitter substance which could be involved in the regulation of the increase of cGMP concentration in cerebellum of rats exposed to cold we turned our attention to the putative aminoacids neurotransmitters. Since in cerebellum many neurons are inhibitory in nature we decided first to study the role of inhibitory aminoacids. In particular our attention was focussed on GABA, taurine and glycine. Of these amino acid taurine is present in cerebellar in concentrations that are about 5 times higher than those of GABA and 10 times higher than those of glycine.

When GABA or taurine were injected intraventricularly they decreased cGMP but they failed to influence the cAMP content. In contrast glycine, like glutamic acid, increased cerebellar cGMP concentration. Moreover GABA and taurine injected intraventricularly in small doses (2.5 or 5 μ moles) before exposing the rats to cold abated the increase of cGMP elicited by cold exposure. The possibility that GABA regulates cerebellar cGMP content was supported by the following finding: 1) Aminooxyacetic acid, hydroxylamine or hydrazine which increased by a different extent the cerebellar content of GABA antagonized the increase of cerebellar cGMP elicited by cold, their potency was related to their action in increasing GABA content; 2) Picrotoxin, a specific GABA receptor antagonist and isoniazid, a drug that decrease GABA levels by inhibiting glutamic acid decarboxylase activity, injected in rats in subconvulsant doses also increased cGMP but not cAMP content in cerebellum; 3) Strychnine, a glycine receptor blocker, injected in subconvulsive doses increased neither cerebellar cGMP nor cAMP content; 4) Intraventricular injection of GABA blocked the increase of cGMP elicited by isoniazid. This increase was not blocked by intraventricular taurine.

The results of these experiments strongly indicate that GABA inhibits the activation of guanylcyclase in rat cerebellum. These findings neither clarify whether the climbing fibers are involved in the activation of cerebellar guanylcyclase nor indicate the site of action of GABA and taurine. This site may be located in brain areas that regulate climbing or mossy fibers excitation. It has been s hown that harmaline tremor is mediated by a selective activation of the inferior olivary neurons which through their axons (climbing fibers) innervate Purkinje cells dendrites in the molecular layer of cerebellar cortex. Tremorigenic doses of harmaline increase the cGMP content of cerebellar cortex by 5 or 6 fold. To test whether the increase of cGMP after harmaline was due to an activation of the climbing fibers. Purkinje cells synapses, harmaline was injected in rats pretreated with 3 Acetylpyridine. A recent report shown that in rat 3-Acetylpyridine produces a total distruction of the olivo-cerebellar pathway (Desclin, 1974). As a consequence a large number of climbing fibers undergo degeneration over extended areas of cerebellar cortex. In rats injected with harmaline 72 hrs after 3-acetylpyridine (70 mg/kg ip) the increase in cerebellar cGMP content and the tremor were prevented. A complete block of the increase of cerebellar cGMP was also observed when the animals were treated with 3-acetylpyridine before exposure to cold. However the increase of cerebellar cGMP elicited by isoniazid was not blocked in rats receiving equal doses of 3-acetylpyridine. Thus these experiments suggest that GABA may regulate cerebellar cGMP content by acting in sites different from the olivo cerebellar pathway.

In postsynaptic cells the cGMP and cAMP content can be regulated transsynaptically. The molecular mechanisms whereby transmitters activate adenylate and guanylate cyclases floating in the lipoids of postsynaptic membrane is not understood. Our studies show that the second messenger concept of Sutherland can be of value in elucidating transmitter interactions at synaptic level. We hope to use the clues emerging from these studies to obtain an identification of the transmitters involved in climbing fiber function.

Our proposed course is:

1) to initiate in vivo and in vitro studies to define the

molecular nature of the exitatory transmitter released from the climbing fibers into the Purkinje cells.

2) to define the molecular nature of the messages mediated by the increase of cGMP elicited in Purkinje cells by the climbing fiber activation.

3) to study the molecular nature of the inhibition elicited by GABA on the increase synthesis of cGMP elicited by the climbing fibers.

Keyword Descriptors:

Neurohormones, cyclic GMP, cyclic GMP, gamma aminobutyric acid, glutamic acids, sulfuraminoacids, cerebellar cortex, cerebellar nuclei, convulsants, anticonvulsants, and harmaline.

Publications:

Mao, C. C., Guidotti, A., and E. Costa: Interactions between γ-Aminobutyric Acid and Guanosine cyclic 3', 5'-Monophosphate in Rat cerebellum. Mol. Pharmacol. 10: 736-745, 1974.

Mao, C. C., Guidotti, A., and E. Costa: The regulation of cyclic guanosine monophosphate in rat cerebellum: possible involvement of putative neurotransmitters. Brain Res. 79: 510-514, 1974.

Mao, C. C., Guidotti, A., and E. Costa: Inhibition of diazepam of the tremor and the increase of cerebellar cGMP content elicited by harmaline. Brain Res. 83: 516-519, 1975.

Mao, C. C., Guidotti, A., and S. Landis: Cyclic GMP: Reduction of cerebellar concentrations in 'nervous' mutant mice. Brain Res., in press.

Costa, E., Guidotti, A., and C. C. Mao: Diazepam, Cyclic nucleotides and aminoacid neurotransmitters in rat cerebellum Collegium International Congress of Neuropsychopharmacology, Paris, France, 1974.

Costa, E., Guidotti, A., and C. C. Mao: Evidence for involvement of GABA in the action of benzodiazepine: Studies on rat cerebellum. American College of Neuropsychopharmacology, San Juan, Portorico, 1975.

Costa, E., Guidotti, A., Mao, C. C. and A. Suria: New concepts on the mechanisms of action of benzodiazepines. Life Sciences, mini review, in press.

Costa, E., Guidotti, A., and C. C. Mao: A GABA hypothesis for the action of benzodiazepines. In: GABA in nervous system function, edited by E. Roberts, T. N. Chase and D. Tower, Raven Press, International Symposium on GABA.

Guidotti, A., Biggio, G., Naik, S., and C. C. Mao: Action of taurine on the regulation of cGMP content in rat cerebellum. International Symposium on Taurine. Tucson, Arizona, 1975.

Mao, C. C., Guidotti, A., and E. Costa: Evidence for GABA mediation in the decrease of cerebellar cGMP and in the anticonvulsant action of diazepam. N-S. Arch. Pharmacol., in press.

Mao, C. C., and A. Guidotti: Simultaneous isolation of adenosine 3'5' cyclic monophosphate (cAMP) and guanosine 3'5'-cyclic monophosphate (cGMP) in small tissue samples. Analyt. Biochem. 59, 63-68, 1974.

Project No. Z01 MH 01516-03 SMRP
1. Division of Special Mental Health Research
2. Laboratory of Preclinical Pharmacology
3. Saint Elizabeths Hospital

PHS-ADAMHA-NIMH
Individual Project Report
July 1, 1974 through June 30, 1975

Project Title: Biochemical Pharmacology of Minor Tranquilizer.

Previous Serial Number: M-SMR-P-28

Principal Investigator: S. Naik, G. Biggio

Other Investigators: C. C. Mao, A. Guidotti and E. Costa

Cooperating Units: None

Man Years:

Total: 0.6
Professional: 0.6
Others: 0

Project Description:

The mode of action of benzodiazepines, which are the most widely prescribed drugs is still unknown. We intended to single out the transmitter that mediates the therapeutic action of these drugs. As a strategy we followed the study of the anticonvulsant action of benzodiazepines against convulsion elicited by blockers of specific transmitter receptors. Once identified, some specific trends in the anticonvulsant action of benzodiazepine we planned on in depth study of the biochemical mechanisms involved.

The anticonvulsant activity was studied by injecting subcutaneously different convulsant drugs which were followed at different times by intraperitoneal or intravenous injection of various benzodiazepines or other anticonvulsants as indicated in Table 1. Both the convulsant doses in 85% of the rats (CD85) and the median anticonvulsant dose (ED_{50}) for the different drugs were calculated according to the method of Lichfield and Wilcoxon, JPET 96: 99-113 (1949) by using 10 rats at each of five dose levels. cAMP and cGMP were assayed in cerebellum as previously reported (Mao, Guidotti, Analytical Biochem., 59: 63, 1974) GABA was assayed by the enzymatic method of Okada et al

(Exp. Brain Res. 13, 514, 1971).

The data reported in the table show that different benzodiazepines, in extremely low doses (Table 1) antagonize the seizures induced by isoniazid. Isoniazid is a drug, that decreases GABA brain content by blocking the glutamic acid decarboxylase. The observation that benzodiazepines could counteract a GABA deficiency prompted us to study whether benzodiazepines could mimick other biochemical and pharmacological actions elicited by GABA. Other studies (Project No.) had shown that GABA could lower cGMP in cerebellum and that it could counteract the tremor elicited by climbing fiber activation. The use of the cerebellum as a model to investigate the action of benzodiazepines possessed some additional attraction because: 1) benzodiazepines injected in large doses produce ataxia that probably reflect a cerebellar action of the drugs; 2) the cerebellum represent a well studied model in which GABAergic nerve terminals play a dominant inhibitory role on the excitation of Purkinje cells; 3) Mutant strain of mice were available which were devoid of cerebellar Purkinje cells.

We measured GABA and cGMP contents in cerebella of rat or mice receiving either diazepam or some of its pharmacological analogues.

We found that flunitrazepam and diazepam were at least 500 and 50 times respectively more potent than pentobarbital in lowering cerebellar cGMP content. Neither of the two benzodiazepines changes the GABA content of cerebellum. When diazepam was injected in a mutant strain of mice with a selective loss of 90% of cerebellar purkinje cells, it failed to decrease cGMP content (Mao, Guidotti, and Landis, 1975). Diazepam not only antagonized the convulsions elicited by picrotoxin and isoniazid but also antagonized the increase of cGMP elicited by these two convulsants. Both convulsant increased cGMP content of cerebellum even when they were injected in subconvulsive doses. Diazepam in doses that do not affect per se GABA or cGMP content (50 μg/kg ip) blocked the increase of cGMP by isoniazid but doses 3 to 4 times higher were necessary in order to block the increase of cerebellum cGMP elicited by picrotoxin.

These results indicate that the action of benzodiazepines may be mediated by their capability to increase in the availability of GABA at receptors. The small doses of diazepam used to obtain these effects are very close to that used in man in order to obtain antianxiety and anticonvulsant effects.

The benzodiazepine have been proved particularly successful

in psychiatry because they reduce anxiety while they produce very little sedation.

Several biochemical mechanism have been suggested to participate in the anticonvulsant and antianxiety effects of benzodiazepine. From time to time, acetylcholine, catecholamines, 5HT, have been implicated. More recently has been proposed that benzodiazepines can work atthe level of glycine receptor. Our data suggested that the pharmacological and therapeutical action of benzodiazepines may be mediated by an action of benzodiazepines on GABAergic neurones.

The importance of these observations may go beyond the immediate explanation of the mode of action of benzodiazepines and may represent the beginning of a better understanding of the role of GABAergic neurones in anxiety and in other mental disorders.

We plan to study the molecular mechansim whereby diazepam increases the availability of GABA at synaptic receptors: we plan to explore whether GABA is displaced from specific binding sites into GABAergic neurones or whether diazepam facilitates the release of GABA by nerve impulses. Cerebellum will be the area of brain in which most of the studies will be conducted because of the present state of our neuroanatomic knowledge in this tissue. On the basis of the results in these organ the observation will be extended to other GABA rich areas.

In particular we plan to study the role of benzodiazepines and other minor tranquillizers on the turnover rate of GABA in GABAergic neurones. The possible interaction of these drugs with postsynaptic cells receptor and with the release of excitatory transmitter from the presynaptic elements.

Keyword Descriptors:

Psychopharmacological agents, benzodiazepine as tranquilizers, anticonvulsants, cGMP, gamma-aminobutyric acid (amino acids), cerebellum, and cerebellar degeneration hereditary.

Publications:

Mao, C. C., Guidotti, A., and Costa, E.: Evidence for an involvement of GABA in the mediation of the cerebellar cGMP decrease and the anticonvulsant action of diazepam. Naunyn Schmiedeberg's Arch. Pharmacol., in press.

Mao, C. C., Guidotti, A., and S. Landis: Cyclic GMP: reduction of cerebellar concentrations in nervous mutant mice. Brain Res., in press.

Costa, E., Guidotti, A., and Mao, C. C.: Diazepam, cyclic nucleotides, and aminoacid neurotransmitters in rat cerebellum. Collegium International Neuropsychopharmacology, Paris, France, 1974.

Costa, E., Guidotti, A., and Mao, C. C.: Evidence for involvement of GABA in the action of benzodiazepines. Studies on rat cerebellum. American College of Neuropsychopharmacology. San Juan, Portorico, 1975.

Costa, E., Guidotti, A., Mao, C. C., and Suria, A.: New concepts on the mechanisms of action of benzodiazepines. Life Sciences, mini review, in press.

ED_{50} OF VARIOUS BENZODIAZEPINES AND OTHER ANTICONVULSANTS TO ANTAGONIZE THE SEIZURES ELICITED BY ISONIAZID, PICROTOXIN, PENTYLENETETRAZOL AND STRYCHNINE

Anticonvulsant	ED_{50} (μmol/kg i.p.) against			
	Isoniazid	Picrotoxin	Pentylenetetrazol	Strychnine
Diazepam	0.14	1	3.5	6.0
Desmethyldiazepam	0.29	2.6	5.1	8.5
Chlordiazepoxide	0.66	6.9	15	25
Oxazepam	1.7	14	20	39
Phenetharbital	54	76	71	68
Phenobarbital	60	73	61	52
Diphenylhydantoin	229	>354	>354	290

The anticonvulsant drugs were injected intraperitoneally 25 minutes after isoniazid (3.3 mmol/kg s.c.), 15 minutes after picrotoxin (7.46 μmol/kg s.c.), 5 minutes before pentylenetetrazol (289 μmol/kg i.v.), and then after with strychnine (4.49 μmol/kg s.c.)

Project No. Z01 MH 01517-01 SMRP
1. Division of Special Mental Health Research
2. Laboratory of Preclinical Pharmacology
3. Saint Elizabeths Hospital

PHS-ADAMHA-NIMH
Individual Project Report
July 1, 1974 through June 30, 1975

Project Title: Development of a high power microwave oven

Previous Serial Number: None

Principal Investigator: A. Guidotti

Other Investigator: E. Costa, D. L. Cheney and C. Wang

Cooperating Units: None

Man Years:

Total:	0.2
Professional:	0.2
Others:	0

Project Description:

Transmitters and second messengers content of brain structure undergoes rapid fluctuation post mortem. To measure concentrations and turnover rate of these regulatory molecules of the synaptic event it is necessary to stabilize the enzymes that synthesize or metabolize these molecules. In order to preserve structures and allow for dissection the microwave radiation has been proposed as a method for killing the animals. To ascertain that this technique is suitable for this purpose the concentrations of various constituents in brain parts of rats killed with microwaves focused to the skull was compared with those of rats killed with the rapid freeze blowing technique.

A metal wave guide channels the microwave power from the microwave generator (2 KW, 2.45 GHz) to a power window opening. A rat or mouse is placed in a special animal holder made of plastic which is mounted on the wave guide. The animal head is mounted inside the power window. The maximum wave intensity will then impinge directly on the head of the rat or mouse. An electronic system precisely controls the duration of radiation (0.5 sec for mice and 2 sec for rats).

The freeze blowing technique used for comparison was

described by Veech, Harris, Veloso and Veech, (J. Neurochem. 20: 183-188, 1973). This method uses high pressure liquid N_2 to blow the brain out of the cranial cavity. This tissue is out and frozen within 0.5 sec. Cyclic AMP, cGMP, acetylcholine, choline, creative phosphate, ATP, ADP, AMP, lactate pyruvate, 2-oxyglutarate, glutamate, the NAD/NADH ratio and the enzymes were measured by methods that have been previous described.

Adenylate cyclase, cyclic nucleotide, phosphodiesterase, and choline acetyl transferase were completely inactivated after 2 sec of focused microwave radiation. The concentrations of cAMP, cGMP, neurotransmitters and their metabolites in rat brain killed by microwave radiation were comparable to those found after freeze-blowing (see Table)

The microwave fixation technique has the significant advantage that·allows recognitiion and dissection of brain nuclei. This offers a unique possibility of measuring the effect of drugs on the steady state and the turnover rate of neurotransmitters or metabolites in small brain nuclei. Inactivation of enzymes is particularly important to measure the concentrations of choline acetylcholine and of cyclic nucleotides.

1) The microwave we have developed can promptly inactivat enzymes in the brain of small rodents. We are attempting to modify our device to inactivate instantaneously the enzyme in spinal cord and in the brain of cats and rabbits.

2) To develop a device that will allow to focus the microwave on the skull of a free moving animal.

3) We are developing a microwave device to inactivate enzymes in vitro in a very short time (1/10 1/100 of a sec.).

Keyword Descriptors:

Microwave heating, brain, temperature, heat stability-lability, enzymes, cyclic GMP, cyclic AMP, choline, glucose.

Publications:

Guidotti, A., Cheney, D. L., Trabucchi, M., Doteuchi, M., Wang, C. T., and R. A. Hawkins: Focussed microwave radiation: A technique to minimize post mortem changes of cyclic nucleotides, dopa, and choline and to preserve brain morphology, Neuropharmacol., 13: 1115-1122, 1974.

TABLE

A COMPARISON OF cAMP, cGMP NEUROTRANSMITTERS AND METABOLITES CONTENT OF RAT BRAIN AFTER FIXATION BY FREEZE BLOWING AND MICROWAVE TECHNIQUE

	Unit/g w.w.	Freeze blowing		Microwave Irradiation	
cAMP	nmoles	1.1 ± 0.08	(8)	1.0 ± 9.96	(8)
cGMP	nmoles	0.037 ± 0.0010	(8)	0.041 ± 0.0018	(8)
GABA	μmoles	2.0 ± 0.080		1.9 ± 0.062	
Glutamate	nmoles	11.5 ± 0.33	(4)	11 ± 0.12	(5)
Dopa	nmoles	0.26 ± 0.021		0.27 ± 0.026	
Acetylcholine	nmoles	12 ± 1.8	(4)	11 ± 1.4	(4)
Choline	nmoles	28 ± 5.4	(4)	33 ± 4.2	(4)
Glucose	μmoles	1.8 ± 0.070	(4)	1.7 ± 0.0030	(5)
Glucose 6 p	μmoles	0.14 ± 0.063	(4)	0.15 ± 0.0020	(5)
Pyruvate	μmoles	0.082 ± 0.0040	(4)	0.0065 ± 0.0020	(5)
Lactate	μmoles	1.2 ± 0.06	(4)	1.2 ± 0.03	(5)
α -oxyglutorate	μmoles	0.20 ± 0.008		0.19 ± 0.003	(5)

Values represent the mean ± S.E.M. In parenthesis the number of animals.

Lightning Source UK Ltd.
Milton Keynes UK
UKHW011628231118
332790UK00013B/1935/P

9 780428 747664